CASTE, CLASS, AND RACE

A Study in Social Dynamics

by Oliver Cromwell Cox, Ph.D. ——————

PROFESSOR OF SOCIOLOGY, LINCOLN UNIVERSITY——————

CASTE, CLASS, & RACE

A Study in Social Dynamics

—————————————— *Introduction by Dr. Joseph S. Roucek*

————————————— PROFESSOR OF SOCIOLOGY, HOFSTRA COLLEGE

MODERN READER PAPERBACKS
NEW YORK AND LONDON

Originally published in 1948 by Doubleday & Company, Inc.
First Monthly Review Press Edition 1959
First Modern Reader Paperback Edition 1970
Fifth Printing

Library of Congress Catalog Card Number: 59-8866
Standard Book Number: SBN-85345-116-8

Published by Monthly Review Press
62 West 14th Street, New York, N.Y. 10011
21 Theobalds Road, London WCIX 8SL

Manufactured in the United States of America

To the memory of
WILLIAM RAPHAEL COX

THE HARVEST *truly is plenteous but the labourers are few; pray ye therefore the Lord of the harvest, that he will send forth labourers into his harvest.*

*C*ASTE, CLASS, AND RACE ARE SOCIAL CONCEPTS WIDELY EMPLOYED in discussions of current social problems, and yet neither the theoretical meaning nor the practical implications of these concepts, as they apply to concrete situations, have been satisfactorily examined. In the past these terms have been used promiscuously and interchangeably, with the result that the literature on the subject is exceedingly involved. Among these involvements two seem to stand out: that between caste and race relations, and that between social class and political class.

An understanding of the characteristics of a caste system is so important as a basis for an understanding of other types of social systems that we have devoted the entire first part of this study to it. A distinction having been made, we could then discuss feudal, capitalist, and socialist systems without distracting suggestions about caste. To some readers this discussion on caste may seem too elaborate and labored. When, however, we consider the hundreds of books written on this subject, the continued, almost universal, misconceptions about the sociology of caste, and the significance of these misconceptions to the student of the social sciences, the space given to it is likely to seem small indeed. Although the writer spent some months observing the partial operation of caste among the thousands of East Indians in Trinidad, British West Indies, his data have been taken almost entirely from published materials on the Hindus in India.

It is not ordinarily realized that, of all the great mass of writing on race relations, there is available no consistent theory of race relations. The need for such a sociological explanation is so great that recently, when one author succeeded, with some degree of superficial logic, in explaining the phenomena in terms of caste relations, the college textbooks and social-science journals, almost unanimously and unquestioningly, hurriedly adopted his theory. The situation appears to be similar with the concept class, especially in the sense of a power-group phenomenon. With the exception of the contributions of some of the "radical authors," the present writer could find very little material which discusses the modern class struggle realistically. As a matter of fact, even the Marxian writers have not made very clear for us their meaning of class, and this is probably one of the reasons for their having been consistently rejected by the orthodox social scientists. Yet, openly, the class struggle goes on with increasing fury.

There is no single hypothesis which serves to explain the functioning of caste, class, and racial systems; therefore, it has not been possible to state one in the beginning. However, we should make it clear that this is no desiccated, academic dissertation. In fact, it may be thought of as partly a reaction to that massive output on this subject which has little or no theoretical content and which is often irritatingly evasive and circuitous in style. Since we have not followed this tradition of tentative expression, we may expect, from some very respectable quarters, the criticism of dogmatism. To be sure, it is well to keep our heads while the world is in convulsions, yet we may become inane if we discuss them as if we were describing an Egyptian mummy. At any rate, in the handling of these vital social problems we have deliberately tried to write clearly and unequivocally rather than tentatively and impressionistically.

Moreover, in an examination of the functioning of modern political classes one enters a field in which sides have already been taken; consequently it would be presumptuous to expect a unanimous acceptance of conclusions derived from even the most objective treatment of the data. Surely we do not assume that the final word has been said on any of the larger problems considered in this study. Most of them are only beginning to become vital in the social sciences; thus we should expect views to remain fluid for some time. In the words of Hans Kohn, "a work of this kind is never a monologue—it is an uninterrupted conversation with those of the past whose thoughts we study, and with those whose task it still is to build the future out of the heritage of the past. And this conversation goes on after the work has been completed."

In considering the behavior of "political classes" it has been practically impossible to ignore the work of Karl Marx and that of some of his associates; indeed, there should be no need to ignore them. In capitalist societies, however, the very name of Karl Marx is ordinarily anathema; consequently, unless the writer takes a position opposite to that of Marx, he is likely not to be heard. Nevertheless, it seems that interpretations of social data should be allowed to stand on their own merits—and this regardless of whether Marx ever lived. If social science has any claim at all to be science, it should at least refrain from distilling social data through a context of designedly developed, popular prejudices. We may be able, for instance, to demolish a certain chain of social logic merely by stereotyping it "Marxian," yet this achievement shows neither that the reasoning is untenable nor even that we have taken the trouble to understand it.

When, for example, Professor Louis Wirth asserts, in an article published as recently as 1947 in the *Annals of the American Academy of Political and Social Sciences,* that "research in the social sciences will remain stunted and inadequate until it includes the search for knowledge on power relations among men and the means for generating the will and the capacity for action directed toward the achievement of a good society," we have an observation by a distinguished sociologist, the accuracy of which should certainly not be impaired simply because we recognize in it a restatement of the position that has been the very driving force behind the colossal intellectual output of Karl Marx. In the interest of historical perspective it is important that the assertion be known to have been emphasized by Marx; but, in so far as its scientific validity as a social fact is in question, Marx has nothing whatever to do with it. At best, Marxian hypotheses are "servants, not masters." Indeed, it has been said that Karl Marx himself was not Marxian because in his studies he strived to understand modern society, while the religious Marxists, in their exegetical discussions, center their attention not upon the ongoing social system but rather upon an explanation and criticism of Marx—a sort of rumination of his conclusions, incidental errors and all. If, therefore, parts of this study seem Marxian, it is not because we have taken the ideas of this justly famous writer as gospel, but because we have not discovered any other that could explain the facts so consistently.

The present writer hopes that he is under no illusion about his own "value premise"; it is probably not hidden. He believes that there is serious maladjustment between the technological potentialities of Western society and the possibilities of bringing them into the service of human welfare, and that this maladjustment is an inherent trait of the social order. Moreover, he believes that it is not beyond the present capacity of human beings to devise plans for a satisfactory way of life. "The problem we are confronted with today," as Erich Fromm puts it, "is that of the organization of social and economic forces, so that man—

as a member of organized society—may become the master of those forces and cease to be their slave."

From many points of view Hindu society is exceedingly interesting; it is probably the greatest of "our primitive contemporaries." In many respects the system is unique. So far as we have been able to determine, developed castes exist in no other part of the world. The caste system of India constitutes the social structure of Hinduism, which is Brahmanic society—a social system, to repeat, virtually restricted to the latter area. Thousands of years ago the priests of India achieved social dominance, and in pursuit of their interests they crystallized tradition so effectively that an ancient society of pre-eminent cultural achievements has come down into modern times almost intact. "All through history," says the *Cambridge History of India,* "down to the period of British rule we see one foreign power after another breaking through the north-western gateway, and the strongest of these winning the suzerainty over India. But the result in all cases was little more than a change of rulers—the deposition of one dominant caste and the substitution of another. The lives of the common people, their social conditions and systems of local government, were barely affected by such conquests. Indian institutions have therefore a long unbroken history which makes their study especially valuable." The core of stability in this society is the caste system, which orders the society essentially according to the function of different groups, and which order is traditional, sacred, and therefore presumptively changeless.

All the tremendous literature of the Hindus, save the very earliest, is vitally concerned with this order, so that in Brahmanic India—that is to say, in unwesternized India—the social rules of some two thousand years ago still obtain both in letter and in spirit. Probably the most significant element in the stability of Hinduism is the phenomenal literary achievements of the early Brahmans, the Hindu priests. This preoccupation with literature is a cultural trait brought into India by the Aryans, a Central Asiatic people who spoke Sanskrit and probably lived for some time in the area northwest of the Hindu Kush Mountains. They have made the cornerstone of authority in Hinduism the sacred books of the Hindus.

The early history of the Aryans had to be ferreted out by modern scholars, because the Aryans themselves left no history of their origin or of the dates of their migrations into India. They came into India in a number of tribal waves through the passes of the Hindu Kush over a period probably centering about the year 2000 B.C. There they met and conquered the native Dravidian tribes, who were darker in complexion than themselves and who had a different culture. But the Aryans seem to have amalgamated rather rapidly with the native population, and they finally settled down as one people to evolve the caste system of India.

There is a tremendous amount of exegetical writing on the Sanskrit literature of India, very much of which is due to the state of the material itself. There is little if any certainty about the dates, the authors, or the places of the various compositions. As J. N. Farquhar says, "Indian history in the stricter sense opens with Alexander the Great's invasion of the Punjab in 326 B.C.; so that all previous events possess only a relative chronology." Indeed the chronology of many succeeding events is also relative. We shall, however, attempt to say a word about the early literature which we have used in this study, but for anything approaching an adequate discussion the reader will have to turn to the authorities. Among these are: the article "Sanskrit Language and Literature" in the eleventh edition of the Encyclopaedia Britannica; the *Cambridge History of India,* Vol. I; A. A. Macdonell, *A History of Sanskrit Literature;* J. N. Farquhar, *The Religious Quest of India: An Outline of the Religious Literature of India;* and Herbert H. Gowen, *A History of Indian Literature.*

In the study of the caste system, probably the most important of the early literature are: the Vedas, the Brahmanas, the Upanishads, the dharmashastras, the epics, and the puranas. All this is Hindu literature which has been either composed or edited by Brahmans and consequently it is sacred.

The Vedas are the fundamental religious work of the Hindus, their earliest literature. One of the Hindu law books (Manu) conceives of them in this way: "In whatever [condition] a man who knows the true meaning of the Veda-science may dwell, he becomes even while abiding in this world, fit for the union with Brahman [God]." There are four Vedas, each of which is a collection, a *samhita,* of sacred texts: (1) the Rig-Veda, or lore of praise (or hymns); (2) the Sama-Veda, or lore of tunes (or chants); (3) the Yajur-Veda, or lore of prayer (or sacrificial formulas); and (4) Atharva-Veda, or lore of the Atharvans (a mythic priestly family). The Rig-Vedic collection of 1,017 hymns is the earliest and basic religious text, but in all these collections there is surprisingly little of significance for an understanding of the social conditions of the early Aryans. The Rig-Veda was probably composed about the middle of the second millennium B.C.

The Brahmanas are intended for the sacrificial priests, the Brahmans; they explain the relationship of the Vedic texts to the sacrificial ceremony. Each Veda has its Brahmana or Brahmanas. It is in the Brahmanas that the priests developed their tradition of social importance most naïvely and made of the sacrifice an exceedingly complicated and mystical ritual.

The philosophic treatises forming a third division of the Vedic literature are called Upanishads. They deal with the meaning of human existence and the nature of the supreme being. In describing the Vedic literature, A. A. Macdonnel says: "In the Vedic period three literary strata can be distinguished: the first is the four Vedas, which consist of hymns, prayers, and spells addressed to the gods; the second, that of the Brahmanas or ritual treatises; the third, that of the Upanishads or the theosophical works, the basis of much of the later Indian philosophy." There are some 170 Upanishads.

For an understanding of Hindu society the dharmashastras or law books are most important. They deal specifically with the practical, everyday behavior and conduct of persons. And by far the most significant of these law books is the Manava Dharmashastra or the Laws of Manu, which is closely related to the Laws of Vishnu. These two codes duplicate a number of verses, some 160 of them, but the authorities seem to think that Manu is the original. Manu and Vishnu, of course, are mythical authors. The period of development of the Laws of Manu was probably during the last two or three centuries B.C. The Laws, however, are considered a divine revelation.

It is from a reading of the law books that one gets a feeling that the existence of Hindus is regulated by the sacred books. The latter illustrate most vividly the extent to which religion, rules, and order enter into the minutest act of the individual's life. As the Code of Manu itself declares: "In this work the sacred laws have been fully stated as well as the good and bad qualities of human actions and the immemorial rule of human conduct, to be followed by all the four castes."

The two great Hindu epics, the Mahabharata and the Ramayana, throw considerable light upon the social life of the ancient community. These epics, which apparently began with the story of a feud between the Kurus and the Pandus, two royal families, the descendants of Bharata, and the story of the life of Rama, respectively, finally grew into great encyclopedic works with additions by unnumbered authors. "The complete work," say the authors of the Britannica article referring to the Mahabharata, "consists of upwards of 100,000 couplets—its contents thus being nearly eight times the bulk of the *Iliad* and *Odyssey* combined. It is divided into eighteen books, with a supplement, entitled Harivamsa, or genealogy of the god Hari (Krishna-Vishnu). The portion relating to the feud of the rival houses constitutes somewhere between a fourth and a fifth of the work; and it is by no means improbable that this portion once formed a separate poem, called the Bhārata." Some authorities assign the date for the growth of this "huge encyclopedia of theology, philosophy, politics, and law" to the period between 600 B.C. and 200 A.D., or even later.

Within the Mahabharata itself there is a long religious poem, the Bhagavad-Gita or the Lord's Song, which has had considerable influence upon the religious thinking of the Hindus. Concerning its importance, Farquhar observes: "There is no other piece of literature that is so much admired and used by thinking Hindus; and it has won very high praise from many Western . . . scholars." And in speaking of the heterogeneity of the compositions in the Mahabharata, A. A. Macdonnel declares, "While the two armies are drawn up prepared for battle, a whole philosophical poem, in eighteen cantos, the Bhagavadgita, is recited to the hero Arjuna, who hesitates to advance and fight against his kin."

The puranas are collections of ancient or "old world" stories, legends, genealogies, cosmologies, and so on. There are some twenty recognized puranas, and they date from the later Vedic period downward. Concerning the significance of these works, Farquhar says: "It would be difficult to exaggerate the popularity and importance of the religious poems known as Puranas. They are very widely used among the common people both in the original and in numerous vernacular versions and adaptations. Indeed the epics and the Puranas are the real Bible of the common people, whether literate or illiterate."

Although the early Hindu literature is indispensable for an understanding of the caste system, it should be supplemented by actual studies of Hinduism. For instance, the early literature has consistently referred to "the four castes"—laws have been declared to govern the social relationships among "the four castes"—and yet there were probably never only four castes constituting Hindu society. It appears that the early Aryans conceived of their society as being divided into four estates and, when the caste system actually came into being, there was a carry-over in thinking to the new social situation with its very large number of castes and subcastes. In Chapter 2 we have stressed the importance of the caste-subcaste distinction for a comprehension of the nature of the caste system.

Since this essay is not of the nature of a survey, we have not attempted to examine and to list the various sources from which valuable data, especially on race relations, may be obtained. In our discussion of previous contributions in this field, for instance, we have been concerned only with showing how the approach of certain leading authorities has apparently limited their chances of developing a convincing theory. However, no study of race relations could be considered adequate without a knowledge of the contributions made by such works as Ray Stannard Baker, *Following the Color Line;* John Dollard, *Caste and Class in a Southern Town;* Hortense Powdermaker, *After Freedom;* Gunnar Myrdal, *An American Dilemma;* St. Clair Drake and Horace R. Cayton, *Black Metropolis;* W. E. B. Du Bois, *The Souls of Black Folk;* and Stetson Kennedy, *Southern Exposure.*

It may be well to reiterate that this study may sometimes appear to be overlively. In times of revolutionary social change, conclusions of even the physical scientists may appear to have radical social consequences. Moreover, in such times there are no means of preventing large numbers of men from becoming either cynics or advocates. The cynics are blinded by the swirling dust of a passing civilization and, therefore, they have hardly any vision of a more glorious rebirth; they are, men of little faith. On the other hand, the advocates are either afraid of or zealous for the emergent social order. In this situation the business of the social scientist is supposed to be that of standing off in cold objectivity while he analyzes the social convulsions, or, more preferably, that of ignoring them entirely until such time as a societal post-mortem could be safely performed.

And yet inevitably he will either deal with totally inconsequential subjects or suffer himself to be categorized either as advocate or cynic in consequence of his meddling with significant social questions that are always "hot to handle." Stefan Zweig's observation in reference to another revolutionary period and in criticism of the Erasmian attitude seems in point: "There are epochs wherein neutrality is stigmatized as a crime; during times of extreme political excitement the world insists upon a clear Yes or No, an affirmation of support or of disapproval, a distinct declaration of 'I am for Luther or I am for the Pope.' " Clearly, the social scientist should be accurate and objective but not neutral; he should be passionately partisan in favor of the welfare of the people and against the interests of the few when they seem to submerge that welfare. In a word, the reason for the existence of the social scientist is that his scientific findings contribute to the betterment of the people's well-being.

To some readers this essay may seem uneven in its level of sophistication. Certain chapters—those on the class struggle, for instance—may seem too simplified. However, it is the opinion of the writer that one reason why this subject has been kept almost completely out of the social-science textbooks is that the monographic discussions of it have been too highly philosophical and abstract.

Then, too, it is intended that the book may be read not only by the specialist but also by any intelligent reader with interest in the field— the journalist, the missionary, the social worker. Probably no part of the discussion is beyond the comprehension of the average junior or senior college student, while the mature graduate student in the social sciences may find a critical approach stimulating.

From the very nature of this work one necessarily feels indebted to so many teachers that, in accordance with ordinary gratitude, it becomes wholly impracticable to mention them all. The citations will probably indicate most of those upon whom I have put some immediate reliance. Many persons among the white, colored, and East Indian people of Trinidad have made my interviews not only a pleasure but also a source of certain germinal ideas on race relations. For face-to-face discussion and criticism of the substance of the book, I should like particularly to thank my colleagues, Professors Melvin B. Tolson, Andrew P. Watson, V. E. Daniel, and Alonzo J. Davis; George V. Bobrinskoy, Professor of Sanskrit Literature at the University of Chicago; and Dr. Werner Cahnman, formerly of Fisk University. Some parts of this book have already appeared as articles, and for permission to reprint these I thank the editors of *The American Journal of Sociology, The American Sociological Review, Social Forces, The Journal of Negro Education,* and *The Aryan Path.* In typing the manuscript, Mrs. Marie Smith took more than ordinary care and interest. For the many courtesies extended to me by the reference librarians at the University of Chicago and in Tuskegee Institute, I am also thankful. I alone, of course, am responsible for the way in which the materials are analyzed and presented.

OLIVER C. COX

Chicago, July 18, 1947

Contents

Part One: CASTE

Part Three: RACE

Introduction

NOTHING has been more provocative of international ill will than problems springing from, and directly and indirectly related to, the phenomena of caste, class, and race. From one point of view, World War II was fought to decide the validity of the claims of Hitler's gang that their "racial" background entitled them to reorganize Europe and the world under the leadership of the "superior" Nazi Aryans. Similarly, the Japanese Jingoists fought the war in order to prove to themselves and to the rest of the world that they had the right to dominate the Asiatic continent as a "super-race."

Important though the racial differences between the Occident and the Orient may be, the peoples of the world, and especially the American people, might also give greater consideration to problems closer home. These may not have the dramatic interest that international relations possess, but they come closer to precipitating actual trouble. The most challenging aspects of these racial, religious, and linguistic groups, which constitute "minorities" in the midst of more numerous and dominating populations, have much to do with the underlying hatreds and machinations that furnish the background of the bitter social conflicts of the post-World War II years. They remain—tragic though it seems at the beginning of the first post-World War II decade—a continued source of trouble. Though frontiers have changed, their alteration far too often has resulted only in the accentuation of the general problem which confronts the world today. And the revolt of the millions of the non-Europeans against the rule of the white man, as especially exemplified in India, indicates that the old formula of domination, utilizing the old-fashioned concepts of the arrangements benefiting the ruling cliques of a few imperialistic nations, has to be drastically revised.

Obviously, while we are prone to regard the questions of caste, class, and race as almost exclusively non-American problems, there is an aspect of these problems which confronts the American people as a challenge to the democratic principles and practices which, we insist, should serve as substantial and living examples to the other peoples as the best ways of life. Yet our difficulties in this field have not been solved and the gigantic Negro problem needs not only to be considered but also solved as America's burning question *par excellence*. The need of dealing with them is overwhelmingly pressing. The development of greater knowledge of the world significance of the question becomes of prime importance to domestic and international good will.

This approach to the problem makes the present examination of the issues of caste, class, and race relations most opportune. The point of view—that of an American familiar with actualities yet given the detachment of American scholarship—should commend itself to those who seek enlightenment. The treatment corrects many minor errors of other writers and presents a clear and straightforward picture of its subject. Those who have never found time to go through other books on the topic will learn from it much they never knew.

In other words, this is a lively book with virtues of more than ordinary degree. An astonishing amount of research has gone into its making and in its wider implications the volume opens vistas not yet scanned. At a time of enforced re-evaluation, such as we are at present undergoing, however unconscious we are of it, this book is greatly needed not only in our schools but also by all Americans who can bear the unpleasant truth about the world-wide implications of the acute problems of caste, class, and race facing us and the globe.

JOSEPH S. ROUCEK

Hofstra College, Hempstead, Long Island
July 1947

Prologue

GREAT WARS ARE CRISIS SITUATIONS WHICH SEEK TO RESOLVE summatory antagonisms between peoples and which always result in more or less accommodation between them and more or less significant internal social changes. There are certain characteristics of war which may be found to be typical in all great national struggles, even as far back as the conquests of the major dynastic Pharaohs of Egypt. Indeed, it is possible to think of war as having its basis in some instinctual residue of human nature. These apparently common traits of war, however, do not tell us very much about it as an immediate social problem; they are likely to lead to pessimistic generalizations about its inevitability.

Wars are significantly functions of social systems, and it is especially by a study of these systems that we can know something about their peculiar nature and social determinants. Peoples in Western society do not go to war for the same causes as those which actuated the early Hindus; in fact, with the rise of capitalist civilization, the nations of Western society began to go to war on different grounds from those which incited the rulers of medieval society. World War II initiated a new era in international sensitiveness, because the primary irritants had never existed in the world before. Feudal wars may be thought of as involving typically the personal power and prestige of great landed rulers, capitalist wars as mainly nationalistic conflicts over markets and exploitable resources; but the era centering about World War II began the fateful period of political-class wars, or the struggle for dominance of the capitalist world by the democratic masses.

This latest period involves, moreover, the struggle between social systems, one of which is new in the world and thus presents a new basis for the next great war. Since the pith of the new antagonism is political-class interests, we should expect to find the conflict as perilously domestic as it is international. Thus, World War II began and ended, although the war in China continues; even today the very word Spain is charged with violent emotion; and imminent civil strife in almost every European country concerns immediately the fate of the political-class adjustment within the three major powers of the world. This is not the old relatively static, imperialistic era; it is something new in history.

The continuance of an exceedingly viable civilization is here in-volved. Frequently, in current discussions, it has been asserted that "the next war will end civilization." The meaning is probably that the next war will end *this* civilization. Although a recognition of the fact may be distasteful, it is necessary to realize that capitalist civilization received a tremendous shock from World War I, and, at the same time, the democratic movement was invigorated. World War II concluded another capitalist crisis, still worse—so much so, indeed, that in all the world only the system as it now exists in the United States can stand unaided upon its own feet. And yet so paradoxical a thing is the intellectual dynamics of capitalism that it is currently believed by some leaders of great political power that only World War III could restore the system to a healthy, peaceful existence.

Perhaps, if we can see exactly what a modern political class is and how it functions, we may not be so certain that the passing system can be restored by another world war. The social ferment now at work is as old as capitalism itself—it is inherent in capitalism—therefore violence cannot destroy it. From a beginning so feeble that it could be almost completely disregarded, democracy has now become a formidable threat to the modern system of power relationship. We cannot liquidate this historical fact either by ignoring it or by calling it names, for it is the unavoidable subject of modern domestic and international conflict; it is, indeed, the question of who shall rule the social system, the few or the many. And the predictable decision involves not simply a political coup d'état, but rather the substitution of a new social order, a new way of life with distinctly different social ends. Thus the class struggle is not a myth; it is as real as the human lives that are being daily sacrificed all over the world in its interest.

Racial antagonism is part and parcel of this class struggle, because it developed within the capitalist system as one of its fundamental traits. It may be demonstrated that racial antagonism, as we know it today, never existed in the world before about 1492; moreover, racial feeling developed concomitantly with the development of our modern social system. Probably one of the most persistent social illusions of modern times is that we have race prejudice against other people because they are physically different—that race prejudice is instinctive. From the point of view of Anglo-Saxon, gentile, well-to-do people, we may hate peoples of other nationalities, hate Jews, hate all colored peoples, and hate union workers. Yet we can safely say that these are not all an identical social attitude.

Our feeling against, say, the Italians may vanish if they become our allies in war; feeling against the Jews may subside as we begin to discount the importance of religion in determining social phenomena; if Negroes do our work contentedly and help to break strikes for us, we may defend and even treat them amiably; we may see considerable virtue in union workers if they insist that the company union has more merit than the outside organization. Human beings have the capacity for "social hatred" or antagonism; yet in any given social situation of inter-group antagonism, we do not seek an explanation by referring to this capacity. The social antagonism is as stable and as different as the inciting cause—the interest—behind the antagonism. Human nature itself is probably the most plastic and malleable of all animal nature.

The interest behind racial antagonism is an exploitative interest— the peculiar type of economic exploitation characteristic of capitalist society. To be sure, one might say this cannot be, for one feels an almost irrepressible revulsion in the presence of colored people, especially Negroes, although one never had any need to exploit them. It is evidently the way they look, their physical difference, which is responsible for one's attitude. The assumption here must be, however, that one's own looks are naturally attractive to all people of color, since it can hardly be shown that any people of color ever had race prejudice before contact with Western civilization. Race prejudice is not an individual idiosyncrasy; it is a social attribute. Ordinarily the individual is born into it and accepts it unconsciously, like his language, without question. In the Deep South, for instance, it is the custom for the different sexes of the two races to look at each other as if they were asexual objects, yet it would be utter nonsense to say that the difference in color has eliminated all chances of arousing sexual appetite between them.

Negroes—to consider the United States specifically—must not be allowed to think of themselves as human beings having certain basic right₂ protected in the formal law. On the whole, they came to America as forced labor, and our slavocracy could not persist without a consistent set of social attitudes which justified the system naturally. Negroes had to be thought of as subsocial and subhuman. To treat a slave as if he were a full-fledged human being would not only be dangerous but also highly inconsistent with the social system.

However, it should not be forgotten that, above all else, the slave was a worker whose labor was exploited in production for profit in a capitalist market. It is this fundamental fact which identifies the Negro problem in the United States with the problem of all workers regardless of color. We can understand, therefore, the Negro problem only in so far as we understand their position as workers. Moreover, their status as workers has been categorically like that of white workers; indeed, with the crystallization of social forces, the real position and problems of both Negro and white workers are beginning unmistakably to converge.

As a race primarily of exploited and exploitable workers, then, we may predict certain trends of the Negro population. In the future, Negroes will probably become more highly urbanized than any other native-born population group in the country. Although they were originally the principal source of "cheap, docile labor," best suited to plantation production, with the coming of freedom and greater knowledge of the labor market we should expect them to seek to sell their labor—practically the only significant economic resource they have—in the best markets. The best labor markets are ordinarily found in the cities; therefore, Negroes have been moving in on the cities. Today Negroes in the United States are less urbanized than native white people, but Negro urbanization has been increasing at a much faster rate than that of whites. In 1910, 27.3 per cent of the Negroes lived in cities, but in 1940 the percentage increased to 48.6. For the same two periods the figures for native whites were 43.6 and 55.1, respectively.

As Negroes become more urbanized they also become a more significant group in the organizable labor force of the nation. Moreover, with the ascendance of industrial unionism, their organization has been greatly facilitated. This, however, is the sensitive spot of race relations in the United States; here the struggle against racial discrimination and prejudice is given its true political-class orientation, and the Negro problem tends to become lost in the major struggle for power that is actually in process in all capitalist countries of the world.

Both the AFL and the CIO are increasing their activities in the South—both are organizing Negro workers—but it is the system of industrial unionism of the CIO, with its inevitable tendency democratically to identify the interests of all workers regardless of color, that threatens to be the Nemesis of racial hatred in the South. In a circular entitled *The Kiss of Death,* sent out on April 29, 1946, by the Southern States Industrial Council, with headquarters at Nashville, Tennessee, the political-class, race, and labor relationships are clearly expressed. Thus this organization of Southern employers declares:

One of the most pitiful, and at the same time *most dangerous* features of this drive to organize the South is the way the Negroes are being misled and used by these Communist groups. By advocating a system of social and economic equality, and by arousing ill-will and hatred between the White and Negro races, these people are promising the Negro an *earthly Utopia* which they know they cannot deliver, and which they really have no intention of attempting to deliver. . . .

I predict that the ones who will suffer most from the abortive efforts of this group of carpet-baggers will be the Negro who permits himself to be used in this unholy effort. *He will have no friends among his own race, and certainly he will have none among the Whites.* . . .

Why this organized effort in the South? Because the Communist-CIO-PAC-SCHW [Southern Conference of Human Welfare] know that as long as the South remains free, there can never be a Communist dictatorship in America. They know that the free Southern worker, who believes in freedom of contract, in the open shop, and in the right to bargain individually or collectively with his employer, must be subjugated and his freedom destroyed before there can be a Communist dictatorship in America. They know that in the South the hearts and minds of the people are strong and reliant in a faith that has been made possible by the right to worship Almighty God according to the dictates of their own conscience, and they know this faith in God must be destroyed before there can be a Communist dictatorship in America. . . . This is no labor movement, unless it is also an effort to destroy the A.F. of L.

This, then, is the offense of all offenses—the attempt to organize the black labor supply of the South. To be sure, the AFL has never been particularly loved by Southern businessmen, but in this situation it is decidedly considered the lesser of two evils. Its past policy of organizing only the upper crust of strategic workers left the masses, in which the Negro workers belong, wholly at the disposal of "free" enterprise.

It is remarkable that some of the most precious rights of human welfare are attributed to the advocacy and practice of communists; and yet, in the same breath, we are asked to hate communists. There must be something wrong about this. It was President Franklin Roosevelt, in fact, and not the CIO, who initiated and won the struggle for the unionization and improvement of the economic condition of the masses of workers; and it is the National Labor Relations Act which guarantees to these masses an American right to organize into labor unions. But since Roosevelt, in spite of all the attacks of the ruling class, has remained the great champion of the people, his name cannot be effec-

tively mentioned. Instead, the CIO is identified with the negative—
stereotype—communism, and is attacked as such.

Of especial significance is the fact that these employers feel that
"one of the most dangerous features of this drive" is the attempt to
organize Negro workers. This is the white, ruling-class conception of the
Negroes' "Utopia"; in the labor union the Negro has his promise of
"social equality." This is indeed so dangerous that, should he join the
workers' organization, "he will have no friends among his own race,
and certainly he will have none among the whites." Moreover, it is
clearly inferred that as long as the South can maintain its racial system
the country as a whole can be effectively inhibited from achieving its
democratic ends. Stetson Kennedy, in his *Southern Exposure,* went to
great pains in making a detailed analysis of this.

The CIO, to be sure, is admittedly dangerous to the racial system
of the South. In order to facilitate and strengthen its organizing activities among the masses of workers, it carries on an intense, anti-
prejudice campaign. This campaign is not the ordinary moralistic
lesson about man's inhumanity to man. It is an indoctrination of the
workers on the very basis of racial antagonism and its effect in keeping
all workers in subjection. At its 1939 Convention the CIO adopted the
following resolution:

Whereas, employers constantly seek to split one group of workers from
another, and thus deprive them of their full economic strength, by arousing prejudices based on race, creed, color or nationality, and one of the
most frequent weapons used by employers to accomplish this is to create
false conflicts between Negro and white workers, Now, therefore, be it—
Resolved, that the CIO hereby pledges itself to uncompromising opposition to any form of discrimination, whether political or economic, based
on race, color, creed or nationality.

Resolutions of this kind have been common in the yearly conventions
of other labor organizations; they are ordinarily paraphrases of a certain amendment to the constitution and are seldom offensive to anyone.
However, it is the determined intent of the CIO to put its anti-dis-
crimination decisions into practice which makes it a particularly
"communist" labor movement. Openly, this union takes pride in an-
nouncing: "In every case, the CIO makes sure that Negro workers receive the same benefits. In every union, the Negro worker and his
family have the same chance to win the better life that the white
worker has." In an educational pamphlet, *The CIO and the Negro
Worker,* it is pointed out: "The CIO has organized Negro and white
workers alike because that is the only way strong labor unions can

be built. For a union to practice discrimination is to hand over half its strength to the employer, who uses it to weaken and divide the workers." The "CIO Committee to Abolish Racial Discrimination" is an active educational and juridical group.

Of course Negro workers have already been beaten and killed for joining the unions, but they have not been completely intimidated. Now and then one reads newspaper accounts such as the following, from the New York *Times* (June 30, 1946):

> Last month a Negro union worker (a recent convert) was taken from his job in Twiggs County, a rural section of Georgia, and beaten soundly by four individuals who said they were knights of the Ku Klux Klan. This was supposed to be a lesson to him and his friends about joining unions.

These stirrings among the workers of the South, however, are merely an insertion of the very thin edge of a wedge which has certain splitting potentialities; progress will be rough and halting, for the system is by no means disintegrated. At any rate, although the democratic forces cannot at present count upon a break-through, World War II has created certain opportunities for enthusiastic activity. Besides the Political Action Committee of the CIO, the National Association for the Advancement of Colored People, the American Civil Liberties Union, the Southern Conference of Human Welfare, all the Negro newspapers, some white, liberal newspapers, and a host of minor organizations and publications have increased their efforts to secure the suffrage for Negroes in the South. Even the Supreme Court of the United States is beginning to feel the time has come to do away with the subterfuges which have circumvented the Constitution in denying Negroes the right to vote. Led by the Texas white primary case, the Court has recently been putting the anti-Negro voting system in the South to probably its severest test in history.

The reaction naturally has been frantic and determined; the big guns of "white supremacy" have been brought into play. A revived Ku Klux Klan, with flaming crosses bigger and more visible than ever, spearheads the movement, while great champions of Southern economic interests such as James Eastland, John Rankin, the successors of Eugene Talmadge, and Theodore Bilbo whip up the white masses into a hysteria of racial fear and hatred—nor has the powerful National Association of Manufacturers been asleep. A number of "Christian" and "veteran" anti-racial organizations have mushroomed in the region, and such anti-labor sheets as *The Trumpet* and *Militant Truth* are finding increasing support. Riots have spread, and Negroes have been driven out of communities and lynched in new demonstrations of refined brutality.

All this is likely to seem confusing if we think of it as an incorrigible racial trait of "Southern white people." It is, in fact, part of a political-class war, the final outcome of which could hardly be mistaken. Poor whites, it is true, are mostly in evidence at the great man hunts and lynchings, yet it would be an egregious error to think of them as initiators of racial antagonism in the South. Surely it must seem paradoxical that, while General Douglas MacArthur, himself a Southerner, with the backing of the United States Army strives with all the sanctimony of a savior to introduce and maintain popular suffrage in Japan, a distinguished United States senator declares to the people of Mississippi that "if a few Negroes vote in the Democratic primary this year, more will vote in 1947, and from then on it will go into a mighty surge . . . [that] every red-blooded, Anglo-Saxon man in Mississippi must resort to any means to keep hundreds of Negroes from the polls."

And the means which this leader advocates are sometimes terrible indeed. For example, *Time,* August 5, 1946, reports one case as follows:

> In Rupert District of South Georgia's Taylor County, Macie Snipes was the only Negro to vote. The day after election four white men called him out from supper. Macie Snipes staggered back into the house with blood gushing from the bullet wounds in his belly. A coroner's jury solemnly reported that he had been killed by one of his visitors in self-defense.

The Negroes who were beaten for attempting to vote in the Mississippi State Democratic primary on July 2, 1946, did not stir up any particular anti-ruling-class sentiment in the United States. However, this does not mean that the entire nation has given its acquiescence. The struggle is far deeper than racial; it is, in reality, a struggle for democracy not only in the South but also in practically every other country of the world. Observe, in illustration, how one Southern letter writer to the Chicago *Sun* (July 23, 1946) ties up outstanding national liberals with the late Governor Eugene Talmadge's white-supremacy campaign in Georgia:

> The radical left-wing combination of Wallace and Arnall suffered a great loss in their plan to revolutionize the South. Eugene Talmadge and decency have won a great victory in Georgia. . . . Talmadge has given America's Communists a warning that Georgia shall be for Georgians.

Probably it is a recognition of this paradox which prompted Chancellor Robert M. Hutchins to say that the United States is not yet morally ready to assume world leadership. What this really means is undoubtedly that we have not yet reached that stage of democratic advancement which is strong enough to condemn certain glaringly anti-democratic acts as crimes. In a democracy, race hatred, advocated by a public official, would be a crime; and this, especially because it would have no positive social or economic value. Orson Welles seems to have sensed this when in August 1946, on a national radio broadcast, he said: "In a people's world, the incurable racist has no rights. He must be deprived of influence in a people's government. He must be segregated, as he himself would segregate the leper and the insane. . . . Tomorrow's democracy discriminates against discrimination." To the same effect Wendell L. Willkie asserted in a speech on May 25, 1944: "Every time some race-baiter ill-treats some man in America he lessens the ability of America to lead the world to freedom."

Today, however, such men as Senator Bilbo, in both the North and the South, should not be thought of as insane or diseased. The tremendous political power and influence which they possess did not come to them simply by accident or chance. Their politics reflect significantly the wishes and interest of that class which holds the actual power of the nation. For that reason, at any rate in so far as it affects their careers, Welles's fulminations are like raindrops on a duck's back. Consider, for instance, the stark reality of the following campaign declaration of Senator Bilbo, reported in the New York *Times,* June 30, 1946. He is describing graphically the actual state of democracy in the capital of the United States:

Some niggers came to see me one time in Washington to try to get the right to vote there. The leader was a smart nigger. . . . I told him that the nigger would never vote in Washington. Hell, if we give 'em the right to vote there, half the niggers in the South will move into Washington and we'll have a black government. No Southerner could sit in Congress under those conditions.

Sometimes Theodore Bilbo is ridiculed, especially in the North, not so much because his description of American democracy is untrue, but because he is so brutally frank in stating the facts. In his crudity he exposes the motivation and nature of the ruling class which he represents. The group of political leaders whom he characterizes know, as did Adolf Hitler and his group, that they are exploiting a real social opportunity—a national or international need—for in the Congress of the United States they are, in addition to their own concern, a decided asset to the great business interests of the North.

Moreover, the anti-democratic violence which they control is not merely that sufficient to secure the seeming illegal, sporadic beating and lynching of a helpless Negro; it is in substance the organized militia of the states and the Army of the United States. To recognize this, one has only to imagine an actual situation. Suppose a number of Negroes, in the interest of "law and order," had come upon the scene in Monroe, Georgia, when two men and two women were being lynched and, finding themselves with the necessary force, had beaten down the lynchers. The result would have been a riot call to restore "law and order," which would have meant the armed police and sheriffs against the Negroes. Had the Negroes increased in number, the militia would have been called against them, and, if we could conceive of their increasing still, then the nearest United States armed forces would have been sent against them. The recent Columbia, Tennessee, riot followed somewhat a similar pattern.

It is this assurance of the continuing availability of the armed violence of the nation which gives confidence and authority to the antidemocratic class, while it produces inaction and irresoluteness in the advocates of democracy. Organized violence is practically all on one side of the table.

Quite frequently during World War II, President Roosevelt declared there should be no "master race" in the world as the Germans claimed to be, and the Secretary of State, Cordell Hull, stated explicitly that one principal purpose of the war was to eliminate fascism wherever found in the world. Both the "master race" ideology and fascism, however, are social attributes of a particular social system. They may not be eliminated by international war. It would seem quite obvious that countries like Great Britain and the United States, whose ruling classes are in fact master races, may not be ready to eliminate this reality in the world. The master-race idea and fascism can be purged from the social system only by a change in the system itself; and, for great powers, this is ordinarily a domestic undertaking.

If this is true, then, America has a desperate problem on its hands. Probably in no other country of the world are the philosophies and practices of racial mastery so openly and tenaciously held to as in the South. In this case the South is not a backwood country of the United States; it is, in fact, to a very considerable extent, at the very head of the diplomatic and political destiny of the nation. It seems, therefore, that as the nations prepare again for war, the nature of the social systems that are actually in question should be as clearly understood as possible. Perhaps it is time that the people, who finally pay the cost of war in lives and wealth, should be ready to examine the crucial subject at issue.

Part One

CASTE

1. The Nature of Caste

*I*N ATTEMPTING A DISCUSSION OF THE CASTE SYSTEM, ONE IS USU-
ally confronted at the very outset with the persistent query: What
is a caste? Many earnest inquirers will not listen further to the caste theorist unless he states precisely, in the beginning, what he means by the
word "caste." The expert, thus cornered, is naturally tempted, in the
interest of the discussion, to submit some hastily considered definition,
hoping that it will be forgotten forthwith. But he seldom settles the
matter so lightly. His abbreviated picture of caste usually remains to
haunt all future commitments about the phenomenon. We shall not
try to escape this situation, but first we shall attempt to point out certain difficulties with respect to the formulation of a proper definition
of caste.

A caste cannot be defined as if it existed in social isolation or suspension, because it is in fact an inseparable element of the society.[1] The
social relationships of any caste interpenetrate the social matrix of the
caste system; and the caste system constitutes a type of society—the
structure and substance of a society. Hence to think of castes as we
would of such institutions as labor unions, churches, or guilds is to begin with a false conception. One caste cannot exist in an otherwise
casteless society, for castes are interdependent social phenomena. Indeed, some question has arisen as to whether a two-caste system is possible. We may, of course, speak of "a caste" as of "a person," but we
should be under the same necessity for mental reservation with respect
to the social isolation of the phenomenon.

When our interest is an understanding of the nature of the caste
system, then some definition of *a caste* is likely to be cumulatively misleading. A description of the more inclusive caste order promises to be

---

[1] We are assuming, for the moment, that a caste system exists in India only.

the more fruitful approach. The problem now becomes one of defining a caste society; this, however, presents not only the difficulty of distinguishing the concept but also that of achieving a satisfactory meaning of the term *society* itself.

The following are some noted definitions of caste or the caste system:

. . . a corporate group, exclusive and, in theory at least, rigorously hereditary. It possesses a certain traditional and independent organization, a chief and a council, and as occasion demands it meets in assemblies endowed with more or less full authority. Often united in the celebration of certain festivals, it is further bound together by a common profession and by the practice of common customs which bear more especially upon marriage, food, and various cases of impurity. Finally, it is armed, in order to assure its authority, with a jurisdiction of fairly wide extent, capable by the infliction of certain penalties, especially of banishment, either absolute or revocable, of enforcing the power of the community. Such, briefly, is the caste system.[2]

A caste may be defined as a collection of families or groups of families bearing a common name; claiming common descent from a mythical ancestor, human or divine; professing to follow the same hereditary calling; and regarded by those who are competent to give an opinion as forming a single homogeneous community. The name generally denotes or is associated with a specific occupation. A caste is almost invariably endogamous in the sense that a member of the large circle denoted by the common name may not marry outside of that circle, but within the circle, there are usually a number of smaller circles each of which is also endogamous.[3]

The first definition by Senart does not seem to distinguish between caste and the caste system; indeed it appears to confuse the concepts. Othewise it is much like Risley's, in that they both seek to circumscribe the operating unit of the caste system; and the result is somewhat artificial. The following three definitions recognize more or less the broader social context of castes:

Repulsion, hierarchy, and hereditary specialization: caste includes these three elements. It is necessary to consider all three if one is to have a complete definition of the caste system. We say that a society is characterized by such a system if it is divided into a large number of hereditarily specialized groups, hierarchically superposed and mutually opposed; if it does not tolerate the principle of rising in status, of group mixture, of changing occupation; if it is opposed altogether to the mixture of blood, to advancement in social status, and to a change of vocation.[4]

---

[2]Emile Charles Marie Senart, *Caste in India,* trans. by E. Denison Ross, p. 20.
[3]Herbert Hope Risley, *The People of India,* p. 67.
[4]C. Bouglé, *Essais sur le régime des castes,* 3d. ed., p. 4.

A caste may be defined as an endogamous and hereditary subdivision of an ethnic unit occupying a position of superior or inferior rank of social-esteem in comparison with other such subdivisions.[5]

A society subjected to a caste system consists of a number of subdivisions or castes which are exclusively endogamous, which show a strong tendency to be socially exclusive, which perpetuate themselves hereditarily, which are hierarchically superposed on a basis of standard supposedly cultural, and which by the working of these four tendencies within the social field of their own delimitations may split up into more and more castes indefinitely.[6]

Dr. Mees says that his definition, immediately preceding, is based upon a study of definitions by previous writers. Had it included the characteristic of a tendency toward functional specialization, it might have been as serviceable as any. At any rate, definitions are seriously limited as means of describing societies. They can be, at most, suggestive. Hence, we shall not add another to the already large assortment available. As an alternative, we shall attempt to point out certain salient characteristics of a caste system.

Caste, a Cultural Phenomenon

There seems to be a quite settled belief among the Hindus that an individual is born with his caste status and that he can no more change this than can the proverbial leopard rearrange its spots. A powerful myth explaining the creation of man has served to support some belief in biological differentiation among castes, while a number of Western and East Indian writers, led by Risley, have also sought to develop a biological explanation of caste. The early Hindus, however, although their emphasis upon caste rigidity favored a logical conclusion of physical concomitance, never attached the common present-day significance of physical differences as cultural determinants.

Moreover, the Hindus believe that a man's caste is irrevocably and functionally dependent upon his past lives. Any possible inference of biological determinism, therefore, must be sharply distinguished from the static modern concept based upon differences in brain weight, pigmentation, nasal index, and so on. No visual technique has ever been developed among the Hindus as a means of allocating caste membership; and of course laboratory methods for this purpose were unknown among them. Thus, although the individual is born heir to his caste, his identification with it is assumed to be based upon some

---

[5] A. L. Kroeber, "Caste," *Encyclopedia of the Social Sciences.*
[6] Gualtherus H. Mees, *Dharma and Society*, p. 71.

sort of psychological and moral heritage which does not go back to
any fundamental somatic determinant. For example, in one of the
early books of the Hindus we observe this moral emphasis: "When evil
happens to a Kshatriya, there is born in his offspring one like a
Sudra. . . ."[7]

In spite of the rationalizing beliefs of some modern Hindus, the determining force of cultural change is everywhere manifested in caste
relationship:

> When one section of a caste develops peculiarities of any kind—a differ-
> ent occupation, habitat or social practice, or more rarely, a different re-
> ligious cult—the tendency is for it to regard itself and to be regarded by
> the rest of the caste as something different. This feeling grows stronger
> with time, until at last it, or the main body of the caste, withdraws from
> the marriage league. The result is a new subcaste, and often in the end
> a new caste. On the other hand, when a section of one caste adopts the
> occupation characteristics of another the tendency is for it to become ab-
> sorbed in the latter.[8]

Bouglé puts it graphically in saying that the caste system "has divided
Hindu society into a considerable number of diminutive societies in
opposition."[9]

Caste Stereotypes the Society

The caste system provides for the ordering of groups in society once
and for all time. There is no provision for initiating change; and when
change becomes inevitable it must be explained away. Conscious striving among persons to enter new functional fields or to achieve advanced
social position is taboo. The idea of progress is almost entirely absent
in the philosophy of Hinduism. It is inimical to the caste system and
its rationale. "The Indian, as long as he was left to himself, never knew
progress."[10] Moreover, the social order is sacred and naturally must
not be questioned. On the subject of inertia in Hindu society William
Crooke observes:

> The main result of the caste system is to stereotype existing conditions,
> to repress the desire of the individual to advance his own interest at the
> expense of, or in opposition to, those of the community in which he is
> included.[11]

---

[7]*Aitareya Brahmana,* VII, 29.
[8]*Census of India, 1911,* Vol. I, Pt. 1, p. 371.
[9]C. Bouglé, op. cit., p. 32.
[10]Ibid., p. 15.
[11]William Crooke, *Things Indian,* p. 89. See also *The Laws of Manu, The Sacred
Books of the East,* Vol. XXV, II, 10.

The early Hindus sometimes went to great lengths in accounting for the naturalness of one's caste position. Note, in illustration, the strength of Manu's position: "A Sudra, whether bought or unbought, may be compelled to do servile work; for he was created by the Self-existent to be the slave of a Brahman. A Sudra, though emancipated by his master, is not released from servitude; since that is innate in him, who can set him free from it?"[12] Even today among westernized Hindus some of the most powerful appeals are couched in regressive attitudes.[13] Such phrases as "our ancient civilization," "Hindu culture and glory," "our past greatness," "back to the Vedas," and so on, run like a refrain through the literature. Some of it, of course, is nationalistic, but it is principally based upon an extreme respect for tradition and abhorrence for social change. The eyes of Hindus are turned toward the past; some of the most zealous among them see in the best of Western culture merely a rediscovery of certain aspects of ancient Hindu civilization.

Social Mobility Inevitable

Although there is a cultural presumption of fixity of social position within the caste system, some movement is not only possible but also inevitable.[14] Movement may be by the individual or by the caste as a whole, and vertically or laterally within the system. Individual mobility, however, is rarer and more difficult. According to Ibbetson,

The classification being hereditary, it is next to impossible for the individual himself to rise; it is the tribe or section of the tribe that alone can improve its position.[15]

---

[12]Manu, VIII, 413–14.

[13]René Maunier, *Sociologie coloniale*, p. 78.

[14]Nesfield concludes that "the number of castes in India is constantly changing, because every marriage union [caste] may admit new constituents or expel old ones. The circle of marriage unionship is not, nor ever has been, immutable. It might rather be compared to a circle, whose center can change its point, and whose radius is perpetually liable to being lengthened or contracted. This process of extension in one direction, followed as it usually is by contraction in another, has been at work for the last two thousand years at least; and thus while some castes once prosperous, such as the Kathak and the Bhat, are surely but slowly dying out, and while others, such as the Baidya, have died out altogether, other castes, such as the Khattri and Kayasth, have been rising into importance in their places. When . . . a caste is said to die out, this does not mean that families which belonged to it have died or been exterminated, but either that the function peculiar to this caste has become useless to the outside community, in which case the families constituting the caste are gradually dispersed into other functional or marriage unions, or if the function is still useful to the outside world, that some new or more energetic centre of activity giving rise to a new marriage circle and assuming a new title, has supplanted the old one. The Baidya, as Baidya, has disappeared, but his descendants are still alive under other names." John C. Nesfield, *The Caste System of the North-Western Provinces and Oudh*, p. 113.

[15]Denzil Ibbetson, *Panjab Castes*, p. 9.

Yet instances of individuals rising into higher castes, either by their own effort or with the aid of others, are by no means unknown. Their falling into lower castes has been common. Under certain conditions, then, individuals may either rise or fall in caste position. "Under Hindu rulers persons were sometimes promoted by the Raja from one caste to another. This power was exercised by the Rajas of Cochin, who often raised men of lower caste to the rank of Nayar. A former Raja of Talcher in Orissa compelled his Chasa subjects to admit certain Goalas to their community."[16] Even marrying up as a means of personal advancement has been possible. E. A. Gait observes:

Cases sometimes occur of men procuring as their wives women of a higher caste with a view to raising their own status. In Kumaon a Dom may, for a sufficient consideration, obtain as wife the daughter of a Rajput Khasiya. In Bombay a Kumbi who has got on in the world may by sufficient payment marry into Maratha families.[17]

Indeed, instances may be cited where not only women but also gifted low-caste men, Sudras, have been able to work their way up into high-ranking castes.[18] These upward movements, however, though very important for an understanding of the caste system, are highly exceptional. Quite frequent, on the other hand, is the occurrence of an individual's falling in caste position. "A considerable number of castes of inferior status are willing to admit outsiders of higher social position who may wish to join their community. In such cases, the newcomer is adopted formally as a caste-brother, much in the same way as a man who has no son of his body takes one by adoption."[19] The fall, of course, is almost never a voluntary matter; it is at most a form of personal adjustment when the alternative may be a life without any caste at all—terrible business at its best. The possibility of losing status by caste de-

---

[16]*Census of India, 1911,* Vol. I, Pt. 1, p. 337. "Men of every caste have been known to be made Brahmans by the caprice of a chief." Senart, op. cit., p. 81.

[17]*Census of India,* op. cit., p. 378.

[18]G. S. Ghurye, *Caste and Race in India,* pp. 41, 59.

[19]"Caste," *Encyclopedia of Religion and Ethics:* "And according to the Census of 1911, in the Punjab the process of degradation from Rajput to lower rank is too common to require proof of its existence. . . . It is not uncommon to find low castes admitting to their community persons of higher castes who have been excommunicated. . . . Members of any Hindu caste except Dom, Dhobi, and Chamar may gain admission to the Dosadh community by giving a feast to the heads of the caste, and eating pork and drinking liquor in token of their adoption of Dosadh usage. In the Central Provinces many of the lower castes will admit men of other castes of a similar social standing who wish to marry a girl of their community." *Census of India, 1911,* op. cit., p. 378. See also Senart, op. cit., p. 14, and H. H. Risley, op. cit., p. 83

motion is a characteristic evidently as old as the caste system itself, for it is referred to everywhere in the early literature.[20]

A still more important characteristic of caste mobility is the movement of the whole or organized parts of the caste itself. The caste as a whole may degenerate because it adopts an occupation of lesser purity or some practice generally believed to be degrading.[21] Between caste and caste, especially between those that approximate each other in social status, there is a tendency to make claims and counterclaims to superior position. Usually the resolution of these attitudes leaves some new mark on the status of the castes involved. Sometimes, however, a caste, of its own volition, deliberately climbs a rung or two in the status hierarchy.

When a caste is prosperous beyond its neighbors, its members often become discontented with the rank assigned to them, and seek to change it. They cannot dispute the theory that caste is permanent and immutable, for Hindu society will never listen to such a heterodox idea. They, therefore, enlist the aid of fiction. They claim to be descended from some source other than that previously assigned to them; and if they can induce the Brahmans to endorse their claim, they often end by gaining general recognition for it, in spite of the opposition of rival castes who are adversely affected by their changed status.[22]

The adoption of "purer" habits by a caste may also raise it in public estimation. We shall revert to this in a later section.

Castes May Combine or Divide

Since the caste system rests upon cultural and not physical variates, two or more castes may fuse, or one caste may divide without threatening the stability of the system. "A section of a caste [say, Saraks] takes to a new occupation, such as weaving, in some locality where the number of members of the Tanti, or regular weaving caste, is insuffi-

---

[20]Manu, for instance, sees many situations in which a man may lose his caste status: "He who does not worship standing in the morning, nor sitting in the evening shall be excluded, just like a Sudra, from all duties and rights of an Aryan." II, 103. ". . . men of these three castes who have not received the sacrament [initiation] at the proper time, become Vratyas outcasts, excluded from the savitri initiation and despised by the Aryans." II, 39. "A Brahman who always connects himself with the most excellent ones, and shuns all inferior ones, himself becomes most distinguished; by an opposite conduct, he becomes a Sudra." IV, 245. "Killing a donkey, a horse, a camel, a deer, an elephant, a goat, a sheep, a fish, a snake, or a buffalo, must be known to degenerate the offender to a mixed caste." XI, 69.

[21]Denzil Ibbetson, op. cit., p. 6. See also Gulshan Rai, "The Caste System of the Hindus, and Absorption of Foreign Elements Among Them," *Hindustan Review,* July 1935, pp. 8 ff.

[22]"Caste," *Encyclopedia of Religion and Ethics.*

cient to meet the needs of the community. This section of the Saraks gets known as Saraki Tanti. In course of time the persons concerned come to regard themselves as a subcaste of Tanti, and assimilate their practices to those of that caste."[23]

Division is even more common than fusion. The sensitiveness of castes to internal cultural inconsistency is exemplified by the classic case of the oil pressers of Bengal. The Gachua Talis and Kolus are both oil pressers. They became separate castes when the Kolus left the traditional practice of soaking up the pressed oil from their mortars with a rag and adopted the device of making a hole in the bottom of the container, through which the oil was drawn off. The status of the Kolus is now very much lower than that of the Gachuas.[24] Among the many causes of caste division are migration, change of occupation, the adoption of new religious practices, and internal group dissension.

Classes within Castes

With respect to other castes, the status of all members of a given caste or subcaste approaches equality; but within castes of any appreciable size, the statuses of different individuals are never all equal to one another. The caste is not a unity of colorless, undifferentiated individuals. Indeed, the very nature of its organization entails internal differentiation. Castes of any size always have their superior and privileged families. Individuals within the caste may differ in wealth,[25] in occupational efficiency,[26] in physical attainments,[27] in choice of vocation among those to which the caste is limited,[28] in political position,[29] in number of Vedas read, or in number of knots in the sacred cord,[30] and so on.

Most caste men are permitted and even encouraged to develop efficiency and dexterity in the specialty of the caste; individuals may also accumulate and bequeath wealth. But innovations are usually frowned upon. The customary ways are sacred, and it is not uncommon for

---

[23]Ibid.

[24]See H. H. Risley, *Tribes and Castes of Bengal*, Vol. II, p. 307.

[25]Edward W. Hopkins, "The Social and Military Position of the Ruling Caste in Ancient India," *Journal of American Oriental Society*, Vol. XIII, 1888, pp. 79–80, 97, 103; George W. Briggs, *The Chamars*, pp. 55, 224.

[26]Radhakamal Mukerjee, *The Foundations of Indian Economics*, p. 40.

[27]Abbé Jean Antoine Dubois, *Hindu Manners, Customs, and Ceremonies*, 3d ed., p. 236.

[28]Ibid., p. 292.

[29]Shri Shridhar Nehru, *Caste and Credit*, p. 148.

[30]M. A. Sherring, *Hindu Tribes and Castes*, Vol. I, p. 9.

individuals to be punished for seemingly slight deviations in methods of production. "The weaver's panchayat, for instance, in some parts of the country prohibited for several years the use of . . . artificial dyes, and excommunicated artisans who dyed clothes in these colours."[31]

Variation in status within the caste, then, is ordinarily to be expected. Should any group within the caste become competitive, however, and attempt to distinguish their common interest, the caste will be quickly sundered.

The Caste Hierarchy

It has been repeatedly emphasized that the caste system constitutes a hierarchy of social-status ranks. This hierarchy may be called the "structure" of the system; it is self-regulating and graduated all the way from top to bottom. Each caste "has its particular rank, defined by tradition and public opinion, and each one maintains it at all costs, or strives to advance itself."[32] This defensive-offensive, intercaste relationship constitutes the basis of caste rivalry. Thus we may think of the caste system as a number of cultural unities invidiously juxtaposed; and the greater the struggle for position, the more secure the structure as a whole.

The significant fact of caste-status stability is not that every caste is ensconced in an unchallengeable social niche, but rather it is the unswerving faith in a conviction that every caste has a *right* to such a position. Thus, says Bouglé: "These incertitudes of the fact leave the principle intact; the contests themselves and the long-drawn-out struggles prove to what point these units of Hindu society are obsessed with the idea of right to be organized hierarchically."[33] To be sure, the system itself is never in question.[34]

Mutual jealousy provides the connective fabric of the caste structure, and its strength cannot be determined by the status of the castes in which it finds expression. We should expect, however, that spatial propinquity and proximity of status between castes will tend to intensify the relationship.

A scavenger, the lowest of the castes, is as proud of his birthright, and almost more punctilious about its rules, than a Khattri or a Kayasth. His arrogance has even led to a disruption within his own fraternity: for some

---

[31]Radhakamal Mukerjee, op. cit., p. 45.

[32]Emile Senart, op. cit., p. 18.

[33]C. Bouglé, op. cit., p. 25.

[34]Unless we call attention to it, we are not here concerned with the caste system under the impact of Western culture.

Bhangis will no longer eat what comes from their master's table, and these men have formed themselves into a distinct sub-caste on that basis. Every Bhangi despises the Chamar because he earns his living by collecting refuse. The lower castes, having no valuable monopoly to defend, have set up the most frivolous distinctions as grounds for despising their neighbors.[35]

Caste rivalry usually ends in a sort of mutual antagonism rather than progressive advancement in the hierarchy. Indeed, any idea of such advancement is inimical to the system itself; hence, each caste is a "natural" guardian of the status of the positions immediately about it.

The rights and privileges for which the Hindus are ready to fight such sanguinary battles appear highly ridiculous, especially to Europeans. Perhaps the sole cause of the contest is the right to wear slippers or to ride through the streets in a palanquin or on horseback during marriage festivals. Sometimes it is the privilege of being escorted on certain occasions by armed retainers, sometimes that of having a trumpet sounded in front of a procession, or being accompanied by native musicians at public ceremonies. Perhaps it is simply the particular kind of musical instrument suitable to such occasions that is in dispute; or perhaps it may be the right of carrying flags of certain colours or certain devices during these ceremonies. Such, at any rate, are a few of the privileges for which Hindus are ready to cut each other's throats.[36]

Sometimes caste distinctions are based upon very slight cultural differences. Chungia Chamars smoke their pipes differently from other Chamars; Ekbaile and Dobaile are subcastes of Telis who yoke one and two bullocks, respectively, to their oil presses; while the Nadha are distinguished by the fact that they live on riverbanks, and the Goria are known to make white pots but not black ones.[37]

The shape of the caste hierarchy is unpredictable, because there is no universally accepted norm for judging the position of all castes in Brahmanic India; and the size of any caste may depend upon the population trend in that caste. Moreover, according to their tribal circumstances, persons entering the system may do so at various social levels. It is more accurate to think of the caste system as constituting a

[35]John C. Nesfield, op. cit., p. 104. See also M. D. Altekar, "Caste System and Its Relation to Social and Economic Life," *Annals of the American Academy*, Vol. CXLIV, Pt. 2, p. 183. To the same effect, M. A. Sherring says: "In adhering to certain important caste rules and distinctions, many of the lower castes are much more rigid than the higher castes. . . . The Chamar . . . are every whit as stringent and exclusive on the subject of marriage." Op. cit., Vol. I, p. xxii. See also Abbé J. A. Dubois, op. cit., p. 60.

[36]Ibid., p. 26.

[37]G. S. Ghurye, op. cit., pp. 36–38. "The Kumbar, potters of the Maratha country, distinguished those who make pots by hand without the wheel as Hatghades . . . those who use a big wheel as Thorchake . . . and those who use a small wheel as Lahanchake." Ibid., p. 36.

multiplicity of hierarchies determined by custom within various geographical areas of organization. Certain Brahmans are always at the
top of each hierarchy, but not all varieties of Brahmans will be always
considered as superior to all other castes in the area. The Maha-Brahman, for example, is particularly inferior.[38] Risley gives the following
broad ordering of castes in a specified region:

In Bihar or the United Provinces the casteless tribes, Kols, Korwas,
Mundas, and the like, who have not yet entered the Brahminical system,
occupy the lowest place. . . . Then come the vermin-eating Musahars
and the leather-dressing Chamars. The fisher castes, Bauri, Bind, and
Kewat, are a trifle higher in the scale; the pastoral Goala, the cultivating Kurmi, and the group of cognate castes from whose hands a Brahman
may take water follow in due order, and from them we pass to the trading
Khatris, the landholding Babhans, and the upper crust of Hindu society.[39]

For an understanding of the caste system, it could hardly be too
strenuously emphasized that possible physical differences among castes
do not constitute significant status indices. Hindus do recognize individual physical difference, but they have never developed a method of
identifying castes according to their physical variations. "The Subar-
nabaniks are a mercantile caste peculiar to Bengal Proper, who claim
to be the modern representatives of the ancient Vaisya. In spite of their
wealth and influence, their high-bred appearance, and the celebrated
beauty of the women of the caste, their claim to this distinguished
ancestry has failed to obtain general recognition. They are excluded
from the ranks of Navasakha, of the nine clean Sudra castes, and none
but Vaidik Brahmans will take food from their hands."[40]

Since it is not physical differences of groups that determine their
position in the caste hierarchy, nor is it difference in wealth or "religion," then what might the criterion of status be? The basis of status
differentiation among castes appears to be caste dharma, or the way
of life of the caste, estimated finally by the expressed or assumed opinion of Brahmans.[41] Each caste has a presumptive, inherited dharma in
which vocation plays a major role. Among the incidences affecting

---

[38]John C. Nesfield, op. cit., p. 69.
[39]H. H. Risley, *The People of India,* p. 28.
[40]H. H. Risley, op. cit., p. 116.
[41]"Brahmans do not *police* the caste system; their influence is indirect. According
to E. A. Gait: "The first test of the social position of a caste is whether Brahmans
will act as its priests, and if so, what their status is in the hierarchical community.
A Brahman loses in social estimation if he acts as a priest to any but those of
'twice-born' rank, but he is not actually degraded from performing the priestly
office for castes regarded as clean Sudras. Castes that enjoy the services of good
Brahmans may thus at once be separated from those whose Brahmans are degraded.
Similarly, those that are ministered to by degraded Brahmans rank higher than

caste mobility, Risley observes that "the status of certain castes has been
raised by their taking to infant-marriage or abandoning the remarriage
of widows; . . . [that] the status of some castes has been lowered by
their living in a particular locality; . . . [that] the status of others has
been modified by their pursuing some occupation in a special or peculiar way."[42] Change in occupation itself is a most revolutionary venture
in the life of a caste.

Social inequality is a keynote of the caste system; it is the theme of
the social etiquette of the Hindus.[43] Therefore, we shall attempt to
illustrate the significance of this superiority-inferiority adjustment.

Caste Superiority

Although there might be some question concerning the means by
which Brahmans gained ascendancy in the caste system, it is undoubtedly established that they are superior people—not superior in
the sense that some modern Teutonic "Aryans" claim to be, but in a
culturally hereditary sense. Group superiority and inferiority are obviously obverse sides of the same social phenomenon, but this fact does not
imply a bipartite organization of the whole society. In the caste system
Brahmans and outcastes represent the zenith and nadir, respectively,
of this relationship; their distance presents a social spectacle. However,
the numerous intermediate steps of superior-inferior caste positions are
as significant to the system as the spectacular extremes. The extremes
are possible only because of the middle.

Too often writers on caste discuss the system as if it constituted
merely one superior-inferior relationship. It is very likely that if the
latter were the case the system could never have become stabilized; the
society would have remained divided against itself. As it is, at any rate,
the castes as a whole are "socially satisfied."

Although there is an interrelationship of superior-inferior attitudes
all the way from the dark roots to the topmost blooms of the system, the

---

those that have no Brahmans at all. Another general criterion is whether the higher
castes will take food or water from a man of the caste under consideration."
"Caste," *Encyclopedia of Religion and Ethics.*

[42]H. H. Risley, op. cit., p. 109.

[43]By keynote we mean that there is a fundamental creed or presumption in Hindu
society that persons are born unequal in status according to the caste to which
they belong; this is the antithesis of the Stoic doctrine of human equality, adopted
in Western democracies. If, in the caste system, we find subcastes with apparently
very little, if any, difference in status, or, on the other hand, persons of vastly different status in a social-class system, we should probably not conclude that the presumption is non-existent. It is this presumption of inequality in the caste system
which sometimes sets the emotional tone for bitter subcaste rivalry on a collateral
plane.

nature of these attitudes might be more easily perceived by describing particularly the extremes. The superiority of one caste over the other does not necessarily mean domination of one caste by the other. Once established, it becomes a situation of mutual expectation and willing, almost happy, yielding of definite privileges and deference. The relationship is spontaneous. From this point of view the system is at peace with itself. Brahmans do not struggle to maintain their position; they *are* superior. On this point Dubois observes:

The Brahmin's superiority is inherent in himself, and it remains intact, no matter what his condition in life may be. Rich or poor, unfortunate or prosperous, he always goes on the principle engraved in him that he is the most noble, the most excellent, and the most perfect of all created beings; that all the rest of mankind are infinitely beneath him, and that there is nothing in the world so sublime or so admirable as his customs and practices.[44]

Indeed, Brahmans have gone beyond the purview of mortals and have probably succeeded in rising superior to the gods themselves. Not infrequently the gods have been made to dance to their tune:

It is by no means uncommon to hear Brahmins speak of their gods in terms of the most utter contempt. When they are displeased with their idols they do not scruple to upbraid them fiercely to their faces, at the same time heaping the grossest insults upon them, with every outward gesture and sign of anger and resentment. . . . There is absolutely no limit to the blasphemies, curses, and abuses which they hurl at them under these circumstances.[45]

The early Hindu literature is particularly insistent on the superiority of Brahmans. Manu explains the basis of Brahman superiority thus: "From priority of birth, from superiority of origin, from a more exact knowledge of sacred science, and from a distinction in the sacrificial thread, the Brahman is lord of all classes."[46] Other castes are graded

---

[44]Abbé J. A. Dubois, op. cit., p. 304. See also C. Bouglé, op. cit., pp. 23 and 182. "Brahmans find it unnecessary to proclaim their authority as Brahmans. But, if anyone fails to recognize the existence of this authority, he is reminded of it so effectively that he does not err again." Charlotte V. and William H. Wiser, *Behind Mud Walls,* p. 20.

[45]Dubois, op. cit., pp. 295–96.

[46]This authority elaborates further: "Man is stated to be purer above the navel than below; hence the self-existent (Svayambhu) has declared the purest part of him to be his mouth. As the Brahmana sprang from Brahman's mouth, as he was first-born, and as he possesses the Veda, he is by right the lord of the whole creation. What created being can surpass him, through whose mouth the gods continually consume the sacrificial viands? . . . The very birth of a Brahmana is an external incarnation of the sacred law; for he is born to fulfil the sacred law, and becomes one with Brahman. A Brahman, coming into existence, is born as the highest on earth, the lord of all created beings, for the protection of the treasury of the law. Whatever exists in the world is the property of the Brahmana; on account

downward from the Brahmans in definite decrements of superiority, the equivalent of some stage of inferiority.

There are, however, two marked steps in the system: the one between the twice-born castes (those who may be initiated) and those who cannot be initiated; the other between the uninitiated caste, the Sudras, and the outcaste castes.[47] It is in the character of status of the latter castes that the nature of caste inferiority becomes most evident. As one descends the hierarchy, traits of superiority decrease and those of inferiority increase, until at length the base, the unsightables who defile by permitting themselves to be seen, is reached. Thus, the lower the caste, the fewer the number of castes from which it can expect deference. This does not mean, of course, that intercaste invidiousness on given levels diminishes directly with inferiority of caste position.

Caste Inferiority

Inferiority must necessarily be as much a social fact as superiority. Inferiority is inherent and accepted with equanimity. The poor and degraded in most parts of the world have seldom been able to champion their own cause; and in Brahmanic India, an articulate upper-caste champion of, say, the outcastes, the least of caste-men, has never been known.[48] Such a person could not be heard in the caste system when it is functioning normally.

As a matter of fact, these low-caste people are not seeking a liberator; they are almost always able to find a group lower than themselves, and their preoccupation becomes that of making the latter feel its position of even greater inferiority.[49] It is a virtue to leave low-caste people to their fate, for to question the justice of inferiority among the lowest increment of the population is to question the caste system itself. Unnumbered generations, living in unrelieved grossness, have produced human beings in Brahmanic India who can scarcely believe that a better state is possible for them. According to the Abbé Dubois:

Notwithstanding the miserable condition of these wretched Pariahs, they are never heard to murmur or to complain of their low estate. Still

---

of the excellence of his origin the Brahmana is, indeed, entitled to it all. The Brahmana eats but his own food, wears but his own apparel, bestows but his own alms; other mortals subsist through the benevolence of the Brahmana." I, pp. 92–93, 95, 98–101. "A wise man should . . . never threaten a Brahmana, nor strike him even with a blade of grass." IV, 169.

[47]Vincent A. Smith, *The Oxford History of India*, p. 35. See also *Census of India, 1931*, Vol. I, Pt. 1, pp. 399, 471.

[48]Again we do not speak of westernized Hinduism.

[49]Emile Senart, op. cit., p. 19; John C. Nesfield, op. cit., p. 104.

less do they ever dream of trying to improve their lot, by combining together, and forcing the other classes to treat them with that common respect which one man owes to another. The idea that he was born to be in subjection to the other castes is so ingrained in his mind that it never occurs to the Pariah to think that his fate is anything but irrevocable. Nothing will ever persuade him that men are all made of the same clay, or that he has the right to insist on better treatment than that which is meted out to him.[50]

Thus, attitudes of social inequality are not only strongly impressed upon the culture, but they are also binding upon the least privileged Hindus.[51] One reason for the strength of these attitudes is that they do not involve social conflict; they are not indoctrinated by pressure from some ruling power; they belong to the substance of the caste system. Attempts to disregard this powerful social orientation have resulted in confusion, as the British discovered more than once in their military experience. During the Mutiny of 1857, ranking in the army, on being confronted with caste ranking, was practically reversed. "The predominance of men of high caste, or, at least, the deference that was yielded to their prejudices, was fatal to discipline. A native officer of low caste might often be seen crouching submissively before the Brahman recruit whom he was supposed to command."[52]

Even at the dawn of the stabilization of the caste system these principles of differential respect were laid down in meticulous detail. In one of the law books, for instance, it is proclaimed:

Know that a Brahmana of ten years and a Kshatriya of a hundred years stand to each other in the relation of father and son; but between these two the Brahmana is the father. Wealth, kindred, age, the due performance of rites, and fifthly, sacred learning are titles to respect; but each latter-named cause is more weighty than the preceding ones. . . . The seniority of Brahmanas is from sacred knowledge, that of Kshatriyas from valor, that of Vaisyas from wealth in grain and other goods, but that of Sudras alone from age.[53]

---

[50]Abbé J. A. Dubois, op. cit., p. 50. See also John P. Jones, *India, Its Life and Thought*, p. 209, and William S. Hunt, *India's Outcastes*, pp. 23–24. To the same effect, Wiser and Wiser observed during their recent study that the low-caste Bhangis "become so accustomed to being creatures to be avoided that they feel no resentment. Many a time when we have winced under the scorn or rebuffs which we have suffered because of the Bhangis we had in our tent or motor, we have observed that those who gave rise to the scorn accepted the situation complacently." Op. cit., p. 62.

[51]". . . the Hindu of lower caste, even when highly educated, will still be in a subconscious state of sitting on the edge of the chair in the presence of a man of higher caste." *Census of India, 1921*, Vol. I, Pt. 1, p. 233.

[52]*Cambridge History of India*, Vol. VI, pp. 171–72.

[53]Manu, II, 135–36, 155.

The inferiority of the lowest Brahmanic caste always comes in for particular emphasis,[54] and the farther down we go the more certain the degradation.

Caste as a Fraternity

It is not only birth—that is to say, direct blood relationship—which earns caste membership for the individual. The caste member is a person consciously participating in an in-group with common expectations of reciprocal service. The destiny of the individual is bound up with that of the caste. The caste, in consideration of its welfare, may include or exclude any person—and this notwithstanding birth outside of the caste. Indeed, it is emphasized particularly among the upper castes that birth alone is insufficient for full caste membership. The child must be initiated.[55] Hence, strictly speaking, among upper castes initiation is more significant for caste membership than birth, for, while any individual of alien birth may be included by initiation, native birth without initiation may not signify membership.[56]

The latter fact also contributes to the proposition that physical characteristics are no final determinant of a man's caste affiliation. "The unwritten law of Indian society requires that every Hindu, when asked, must mention not only the names of his paternal and maternal ancestors, but must give also every point of information that he can about such queries as the following: (1) What is your caste? (2) What is your class? (3) What is your Gotra? (4) What is your Pravara? (5) What is your Veda? (6) What is your Sakha? (7) What is your Sutra?"[57] Not all these questions, of course, will be asked of caste-men indiscriminately; low-caste men, for example, will not have a Veda.

---

[54]"Let him not give a Sudra advice, nor the remnants of his meal, nor food offered to the gods; nor let him explain the sacred law to such a man, nor impose upon him a penance. For he who explains the sacred law to a Sudra or dictates to him a penance, will sink together with that man into the hell called Asamvrita." IV, 80–81. "But let a Sudra serve Brahmanas, either for the sake of heaven, or with a view of both this life and the next; for he who is called the servant of a Brahmana thereby gains all his ends. The service of Brahmanas alone is declared to be an excellent occupation for a Sudra; for whatever else besides this he may perform will bear him no fruit." X, 122–23. "No collection of wealth must be made by a Sudra, even though he may be able to do it; for a Sudra who has acquired wealth, gives pain to Brahmanas." X, 129. ". . . the sacrificer may take at his pleasure two or three articles required for a sacrifice from the house of a Sudra, for a Sudra has no business with sacrifices." X, 13. All from Manu.

[55]Manu, II, 39. See also Emile Senart; op. cit., p. 120.

[56]This, of course, should not be taken to imply that the membership of castes consists largely of alien initiates. The concept of initiation is valuable here mainly for an understanding of the nature of the caste association.

[57]J. H. Bhattacharya, *Hindu Castes and Sects,* p. 30.

But the significant fact is that the many indices of belonging are associational in character.

In one sense, then, a caste may be conceived of as a brotherhood in which the individual is able to realize a satisfactory way of life.[58] Denied caste affiliation, the individual becomes a rudderless ship; whereas, in good standing, he is never left alone to bear the full weight of possible misfortune. "A member of the caste, even if he is an orphan, is not helpless, for the caste will feed and protect him and train him in his craft till he can earn his livelihood. . . . It is the caste on which he depends for help at the time of a death in the family. The caste-men are really his friends in need."[59]

It is this heightened emotion of interdependence, which amounts to almost familial concern for the welfare of one another, that accounts in large measure for caste stability. Although the caste is, under certain conditions, sensitive and temperamental, it ordinarily coheres under considerable hardship and vicissitude. It may even change its vocation, its religious orientation, even lose much of its juridical function, and yet remain intact, so far as its membership is concerned.

Caste, Not Slavery

The relationship of one caste to another is not similar to that which exists between master and slave. Slavery implies domination and force. Slavery puts the bondsmen outside the field of social competition; the individual becomes chattel. Under ideal conditions "the slave is not a person."[60] Unlike caste-men, slaves cannot have a common purpose or interest; they cannot have plans or leaders; they cannot conceive of themselves as having a claim or right to any given status. They are auxiliary to their master's interest and contributory to his status.[61]

---

[58]"Caste adds greatly to general contentment. Everyone is pleased and proud of his caste; no one will part with it on any account. It may well be said that no man in any country has more friends in need than Indian caste-men. All the men of the caste, it may be considered, are their brothers' keepers. . . . By the very name of his caste an Indian carries with him, as it were, a certificate of character and reputation of a certain value wherever he goes. He needs no introduction wherever there are caste brethren. He can depend on a hospitable reception. Caste people consider it a binding duty not only to provide for kinsmen and friends, but for all brethren in distress." A. H. Benton, *Indian Moral Instruction and Caste Problems,* p. 17.

[59]R. Mukerjee, op. cit., pp. 45–46. See also Warren H. Wilson, "The Family and Village in India," *Publications of the American Sociological Society,* Vol. XXV, No. 4, November 1931, p. 54.

[60]Goetz A. Briefs, *The Proletariat,* p. 28.

[61]Cf. Gunnar Landtman, *The Origin of the Inequality of the Social Classes,* p. 229.

Slaves are personally, spatially immobile and cannot become organized. Their only possible common purpose is that of revolt. They can, indeed, unite for purposes of insurrection, but then they become a power group and not a caste. Neither do masters constitute a "caste," for masters may be a heterogeneous group, having in common only the circumstance that they possess the wherewithal to purchase and maintain a large or small number of slaves.

Slaves are not the lowest class in a society; they are "out-classed"; that is, they are completely without class status. Moreover, slaves are neither the lowest caste nor outcastes. If the culture is compatible with slavery, as it was not in America, slaves may become highly accommodated, but they will always be kept from organizing as an interest group. While a slave society is based upon some form of coercion, the caste system is maintained by consensus. The one is, at most, an accommodation situation; the other is an agglomeration of assimilated cultural entities.

2. *The Nature of Caste, Continued* ———

Caste Assimilated

BRAHMANIC INDIA CONSTITUTES A CASTE SOCIETY, AND THE LIFE of unwesternized Hindus is so closely geared to it that any other social arrangement is inconceivable. No one ever discusses, far less questions, the caste system. Caste is the "bedrock" of Hindu life.[1] "An Indian considers his caste as the thing of all things to him of the most importance. Any lively fear of interference with it will arouse him, without hesitation and without waiting to count the cost, to take the most desperate measures."[2] Caste in India, then, is right—not right for Brahmans only, but right and proper for all caste-men regardless of status.[3]

When one uses the norms of Western society as a basis of judgment, caste may seem partial or even unjust—indeed, wholly intolerable.[4] But far from being intolerably burdened, seemingly underprivileged caste-men are actually proud of their caste. Consider, in illustration, the following observation by J. H. Bhattacharya:

> While the Brahman guests eat, the Sudras have to wait in a different part of the house. It is not, however, to be supposed that Sudras take offense at such treatment. On the contrary, they not only wait patiently, but in some places, insist upon eating the leavings of the Brahmans, and refuse to eat anything from clean plates.[5]

[1] Cf. Shri Shridhar Nehru, op. cit., p. 2.

[2] A. H. Benton, op. cit., p. 26.

[3] We are not thinking here of caste under the impact of Western civilization.

[4] The following poetic flight of Arnold J. Toynbee shows to what extent the outsider might go in his criticism: "Caste is always on the verge of being a social enormity; but when caste is 'keyed up' by receiving a religious interpretation and a religious sanction in a society . . . then the latent enormity of the institution is bound to rankle into a morbid social growth of poisonous tissue and monstrous proportions." *A Study of History,* Vol. IV, p. 230.

[5] Op. cit. "The Hindu does not feel caste a burden as the individualistic occidental might. To him it seems both natural and desirable, its deliberate breach unnatural, perverse and unforgivable. Whatever his caste, the Hindu is proud of it, as Westerners are of their nationality. It gives him a sense of solidarity, and he does not seek to escape it." A. L. Kroeber, op. cit.

The caste system does not represent a social order in unstable equilibrium; it represents rather a powerful norm toward which social variations tend to gravitate; it is capable of perpetuating itself indefinitely. Its practice and theory are in complete synchronism; it does not rationalize its position; its scriptures are outspoken on the point of man's inequality to man; it has no shortcomings; it does not excuse itself; it is totally excellent.

The caste system is in the mores of all caste Hindus, not in those of Brahmans only; hence a man's caste is normal and natural for him. It is sufficient for the realization of his spiritual and social ideals; there is no individual striving or aspiration to move beyond its bounds. A man's acceptance of his caste does not amount to despairing resignation to an ill fate; indeed, opportunity considered, it is taken with less scruple or thought than Occidentals accept Christianity. Resting securely upon universal consensus, the system is taken for granted, and it cannot be legislated out of existence or defeated on the battlefield.[6]

Yet the caste system is a cultural phenomenon and, as such, capable of and subject to change. What the sword cannot do, another culture might. Even in India cultures may match their strength and struggle for ascendancy. Before the impingement of Western culture upon the system there was no "caste question" in India.[7] Today, however, and for many years since the invasion of Western ideas and artifacts, some Hindus are beginning to doubt or, at any rate, to discuss the principles of caste. The area of greatest disorganization is about the cities, the centers of communication. As would be expected, the leaders of social change are moved by different degrees of enthusiasm:

We find progressive opinion taking two distinct positions. First, there are those who consider . . . caste an evil which must be overthrown and a better social order substituted. . . . To this class belong the Brahmo Samajists and a few leaders of prominence. . . . The other position is held by those who would retain caste as a system, believing it to be an essential part of Hindu culture, but who would abolish the practice of "untouchability". . . . They hold that Hinduism as a system is simply caste, and that in abolishing caste they would also be destroying Hinduism. . . . To the orthodox Hindu, caste is religion.[8]

---

[6]Cf. G. S. Ghurye, op. cit., pp. 95, 161.

[7]Merciless as some of the Mohammedan rulers were toward Hinduism as a religion, they nevertheless yielded finally to the power of caste. It might have conquered them completely, had it not been for the coming of Western culture. The early Greek invaders did not even so much as make the system self-conscious.

[8]Martin Luther Dolbeer, "The Movement for the Emancipation of Untouchable Classes in South India," Master's Thesis, University of Chicago, 1929, pp. 124, 125, 135. See also William Crooke, *Things Indian,* p. 68, and A. C. Underwood, *Contemporary Thought of India,* p. 139. The advocates of "Varnashrama Dharma"

One probable sign of the weakening of the theoretical basis of caste in the light of Western culture is the defensive, rationalizing, and apologetic attitude of many educated Indians in their discussion of the system. One of their most satisfying approaches is to compare "a caste" with some institution in Western society, such as the old guilds, or with social classes. The lower class, the untouchables, will then be seen as only somewhat worse off than slum dwellers. And of course the implication must follow that the evil may be remedied by giving somewhat more attention to the development of social-service organization.

Probably another sign is an unwillingness to make records of caste membership. Official recognition of the existence of castes may tend to give them undesirable prestige:

On the occasion of each successive census since 1901, a certain amount of criticism has been directed at the census for taking any note at all of the fact of caste. It has been alleged that the mere act of labeling persons as belonging to a caste tends to perpetuate this system, and . . . a campaign against any record of caste was attempted in 1931. . . . On the whole, it is fair to conclude that there is a tendency for the limitations of caste to be loosened and for the rigid distinctions to be broken down.[9]

The indices of cultural change in India are indeed numerous; we make reference here, however, merely to indicate the fact that at certain points the system is in disintegration; and, naturally, where this is so, we may not have representative instances of the system functioning normally.

Inequality of Man Fundamental

In all societies of any considerable degree of complexity, it will be found that there has developed some means of differential treatment of individuals.[10] In class societies, social equality at birth is obviously ruled out. In many societies, there has not even been a presumption of equality in the law.[11] Obviously, were groups to stand to each other in the relation of conqueror and conquered, or of master and slave, there could be no social equality. In no society, however, is the idea of social inequality so thoroughly organized as in the caste system.

Not by accident are men here unequal, not by luck or by variations in personal effort, not because of differences in race or defeat in war,

---

(the caste way of life of which Mahatma Gandhi is a sympathizer) are devoted to a policy in defense of the system against the attacks of Western ideas. See Romain Rolland, *Mahatma Gandhi,* pp. 45ff., and G. S. Ghurye, op. cit., pp. 182–83.

[9] *Census of India, 1931,* Vol. I, Pt. 1, pp. 430, 432.

[10] Gunnar Landtman, *The Origin of the Inequality of the Social Classes.*

[11] E. A. Ross, *New-Age Sociology,* p. 272.

but because of the Divine Plan in the creation of the social order. Society rests upon group inequality—stable inequality; without it the caste system could not exist. We could not conceive, for example, of a situation in which lower castes moved progressively up in social status until the status of all castes approximated each other, and, at the same time, have a caste system. Long before such a possibility could be achieved, the caste system would have destroyed itself.

In the caste system, group inequality is a social virtue appreciated by the whole hierarchy of castes; it is the only means by which the low castes as well as the high can survive; and caste survival is a preoccupation of all castes.

Therefore, in the operation of Brahmanic law, caste-men are carefully distinguished. Manu declares thus:

A Sudra who has intercourse with a woman of a twice-born caste, guarded or unguarded, shall be punished in the following manner: if she was unguarded he loses the part offending and all his property; if she was guarded, everything, even his life. For intercourse with a Brahmani, a Vaisya shall forfeit all his property after imprisonment for a year; a Kshatriya shall be fined one thousand (panas) and be shaved with the urine of an ass. . . . A Brahmana who carnally knows a guarded Brahmani against her will, shall be fined.[12]

Although the caste system does not depend upon force for its maintenance, breaches of caste etiquette are liable to be followed by terrible punishment. "A once-born man, who insults a twice-born man with gross invective, shall have his tongue cut out; for he is of low origin. If he mentions the names and castes of the twice-born with contumely, an iron nail, ten fingers long, shall be thrust red-hot into his mouth."[13] Today, of course, the British will have none of this in India, but the present awful fear on the part of low-caste men of the judgment of their superiors may be indicative of a frightfully brutal past.

It is the law that high-caste men may punish their inferiors at will or have them punished on the spot for breaches of caste etiquette. "When the Kshatriyas become in any way overbearing towards the Brahmanas, the Brahmanas themselves shall duly restrain them."[14]

---

[12]Manu, VIII, 374–75, 378. See also 279–82, and Vishnu, V, 19–25. "I will next propound the manner of deciding cases of defamation. A Kshatriya having defamed a Brahmana, shall be fined one hundred (paras) ; a Vaisya, one hundred and fifty or two hundred; a Sudra shall suffer corporal punishment. A Brahmana shall be fined fifty (paras) for defaming a Kshatriya; in the case of a Vaisya the fine shall be twenty-five (paras) ; in the case of a Sudra, twelve." Manu, VIII, 266–68. Incidentally this is a Hindu form of wergild.

[13]Manu, VIII, 270–71.

[14]Manu, IX, 320. See also XI, 31–35.

Even to this day it is well within the prerogative of high-caste men to administer corporal punishment to their inferiors.

Eating Habits

Among the many marks which distinguish castes, eating habits are significant. The ritual of eating is both religious and social. What a man eats and how he eats it affect not only his status as a caste-man but also the welfare of his soul. "The foolish man who, after having eaten a Shaddha-dinner, gives the leavings to a Sudra, falls headlong into the Kalasutra hell."[15] Persons of some of the lower castes may pollute the meal of other caste-men by merely looking upon it;[16] and conversely, foods may be utterly ruined if at mealtime men of certain upper castes happen to see certain low-caste men, or a dog, for example. "There are abundant proofs that the repast has kept a religious meaning for the Hindus. The Brahman avoids eating at the same time or out of the same vessel not only with a stranger or an inferior, but even with his own wife and his yet uninitiated sons."[17]

The status of commensals, of course, is of prime importance. The rule is that persons of different castes may not eat together.

A Kshatriya who comes to the house of a Brahmana is not called a guest. . . . But if a Kshatriya comes to the house in the manner of a guest, the householder may feed him . . . after the above-mentioned Brahmanas have eaten. Even a Vaisya and a Sudra who have approached his house in the manner of guests, he may allow to eat with his servants, showing thereby his compassionate disposition.[18]

There is a tendency for social distances to become narrowed among persons who eat together, and this fact is not limited to Hindu society. But it has been recognized from earliest times in Brahmanic India, and every device and fiction have been developed to keep tables apart. However, there may be breaches of the rules of commensality, especially among the lower castes, without resulting in loss of caste identity.

---

[15]Manu, III, 249.

[16]Emile Senart, op. cit., p. 93.

[17]Ibid., p. 181. The practice of separate eating may assume an aspect so deeply religious as to constitute in itself the principal overt barrier between social groups. "Ordinarily, no doubt, when people will not eat together, still less will they intermarry. But this is not always the case. Among the Agarwals, for instance, members of different religious sects intermarry but do not eat together. At marriage the wife is formally admitted into her husband's sect, and must in future have her food cooked separately when she stays with her own people." H. H. Risley, op. cit., p. 153.

[18]Manu, III, 110–12.

In comparing the rigidity of these rules with those against intermarriage, Senart says:

> Speaking generally, we may take it that only those may eat together who are allowed to intermarry. . . . The twelve sections of the Kayasths of Bengal may no more eat in company than they may permit alliances with one another. However, all things considered, the prohibition here is less strict. Many sections of castes between which marriage is unlawful do not refrain from sharing meals together. Moreover, custom in this respect varies from one part of the country to another, still more than marriage laws.[19]

Furthermore, what a caste-man eats may be a mark of his general caste position. Only low-caste men eat meat and drink liquor. Among some orthodox castes there is probably no greater offense than that of eating beef. This has been known to be the one act which may result in final and irrevocable excommunication. Upper-caste Hindus are vegetarians; but, while many castes eat animal flesh, the lowest alone eat beef. "There are castes whose touch defiles the twice-born, but who refrain from the crowning enormity of eating beef; while below these again, in the social system of Upper India, are the people like Chamars and Doms who eat beef and various sorts of miscellaneous vermin."[20] We may repeat, then, that both the kind of food and his table companions may be of vital concern to a man's caste.[21]

Caste and Subcaste

Failing to differentiate between the caste and the subcaste has resulted in no little confusion in discussions of the caste system. The caste and the subcaste may be so significantly different that reference to one when the other is meant may be totally misleading. The caste includes the subcaste; ordinarily the subcaste, not the caste, is the endogamous unit; usually the subcaste, not the caste, is organized; the individual is mainly identified with the subcaste.

One caste may include more than a thousand subcastes, or it may be without any subcaste whatever. When the latter is the case, the caste, as a social phenomenon, is identical with the subcaste. The larger the number of subcastes and the larger the geographical area over which

---

[19]Emile Senart, op. cit., p. 39.

[20]H. H. Risley, op. cit., p. 112. See also Senart, op. cit., pp. 47–50. Upper-caste Hindus also "severely disapprove" the use of spiritous liquors.

[21]Like many other caste practices, the application of eating restrictions may be reciprocal: "Their authority is so absolute that Santals—a very low caste in Bengal —have been known to die of hunger in times of famine rather than touch food even prepared by Brahmans." Ibid., p. 39.

they are spread, the more the caste tends to be destitute of those attributes which characterize the subcaste. In order, consequently, that this discussion may not be burdened with modifying statements, we shall assume that all castes have subcastes, or that castes without subcastes are in fact sociological subcastes.

The caste is a potential interest group which may become organized for political action. This interest may be so vaguely operative that it is possible for a caste to have had a history of hundreds of years without ever knowing, precisely, the number and distribution of its subcastes, far less ever coming together for any concerted purpose. It is also true that subcastes may hold subcastes of the same caste in greater social disdain than subcastes of other castes. However, in any given area of communication, social change may affect the common occupation of many subcastes, or the status of all subcastes claiming a common original heritage may be threatened,[22] in which case the caste or part of it comes together to defend itself. Indeed, it may come together as an interest group for aggressive purposes also.

We should expect the status of all subcastes to approximate each other, but this is not always so. Some of the larger castes have subcastes over large areas of India, and these subcastes may have widely different positions in the different district hierarchies.[23] Moreover, within the same hierarchical area a large caste, such as the Brahmans, may have subcastes with statuses varying almost as widely as the status amplitude of the social hierarchy itself.[24]

---

[22]"The decision as to what does, and what does not, constitute a caste is largely a matter of degree. In practice, cases will arise where it is difficult to come to a decision. The word Brahman is a case in point. There are numerous communities claiming this designation which not only do not intermarry, but are widely separated from each other in respect of race, status, and social customs. But they all have the same *traditional occupation* and the same *reputed origin;* and there can be no doubt that, both in their own eyes and in those of the public, these links constitute a bond which, when a broad view is taken, overshadows the secondary distinctions that actually exist." *Census of India, 1911,* Vol. I, Pt. 1, p. 367. (Italics added.) The use of the word "secondary" here may be misleading. In saying "these links," traditional occupation and reputed origin, "constitute a bond which overshadows the secondary distinctions," the meaning is that even the distinctions derived from the powerful elementary forces of subcaste cohesion: endogamy, status, and custom —particularly the actual occupation—may not be sufficient to nullify such indices of reputed *caste* membership as common origin and traditional occupation. In this citation the subcaste ties are taken for granted, while emphasis is put upon those apparently nebulous symbols of belonging which give the subcaste its claim of inclusion within the caste.

[23]On this point G. S. Ghurye may be misleading in holding that "the status, in the hierarchy, of any sub-caste depends upon the caste." Op. cit., p. 20.

[24]"The social position of Brahmans is . . . infinitely varied, and it is extremely difficult to arrange in order of respectability people who practice such diversity of function. The highest in the list of those devoted to religious functions are those priests who profess to celebrate the purest Vedic ritual; next come those who pre-

The caste has no established form of government or organization for control of the subcaste; it neither limits nor directs the formation of new subcastes.

The caste, unless it has no subcastes, is not endogamous; the subcaste is the endogamous unit. In some localities, however, intermarriage restrictions across subcaste lines are less rigid than across caste lines.[25] Yet the fact remains that endogamy is of prime importance to the subcaste and relaxation of this rule is exceptional. Referring to the Brahmans, Crooke observes:

> It would . . . be an error to suppose that all Brahmans form one homogeneous caste . . . a group the members of which freely intermarry and dine together. On the contrary, the subordinate groups classed under the general name of Brahman are practically independent of each other, and occupy very different positions in the social scale. . . . In Bombay . . . the Brahmans number slightly over a million, and have more than two hundred groups, none of which intermarries with another. In Madras the Brahmans fall into six linguistic groups, each speaking a different tongue, and no member of any one group will marry or eat with a member of another.[26]

---

tend to perform any priestly function of the higher class. In the third grade come astrologers, family priests, and the lower class of instructors in the mysteries of Hinduism. The fourth group includes the sorcerer, the fortune-teller, the river-priest, who all frequent places of pilgrimage, and the temple priest. In the lowest rank of all comes the funeral-priest, who is an object of abhorrence to all respectable Hindus." William Crooke, op. cit., p. 24. See also John C. Nesfield, op. cit., p. 49. Manu's declaration that a Brahman is a Brahman regardless of circumstances might be a factor responsible for that more or less vague sense of solidarity which we call a common interest, but it has not been able to identify the status of all Brahmans. The Lawgiver says: "A Brahmana, be he ignorant or learned, is a great divinity. . . . Thus, though Brahmanas employ themselves in all sorts of mean occupations, they must be honored in every way, for each of them is a great deity." IX, 317, 319.

In a discussion of this point the question was put to the writer: "Is any Kshatriya or Vaisya subcaste ever of higher status than the lowest Brahman subcaste?" The evidence of the data seems to indicate an affirmative answer. But we should remember that this classification is mythical or at most suggestive only. There are no *four* castes in India in which all the other subcastes can meaningfully claim membership. The Maha-Brahman and the funeral-priest are apparently not higher in status than, say, subcastes of landowners or of writers. Certain subcastes of Brahmans are always on top, but there are those called Brahman who are virtually untouchable.

Thus, according to Danzil Ibbetson, ". . . there are Brahmans who are looked upon as outcasts by those who under the fourfold classification would be called Sudras. . . . The Maha Brahman, so impure that in many villages he is not allowed to enter the gates, the Dakaut and Gujrati, so unfortunate that other Brahmans will not accept offerings at their hands, are all Brahmans, but are practically differentiated as distinct castes by their special occupations." See the *Census of India, 1901,* Vol. I, ethnographic appendices, pp. 234, 237.

[25]*Census of India, 1911,* Vol. I, Pt. 1, p. 368.

[26]William Crooke, op. cit., p. 63. M. A. Sherring listed more than 1,880 subcastes of Brahmans and about 600 subdivisions of Rajputs. Op. cit., xxii–xlvi. See also Emile Senart, op. cit., p. 15.

The individual's devotion and loyalties go to the subcaste. The subcaste, then, is the unit of social organization within the caste system. By unit of social organization we mean the fundamental point of social reference in the individual's life organization; in so far as his caste status is concerned, his subcaste is what he is. The caste has a greater variety of occupations than the subcaste; indeed, we should expect it to be more heterogeneous with respect to any given characteristic than the subcaste. The latter is the more responsible entity, and it is to the subcaste that we most commonly refer when discussing the characteristics of the caste system. Elsewhere in this study also, when we speak of "the caste"—unless we modify the statement, or it is clearly apparent that a subcaste could not be meant—we shall be referring to the subcaste.

Social Distance and Purity

Social distance, or the tendency of individuals or groups to keep other individuals or groups outside of a certain socio-psychological aura of the former's individuality, is intensified in India by the idea of impurity or defilement. Social distance has become an important part of Hindu religious ritual. It is the individuating factor among castes; it formalizes their interdependence. Says Bouglé: "These specialized groups are not only superposed, but opposed. The power which animates the Hindu is a force of repulsion which holds the bodies separate and causes each to fall back within itself."[27] Max Weber puts it strongly: "Caste means, from the point of view of the group, the enhancement and carrying over of the idea of social distance into religion or, more particularly, magic."[28]

The doctrine of purity has given to social distance among castes an important physical aspect as well. The violence with which the integrity of the body of one caste-man has been protected from the contaminating presence of other caste-men is curtly suggested by Manu: "A low-caste man who tries to place himself on the same seat with a man of high caste shall be branded on the hip and banished, or the king shall cause his buttock to be gashed."[29]

Thus, in Brahmanic India social distance is involved with the idea of impurity and means more than a psychological barrier which limits the possibility of certain individuals identifying their aspirations and problems; it is also a prophylaxis against spiritual and bodily defilement. Of significance for an understanding of the caste system is the fact that the

[27]C. Bouglé, op. cit., p. 25.
[28]Max Weber, *Gesammelte Aufsatze zur Religionssoziologie,* Vol. II, p. 44.
[29]Manu, VIII, 281.

power of one man to pollute another depends upon the number of degrees below, in caste position, the former is from the latter.

It is not always clear whether a man's power to pollute establishes his caste status, or whether it is his position which renders him contaminative. In some communities, however, a man's ability to pollute is known to the nearest foot. "The lower a man's caste the more polluting he is, and the higher he is, the more sensitive he is to pollution. A Brahman in Malabar is polluted if an outcaste comes within ninety paces of him, but a man a little lower is not polluted if the outcaste keeps fifty paces away."[30] Even among the lowest castes, the outcastes, pollution may result from intercaste contact.[31] Under these conditions, of course, communal segregation becomes a necessity; indeed, the use of a common road is frequently impossible.

The inferior-superior relationship of a caste, then, may be stated in terms of its purity. A caste is pure or impure according to its hierarchical position.[32] Our purpose here is not to indicate that one group of Hindus is considered pure and another impure. Such a concept would not only be contrary to fact, but also inconsistent with principles of caste. The feeling for purity is atomized and interlays the numerous castes of the hierarchy. It is this idea of a purity-impurity matrix rather than that of a dichotomy which is significant for an understanding of the system.

Further, it should be made quite clear that purity among Hindus, so far as it concerns human beings, does not mean purity of blood or purity of "race"; it means purity of caste.[33] Therefore, there can be no ocular proof of purity, unless the whole circumstance of the individual indicates his caste or bodily state.[34]

---

[30]William S. Hunt, *India's Outcastes,* p. 19. Risley states further that: "In Madras, especially, the idea of ceremonial pollution by the proximity of a member of an unclean caste has been developed with much elaboration. Thus the table of social precedence attached to the Cochin report shows that while a Mayar can pollute a man of a higher caste only by touching him, people of the Kammalan group, including masons, blacksmiths, carpenters, and workers in leather, pollute at a distance of twenty-four feet; toddy-drawers at thirty-six feet; Pulayan or Cheruman cultivators at forty-eight feet; while in the case of the Paraiyan (Pariahs) who eat beef, the range of pollution is stated to be no less than sixty-four feet." Ibid., p. 112.

[31]Ibid., p. 33.

[32]Shridhar V. Ketkar, *The History of Caste in India,* Vol. I, p. 23.

[33]"The darker complexioned 'southern' Brahman claims to enjoy a higher rank of purity than his brethren of northern India. Unlike the Brahman of the North, there is no lower caste from whose hands he will take water. The reason which he will assign for this is that Hinduism in the North has been defiled by one conqueror after another, while, isolated in the South, it has remained untouched by foreign influence." William Crooke, op. cit., p. 65. See also John C. Nesfield, op. cit., p. 108.

[34]Modern literature on caste, however, is overburdened with allusions or explicit statements to the effect that upper castes have been contriving to keep their "blood

The feeling for social purity probably got its impetus during the early struggle for superiority and pre-emption of function between Brahmans and Kshatriyas; it evidently has its rationale in the Brahmanic argument for exclusiveness at the sacrifice. A good deal of the Brahman's importance was achieved by comparing his position with the extreme inferiority of other persons:

> The Brahmanical law-books . . . repeatedly emphasize the law that members of the lowest castes (the Sudras and the Chandals) may not learn the sacred texts; for impure as a corpse, as a burial place, is the Sudra, therefore the Veda may not be recited in his vicinity.[35]

One significant aspect of the purity belief is that certain persons and objects considered holy may be defiled by bringing them into contact with the vulgar. The priests had achieved not only blessedness for themselves but also inviolability for all that they could call theirs; moreover, they capitalized their position by developing a "science of purity" for all society.[36] In connection with the sacrifice, the early Vedic literature is critical about the possible participation of different castes, while it ostracizes low-caste persons altogether:

> The Sudra is prohibited from milking the cow for the milk required at the . . . oblation to Agni; and the Satapatha Brahmana forbids a man who has been consecrated for a sacrifice to speak to a Sudra at all . . . At the sacrifice itself the Sudra could not be present in the "hall"; he is definitely classed in the Satapatha Brahmana as unfit for sacrifice. . . . At the Pravargya rite the performer is not allowed to come in contact with a Sudra.[37]

Thus, the spirit of exclusiveness is sanctioned in the religious attitudes of the people. Purity is ceremonial rather than hygienic;[38] and

---

pure," meaning, of course, their "white blood." The great emphasis upon purity in the sacred books of the Hindus is assumed to refer willy-nilly to purity of racial stock. See, for example, Shridhar V. Ketkar, op. cit., Vol. II, p. 92.

[35]Maurice Winternitz, *A History of Indian Literature,* trans. by S. Ketkar, Vol. I, pp. 35–36.

[36]"Their code is a part of the Vedas, which none but the Brahmans may teach; the secret of uncleanness is therefore in their possession, and forms by no means an inconsiderable branch of their trade, as it is requisite for the inhabitants on every emergency to apply to some expounder of the Vedas. The Brahmanic expounder of the laws of impurity is therefore a person of no little consequence in the commonwealth, his aid being required much more frequently than that of a physician." *Essays Related to the Habits, Character and Moral Improvement of Hindus,* pp. 256–57.

[37]Arthur Anthony Macdonell and Arthur Berriedale Keith, *Vedic Index,* Vol. II, pp. 389–90. See also *Census of India, 1931,* Vol. I, Pt. 1, p. 496. Compare the Mosaic law in Numbers 1:49–54, where the Levites are given exclusive charge of e tabernacle, with the injunction: "The stranger that cometh nigh shall be put death."

[38]On this point the Abbé Dubois is clear: ". . . to complete his purification, he is made to drink the *panchagavia*. These words . . . signify literally *the five things*

the state of impurity may exist either between members of one caste, between members of different castes, or between human beings and any other objects. Intercaste impurity is permanent, but intracaste impurity may be cleansed.[39] A Pariah, as the outcaste person is sometimes called, could not wash himself clean; no ceremony could remove his taint; he is unalterably unclean. Indeed, Vishnu insisted that he must do nothing to make it appear that he considers himself clean; his clothes must be the discarded raiment of the dead.[40] "A healthy, clean-minded outcaste would have to keep the prescribed distance from an immoral and leprous Brahman, so as to prevent the latter from being polluted by him."[41]

On the other hand, individual uncleanness within the caste may be removed by religious acts and ritual. Of particular interest from the point of view of caste relationship is the fact that the lower the polluting caste, the more difficult it is to rid oneself of the pollution. For instance:

When a Brahman follows the corpse of another Brahman of different kindred, he must purify himself by bathing, touching fire, and eating clarified butter. If the corpse belongs to the military caste, the Brahman

---

or substances derived from the body of the cow: namely, milk, curds, ghee, dung and urine, which are mixed together. The last-named, urine, is looked upon as the most efficacious Hindus for purifying any kind of uncleanness. I have often seen superstitious Hindus following the cows to pasture, waiting for the moment when they could collect the precious liquid in vessels of brass, and carrying it away while still warm to their houses. I have also seen them waiting to catch it in the hollow of their hands, drinking some of it and rubbing their faces and heads with the rest." Op. cit., p. 43. "Nothing can equal the supposed virtues of this mixture. Brahmins and other Hindus frequently drink it to remove both external and internal defilements." Ibid., p. 153. See also p. 125 and Manu XI, 92.

Another possibility, especially from the point of view of complacency in the lower-caste man, is exemplified in the following admonition: "He shall not ordinarily give the residue of his food to a person who is not a Brahman. When he gives it to such a one, he shall clean his teeth and give the food after having placed in it the dirt from his teeth." *Sacred Books of the East,* Vol. II, Pt. 1. Apastamba I, 11, 31, 24.

"Among the Hindoos health is scarcely affected [by ceremonial uncleanness]; its chief effect is to incapacitate the individual for performance of religious duties. Ceremonial impurity is defined [as] *that which invisibly occasions a suspension of the duties commanded in the Vedas.* While a person is unclean, he can neither perform his religious duties, nor partake of food with those of his own caste, nor receive or bestow either presents or instruction." *Essays Related to the Habits, Character and Moral Improvement of the Hindoos,* p. 245.

"It must . . . be remembered that the Hindu is given much more to seeking ceremonial than sanitary cleanliness. It matters not how filthy the water may be, chemically; if it be ceremonially clean, he uses it freely. If it be ceremonially polluting, it is eschewed." John P. Jones, *India, Its Life and Thought,* p. 267.

[39]It may be well to recall that we are referring here to the subcaste. There is impurity between subcaste and subcaste within the same caste (e.g., among Brahmans).

[40]Vishnu, XVI, 14.

[41]William S. Hunt, op. cit., p. 17. See also p. 20.

who follows it is unclean for one day; if to the commercial class, he is unclean two days . . . if the deceased be of the servile class, for three days, after which he must perform one hundred Pranayamas. A Pranayama is performed by closing each nostril successively, and exhaling breath . . . accompanied with internal meditation.[42]

The situations in which one person may pollute another are exceedingly numerous; therefore, we shall not attempt to list them. In the case of objects, the ritual of purity is also delicate and complicated. The cow, dog, pig, snake, monkey, water, bread, milk, ghee, clothing, leaves, and a host of other objects come in for specific ritualistic attention, breaches of which may result in states of impurity.[43]

This belief in impurity, this cultural trait which ramifies Hindu society, attains an extreme in the phenomenon of untouchability. The high-caste man will be veritably horror-stricken if by accident he should come into contact with a Pariah.[44] But the sense of untouchability is not limited to two groups; it pervades the system. There is untouchability among untouchables. "The exterior castes themselves are . . . guilty of similar treatment to each other, and an exterior caste which considers itself to be on a higher social level than another exterior caste adopts exactly the same attitude as the higher castes do towards the exterior castes."[45] Untouchability, then, is a deep-seated cultural trait of Hinduism. Ghurye thinks that it is the characteristic fact of Hindu society.[46]

The indication seems to be, however, that untouchability is merely a heightened manifestation of the larger attitude of impurity, or social distance made sacrosanct. The untouchable is not hated primarily; he is feared for his power to defile any of certain classes of men with whom he may come into contact; and the unregenerated untouchable sin-

---

[42]*Essays Related to . . . Hindoos,* op. cit., p. 254.

[43]"There are some varieties of food which would be very easily polluted, e.g., bread made in water. Such a bread a man cannot eat at any time. He should eat it only after bathing and wearing a special consecrated cloth. The bread also must be especially prepared with such ceremonial purity. If any bread is to be left over for another meal, it should be kept in a select and ceremonially pure place in the house by a man who may be in the pure condition. . . . Bread made in milk does not demand so many formalities in order to guard against pollution. You can make the bread in milk, put it in a can of tinned brass, put it in your pocket, and go any place, even wearing a shoe·made of cowhide; but still the bread could not be polluted. Articles like Pedha, which are made of milk and sugar only, would not be polluted even if a Mohammedan, Christian or low-caste Hindu touched them." Shridhar V. Ketkar, op. cit., Vol. II, p. 90, note.

[44]Bouglé, op. cit., p. 26.

[45]*Census of India, 1931,* Vol. I, Pt. 1, p. 498.

[46]"It would seem that the Hindu system is unique only in this: that it alone classified some groups as untouchable and unapproachable." G. S. Ghurye, op. cit., p. 142. Cf. *Cambridge History of India,* Vol. I, p. 234.

cerely believes that his presence pollutes other men. Just as the intelligent, tubercular person knows that it is right to keep children away from his bedside, so, also, the untouchable recognizes the danger in other men's coming too near him. Indeed, in order to cause as little suffering to high-caste men as possible, he would willingly announce his approach when walking abroad.

The social continuity of the phenomena of untouchability and impurity is illustrated in Dr. Ghurye's observation:

> In the Maratha country a Maha—one of the untouchables—might not spit on the road lest a pure-caste Hindu should be polluted by touching it with his foot, but had to carry an earthen pot, hung from his neck, in which to spit. Further, he had to drag a thorny branch with him to wipe out his footprints and to lie at a distance, prostrate on the ground, if a Brahmin passed by, so that his foul shadow might not defile the holy Brahmin.[47]

Thus the impure caste-man or anything associated with him is untouchable; and, of course, the greater the impurity of his caste, the more contaminating is his touch. Therefore, we may conclude that untouchability is not a unique phenomenon; it is part of a general attitude which serves to limit association between caste and caste; it is not a conflict attitude. "They may be untouchables to the rest of their co-religionists, but among themselves they have degrees of untouchability and superiority."[48] This being so, one wonders about Mahatma Gandhi's position:

> If untouchability was a part of the Hindu creed, I should decline to call myself a Hindu and most decidedly embrace some other faith if it satisfied my honest aspirations. Fortunately for me, I hold that untouchability is not a part of Hinduism.[49]

Of course a good question for debaters would be whether Hindus have a "creed." We agree with the consensus of opinion that they have not.[50] Further, it seems that untouchability is very much a part of Hinduism; in fact, it belongs to the very tissue of the social structure.[51]

---

[47]G. S. Ghurye, op. cit., pp. 11–12.

[48]M. D. Altekar, "Caste System and Its Relation to Social and Economic Life," *Annals of the American Academy,* Vol. CXLIV, Pt. 2, p. 186.

[49]Mahatma Gandhi, *Young India, 1924–1926,* p. 12.

[50]See A. C. Underwood, *Contemporary Thought of India,* p. 140.

[51]Says W. S. Hunt: "We must not suppose that Hindus avoid pollution merely because of the expense it causes. To the orthodox it really matters. It has for them 'the nature of sin.' It affects their karma, and therefore, their status in their next life. The high-caste lady would genuinely believe that she had been made unclean, that her ceremonial purity had been besmirched, by the propinquity of those unclean outcastes if they had dared to come too near her. Ceremonial purity is, indeed, for

It is an indispensable complement of the religion of caste, by which alone the psychic stability of the caste hierarchy has been achieved.

Some twenty-five hundred years ago Manu had a system of purity worked out with almost mathematical exactness. In order that Brahmans might attain their extreme superiority, there had to be extremely inferior men. We might mention that Gandhi himself, who knows the Christian Gospels well, is still unable to rise very far beyond the principles of impurity and its logical extreme, untouchability. The Mahatma would probably do the impossible: remove untouchability but otherwise maintain the caste system intact.[52]

---

the reason just mentioned, the Hindu's most prized possession." *India's Outcastes,* p. 16.

[52]"I do not regard inter-dining and inter-marriage as an essential to the removal of Untouchability. I believe in Varnashram Dharma [caste principles]. . . . In my Ashram, Dudhabhai, one of the 'untouchable' inmates, dines with the rest without any distinction. But I do not recommend to anybody outside the Ashram to follow this example. . . . the reform contemplated in the untouchability movement does not obliterate the restrictions as to inter-dining and inter-marrying. I cannot recommend wholesale abolition of these restrictions. . . . I want to remove untouchability because its removal is essential for Swaraj [home rule], and I want Swaraj." Mahatma Gandhi, op. cit., pp. 649–51.

On April 29, 1947, the Indian Constituent Assembly "outlawed untouchability." It should be interesting to observe the way in which this law affects caste-men of different degrees of orthodoxy.

3. Religion and Caste

*R*ELIGION IN INDIA IS SO THOROUGHLY INTERMESHED IN THE fabric of Hindu culture that some special consideration of it seems indispensable. It is well known that India is a country of religions, and that not only contradictory beliefs but also primitive and advanced systems exist side by side. There is thus no such thing as *the* Hindu religion. There are certain aspects of Hinduism, however, which remain fairly stable throughout the culture.

The Meaning of Hinduism

In Brahmanic India there is no word for religion because everything is religious. Hinduism is the customary way of life of the Hindus made sacrosanct. Art, technology, law, science, and learning are inseparable from religion; and from this point of view, Indian culture is primitive.[1] According to the Abbé Dubois:

There is not one of their ancient usages, not one of their observances, which has not some religious principle or object attached to it. Everything, indeed, is governed by superstition and has religion for its motive. The style of greeting, the mode of dressing, the cut of clothes, the shape of ornaments and their manner of adjustment, the various details of the toilette, the architecture of the houses, the corners where the hearth is placed and where the cooking pots must stand, the manner of going to bed and of sleeping, the forms of civility and politeness that must be observed: all these are severely regulated.

During the many years that I have studied Hindu customs I cannot say that I ever observed a single one, however unimportant and simple, and I may add, however filthy and disgusting, which did not rest on some religious principle or other. Nothing is left to chance; everything is laid down by rule, and the foundation of all their customs is purely and simply

---

[1]Emile Senart, op. cit., p. 8.

religion. It is for this reason that the Hindus hold all their customs and usages to be inviolable, for, being essentially religious, they consider them as sacred as religion itself.[2]

The caste system constitutes the structure of Hinduism. Each caste has its own God-given dharma, its religious way of life and natural priesthood. Indeed, we may think of caste dharma as Hinduism in microcosm. An individual or group may become a Hindu by adopting the customary behavior of the Hindus rather than by being converted. In fact, it is practically impossible for an individual to become "a Hindu," for Hinduism does not recognize individuals; it is preoccupied with customs, not with habits.

The individual, entering the system as a member of a group, may take up his position as a member of a new caste. He becomes Hindu when his caste comes to realize its particular cultural variation as God-given and sacred. Hinduism becomes conscious of itself not as a cultural homogeneity, but rather in interaction among an unlimited number of dharmaic groups. Thus, a person becomes Hindu when he sees himself as a member of an in-group with a magico-religious way of life and all other groups about him as inherently different from his own—in other words, when his beliefs are determined by caste principles.[3]

Of course a mere verbal denial of caste may not mean that an East Indian is no longer a Hindu, any more than a westerner in India who advocates the caste system becomes a Hindu. Moreover, the outcasting of a hereditary Hindu does not of itself make him non-Hindu; Hinduism has made status provisions for outcastes. The very act of treating the outcaste as a despised non-entity is a factor determining caste solidarity, the *sine qua non* of Hinduism.

The power of Hinduism to absorb peripheral groups lies paradoxically in its self-centered disregard of them. It cares little, if at all, about the beliefs of an out-group or even about its culture; but the group which seeks a position of consequence in the caste hierarchy must carefully respect the opinion of Brahmans or suffer the slights, ridicule, and, finally, the boycott of reputable castes. In this very power of repulsion lies the attractional force of Hinduism; in other words, the ability of the organized individuals to ignore, to cut alien groups dead as of no consequence, tends to set up a desire in the latter to assume those practices which compel recognition. In India probably nothing but strong Western connections could keep such a group as the Christian mission-

---

[2]Op. cit., pp. 30–31. See also C. Bouglé, op. cit., p. 184.

[3]On this point Risley is rather explicit. He concludes: "Caste rules are rigid and no individual can become a Hindu." Op. cit., p. 238.

aries from becoming gurus and castes of Brahmans with Jesus as their principal god.[4]

Hinduism as a Religion

Although the entire culture of the Hindus is sacred,[5] there are certain aspects of it which contribute directly to their spiritual aspirations. Hinduism as a religion is a system of beliefs and doctrines developed about the basic principles of karma and samsara, judgment after life and metempsychosis. Hindus may be said to live ritualistically, but their lives are oriented toward these two fundamental ideas; they are the Hindu's answer to that question which must confront all mankind: What is the end and purpose of life? They embody his essential eschatological insight. An outstanding characteristic of this religion is its divorcement of ethics from its system of beliefs and practices; in fact, in so far as a system of ethics is concerned, Hinduism is barren.

As we have seen, the religion of the Hindus is by no means uniform. It is a far cry from the highly refined polytheistic religion of the Rig-Veda, with its complicated sacrifices and oblations of soma juice and melted butter to the gods, to the primitive animism of low-caste men. "Hinduism is an amorphous thing; it has been compared to a many-colored and many-fibered cloth, in which are mixed together Brahmanism, Buddhism, Demonolatry, and Christianity."[6]

---

[4] "That Hindus should be able to pay this reverence to Jesus Christ, and no objection raised by their co-religionists, is due to the tolerance and fluidity of Hinduism. A Hindu can be a Christian at heart provided he is faithful to the social system which is Hinduism's characteristic expression. . . . No Christian missionary can be content with this willingness on the part of so many Hindus to give Jesus Christ a place, and even a high place, in their pantheon, for the missionary enterprise stands or falls with the uniqueness and indispensability of Jesus Christ." A. C. Underwood, op. cit., p. 147. See also S. V. Ketkar, op. cit., Vol. II, p. 33. The omnibus cultural capacity of Hinduism has been frequently referred to. See, for example, John P. Jones, op. cit., pp. 375–76.

The following is said of the early Roman Catholic missionaries who sought to compromise with the caste system: "One missioner would be seen moving about on horseback or in a palanquin, eating rice dressed by Brahmans, and saluting no one as he went along; another, covered with rags, walked on foot surrounded by beggars, and prostrated himself as his brother missioner passed, covering his mouth lest his breath should infect the teacher of the great." W. Strickland and T. W. M. Marshall, *Catholic Missions in Southern India to 1865*, quoted by L. S. S. O'Malley, *Modern India and the West*, p. 52.

[5] John P. Jones, op. cit., p. 92.

[6] John P. Jones, op. cit., p. 194. W. Crooke's statement on this subject helps to emphasize the fact that Hinduism is leaderless: "All these multitudinous forms of belief are left without any official control from its leaders. Hinduism has never dreamed of a Council or Convocation, a common Prayer-book, or a set of Articles of Belief. Each sect goes its own way, preaching its peculiar tenets, converting to its own standard the animists by whom it is surrounded, never combining for action except under the influence of some outburst of fanaticism." Op. cit., p. 252.

The religion in its upper reaches is magical and introspective, and it is not available to mankind as such. Brahmans have a vested interest in it, and its blessings cannot reach men of low status. It has no creed, no central power, no church; and its multiplicity of practically individuated temples is built about community priests.

Mysticism, an Indispensable Factor

Through meditation and self-induced projection of personality and soul, the Hindu seeks integration with the universal soul substance. The attainment of this is his highest possible achievement;[7] it involves a method,[8] the knowledge of which need not include respect for ethical principles.

The Hindu "studies the Universe to discover whether he can apprehend and become one with the mysterious will which governs it. Only in spiritual unity with Infinite Being can he give meaning to his life and find strength to suffer and to act."[9] Thus in isolation, oblivious of men and the world, the individual attempts to move directly toward final salvation and bliss. Of the Brahmans, Schweitzer says: "Their whole endeavour was directed to piercing deeper into the secret of the supra-sensuous to which they drew near as priests by means of the incantations of sacrifice, and with which they became one in the state of ecstasy."[10]

Mysticism is particularly adapted to Brahmanic culture. The final reabsorption of man into the super-soul is achieved by a "pure act of the spirits," and the question of a man's regard for his fellow men is of no particular significance. This is consistent with the functional aspects of the caste system. "The mystic," observes Nehru, "tries to rid himself of self, and in the process usually becomes obsessed with it."[11]

---

[7] "Our rituals and sacraments, our fasts and feasts, our social regulations and religious liturgies, all have had, from time immemorial, this one end in view, namely, to help the realization of the Absolute through the conscious spiritual identification of the individual self with the Universal. Our highest conception of salvation is, therefore, called *Brahma* Nirvana, which means . . . the conscious identification of the individual with the Universal." Bipin Chandra Pal, *The Soul of India*, p. 23.

[8] On this general fact of mysticism it has been recognized that "the mystic strives toward a definite spiritual state and for its attainment utilizes various psychotechnical methods; these methods may, however, as with the Yogis and the later Buddhists, acquire a special importance and as pure psychotherapy may play a significant role in individual and social life." "Mysticism," *Encyclopedia of the Social Sciences.*

[9] Albert Schweitzer, *Indian Thought and Its Development,* New York, 1936, p. 11. "But if we regard the contents, all mysticism down to the present is unsatisfying, because it denies the world and life, and has no ethical content." Ibid., p. 12.

[10] Ibid., p. 28. See also p. 117.

[11] Jawaharlal Nehru, *Toward Freedom,* p. 243.

Of course the difference in mystical tendency between Hinduism and other great religions is one only of degree. Even so, however, India is the great home of ascetics, holy men, and *sannyasis*. It is here that spiritual rumination and introspective living are developed even among the masses. B. Groethuysen observes the universal association of mysticism and religion but differentiates Indian mysticism from that of other cultures:

Quite different is the position of mysticism in Jewish, Christian, and Moslem cultures, for here mystical tendencies conflict with other spiritual orientations. Scientifically grounded philosophy and the religion of faith oppose, each in its own way, their respective authorities to the force of mystical tendencies. . . . Mysticism . . . was . . . always in conflict with the Philosophico-scientific spirit and its striving for objectivity as well as with religion. The faith religion of the West was a strong bulwark against the penetration of any tendency to pure mysticism.[12]

Karma and Caste

The doctrine of karma maintains that every action of an individual has a moral significance; that all bad behavior is laid to his account; that after death his behavior account is balanced and judgment pronounced. The individual reaps his reward either in spiritual well- or ill-being, in favorable or unfavorable rebirth, or in both spiritual and rebirth recompense. The highest spiritual achievement of man is that of reaching the abode of the gods, thus ending the cycle of rebirths;[13] the depths of misfortune are reached by those individuals whose souls re-enter the world as living insects, vermin, or even inanimate objects.[14]

Although they did not always corroborate each other, the authors of the sacred scriptures had a detailed knowledge of the processes of transmigration. Consider, for instance, Manu's eschatology:

In consequence of many sinful acts committed with his body, a man becomes in the next birth something inanimate; in consequence of sins committed by speech, a bird or a beast; and in consequence of mental sins, he is reborn in a low caste. . . . Those endowed with goodness reach the state of gods, those endowed with activity the state of men, and those endowed with darkness even sink to the condition of beasts; that is the

---

[12]"Mysticism," *Encyclopedia of the Social Sciences.*

[13]Manu says: "A Brahman who thus passes his life as a student without breaking his vow, reaches after death the highest abode and will not be born again in this world." II, 249. For a discussion of the origin of the idea of transmigration and karma as indicated in the Upanishads, see J. N. Farquhar, *The Religious Quest of India,* London, 1920, pp. 33ff.

[14]Thus "A Brahmana who drinks the spirituous liquor called sura shall enter the bodies of small and large insects, of moths, birds, feeding on odure, and of destructive beasts." Manu, XII, 56.

threefold course of transmigration. . . . Elephants, horses, Sudras, and despicable barbarians, lions, tigers, and boars are the middling states, caused by the quality of darkness.[15]

The doctrines of karma and metempsychosis explain the justice of the distribution of individuals within the social structure; it sees social relationship as having a divine purpose and brings the individual face to face with the omniscient judgment of the deity. Confronted by this doctrine, the individual stands alone.[16] The doctrine does not explain the caste hierarchy. That originated in the body of the great god Purusha himself, and of course there could be no question about its wisdom. It rather gives the reason for the individual's present position and demonstrates the hopelessness of his trying to question the fairness of his caste status. It disarms him by figuratively lifting him from the security of his caste and making him personally responsible for his actions.

His caste is an imperishable social cyst through which he might pass only by death.[17] At death, however, he has earned entrance into the same or some other caste. Therefore, the Hindu admits caste mobility of the individual only through rebirth. Moreover, birth in a given caste is no accident. The individual, on the basis of his works in a former life, merits his status. Indeed, it may be said that he so lived, then, that he consciously selected his present natal caste.[18]

But good behavior in Brahmanic India is good caste behavior. Therefore, to the question, "What might a man do to be saved from an inferior rebirth?" the Indian answer is: "Follow in minutest detail your caste dharma."[19] The sacred literature has repeatedly emphasized

---

[15]Manu, XII, 9, 40, 43. See also Emile Senart, op. cit., p. 204; in Vishnu, XLIV–XLV, the subject is here treated in great detail; Robert Ernest Hume, *The Thirteen Principal Upanishads*, 2d ed., pp. 52–57, 417–18 *passim;* H. H. Risley, op. cit., p. 243. The origin of this doctrine is not known, but it goes far into India's past. "In its earliest form it appears in the *Satapatha Brahmana,* where the notion occurs that retribution is inflicted in the next world in the guise of repeated births and deaths. It is developed in the Upanishads. . . . The theory of transmigration must have been firmly established by the time when Buddhism arose (500 B.C.), for Buddha accepted it without question. A curious thing, however, is that he also adopted the doctrine of *Karma* or 'actions,' which regulates the new births as dependent on a man's own previous deeds, although he denies the existence of soul altogether." A. A. Macdonell, *India's Past*, p. 48. See also "Brahmanism and Hinduism," *Encyclopedia of the Social Sciences.*

[16]Cf. C. Bouglé, op. cit., p. 175.

[17]This is the religious rationale of the system. It is quite clear, however, that as a social fact the individual may be outcasted and even initiated into other castes.

[18]The ancient lawgiver was explicit on this point: "A twice-born man who recites these Institutes, revealed by Manu, will be always virtuous in conduct and will reach whatever condition he desires." Manu, XII, 126.

[19]A possible exception to this is embodied in the magic of mysticism which might take the individual directly to the deity even before death.

to caste-men, especially low-caste men, that respect for caste duties is a man's primary obligation. A Sudra's hope of rebirth into a higher caste lies in his being a perfect Sudra in this life.[20] The doctrine, then, is ideally pessimistic and other-worldly. It is fatalistic and provides the philosophical basis for caste complacency.

Holding that a man's caste is right from the beginning, one must necessarily conclude that it is futile to rail at its limitations and barriers. In fact, the individual who becomes dissatisfied with his status is pitted against his own caste. He will have to assume that he has been given a deal less just than that of his fellows; or that, while they merit their particular state, he deserves some rung above them. The gravity of such a position makes its occurrence practically inconceivable.

Caste and Hinduism

Shorn of mysticism, Hinduism, as a religious philosophy, is a system of thought developed in explanation and justification of the functioning of the caste system. The caste order is the stuff of Hindu religious thinking. An East Indian may call himself Mohammedan or Christian and, indeed, he may have adopted the latter's ethical philosophy, but if his fundamental beliefs are caste beliefs, he remains at peace in Brahmanic India. "Caste," says Bouglé, "is the very core of Hindu religion."[21] The codes of conduct are in the interest of caste; moral thinking is at the service of caste; hence the tremendous stability of the system. Caste relationships are not only right but also sacred—and sacred to all Hindus, regardless of caste position.[22]

Christianity and Caste

Probably the factor which distinguishes Christianity most vividly from Hinduism is its ethical system. The golden-rule idea and the doctrine of the fatherhood of God and the brotherhood of man could not possibly have unlimited currency in India. Here it is always "we for our caste and may the devil take the lowly"; consequently, it has been said that "selfishness is stamped upon the Hindu faith."

Christianity and Brahmanism go back to different basic premises. The one holds that in the beginning man was created in the likeness of

---

[20]Manu, X, 122.

[21]Op. cit., p. 169.

[22]Cf. John P. Jones, op. cit., p. 199. See also Mildred Worth Pinkham, *Women in the Sacred Scriptures of Hinduism;* H. H. Risley, op. cit., p. 267; A. H. Benton, op. cit., p. 32; and W. E. S. Holland, *The Indian Outlook,* p. 25.

God, while the other maintains that from an original being came men into the world originally unequal, with special emphasis upon the god's conscious purpose that men should forever remain socially unequal.

Christianity is preoccupied with the poor, the sinful, the sick, the lowly, the lost, the downtrodden, the exploited;[23] Brahmanism is concerned with the upper, fortunate crust of society. The blessings of the Hindu gods are not even available to low-caste men. That Sudra who attempts, by prayer, ritual, or recitation of the sacred texts, to reach the ear of the deity not only insults the deity, but also commits an egregious outrage meriting speedy punishment in this world and hereafter.[24]

The deity is concerned only indirectly about the fate of low-caste men; he created them from his feet, or, worse still, he did not even sanction the creation of the outcastes; hence from the beginning he intended that they should be oppressed. On the other hand, Christianity is diametrically opposed to this point of view. Men of low status seem to be particularly beloved of God. On this score the following teaching is revealing: "Inasmuch as ye have done it unto one of the least of these my brethren, ye have done it unto me."[25]

Hinduism is self-centered; its gods are possessed by, and available to, only a certain class of men. It could not produce social reformers championing the cause of mankind, since a movement of this type would strike directly at its foundation—the caste system. The idea of "righteousness" is foreign to it, and it must necessarily be non-proselyting. Moreover, its adherents, particularly those of the upper castes, can seldom be converted to other faiths.

To be converted to Christianity, a man must give up both caste and caste thinking, and in India this is about as difficult a piece of business as one could propose. It calls for the spirit of the martyr. A man must give up his belief in his society while it lives about him, for religion and society are one in India. The high-caste man, unless he can become a paid leader for his conversion, has everything to lose and no earthly thing to gain. "The social system inflicts such tremendous penalties on conversion to Christianity that a convert from the higher caste is truly a miracle."[26]

---

[23]For a good discussion of this subject see George W. Briggs, *The Chamars*, pp. 240-47.

[24]Manu, IV, 81 *passim*.

[25]Recall also the emphasis upon man's spiritual equality: "There is neither Jew nor Greek, there is neither bond nor free, there is neither male nor female: for ye are all one in Christ Jesus. And if ye be Christ's, then are ye Abraham's seed, and heirs according to the promise." Galatians 3: 28–29. This stoic philosophy of St. Paul found an easy place in his conception of the teachings of Jesus.

[26]The Bishop of Madras, quoted by H. H. Risley, op. cit., p. 241.

The Roman Catholics, even from the time of the Abbé Dubois, saw the immensity of the task before the missionaries in India. Christianity seemed to strike at the vitals of the social order; hence the Catholics decided not to drive home their philosophy. The medicine might destroy the patient and probably the doctor also. Dubois believed that the caste system was too well established, too thoroughly ingrained in the lives of the people, to permit of radical disturbance. The social disorganization likely to result might have been too costly in human suffering; thus the Catholics made terms with caste, not without, however, arousing the criticism of many Protestant missionaries.[27]

Christianity is a religion of optimism, altruism, and consolation; it permits the lowliest to rise in spirit above the most successful of wrongdoing men on earth. "Look at the generations of old, and see; did any ever trust in the Lord and was confounded? or did any abide in His fear and was forsaken? or whom did He ever despise, that called upon Him?"[28] In teaching that greatness lies in the power to serve one's fellows, Christianity tends to keep man from rising to unreachable flights of superiority by climbing over his fellows, exploiting and oppressing them.[29]

In contrast, the caste world is made to serve Brahmans. Through mysticism the Hindu may reach the deity directly. Says the Gita: "Even if a very ill-conducted man worships me, not worshiping anyone else, he must certainly be deemed to be good, for he has well resolved." On the other hand, the theme of the gospels is that a man cannot know God if he thinks even that his brother has aught against him. We may conclude, then, that the religious philosophies of Hinduism and Christianity stand upon different grounds and may be basically incompatible.

Western Thought and Hinduism

Brahmanic India has not yet reached its age of rationalism. Everything of importance concerning human life and welfare has already been said by the ancient sages; the sole employment of the reason now

---

[27]"Roman Catholicism, which has still the most numerous native Christian community in India, has largely adopted the Hindu system and tries to utilize it in furtherance of Christianity in the land! No greater mistake was ever made than this of trying to uphold and promulgate the meekness, the humility, the love and the fellowship of Christ by means of the haughty pride, the cruel hate, and the bitter divisiveness of caste." John P. Jones, *India, Its Life and Thought,* p. 143. See also *Census of India, 1931,* Vol. I, Pt. 1, p. 380.

[28]Ecclesiasticus ii: 10. See also Matthew, 23.

[29]The writer is not unmindful of the frequent inconsistencies between the world view of Christianity and its practice.

is interpretation and rumination upon this store of sacred wisdom.[30] The latter answers all their questions; Hindus need only to search carefully enough to find them all revealed. With reference to this Dr. Pinkham observes: "It must be recognized that the acts of many Hindus are the result of blind adherence to the unquestioned authority of the sacred scriptures, rather than of a testing of traditional doctrine by conscience, practical observation, and experimentation."[31]

There is no secular law, hence there can be no reasoning about social problems as such.[32] In fact, in Brahmanic India there is no such phenomenon as "the social" as distinct from "the religious." So far as political thinking is concerned, the Hindu is incorrigibly aristocratic. We could not conceive of his originating the democratic idea, and he could not adopt it except at the expense of a revolution in the social order.

In India the theory of "liberty, equality, and fraternity" could have universal meaning only as a weapon against the foreigners who invented it. Even the depressed classes could not conceive of themselves as aspiring to this state, for the disorganization of the social structure and its religious rationale must at least go hand in hand with the grasping of this idea by the masses.[33] Furthermore, the caste system insists on loyalty to the caste rather than to the nation or people as a whole.

In this chapter our purpose has not been, of course, to make an invidious comparison of the religion and thought of the Hindus. Yet it has been necessary to indicate those differences which seem significant for an understanding of the possibilities of Hindu culture with respect to Western culture. We have attempted to show that the caste system is supported by a system of religious beliefs probably as different from Christianity as the caste system itself is different from the social organization of the West. This done, the problem of cultural evaluation must be left to the reader.

---

[30]Cf. W. E. H. Leaky, *Rationalism in Europe,* Vol. I, p. 88.

[31]Mildred Worth Pinkham, op. cit., p. ix.

[32]See C. Bouglé, op. cit., p. 171.

[33]M. K. Gandhi, very much westernized, of course, is surprised at the undemocratic attitude of Cochin, the Indian state. "There," he writes, "the repeated attempts to bring even a resolution before the Cochin Legislative Assembly asking the Cochin State to remove the ban on the use of public roads by untouchables was disallowed. An assiduous member inquired in the Cochin Legislative Assembly . . . 'On what grounds was the use of certain roads constructed and maintained by the Public Works Department prohibited to untouchables?' Reasons given without any sense of shame on behalf of the Cochin Government were: 'The roads are in close proximity to *temples* and *palaces.* There cannot be a sudden break with the past. Long standing customs have to be respected.' " *Young India,* pp. 725–26.

4. Women, Marriage, and Caste

*F*OR AN APPRECIATION OF THE POSSIBILITIES OF ANY SOCIETY, AT least in so far as social change is concerned, a knowledge of the social position of women is necessary. In Brahmanic India women are at once a most powerful anchor of the caste system and the most fettered of their sex in all the world.[1]

Ascendancy of Man

The Brahmanic Indian family is intensely patriarchal. The woman is an adjunct,[2] significant for her aid to man in working out his destiny. According to the religion of the Hindus, this destiny is unfulfilled at his death; a son is necessary to continue the work of salvation. This is part of the rationale which emphasizes the unquestionable superiority of man over woman even before birth. John P. Jones says: "The greatest disappointment in the life of a Hindu woman is not to be able to present her lord a son to solace him in this life and to assist him through the valley of death."[3]

There is in the Hindu family a strong tradition of idolization of sons. Such a tendency is operative in probably most other societies; however, it evidently reaches an extremity among the Hindus. The following

[1] In this discussion we are interested in the question of how the caste system is possible. Today, in urban India, there are Western tendencies inimical to a caste society. With these instances of caste in disintegration we are not particularly concerned. For a discussion of modern educational progress among East Indian women, see *The Indian Year Book, 1939–40*, pp. 408ff. and for a discussion of great Indian women of ancient India, see Mildred Worth Pinkham, op. cit.

[2] A wife is conceived of as *belonging* to her husband. Manu declares: "A wife, a son, and a slave, these three are declared to have no property; the wealth which they earn is acquired for him to whom they belong." VIII, 416.

[3] Op. cit., p. 274. "Their welfare in the other world depends upon his having a son to take over from himself the sraddha ceremonies." J. N. Farquhar, *The Crown of Hinduism*, p. 85.

excerpt from one of the Rig-Veda Brahmanas may give us some idea of the antiquity of the attitude. Hariccandra Vaidhasa Aiksraka was the son of a king; a hundred wives were his, but he had no son from them. In his house dwelt Pravata and Narada; he asked Narada:

> *"What doth a man gain by a son?"*
> *The latter replied:*
> *"A debt he payeth in him,*
> *And immortality he attaineth,*
> *That father who seeth the face*
> *Of a son born living.*
> *The delights of the earth,*
> *The delights of the fire,*
> *The delights in the waters of living beings,*
> *Greater than these is that of a father in a son.*
> *By means of a son have fathers ever*
> *Passed over the deep darkness;*
>
> . . . .
>
> *The son is a ship, well-found, to ferry over.*
>
> . . . .
>
> *Food is breath, clothing a protection,*
> *Gold an ornament, cattle lead to marriage.*
> *A wife is a comrade, a daughter a misery*
> *And a son a light in the highest heaven."*[4]

From infancy girls are taught man-worship; this constitutes their principal training, for education in a formal sense is ordinarily not allowed them. The ideal of Hindu womanhood is she who lives only to serve her husband—indeed, she who is most successful in deifying her husband.[5]

There is no other god on earth for a woman than her husband. The most excellent of all the good works that she can do is to seek to please him by manifesting perfect obedience to him. Therein should lie her sole rule in life.

Be her husband deformed, aged, infirm, offensive in his manners; let him also be choleric, debauched, immoral, a drunkard, a gambler; let him frequent places of ill-repute, live in open sin with other women, have no affection whatever for his home; let him rave like a lunatic; let him live without honor; let him be blind, deaf, dumb or crippled; in a word,

---

[4] *Harvard Oriental Series,* Vol. 25, Rig-veda Brahmanas, pp. 299–300.
[5] See *Indian Legislative Assembly Debates, 1925,* Vol. V, Pt. III, p. 2884. Quoted in Katherine Mayo, *Mother India,* pp. 37–38.

let his defects be what they may, let his wickedness be what it may, a wife should always look upon him as her god, should lavish on him all her attention and care, paying no heed whatever to his character and giving him no cause whatever for displeasure.

A woman is made to obey at every stage of her existence. As daughter, it is to her father and mother she owes submission; as a wife, to her husband, to her father-in-law, and to her mother-in-law; as widow, to her sons. At no period of her life can she consider herself her own mistress.[6]

By comparing woman with "the soil in which seed is sown," Hindu men have further fortified their position of importance. "The seed is declared to be the more important; for offspring of all created beings is marked by the characteristics of the seed."[7] Ministering to the pleasures and desires of man is the only possible legitimate vocation of women, and this goes so far as to make life without such employment a meaningless existence.

The Suttee

Suttee-mindedness is an extreme form of the man-centered attitude of Hindus. The suttee may be said to represent man's supreme achievement in subjugating woman to his service. It is an overwhelming symbol of the meaninglessness of her life apart from his. Climbing onto the waiting pyre which presently will be an inferno, she assumes the stature of a goddess, her shining virtue being that she has fully accepted the brutal fact that her life is an inseparable adjunct to that of her deceased master and god.

Since, regardless of the number of wives he has, a woman's life may be identified with only one man, and, since women were created solely for the service of husbands, a widow is a woman without a purpose. She may not remarry, for to do so would be not only a grave insult but also a possible deprivation to her dead husband.[8] On the other

---

[6]Abbé Dubois, op. cit., pp. 344–45, trans. from the Padma-purana. To the same effect, see Manu, V, 154–60.

[7]Manu, IX, 33–36.

[8]Risley thinks that the social logic behind the custom of a widow s not remarrying is based upon the belief that she cannot be given away twice; or, rather, that her husband being dead, no one can now legitimately give her away. "Her father being out of the question, it may be said that she may give herself in marriage. But this she cannot do, because she never had anything like disposal of herself. When young she was given away, so that the ownership over her was transferred by a solemn religious act to the husband; and he being no more, there is no one to give her away. Since Hindu marriage must take the form of a religious gift, her marriage becomes impossible." Op. cit., p. 176. This idea of the sanctity of a consummate gift seems, however, too fragile a basis for a custom so widespread and stable as the peculiar institution of Hindu widowhood. Indeed, the Law Books seem to be somewhat at variance with Risley's view. "Three years let a damsel wait," says

hand, immolating herself on the funeral pyre of her husband may have a double value: She may continue to be of service to him immediately after his death, thus saving him the inconvenience of having to remain wifeless until her natural death; and the act of extreme submission symbolized in the suttee may be an unforgettable lesson in man-worship to living Hindu women.

Not love but duty is the impelling social force in the suttee.[9] In the case of a husband, the death of one wife creates only the problem of securing another. Indeed, the symbolic meaning of the suttee has been carried so far in some communities that "if a man died during an absence from home in another country, his wife was recommended to take his slippers or any other article of dress and burn herself with them tied to her breast."[10]

Sometimes the suttee was voluntary, but the horror of the occasion frequently terrified even the most convinced Hindu woman.[11] Today suttee is practically abolished in India. We should expect suttee-mindedness, however, to linger much longer, for it is a part of Hinduism. A free life among women is not compatible with a caste system.

Conception of Woman's Nature

With the subjugation of woman it became necessary to guard her, for if lower-caste men were to gain access to submissive women of upper

---

Manu, "though she be marriageable; but after that time let her choose for herself a bridegroom of equal caste and rank. If, being not given in marriage, she herself seeks a husband, she incurs no guilt, nor does he whom she weds." IX, 90–91.

[9]The following is one of the earliest accurate accounts of the suttee by a Western observer: "When the Bramenes die, all their friends assemble together, and make a hole in the ground, wherein they throw much wood and other things: and if the man be of any accompt, they cast in sweet sanders, and other spices, with rice, corne, and such like, and much oyle, because the fire should burn the stronger. Which done they lay the dead Bramenes in it: then cometh his wife with musike and many of her neerest friends, all singing certain prayses in commendation of her husband's life, putting her in comfort, and encouraging her to follow her husband, and goe live with him into the other world. Then she taketh all her jewels, and parteth them among her friends, and so with a cheerful countenance, she lapeth into the fire, and is presently covered with wood and oyle: so she is quickly dead, and with her husband's bodie burned to ashes: and if it chance, as not very often it doth, that any woman refuseth to burn with her husband, then they cut the haire cleane off from her head: and while she liveth she must never after wear any jewels more, and from that time she is dispised, and accounted a dishonest woman. This manner and custome of burning is used also by the nobels and principallest of the countrey, and also some marchantes." Arthur Coke Burnell, ed., *The Voyage of John Huyghen van Linschoten to the East Indies,* from English trans., 1598, Vol. I, pp. 249–50.

[10]R. V. Russell, *The Tribes and the Castes of the Central Provinces of India,* Vol. II, pp. 369–70.

[11]For a discussion of coercive factors in the suttee, see *Essays Related to . . . Hindoos,* op. cit., pp. 10ff. See also Abbé Dubois, op. cit., pp. 355–67.

castes the system would be speedily disrupted. Thus the society had to be definitely convinced about the inborn untrustworthiness of women. Manu says with assurance:

Through their passion for men, through their mutable temper, through their natural heartlessness, they become disloyal toward their husbands, however carefully they may be guarded in this world. When creating them, Manu allotted to women a love of their bed, of their seat and of ornament, impure desires, wrath, dishonesty, malice, and bad conduct. For women no sacramental rite is performed with sacred texts; thus the law is settled.[12]

The aim is to keep a constant watch over the woman, to give her no opportunity to act independently,[13] and to limit very carefully her spatial mobility. "Carefully watch the procreation of your offspring, lest strange seed fall upon your soil."[14] It is, then, a sacred duty of Indian caste-men to guard the women of the caste; and so to this day there is a basic suspicion about Indian women, while not a little of their caste difficulties is due to reports and rumors about their sexual deviations. "Among the higher classes, where we might expect more liberality, we find less. Women are not permitted to pay visits and never leave home except for the house of a relative, and these journeys are rare, and attended with much anxiety."[15]

In order to emphasize the perfidy of women the authors of the sacred literature of the Hindus warned men to guard themselves against seductions; indeed, in this respect one may not trust even his own relatives. Says Manu: "It is the nature of women to seduce men in this world; for that reason the wise are never unguarded in the company of females. For women are able to lead astray in this world not only a fool, but even a learned man, and to make him a slave to desire and anger."[16]

---

[12]Manu, IX, 15–18.

[13]"By a girl, by a young woman, or even an aged one, nothing must be done independently, even in her own house. In childhood a female must be subject to her father, in youth to her husband; when her lord is dead, to her sons; a woman must never be independent. She must never seek to separate herself from her father, husband or sons; by leaving them she would make both her own and her husband's families contemptible. Him to whom her father may give her, or her brother, with her father's permission, she shall obey as long as he lives, and when he is dead, she must not insult his memory." Manu, V, 147–51. "Day and night women must be kept in dependence by the males of their families." IX, 2. See also Vishnu, XXI, 1, 12–15.

[14]*Sacred Books of the East,* Vol. II, Pt. 2; Baudhayana, II, 2, 3, 35.

[15]*Essays Related . . . to Hindoos,* etc., op. cit., p. 170.

[16]Manu, II, 212–15.

The Problem of Divorce

A good example of the hypothesis that the number of divorces in a country need not be an index of "familial happiness" is presented in the stability of the Hindu family. There is no divorce in Brahmanic India, but desertion is man's prerogative. There is a powerful social coercion against women leaving their husbands, for, should they do so, their future life will be defined as purposeless—a punishment extreme, indeed. For any action of a wife against a husband which interferes with the solidarity of the family, the wife will be held blamable, and this regardless of the role of the husband.[17] "She would rather undergo any suffering than testify against him in a court of law, especially as social opinion may not uphold her."[18]

It has been said that in India a man marries "for his own convenience, without any view to his wife's happiness."[19] It may be, however, that this end can be facilitated by looking to the happiness of his wife. And, in fact, Indian women are overburdened with jewelry, while family ritual sometimes throws a halo of honor about the wife.[20] Thus, though they are objects of restraint and distrust, enlightened self-interest calls for a certain pampering of Hindu women.

Women Not Slaves

Of course we should be very much in error if we supposed that women in India consider themselves unfortunate. A social condition of itself is never sufficient to create unrest among a group. Poverty, hunger, misery, seeming oppression, and so on, may be endured, without social definition to the contrary, in social complacency and contentment. Like

[17] On the question of what might be done for serious wrongs of husband to wife, the Age of Consent Committee concluded: "After conviction, even if the punishment does not amount to imprisonment, it is not unlikely that the relations between the husband and the wife would be unhappy; and it may even happen that the husband may discard her and take another wife. Among Hindus generally there is no custom of divorce; and girls cannot remarry even if discarded. Moreover, if the husband goes to jail, the girl and her people must always bear the stigma of being instrumental in putting him in prison." *Report of the Age of Consent Committee, 1928–29,* p. 19.

[18] Ibid.

[19] *Essays Related . . . to Hindoos,* op. cit., p. 174.

[20] This truth of reflective happiness was recognized early: "Women must be honoured and adorned by their fathers, brothers, husbands, and brothers-in-law, *who desire their own welfare.* . . . Where the female relatives live in grief, the family soon wholly perishes, but that family where they are not unhappy ever prospers. . . . Hence men who seek their own welfare should always honour women on holidays and festivals with gifts of ornaments, clothes, and dainty food." Manu, III, 55, 57, 59. (Italics added.)

the least of the outcastes, persons who never knew freedom or have never been taught to expect it obviously cannot be oppressed by its denial. The group must first define the situation as socially wrong and inadequate before it can be so conceived by the individual.[21]

At any rate, the place of women in Brahmanic India is everywhere— westernized areas excluded—considered right. On this score the society has attained peace with itself, and naturally no one is able to formulate a question about it. In fact, we should expect Hindu women themselves to lament the social condition of women, say, in Western society, as unfortunate. According to William Crooke:

> She, no less than her husband, would resent the belief that she is down-trodden and degraded. In a land where the affairs of life are regulated by custom, she is quite content to repeat the experiences of the heroines of old times, whose docility and reverence for the men with whom they were linked are an ideal which she is proud to follow.[22]

Another indication of the strength of the culture may perhaps be illustrated by the following: Out of respect for husbands, wives may not mention their names. Some such title as "master" or "lord" may be used. "In no way," says Louis H. Gray, "can one of the sex annoy another more intensely and bitterly than by charging her with having mentioned her husband's name. It is a crime not easily forgiven."[23] Among women themselves, then, as might have been expected, man's superiority is propagated. Even the supreme effort at self-subordination, the suttee, has been claimed by Hindu women as a right and privilege, and there are cases where considerable restraint by foreign officials had to be exercised in order to prevent it.[24]

The Stabilizers of the Culture

Hindu women tend to be the keepers of custom in its pristine simplicity. Their almost universal illiteracy and the overwhelming social emphasis upon limitations to their emotional life leave them yet another avenue for passionate preoccupation. The Hindu woman is the

---

[21] With reference to the individual, the Stoic Seneca puts the converse of this moralistically: "If what you have seems insufficient to you, then, though you possess the world, you will yet be miserable." Will Durant, *The Story of Philosophy*, p. 109.

[22] Op. cit., p. 522. "Nowadays the most obvious evidence of a man's rise in social estimation is that he secludes his wife." Ibid., p. 524.

[23] "Names," *Encyclopedia of Religion and Ethics.*

[24] "Tavernier records a case of a woman at Patra who asked permission from the Dutch governor to burn herself, and allowed her arm to be severely burned in proof of her courage. General Sleeman states that in 1829 he was reluctantly forced to allow a woman to become a suttee, because she would otherwise have starved herself to death." William Crooke, op. cit., p. 451.

arbiter of custom for custom's sake, the unyielding anchor of Hinduism, the strict rote mistress of daughters-in-law, and the cryptic power behind the meticulous, irrational life of the Hindu home. Her knowledge of what is right is critical and fastidious; and custom, which is religion in India, is usually stronger than any possible novel ideas of a father or husband.[25] "These illiterate women," Underwood comments, "are a drag upon progress because the women of India exert a great influence within their homes. They dominate their husbands and sons even when these have received a western education."[26] Ketkar attributes the influence of pundits in present-day India to their following of women and men of little education.[27]

Hindu men have struggled in the past to produce a quiescent womanhood unschooled in intellect.[28] Believing her to be of a low order mentally and innately irresponsible, they have limited her mobility and ruled out the slightest possibility of romantic love. All this is consistent with a caste culture. At length, however, she has become a power with which even the most ambitious leader of social change in modern India must reckon. The educated man may now be ready for reform, but his womenfolk, among others, are the unlimited heirs to a system that brooks no progress.[29]

The Meaning of Marriage as a Factor in Caste Relationships

It is a fact well known to students of Indian society that marriage is an indispensable consideration among castes. The question of the role of marriage in caste relationships, however, is by no means settled. The

---

[25] Cf. John P. Jones, op. cit., p. 258.

[26] A. C. Underwood, op. cit., p. 119. Says Mohandas K. Gandhi: "I have adopted an untouchable child as my own. I confess I have not been able to convert my wife completely to my view. She cannot bring herself to love her as I do." *Young India,* p. 652. Another great leader of social change in India, Ram Mohan Ray, found stout opposition from his women relatives when he broke with Hindu orthodoxy: "From this time onward his mother opposed and persecuted him, and for some considerable time his wives refused to live with him on account of his heterodoxy." J. N. Farquhar, *Modern Religious Movements in India,* p. 31.

[27] Shridhar V. Ketkar, op. cit., Vol. II, p. 84.

[28] For a statistical commentary on the exceedingly small percentage of literate women, and on obstacles to the spread of female education, see *Cambridge History of India,* Vol. VI, pp. 345, 350.

[29] J. N. Farquhar, *The Crown of Hinduism,* p. 109. "Perhaps the strongest restraining influence hitherto has been that of the female members of the family. Brought up in seclusion and without much education, and seldom leaving home, the women of the family are tenacious of the old observances and restrictions, and regard any departure from them with greatest disfavor." "Caste," *Encyclopedia of Religion and Ethics.*
We should mention again that while this social trait of woman's subordination reaches some extreme in the caste system, it is not unknown in Western society. In the static medieval society of Europe women were also highly subordinated.

caste is endogamous; if the caste includes subcastes, then the subcastes will be endogamous. So persistent is this characteristic of castes that sometimes they have been referred to as marriage circles. We know that intermarriage is a most potent leveler of cultures and races; so much so, indeed, that we might assume that no group can maintain its identity or solidarity if it permitted free intermarriage with out-groups.

We may observe further that endogamy is a protective device utilized by social groups that feel they have some biological or cultural heritage to preserve. *The caste prevents intermarriage so that it may isolate itself,* and not vice versa. In India endogamy serves as a means of maintaining unnumbered little cystlike cultural variants invidiously juxtaposed. We should probably be grossly misled, however, if we were to think of endogamy, rather than that which its prohibition is intended to protect, as of primary significance. Edward Westermarck says with finality: "Endogamy is the essence of the caste system."[30]

This point of view has actually resulted in many questionable conclusions. A. H. Benton sees the social utility of sex as providing the need for marriage restrictions. To him, sex itself, the value of women to men secured in marriage, is the advantage which one caste gains over another in its practice of endogamy. In other words, marriage per se is the essential circumstance. Says this writer:

My contention is that the system at the outset had had for its object the due adjustment of sexual relations. . . . The basis and starting point of the whole system are obviously the fact that the community consists of sections, the members of which are under agreement to exchange brides with each other on certain customary conditions. . . . All men must find their brides, each in that section of the population which has arranged for mutual interchange.[31]

Thus a sort of contractual conservation of women, a struggle for sex satisfaction among men, appears to be here a dominant purpose of caste. Equally misleading is the idea of natural antipathy between man and man, which becomes explicit in a superior group's refusal to give its women to inferior men.[32]

---

[30]*The History of Human Marriage,* Vol. II, p. 59.

[31]*Indian Moral Instruction and Caste Problems,* pp. 17–18.

[32]Bryce's theory that "nothing really arrests intermarriage except physical" difference will not bear critical examination. In fact, Bryce himself says: "In Morocco one sees every type of feature and every shade of colour, from the light yellowish brown pure Arab to the jet-black Negro, and all seem to stand on the same social level." However, "when Muslims and Christians or Jews dwell side by side, each race [sic] so cleaves to its own faith as to stand sharply apart from the other. Thus in the Turkish and Persian and Arab East there is practically no intermarriage." James Bryce, *The Relations of the Advanced and Backward Races of Mankind,* 2d ed., pp. 18–22.

Evidently it is not the absence of intermarriage between group and group which is the test of caste, but rather the type of phenomenon which marriage restrictions seek to isolate. The cultural values are developed first; endogamy is primarily an isolating contrivance.[33] Therefore, we cannot know whether caste exists until we have studied and identified the form of social organization isolated. In fact, Risley has observed some religious sects that have succeeded in maintaining their integrity not by endogamy but by extremely rigid non-commensal practices.[34]

However castes might have originated, it is true that caste rules and customs are vital. Confusion of these rules results in ill-being to all caste members. "Their special caste rules make of their community, in effect, a distinct species."[35] We should make it clear that caste bastardy is not a matter of blood but rather a disruptive mixture of the ordered life of the community. It is a consummate cultural cross in a society whose continuity is based upon cultural individuation. Castes, indeed, are cultural sanctuaries preserved from defilement by endogamy. Each caste has a sacred way of life, a dharma, which it calls its own, and this is what it seeks to protect.

H. H. Risley and E. A. Gait conclude that "marriage is the most prominent factor in the caste system."[36] From the same point of view, however, marriage is also the most prominent factor in the social-class system, or the race system, or any other system of group isolation. It may be revealing to recall that a former European king was allowed every social familiarity with a certain woman of plebeian descent, but on his marrying her was forthwith induced to abdicate. The principle which operated so decisively in this case is also more or less operative throughout the whole social-class hierarchy.[37] The greater the disparity in social-class status, the more rigid the sanctions against intermarriage.

Endogamy, then, is a sort of fence behind which a variety of social interests and types of social organization may be protected. The group

---

[33]An imperfect realization of this fact has led Romanzo Adams to state that: "Any sort of social control able to prevent interracial marriage for a long time cannot fail to create a caste system." See *Interracial Marriage in Hawaii*, p. 45.

[34]Op. cit., p. 153.

[35]Vincent A. Smith, *The Oxford History of India*, p. 35.

[36]*Census of India, 1901*, Vol. I, Pt. 1, Sec. 692.

[37]Thus, in the case of class relations, A. C. Mace emphasized the importance of marriage: "Apart from the commission of crimes there are few things that are so *degrading* as the inappropriate marriage. It is a much more serious matter if a youth marries out of his class than if he marries a woman of a different nationality or of a different religion." "Beliefs and Attitudes in Class Relations," in *Class Conflict and Social Stratification*, ed. by T. H. Marshall, pp. 157–160.

first becomes organized about some vital social interest before it decides upon its protection by non-intermarriage isolation. The interest
may be political, as in the case of conquerors desiring to maintain ruling status. "Government minorities, even when of the same race and
approximately the same cultures as the governed, hold themselves
aloof; and when their status is threatened by intermarriage they enact
against it—the Statute of Kilkenny (1366) forbidding the English of
the Pale to intermarry with the Irish is typical of such legislation."[38]
Or the interest may be nationalistic as, for example, the German Nazi
laws against intermarriage with Jews and Poles. The interest may be
religious, as that between sect and sect. "The marriages of the faithful
with aliens to the Catholic Faith were . . . universally forbidden at
the close of the fourth century. . . . All marriages with those outside
the Church were forbidden."[39] Among some groups such as the Jews,
it is a religio-cultural interest which is to be preserved. "With them the
problem has been and is still primarily one of the integrity of Jewish
home life, and therefore of the social solidarity of the Jewish people."[40]
The Jews, partly because of some "deep-seated dread of extinction,"
have achieved solidarity by isolating themselves through marriage restrictions; the fact of being Jewish, however, does not tend to give them
internal status homogeneity.

The interest may be mainly economic as, for example, that protected
by social-class sanctions against marriage between persons of different
classes, or between persons of different estates.[41] It may be racial, in an
immediate or proximate sense, as in the case of blacks and whites in
South Africa. Finally, it may be a composite of cultural factors, as in
the case of marriage restrictions between caste and caste in India, or of
the ethnocentric isolation of certain foreign groups in the United States.

Marriage restriction, then, is a dependent social phenomenon having
as its determinant some primary social interest, which interest may

---

[38]Bernhard J. Stern, "Intermarriage," *Encyclopedia of the Social Sciences.*

[39]Francis J. Schenk, *The Matrimonial Impediments of Mixed Religions,* p. 24.

[40]Julius Drachsler, *Democracy and Assimilation,* p. 127, note. For Jewish declarations against intermarriage see Bernhard J. Stern, loc. cit. For a discussion of endogamy among various social groups see Edward Westermarck, op. cit., Chap.
XVIII.

[41]"In Madagascar there was not only clan but class endogamy. Thus among the
Hovas the three great divisions—the nobles, the commoners, and the slaves—with
few exceptions, could not intermarry; nor did the three different classes of slaves
marry into one another." Edward Westermarck, op. cit., p. 61. See also Ruby Reeves
Kennedy, "Premarital Residential Propinquity and Ethnic Endogamy," and Lowry
Nelson, "Intermarriage among Nationality Groups in a Rural Area of Minnesota,"
The American Journal of Sociology, Vol. XLVIII, March 1943, pp. 580–84, 585–
92, respectively.

vary with the situation. The group initiating the restriction ordinarily has some apparent advantage which it seeks to preserve. In his discussion of caste formation Risley says, "The first stage is for a number of families, *who discover in themselves some quality of social distinction,* to refuse to give their women in marriage to other members of the caste."[42]

The sanction of the dominant group is seldom, if ever, against intermarriage as such; but rather against equal cultural participation. Where each group has *de facto* equal freedom to participate in the culture, intermarriage will not be a social problem, and of course there will be no social sanctions against it. Endogamy obviously may be an imposition. In the United States peoples of color are not endogamous by election.

Caste-women may marry up without disturbing caste integrity; such a relationship has been called hypergamy.

Hypergamy, or "marrying up," is the custom which forbids a woman of a particular group to marry a man of a group lower than her own in social standing, and compels her to marry in a group equal or superior in rank. . . . The men of the division can marry in it or below it; the women can marry in it or above it.[43]

Hypergamy is possible because of the cultural nature of caste, the position of women in India, and the custom of early marriage.

Marriage, a Parental Problem

In Brahmanic India the marriage contract is a religious one, and the bride and groom ordinarily have no part in its negotiation. The problem of contracting for marriage is left solely in the hands of parents or guardians; therefore, no possible interest of the marital pair could contravene that of the parents. The interest of the parents is that of the family and the caste and, of course, not sex. Thus romantic love is virtually ruled out in India. Says the Abbé Dubois, "What we call love-making is utterly unknown amongst the Hindus."[44] Children are ordinarily married before they reach the age when meaningful love is possible, and naturally:

The inclinations of the persons about to be married are never consulted. In fact, it would be ridiculous to do so amongst the Brahmins, seeing the age at which they marry their daughters. But even the Sudras, who often

[42]Op. cit., pp. 252–53; see also p. 70. (Italics added.)
[43]Ibid., p. 163.
[44]Abbé Dubois, op. cit., p. 313.

do not marry their daughters until they have attained full age, would
never dream of consulting the tastes and feelings of their children under
these circumstances. The choice is left entirely to the parents. That which
chiefly concerns the young man's family is the purity of the caste of his
future wife. Beauty and personal attractions of any kind count for nothing
in their eyes. The girl's parents look more particularly to the fortune of
their future son-in-law, and to the character of his mother, who after the
marriage becomes the absolute mistress of the young wife.[45]

In most castes parents are under strict obligation to marry their children early, and allowing a child to reach maturity unmarried may
result in serious caste penalties. We should expect this, for Hindu adults
are very much concerned with keeping their community closed. They
cannot permit romantic marriage.[46] We should also expect to find that,
as the system developed and castes multiplied, there would be a greater
necessity for child marriage. Cultural differences becoming less distinct, they would naturally tend to be less convincing as barriers to
Hindu youth. Geographically, too, we should expect the custom of child
marriage to expand coterminously with Hinduism.[47]

Early Marriage

In India early marriage is prescribed particularly for females. The
Law Books put the age of marriage for reputable men rather high, but
for women it seems inordinately low. Manu says, for instance: "A man,
aged thirty years, shall marry a maiden of twelve who pleases him, or a
man of twenty-four a girl of eight years of age; if the performance of
his duties would otherwise be impeded, he must marry sooner."[48]
Moreover, the fact that widowers may remarry at will makes possible
the marrying of older men. "It is no uncommon thing," observes Abbé
Dubois, "to see an old man of sixty or more, having lost his first wife,
marry for the second time a little child five or six years old, and even
prefer her to girls of mature age."[49]

---

[45]Ibid., p. 213.

[46]See H. H. Risley, op. cit., p. 149.

[47]"The Hindu youth has to maintain an attitude of utter indifference about every
proposal regarding his marriage, and when any arrangement in that respect is made
by his parents, grandparents, uncles, or elder brothers, he has to go through the
ceremony out of his sense of duty to obey or oblige them. The selection being, in
all cases, made by the guardian in accordance with his sober judgment, and never
by the parties themselves in accordance with their impulses. For the time being,
marriage out of caste is almost impossible in Hindu society." Bhattacharya, op. cit.,
p. 12. See also Senart, op. cit., p. 52; Hari Singh Gour, "Marriage Reform in India,"
Indian Affairs, Vol. I, p. 11; and "Caste," *Encyclopedia of Religion and Ethics.*

[48]Manu, IX, 94.

[49]Op. cit., p. 212.

Ordinarily, however, both boy and girl are married before puberty;[50] and, as we have seen, therein lies a significant means of controlling the caste system. In Brahmanic India the control of marriage by adult members of the family provides an effective guard against out-marrying, while the subjugation of women secures to men the final decisions about caste interests. Both hypergamy and permanent widowhood contribute also to the social ascendancy of males.

Married State Universal

Among Hindus marriage is not only a sacrament of primary importance but also a lifelong concern of the individual, the family, and the group to which he belongs. As we have already stated, the Hindu woman outside the married state is a rather meaningless entity, while an unmarried man is both socially inconvenienced and spiritually blamable. Marriage is not looked upon as a matter of personal predilection but as a necessity—so much so, indeed, that "among a number of Hindu castes, as also among the Todas of southern India, the corpse of a person dying unmarried is married before cremation as a necessary qualification to future happiness."[51] In India, then, every adult and a goodly proportion of infants are supposed to be married. Says one writer of wide experience:

The first point which strikes the observer is the almost universal prevalence of the married state. . . . Religion . . . which in the West makes in the main for celibacy, throws its weight in India almost wholly into the other scale. A Hindu man must marry and beget children to perform his funeral rites, lest his spirit wander uneasily in the waste places of the earth. If a high class Hindu maiden is unmarried at puberty, her condition brings social obloquy on her family, and on a strict reading of certain texts, entails retrospective damnation on three generations of ancestors.[52]

Marriage itself, then, constitutes a social condition of extreme importance—a fact which is of some significance when comparing marriage among castes with the marital relationships existing in other parts of the world.

---

[50]According to H. H. Risley, "Infant marriage is now so widely diffused as to have almost entirely displaced adult marriage within the limits of the caste system." Op. cit., p. 179.

[51]*Census of India, 1931,* Vol. I, Pt. 1, p. 405.

[52]H. H. Risley, op. cit., p. 148.

5. *Occupation and Caste*

*I*T HAS BEEN QUITE GENERALLY RECOGNIZED THAT OCCUPATION has some significant connection with caste organization, but its importance to the system seems to be still an open question. Perhaps a good deal of the difference of opinion may have its basis in the way the question is put. Thus we may ask: (a) Is it necessary that each caste have an occupation? or (b) Must every occupation have a caste? The problem, then, may be approached with these two points of view in mind. Let us consider some commitments of the early authors.

Natural Occupations

In perusing the early literature one is struck, first of all, by the settled way in which the authorities conceive of caste and occupation as naturally associated. Describing the creation of man, Manu says: "But for the sake of the prosperity of the world, he caused the Brahana, the Kshatriya, the Vaisya, and the Sudra to proceed from his mouth, his arms, his thighs, and his feet. . . . But in order to protect this universe he, the most resplendent one, assigned separate duties and occupations to those who sprang from his mouth, arms, thighs, and feet."[1] This, then, is no casual, fanciful business; the occupation of a caste is assumed to be as fundamental and as ancient as the social order itself.

[1]Manu, I, 31, 87.
In the last quarter of the sixteenth century a Dutch traveler and adventurer, who lived some years among the Portuguese at Goa, wrote: "The Indian heathens have a custome that no man may change nor alter trade or occupation, but must use his father's trade, and marrie men's daughters of the same occupation, trade or dealing, which is so nearly looked into, that they are divided and set apart, each occupation by it selfe, as countries and nations are, and so they call one another: for if they speake to a man, they aske him of what trade he is, whether hee bee a goldsmith, barber, merchant, grocer, fisherman, or such like." Arthur Coke Burnell, ed., *The Voyage of John Huyghen van Linschoten to the East Indies,* Vol. I, p. 231.

Moreover, the occupation of a group is considered a divine *duty* of that group. Hence, "a man, who is intent on his own natural work, attains perfection"; and the sacred books continue to admonish the group that "the inborn work . . . though defective, ought not to be abandoned."[2] Some of the most respected authorities hold that the association of a group with its occupation is inherent. Thus the Gita declares: "The work of the Brahmins, Kshatriyas, Vaishyas, and Sudras is divided according to qualities born of their own inner nature."[3] Indeed, this authority clearly identifies virtue with function. Certain types of work are considered to belong to certain groups, and an individual may descend to the status of a lower group by merely following its occupation.[4] Although the reverse of this—that is, upward mobility—is not so common, "there is [today] a tendency . . . to relax the rule of pollution by touch in the case of members of the untouchable castes who do not pursue *untouchable avocations.*"[5]

Sometimes the authorities discard all myths and come out with a bold insistence that the very continuity of the social order depends upon each caste's holding faithfully to its occupation. Says Manu: "The king should carefully compel Vaisyas and Sudras to perform the work prescribed for them; for if these two castes swerved from their duties, they would throw this whole world into confusion."[6] It may be that an understanding of the significance of occupational specialization in the caste system will shed further light upon the nature of Brahmanic Indian culture. Indeed, it may be that we are observing here the effects

---

[2]*The Message of the Gita,* interpreted by Sri Aurobindo, ed. by Anilbaran Roy, 18. 45, 48. See also John P. Jones, op. cit., p. 178; and Vishnu II, 1–17.

[3]The Gita, 18. 41. "Calm, self-control, askesis, purity, long-suffering, candor, knowledge, acceptance of spiritual truth are the work of the Brahmin. . . . Heroism, high spirit, resolution, ability, not fleeing in battle, giving, lordship . . . are the natural work of Kshatriya. Agriculture, cattle-keeping, trade inclusive of the labour of the craftsman and the artisan, are the natural work of the Vaishya. All work of the character of service falls within the natural function of the Sudra." Ibid., 18. 42–44.

[4]"To Brahmans he assigned teaching and studying the Veda, sacrificing for their own benefit and for others, giving and accepting alms. The Kshatriya he commanded to protect the people, to bestow gifts, to offer sacrifices, to study the Veda, and to abstain from attaching himself to sensual pleasures. The Vaisya to tend cattle, to bestow gifts, to offer sacrifices, to study the Veda, to trade, to lend money, and to cultivate the land. One occupation only the lord prescribed to the Sudra, to serve meekly even these other three castes." Manu, I, 88–91. See also X, 1, and Vayu Purana, VIII, 166–72.

[5]*Census of India, 1931,* Vol. I, Pt. 1, p. 399. (Italics added.)

[6]Manu, VIII, 418. "The observance of one's own duty leads on to infinite bliss. When it is violated, the world will come to an end owing to confusion of varnas and duties. Hence the king shall never allow people to swerve from their duties, for whoever upholds his own duty, ever adhering to the custom of the Aryas . . . will surely be happy both here and hereafter." Artha-Sastra, I, 3, 13–14.

of the giving of religious sanction to a form of social organization which appeared ideally harmonious because of the ordered distribution of function and the apparent absence of competition among groups of workers—a stereotyping of division of labor.[7] "The chief economic significance of the system," says Pramathanath Banerjea, "is that it fixes absolutely the supply of any kind of labor. The scope given for the play of competition thus becomes limited, and consequently the law of demand and supply is rendered either inoperative or oppressive in its operation. When any change takes place in the economic world, labor is unable to adjust itself. . . . Wages and prices have very often to be regulated by custom or some other artificial means."[8] Caste specialization is specialization by trade, not specialization by task.[9]

From this point of view the necessity for conceiving of Hindu society as a system of castes becomes very obvious. There can be no caste isolated outside of a caste system. Castes are interdependent entities, and where there is imbalance among them hardship results. It is this functional ordering of castes which has evidently inspired and given so much permanence to the Purusha myth explaining the origin of the system from a primeval organism. The Sudra caste is inferior but none the less essential. "Feet are made to serve the rest of the body; they are inferior to the head," but a body without feet is seriously handicapped—so much so that it may even perish without them.

The Traditional Occupations of Castes

Having discussed the early belief in the necessity for maintaining the caste-occupation relationship, we hasten to add that there is no certainty as to whether there ever were only four castes in India. As we shall attempt to show in another chapter, it seems likely that there were always much smaller and more numerous divisions. The occupational caste names of great antiquity tend to indicate this. However, a caste may follow an occupation other than its traditional calling. Bouglé asserts that today it is only rarely that we find a caste practicing the occupation designated by its name.[10]

---

[7] In the caste system, division of labor is the basis of economic organization; and the economic organization is in the interest of community welfare. In Western society, division of labor and specialization are competitive contrivances adopted with a view of maximizing profits. Hindu society could not exist without castes because the social order depends upon specialization; in Western society, however, economic specialization is simply an expedient of individual enterprisers. Cf. Alexander Gray, *The Development of Economic Doctrine*, p. 17.

[8] *A Study of Indian Economics*, 2d ed., p. 41.

[9] Cf. B. H. Baden-Powell, *Village Communities in India*, London, 1899, pp. 9–10.

[10] Op. cit., p. 18.

In time, then, castes may change their occupation.[11] *The Report on the Census of British India* for 1881 states that "caste, beginning with being a bond between persons of the same occupation, had then become a hereditary qualification for that occupation; as society outgrew, from a commercial point of view, the sphere of a monopoly of that sort, the caste began to expand into a variety of occupations."[12]

Thus one caste claiming an eponymic occupation may, in fact, have many subcastes with different occupations, and the status of the caste does not seem to be a factor limiting variety of subcaste occupations. "It is perhaps among the Brahmans," says Senart, "that there occurs the most complicated mixture of occupations and confusion of trades. . . . As a matter of fact, people who proudly bear the title of Brahman and to whom everywhere this title assures great respect, may be found engaged in all sorts of tasks."[13] It must not be supposed, however, that the status of all Brahmans is the same, regardless of occupation. Nothing is farther from the truth. From the Sanauriyas, the thieving Brahmans of Bundelkhand, and the untouchable Maha Brahmans, to the sacrificial priests and gurus, there is an unbridgeable status chasm.[14]

Caste as a Function of Occupation

A number of eminent caste theorists have questioned the conclusion that occupational specialization is essential to the caste system. All these, however, have viewed the system in reverse. They have

---

[11]"A general examination of the castes tabulated by occupation enables the position to be roughly summarized as follows: In the majority of castes, about half the males tabulated retain their traditional occupation; while varying numbers up to, but rarely exceeding, a quarter have subsidiary occupations. About a quarter or less of the half that have abandoned their hereditary occupations as their means of subsistence retain them as subsidiary. One or two occupations are worth stating: Of the Chamars, hardly more than one in thirteen retain their traditional occupation as the principal means of subsistence, and only one in forty as the subsidiary means. The Bhats again form a similar exception and not unnaturally, as the demand for genealogists is probably less than that for tanners. . . . On the other hand, the agricultural communities of Jat and Kurmi have not gone nearly so far as to abandon their hereditary occupation to the extent of fifty per cent." *Census of India, 1931,* Vol. I, Pt. 1, p. 296.

[12]Vol. III, Appendix H, Sec. cxvi. See also *Census of India, 1911,* Vol. I, Pt. 1, pp. 428–29.

[13]Op. cit., pp. 35–36. See also William Crooke, op. cit., p. 63, and G. S. Ghurye, op. cit., p. 16.

[14]See John C. Nesfield, op. cit., p. 74. "The Maha Brahman, so impure that in many villages he is not allowed to enter the gates; the Dakaut and Gujrati, so unfortunate that other Brahmans will not accept offerings at their hands, are all Brahmans, but are practically differentiated as distinct castes because of their occupations." Denzil Ibbetson, op. cit., pp. 6–7.

argued that since each occupation does not have a caste monopolizing it, there could be no principle identifying occupation with caste. "If the current idea were correct," Risley maintains, "all cultivators, all traders, all weavers, ought to belong to the same caste, at any rate, within the same area. But everyone knows that this is not the case; that the same occupation embraces a whole crowd of castes, each of which is a closed corporation."[15] This point of view clearly inverts thinking about the ongoing social process.

Each caste must have a God-given function, which fact need not necessarily exclude all others from so occupying themselves for all time and in all places. Moreover, we should also expect that over long periods of time old occupations may be lost and new ones developed; hence, no permanent group-occupation monopoly could have been originally formulated. There is only a strong presumption of unchangeability. None of these changes incident to social dynamics seems to contravene the principle that each caste must perform its sacred duty. Here, too, we must be careful not to confuse the idea of caste and subcaste; it is the latter which strives to maintain its occupational integrity. Bouglé is rather explicit on this point. He concludes that the fact that members of the same castes sometimes exercise different occupations does not in any way vitiate "the rule that each caste must have an occupation. Possible exceptions to this do not eliminate the obligation."[16]

There are some occupations that are so difficult to control and so obviously generalized callings that they tend to be avocational and subsidiary. They may serve as specialties, catchalls to failures, or staples

---

[15]H. H. Risley, op. cit., p. 259. See also the *Imperial Gazetteer of India,* new ed., Vol. I, p. 342, where Risley quotes Senart to this same effect, and Nripendra Kumar Dutt, *Origin and Growth of Caste in India,* Vol. I, p. 25, an echo of Risley. On this score the *Census of India, 1901,* is rather emphatic: "These figures are of much interest. They will, in the first place, effectively demolish any vestige which may remain of the idea that the functions of the South Indian castes are still confined to the narrow limits laid down for them in Manu and the Vedas or by tradition, and that the Brahmans are still exclusively engaged in priestly duties, the trader castes in commerce . . . that the cobbler and smith still stick exclusively to the last and the anvil at which their forefathers worked for so many generations." Vol. I, Pt. 1, Sec. 363. These figures, however, do not show the significance of the relationship between occupation and the *true caste.* In India, Brahmans are not a caste, they are an estate. Probably there never was an agricultural or trader caste in India. The conclusions here necessarily confuse the idea of caste and subcaste. The data do not show what percentage, if any, of the members of the marriage union, the subcaste, follows independent occupations.

For a rather extensive list of castes according to occupations, but not refined with respect to the subcastes, see E. A. H. Blunt, *The Caste System of Northern India,* pp. 247–52.

[16]Op. cit., p. 41.

for groups in transition; they may serve as supplements to other occupations. Among them agriculture and trading are common examples.[17] On the other hand, castes whose vocations call for specialized training and skill are able to maintain a high degree of occupational stability. "In these . . . the industries have continued for the most part hereditary up to the present day."[18]

It is possible, then, for two distinct castes or subcastes to follow the same occupation—say, for example, agriculture. The significant fact is, however, that, no matter how many castes follow the same occupation, each conceives of its work as belonging to itself; each conceives of its calling as a duty. Furthermore, agriculture and trade are fairly meaningless categories among castes. The basis of occupational division is far more subtle than these. The kind of crops, the method of planting, the nature of goods traded, the system of measure used are among the many sufficient reasons for distinction between caste and caste.[19]

We do not mean to imply here, of course, that any group which follows a common occupation is, because of that fact, a caste. This seems to be Ketkar's belief. According to him: "The fact that the Chinese are a caste of laundrymen is something every American knows. There are also occupational castes of Negro porters and of Japanese

---

[17] "Any trading caste in this country may deal in any kind of commodity that it prefers, and hence within the same caste every variety of trade will be found to exist. Thus, the element of specialty which in the case of all the Indian castes previously named has been the mainspring of their existence . . . is here entirely wanting. . . . No restrictions have ever been imposed by the laws or customs of the Hindus through which a man belonging to any of the landed or artisan castes could be debarred from setting up as a trader, if it pleased him. The business of the trader has always been open to all comers alike. . . . Consequently, there has been a continual influx of families from the various industrial castes who have detached themselves from the ancestral caste and calling, but have not coalesced with each other so as to form a compact trade union of their own. . . . The consequence has been that, while in the case of artisans, etc., there is a system of clearly defined castes, each distinguished from the other by some hereditary peculiarity of craft, in the case of traders, almost every distinction of caste that can be said to exist is a distinction without a difference." John C. Nesfield, op. cit., p. 34. See also "Caste," *Encyclopedia of Religion and Ethics.*

[18] John Nesfield, op. cit., p. 103.

[19] Charlotte V. and William H. Wiser report an interesting incident which may help to throw some light upon the place of occupation in the thinking of Hindus. Speaking of their Hindu automobile helper, Prem, they relate: "This same boy was walking from Mainpuri out to our camp. A cart passed him on the road, and one of its two occupants called to him to ride. The speaker was a Brahman of Karimpur. The second man, a Brahman of another village, demurred: 'But is he not a Chamar?' The first man agreed that Prem's people were Chamars, but added that Prem himself could hardly be called one in our village. He explained, 'Here he has become watchman of the Sahib's motor, and that is a job which has no caste!' No further objection was raised and Prem was taken in." *Behind Mud Walls,* pp. 55–56. Of course a whole caste of Chamars could not change its status thus easily; yet the incident reveals a type of spontaneous reasoning in which the fact of occupation itself defined the immediate personal relationship.

butlers."[20] These groups, which may have absolutely no organization, consensus, or common purpose, but may simply find themselves, through competition, gravitating individual by individual into certain occupations, are not castes at all. Castes do not compete for occupations. Such errors as the latter are likely to occur because of over-emphasis upon an inverted view that occupation is a determinant of caste. It is an attempt to see castes outside of a caste system. Even in India vocational specialization alone will not bring a group within the caste system. "The Jews of Kolaba monopolize the local oil industry to such an extent that they are generally known as Telis, but no one will dream of affiliating them to the ordinary Teli caste."[21]

It is not occupation as such which alone characterizes the caste. Such a simplification will lead us to include trade unions and guilds in the definition of caste. The vocation of a caste is one aspect of its way of life, possibly the most significant aspect; but even the earliest authorities did not hold that variations of occupation always meant variations of caste. Personality, virtue, and function are associated, and a change of one of these may not involve a coincident change of the others. Yet each caste has a sacred duty not to deviate from its occupation, for the social order depends upon occupational permanence. Thus says Nehru:

> To assess the significance of caste properly it may be essential to examine their functions. These may be (1) ordinary and (2) extraordinary. The ordinary functions or occupations of different castes are familiar to all. According to his peculiar caste, every man must drive his plough, or awl, or team, or goad, or reed, or whatever the instrument he handles in the discharge of his business. Thereby labour in the rural area is *subdivided, specialized, standardized, integrated, stabilized.* . . . The extraordinary functions of certain castes regulate the mechanism of rural life on important social, religious, and financial occasions. . . . The village Nai, who is an itinerant barber, is also the local gossip . . . publicity man, and general busybody of the village.[22]

---

[20]S. V. Ketkar, Vol. I, p. 102, note.

[21]*Census of India, 1911,* Vol. I, Pt. 1, p. 367.

[22]Shri Shridhar Nehru, *Caste and Credit,* p. 19. (Italics added.) W. H. Wiser, who lived as a participant observer in an Indian village, says, "Every man has his God-appointed function and recognized obligations, and at the same time his rights and privileges. Each man is a member of some caste and each caste is an essential organ of the whole, discharging a function at once peculiar to itself and necessary to the full life of the caste system. Only through his participation in this group life can the individual attain his own ends, and conversely, only with the aid of every individual and every group can the caste system afford the appropriate setting for the fullest life of its individual members. All men exist in and for each other and are bound to each other by an intricate network of mutual obligations." *Social Institutions of a Hindu Village of North India,* an abstract of a Doctor's Thesis, Cornell University, p. 3.

It is, then, not that every occupation has a caste, but that each caste has an occupation or group of related occupations. The caste structure is fundamentally a labor structure, a system of interrelated services originating in specialized groups and traditionalized in a religious matrix.

From time immemorial upper-caste persons have been permitted, in periods of stress, to take the occupations of castes next below them, and this process is a consequence of inevitable social change; it has not contravened the principle of hereditary vocation and respect for one's traditional work.

Substituting Occupations

However, there is no provision in either the custom or the law of the caste system for voluntary change of occupation. It has been recognized that through circumstances which cannot be controlled a caste may not always be able to live by its hereditary work. In such cases the caste is allowed to find some other employment. But a caste in distress may not look for relief to the vocations of superior castes; it may resort only to those of castes inferior to itself. Indeed, the system, in recognizing any sort of social change, will generally admit only degradation. "A Brahman, unable to subsist by his peculiar occupations . . . may live according to the law applicable to Kshatriyas; for the latter is next to him in rank. . . . A Vaisya who is unable to subsist by his own duties may even maintain himself by a Sudra's mode of life. . . . But a Sudra, being unable to find service with the twice-born and threatened with the loss of his sons and wife through hunger, may maintain himself by handicrafts."[23]

Most specifically, no man has the right to take the work of a Brahman—that is to say, become a priest. And this must necessarily be so in the caste system, for if, upon any excuse whatever, individuals or castes are permitted to covet superior occupations, competition will speedily reduce the social order. The rationale of this is that the position of all men is known, karmic, and guarded by the gods. To suffer through the operation of natural economic forces or ill conduct must be interpreted as being consistent with the divine will.[24]

---

[23]Manu, X, 81, 98–99.
[24]See Martin Luther Dolbeer, *The Movement for the Emancipation of Untouchable Classes in South India*, Master's Thesis, University of Chicago, 1929, p. 60. Abbé Dubois, op. cit., p. 295; S. V. Ketkar, op. cit., Vol. I, pp. 136–37.

Nature of Occupational Change

In Brahmanic India the individual normally takes the occupation of his father; there are no provisions for personal choice in this matter. The occupation of the caste is an "obligatory monopoly, the continuance of which is for the child not only a right but also an hereditary duty."[25] Hence, at the very outset, the individual finds the system set against occupational predilections. He learns to have great respect and reverence for the vocation of his caste. Thus, in India one speaks of the "traditional occupation" of his caste, a loyalty which may constrain him even when that caste has partly or wholly changed its occupation.

A man's caste function is important to him. With consummate contentment he will be a criminal or a beggar as well as a productive worker according to the interest of his caste. Says the Gita: "One should not abandon a natural duty though it be tainted with evil."[26] Able-bodied men beg or steal religiously as a vocation because these are legitimate traditional functions of their caste. Even though they, as individuals, should wish to change, the system offers practically no escape.

Occupational mobility, then, is collective rather than individual. Part of a caste may be detached from the parent body, but within this segment the rigidity of the rule against individual occupational choice is maintained.[27] However, we must not suppose that the caste either changes its occupation frequently or thinks lightly about the matter. Dubois gives his personal experience on the desperate reluctance of workers to leave their vocation:

I travelled through some of the manufacturing districts, and nothing could equal the state of desolation prevailing in them. . . . All the workrooms were closed, and hundreds of thousands of the inhabitants, com-

---

[25]C. Bouglé, op. cit., p. 3. See also p. 22. In urban centers today, where caste is under the impact of Western civilization, children are being given much greater latitude in selecting occupations. For a broad account of this, see Atul Chatterjee, "Social Change in India," *Great Britain and the East,* Vol. LV, November 1940, p. 368.

[26]*Sacred Books of the East,* ed. by F. Max Muller, Vol. VIII; the Gita, 18. 51.

[27]C. Bouglé, op. cit., p. 20. "In places where the demand for a particular service is greater than the numbers of the caste ordinarily associated with it are able to meet, or the profits are unusually high, it often happens that persons belonging to some other community adopt the occupation. At first the regular members of the caste refuse to have anything to do with them, but in time their attitude undergoes a change. Community of occupation involves community of interest. The newcomers lose touch with their former associates and withdraw, or are ejected, from their old marriage circle; and they gradually come to be regarded by the general

posing the weaver caste, were dying of hunger; for through the prejudice of the country they could not adopt another profession without dishonouring themselves.[28]

There is always a danger of the caste's losing status permanently by changing its occupation, for, although it may fairly easily adopt an inferior occupation, there may be insurmountable difficulties in the way of returning to the original status.

The Bhuinhars are now chiefly tillers of the soil; but apparently the original cause of their being lowered in the scale of caste [from Brahmanhood] was the adoption of the military profession, and their subsequent practice of agriculture has served only to degrade them a little further.[29]

Notwithstanding the sacred law, it is seldom, if ever, a simple matter to assume a new occupation. Caste-men know the value of their vested interests, and not infrequently they offer newcomers considerable opposition. Therefore, it may be not only the moral inhibitions of one's caste which tend to limit occupational mobility but also the resistance of other castes to occupational encroachments.[30]

With respect to the formation of new castes, the entering of new groups into the caste system, vocation has a dominant role. Not all castes attain position on the sole basis of functional specialization, but in time all come to be looked upon as having some traditional duty. Ordinarily tribes enter the caste system in fragments. The tribe disintegrates, occupation by occupation, and gradually enters the system at status levels functionally determined. Thus, it is not the whole tribe which ordinarily becomes a caste; the breakdown of a tribe may contribute caste members to many different rungs of the caste hierarchy.[31] In conclusion, then, we may add that although vocational specializa-

---

public as a section of the caste whose occupation they have appropriated, and to be called by the same name. Later on, members of that caste come to look upon them as belonging to their community, though of a separate sub-caste, and they themselves take the same view." *Census of India, 1911*, Vol. I, Pt. 1, p. 375.

[28]Op. cit., pp. 94–95; see also C. Bouglé, op. cit., p. 21.

[29]J. H. Bhattacharya, *Hindu Castes and Sects*, p. 131.

[30]See G. S. Ghurye, op. cit., pp. 15–16.

[31]See "Caste," *Encyclopedia of Religion and Ethics*. Says John C. Nesfield: "Castes act as a solvent of tribes. The formation of a caste implies that clans or fragments of clans, possessing some craft or occupation in common, but belonging to different tribes, have been seceding from their respective tribes and forming themselves into a new group united by the common craft or industry. The new group thus formed is a caste. . . . The tribe . . . begins to crumble away . . . and groups of men associated in hereditary professions, trades, or crafts, succeed to its place. . . . When two or more fragments, drawn from different tribes, have thus cemented by marriage into a single group, and when marriage within the group has been made a condition of membership, the caste has been completely formed." Op. cit., p. 105.

tion alone may not assure us of the presence of caste, hereditary specialization is none the less essential to the caste system.[32]

---

[32]It has been suggested to the writer that "it is significant that the caste system
has been particularly subjected to strain in industrial centers where modern factory organization cannot be efficiently geared into the caste system, therefore an
examination of the impact of industrialization on the caste system would clarify
considerably the place of occupation in that system." There is very much truth in
this. But Western civilization attacks and substitutes more than the occupational
basis of caste. Not only the caste system but all other systems of social organization
in the world bow to it. In so far as the caste system is concerned, it is probably the
powerful strain toward individualism which saps its vitality.

6. Caste Organization

No Central Government

THERE IS SO LITTLE GENERAL POLITICAL ORGANIZATION AMONG THE Hindus that Brahmanic India may be called a society without an organized state. Hindu society consists of a large aggregation of practically autonomous small communities held together by mutual dependence. There have been kings among the Hindus from time immemorial, but, so far as we know, these have always governed in the interest of a ruling caste or estate. In days of native rule, strong rajas here and there have exercised considerable authority in the affairs of castes;[1] their administration, however, has been despotic and capricious. Law has never attained the objectivity of the secular. According to the Abbé Dubois:

There has been no legal code; neither has there been any record of legal usage. There are, it is true, a few works containing general legal principles, and a few wise legal maxims which have helped to guide the judges in their decisions; yet nowhere have there been properly organized courts of justice.[2]

The Idea of a State and Nationality

An organismic theory of society has persisted with great strength among the Hindus. It has filled the need for a rationale of the social order. The individuating influence of caste has probably kept every appearance of collective sympathy from developing into an organized state, and of course Brahmanic India never dreamed of nationalism.

[1] *Census of India, 1911*, Vol. I, Pt. 1, p. 393. For a general discussion of the activities of early kings, see Edward W. Hopkins, "The Social and Military Position of the Ruling Caste in Ancient India," *Journal of American Oriental Society*, Vol. XIII, 1888.

[2] Op. cit., p. 654. For instances of direction and advice to the king in his administration of justice, see Manu, VIII, 1, 41, 45, 310.

The system limits the opportunity both for concerted action and of achieving a common purpose. Hindu society, says Senart, "has given rise to no state which is comparable even with the narrow government of the cities of antiquity, still less with our modern state."[3] And Risley observes further: "There is consequently no national type and no nation or even nationality in the ordinary sense of the words."[4]

The Hindus, then, never attained a conception of nationality. Possible national patriotism has been absorbed in caste patriotism. Nationalism calls for some degree of popular identification of aspirations, memories, and sympathies, but the caste system is antipathetic to such a tendency. René Maunier has put considerable emphasis on the point that "the idea of nationality takes birth everywhere by the putting of peoples in contact with strangers."[5] A people does not gain a national conception of itself in isolation; the feeling for group unity and the idea of a common fortune result from its reaction to competitive incursions of strangers who conceive of themselves as having a common destiny.[6] India has had its share of invasions, but up to recent times it was still possible to say that "the vast majority of the people of India are as yet untouched by the idea of nationality."[7] However, as the country begins to get its bearings in the arena of capitalistic competition, nationalistic sentiment crops up sporadically.

Many Hindus have mistaken the general absence of concern of one caste about the affairs of another for "the democratic spirit." In a system where sympathy for man as man is at its nadir, groups, at a prescribed distance, may live very much as they please; but this situation is hardly democratic. To think of others as being unworthy of notice is not necessarily tolerance. Intercaste indifference and apathy do not mean democracy. "True citizenship [is] impossible under a caste system which all but deified the priestly class, condemned great multitudes [the Sudras] to a life of contempt, and banished the untouchables beyond the social pale."[8] The concept of a civic ideal, then, becomes practically impossible; for the individual, the welfare of the nation must always be subordinated to the welfare of the caste.

No possible qualification of an "other-caste" individual could be

---

[3] Op. cit., pp. 8–9. See also p. 198.

[4] Op. cit., p. 25. To the same effect, see pp. 272, 289. See also G. S. Ghurye, op. cit., pp. 182–88, for a discussion of caste as a barrier to the development of an Indian nation.

[5] *Sociologie coloniale,* p. 76.

[6] Ibid., pp. 75–76.

[7] H. H. Risley, op. cit., p. 288.

[8] H. N. Brailsford, "Indian Question," *Encyclopedia of the Social Sciences.*

sufficient to attract a voter against the wishes of his caste. In fact, under the caste system, voting by caste may be the only possibility, and what this would mean politically is difficult to say. The caste system is probably the "completest denial of democracy."[9]

Spatial Organization

The village is the geographical unit of caste life. Caste occupational specialization tends to be limited by the size of the village. In India today there are well over half a million villages, and these are informally divided into natural districts of one or more villages, each having its hierarchy of castes.

Caste and village organization are complementary to one another, two closely adjusted parts of one total situation. . . . Economically the village is a unit, self-sufficient and largely self-governing, completely equipped with farmers, merchants, artisans, and menials. . . . The duties and remunerations of each group are fixed by custom, and the caste rules strictly prohibit any man from entering into competition with a fellow-caste member.[10]

Money is seldom used in the village because payments are ordinarily made in kind.[11] These diminutive economic systems tend not only to secure the interdependence of castes but also to bar strangers from community participation. The village provides its own communal services—its roads, temple, school, water, courts, and so on. Village life helps to stabilize the caste system. The primary group relationship which it facilitates permits the easy identification of caste members, and since generation after generation lives in the same limited areas, family histories become common knowledge. Consequently there is seldom any mistake about a man's caste affiliation.

Brahmans, a Factor

The primary organizing social force in Hindu society is a prestige-social-distance complex. What the public thinks of a man or the group to which he belongs appears to be a more powerful source of social control in India than in most other parts of the world. We recognize it in the plight of the outcaste and in the ceaseless struggle for mainte-

[9]See *The Cambridge History of India,* Vol. VI, pp. 594–95, and H. H. Risley, op. cit., p. 275.
[10]Martin Luther Dolbeer, op. cit., pp. 12–13.
[11]R. Mukerjee, op. cit., pp. 3–4, 12. See also "Indian Question," *Encyclopedia of the Social Sciences.*

nance or advancement of caste position. The norm of public opinion is the attitude of the Brahman.

Groups organized principally about some occupation hold each other in equilibrium by scrutinizing any claim to rights and privileges, by exacting or withholding customary dues and services, and by controlling rigidly the intracaste practices and behavior of each caste member. The greater the proximity of castes, both in space and status, the greater the intercaste pressures toward conformity to expected patterns of behavior. Thus we may think of the system as self-regulating—that is to say, it is not policed.

The dharma, or way of life, of a caste is traditional; it is grounded in the static doctrine of karma and transmigration, and attempts by lower castes to appropriate it by imitation provoke considerable envy and ill will. The effectiveness of these controls developed among the castes has led some writers to conclude that the Brahman plays but an insignificant part in the determination of intercaste relationships.

The role of the Brahman, however, is subtle; we must not expect to see him as the policeman of the system. Brahmans are the traditional keepers of knowledge and wisdom; the gurus have earned the unquestioned respect of all other castes, and their very attitude toward caste tends to determine caste rank. The Brahman is not capricious in judgment, for he is himself the personification of tradition. Intercaste behavior tends to be in terms of what each caste believes Brahmans will sanction, while Brahmans are controlled reflectively by the exalted opinion which the community holds of them.

The services of the Brahman are indispensable to the system; there is no substitute for him.

By the people generally, he is regarded as a pure, stainless, twice-born being, divine as well as human, worthy of unbounded admiration and worship. He is the priest of the Hindu religion, directing the ceremonies performed at the temples, sacred wells, sacred tanks, sacred rivers, and at all other hallowed places throughout the land. He is present to sanction and give effect to the great social festivals of his countrymen, held at marriages, at births of sons, and at deaths. He casts the horoscope, tells the lucky days, gives spiritual counsel, whispers *mantras* or mysterious words, executes magical incantations and charms; and is at once household god, family priest, and general preceptor and guide, in behalf of the many millions of Hindus residing in the vast country lying between the Himalayas and Cape Comorin.[12]

No other caste covers the territory so completely as the Brahman. These priests are indeed the hubs of the hundreds of thousands of small

[12]M. A. Sherring, op. cit., Vol. I, p. 3.

communities which compose the system. "India, as a whole, is the home of the Brahmans; but only a portion of it is the home of Rajpoots [the military caste]. A district in India without Brahmans would be like *Hamlet* with its leading character withdrawn; yet there are many districts in which no Rajpoot has ever dwelt."[13] The caste system, then, is essentially a religious rather than a political social order. Quite early in the history of the Hindus the Brahmans defeated the Kshatriyas in a struggle for social precedence, and, though they have never taken to the sword, their spiritual influence over the people is probably stronger than any military control ever exercised by a secular ruler.

"The supremacy of the Brahmans has now become one of the cardinal doctrines of Hinduism; so much so, that orthodox Sudras of the old school will not break their fast until they have sipped water" which has been sanctified by a Brahman's dipping his toe into it.[14] According to Bouglé, the sole organizing force which has kept the caste system from crumbling is an unquestioned acceptance of a religious conception of life and a belief in the omnipotence of the sacerdotal body.[15] Nripendra K. Dutt asserts that "the prestige of the Brahman is the corner-stone of the whole organization."[16]

Ordinarily Brahmans are competent to administer any phase of Hindu law; indeed, all law in Brahmanic India is "canon law." Hence any breach of custom or written rule is considered a violation of a divine mandate, and, consequently, any punishment meted out by Brahmans is accepted as a sacred judgment.[17] Even when Brahmans leave the actual administration of the law to the king they never concede the right to advise him in reaching decisions.[18]

Formerly, Hindu kings, under instruction from their pandit ministers, would enforce caste observances. But under the present non-Hindu state, no such action could be expected. In many instances, pandits have to be consulted both as to whether a member has really violated *Shastraic* injunctions and as to the penalty which should be inflicted in that special case.[19]

Usually, however, each caste is competent to deal with infractions of its own rules; and the judgments of its council or panchayat are usually final.

---

[13]Ibid., Vol. II, p. lxviii.
[14]"Caste," *Encyclopedia of Religion and Ethics.*
[15]Op. cit., pp. 172, 179, 182.
[16]*Origin and Growth of Caste in India,* Vol. I, p. 3.
[17]C. Bouglé, op. cit., pp. 179, 189.
[18]See, for example, Manu, VIII, 1.
[19]John P. Jones, op. cit., p. 123.

The Panchayat

Probably no single institution of the caste system so clearly illustrates the fact that a caste is a corporate unity as the panchayat. Not all castes have a panchayat (literally, a tribunal of five), but they all have some means of constituting a body capable of exercising its functions. It is upon the panchayat that the business of maintaining order within the caste and the settling of intercaste questions devolve. Indeed, it has been said that "the caste is its own ruler."[20] Of course we should expect methods of procedure to vary from caste to caste, but an examination of some of the features of this council may give us a fair understanding of its character.

But before describing the panchayat it may be well to differentiate some of the more important judicial bodies of the system. The panchayat proper is a permanent or temporarily constituted governing body of a caste. It is seldom, if ever, composed of fewer than five members, although a larger number is not uncommon.[21] The *parishad,* or village panchayat, is a village council composed of representatives from the leading castes in the village. It is concerned mainly with inter-caste questions, and "questions concerning which the law is silent or doubtful."[22] George W. Briggs has observed some of these in the Punjab and the United Provinces.[23] It seems, however, that the village panchayat is very uncommon. "Whatever may have been the case in the past, the village panchayat is rarely found at the present day."[24] More recently public officials have been working to revive the village panchayat as an institution of village government.

Sometimes a powerful headman or guru may act as sole arbiter on questions arising in the caste, or a general assembly of all the adult male members of the caste may sit in judgment upon the affairs of the caste. Of more recent development is the *sabha,* or general meeting of regional representatives from the subcastes of a caste. It settles matters of interest to the whole caste.[25] In this discussion we shall be concerned mainly with the panchayat.

---

[20]"Every caste has its own laws and regulations, or rather, we may say, its own customs, in accordance with which the severest justice is meted out." Abbé Dubois, op. cit., p. 32.

[21]Ibid., p. 655.

[22]*Census of India, 1911,* Vol. I, Pt. 1, p. 395, where Manu is cited as authority for assigning the function of this tribunal.

[23]*The Chamars,* p. 49.

[24]*Census of India, 1911,* Vol. I, Pt. 1, p. 395.

[25]George W. Briggs, loc. cit.

The juridical functions of most castes are in the hands of the head-man, the panchayat, and the caste assembly. The headman calls the panchayat, presides at its deliberations, and pronounces the decision of the group.[26] In most castes supreme authority is in the hands of the panchayat, a body numbering five or more men, and sometimes in-cluding the older women of the caste.[27] In others, however, final authority is reserved to the caste assembly.[28] "Panchayats, as a rule, do not allow persons of other castes to take part in their deliberations, but in case of difficulty they sometimes refer the matter to some out-sider of local dignity or experience, whether he be a Brahman or be-long to some other caste of good status."[29]

The caste panchayat has jurisdiction over all matters concerning its welfare; it is not at all concerned with questions of a civic nature. It organizes boycotts, regulates the occupational activities of its caste members, upholds rules concerning commensality, settles questions of marriage, and assumes responsibility for general intercaste relation-ships.[30] Of particular interest to the panchayat are those relationships

[26] In summarizing the Report from the Central Provinces and Berar, the *Census of India, 1911,* describes the procedure of the council: "The constitution and pro-cedure of the panchayat are the same in most of the castes. As a rule, the pan-chayats are not permanent bodies, but are called together when required. It is the business of the man who, for any reason, requires the decision of the panchayat, after consulting the headman of the caste, to collect the members of the caste at the ap-pointed place, his own house, a temple, a pipal tree, a specially built meeting place or the headman's house. The headman is in most cases a hereditary office-bearer, but has usually no independent powers, unless he is far superior in wealth and power to his caste fellows. In the latter case he may have the absolute position of dictator. . . . On the appointed day the members meet at a fixed place, and the headman or one of the elders explains the nature of the offense committed, and calls upon the offender to admit it or make his defense." Vol. I, Pt. 1, p. 389.

[27] Ibid.

[28] Emile Senart, op. cit., p. 64.

[29] Ibid. Senart elaborates upon this point: "Sometimes . . . the Brahman appears to act alone; in fact, a more or less tacit delegation takes place." Moreover, "the mere circumstance of their assistance is enough to make the caste vastly superior to those who do not enjoy the Brahman's administration." Ibid., pp. 73, 85. See also "Caste," *Encyclopedia of Religion and Ethics.*

[30] The *Census* lists the following chief offenses of which a panchayat takes cogni-zance: "(1) Eating, drinking, or smoking with a person of another sub-caste or caste. (2) Killing sacred animals, such as the cow, squirrel, cat, etc. (3) Homicide or murder. (4) Getting maggots in a wound. (5) Having the ear or nose torn. (6) Abusing relatives held in reverence, or beating parents. (7) Following prohibited occupations; e.g., a Mang sweeping a road, a Darji stitching leather, a Kirar selling shoes, a Kurmi serving as a syce, an Ahir cleaning pots, a Maratha washing clothes, and so on. (8) Breach of caste etiquette; e.g., leaving a dinner before others have finished. (9) Naming or touching relatives who should not be so named or touched; e.g., a wife should not name her husband, an elder brother may not touch his younger brother's wife." *Census of India, 1911,* Vol. I, Pt. 1, pp. 392–93.
Other matters which a panchayat may deal with are: (1) finding a suitable mate for a marriageable boy or girl; (2) widow remarriage; (3) partition of property, the decision of minor quarrels, and, occasionally, the adjudication of thefts. Ibid.,

of the individual with the community which tend to affect the status of the caste.

The highest castes do not ordinarily have panchayats. "When a case comes up for decision, a special meeting has to be convened for the purpose."[31] Not infrequently the most influential men of the caste or the gurus of the community decide caste affairs and pronounce judgments which are followed by the entire caste or subcaste.[32]

The caste has power to punish its members. This apparently simple fact tells a big story about the sociology of caste. Caste punishment is not merely ridicule or exclusion; it involves rather the infliction of specific sentences upon an individual or group of individuals. The power of a caste to punish is indispensable. It is the basis upon which the corporate responsibility of the group rests. It indicates, moreover, the extent of dependence of the individual upon his caste for existence. The caste had power (before British rule) to mete out penalties even of death to its members; it may impose fines, castigate, banish, subject to ignominy, and excommunicate.[33] There is no appeal from the decision of the caste. Today, in areas where the British courts are established, the panchayat has been forced to contract its criminal jurisdiction; but offenses specifically against the interests of the caste are still within the purview of caste judgment.

Control over the Individual

The security which the caste gives its adult members is of the same kind of fearful indispensability as that which the family provides for its young children. The competence of the caste does not end with the exercise of organizational and juridical functions; it is also intimately concerned with the domestic life of the individual. After long personal

---

p. 392. On this subject see also Risley, op. cit., p. 76, and George W. Briggs, op. cit., pp. 49–50.

[31]*Census of India, 1911,* Vol. I, Pt. 1, p. 388; and G. S. Ghurye, op. cit., p. 3.

[32]Abbé Dubois, op. cit., p. 284.

[33]The Abbé Dubois puts the situation graphically: "Although the penalty of death may be inflicted by some castes under certain circumstances, this form of punishment is seldom resorted to nowadays. Whenever it is thought to be indispensable, it is the father or brother who is expected to execute it, in secrecy. Generally speaking, however, recourse is had by preference to the imposition of a fine and to various ignominious corporal punishments. As regards these latter, we may note as examples the punishment inflicted on women who have forfeited their honor, such as shaving their heads, compelling them to ride through public streets mounted on asses and with their faces turned towards the tail; forcing them to stand a long time with a basket of mud on their heads before the assembled caste people throwing into their faces the ordure of cattle, breaking the cotton thread of those possessing the right to wear it, and excommunicating the guilty from their caste." Op. cit., p. 37. See also George W. Briggs, op. cit., pp. 50–51.

contact with the system John P. Jones comes to the conclusion that the caste "so completely hems in the life of a man, imperatively prescribes for him the routine of life, even down to the most insignificant details, and thus shuts him up in his own clan and with equal completeness cuts him off from the members of other castes, that it can reduce any recalcitrant member to certain and speedy obedience, simply because there is no one to whom he can flee for sympathy and refuge."[34]

A satisfactory way of life for the individual is practically impossible outside of his caste. He "depends probably more than any other peasant in the world on the sympathy and co-operation of his brethren. . . . All the affairs of his life are regulated by the opinion of the [caste] in which he is born, and severed from that group he finds himself a hopeless outcaste."[35] There are, then, no actions of the individual which he may reserve to his own discretion, even on the ground that they are private.

Yet we should not think of a man's caste as constituting a tyrannical clique. In the caste system, caste members are passionately devoted and attached to their caste. Probably one factor naturally limiting spatial mobility among Hindus is the extreme nostalgia which usually develops among migrants. A man's allegiance to his caste is natural. He has, so to speak, inherited it. Therefore, we should not conceive of the caste as a sadistic institution. It has the definite function of protecting the welfare of all its members, and it cannot permit the possible devious acts of any one of them to subordinate this.

The shame which would reflect on the whole caste if the faults of its individual members went unpunished guarantees that the caste will execute justice, defend its own honour, and keep all its members within bounds of duty.[36]

The individual looks to the opinion of his caste as a comforting arbiter of right and wrong; he is subordinated to the group, a fact which works neither spiritual nor physical hardships. His rights and immunities against the world are secured for him by his caste, while outside of his caste he is destitute of social influence and disconsolate.

---

[34]Op. cit., pp. 115–16.

[35]William Crooke, op. cit., p. 177. See also Godfrey E. Phillips, *The Outcastes' Hope*, p. 20.

[36]Abbé Dubois, op. cit., p. 32.

Dharma

Caste dharma is the customary norm of behavior accepted and developed by a caste as its sacred way of life; it is caste usage made sacrosanct.[37] The dharma of a caste is a complex cultural whole, an atomized variant of the total culture. Ordinarily the dharma of a caste does not differ in every aspect from that of other castes, yet the slightest variation in some peculiar aspect may be sufficient to distinguish the whole.

It is the sacred duty of every member of a caste not only to follow religiously the dharma of his caste, but also to protect it against infringement or appropriation by other castes. Thus, respect for one's caste dharma, be that what it may, constitutes a greater source of divine favor than a desire to covet any other. "This strict and universal observance of caste and caste usage forms practically the whole sacred law."[38] Furthermore, the necessity of protecting caste dharma may be thought of as a factor contributing to caste stability and inter-caste invidiousness.

The Boycott

Another means of social control of which the Hindus are past masters is the boycott. Short of open conflict, it is the most powerful weapon which they possess. The use of the boycott is ingrained deeply in the immemorial practices of the people. Outcasting is itself a form of boycotting, and the effectiveness with which the latter may be employed against individuals or groups is universally attested to by observers in India.

A whole village may close up tight against anyone attempting to break with the social order. Again we refer to the Abbé Dubois for

[37]For a good discussion of the various uses of the term "dharma" in Hindu literature, see Gualtherus Mees, *Dharma and Society*, pp. 3ff. In his elaboration of the subject, however, Dr. Mees seems to have developed a sort of metaphysical eulogy of the concept. After lamenting the probable loss of dharma in human affairs the author inquires: "How does a man become aware of Dharma? . . . He becomes aware of an urge within himself, and, because it demands satisfaction, he follows, he obeys. The religious man will call it listening to the voice of God and obeying it. The ethical man will call it doing his duty and obeying his conscience. The practical sociologist will call it following his calling." P. 24. Again: "The ethical, the religious, the mystical, and the ideal aspects of Dharma are really aspects of what we might call the 'first aspects of Dharma.' Dharma, economic, political, racial, professional, etc., appertains to the 'second aspect'. . . . The 'first aspect of Dharma' accounted for the birth of the theory and ideal of Varna. The 'second aspect of Dharma' created caste in India." P. 90.

[38]Abbé Dubois, op. cit., p. 41. See also Vincent A. Smith, op. cit., pp. 34, 37.

a classic statement: "Sometimes one may see, as a result of a caste order, the tradesmen and merchants of a whole district closing their shops, the laborers abandoning their fields, or the artisans leaving their workshops, all because of some insult or of some petty extortion suffered by some member of their caste; and the aggrieved people will remain obstinately in this state of opposition until the injury has been atoned for and those responsible for it punished."[39] When applied to a caste-man, it is punishment feared even as a death sentence.

---

[39]Op. cit., p. 33. See also M. L. Dolbeer, op. cit., pp. 216ff.

7. The Origin of Caste

*T*HE TITLE OF THIS CHAPTER IS TOO PRETENTIOUS; WE COULD never hope to bring its content up to the expectations which are most likely aroused. When we put the question, "How did caste originate in India?" we are really asking, "How did Hindu society originate?" In the latter form, the magnitude of our assignment becomes clearly apparent. Had it not been that we are today, as ever, convinced by stories of origins, it would indeed be a thankless task to undertake a discussion of *the origin* of caste. Yet our discussion may not be entirely without fruit, for the various points which we shall consider will probably give us a clearer insight into the nature of Hindu society.

The racial theory of the origin of caste has tended to give new meaning to some Hindus' conception of themselves. Castes are now claiming to be "true Aryans" with a recently discovered sense of tentative Nordic arrogance.[1] Then, too, there are probably hundreds of popular and scientific writers who predicate axiomatically a racial origin of caste. This, of course, should be a rather harmless matter involving only an academic question of historical accuracy, did not the authors use the point as a postulate either in explaining the nature of the caste system in India or in justification of some form of modern race relationships. Consider, for example, Professor Pitirim Sorokin's conviction:

> The factors of race, selection, and heredity were known long ago. . . . In the *Sacred Books of India,* we find the theory that the different castes

[1] See S. V. Ketkar, *History of Caste in India,* Vol. I, pp. 77–82. "This noble pride has prevented the members of different communities from holding free intercourse and from intermarrying with foreigners and invading nations, and has thus kept the *Aryan blood pure and unadulterated.* If they had not possessed that *tremendous national pride* and had mixed freely with all people by whom they were overrun, we should not find in India today the full-blooded descendants of the *pure Aryan* family." Swami Abhendananda, *India and Her People,* p. 90. (Italics added.)

were created out of different parts of the body of Brahma, and that they are innately different; consequently, any mixture of blood, or cross-marriage, or even any contact of the members of different races is the greatest crime, and the social status of every individual is entirely determined by the "blood" of his parents. . . . Eugenics was well known and widely practiced in ancient societies. "Twice-born men (of the higher castes) who, in their folly wed wives of low caste, soon degrade their families and their children to the state of Sudras."[2]

The concluding quotation is from the Laws of Manu. It is clear that Professor Sorokin believes that ideas of racial purity, similar to those now current, and political biologists, usually called eugenists, were common among the Hindus some three thousand years ago. Though charged with error, such easy transitions from an ancient myth to conclusions about modern theories of racial purity are not uncommon. The author uses this as a basis for explaining the naturalness of race relations today. Harry Elmer Barnes and Howard Becker, without specific implications for modern situations, may yet be misleading in conclusions such as the following. They write:

It is significant that the four varnas providing the main scaffolding of Indian caste structure mean the four "colors." The castes shade from light to dark, with the priestly Brahmans, purest blooded and most jealously endogamous descendants of the "Aryan" invaders of about 3000 B.C. and therefore, at the highest and lightest part of the framework.[3]

It would be indeed remarkable if the thousands of castes in India really shaded off into a distinguishable gradation of tints from dark to light, and if each tint faithfully reproduced itself, protecting its "purity" all the while by endogamy from incursions of darkness. We shall refer again to this tendency to transfer one's own cultural attitudes to other social situations.

Seeking social origins is a particularly unproductive type of endeavor. The following ancient Hindu text seems to suit the occasion: "The origin of seers, rivers, great families, women, and sin is not to be found out."[4] With respect to the origin of castes, the difficulty probably

---

[2] *Contemporary Sociological Theories,* pp. 219–20; also p. 669.

[3] *Social Thought from Lore to Science,* Vol. I, pp. 71–72. Some popular writers as B. L. Putnam Weale put it vulgarly: "It is a fact certainly well worth always remembering that *castes* in Sanskrit are called *colours,* thus proving that race-prejudice is absolutely ingrained in human beings, no matter in what part of the world they may live." (Italics Weale's.) *The Conflict of Colour,* p. 229. For a Nazi-like vulgarization of this belief in ancient Aryan race prejudice, see the anti-color book by Stuart Orner Landry, *The Cult of Equality,* pp. 238–39.

[4] Quoted by Edward W. Hopkins, op. cit., p. 135. And the wise authors of Ecclesiastes (3:11) saw that "no man can find out the work that God maketh from the beginning to the end."

lies in the fact that the caste system did not *originate*. A social order does not originate; it evolves. Hence, that which we might discover as the origin is most likely not the social organization which we are seeking to describe.[5] At any rate, with this in mind we shall go as far back as history permits us.

If we were to ask ourselves what in Hindu society differentiates it from other advanced societies, we cannot help concluding that it is principally the dominance of priests. If, then, we are able to follow the circumstances which led to the ascendancy of priests, we might be able to achieve some insight into the development of the type of society which they influenced and helped to fashion. The presence of the Dravidians, a people distinguishable physically and culturally from the Aryans, must certainly have been a factor determining the kind of society which evolved in India. We should assume that they contributed to the system at every stage of its development.

The pure-blood theorists have discovered the origin of caste in Aryan racial antipathy, which is supposed to be an inherent attribute of Aryans. The caste system, as we know it today, however, is admittedly not based upon Aryo-Dravidian racial antagonism. It is a social system of an entirely different nature. Hence, it is the origin of the latter system and not of the postulated race-caste system, which we are interested in determining. Those who adduce the racial theory of caste always assume that there were at first two castes, the Aryans and the Dravidians, conquerors and conquered, white and black.[6] Their discussion of the relationship between these two peoples is always deductive and inferential, based upon the type of race relations with which we are now familiar among whites and peoples of color.[7] However, these writers have never succeeded in making a convincing

---

[5]"It is often said that the origin of a thing can never explain it; and this is true enough. Its origin is but one fragment of its history, even as its present activity is another fragment." G. D. Cole, *What Marx Really Meant,* p. 10.

[6]For instance, in comparing the culture of the Aryans and their conquered people, Arnold J. Toynbee says with assurance: "The relative material power of the two castes was in inverse ratio to their relative civilization. The Aryan conquerors of the Indus Basin . . . were barbarians." *A Study of History,* Vol. IV, pp. 229–30; and Edward Westermarck declares: "India was inherited by a dark people before the fairer Aryans took possession of it . . . the domineering spirit of the conquerors, their bitter contempt for foreign tribes, and their strong antipathies of race . . . found vent in the sharp distinction which they drew between themselves and the conquered population, the Sudras." *The History of Human Marriage,* Vol. II, p. 66.

[7]Almost without exception these authorities refer to the social situation which has developed between whites and Negroes in South Africa and in the Southern states of the United States in support of their theories. Always the African and American citations are more cogent than the point which they propose to establish about caste in India.

transition from such a pattern of race relationship to the caste system which we know in India. They either skip the difficulty or gloss it over with new theories about occupations and religion. Observe, for instance, the following conclusion of Dr. Ghurye:

The three first castes were first enjoined not to marry a Sudra female before any other restriction of an endogamous nature was tried to be promulgated. . . . The various factors that characterized caste-society were the result, in the first instance, of the attempts on the part of the upholders of the Brahmanic civilization to exclude the aborigines and the Sudras from religious and social communion with themselves.[8]

The three first castes were, so far as certain statements in the literature are concerned, Aryans. It would be consistent with modern thinking to pit them against the Sudras of questionable race and the Dravidians. But in order to do this Dr. Ghurye had to go to the extent of implying that the Brahmans, the Kshatriyas, and the Vaisyas were developed castes intermarrying among themselves but endogamous only with respect to others! This, of course, is not only opposed to the logic of the caste system but is also without a scintilla of historical support. Clearly it is absurd to say that the three first castes were endogamous among themselves.[9]

The second proposition of the Brahmans defending their civilization is a type of gloss which we usually find in the form of a corollary to these theories. In the following sections we shall consider in more detail various attempts to account for the system.

Traditional Theories

There are many stories and variations of stories of creation in the literature of the Hindus, but the one which occurs most frequently and which is most generally accepted is the famous Purusha myth of the Rig-Veda. In Book X, hymn 90, verses 11–12, an account is given of the creation of the four castes from the body of the great god Purusha; it is the earliest of all accounts. We cite it here at the risk of some repetition:

When they divided Purusha, how many portions did they make?
What did they call his mouth, his arms?
What did they call his thighs and feet?

---

[8] Op. cit., pp. 143–44.
[9] Cf. Stanley Rice, *Hindu Customs and Their Origins,* pp. 39–40.

> *The Brahman was his mouth,*
> *Of both his arms was the Rajanya made;*
> *His thighs became the Vaisya,*
> *From his feet the Sudra was produced.*[10]

The Rig-Vedic description is as limited as that; without elaboration or further explanations it stands in stark finality, one of the most powerful bits of philosophy in Hindu culture. This story of creation is valuable, not so much as an accurate description of the origin of caste, but rather as an indication of the fact that, even at so early a period (about 1000 B.C.), the most thoughtful men had been so far removed from the true social basis of castes or of social estates that it had become possible for them to accept a mythical explanation. The myth may be also indicative of the crescive nature of the caste system. Since the Hindus do not have a historical theory of caste, we shall pass on to some of the modern explanations.

There are, as we have noticed, many modern theories[11] of the origin of caste, but they may all be classified broadly into two categories: (a) those having a cultural explanation, and (b) those having a racial explanation. The number of writers accepting the latter type of explanation is probably many hundreds. All, however, have some variation of the idea that the early Aryans were determined to keep their white blood pure and that caste was their most effective method. Fewer theorists rely on a cultural hypothesis, but among them there is greater diversity of opinion. We shall consider the racial approach first.

Pure-Blood Theories

We shall have to quote fairly lengthy passages, for a paraphrasing of the authors may do violence to their thoughts. The early social life of the Hindus is obscure because there is very little historical record of it;

---

[10]*Hymns of the Rigveda,* translated with a popular commentary by Ralph T. H. Griffith, 2d ed., X, 90:11–12. For other later stories of creation, see John Muir, *Original Sanskrit Texts on the Origin and History of the People of India,* Vol. I.

[11]"Roughly speaking, there may be said to be five important theories of the origin of caste. Apart from minor variations and combinations of these five, there is first the traditional view of the origin of caste typified in the Code of Manu; there is the occupational explanation of which Nesfield was the best-known exponent; the tribal and religious explanation of Ibbetson; the family or gentile explanation offered by Senart; and the racial and hypergamous explanation of Risley." *Census of India, 1931,* Vol. I, Pt. 1, p. 433.

For a well-taken criticism of Senart's theory, see Macdonell and Keith, op. cit., Vol. II, pp. 268ff. See also for a recent discussion of the origin of caste: J. H. Hutton, *Caste in India,* pp. 117–66.

hence, attempts to ferret out social situations usually involve deductive reasoning.

It is generally recognized that Sir Herbert Risley has been the most insistent advocate of the racial theory of caste. He did considerable anthropometrical research among the Hindus, using his racial hypothesis as a guide. However, the reliability of his data and the validity of his conclusions have been questioned by later observers.[12] There remains, then, only his hypothesis supported by deductive reasoning. Risley puts his theory in the form of a law of race contact.[13] It runs roughly as follows: White men in contact with people of color will take women from the colored group but will not give their own women. When the whites have bred enough white women, "they will close their ranks" and form a superior caste. The mixed bloods will then close their ranks, forming additional castes with degrees of superiority based upon lightness of color.

This hypothesis covers considerable ground, hence we shall postpone consideration of it. In fact, what Risley has really achieved is an explanation of caste in terms of race relations and, having done so, he called race relations caste. Nripendra Kumar Dutt, writing more recently on the origin of caste, presents a variation of Risley, but his approach is somewhat more historical. Let us consider this:

That the color question was at the root of the varna system is apparent from the meaning of the word *varna* (complexion) and from the great emphasis with which the Vedic Indians distinguished themselves from the non-Aryans in respect to color. The class which retained the utmost

---

[12]"Risley's conclusions, based on measurements made by him in Bengal, have been called in question by Crooke in the United Provinces, Enthoven in Bombay, and Thurston in Madras, while O'Donnell has argued that even in Bengal measurements are often at variance with it." *Census of India, 1911,* Vol. I, Pt. 1, p. 381. For further criticism, see *Census of India, 1931,* Vol. I, Pt. 1, pp. 439ff., and Vol. V, Pt. 1, pp. 432ff.

[13]"Wherever in the history of the world one people has subdued another, whether by sudden invasion or by gradual occupation of their territory, the conquerors have taken the women of the country as concubines or wives, but have given their own daughters in marriage only among themselves. Where these two peoples are of the same race, or at any rate of the same color, this initial stage of hypergamy soon passes away and complete amalgamation takes place. Where, on the other hand, marked distinctions of race and color intervene, and especially if the dominant people are continually recruited by men of their own blood, the course of evolution runs on different lines. The tendency then is toward the formation of a class of half-breeds, the result of irregular unions between men of the higher and women of the lower, who marry only among themselves and are to all intents and purposes *a caste.* In this literal or physiological sense, caste is not confined to India. It occurs in a pronounced form in the Southern States of the American Republic, where negroes, and the various mixed races, mulattoes, quadroons, and octoroons, each have a sharply restricted *jus connubi* of their own and are practically cut off from legal unions with the white race. The same set of phenomena may be ob-

purity of color by avoiding intermixture naturally gained precedence in the social scale. The Brahmans were white, the Kshatriyas red, the Vaisyas —because of large absorption of black blood—were yellowish like the mulattoes of America, and the Sudras black, as is described in the Mahabharata.

In the first stage the Indo-Aryans were divided into three orders or varnas. They had no scruple in marrying indiscriminately among themselves, while racial hatred made them avoid contact with the non-Aryan Sudras. The memory of this age is preserved in the Mahabharata, Anushasana Parva, where it is stated that "The son of a Brahman by wives of the three varnas is a Brahman. Only four varnas are known to exist; a fifth does not exist." In other words, the son invariably belonged to the order of his father, whatever might be the rank of his mother. Such a statement is not subscribed to by any of the Dharmasastras. As, however, the Vaisyas came into greater association with the Sudras and became more *polluted* with non-Aryan blood than the two other classes, aversion came to be felt towards the union in marriage with a Vaisya girl.

This state of caste development is represented in a *sloka* of the same Anushasana Parva which states that: "of the four wives of four orders of a Brahman, in the two higher he himself (i.e., a Brahman) is born, in the two lower less pure sons are born who belong to their mother's varna." This state of things evidently continued till about the time of Manu, who also does not assign a separate caste to the son of a Brahman father and a Kshatriya mother. With the hardening of caste rules in the course of time, even this freedom was restricted. In the later Dharmasastras we find that none could become a Brahman who was not born of Brahman parentage on both sides. When the *marriage with a Sudra woman was so much abhorred and blamed,* we can easily conceive of the horror and detestation which a Brahman in his *racial pride* would feel at the sight of a Brahman woman marrying a Sudra. No words are too strong to condemn such a marriage, and as a deterrent it is enacted that the issue of such a union should occupy the humblest position in society. Thus we see that the development of inter-caste marriage restrictions was principally due to the racial difference between white conquerors and the black, and the desire of the former to preserve their purity of blood.[14]

Dutt's hypothesis contains just about the whole gamut of spurious reasoning on this problem; therefore, it is particularly appropriate as a model for discussion. We shall first mention broadly some of the points which come into question and then discuss their significance in other sections of this chapter.

---

served among the half-breeds of Canada, Mexico, and South America, and among the Eurasians of India, who do not intermarry with the natives and only occasionally with pure-blood Europeans." *Imperial Gazetteer of India,* Vol. I, new ed., p. 345. See also *The People of India,* 2d ed., pp. 56 *passim.* G. S. Ghurye has criticized Risley's explanation but has himself presented a similar racial theory; see *Caste and Race in India,* p. 108.

[14]*Origin and Growth of Caste in India,* Vol. I, pp. 21-23. [Italics added.]

Probably the most common explanation of the origin of caste is based upon beliefs that the word "varna" means color; hence, caste must have originated in the Aryan's passion for protecting their light Asiatic color from intermixture with the dark color of the Dravidians. However, as we shall attempt to indicate below, the early literature of the Hindus does not show this to be the case.

It becomes necessary for Dutt to rely upon even such remote metaphorical descriptions of the castes as *white, red, yellow, and black*. There is understandably some silence about explaining why the blood of the princes had already become "red" and only that of the priests had remained white—and this in spite of the fact that the Brahmanas and the Kshatriyas intermarried freely. In fact, Professor Hopkins has shown that in the Vedic period the Kshatriyas were the ruling caste in India.[15] If we take these disconnected references to color as implying superiority, then "red" must have been superior to white. As we shall see below, the term "varna" has other meanings besides color.[16] The analogy with the mulattoes in America is rather astonishing but characteristic of these theories.

One assumption which seems fatal to these theories is that there were two color castes before there were castes within any one color group. Not only is this position unrevealed in the data, but also reliance upon it has led to such confused statements as: "The class which retained the utmost purity of color by avoiding intermixture naturally gained precedence in the social scale." Why "naturally"? What does our writer mean by "class"? If it means caste, then castes were formed before they began to avoid color mixture.

Let it be said that we have no record of the racial composition of the Sudras. The term "Sudra" is not synonymous with "Dravidian." Neither do we have any authority for the statement: "Indo-Aryans had no scruple in marrying indiscriminately among themselves." The period is not known when a Vaisya man could freely marry a Brahman woman or even a Kshatriya woman. Only in the legendary narratives do kings wed the daughters of priests, but it is a platitude of the Mahabharata that no woman could marry into the caste beneath hers. Hopkins quotes the epic story of a Brahman woman and a king. Says the king: "Thou

---

[15]Edward W. Hopkins, "The Social and Military Position of the Ruling Caste in Ancient India," *Journal of American Oriental Society,* Vol. XIII, 1888.

[16]It should be remarked that the criterion of a single word, "varna," could never be accepted as adequate evidence of racial antagonism among Vedic Indians. Racial antagonism is a peculiar and complicated form of intergroup relationship, and it is this relationship which must be identified. We might just as well conclude that the Indo-Aryans ran locomotives in northwestern India because, let us say, the word "steam" is frequently used in the Vedas.

canst have no connubial connection with me, for thou shouldst not make a caste mixture."[17]

Then, too, in spite of the assumed "horror" of mixture with the darker race, Brahman men were privileged to have wives from all three castes below them, Kshatriyas from the two lower ones, and Vaisyas from the Sudras. Therefore, Brahmans may be said to have been the most flagrant mixers of blood in India. If color were indeed the determining factor, is it possible to say that if a person happened to be white he *ipso facto* became a Brahman, if black, a Sudra, so that one might look upon a man and classify him unquestionably? The historical data do not sustain this possibility.

The usual way of making the evidently impossible transition from the racial origin of caste to the non-racial caste system as we know it is to employ some such phrase as "with the hardening of caste rules in the course of time." Yet why should caste rules "harden"? We should expect them to have been relaxed, for as the population became increasingly mixed—so much so that today Brahmans are not infrequently darker in complexion than lower-caste persons—the *raison d'être* of caste should have vanished. Should we say that the *memory* that at one time Aryans protected themselves from intermixture by preventing their women from marrying darker persons is sufficient to perpetuate the caste system with increasing rigidity? It would be indeed difficult to accept such a proposition.

Moreover, if it is true that the Vaisya became so mixed that they were classed with the Sudras, how is it that they were able to maintain the "purity" of their caste as against the Sudras? Could it be that these people were so homogeneously "yellow" that they were able to maintain themselves intact, and this considering the fact that Vaisya men married Sudra women? Finally, if color were really the test of caste, how was it possible to make the cross between a Sudra man and a Brahman woman the most despised of all castes? The status of the offspring of Vaisya men and Brahman women was considered to be lower than that of Sudras. Certainly both these crosses must have resulted in offspring very much lighter in complexion than that of the lower-caste men. Is it possible that a system as permanent and as rigid as the caste order of India could be built upon skin color—distinguished not by color as such but by the parentage of the color groups? We might have castes of very light people occupying a position much below that of black Sudras merely because they originated from higher-caste mothers and lower-caste fathers. The pure-blood theories leave these questions unanswered.

---

[17]Op. cit., p. 352.

The writers who use modern ideas of race relations for the purpose of explaining the origin of caste make an uncritical transfer of modern thought to an age which did not know it. The early Indo-Aryans could no more have thought in modern terms of race prejudice than they could have invented the airplane. The social factors necessary for thinking in modern terms of race relations were not available. It took some two thousand years more to develop these ideas in Western society, and whatever there is of them in India today has been acquired by recent diffusion.

The Aryans could not have known the world position of white people. Says Manu: "All those tribes in this world, which are excluded from the community of those born from the mouth, the arms, the thighs, and the feet of Brahma are called Dasyus."[18] Like most primitive peoples, their world was limited to the known environment. Evidently the Dasyus were the Dravidians and aborigines who had not yet entered the caste system. Yet it is astonishing how many writers interpret these references to the Dasyus as indicating a bipartite race-caste system. The fact that the early authorities usually mention four castes already developed among the Aryans seems to have slipped them altogether.[19]

---

[18]Manu, X, 45. The Dasyus, or Mlechchhas, were evidently the Dravidian warriors, "the unsubdued foreign tribes who did not speak Sanskrit and had not been influenced by Aryan culture." W. Crooke, "Sudra," *Encyclopedia of Religion and Ethics.* The Dasyu, of course, should not be thought of as constituting a caste. The following excerpt from *The Cambridge History of India* indicates further the simple reasoning employed in developing a theory of the racial basis of caste: "The distinction between the Aryan colour (varna) and that of the aborigines is essential and forms the basis of caste. The question is thus narrowed down to the consideration of the arguments for and against the view that in the Aryans themselves caste divisions were appearing." Vol. I, p. 92. This statement is indeed surprising when one considers that all the author has in support of his conclusion is his belief that the word "varna" means color of skin. How this assumed two-caste system developed into the great multiplicity of castes, of course, is not explained.

[19]In this discussion we do not mean to say that the Aryan invaders did not recognize that they were of different color and culture from the native Indians, the Dasas or Dasyus; indeed we should assume that the latter made a similar recognition. Yet it is conclusions like the following for which we do not find support: "The main distinction between the Aryan *varna*, colour, and the black colour is unquestionably one of the main sources of the Indian caste system. The overthrow of the black skin is one of the most important exploits of the Vedic Indian." A. Berriedale Keith in *The Cambridge History of India,* Vol. I, p. 85. And this authority has no conflict of reasoning when, from the threads of history, he is led to conclude: "in the age of the Rigveda there was going on a steady process of amalgamation of the invaders and the aborigines, whether through the influence of intermarriage with slaves or through friendly and peaceful relations with powerful Dasa tribes." Ibid., p. 86. For a similar view, see Herbert H. Gowen, *A History of Indian Literature.* Gowen describes the Aryans in this way: "They are tall men, proud of their white skins to the disdain of others." Ibid., p. 43.

The term "Dasyus" seems to have been used by the Aryans in the same sense that the Greeks use the term "barbarian" to mean all those people whose culture

Even if it were possible for the Aryans to know the world condition of light-complexioned peoples, there would have been no particular cause for pride in identifying themselves with, say, the ancestors of the haughty Teutons of today. At that time the Dravidians evidently had a higher culture than that of the Aryans. The error made by the over-enthusiastic comparative philologists of the nineteenth century in identifying the Aryan family of languages with an Aryan race bears no little part of the responsibility for confusion in the study of caste. In referring to this general tendency to identify culture and race, Marcellin Boule writes:

It must be fully understood that race, representing the continuity of a physical type, stands for an essentially natural grouping, which can have nothing and in general has nothing in common with the people, the nationality, the language, or the customs corresponding to groupings that are purely artificial, in no way anthropological, and due entirely to history, whose actual products they are. Thus there is no Breton race, but there is a Breton people; no French race, but a French nation; no Aryan race, but Aryan languages; no Latin race, but Latin civilization.[20]

The Indo-Aryans have left no account of their pre-migration homeland, and it has not yet been determined. Some writers, however, have stated that the Indo-Aryans were the first white people who were faced with the problem of keeping their blood free from admixture with that of darker peoples. But this seems to be a pyramiding of assumptions. In the first place, we do not know when the Aryans entered India;[21] hence it may be futile to embark upon a discussion, the validity of which can depend only on definite knowledge of the date of Aryan immigration.

But suppose we grant priority of contact for the moment; it yet does not appear why the mere fact of first meeting of whites and peoples of color should be more favorable to the formation of a caste system than the second or third meeting. Obviously the Aryans did not know they were making the first contact; hence they could not have taken this into consideration. Moreover, it is certain that quite early different races lived together about Egypt and North Africa without developing a form of social organization similar to that of Brahmanic India:

Champollion has given the well-known picture of the human races of ancient Egypt after the paintings in the royal tombs of Biban el Molûk

---

differed from their own. Thus J. N. Farquhar observes: "The differences between [the Dasyus] and the Aryans on which the hymns [the earliest literature of the Aryans] lay most stress are religious." *The Religious Quest of India: An Outline of the Religious Literature of India,* p. 5.

[20]Quoted in *Race and History,* by Eugene Pittard, p. x.

[21]See Ibid., p. 289, for various estimates of the date of entry.

(The Valley of the Kings). These men, led by the shepherd of the Horns people, belonged to four distinct families. The first, nearest to the god, were of a dark red colour. . . . There can be no doubt whatever about him who comes next: he belongs to the Negro race known under the general name of *Nehasi*. The next one presents a different aspect: his skin is fresh-coloured, verging on yellow; he is bronzed with a strong aquiline nose. . . . This race bears the name of *Aamu* (Asiatics). Finally, the last has the skin colour we call fresh-coloured or white-skinned in its most delicate tint, and a straight, slightly arched nose, blue eyes, fair or ruddy beard. . . . He is clothed in an undressed bullock-hide, a veritable savage, tattooed on different parts of his body; this race is called Tamahu (Europeans).[22]

The period of itself, then, does not seem to be a factor determining caste.

With respect to the question of identifying race relations in other parts of the world with the origin of caste, we may observe an interesting cycle in thinking. The theorists usually begin by comparing the origin of caste with the modern white-black pattern of race relationships. An identification of the phenomena having been made, they proceed to establish their racial theory of caste; then they return forthwith to identify present-day race relationship with caste. In the meantime, they remain oblivious of the ongoing caste system as we know it in India. Therefore, *their* origin of caste, and not that of caste in action, becomes the standard. In other words, they must assume race relations today to be caste relations only as they conceive of the latter in their origination.

Color as a Factor

The word "varna" is practically all that the pure-blood theorists have in support of their position. Observe with what assurance H. D. Griswold reaches his conclusion: "The difference in colour was one of the causes that lay at the foundation of caste, for the very name of caste is *varna*, 'colour.' "[23] As a matter of fact, however, Böhtlingk and Roth state in their *Sanskrit-Wörterbuch* that the word "varna" means appearance, exterior, color, kind, species, caste; and Manu has used "varna" synonymously with "jati," which means birth—the form of existence determined by birth, position, rank, family, descent, kind, species.

[22]Eugene Pittard, op. cit., pp. 413–14. See also Edward Eyre, *European Civilization*, Vol. I, pp. 289, 359.

[23]*The Religion of the Rigveda*, p. 40. And, as is commonly done, this author found a satisfying analogy between the Indian situation and the "color line" developed in Africa and America.

But dictionary definitions are rather limited; hence we shall have to examine the application of the color concept in the literature. The following is the celebrated passage in the Mahabharata, so much relied upon by some students of caste. We quote it at length:

Bhrigu replied: "The Lord . . . also formed . . . men, Brahmans, Kshatriyas, Vaisyas, and Sudras, as well as other classes of beings. The colour of the Brahman was white; that of the Kshatriyas red; that of the Vaisyas yellow; and that of the Sudras black." Bharadvaja here rejoins: "If the caste of the four classes is distinguished by their colour, then a confusion of all the castes is observable." . . . Bhrigu replies: "There is no difference of castes: This world having been first created by Brahma entirely Brahmanic, became separated into castes in consequence of works. Those Brahmans who were fond of sensual pleasure, fiery, irascible, prone to violence, who had forsaken their duty, and were red-limbed, fell into the condition of Kshatriyas. Those Brahmans who derived their livelihood from kine, who were yellow, who subsisted by agriculture, and who neglected to practice their duties, entered into the state of Vaisyas. Those Brahmans who were addicted to mischief and falsehood, who were covetous, who lived by all kinds of work, who were black and had fallen from purity, sank into the condition of Sudras. Being separated from each other by these works, the Brahmans became divided into different castes. Duty and the rites of sacrifice have not always been forbidden to any of them."[24]

It is from this passage that authority has been derived for many conclusions about racial antagonism among the early Indo-Aryans. Pratapa C. Roy, translator of the Mahabharata, says, "The commentator explains that the words expressive of the hue of color really mean attributes. What is intended to be said is that the Brahmans had the attribute of goodness; the second order the attribute of passion; while the lowest order got the remaining attribute, viz., darkness."[25]

Consider, on the other hand, the meaning which G. S. Ghurye reads into the same passage: "The colour connotation of the word was so strong that later on when the classes came to be regularly described as varnas, four different colours were assigned to the four classes, by which their members were supposed to be distinguished."[26] The author, of course, does not show by historical data that varna really symbolized

---

[24]Santiparvan, verses 6930ff., quoted by John Muir, op. cit., Vol. I, pp. 139–41. According to this version, "The commentator . . . explains the different colours mentioned . . . as follows: red (rakta) means 'formed of the qualities of passion' . . . yellow (pita) 'formed of the qualities of passion and darkness' . . . and black 'formed of darkness only.' " Ibid., note pp. 140–41.

[25]Mahabharata, Vol. II, Santiparvan, p. 48, note.

[26]Op. cit., p. 42. Cf. Vincent A. Smith, *Oxford History of India,* p. 26.

racial antipathy between Aryan and Dravidian; reference to this four-fold color scheme is his sole reliance.

The metaphorical use of color in the Mahabharata seems to be closely identified with some sort of incipient dharma, a way-of-life virtue complex. Vishnu uses it somewhat in the same sense: "What has been acquired by the mode of livelihood of their own caste, by members of any caste, is called 'white.' What has been acquired by the mode of livelihood of the caste next below in order of their own is called 'mottled.' What has been acquired by the mode of livelihood of the caste two or more degrees lower than their own is called 'black.' "[27] In other uses, color seems to be "a symbol of the inherent qualities of nature." Thus in the Varnapavan of the Mahabharata a god says of himself: "My color in the Krita age is white, in the Treta yellow; when I reach the Dvapara, it is red, and in the Kali black."[28] And in the Taittiriya Brahmana, ii: 3, 8, 1, it is related: "Prajapati desired, 'May I propagate.' He practiced austerity. He became pregnant. He became yellow-brown. Hence a woman when pregnant, being yellow, becomes brown. Being pregnant with a foetus, he [Prajapati] became exhausted. Being exhausted, he became blackish-brown. Hence an exhausted person becomes blackish-brown."[29] Again in the same book of the Mahabharata from which the preceding color scheme is taken, the following explanation appears: "Six colours of living creatures are of principal importance, black, dusky, and blue which lies between them; then red is more tolerable, yellow is happiness, and white is extreme happiness. White is perfect, being exempt from stain, sorrow and exhaustion; possessed of it, a being goes through various births, arrives at perfection in a thousand forms."[30]

We are not even certain which skin color, if any, was always preferable among the early Aryo-Dravidians. As Dr. Mees points out:

The white complexion was not always the most popular and the most admired one. Shri-Krishna, the greatest Hindu Divine Incarnation and human hero, was always being called the "dark-cloud-faced one" or the "dusky-one" or the "dark-blue-one," and Rama, the divine hero, usually being represented as dark or blue or green. These two were the ideal of all that was most beautiful in a man. In the Bhagavata the beauty of Suka,

---

[27]Vishnu, LVIII, 6–8.

[28]Verse 12981, quoted by John Muir, op. cit., p. 145, note.

[29]Quoted, ibid., p. 23.

[30]Mahabharata, Santiparvan, 10058–59. See also Vishnu Purana, ii: 4–12, where, in describing worlds unknown, reference is made to the color of castes: "The castes which dwell there are severally the Kapilas, Aruneas, Pita, and Krishnas, or the Tawny, the Purple, the Yellow, and the Black." Quoted in John Muir. op. cit., Vol. I, pp. 498–99.

the "glorious son of Vyasa," is described at length. He is said to be of dark complexion.[31]

Mees continues to observe that "as regards physical beauty, the Indo-Aryans and the cultured Dravidians were equally handsome."[32] Nor was the literature always consistent in the figurative use of color as applied to human beings. Professor Weber quotes a passage from the Kathaka Brahmana which reverses somewhat the color scheme of the Mahabharata: "Since the Vaisya offers an oblation of white (rice) to the Adityas, he is born as it were white; and as a Varuna oblation is of black (rice) the Rajanya is as it were dusky."[33] The case for color as a dominant factor in the development of caste, then, does not seem to be supported by the use of the word "varna" in the literature. We shall now consider two well-known cultural theories of caste.

The Theories of Ibbetson and Nesfield

Both Denzil Ibbetson and John C. Nesfield worked officially with the 1881 census of India; they both developed occupational theories of caste, but Nesfield's is the more elaborate. Briefly, Ibbetson holds that caste is little more than an ordinary class society made rigid. His approach to the problem of origin is rather deductive. Laying down a principle of social differentiation for all societies, he dispenses with the necessity of treating the Hindu situation as a special case.[34] This ex-

---

[31]Gualtherus H. Mees, op. cit., p. 58. See also *Indian Year Book, 1939–40,* p. 16.
[32]Ibid., p. 68.
[33]Quoted by John Muir, op. cit., Vol. I, p. 140.
[34]The substance of Ibbetson's theory follows: "In every community which the world has ever seen, there have been grades of position and distinctions of rank; and in all societies these grades and distinctions are governed by two considerations: descent and calling. As civilization advances and the ideas of the community expand in more liberal growth, the latter is ever gaining in importance at the expense of the former; the question what a man is, is ever more and more taking precedence of the question what his father was. But in no society that the world has yet seen has either of these two considerations ever wholly ceased to operate; in no community has the son of the coal-heaver been born the equal of the son of the nobleman . . . while in all the son has begun where the father left off. The communities of India in whose midst the Hindu religion has been developed are no exception to this rule; but in their case special circumstances have combined to preserve in greater integrity and to perpetuate under a more advanced state of society than elsewhere the hereditary nature of occupation, and thus in a higher degree than in other modern nations to render identical the two principles of community of blood and community of occupation. And it is this difference, a difference of degree rather than of kind, a survival to a later age of an institution which has died out elsewhere rather than a new growth peculiar to the Hindu nation, which makes us give a new name to the old thing and call caste in India what we call position or rank in England. The whole basis of diversity of caste is diversity of occupation. The old division into Brahman, Kshatriya, Vaisya, Sudra, and Mlechchha or outcaste who is below the Sudra, is but a division into the priest, the warrior, the husbandman, the artisan, and the menial; and the more modern

planation, however, is so generalized and ideally constructed that it must be of little value for an understanding of the early history of caste. Because of this fact we shall not examine it critically.

The most carefully developed cultural theory of caste is that of John C. Nesfield. It has been called the occupational theory, in a very limited sense, by most authorities who wish to differ with it.[35] Nesfield insists that no racial theory of caste can stand, because before the system became organized the population had already become inseparably mixed:

> The restrictions of marriage which are *now* imposed by rules of caste did not begin to exist until at least a thousand years after the Aryans had come into the country, and by this time the Aryan blood had been absorbed beyond recovery into the indigenous. It was not till the time of Manu, that is, about 200 B.C. or later, that the caste rules in regard to marriages were coming into force. Even then, as his own writings show, they were not universally accepted by Brahmans themselves: for he waxes very wroth with certain Brahmans of his own day who persisted in the habit of taking Sudra or low-caste women as their first wives. . . . It is clear, then, that prior to his time, that is, ever since the Aryan invader had set foot on Indian soil, which must have been more than a thousand years before his code was compiled, a Brahman or professional priest (for Brahman *caste* did not then exist), could marry any woman that he liked.[36]

Besides emphasis upon the point that the population had become amalgamated quite early, Nesfield asserts that even today "a Bengali Brahman looks like other Bengalis, a Hindustani like other Hindustanis, a Mahratti like other Mahrattis, and so on, which proves that the Brahmans of any given nationality are not of different blood from the rest of their fellow-countrymen."[37]

Briefly, the theory runs as follows: The priesthood was not at first an exclusive monopoly of Brahmans; sacrifices were performed and invocations composed by the military chiefs. But when the hymns were

development which substituted trader for husbandman as the meaning of Vaisya or 'the people' did not alter the nature of the classification. . . . I have attempted to show in the preceding paragraphs that pride of blood, especially in the upper, and shame of occupation, especially in the lower classes, are in all societies the principal factors which regulate social rank; and that when Brahmanism developed caste, all that it did was to bind the two together, or at least to prevent the dissolution of the tie which bound them and which would have broken down in the ordinary course of social evolution, and while thus perpetuating the principle of the hereditary nature of occupation and social status, to hedge it round and strengthen it by a network of artificial rules and restrictions which constitute the only characteristic peculiar to the institution of caste." *Panjab Castes*, p. 13.

[35] For a mistaken presentation of Nesfield's theory, see, for example, J. D. Anderson, *The Peoples of India*, pp. 13ff.

[36] John C. Nesfield, op. cit., p. 76.

[37] Ibid., pp. 75-76.

collected into liturgies and the sacrifices became more complicated, specialization became a necessity. The importance of the sacrifice to the well-being of society gave the priesthood a position of great honor; the tendency was for the priesthood to become hereditary, like royalty. "When the Brahman had thus set the example of forming himself into an exclusive and highly privileged caste, the other classes in the community were compelled to take what precaution they could for securing privileges as were within their reach; and they did this, not merely in self-defense, but in imitation of a class of men whom they had been accustomed for centuries to regard with deepest veneration. If Brahmans had been a celibate order, like the Roman Catholic priesthood in western Europe . . . the example which Brahmans gave of setting up caste barriers against outsiders, might have had no effect upon the general structure of society."[38]

This, then, is Nesfield's account of the beginnings of caste in India. The author concludes by saying: "The main contention urged in this paper remains unshaken, that the Indian race is practically one in blood, character, traditions, and sympathies, and that caste is not a question of blood but of function."[39] The latter statement is broad indeed; it shares no little part of the responsibility for other students discarding the whole theory. Moreover, his explanation might have been much more acceptable had he not marbled into it an almost distinct theory based upon Herbert Spencer's "stages of civilization." Reliance is put upon a universal evolutionary theory of culture, of which the four stages are the hunting, the pastoral, the agricultural, and the industrial stage. Thus he asserts:

Each group of castes represents one or other of those progressive stages of culture which have marked the industrial development of mankind not only in India, but in every other country in the world, wherein some advance has been made from primeval savagery to the arts and industries of civilized life. The rank of any caste as high or low depends upon whether the industry represented by the caste belongs to an advanced or backward stage of culture; and thus the natural history of human industries affords the chief clue to the gradations as well as the formation of Indian castes. Such in rough outline is the theory of caste advocated in these pages.[40]

It should be easily evident that this is too nice a formulation to be accepted without question. It has resulted in some confusion of an ex-

---

[38]Ibid., p. 100.
[39]Ibid., p. 39.
[40]John C. Nesfield, op. cit., p. 88.

ɔlanation of the caste system which otherwise seems to have considerable merit. We shall refer again to Nesfield.

The Varna Theory

Dr. Gualtherus H. Mees has developed a varna theory of caste based
upon the idea of a morally stratified society. As a general premise the
author says: "Caste or class differences, in East and West equally, were
at first based on merit and social usefulness, and later tended to become hereditary and economic."[41] This hypothesis has met with much
favor, especially in the East, for it tends to give especial dignity to the
ancestors of high-caste groups. To Mees, a man's varna is his *natural*
and *right* position in society; it was the early Hindu ideal. "Varna . . .
is the Hindu ideal and theoretical picture of class based upon
Dharma,"[42] the good life. "We have not rendered 'Varna' as 'class' because 'Varna' presents the theory and ideal of 'class,' and the word
'class' at once suggests historical and actual classes. . . . We have
translated Varna as 'natural class.' "[43]

According to the author, the varnas are a population gradient of
social usefulness. "The four Varnas represent degrees of sociality from
the most highly social to the extreme non-social. . . . In a healthy and
harmonious society the population classes correspond to the Varnas."[44]
And Mees believes further that "the ancient Hindu Sages were far
wiser than we now think,"[45] because they planned a "varna society."
In support of this contention he cites the religious rationalization of
the social order from the Mahabharata:

A man, whether he be a Brahman, Kshatriya, Vaisya, or Sudra, is such
by nature, this is my opinion. By evil deed a twice-born man falls from
his position. . . . The Kshatriya or Vaisya who lives in the condition of a
Brahman, by practicing the duties of one, attains to Brahmanhood. . . .
By practicing the following good works, a Sudra becomes a Brahman.[46]

Literally, and out of its context, the foregoing passage would seem to
abandon completely many principles of caste. The reference, however,
seems to indicate a karmic ideal, for it is not only inconsistent with the

---

[41]*The Hindustan Review,* April 1937, p. 652.
[42]G. H. Mees, *Dharma and Society,* p. 51.
[43]Ibid., p. 52.
[44]Ibid., pp. 143–45.
[45]"Caste and Class and Ideals of Equality," *Hindustan Review,* July 1937, pp.
30–34.
[46]Ibid., August 1937, p. 85.

theme of the Epic but also incompatible with the closed-group cultural development of India. We have only to put the thought positively to recognize its imperfections. Thus we may not say: "In the Epic period persons born Sudras had only to live like Brahmans in order to attain full-fledged Brahmanhood."[47]

Mees conceives of his varna hierarchy as a gradient of socio-physiological groups. He compares this "natural hierarchy" to the organs of the human body, functioning with varying degrees of excellence.[48] The early authorities, however, thought that although the mouth was superior to the foot, each was, in its own way, equally efficient. So far as this life was concerned, there was no insistence on the possibility of group improvement to a higher status.

But this theory of "natural class" is even more foreign to anything that we know to have ever existed in India. It is in reality a variation of the Platonic-Aristotelian philosophy of superiority of "inner nature" at birth, and the desirability of fashioning a society that will permit the finest natures to gravitate to their *natural* positions. "Every man," says Dr. Mees, "belongs to a certain Varna in accordance with his character, social behavior, and function . . . and as he *unfolds* and *grows* he may himself raise his status to a higher Varna."[49] Originally in India, Mees thinks, there was a social hierarchy based upon virtue: "Does his class and position correspond to his Varna? His *conduct* indicates it."[50] The latter possibility has always been a desideratum in social life; however, such a hierarchy still remains to be developed on this earth.

So far as social stratification is concerned, it is ceremony and ritual, not character, which are the determining factors. Says Abbé Dubois:

A Brahman would be degraded and banished from his caste for having eaten food which had been prepared, or drunk water that had been drawn, by a person of lower caste, but were he convicted of stealing, or uttering vile calumnies, of attempting to take another man's life, or of betraying his prince or country, none of these offenses would prevent his appearing without fear or shame in public, or would hinder his being well received everywhere.[51]

---

[47]The sense in which the early authorities thought of personality is shown in the following passage from Manu: "From a Kshatriya and the daughter of a Sudra sprang a being, called Ugra, resembling a Kshatriya and a Sudra, ferocious in his manners and delighting in cruelty." X, 9.

[48]*Dharma and Society,* pp. 143–45.

[49]Ibid., p. 136. (Italics added.)

[50]Ibid., p. 150.

[51]Op. cit., p. 661.

To the same effect Holland writes: "He is a good Hindu who observes the rules of caste and the dictates of religious ceremonial, be his moral character what it may. No Hindu is ever out-casted for theft or lying."[52] And Landtman concludes further: "Philosophers of all ages have pronounced true human merit and virtue to be independent of rank and class."[53] Furthermore, it should be quite a problem for Mees to show how virtue finally became hereditary.

However, Dr. Mees believes that this attribute of "natural classes" was not peculiar to the early Indo-Aryans: "We cannot escape from the conclusion that Christ also distinguished grades of morality and sociality, and organs with different social functions."[54] But what Christ did not say is that virtue is directly correlated with social status. Indeed, He was inclined to show an inverse relationship between the two. The difficulty with Mees's "natural hierarchy" is that it is highly unnatural. Ordinarily we do not find social classes based upon virtue. Although merits and demerits may tend to determine the place of the individual in society, social classes need not consist of individuals of uniform merit. What individuals believe privately—their character— has never been a determining factor in social stratification. "Behold," sings the Psalmist, "these are the ungodly, who prosper in the world; they increase in riches."[55]

If one has an upper-class job or is born within a given class and behaves according to the rules of that class, he may leave the practice of such things as purity, truth, and kindness to members of any class; therefore, "true gentlemen" and "Honest Abes"[56] are not to be thought of as constituting a social stratum of society. In the 23rd chapter of Matthew, to illustrate further, Jesus rebukes those who sit in high places and yet lack basic virtues; nonetheless, there they sit.[57]

---

[52]W. E. S. Holland, *The Indian Outlook,* p. 18; see also Godfrey E. Phillips, op. cit., p. 29.

[53]Gunnar Landtman, *The Origin of the Inequality of the Social Classes,* p. 1. "The equality which is the principal object of sociological interest is not inequality of capability and attainment but of conditions and circumstances. The inequality in question here is not inequality of personal gifts but of established social gradations." Ibid., p. 3.

[54]Op. cit., p. 148.

[55]Psalms, 73:12.

[56]Mees, op. cit., pp. 144–45.

[57]Thorstein Veblen puts it this way: "Manners presently come, in popular apprehension, to be possessed of a substantial utility in themselves; they acquire a sacramental character. . . . There are few things which so touch us with instinctive revulsion as a breach of decorum. . . . A breach of faith may be condoned, but a breach of decorum cannot. 'Manners maketh the man.' " *The Theory of the Leisure Class,* p. 48. In his advice to him who would be a successful tyrant Aristotle declares: "[The tyrant should be concerned] always *to seem* particularly attentive to

An overemphasis on the spiritual nature of the early Indo-Aryan system of social stratification leads Dr. Mees to the conclusion that the Brahman-Kshatriya-Vaisya-Sudra relationship was a logical one; thus he concludes: "Quite in accordance with the theory of Varna one would expect mostly Kshatriyas to become Brahmans. . . . From the pinnacle of the hierarchy, people are drawn up step by step, each being the example of the man next below, and forming the ideal for a group farther below."[58] This, indeed, is what should have been; it is as natural, however, for the "pinnacle" to be corrupt as it is for it to be a beacon of integrity.

The tendency of persons of lower status to accept the way of life of those above them as their ideal of decorum does not mean that such acceptance will, *ipso facto,* result in an advance in status or that the ideal will necessarily be judged meritorious for all times and places. In fact, the very position of Brahmans at the head of the social structure tends to contravene Mees's belief that "man has largely lost the capacity to recognize Varnas."[59] The pinnacle of a society is ordinarily reserved for Caesar, the military class. And so it was in India. Only after a long and unparalleled struggle for power did the priests secure that position to themselves.[60]

We have no reason to believe that early Dravido-Aryans were more "virtuous" than modern Hindus. The "good old Krita Age, the age of virtue," belongs to the system of Hindu mythological chronology. The Kali Age of human strife, selfishness, and discord, the age which the Hindus actually know, is the only age that they have ever known. The Aryans came into India not as missionaries of virtue but rather as conquering, bloodshedding, plundering, wine-drinking, meat-eating, gambling, enslaving, internecine, polytheistic hordes—and this notwithstanding sporadic flights of idealism in their early literature. This array of descriptive terms is by no means intended to derogate from the early cultural achievements of the Indo-Aryans; it may appear to do so only if we impute modern standards to that period, a transfer which some writers are unfortunately too prone to make.

Let us say, then, that the early God-fearing Aryo-Dravidians never attained that form of social organization necessary to allow meritorious

---

the worship of the gods; for from persons of such a character men entertain less fears of suffering anything illegal while they suppose that he who governs them is religious . . . but this must be done so as to give no occasion for any suspicion of hypocrisy." *Politics,* William Ellis, trans., p. 178.

[58]Op. cit., pp. 137, 177.

[59]Ibid., p. 144.

[60]See infra, p. 113ff.

persons to pass easily up to the top regardless of inherited rank. We might err seriously if we rely upon glimmerings of religious ideal:sm in the early literature as representative of forms of social organization. The varnas were mixed concepts. They included the idea of estate and of caste.

The Brahmans, authors of the varna myth, were never very much interested in describing in detail individuals far from themselves in status; hence, they, like the Kshatriyas, were defined functionally, while the Vaisyas and Sudras were left as functionally heterogeneous groupings. All the rest of humanity, besides these four categories, were classed as one, the Mlechchhas.[61] The farther away in status the group to be classified, the less careful the Brahmans were about their definition and the more inclusive their classes.[62] Even to this day Brahmans are not particular about distinguishing low-caste people. The latter are generally referred to by class terms such as "Sudra" or "Panchama."[63] We shall revert to this point in a later section.

Early Amalgamation of Population

In a previous section reference was made to Nesfield's contention that Indian peoples in contact became mixed before the caste system developed; the obvious importance of this position has led us to a further consideration of it. We should understand clearly that it has never been shown that the Indo-Aryans conceived of themselves as part of a white race. "White-race psychology" is a modern phenomenon. The Aryans thought of themselves as culturally different from the Dravidians, but not culturally superior. They did not think of themselves as a branch of a race, the world distribution and status of which they could not possibly have known.

In India they were quickly isolated and, by the time they had developed a literature, they had lost all memory of their geographical origin. Their mixture with the native population was rapid at first, and

---

[61]"All those tribes in the world, which are excluded from the community of those born from the mouth, the arms, the thighs, and the feet of Brahman [the god], are called Dasyus, whether they speak the language of the Mlechchhas [barbarians] or that of the Aryans." Manu, X, 45.

[62]"The division of Aryans into three classes, while all the non-Aryans except the untouchables are lumped together in one, is explained by the fact that the classification was made by the members of the former community and that differences amongst themselves naturally loomed more largely in their eyes than those amongst the Anaryas." *Census of India, 1911,* Vol. I, Pt. 1, p. 366.

[63]"To the Brahman . . . it is immaterial whether a man is a Teli, a Kahar, or a Nai; the important question for him is whether water can be taken from him or not, whether his touch does or does not cause pollution." Ibid.

when the caste system came with its retarding effects upon amalgamation, neither race nor color was its principal motivation. Retardation
of complete amalgamation was evidently a by-product rather than a
main purpose of caste. Our recently developed[64] white-colored pattern
of race relations has been one of the most stubborn distractions to an
understanding of caste. Ketkar recognized the limiting influence of this
race hypothesis for the study of Hindu society and remarked:

> Till the arrival of European scholars on Indian soil, the people of
> India never meant by the word "arya" that race of invaders who reduced
> the natives of the soil to servitude. The word indeed probably had such a
> meaning, but only for a short period antedating the concrete beginnings
> of civilization in India. . . . All the princes, whether they belonged to the
> so-called Aryan race or the so-called Dravidian race, were Aryas. Whether
> a tribe or a family was racially Aryan or Dravidian was a question which
> never troubled the people of India until foreign scholars came in and
> began to draw the line.[65]

Respect for status determined by some cultural mark of superiority
rather than race seems to have been the concern of the society. The
Aryans "warred and made alliances indiscriminately with one another
and with those Dravidian states surrounding them that still maintained
their independence."[66] Indeed, it appears that the designation
"Kshatriya" included all the nobility, whether Aryan or Dravidian.[67]
Of course the Kshatriyas intermarried freely, while Brahmans always
had the option of taking Kshatriya women as wives. There is very
little direct reference in the literature to the process of amalgamation;
however, there are no white castes in India today. "Its early conquerors: Aryans, Greeks, Pathans, and Moguls, settled in the country,
intermarried, lost their white skins, and became Indians."[68] Race

---

[64] Says Ralph Linton: "Prior to the sixteenth century the world was not race-
conscious, and there was no incentive for it to become so. The ancient world was
a small world and because of the gradual transition in physical types which is to
be found in all continuous geographic areas, the physical differences between the
classical and the barbarian peoples were not very marked. . . . Even when the
existence of such physical differences was recognized, they had no immediate social
connotations. . . . Even the Crusades failed to make Europe race-conscious. . . .
It is only with the discovery of the New World and the sea routes to Asia that race
assumed a social significance." *The Study of Man,* pp. 46–47.

[65] Op. cit., Vol. I, pp. 79, 82.

[66] H. J. Fleure, *The Dravidian Element in Indian Culture,* 1924, p. 61.

[67] A. A. Macdonell and A. B. Keith, *Vedic Index of Names and Subjects,* 2 vols.,
London, 1912.

[68] H. N. Brailsford, "Indian Question," *Encyclopedia of the Social Sciences.* According to H. D. Griswold, "The Kashmiri and Punjab Brahmans represent probably the purest Aryan blood, but the whole population . . . is to be regarded as
more or less a mixture. Thus the Vedic antithesis between Aryan and Dasyu has
been resolved into a higher synthesis consisting of the blending of the two races."
The Religion of the Rigveda, p. x.

crossing, so far as it affected physical appearance, seems never to have been a problem of the Hindus.

The following remark of a Hindu scholar, which is obviously a composite of fact and apprehension, may throw more light on the subject:

The Brahman orthodoxy does not know what Aryan or Dravidian means, nor does it care to inquire into it for its purpose. All that the Brahmans care to inquire about is Sanskara (the sacraments) and Karman (the aggregate of a man's actions as determining his future fate-character) . . . But the Hindu of English education is quite different. Hearing of the conditions in the United States, those Hindus who think themselves to be Aryans wish to demark themselves sharply from those whom they think to be Dravidians. . . . I shall be very sorry if a superficial acquaintance with a half-developed and hybrid ethnology, a wrong interpretation of ancient documents, and an invented tradition should result in magnifying racial differences and in making future consolidation and amalgamation of India more difficult and distant.[69]

Vaisyas and Sudras

Belief in the fourfold division of caste in India has persisted from the Vedic period to this day, yet it appears never to have existed in fact. The persistence of this belief is probably due to the influence of Brahmans in the system. Quite obviously this ancient classification of castes is not the result of an objective study of Hindu society; rather, it represents a picture of society as seen from the point of view of Brahmans. And, since Brahmans were the authors of practically all the early literature, their insights had more than an even chance of becoming generally accepted. As we have mentioned above, the concept "Aryan-Anaryan" does not imply a white-caste versus black-caste relationship.

The three Aryan castes were supposed to be the Brahman or priestly caste; the Kshatriya, comprising the "king, his great lords and vassals, together with the knightly part of the army"; and the Vaisya or caste of the people. In infancy, individuals born in these three castes had the exclusive right to receive the sacrament of initiation, after which they were called twice-born. And because of this right these three were designated the twice-born castes. The Sudras were the servant caste, while all the other people of the world were outcastes.[70] At most, the early system might have been in an *estate* stage of development, when large strata of society had attained legal distinction.[70a]

At any rate, the fourfold classification is particularly inaccurate in its

---

[69] S. V. Ketkar, op. cit., Vol. I, pp. 78–79, note.
[70] See Manu, X, 4.
[70a] See J. H. Hutton, *Caste in India,* p. 59.

description of the Vaisya, Sudra, and outcastes. These three never formed castes in the sense that the priests and royalty were castes. The two latter were identified with specific functions and interests; the three former were heterogeneous categories. The fact that Vaisyas and Sudras were classified without internal distinction may indicate the supercilious disregard in which the military and priestly groups held the people in general. This attitude seems to have persisted through the ages.

The people never had a limited occupation in the sense that the Brahmans had one. Macdonell and Keith mention more than a hundred different occupations and skills as they appear at random in the Vedic literature;[71] undoubtedly a census would have shown many more. Thus, only by some Procrustean device would it be possible to include all these in one caste. One hardly needs to labor the point that the *rathagrtsa,* or skilled charioteer, must have had a different social position from the *malaga,* or washerman; the *vanij,* or merchant, from the *sauskala,* or seller of dried fish; the *manikara,* or jeweler, from the *dasa,* or fisherman. In the law books the duty of the Sudra is repeatedly emphasized, but this seems to have been an emphasis on what ought to be rather than an exact description of what was actually the case. The margin between Sudra and Vaisya classes seems to have been always obscure. Not only are the real limits of occupation between them vague, but also these two groups are frequently classed together for social distinction. Furthermore, they appear to have been highly amalgamated, a situation which contravenes the race-caste hypothesis. According to Hopkins: "Such co-mingling of Aryan and un-Aryan must have been very early.; and I fancy that in the earliest period of the Epic, the people-caste had already a more and more uncertain line dividing it from the vulgar."[72]

The Brahmans and the Kshatriyas have been the immemorial castes, the stabilizers of the system. Within the Vaisya and Sudra classes, however, there have been many castes. Some authorities have doubted whether even the Kshatriyas ever constituted a caste;[73] it seems, however, that the repeated specific reference made to Kshatriyas in the early literature and the natural tendency for royalty to be endogamous favor the conclusion that they were at least as much a caste as the Brahmans. On the other hand, Vaisyas are mentioned only infrequently and

---

[71] *Vedic Index,* Vol. II, pp. 585–86.

[72] Edward W. Hopkins, op. cit., p. 80. See also G. S. Ghurye, op. cit., pp. 58–59.

[73] See S. V. Ketkar, op. cit., Vol. I, pp. 96–99; Emile Senart, op. cit., p. 117; Vincent A. Smith, op. cit., p. 35.

Sudras almost not at all. Say Macdonell and Keith: "The Vaisya plays singularly little part in Vedic literature, which has much to say of Kshatriya and Brahmin."[74]

However, as the Kshatriyas tended to lose their ruling-class status by their being reduced from time to time by foreign conquerors, their status became increasingly nebulous. In an analysis of the census data of 1881, Ibbetson explains:

> There is no such thing as a Vaisya now existing; . . . it is very doubtful indeed whether there is such a thing as a Kshatriya, and if there is, no two people are agreed as to where we shall look for him; and . . . Sudra has no present significance save as a convenient term of abuse to apply to somebody else whom you consider lower than yourself; while the number of castes which can be classified under any one or under no one of the four heads, according as private opinion may vary, is almost innumerable.[75]

Purport of Anthropometry

Many attempts have been made to study caste relationship by comparing the physical measurements of different castes. In the *Census of India, 1901,* Herbert Risley, who conducted extensive anthropometrical research, reviewing the aim of ethnology, states quite broadly:

> The modern science of ethnology endeavors to define and classify the various physical types, with reference to their distinctive characteristics, in the hope that when sufficient data have been accumulated, it may be possible, in some measure, to account for the types themselves, to determine the elements of which they are composed, and thus to establish their connexion with one or other of the great families of mankind.[76]

With these possibilities in mind, Risley set out to develop experimental techniques for explaining both the origin of caste and modern caste relationships. The following classic statement on the subject sums up his position: ". . . it is scarcely a paradox to lay down as a law of caste organization in Eastern India that a man's social status varies in inverse ratio to the width of his nose."[77] We have already mentioned that both the data and the findings of Risley have been called into question; we revert to his conclusions here so that we might discuss the potentialities of the method. It has helped him to the belief that caste originated in Aryo-Dravidian racial antagonism.

We may well ask, then, What does anthropometry seek to discover

---

[74]Macdonell and Keith, "Vaisya," *Vedic Index.*
[75]Op. cit., p. 2.
[76]Vol. I, Pt. 1, Sec. 765–66.
[77]Herbert H. Risley, *The Tribes and Castes of Bengal. Ethnographic Glossary.* Calcutta, 1891, p. xxxiv.

about the origin of caste? Suppose, indeed, it is determined that physical measurements correlate with caste position; would this fact show that caste had its inception in racial antipathy? Caste might have had other beginnings, while thousands of years of inbreeding might have resulted in distinguishable physical types. In India the number of castes runs into thousands; is it possible that even, say, twenty castes should have selected common nose widths and maintained them intact over the years? That this should be so, of course, is highly absurd. Yet such must be the implications of these physical measurements. For, if the caste did not purposely select the physical trait which has been protected by caste isolation, it must be assumed that the castes have jealously guarded their blood for probably thousands of years without actually recognizing the physical trait which distinguished them.

The hypothesis seems to be that, even though in modern times it cannot be shown that race difference is a factor determining caste position, the fact that the physical measurements of castes vary should be sufficient proof that race must have been a factor in the past. It must follow, therefore, that castes have forgotten their initial motivating force; they do not know that their rigid exclusiveness depends in reality upon an ancient technique for preserving racial purity. And since, let us say, in southern India today the population is physically homogeneous, modern castes must be considered useless vestiges.

We need not labor the fallacy of this trend of thought. It should be sufficient to determine from actual inquiry the social role of physical variation in the system, for it could have been neither necessary nor possible for the ancient Hindus to use anthropometrical data in setting up their social hierarchy. If race were a factor, simple visibility should have answered the purpose.

We may mention finally that all attempts to rank castes in India according to physical criteria have been fruitless and that none of the researchers has been able to state his hypothesis clearly, nor has he been able to show the significance of the same for an understanding of the caste system.[78]

Brahman-Kshatriya Struggle for Power

It is the thesis of the eminent student of early Indo-Aryan society, Edward W. Hopkins, that priests did not always constitute the highest

---

[78]See "Caste," *Encyclopedia of Religion and Ethics;* G. S. Ghurye, op. cit., pp. 106–07; C. Bouglé, op. cit., pp. 141ff.; Emile Senart, op. cit., p. 169; Edgar Thurston, *Castes and Tribes of Southern India,* Vol. I, pp. livff.; D. N. Najundar, "Blood Groups and Castes," *Nature,* Vol. 145, p. 1025.

caste.[79] Only after a long and pertinacious social struggle did the Brahmans succeed in achieving undisputed primacy in the system. In that protracted dispute, each side chose its weapons, but the Brahmans' proved to be the more potent. The Brahmans readily conceded to the Kshatriyas the full expression of temper and of physical prowess over mundane matters, but they virtually exhausted the possibilities of ingenuity, tact, and subtlety in demonstrating to the Kshatriyas that Brahmans controlled the very will of the gods. There was never any open encounter between these two powerful groups which settled decisively the place of each in society; notwithstanding this, however, the haughty Rajanyas were slowly and imperceptibly subdued.

The Brahmans, never having been centrally organized, presented no common front which might have been attacked by the military class. They fought individually; therefore, an occasional defeat was more a personal matter than a reverse for the Brahman caste as a whole. "It is true that they formed an association, that they were an exclusive and distinct class. But they formed no corporate body, and had no head. They worked as individuals."[80]

The Brahmans never sought to rule the people by taking over the powers of the Kshatriyas. They were always willing for—indeed they encouraged—the king to administer the law. They recognized the necessity of the military power; they themselves could not prosper without it. Yet they wanted this natural ruling class to realize that it held its position at the pleasure of Brahmans; hence, the king must be humbled in the presence of Brahmans even as he would before the gods.

The following verses from the Institutes of Vishnu show what the Brahmans wanted: "Let the king in all matters listen to the advice of his astrologers; let him constantly show reverence to the gods and to the Brahmans; let him bestow landed property upon Brahmans."[81] Thus they wanted to be supreme arbiters of social policy, to be immune from punishment by the king, and to be assured of economic security. All these things, indeed, the Brahmans finally achieved, but not without a struggle. The great Epic "recounts a scene wherein a king meeting a priest calls out to him 'Get out of the way' . . . and when the priest repeats the 'law eternal' . . . it is without effect, and the king even smites him with his whip."[82] By the time Book IX of Manu was com-

---

[79]"Social and Military Position of the Ruling Caste in Ancient India," *Journal of American Oriental Society,* Vol. XIII, 1888.

[80]Ibid., p. 72.

[81]Vishnu, III, 75, 76, 81.

[82]Edward W. Hopkins, op. cit., p. 73, note.

posed, however, the Brahmans were able to say: "When the Kshatriyas become in any way overbearing towards the Brahmans, the Brahmans themselves shall duly restrain them; for the Kshatriyas sprang from the Brahmans."[83]

The priests were the intellectual specialists of the time, and they seldom failed to use their ability to advantage. They couched their religio-political arguments in favor of their superiority in unnumbered wily aspects, until at last they convinced the people.[84]

---

[83]Manu, IX, 320.
Both Jainism and Buddhism were religious movements initiated by Kshatriyas partly as reactions to the pretentions of Brahmanism. But since these movements did not seriously change the course of Hindu society—Buddhism itself having been almost banished from India—we have not considered them in this discussion.

[84]One of the many legends and allegories emphasizing Brahman superiority over Kshatriyas appears in the Bhagavata of the Mahabharata, verses 7196 and following. It demonstrates the capitulation of Arjuna, a king, who dares to question the authority of Brahmans: "Then ascending his chariot glorious as the resplendent sun, he exclaimed in the intoxication of his prowess, 'Who is like me in fortitude, courage, fame, heroism, energy, and vigor?' At the end of his speech a bodiless voice in the sky addressed him: 'Thou knowest not, O fool, that a Brahman is better than a Kshatriya. It is with the help of the Brahman that the Kshatriya rules his subjects.' Arjuna answered: 'If I am pleased, I can create, or if I am displeased, annihilate, living beings; and no Brahman is superior to me in act, thought or word. . . . The Brahmans are dependent on the Kshatriyas, and not the Kshatriyas on the Brahmans, who wait upon them and only make the Vedas a pretence. . . . I shall subdue all those unruly Brahmans clad in hides. . . .' Hearing this speech of Arjuna, the female roving in the night became alarmed. Then Vayu, hovering in the air, said to Arjuna: 'Abandon this sinful disposition, and do obeisance to the Brahmans. They will subdue thee; those powerful men will humble thee, and expel thee from thy country.' The king asked him, 'Who art thou?' Vayu replied: 'I am Vayu, the messenger of the gods, and tell thee what is for thy benefit.' Arjuna rejoined, 'Oh, thou displayest today a great warmth of devotion to the Brahmans. But say that a Brahman is like any other earth-born creature. Or say that this most excellent Brahman is something like the wind.'"
Vayu, however, goes on to answer this spirited banter by adducing various instances in which the superiority or terrible power of the Brahmans had been manifested. . . . The story continues: "When the gods, including Indra, were enclosed within the mouth of Mada, the earth was taken from them by Chyavana. The gods then considering that they had lost both worlds, in their distress resorted to Brahma, and said, 'Since we have been swallowed up in the mouth of Mada, the earth has been taken from us by Chyavana, and the heaven by the Kapas.' Brahma answered, 'Go speedily, ye gods, with Indra, to the Brahmans for help. After propitiating them, ye shall regain both worlds.' They did so and the Brahmans, after ascertaining that the gods would themselves deal with those of their enemies who were on earth, began a ceremony for the destruction of the Kapas. The Kapas upon this sent a messenger to the Brahmans, to say that they themselves were all, like them, skilled in the Vedas, learned, and offerers of sacrifice. . . . How then should the Brahmans be able to conquer them? It would be more for their interest to desist from the attempt. The Brahmans, however, would not be persuaded; and when in consequence, the Kapas assailed them, they hurled forth fires by which the Kapas were destroyed.
"Hearing all these testimonies . . . Arjuna at length gave in, saying: 'I live altogether and always for the sake of Brahmans. I am devoted to the Brahmans, and do obeisance to them continually. And it is through the favor of Dattattreya [a Brahman] that I have attained all this power and high renown, and that I have practiced righteousness. Thou hast declared to me truly all the acts of the Brahmans.

They employed extended allegories such as the celebrated Parasurama myth, wherein the great Rishi destroyed all the Kshatriya men and, but for the benevolence of Brahmans in siring the offspring of the Kshatriya women, the whole Kshatriya caste would have gone out of existence;[85] or they used cryptic little invidious assertions such as: " 'A Brahman is higher than a Kshatriya,' Varuna said";[86] or hedged themselves about with mystery, such as the elaborate proof, in the Aitareya Brahmana, that the king must not drink the soma, a prerogative of Brahmans only.[87] By patient persistence, disdain for the sword, and a dispersed army of religio-political propagandists, then, the priests of India accomplished what their fellow workers in other parts of the world frequently attempted but usually failed to realize.

Brahmans, the Keepers of Knowledge

Almost always the priests of a society tend to become the oracles of the people, and Hindu society is not an exception. In fact, Hinduism offers a classic example of this. Brahmans were probably the most learned priesthood of the ancient world. There may be some question about the social value of their learning, but, so far as volume of literary production and zeal for conserving it are concerned, they were unsurpassed. One is amazed when one considers the great quantity of matter held in the minds of these men and transmitted precisely from generation to generation.

There were evidently no written books in ancient India. Instead of libraries, the memories of the learned priests were "the repositories of literature,"[88] while orally transmitted knowledge was the only means of bestowing this heritage. In regard to this Professor Maurice Winternitz writes:

Even today, the whole of the literary and scientific intercourse in India is based upon the spoken word. Not out of manuscripts or books does one learn the texts, but from the mouth of the teacher, today as thousands of years ago. . . . If all the manuscripts in print were to be lost, that would by no means cause the disappearance of Indian literature from the face

---

and I have listened intently.' Vayu then said to him: 'Protect the Brahmans, fulfilling a Kshatriya's function; and restrain your senses!' " Thus the Brahmans won another battle. See John Muir, op. cit., Vol. I, pp. 463–73. Another famous legend is that of Vasishtha and Visvametra, which represents the complete victory of Brahmans over the Kshatriyas. Ibid., pp. 296–426.

[85]See R. C. Dutt, *The Epics and Lays of Ancient India,* Vol. I, p. 153. Mahabharata, Adi Pava, I. 104. 5–7; and Muir, op. cit., Vol. I, Sec. XVIII.

[86]*Harvard Oriental Series,* Vol. 25, Rig-Veda Brahmanas, p. 303.

[87]Ibid., p. 29ff.

[88]A. A. Macdonell, *India's Past,* p. 52.

of the earth, for a great portion of it could be recalled out of the memory of the scholars and reciters.[89]

It is true that the Brahmans had a monopoly on learning; in one sense, however, it was a natural monopoly. After the literature had accumulated to such large quantities it became necessary for the individual to devote virtually his whole life to committing it to memory. He had to start as a child, and the unfailing interest of schooled parents became the best means of leading him into the arduous tradition. Hence the transmission of the sacred knowledge from father to son, and consequently a hereditary priesthood, became natural. But the priests capitalized this normal situation and ruled out the possibility of any outsiders entering the field.

Whatever material emoluments accrued to their office were reserved to themselves and their children. Indeed, even when writing became available, they were loath to transmit their knowledge by manuscripts. Says Winternitz:

It was to the interest of priests . . . that the sacred texts which they taught in their schools, should not be committed to writing. By this means they kept a very lucrative monopoly firmly in their hands. He who wished to learn something, had to come to them and reward them richly; and they had it in their power to withhold their texts from those circles whom they wished to exclude from sacred knowledge.[90]

Although the three twice-born castes had the privilege of studying the Vedas, the sacred law ruled that only the Brahmans should teach them.[91] It is clear that this arrangement not only insured the authority of Brahmans but also provided a sufficiently large number of students for their schools. Brahmans, then, became the sages of the land, and we can see how, especially in times of social unrest which ordinarily indi-

---

[89]*A History of Indian Literature,* trans. by S. V. Ketkar, op. cit., Vol. I, p. 34; see also Albert Schweitzer, op. cit., pp. 33–34.

[90]Op. cit., p. 35. Attempts to keep the sources of religious knowledge out of reach of the people are, of course, well known in Western society. The violent resistance of the Roman Catholic Church to the translation of the Bible is the classic instance. But Brahmans had such incontestable control over the minds of Hindus that even when the sacred compositions were written they were able to keep them out of the hands of laymen. Thus the Abbé Dubois remarks that it is so much to their interest to maintain a monopoly on the material that "the Brahmans have inculcated the absurd theory, which is implicitly believed, that should anybody of any other caste be so highly impudent as even to read the title page, his head would immediately split in two. The very few Brahmans who are able to read these sacred books in the original do so only in secret and in a whisper. Expulsion from caste, without the slightest hope of re-entering it, would be the lightest punishment for a Brahman who exposed these books to the eyes of the profane." Abbé Dubois, op. cit., p. 172.

[91]Manu, II, 172 *passim.*

cated the displeasure of the gods, they whittled away the pretensions of the Kshatriyas.

Dominant Factors in Caste Development

In this section we shall consider what seem to be determining factors in the rise of the caste system. The hypothesis is roughly this: that the caste order arose not in a conflict situation between Aryans and Dravidians, nor was it motivated from the lower social rungs of society, but rather it had its incipience in rivalry between Brahmans and Kshatriyas for primacy in the social order. Since, however, it has been repeatedly shown that the priests were the social aggressors and that they finally emerged victorious, it seems advisable to approach the subject from their point of view. Moreover, as we have attempted to show above, the caste system is under the paramount influence of Brahmans; we have no data indicating that it has ever been dominated by "Aryans." We might reiterate also that the idea of an Aryan and a Dravidian caste standing in opposition to each other is entirely without historical support.

Almost to the exclusion of all others in the early literature, we come upon two groups, the Kshatriyas and the Brahmans. And concerning them two facts seem to stand out: the one that Brahmans were not initially organized into a closed corporation with priestly functions entirely for themselves; and the other that, although their position was highly esteemed, they were amenable to the will of royalty, the early ruling class. We do not imply, of course, that the priesthood was not hereditary. In that period we should expect not only priestcraft but also all other occupations calling for some degree of skill to be jealously guarded and transmitted as a heritage from father to son. Our meaning is rather that it is only gradually that rigid occupational exclusiveness developed.

Persons of both the military and the artisan classes performed all the Vedic rites. "Any such person, therefore, and consequently a person not a Brahman might . . . have been called, though no doubt figuratively, a priest."[92] There was a priesthood, a hereditary priesthood, but the functions of the priest were not completely monopolized. During the years, however, the religious literature was augmented and the sacrifice increased in complexity and importance; therefore, of necessity the priesthood became more and more specialized.[93]

---

[92]John Muir, op. cit., p. 245. To the same effect see also pp. 265ff.

[93]The state of complexity which the sacrifice had reached is indicated by the following statement by A. A. Macdonell: "Of the sacrifical priests there were several,

Concomitant with this development, Brahmans increased their grasp upon public opinion. They demonstrated their indispensability in the social order by taking complete control of the sacrifice. Endogamy and ascendancy over the Kshatriyas were all that were necessary to give momentum to the system. Endogamy, like other tendencies, developed gradually; we should expect the feeling for it to have increased with emphasis upon distinctiveness. It was the means by which functional groups protected their heritage.

While the struggle for position was in process, the masses of the people—Aryan, Dravidian, and their mixed offspring without distinction—looked on and listened. That they had to be reckoned with is illustrated by the following story of a theological argument between a group of Brahmans and King Janaka:

The Brahmans said among themselves, "This Rajanya has surpassed us in speaking; come, let us invite him to a theological discussion." Yajnavalkya, however, interposed, "We are Brahmans, and he a Rajanya; if we overcome him, we shall ask ourselves, whom have we overcome? but if he overcome us, men will say to us, a Rajanya has overcome Brahmans. Do not follow this course."[94]

An indication of the involvement of the people is also brought out by a verse from the Mahabharata expressing the concern, "From the dissensions of Brahmans and Kshatriyas the people incur intolerable suffering."[95] However, the priests never failed to see the value of cooperation with the military class; and it is evidently in this situation that the pattern of antagonistic co-operation among castes was nurtured for the system. Says Hopkins, "The priestly and knightly castes were always together, for ill or good. . . . They fought bitterly, and learned each other's strength. They became friendly, and joined on the basis of mutual advantage, and from that time on were as one, above the lower order."[96]

---

with definite functions and technical names, the chief being the Hotr or 'invoker,' the Udgatr or 'chanter,' the Adhvaryr or officiating 'sacrificer,' and the Brahman or superintending priest; in the period of the Rigveda, the Hotr was the most important; later the Brahman became so. The Purohita was probably not any one of these, though he might be employed to perform the functions of one of them." "Vedic Religion," *Encyclopedia of Religion and Ethics.*

[94]From the Satapatha Brahmana, quoted by Muir, Vol. I, p. 428.

[95]Santiparvan, 2802, ibid., p. 129. See also Macdonell and Keith, *Vedic Index,* Vol. I, p. 204.

[96]Edward W. Hopkins, op. cit., p. 76. The Brahmans insisted that no king should be acceptable to the people if he did not maintain a purohita, or Brahman adviser. "The gods do not eat the food offered by a king who has no purohita. Wherefore even when not about to sacrifice, the king should put forward a Brahman as his domestic priest." Aitareya Brahmana, VIII, 24, 27, quoted in John Muir, op. cit., p. 367.

The Brahmans did not seek to gather the Vaisyas, the supposedly Aryan-race people, to themselves. Had a racial sentiment existed, we should have expected this. But they left them to guard their own status, so that "in the course of time the Vaisya fell more and more in position" until they were frequently on a social parity with the Sudras.[97] Notwithstanding this, the Vaisyas did not permit themselves to be degraded in a body. They, too, with the blessing of Brahmans, organized about the hereditary interest which occupation provided,[98] and imitated the exclusiveness of the upper castes. Indeed, as Nesfield remarks, "the principle of caste arrogance, once set in motion by the most influential class in the community, has been extended downwards from the Brahman to those immediately next him in rank, till it has at last taken possession even of those inferior and backward classes which had no privileges or functions that are worth defending."[99]

It may be well to observe that the purpose of the Brahmans was not to dominate the people by force; they wanted rather to obligate paternally the society to them for all time. For instance, after monopolizing the teaching of the Vedas, they set out forthwith to advertise this function as infinitely more important than that of any other group of men. Says Manu, "Of him who gives natural birth and him who gives the knowledge of the Veda, the giver of the Veda is the more venerable father. . . . That Brahman who is the giver of the birth for the sake of the Veda and the teacher of the prescribed duties becomes the father of an aged man, even though he himself be a child."[100] Therefore, even Kshatriyas, who could not teach the Vedas, must respect Brahmans even as a child holds its parents in reverence. Once this natural ruling class accepted such a pretention, the rest of the lay society followed suit as a matter of course.

The priests did not end with rivalry among mere men; they went beyond the earth to achieve superiority to the gods themselves. If nothing else did, this was calculated to overawe the earthly princes. Dubois refers to a popular Sanskrit verse which illustrates the cogency of their logic. "The universe is under the power of the gods; the gods are under

---

[97]Macdonell and Keith, op. cit., p. 256.

[98]Writing in the latter part of the last century, John Nesfield observed: "In more than nine-tenths of the industries of India at the present day, oral transmission, through the example and teaching given by the father, is the sole means, both among Hindus and Muhammadans, by which a boy can acquire his father's craft, and this is no doubt one reason for the hold which caste has had on the people of this country through all the vicissitudes of creeds." Op. cit., p. 95.

[99]John C. Nesfield, op. cit., p. 101. See also William Crooke, op. cit., p. 65; H. G. Rowlinson, *India, A Short Cultural History*, p. 25.

[100]II, 146, 150. See also IV, 233.

the power of *mantrams* [incantations], the *mantrams* are under the power of Brahmans; therefore the Brahmans are our gods."[101] Again they proclaimed in the great Epic: "The world cannot be ruled in opposition to Brahmans; for the mighty Brahmans are the deities even of the gods. If thou desire to possess the sea-girt earth, honor them continually with gifts and with service."[102]

With this achievement, it became necessary to develop a philosophy of the social order which would give to other men some self-respect regardless of their function. Hence we have the paradoxical doctrine that some social functions are superior to and purer than others, but that the greatest blessing which could come to man is inspired by the performance of his hereditary duty without murmur or envy of another. This gave the stronger groups of men in society both security and some degree of respect from lower groups, which the former found acceptable in exchange for their right to question the pretentions of Brahmans.

Gradually, then, the caste system became orderly and stabilized, with priests giving a religious interpretation to all questions of moment. Brahmans were never centrally organized, and so, too, the caste system has remained decentralized, for it is built about priests. Brahmans constitute the only indispensable caste in the system.

Perhaps the age of the priest-kings in ancient Egypt provides the best analogy to the Brahman-Kshatriya struggle for power; however, a caste system did not emerge in Egypt. In Egypt, the contest developed mainly between the chief priest of the sun-god, Amon, and the king. With the decline in power and heroism of the Pharaohs of the Nineteenth Dynasty, the prestige of the high priest of the temple of Amon at Thebes became magnified. The high priest, through many crafty devices, sapped the dwindling power of the decadent Ramesside Pharaohs until "in the reign of the last Ramses the crown passed from the head of the Pharaoh to that of the chief priest of Amon."[103] Thus, in about the year 1100 B.C. the high priest made himself king and thereupon began a long rivalry between a succession of high priests and more or less weak Pharaohs for the rulership of Egypt.[104]

But the difference between the Egyptian situation and that in Vedic India is significant. In Egypt the high priesthood, a single office, became hereditary; in India, on the other hand, it was the entire priesthood

---

[101]Op. cit., p. 139.
[102]The Mahabharata, Anusasanap, 2160, quoted in John Muir, op. cit., p. 130.
[103]*The Cambridge Ancient History,* Vol. II, p. 209.
[104]Ibid., Vols. II, III, pp. 164–210 and 251–88, respectively.

which became hereditary. In Egypt the high priest sought to become the king; in India the Brahmans never usurped the functions of the Kshatriyas. The Brahmans willingly left the occupation of government to the Kshatriyas, but they claimed exclusive right to the duties of the priesthood and, in addition, pre-eminence for those duties. In other words, instead of seeking to elevate the function of the priesthood above that of the military rulers, the high priest of Egypt envied that function and sought to usurp it. The result was frequently a mixture of function with at least tacit admission of the inferiority of the priesthood. The Brahmans, on the contrary, kept the function of the priesthood as a whole separate and exclusive, and finally dignified it beyond that of the nobility. It is in this exclusiveness of group function that we recognize some basic trait of the caste system.

Later Caste Formation

It is necessary to distinguish between discussions concerning the origin of the caste system and those which seek to explain the means by which "a caste" is constituted. The system, once in motion, develops into an assimilating force whose action upon attracted groups tends to be determined by the latter's previous vocations. In the end they all become castes with some cultural variations which mark them for caste distinctions. It may be well to say again that, of all factors influencing the entrance of groups into the caste system, color or race is not one. Indeed, the very ways by which entrance is achieved negate the possibility that race plays a significant role.

New converts to the caste system come mainly from the tribes on the periphery of the culture. In entering the caste system a tribe disintegrates gradually along functional lines and ordinarily contributes its members along the gamut of the status system. Thus the priests of the tribe become Brahmans, those who are able to acquire "territorial sway" become members of the Chattri caste, the tribal artisans go into the castes of their specialty, while the dross of the tribe become the sweepers, burners of corpses, or "executioners of the living," repulsive eaters of dogs and carrion.[105]

Although we are not now discussing specifically the beginnings of the caste system, it may be significant to observe that this explanation of caste formation serves to refute the popular pure-blood theory of the origin of caste. It holds that the system arose as a prophylaxis against

---

[105]See "Caste," *Encyclopedia of Religion and Ethics;* M. A. Sherring, *Hindu Tribes and Castes,* Vol. II, p. lxvii; John C. Nesfield, op. cit., pp. 17–18, 106.

the incursion of dark-colored tribes surrounding the Aryans. But so far as we know, persons of high status in the Dasyu tribes always had high status in the caste system.[106] Even from Rig-Vedic times Brahman *rishis* associated with or went into the service of the Dravidian princes.[107]

New castes may also be formed by groups separating from the parent body and migrating to areas out of range of normal communication, or by occupational changes within the caste, by religious schisms, by fragments from other castes grouping about some common objective, by the offspring of crossings between two or more castes, by sects, and so on. When the caste is established it will ordinarily claim specialty in some vocation, and it will claim distinction on the basis of some fictitious or real cultural heritage, which it will guard jealously.[108]

---

[106]So far as culture is concerned, it is believed that the Dravidians were more advanced than the Aryans. According to H. J. Fleure: "There was in India at the time of the Aryan invasions a Dravidian civilization of a more elaborate and developed character than the civilization, if civilization it can be called, of the Aryans." *The Dravidian Element in Indian Culture,* p. 80. See also "Indian Question," *Encyclopedia of the Social Sciences.*

[107]Ralph T. H. Griffith, op. cit. Rig-Veda, VIII, 32, 46.

[108]See H. H. Risley, op. cit., pp. 75–79; Emile Senart, op. cit., pp. 16, 78; G. S. Ghurye, op. cit., pp. 28–38; "Caste," *Encyclopedia of Religion and Ethics;* John C. Nesfield, op. cit., p. 109.

Part Two

CLASS

Introduction

*F*ROM A PRELIMINARY DISCUSSION OF CASTE WE PROCEED TO EX-
amine and compare certain commoner systems of social stratification, social status, and social division. These are estates, social classes,
political classes, ethnics, and their interrelations. The literature on this
subject is not very considerable in quantity. In fact, these important
means of channeling currents of social behavior have been given relatively scant attention by sociologists. Attempts have been made, mainly
among European scholars, to distinguish between the social functioning of estates and classes;[1] but these analyses for the most part have
been insufficiently detailed and clear. Professor Pitirim Sorokin reports
a collection of thirty-two "forms" of definitions of "social class";[2] and
Charles Hunt Page has combed the materials for the statements on
social class by six leading American sociologists.[3] However, a convincing theory of "class" relations is still not generally available.

In this study we shall attempt to describe briefly the nature and
development of estates particularly in medieval Europe and essay to

---

[1]See especially the German writers, Othmar Spann, "Klasse und Stand," *Hand-
wörterbuch Der Staatswissenschaften,* Vol. 5, and authors there reviewed; Werner
Sombart, "Stände und Klassen," *Der Moderne Kapitalismus,* II, 2; Max Weber,
Wirtschaft und Gesellschaft; "Stände und Klassen," Vol. I, pp. 177–80; also
"Klasse, Stand, Parteien," Vol. II, pp. 631–40, and *passim;* and Hans Freyer,
Einleitung in die Soziologie, "Ständegesellschaft, Klassengesellschaft," pp. 137ff.

[2]*Contemporary Sociological Theories,* p. 543, note. See also Pitirim Sorokin and
Carle C. Zimmerman, *Principles of Rural-Urban Sociology,* p. 60, for a typology of
definitions of class by various authors.

[3]Charles Hunt Page, *Class and American Sociology.* The sociologists are Lester F.
Ward, William G. Sumner, Albion W. Small, Franklyn H. Giddings, Charles H.
Cooley, and Edward A. Ross. For recent discussions, see C. H. Cooley, R. C.
Angell, and L. J. Carr, *Introductory Sociology,* Chaps. 20–21; E. A. Ross,
Principles of Sociology, Pt. VI, *passim;* Kimball Young, *An Introductory Sociology,*
Chap. XXIV. The studies of the Yankee City Series headed by W. Lloyd Warner
are most elaborate.

show their relationship to social classes. The "political class" shall be considered as a distinct social phenomenon, while the term "ethnic" shall be relied upon for wider serviceability as a social concept in the analysis of race relations.

8. Estates

THE TERM "ESTATE" IN THE ENGLISH LANGUAGE, LIKE *Stand* IN the German and *état* in the French, has a variety of meanings. It may be correctly employed to mean status, degree of rank, position in the world, state, public, property, profession, social class, and so on. But the meaning with which we shall be concerned is that of a social order or stratum of society, and we shall mean by an estate system a society divided into estates.

From a political point of view, an estate may be thought of as one of the orders of a body politic, having expressed or implied legal claim to some degree of importance in the government. From the point of view of social structure, an estate may be thought of as one of the generally recognized social divisions of society, standing in relation to other divisions as socially superior or inferior. In other words, in any society a number of persons forming a social-status stratum more or less clearly delimited from other strata in customary or statutory law constitutes a social estate. But for an understanding of an estate society, definitions can serve only a very limited purpose; more detailed characteristics must be looked into.

Estates as Social Structure

An economic order based mainly upon agricultural production provides the ideal foundation of an estate social system. Where land is the basic economic resource and where it may be held by individuals as transmissible property, social status ordinarily correlates directly with the extent of landownership. The individual ordinarily has power and prestige according to his hereditary relationship to the land, and his relationship to the land determines his social estate. In Western society, feudalism, and indeed feudalism wherever it is found, represents this form[1] of estate society.

In this discussion, therefore, we shall direct our attention to the feudal system in Europe, and our purpose shall be to sense, so to speak, the nature of social estates. Ordinarily, feudalism has been dated from the ninth to the fourteenth centuries—from approximately the "breakup" of the Carolingian Empire to the start of the Renaissance.[2] Feudalism, however, did not begin and end in all European countries at the same time; neither did all aspects of its rise and decline, in different countries, occur at the same rate and time. In the England of Henry VII, in the France of Louis XIV, in the Germanies of Frederick the Great, or in the Russia of Alexander II feudalism, or certain significant aspects of it, was very much alive. Moreover, in our attempt to gain some insight into the nature of estates, we are interested not so much in a period of European history as in a social system. It may be possible to learn a good deal about that system during its struggles for survival. When a social system is at the height of its stability its significant social traits are ordinarily taken for granted; some of them begin to appear in discussion only when the system begins to decline. "From the thirteenth century onwards feudal law continued to be appealed to and feudal principles were sometimes formulated even more sharply than before, but the modern State was beginning to assert itself . . . and its influence began to modify the fundamental conceptions of feudalism."[3]

In this discussion of feudalism we do not pretend to submit original historical material. The data are limited and probably much still remains to be uncovered by historians of the period. Notwithstanding this, however, we shall hope to present a fairly clear idea of the sociological concept of social estates.

A feudal system may be characterized as a society living on "frozen capital"; its status structure is consequently static. In this connection Sombart distinguishes between capitalistic and precapitalistic economic

---

[1] Pastoral communities also ordinarily developed estate systems. Among the early Germanic tribes, whose wealth consisted mainly of cattle, four recognized status groups emerged: *nobles, ingenui, liberati,* and *servi.* A contemporary writer, Rudolph von Ems, says: "It is by law established that no order shall in contracting marriage remove the landmarks of its own lot; but noble must marry noble; freeman freewoman, freedman freedwoman, serf handmaid. If any take a wife of different or higher rank than his own, he has to expiate the act with his life." Quoted by William Stubbs, *The Constitutional History of England,* Vol. I, p. 46. See also pp. 21–24.

[2] Cf. *The Cambridge Medieval History,* Vol. I, Chap. I.

[3] Ibid., Vol. III, p. 458.

organization. In the Middle Ages, he says, "the norm of wants was that of the social class, and was fixed by tradition. Consequently, the idea of a sufficiency of existence slowly became permanent in all pre-capitalistic economic legislation and organization."[4] On the land-status relationship of the Middle Ages, Henri Pirenne concludes:

> From every point of view, Western Europe from the ninth century onwards, appears in the light of an essentially rural society. . . . The merchant class had disappeared. A man's condition was now determined by his relation to the land, which was owned by a minority of lay and ecclesiastical proprietors, below whom a multitude of tenants were distributed within the framework of the great estates. To possess land was at the same time to possess freedom and power . . . to be deprived of it, was to be reduced to serfdom. . . .[5]

"Tenancy," then, in some form constituted the material counterpart of status. According to Petit-Dutaillis and Lefebvre, social relations in England rested upon a principle of *tenure* "which was applied to almost the whole of the population from the king, from whom every tenure depended mediately or immediately, down to the humblest serf cultivating the land of his lord. There was not an inch of English soil which was not subjected to this formula . . . being either *tenens in capite* or separated from the king by more or less numerous intermediaries."[6]

As social structure the number of social estates may not only vary from society to society but also, depending on the political fate of the community, their relationship may change.[7] In any society the number of estates tends to be few—seldom if ever more than twelve and usually only three or four. Among an early Frankish tribe, the Merovingians, there may be recognized six status groups sharply differentiated in the

[4]Werner Sombart, *The Quintessence of Capitalism,* trans. by M. Epstein. See also Frederick L. Nussbaum, *A History of the Economic Institutions of Modern Europe,* New York, 1933, pp. 17–28.

[5]*Economic and Social History of Medieval Europe,* trans. by I. E. Clegg, p. 12.

[6]Ch. Petit-Dutaillis and Georges Lefebvre, *Studies and Notes Supplementary to Stubbs' Constitutional History,* p. 55.

"In the form which feudalism had reached at the Norman Conquest, it may be described as a complete organization of society through the medium of land tenure, in which from the king down to the lowest landowner all are bound together by obligation of service and defence: the lord to protect his vassal, the vassal to do service to his lord; the defence and service being based on and regulated by the nature and extent of the land held by the one of the other. . . . In states in which feudal government has reached its utmost growth, the political, financial, judicial, every branch of public administration is regulated by the same conditions. The central authority is a mere shadow of a name." William Stubbs, op. cit., Vol. I, p. 274.

[7]Cf. W. K. Ferguson and G. Bruun, *A Survey of European Civilization,* pp. 231–32.

law: clergy, nobles, townsmen, *coloni,* serfs, and slaves.[8] In medieval society three estates have been commonly recognized. James Westfall Thompson says:

> Medieval society was divided into three strata: clergy, nobility, and servile peasantry . . . the first two were ecclesiastically or politically the ruling class, socially an aristocracy and economically the wealthy classes in medieval society. These distinctions obtained both in social theory and in law. Each of these classes constituted an "estate," whose status was recognized and defended.[9]

But it should not be assumed that these three estates were socially homogeneous. Among the "peasants" there were usually some slaves employed as household domestics, praedial serfs bound to their tenures, serfs not indefinitely bound to the land, villeins who had undertaken to work a servile tenure, free villeins working lands on a share basis, and free peasantry.[10] Furthermore, there were smaller and larger landholders among the nobility, while the upper and lower clergy were distinguished in the law.

> The three estates of the realm [says Stubbs, referring especially to England] were thus divided, but not without subordinate distinctions, cross divisions, and a large residue that lay outside the political body. In the estate of baronage were included most of the prelates, who also had their place in the estate of clergy. . . . Many lines of distinction which separated the baron from the knight, such as relief and other matters of taxation, might have been made to separate the earls from the barons; but these points became more prominent as the ranks of the lords are marked out by new titles, duke, marquess, viscount.[11]

With the rise of towns the burgesses achieved a recognized status for themselves, and in many European countries they formed an estate of their own. By the thirteenth century it had already become common "to speak of peasants, burghers, knights, and clergy as separate estates."[12] In time this estate, the most significant element in what was referred to in England as the Commons, and in France as *le tiers état,* insinuated its ideology into that of all the other estates.

An estate system, then, represents a hierarchy of social groups more or less individually distinguishable both in law and in custom. In con-

---

[8] See James Westfall Thompson, *The Middle Ages,* Vol. I, p. 190.

[9] Ibid., p. 721. The author continues to say that "slavery did not disappear wholly in the Middle Ages, but it largely fused with praedial serfdom." P. 722.

[10] Ibid., pp. 727–28.

[11] William Stubbs, op. cit., Vol. II, p. 201. See also Henri Sée, *Modern Capitalism,* trans. by Homer B. Vanderblue and George F. Doriot, p. 172.

[12] See W. H. Bruford, *Germany in the Eighteenth Century,* p. 47.

sidering the social antecedents of eighteenth-century Germany, W. H. Bruford observes:

In each state big or small, there was a similar pyramid of social groups rising tier on tier to the ruler. At the base in each was the peasantry, not an undifferentiated mass . . . but relatively homogeneous. At the apex was the aristocracy, graded from prince down to the single country gentleman. . . . In between came the middle class of town-dwellers again with many subdivisions overlapping both nobility (in its patricians and higher officials) and peasantry (in its semi-agricultural tradesmen). . . .[13]

Although estates are distinguishable they are functionally co-operative. Their separateness tends to be determined by the type of economic interest common to each. We shall now attempt to examine some of these interests and consequent organization.

Estate Organization

Since estates are co-operative, functional, social-status entities, they ordinarily develop only so much organization as would permit them to exploit their position in society most effectively; indeed, the lower estates may even find an absence of organization most effective. The following is a brief description of the organization of some well-recognized estates.

1. *The Clergy.* To the priesthood of any society, organization tends to come naturally, for besides performing a necessary function it is characteristically institutional. At any rate, in medieval Europe the priesthood achieved a remarkable degree of organization, which facilitated its acquisition of land, power, and social prestige. With the Pope as head, the Church achieved international power frequently superior to that of local kings. "In this strictly hierarchial society," says Pirenne, "the first place and most important belonged to the Church, which possessed at once economic and moral ascendancy. Its innumerable estates [lands] were as superior in extent to those of the nobility, as it was itself superior to them in learning. . . . From the ninth to the eleventh century the whole business of government was in fact in the hands of the Church, which was supreme here as in the arts."[14]

The organization of the priesthood may have indeed shown the way to national organization. Its local synods, provincial convocations, and national councils were examples of effective government in a highly

---

[13]Ibid., p. 46.

[14]Henri Pirenne, op. cit., p. 13. See also Ephraim Emerton, *Medieval Europe, 814–1300*, p. 547.

individuated feudal society. Stubbs describes this organization graphically, declaring:

> We may regard the spirituality of England, the clergy or clerical estate, as a body completely organized, with a minutely constituted and regulated hierarchy, possessing the right of legislating for itself and taxing itself, having its recognized assemblies, judicature and executive; and, although not a legal corporation holding common property, yet composed of a great number of persons, each of whom possesses corporate property by a title which is either conferred by ecclesiastical authority, or is not to be acquired without ecclesiastical assent. Such an organization entitles the clergy to the name of "communitas."[15]

As an estate, then, the clergy as a whole was well organized, rich, learned, and consequently very powerful. But unlike other social estates, the clergy constituted a system which did not reproduce itself. It was at once the most closely knit group and the most heterogeneous; it had to be continually repopulated from the other estates—a fact which forever precluded the possibility of its achieving the solidarity of a caste. Thus, in a peculiar way, the estate of the priesthood belonged to every stratum of society, for all men might aspire to its ranks: "The great nobles and the king's ministers looked on the bishoprics as a provision for their clerical sons. The villein class . . . aspired to holy orders as one of the avenues of liberty . . . and every tradesman or yeoman might live to see his son promoted to a position of wealth and power."[16] Yet, although the least of priests might derive some prestige from belonging to an order with which the most powerful families in the country were affiliated, there were ranks even legally recognized within the clergy. There were great landowners and offices which constituted "ecclesiastical princedoms" as well as poor stipendaries. Politically the baronial priests were usually separated from the ordinary clergy.[17]

2. *The Nobility.* The feudal nobility had no such intricate organization as the clergy; at least it was less apparent. But the nobility, being the normal ruling class—the warrior class—was rather preoccupied with matters of social distance and other methods of maintaining or enhancing its prestige. The relationship between noble and noble was

---

[15]William Stubbs, op. cit., Vol. III, pp. 298–99.

[16]Ibid., p. 380. See also, for a general discussion of the social position of the clergy in France, Henri Sée, *La France economique et social au XVIIIᵉ siècle,* pp. 53ff.

[17]"Everything that we have said about the rights and duties of feudal princes," remarks Ephraim Emerton, "applies with equal truth to the bishops—with one very great exception. The lay fief was, from an early day, hereditary; the ecclesiastical fief passed from one hand to another by virtue of an election." Op. cit., pp. 547–48.

more socially competitive than co-operative, while that between noble and commoner was exploitive. "Feudalism," says James Westfall Thompson, "was based upon an honorable submission of noble to noble, and each party to that relation possessed certain definite specific rights and privileges. Manorialism, on the other hand, was the relation of the noble as a landed proprietor to his servile tenantry. It was a relationship of master and servant. There was neither pride of 'aid' nor fellowship in it. . . . The services exacted were the hard, compulsory labors of a farm tenantry."[18]

Ordinarily the medieval noble was a vassal, holding devisable lands, called a fief, of some other noble. Thus nobles were bound to each other by "ties of vassalage and fidelity" in a sort of gradation of landholding. However, the fact of vassalage did not always imply inferiority, for one noble might hold fiefs of many lords, so that in the end he might become more powerful than any of them.[19] Although the system was regulated by custom and law, continual friction developed between noble and noble over conflicting claims. Private war and strife were a common means of settlement. "The history of feudalism," says Thompson, "is that of constant friction between the rights of lord and those of the vassal."[20] Although it is true that they had a like interest in the society, the nobility was never a unified corporate body working harmoniously toward some common end.[21]

Notwithstanding internal conflict and ranking, however, the nobility represented a distinguished social estate. They kept the commonality at a distance so that aspiration to their status was very small. With reference to the later estate relationship in Germany, Bruford writes: "The nobility were taught from their childhood to look upon themselves as a class apart. They differed from the middle class in legal status, standard of living, social customs and moral code, in their education, their taste in art and literature, in the very language they habitu-

---

[18]James W. Thompson, op. cit., Vol. II, p. 722.

[19]On this point G. G. Coulton observes: "A man's immediate obedience was to his landlord. He might have only one landlord, for the royal estates were considerable, and on those estates the peasant owed homage to the king alone. But, on the other hand, he might have half a dozen landlords, in various degrees of proximity. If his immediate landlord was the lord of the manor, then that squire might be the direct tenant of the king; but, on the other hand, this squire might hold his lands under some other squire, and he under some other, and he under some count or baron or bishop or abbot, so that there were many steps between the actual tiller of the soil and the central government. But the man's immediate loyalty was due to his immediate landlord; he might have many lords but he had only one *liege* lord, the man from whom he held directly. Thus came about the strange paradox, that the peasant owed closer loyalty to his squire than to his king." *The Medieval Scene*, p. 6.

[20]Op. cit., p. 702.

[21]See F. M. Powicke, *Medieval England*, pp. 59, 78.

ally used."[22] The nobility did not eat, sleep, play, sit, or wash together
with the commonality. They dressed distinctively, often secured sumptu-
ary laws to limit imitation, and insisted upon an etiquette which emphasized their superiority.

It was impossible, of course, for the nobility to avoid all intercourse
with the vulgar, but they made every effort on public occasions to keep
social inferiors at a distance. In the theater, they sat apart from the common man, either in the front seats or in boxes. . . . At public concerts too,
a space was left between the chairs of the quality and the rest. . . . In
the village church the local nobility would, of course, have separate pews
and a family vault. In the council chamber and in lecture rooms, where
noble and commoner met for a like purpose, each class was assigned its
separate benches. Even at the few schools . . . where boys of good birth
and others were educated together, they wore distinctive epaulettes, dined
at different tables, slept in separate dormitories and used bathing places
at the river parted by a raised bank. . . . The nobility considered themselves in fact, with rare exceptions, to be of different race from the un-
titled mass.[23]

In fact, the very titles of the nobility served to maintain the prestige
of their estate. Just as *lady* once referred to the wife of a lord, so
Fräulein was the title of a nobleman's daughter. For practically every
rank of nobility there was some title, while the common people were not
mistered at all.[24]

But, although the nobility guarded its rights and privileges with considerable jealousy, it never attained the solidarity of a caste. Even
though very difficult, individuals of lower estates might obtain the
material or official substance of nobility and finally achieve identification. On the decline of feudalism education became one rough road
to success—at least, through the priesthood.[25] Unlike a caste, the

---

[22]W. H. Bruford, op. cit., p. 49. See also, for a discussion of the privileges of the
nobility, Henri Sée, op. cit., pp. 75ff.

[23]Ibid., pp. 57–58. With regard to the German nobility, Bruford continues:
"They could further distinguish themselves by the use of plumed hats—we hear
of many a duel on these points between nobleman and commoner at the universities
—by putting their servants into livery, displaying coats of arms, using special
seals, wearing pink dominoes at masquerades, and a thousand and one such trifles."
P. 54.

[24]See "Titles of Honour," Encyclopedia Britannica.

[25]The registers of the University of Oxford from 1567 to 1622 showed the following classification:

Sons of Noblemen (Earls, Lords, and Barons)	84
Sons of Knights	590
Sons of the Clergy	758
Sons of Esquires	902
Sons of Gentlemen	3615
Sons of Plebeians	6635
Status not given	758

See Mildred Campbell, *The English Yeoman*, p. 271.

estate never became responsible for its members and its limits were international. According to Stubbs:

> The great barons would probably, at any period, have shown a disinclination to admit new men on terms of equality to their own order, but this inclination was overcome by the royal policy of promoting useful servants, and the baronage was recruited by lawyers, ministers, and warriors, who in the next generation stood as stiffly on their privileges as their companions had ever done. The county knight was always regarded as a member of the noble class, and his position was continually strengthened by intermarriage with the baronage. The city magnate again formed a link between the country squire and the tradesman; and the tradesman and the yeoman were in position and in blood close akin. . . . But the most certain way to rise was furnished by education.[26]

3. *The Common People.* Before the rise of towns in western Europe the common people were practically confined to the manors. That is to say, they lived a comparatively sedentary life in villages owned by landlords and they cultivated the adjoining lands on some customary agreement for dividing the produce. "Each manor had its court, composed of peasants, presided over by the bailiff or *villicus,* and giving judgment according to 'the custom of the manor' . . . the traditional usage which, at long intervals, the population, consulted by the lord, declared and set down in the custumals or Weistümer."[27] The manor, indeed, aimed at self-sufficiency.[28] A church was built and a priest was nominated by the lord. The cultivators had no market outside of the manor.

---

[26]William Stubbs, op. cit., Vol. III, p. 625. See also, Bruford, op. cit., p. 59. Observe, however, the point which De Tocqueville makes: "In the eleventh century nobility was beyond all price; in the thirteenth it might be purchased; it was conferred for the first time in 1270." *Democracy in America,* Vol. I, p. xiii.

[27]Henri Pirenne, op. cit., p. 63. See also James W. Thompson, op. cit., p. 722–23. "It is, perhaps, unnecessary to add," says Pirenne, "that the manorial was not imposed on all the rural population. It spared a certain number of small free proprietors, and in isolated districts we meet with villages which more or less escaped its control " Op. cit., p. 59. For a discussion of living conditions of the medieval peasant, see G. G. Coulton, *The Medieval Village,* especially pp. 307ff.

[28]The following is an illustration of the nature of manorial economy: "In some manors the dues are arranged to form a complete outfit for the consumption of the lord's household, a farm of one night, of a week, of a fortnight, as the case may be. The manors of the Abbey of Ramsey were bound to render as a fortnight's farm 12 quarters of flour, 2,000 loaves of bread, 24 gallons of beer, 48 gallons of malt, 2 sesters of honey, 10 flitches of bacon, 10 rounds of cheese, 19 very best sucking pigs, 14 lambs, 14 geese, 120 chickens, 2,000 eggs, 2 tubs butter, 24 gallons of audit ale. . . .
"By the help of these accumulated stores, and funds drawn from money rents and small leases, the lord keeps a number of servants, and hires some labourers for the cultivation of the home farm. . . ." *The Cambridge Medieval History,* Vol. III, p. 475. See also James Harvey Robinson, *Readings in European History,* pp. 181–84; and Mary Bateson, *Medieval England,* pp. 116–17.

Ordinarily the inhabitants of a manor looked to the lord for paternalistic advice, much of their private lives being regulated according to his wishes. Should they leave the estate, he could apprehend and return them. In fact, "they were his men in every sense of the word, and it has been justly observed that seigneurial authority rested more on the attributes of chieftainship which it conferred on its possessor than on his attributes as a landed proprietor. . . . In times of war he defended them against the enemy and sheltered them within the walls of his fortress, and it was clearly to his own advantage to do so, since he lived by their labor."[29] It should be mentioned parenthetically that the manor had none of the significant characteristics of the modern village; the modern village is economically intermeshed in a world-capitalist economy.

Although there were some social differentiations, more or less distinct, among the peasants, they were the least organized of the social estates. Indeed, they had very little to protect by organization. They were administered almost entirely from above, while politically they were never heard unless through their lords. But as villages developed into boroughs, sometimes under the guidance of the lords themselves, an avenue of partial escape was opened to the serf.

4. *The Bourgeoisie.* "From the point of view of the common people of Europe," says Professor Thompson, "the rise of the towns is the most important phenomenon of the history of the feudal age. It was a political, economic, and social revolution of the first magnitude."[30] The medieval town was built from the ground up; the great Roman and Grecian cities had perished and their "people disappeared."[31] Hence the new urban institutions were developed virtually without precedent to meet the needs of the new urban situations. "The new towns may be regarded as markets made permanent."[32] But although this novel way of life gradually wormed its way into the entire fabric of medieval society, town population was never very large. Be-

---

[29]Ibid., p. 64. See also, for a good discussion of the manorial system, Harry Elmer Barnes, *An Economic History of the Western World,* Chap. V, and W. K. Ferguson and Geoffrey Bruun, op. cit., pp. 309–14.

[30]James W. Thompson, op. cit., p. 733. To the same effect see Harry Elmer Barnes, op. cit., Chap. VI, and W. K. Ferguson and G. Bruun, op. cit., Chap. XX.

[31]Cf. Jonathan F. Scott, Albert Hyma, and Arthur H. Noyes, *Readings in Medieval History,* pp. 293–96. Some vestiges of Roman cities did remain in Italy, Spain, and southern France; even so, however, their trading functions became considerably involved with the feudal and religious interests upon which they largely depended.

[32]Friedrich W. E. Keutgen, "Commune," in the Encyclopedia Britannica, 11th ed.

tween the twelfth and fifteenth centuries probably not more than ten per cent of the population was urban.[33]

Before about the twelfth century, then, there was no effective and recognized class of town dwellers. In England "during the Anglo-Saxon period, and even in the eleventh century, the word *burh* had an extremely general signification. It does not even exclusively denote a town, but is also applied to a fortified house, a manor, a farm surrounded by walls."[34]

Once under way, however, commercial towns developed rapidly. They recruited new population from the farms, and it is Pirenne's thesis that the early town people constituted the dross of the country. They were marginal persons in an agricultural society. Landless men, the younger sons of large tenant families, and "the crowd of vagabonds who roamed through the country, going from abbey to abbey taking their share of alms reserved for the poor," were among the first to seek opportunities and fortune in the commercial life of the towns.[35] It was common practice for serfs to run away and hide about the towns seeking casual employment with merchants and craftsmen. "The lords pursued them and brought them back to their holdings, when they succeeded in laying hands on them. But many eluded their search, and as the city population increased, it became dangerous to try to seize the fugitives under its protection."[36]

Although it is customary to speak of the bourgeoisie or burgesses as one of the estates, they finally became a class with social norms fairly distinct from those of the agricultural community at the head of which was the nobility. The bourgeoisie "formed a privileged class in the midst of the rest of the population."[37] And the privilege was a necessity usually bought and paid for by the town dwellers. The institutions which functioned smoothly in the agricultural environs of the towns were found to be totally unsatisfactory in the industrial commercial life of the latter. Hence the burgesses sought rights and obtained charters which would leave them legally to organize their town in a way that facilitated their economic activity. They wanted most of all to be re-

[33]See Henri Pirenne, op. cit., p. 59.

[34]Ch. Petit-Dutaillis and Georges Lefebvre, op. cit., p. 70.

[35]See Henri Pirenne, op. cit., pp. 46–47.

[36]Ibid., p. 49. "The territory of the town was as privileged as its inhabitants. It was a sanctuary, an 'immunity,' which protected the man who took refuge there from exterior authority, as if he had sought sanctuary in a church." Ibid., p. 57. See, however, for a discussion of the struggles for emancipation of the early towns with the feudal lords: Scott, Hyma, and Noyes, op. cit., pp. 297–303.

[37]Henri Pirenne, op. cit., p. 56.

lieved of the restraints of the manor, to be left alone to develop their own institutions. They wanted to be free—free to make business agreements, to own and control property, to buy and sell goods. "Without liberty, that is to say, without power to come and go, to do business, to sell goods, a power not enjoyed by serfdom, trade would be impossible."[37a] Therefore, among the rights which the lords upon whose estate the towns were located sold to the burgesses, the right to be left alone was crucial. In order to keep their business private they carefully avoided individual tax assessment, preferring to pay a lump sum raised by the mayor of the corporation. "Freedom became the legal status of the bourgeoisie, so much so that it was no longer a personal privilege only, but a territorial one, inherent in urban soil just as serfdom was in manorial soil."[38] At length it became a general rule that the runaway serf who lived in the city for a year and a day became thereafter free. In discussions of this fact the German proverb, *Die Stadtluft macht frei,* has been frequently cited.

The organization of the burgesses was, of course, different and separate from that of the other estates. They ordinarily had judicial autonomy with court practices suitable to their practical way of living and they developed new systems of administration and taxation. They provided their own policing and built the town wall as a defense against the thieving knights of the countryside. "The construction of ramparts was the first public work undertaken by the towns and one which, down to the end of the Middle Ages, was their heaviest financial burden. . . . There were no unfortified towns in the Middle Ages."[39] The bourgeoisie, then, were well organized and, in a sense, organized against the

---

[37a]Henri Pirenne, *Economic and Social History of Medieval Europe,* trans. by I. E. Clegg, pp. 51.

[38]Ibid., pp. 51–52. On this point Mrs. J. R. Green says: "In the beginning of municipal life the affairs of the borough, great and small, its prosperity, its' safety, its freedom from crime, the gaiety and variety of its life, the regulation of its trade, were the business of the citizens alone. Fenced in by its wall and ditch—fenced in yet more effectively by the sense of danger from without, and clinging to privileges won by common effort that separated it from the rest of the world—the town remained isolated and self-dependent." *Town Life in the Fifteenth Century,* Vol. I, p. 125.

[39]Ibid., p. 54. In this regard Carl Bucher observes: "Every town . . . presupposes the existence of a defensive union which forms the rural settlements lying within a greater or narrower radius into a sort of military community with definite rights and duties. It devolves upon all the places belonging to this community to co-operate in maintaining intact the town fortifications by furnishing workmen and horses, and in time of war in defending them with their arms. In return they have the right, whenever occasion arises, to shelter themselves, their wives and children, their cattle and movables, within its walls. This right is called the right of burgess, and he who enjoys it is a burger (burgensis)." *Industrial Evolution,* trans. by S. M. Wickett, p. 116.

rest of the rural estates. "Each town formed, so to speak, a little state to itself, jealous of its prerogatives and hostile to all its neighbors. . . . For the burgesses the country population existed to be exploited. Far from allowing it to enjoy their franchises, they always obstinately refused it all share in them."[40] In the city, the clergy were an estate apart. They did not always share in the special privileges of the burgesses, for they had the rights of their own estate.[41] The nobility ordinarily left the city to live in their country castles. The medieval town, then, was the home of the burgesses. "It was in their own interest, and in their own interest alone, that they created its institutions and organized its economy."[41a] In emphasizing the individuality of these townspeople Pirenne writes:

> The medieval burgess . . . was a different kind of person from all who lived outside the town walls. Once outside the gates and the moat, we are in a different world, or more exactly, in the domain of another law. The acquisition of citizenship brought with it results analogous to those which followed when a man was dubbed knight or clerk tonsured, in the sense that they conferred a peculiar legal status. Like the clerk or the noble, the burgess escaped from the common law; like them, he belonged to a particular estate, which was later to be known as the "third estate."[42]

But it must not be supposed that the burgesses constituted a homogeneous status group. In fact, the bourgeoisie were an estate of aristocratic urban oligarchs. There was a more or less distinct cleavage between the upper-class merchants, the small retailers and craftsmen, and the laboring class. "The towns welcomed the serfs who drifted into them from the rural areas, but only because they increased the laboring class within the towns. The serf or the villein met with a cold reception if he tried to buy a plot of ground within the town wall. . . . Freedom from serfdom did not imply political qualification."[43]

---

[40] Henri Pirenne, op. cit., p. 57. "The middle class achieved its aims politically by transformation from within. Instead of making a direct assertive attack, these master-traders usually so developed their own interests within the established institutions that they gained their object quietly and shrewdly. This class established itself against the king and the nobles on the one hand, and against the workers on the other. . . . Already in the fifteenth century the workmen were founding fraternities of their own." Edwin Benson, *Life in a Medieval City,* p. 42. See also Gustav Schmoller, *The Mercantile System,* pp. 7–8, 11.

[41] See Karl Bücher, *Die Bevölkerung von Frankfurt am Main im XIV. und XV,* Chap. V, *passim.*

[41a] Henri Pirenne, op. cit., p. 171.

[42] Op. cit., pp. 56–57.

[43] James W. Thompson, op. cit., p. 738. See also, W. H. Bruford, op. cit., p. 49. The ordinary workers of the town "had neither any share in the government, nor any rights to rent a stall in the market, nor to own shop or workroom in the town. These formed an obscure company of workers without records or history. They

Bourgeois freedom was never intended for everybody. Those who had become wealthy, even the *nouveaux riches,* formed themselves into a closed patriciate, excluding the manual craft workers and small traders.

Town politics was in the hands of an upper class. "Throughout the whole of western Europe, the *haute bourgeoisie* had, from the beginning, monopolized town government."[43a] However, two organized classes in the town were constantly struggling for power: the master craftsmen and the merchants. This struggle took on revolutionary. proportions in the Low Countries and in Italy. Sometimes, as was mostly true of English towns, where the merchants were very wealthy but with ranks not too rigidly closed, the craft guilds were definitely subordinated. They were either suppressed by the merchants or incorporated and regulated.[44] Yet in the long run the city provided a new facility for social mobility; here it was possible for men in relatively large numbers, through their own ingenuity, to acquire the substance of upper-class status. We shall again quote William Stubbs, who makes a graphic comparison between bourgeois and feudal social mobility—indeed, a comparison between a social-class system and an estate system:

There was no such gulf between the rich merchant and the ordinary craftsman in the town, as existed between the country knight and the yeoman, or between the yeoman and the labourer. In the city it was merely a distinction of wealth; and the poorest apprentice might look forward to becoming a master of his craft, a member of the livery company, to a place in the council and aldermanship, a mayoralty, the right of becoming an esquire for his life, and leaving an honourable coat of arms for his children. The yeoman had no such straight road before him; he might improve his chances as they came, might lay field to field, might send his sons to war or the universities; but for him also the shortest way to make one of them a gentleman was to send him to trade; and there even the villein might find liberty and a new life that was not hopeless. . . . The townsman knew no superior to whose place he might not aspire; the yeoman was attached by his ties of hereditary affection to a great

counted among their number ancient burghers who had fallen into low estate and could no longer pay their burgage dues, as well as the poor who had never prospered so far as to buy a tenure or citizenship. But they were not all necessarily poor or miserable." Mrs. J. R. Green, op. cit., Vol. I, p. 193. See also Edwin Benson, op. cit., p. 33.

And Pirenne observes further: "The competition which they maintained with each other in the labor market allowed the merchants to pay them a very low wage. Existing information, of which the earliest dates back to the eleventh century, shows them to have been a brutish lower class, uneducated and discontented." *Medieval Cities,* trans. by Frank D. Halsey, p. 160.

[43a]Henri Pirenne, op. cit., p. 201.

[44]William Stubbs, op. cit., Vol. III, pp. 581, 616.

neighbour whose superiority never occurred to him as a thing to be coveted or grudged.[45]

During the Middle Ages and for long after, social prestige in Europe ranked from the nobility. Even the greatest of the burgesses were not fully accepted by the old ruling class. It took the world-shaking bourgeois revolution of 1789 in France to challenge the position of the nobility. But unless estates are transformed into "political classes" the social structure remains self-regulative and harmonious. The burgeoisie had wealth, but they were too socially mobile to attain the superb style of living of the nobility; hence it became the aspiration of townsmen to be included in the nobility. The dominant society was feudal; hence fashion had to be set by the ruling feudal class. Wealthy merchants either married their daughters to knights, purchased great estates, or bought titles of nobility outright. "The Florentine wealthy classes," says Sombart, "generally strove to obtain patents of knighthood which were coveted so much because they alone enabled the holders to participate in tournaments."[46] And regarding this same method of achieving nobility, W. H. Bruford mentions the large sums of money paid into the imperial treasury in Germany for titles of nobility: "Joseph II made financiers into noblemen by the dozen; in his time it cost in all about 20,000 Gulden to become a count . . . 6,000 to become a baron . . . and 386 Gulden in fees to be a mere Adliger (von)."[47] In England it became common for rich burgesses to intermarry with the knights and gentry; indeed, after the decline in influence of the elder baronage and the expansion of industry and trade under the Tudors, a sort of easy fusion developed between the lower nobility and the richer bourgeoisie.[48] Even so, however, the ennobled bourgeoisie were called "nobility of the robe" as a final personal distinction from those of feudal heritage, the "nobility of the sword."

Up to about the early eighteenth century, then, estates were recognizably distinguished, and each sought increasing organization for the purpose of exploiting its position. Each was jealous of its status and sought exclusiveness from lower estates. Estates did not maintain their position merely by inherent, private authority; they claimed, in addition, political and legal right. The lower estates, which could not obtain the sanctions of formal law, relied upon custom for all that it was worth.

---

[45]Ibid., p. 616.

[46]Werner Sombart, op. cit., p. 134.

[47]*Germany in the Eighteenth Century*, p. 61.

[48]See William Stubbs, op. cit., Vol. III, pp. 569, 614–15; also Henri Pirenne, op. cit., p. 50.

Estate as a Political Concept

"An assembly of estates," says Stubbs, "is an organized collection . . . of the several orders, states, or conditions of men, who are recognized as possessing political power."[49] The king, of course, is not an estate; he is a leader at the head of estates. Thus it is possible to think of estates as only those recognized groups of the population that have a voice in the government. Obviously this attribute is not dissociated from the idea of social status in the community. Power is an attribute of social status; and on the theory that the State is the source of all power, the status of the group will tend to rise according to its importance as a factor controlling the machinery of government.

The great nobles of Europe were powerful individuals before they became the first estate of a larger nation. The breakup of the Frankish Empire resulted in a number of realms with relatively weak kings and strong landholders. These great proprietors armed their retinue not only against strong neighbors but frequently against the king. "When this condition was reached, the great noble was not merely a grand proprietor, he was a local magnate, a petty ruler, exercising in a *de facto* capacity the functions of the government within his patrimonies over all the tenantry, *coloni,* and slaves upon them."[50] But as kings became stronger and as national wars began to be waged, the nobles were increasingly relied upon for financial and personal aid. In England after the Conquest, the Norman monarchy established the English baronage,[51] and "thus the first and oldest medieval estate" emerged. A fraction, and not always the same fraction, of this estate of feudal tenants-in-chief, both spiritual and lay, "was summoned by the king from time to time to his Councils."[52] Politically the baronage was the only estate of the realm; their decision was their own, and only in a very indirect way could they be thought of as representing any other status group below them.[53]

From a political point of view, then, only those groups who have a voice in the government may be thought of as estates. The second great estate to emerge was the clergy. As great landowners, they were

---

[49]William Stubbs, op. cit., Vol. II, p. 170.

[50]James W. Thompson, *The Middle Ages,* p. 690. See also *The Cambridge Medieval History,* Vol. III, pp. 464, 470–71.

[51]See Ch. Petit-Dutaillis and Georges Lefebvre, op. cit., p. 53.

[52]See *The Cambridge Medieval History,* Vol. VII, pp. 672–73, "Medieval Estates," by C. H. McIlwain

[53]Ibid., p. 675.

already included with the baronage, but only later did they begin to share the burdens and privileges of government as an organized group. Other representative groups, such as the knights and burgesses, also developed into significant estates.[54] In England certain interest groups, such as lawyers and merchants, attempted with little success to organize themselves into estates in their own right. There were always persons or groups who were not included in any political estate.[55]

During deliberation in council, the assembled estates did not sit together, and ordinarily their arrangement showed their social rank. "When summoned to parliament, the knights of one county . . . were directed to treat with representatives of the other counties. . . . When burgesses were summoned, they too deliberated together but apart from the other estates and the same was true of the . . . cathedral and the parish clergy. . . . Thus, the parliament was really not one body . . . but often three, four or five, according as the knights, burgesses, cathedral and parish clergy were present or not."[56] There were many formalities of procedure, such as the type of summons used, which served to distinguish the estates.

Furthermore, estates had legal recognition; many of their privileges and obligations were guaranteed by law. Indeed, it may not be incorrect to say, as Max Radin observes, that "to know a person's real position, it was first of all necessary to know 'the law by which he lived.' "[57] The principle at the basis of the wergild (man-money) which provided a scale of monetary values for the life or limb of men of different estates reappeared in some form in all estate relationship.[58]

---

[54]Ibid., pp. 676–77, 679. See also E. William Robertson, *Scotland under Her Early Kings*, Vol. I, pp. 292–93.

[55]The "fourth estate," the nascent proletariat and peasants, never became a recognized political force before the French Revolution.

[56]*The Cambridge Medieval History*, loc. cit., p. 680. See also "Estates General," *The Encyclopedia of the Social Sciences*, and William Stubbs, op. cit., Vol. II, p. 202.

[57]"Status," *Encyclopedia of the Social Sciences*.

[58]E. William Robertson, in his *Scotland under Her Early Kings*, Vol. II, pp. 275–318, discusses the wergild of different peoples. The following is that of Wessex under the Anglo-Saxon King, Ini or Ine:

Twelfhyndman	1200	scillings
Sixhyndman	} 600	"
Wealh with five hydes		
Twyhyndman	} 200	"
King's Horswealh		
Wealh with a hyde	} 120	"
Do Gafolgelda		
His son	100	"
Wealh with half a hyde	80	"
Free wealh without land	60	"
Theow	{ 60	"
	50	"

On this subject Henri Sée asserts that, "during the seventeenth and eighteenth centuries in France, distinctions between the social classes were reinforced by distinctions of a legal or juridical nature."[59] In fact, the functional difference of estates necessitated differential treatment in the law. Distinction was chiefly made in such matters as military service, rates of pay, taxation, rights to office, application of the criminal law, opportunity to own property, political representation, various hereditary rights to command the services of other persons, and so on.

Philosophy of Estates

Every social system has its rationale—its way of looking at the world and its explanation of things as they are. Unless the society is on the brink of great change, the status quo is always right and God is always credited with devising the social plan. Medieval society was no exception to this.

The estate system lent itself admirably to the development of organismic theories of society. It became easy and satisfying to conceive of society as a living organism with each organ or estate performing its necessary function as a contribution to the total good.[60] The basic idea of society thus settled, the function of each estate was assumed to constitute part of an inseparable combination. "The nobility were ordained to defend all, the clergy were ordained to pray for all, and the commons were ordained to provide food for all."[61] The doctrine, of course, presumes a settled order; hence there would be no place for ambition. God has assigned each man to a given estate with which he should be content. The ideal social order was static; the sharper the

---

[59]Op. cit., p. 170. R. H. Tawney puts it strongly: "The special characteristic of the [estate] system in France and Germany had been, in fact, that inequality was not primarily economic, but juristic, and that, in spite of disparities of wealth, it rested on differences, not merely of income but of legal status. Civil, not to mention political, rights were not identical for all men, but graded from class to class." *Equality*, pp. 107–08.

[60]We have mentioned in a preceding chapter the Rig-Vedic theory of the origin of the four orders of society from one great body. See also P. Sorokin, *Contemporary Sociological Theories*, pp. 197–200, for a review of early theories; and also Otto Gierke, *Political Theories of the Middle Ages*, trans. by F. W. Maitland, pp. 102–40, *passim*, for a listing of medieval thought on the subject.

[61]Ruth Mohl, *The Three Estates in Medieval and Renaissance Literature*, p. 316. See also James W. Thompson, op. cit., p. 721.

"As noble service was that of the person in arms and on horseback, so ignoble service was every other form of return for the protection afforded by the lord of the land. And as, primarily, noble service was that of the unpaid soldier, so, primarily, ignoble service was that of the laborer in the soil,' Ephraim Emerton, op. cit., p. 511.

lines separating the estates and the more satisfied they were, the more perfect the social order. In reviewing the literature on estates, Ruth Mohl concludes: "All these more or less voluminous twelfth, thirteenth and fourteenth century moralists saw fit to preach in terms of class society. Most of them classify society in three feudal groups, and agree that these three estates, necessary to the world, were ordained by God to serve Him and each other."[62]

Of course, there had to be some explanation of the misery of the unfortunate lower estates; and here, too, as is common in Christian countries, it was ordinarily attributed to their supposed Hamite curse. Moreover, the folly of persons of lower estate attempting to rise was emphasized and made obvious, for "an ape wyll ever be an ape, though purple garments hyde."[63] Yet the common people had to be constantly sermonized. Robert Crowley, writing in 1550, admonishes them in this way:

> *For what doste thou; if thou desyr*
> *To be a lord or a gentleman*
> *Other than heape on thee God's ire*
> *And shewe thy selfe no Christian.*[64]

But in spite of a static philosophy and indeed a highly static economic order, the estates never disintegrated[65] into castes. Such beliefs and theories emphasizing "the divine origin of the three classes of society, the importance to the state of every class, the obligation resting upon each class to do its duty, the desirability of every man's being content with his degree, and the folly of trying to change his estate"[66] might probably seem to identify the estate system of medieval Europe with a caste system. Yet many elements of caste were wanting and the estates finally evolved in a direction distinctly opposite to caste. Among others, two factors were decisive in turning the medieval social order away from a caste system: (a) the substance of status in Western society was an acquirable tangibility, and (b) the most influential order in the system, the priesthood, was celibate. The possession of property, especially in land, was not only the basis of political and constitutional right but also the *"badge* of social status"; furthermore, the

<hr>

[62]Op. cit., p. 65.
[63]Ibid., p. 199, quoting Barnabe Googe, 1563.
[64]*The Yeoman's Lesson,* quoted by Mildred Campbell, op. cit., p. 43.
[65]We use the term "disintegrate" advisedly, for we mean literally "fall to pieces." To be like the caste system, every slightly differing functional group of an estate stratum will have had to assume a recognizable status. So far as group status is concerned, therefore, the estates would have been atomized.
[66]Mildred Campbell, op. cit., p. 277.

priesthood, naturally, never became hereditary. On this question
Stubbs concludes:

Although English society was divided by sharp lines and broad intervals,
it was not a system of castes either in the stricter or in the looser sense. It
had much elasticity in practice, and the boundries between the ranks
were passable. The ceorl who had thriven so well as to have five hides
of land rose to the rank of a thegn; his wergild became twelve hundred
shillings; the value of his oath and the penalty of trespass against him
increased in proportion. . . . Nor was the character of thriving defined:
It might, so far as the terms of the custom went, be either purchased, or
acquired by inheritance, or the tenure of important office, or the receipt
of royal bounty. The successful merchant might also thrive to thegn-right.
The thegn himself might rise to the rank, the estimation, and status of an
earl.[67]

In this characterization of estates we have limited our discussion to
the European situation, principally because data here are more readily
available. Wherever estates are found, however, we should expect
them to be similarly characterized. Another value of this selection is
that out of the European estates came the modern social-class system,
to which development we shall now address ourselves.

---

[67]William Stubbs, op. cit., Vol. I, p. 180.

9. *From Estate to Social Class*

*I*N THIS CHAPTER WE SHALL SCARCELY BE CONCERNED WITH *the origin* of social classes. We shall hope to indicate only some of the well-known factors in the change from medieval autarchy to modern capitalism. Social-class systems are phenomena peculiar to capitalism;[1] but before giving consideration to this fact, it may be in order to derive briefly some meaning of the concept "social class." By a social-class system we mean some variant of that social-status order which followed the breakdown and atomization of the European estate system. "Social class" should not be confused with "political class," an entirely different concept.

Difference in Economic Organization

Capitalism developed in the urban communities of Europe,[2] and it may be called the way of life of the burgesses. Trade, profit, the indispensability of money, inventiveness, mechanical power, money-making as an end in itself, factory manufacture, efficiency, individualism, competition, bourgeois freedom, utilitarianism, ambition, plutarchy, capital accumulation, exploitation, nationalism, humanitarianism, idealism, and so on, characterize this way of life.[3] Once under way, capitalism is

---

[1]In referring to *a* social-class system or social-class systems instead of *the* social-class system, we have in mind the difference in the pattern of social-class organization in different countries of Western civilization.

[2]There is an immense literature on the rise of capitalism. Our purpose here is merely to indicate the continuity of social estates and social classes and not to discuss capitalism in all its economic ramifications.

[3]Louis M. Hacker suggests the following definition of capitalism: "Capitalism is an economic order based on the profit motive: therefore its leading characteristics are the private ownership of the means of production, their operation for pecuniary gain, their control by private enterprisers, and the use of credit and the wage system." *The Triumph of American Capitalism*, p. 16.

progressive, sometimes in a pathological sense, and naturally it is im-patient of restrictions. We have attempted to show in the preceding chapter that medieval society rested upon a land economy; wants were supplied mainly in kind, and production was largely for immediate con-sumption. This comparatively stationary economic order and its ideology precluded any ideal of "infinite productivity." According to Henri Sée:

The whole idea of profit, and indeed the possibility of profit, was incompatible with the position occupied by the great medieval land-owner. Unable to produce for sale owing to the want of a market, he had no need to tax his ingenuity in order to wring from his men and his land a surplus which would merely be an encumbrance; and as he was forced to consume his own produce, he was content to limit his needs.[4]

The system entailed work in common, and, in a sense, its institutions were communalistic. Since production was largely localized in a num-ber of virtually self-sufficient units, money had a very limited use. Barter and the direct reciprocation of personal services were sub-stitutes for a medium of exchange. "The most essential economic dues, those which were paid on the great domains, upon which the social equilibrium then rested, escaped it almost entirely. . . . Where, more-over, could the villeins themselves have obtained enough money to represent the value of their dues, since they sold nothing outside the estate?"[5] Indeed, this period has been described as the age of "the economy of no markets." The monetary system, then, had its develop-ment in the exchange economy of the city.

Before the industrial revolution, capitalism never gained complete ascendancy over the "natural economy" based upon land. There were great commercial cities, but the agricultural communities were very much greater still and they always dominated the society. Gradually, however, through moneylending especially, the urban financiers brought the landowners into line and finally geared their activities to the business practices of the city. We do not know, of course, when capitalism originated; some form of commercial capitalism—buying and selling rationally for profit—has probably always been known in

[4]*Modern Capitalism,* trans. by Homer B. Vanderblue and George F. Doriot, p. 64.
[5]Ibid., p. 106. See also Frances M. Page, *The Estates of Crowland Abbey,* p. 144. Says Henri Pirenne, "Perhaps the most striking character of the feudal state was its almost absolute lack of finances. In it, money played no role." *Medieval Cities,* p. 234. For a discussion of the limited use of money on an English manor in the late Middle Ages see F. W. Maitland, "The History of a Cambridgeshire Manor," *The English Historical Review,* Vol. IX, 1894, pp. 417–39.

market places.[6] But the capitalism which suffuses the way of life—the thinking—of entire peoples is a modern phenomenon. It has been said, however, that only the machine, with its concomitant technical organization, distinguishes modern capitalism from medieval commercial capitalism.[7]

At any rate, out of the post-medieval cities of Europe sprang a new civilization, a new kind of efficient, rational, individuated people.[8] Without precedent they worked out the new system, which was destined finally to characterize the whole of Western civilization. These builders of cities were hardly "financed" by the great landed proprietors. "Most of them," says Pirenne, "must have built up their first capital by hiring themselves out as sailors, or dockers, or as assistants in merchant caravans."[9]

The Transition

In the preceding chapter we have, according to common usage, considered the bourgeoisie as one of the medieval estates; frequently they have been referred to as the "middle class." Strictly speaking, however, the bourgeoisie never constituted a social estate of the feudal system; consequently they were never a middle class of the estate system. The social-status system—the estate system—based upon the landed economy of feudal society was never able to assimilate the townsmen. The

---

[6]Cf. Henri Pirenne, *Les Périods de l'histoire sociale du capitalisme*, p. 5. On the origin of capitalism, see Harry Elmer Barnes, op. cit., Chap. IX, and Frederick L. Nussbaum, op. cit., pp. 31–56.

[7]See H. M. Robertson, *Aspects of the Rise of Economic Individualism*, p. 42, and Max Weber, *The Protestant Ethic and the Spirit of Capitalism*, trans. by Talcott Parsons, pp. 13–31.

[8]"In the town a new world had grown up with an organization and a polity of its own wholly different from that of the country. . . . Its way of life, its code of manners, its habits, aims, and interests, the condition of the people, the local theories of trade by which its conduct of business was guided, the popular views of citizenship and government" marked and distinguished the town. Mrs. J. R. Green, op. cit., pp. 2–3.

[9]*Economic and Social History of Medieval Europe*, p. 166.

Concerning a somewhat later period Harry Elmer Barnes concludes: ". . . the demands of the bourgeoisie for the recognition of the towns as self-governing urban communities met with strenuous opposition from those in control. Ecclesiastical even more than lay lords were reluctant to surrender their authority. Sometimes a peaceful demand was sufficient. At other times violence in the form of costly and bloody conflicts turned the trick. Twelve times the burghers of Tours were forced to resort to arms. The lesser nobility were cleverly played off against the higher nobility, the Church against the lay lords, the royal power against both. Sometimes the feudal lords, eager for gain, sold charters of freedom to the communes. In some regions, in Flanders, for example, the lords shrewdly discerned in the communes a source of prosperity for the whole locality, and permitted them to develop, granting them many concessions." Op. cit., pp. 60–61.

bourgeois social order was not only different from the feudal order but also antagonistic to it. To be sure, when feudalism was the dominant social system, the ideology of the whole society was feudal and the nascent capitalists had to be conceived of in terms of this ideology. But the bourgeoisie could not accept a stable place in the feudal order; therefore, they struggled against it with increasing effectiveness.

We may attempt to indicate the place of the bourgeoisie in the feudal system by a diagram. If we think of this as representing a typical feudal-urban societal relationship—say, France at about the end of the seventeenth century—then the small pyramid will indicate the divergent growth of the bourgeois system upon the old estate

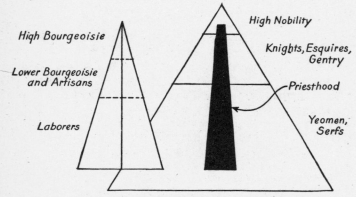

Impingement of Social-Class System upon Feudalism

society. Besides a more or less clearly defined stratification of social estates, the urban system, with no well-defined class barriers, developed. The estate of the priesthood may be thought of as a slender, truncated pyramid extending neither to the top nor to the base of the feudal hierarchy but forming the backbone of moral support for the system.

It has been recognized that the French Revolution represented the climax of the struggle for dominance between the rural and the urban way of life at that time in Europe—that is to say, the feudal and the bourgeois way of life. Says Edmund Burke ruefully: "The whole of the power obtained by this revolution will settle in the towns among the burghers, and the moneyed directors who lead them. The landed gentlemen, the yeoman, and the peasant have, none of them, habits or inclinations, or experience, which can lead them to any share in this the sole source of power and influence now left in France."[10] And Sée declares that "the effect of the Revolution was to destroy the legal distinctions which had divided the social classes and to establish equality of rights among all citizens."[11] The revolution removed all intermediary political loyalties between the individual and the state.[12] This, then, was the supreme organizational triumph of capitalism: the shattering of the social estates and the ascendance of individualism. The estates lost their wholeness, and the criteria of social status became diffused. While there may still be vestiges of the social estates in some Western countries, today the individual in cities especially has no estate; he belongs to a social-class system.

Ideology of Social-Class System

The ideology of the social-class society is the system of beliefs and social theories which support our present social order. Most of these are taken for granted. All our literature, art, textbooks, and "social sciences" presume a social-class society.[13] Even before the revolution, French and English writers had developed the essential ideology of the modern city dwellers. John Locke and the Encyclopedists particularly had perfected a new philosophy of bourgeois freedom, the *sine qua non* of bourgeois life; François Quesnay and particularly Adam Smith had already written its economic theory; scholastics had begun to

---

[10]*The Works of Edmund Burke,* Vol. II, "Reflections on the Revolution in France," p. 464.

[11]Henri Sée, op. cit., p. 171. Speaking of the transition in France, R. H. Tawney says: ". . . estates disappear in a common and equal citizenship. All men, at least in theory, became equal before the law . . . all men may enter all occupations. All men may buy and sell, trade and invest, as they please. Above all, all men may acquire property of all kinds. And property itself changes its nature. The element of sovereignty in it—such, at least, is the intention—vanishes. What remains is the right of exclusive disposal over marketable commodities." Op. cit., p. 112.

[12]Of these intermediary political loyalties, *The Cambridge Medieval History* says: "It is evident in theory that a baron, being a sovereign, could not be subjected to any will but his own, and that therefore such common arrangements as had to be made in medieval society had to be effected on the same lines as modern international conventions. And indeed we find this idea at the root of the feudal doctrine of legislation; in the custom of Touraine-Anju it was expressed in the following way: 'The baron has all manner of justice in his territory, and the king cannot proclaim his command in the land of the baron without the latter's consent; nor can the baron proclaim his command in the land of his tenant without the consent of the tenant.'" Vol. III, pp. 470-71.

[13]Marx and Engels put it pointedly: "Your very ideas are but the outgrowth of the conditions of your bourgeois production and bourgeois property, just as your jurisprudence is but the will of your class made into a law for all, a will, whose essential character and direction are determined by the economic conditions of existence of your class." *Communist Manifesto,* authorized English trans. ed. and annotated by Frederick Engels, 1888, p. 35. See also Nikolai Bukharin, *Historical Materialism,* Chap. VI.

puzzle over the apotheosis of its science; and Condorcet, in the glare of the revolution itself, expressed the new passion for progress in his great dream of infinite perfectibility of man. By the time of the French Revolution, also, the townsmen had a revised religion, a "free market in God," which was in the making for some centuries. The Reformation defied the most powerful estate and its philosophy and provided the necessary sanctions for bourgeois exploitation of *opportunities*.[14]

To be sure, in modern society agriculture and land continue to be indispensable, but land has lost its old character as the economic and social fundament. It no longer makes the man; in other words, it is as much as it is worth in money—a mere factor of production frequently despised by financiers because of its inertness. The individual has been freed from the land, the attractiveness of which must now be proved in an unsentimental market.[15]

Probably the crucial characteristic of a social-class system is individualism. Although it is still true that we explain poverty or wealth by stereotyping large groups with certain attributes, individuals are nonetheless assumed to have willingly chosen the course leading to their station in life. "Individualism," says Robertson, "believes that different individuals have different attributes and that each should be allowed to develop them in competition with others to the best of his ability."[16] Individualism presumes also that one person is as free as another to achieve advantageous social position. It acclaims ambition, progress, and, above all, success. Freedom of the individual means that he should be permitted, at least in theory, to make the greatest progress for himself and that this progress would redound to the greatest good of society.

The greater the distance of flight up the social-status gradient, the greater the social praise of the individual. That man who "minds his own business," adding success to success, until at last he is able to rise

---

[14]See Max Weber, op. cit., for one widely accepted thesis concerning the functional relationship between religion and capitalism, and the foreword by R. H. Tawney in which Weber's view is questioned.

[15]Karl Marx puts it thus: ". . . agriculture comes to be more and more merely a branch of industry and is completely dominated by capital." See *A Contribution to the Critique of Political Economy*, trans. by N. I. Stone, p. 303.

[16]H. M. Robertson, op. cit., p. 34. Speaking of the role of money in the individuation of persons in "the capitalistic system," Georg Simmel points out: "Money has brought it about that one individual may unite himself with others without being compelled to surrender any of his personal freedom or reserve. That is the fundamental and unspeakably significant difference between the medieval form of organization which made no difference between the association of men as men and the association of men as members of an organization." From *Philosophie des Geldes*, quoted by R. E. Park and E. W. Burgess, *Introduction to the Science of Sociology*, p. 554.

above all material necessity or social restriction,[17] so that he might boast himself *"le vainqueur du vainqueur de la terre,"* is the ideal of our social-class system. Moreover, as Thorstein Veblen has emphasized, the bourgeois thirst for achievement is unquenchable, and "invidious comparisons" become a stimulating gauge for ceaseless striving and acquisitiveness.

So long as the comparison is distinctly unfavorable to himself, the normal average individual will live in chronic dissatisfaction with his present lot; and when he has reached what may be called the normal pecuniary standard of the community, or of his class in the community, this chronic dissatisfaction will give place to a restless straining to place a wider and ever widening pecuniary interval between himself and this average standard. The invidious comparison can never become so favorable to the individual making it that he would not gladly rate himself still higher relatively to his competitors in the struggle for pecuniary reputability.[18]

Instead of well-marked-off estates or social ranks, then, we have in our social-class system a constant milling of social-status atoms—that is to say, a circulation of individuals or families as bearers of status. The movement is directed upward and against a powerful "social gravity" that brings down the less efficient competitors relentlessly. The situation is dynamic, and, indeed, so sensitive that the very expectation of success or failure tends to influence the social status of the individual.

A word should be said on the nature of bourgeois freedom of political competition called democracy. Modern democracy is not a revival of Athenian democracy, nor did it spring from Christianity—in practice it has never attained its ideals. In fact, the bourgeoisie never intended that it should. "Nothing was farther from the mind of the original middle classes than any conception of the rights of man and citizen. Personal liberty itself was not claimed as a natural right. It was sought only for the advantages it conferred."[19]

Quite early in the development of towns the Western bourgeois idea

---

[17] "Economic pre-eminence means economic independence, and independence means relative freedom from political control." See *Economic Power and Political Pressures,* Monograph No. 26, Temporary National Economic Committee, p. 22.

[18] *The Theory of the Leisure Class,* pp. 31–32. Benjamin Franklin, sometimes called the pure bourgeois, says in his *Autobiography:* "I experienced, too, the truth of this observation: *'that after getting the first hundred pounds, it is more easy to get the second,'* money itself being of a prolific nature." (Italics Franklin's.) John Bigelow, ed., p. 226. There has been some question concerning acquisitiveness as an attribute of modern capitalism. See, for instance, Max Weber, op. cit., p. 58 and *passim.*

[19] Henri Pirenne, *Medieval Cities,* p. 177. Pirenne declares further: "Freedom, as the middle class conceive it, was a monopoly." P. 221.

of citizenship, the "territorial" idea as distinct from the "personal" or religious basis of association, characteristic of feudalism, came into being. Persons who lived in the town were presumed to benefit from the very fact of "communal" residence; hence they were compelled to take an oath of loyalty to the jurisdiction of the area. Says P. Boissonnade, "It was an association for mutual defense, and it exacted from its members an absolute devotion, sealed by an oath, in exchange for the precious rights which it assured them, above all, in the domain of practical interests. . . . This is the fertile germ out of which . . . there sprang medieval democracy, the mother of all modern democracies."[20] Here, too, we may observe the germ of modern nationalism, which was destined to become the most powerful idée-force in the mature bourgeois state.

It has been said that one of the greatest sins of democracy is hypocrisy. But if reference is to the form of government which has existed for, say, the last hundred years in France, England, and the United States, then the saying might well be changed to mean that hypocrisy is elemental in democracy. And yet in a sense the idea is inappropriate, for a quality that is inherent cannot at the same time be dispensable. This bitter charge has its roots in the unattainable assumption of political democracy that every individual in the system is in fact equally free to achieve, and in the conflict of distinct political-class ideologies inherent in bourgeois society.

Capitalistic freedom means ostensible freedom to compete for the available wealth of the nation, and political democracy is the method of government which purports to assure the commonwealth that every individual will abide by the rules of the game. This freedom, which the eighteenth-century city dwellers died for, requires that he who fails in the competitive struggle be a good sport, for was he not master of his own chances of success? Herbert Hoover expresses the traditional view in characterizing the government as the "umpire in our social system."[21]

---

[20] *Life and Work in Medieval Europe,* p. 197.

[21] *American Individualism,* p. 51. Cf. Joseph A. Schumpeter, *Capitalism, Socialism, and Democracy,* pp. 297–98.

It may be well to mention that this ideology is not so unbiased as it might first seem. In reality the bourgeois government as umpire keeps the rules of a game in which the players are very unequally matched. As one nineteenth-century priest exclaimed: "Be advised, oh, ye who do not already know it; be advised, ye enemies of God and man—by whatever names ye be known—that in matters between the strong and the weak, between the rich and the poor, between master and servant, it is liberty that enslaves and the law which emancipates." Speech delivered April 2, 1848, by the Rev. Father Lacordaire, quoted by Louis Marlio, *Can Democracy Recover?,* p. 27. Here the idea of law is that of control of the powerful instead of *laissez faire.*

Furthermore, from the beginning it was intended that the government should be in fact in the hands of the successful.

The realities of bourgeois government have undergone practically no change. Recently a distinguished American businessman made it quite clear what democracy really means to businessmen. "Businessmen," he declared, "naturally are apprehensive of any unnecessary intervention of government in the functions of private enterprise . . . as undermining the democratic concept of individual liberty. . . . The function of governmental agencies in normal times is that of assisting private enterprise by the removal of barriers to its legitimate undertakings."[22]

It is in the United States that freedom, business freedom, has attained its highest perfection. "This," says John Stuart Mill, "is what every free people ought to be; a people capable of this is certain to be free."[23] Again, that great individualist, Herbert Hoover, even thinks that democracy in America is unique.

Our individualism differs from all others because it embraces these great ideals: that while we build our society upon the attainment of the individual, we shall safeguard to every individual an equality of opportunity to take that position in the community to which his intelligence, character, ability, and ambition entitle him; that we keep the social solution free from frozen strata of classes; that we shall stimulate effort of each individual to achievement . . . while he in turn must stand up to the emery wheel of competition.[24]

This is liberalism, the great antagonist of the feudal estate system.[25] Liberalism is sometimes confused with democracy, which is in fact antagonistic to it. Democratic ideals are proletarian ideals and, in so far as they are allowed expression in bourgeois society, they tend to limit the full expression of liberalism. As Lewis Corey asserts concerning democracy: ". . . the mere ideal is dangerous to capitalism, and

---

[22]From address by E. P. Thomas, President, National Foreign Trade Council, delivered April 27, 1943, at the Thirty-first Annual Meeting of the Chamber of Commerce of the United States. To this Marx and Engels agree: "By freedom is meant, under the present bourgeois conditions of production, free trade—free selling and buying." *The Communist Manifesto*, p. 33.

[23]From *Utilitarianism, Liberty, Representative Government,* cited by Albert R. Chandler, *The Clash of Political Ideals*, p. 106.

[24]Herbert Hoover, op. cit., p. 9. For a studied development of this thesis, see *The American Individual Enterprise System,* by the Economic Principles Commission of the National Association of Manufacturers, New York and London, 1946, 2 vols.

[25]Liberalism, of course, is this and much more. For a discussion see Harold J. Laski, *The Rise of Liberalism;* Guido de Ruggiero, *The History of European Liberalism,* trans. by R. G. Collingwood; L. T. Hobhouse, *Liberalism.*

it is the object of a growing offensive."[26] In a later chapter this point will be discussed more fully.

Another type of social phenomenon, distinct from social class but frequently confused with it, is the "political class." We shall now consider this.

---

[26]*The Decline of American Capitalism,* p. 521.

10. *The Political Class*

*I*N THE LAST TWO CHAPTERS WE HAVE DISCUSSED TWO TYPES OF
social-status systems: estates and social classes. In this chapter we
shall attempt to determine the characteristics of political classes which
do not constitute a system. The term "political class" is used here, for
want of a more suitable one, to distinguish a social phenomenon usually
called "class" or "social class" from that which we have previously described as "social class." Instead of the term "political class," the
designation "economic class"[1] might have been used, but economic
determinants are evidently at the base of social classes also. On the
other hand, to substitute the German word *Stand* for "social class" is
to introduce a concept that is already confused in the literature. At any
rate, the designation may be of less significance than its meaning.[2]

Meaning of Political Class

"Any city, however small," says Plato, "is in fact divided into two;
one, the city of the poor, the other, of the rich; these are at war with
one another."[3] To the same effect, Franklin H. Giddings concludes:
"In every sovereign state there are would-be states. . . . Every would-be
state strives actively to become sovereign. It initiates and foments class
struggle."[4] We could go on citing conclusions about class struggle
almost indefinitely, but they would all tend to be divided into two

---

[1]In this study we shall not discuss economic classes as functional groups. Farmers,
bankers, investors, teachers, and so on, are occupational groups which may be classified into economic classes according to the immediate interest of the taxonomist.
These groups cannot be equated to either social or political classes.

[2]In his speech in Naples, August 11, 1922, Mussolini called the Fascists "a new
political class."

[3]*The Works of Plato*, trans. by B. Jowett, pp. 137–38.

[4]Quoted by Charles Hunt Page, *Class and American Sociology*, p. 165.

main groups: those before, and those after, Karl Marx. Marx himself says:

> The history of all hitherto existing society is the history of class struggle. Freeman and slave, patrician and plebeian, lord and serf, guild-master and journeyman, in a word, oppressor and oppressed, stood in constant opposition to one another, carried on an uninterrupted, now hidden, now open fight, a fight that each time ended either in a revolutionary reconstitution of society at large, or in the common ruin of the contending classes. . . . The modern bourgeois society that has sprouted from the ruins of feudal society has not done away with class antagonisms. It has but established new classes, new conditions of oppression, new forms of struggle in place of the old ones. Our epoch, the epoch of the bourgeoisie, possesses, however, this distinctive feature; it has simplified the class antagonisms. Society as a whole is more and more splitting up into two great battle camps, into two great classes directly facing each other: Bourgeoisie and Proletariat.[5]

In all the voluminous works of Marx, however, there is no definition of class, and, naturally, no clear distinction between the idea of these "two great classes directly facing each other" and that of the social-class system. These are both products of bourgeois economy, and in the literature following Marx both are usually referred to as "social classes." At the outset it should be made clear that political-class action may be found in all organized society, and certainly it is not necessarily limited to the period of the rise of urbanism in Europe. Bourgeoisie-proletariat struggle is one type of political-class action; it is a product of modern capitalistic society. But we may repeat that fully developed social-class systems are also unknown to ancient society; they came into their own only after 1789.

It must be already obvious that political and social classes are distinct phenomena. Social classes form a system of co-operating conceptual status entities; political classes, on the other hand, do not constitute a system at all, for they are antagonistic.[6] The political class is a power group which tends to be organized for conflict; the social class is never organized, for it is a concept only. Although the political class is ordinarily weighted with persons from a special sector of the social-status gradient, it may include persons from every position.[7] Hence we do not speak of political classes as forming a hierarchy; they may con-

---

[5] Karl Marx and Friedrich Engels, *Communist Manifesto*, pp. 12–13.

[6] Cf. Joseph A. Schumpeter, op. cit., pp. 53–54.

[7] The status system of any society, whether it be estate, caste, or social class, always presumes the inclusion of every individual; but, although the outcome of political-class struggle invariably affects the social condition of every individual in the society, the immediate contending political classes may include only a minority of

ceivably split the social hierarchy vertically; therefore, there is here no primary conception of social stratification. In other words, members of the political class ordinarily do not have a common social status. These classes, therefore, are not thought of as social-class strata but as organizations arrayed face to face against each other. Furthermore, unlike the social class, the political class seeks to attract members to itself, and group solidarity is highly valued. Social solidarity is not a characteristic of social classes, for it is expected that persons are constantly attracted upward and away from their social position, while those who fall may be allowed to sink even farther.

Control of the State—a Goal

As a power group, the political class is preoccupied with devices for controlling the state. In emphasizing this point, Lewis L. Lorwin says: "Since the power of the ruling class is always concentrated in the organization of the state, the oppressed class must aim directly against the mechanism of the state. Every class struggle is thus *a political struggle*, which in its objectives aims at the abolition of the existing social order and at the establishment of a new social system."[8] However, political-class action may not be identified with that of political factions, for the faction may have as its purpose nothing more than the acquisition of the spoils of office. Thus different political factions may represent the same political class. Political factions may come into being, disappear, or regroup, "but the fundamental interests of the classes remain. That party [faction] conquers which is able to feel out and satisfy the fundamental demands of a class."[9]

---

the population. In other words, the political classes may have a "phantom public" larger in numbers than themselves. Of course, we do not mean to say that this public is of no importance. It may remain apathetic or it may shift its weight of sentiment toward one side or the other—it is always watched by the contending classes.

[8] See "Class Struggle," *Encyclopedia of the Social Sciences*.

[9] See Leon Trotsky, *The History of the Russian Revolution*, Vol. III, p. 338.

In the United States there is only one effective political party, with two factions: Republicans and Democrats. There is no effective Socialist party, the organized leadership of the opposite political class.

The following is a political-faction, and thus quite misleading, analysis of the modern class struggle: "The important long-run consideration is not what political philosophy or what ideology the present ruling class now holds, but rather to what extent the economic powers, and hence the livelihood of all the people in those countries [Germany, Italy, and Russia], are in the hands of the government. How governments use such important powers will change from time to time depending on what groups of politicians temporarily are in power. And what these groups will be is, in *totalitarian* states as in other countries, to a large extent accidental, and certainly unpredictable." James Harvey Rogers, *Capitalism in Crisis*, pp. 6–7. (Italics added.)

Furthermore, in class-conflict situations the object on trial is not an administration but rather a political system; the whole institutional order may be marked for weeding out. Says Paul M. Sweezy: "Any particular state is the child of the class or classes in society which benefit from the particular set of property relations which it is the state's obligation to enforce."[10] It is this pattern of property relationships which political-class conflict threatens. Hence the goal of a political class is always control of the state. As an instance of this, Frederick L. Schuman, commenting upon the seizure of power by the German Nazis, declares: "The first step in the evolution of the judicial system of the Third Reich was the identification of the [Nazi] Party with the State and the punishment of offences against the Party as crimes against the State."[11]

Method and Procedure

Class struggle is not only a course of action but also a process of winning new adherents to some political ideal or of maintaining old convictions. The political class usually has a policy and a propaganda machine. The ideal of the attacking political class is neither utopian nor merely conflictive; it involves a rational plan for displacing the existing government. "An effective revolutionary ideology," says Alfred Meusel, "must reveal to the rising social class that it is and why it is a class distinct from the society into which it was born; it must offer a critique of the existing order and draw the general outline of the ideal substitute."[12]

No ruling class can be overthrown simply by sporadic conflict; "revolutionism" is ordinarily pointless. Adolf Hitler saw this clearly in his assertion that a new way of life must be presented as superior to the old:

Every attempt at fighting a view of life by means of force will finally fail, unless the fight against it represents the form of an attack for the

---

[10] *The Theory of Capitalist Development*, p. 242.

[11] *The Nazi Dictatorship*, p. 301. Dr. Goebbels had already said: "If in our struggle against a corrupt system, we are today forced to be a 'party' . . . the instant the system crumbles, we will become the State." Quoted by Daniel Guerin, *Fascism and Big Business*, p. 134. And another revolutionist, Leon Trotsky, declares: "A class struggle carried to its conclusion is a struggle for state power." Op. cit., Vol. I, p. 169.

[12] "Revolution and Counter-Revolution," *Encyclopedia of the Social Sciences*. Sombart sees the activities of the aggressive political class definitively: "By a social movement we understand the aggregate of all those endeavors of a social class which are directed to a rational overturning of an existing social order to suit the interests of this class." *Socialism and the Social Movement in the 19th Century*, trans. by Anson P. Atterbury, p. 3.

sake of a new spiritual direction. Only in the struggle of two views of life with each other can the weapon of brute force, used continuously and ruthlessly, bring about the decision in favor of the side it supports.[13]

A political class develops naturally—that is to say, new political classes come into being inevitably with significant changes in the method of economic production and economic distribution. On the other hand, class conflict is consciously developed between the classes. Werner Sombart gives the following stages in the development of class struggle: ". . . first a difference of class, then class interests [consciousness], then class opposition, finally class strife."[14] A political class becomes conscious of itself only through successful propaganda; the objective position of the class and its aims must be focused by its leaders. We may put it in this way: As a function of the economic order, the class has potential existence, but as the result of agitation it becomes organized for conflict. The dominant political class becomes class-conscious—and sometimes with overwhelming vehemence—in response, or as a counteraction, to the developing class consciousness of the subordinate class.

Therefore, no class ever realizes its ideals as a matter of course. "To realize these ideals," says Sombart, "it is necessary to become inspired, to kindle a heart's glow, to develop a fire of enthusiasm."[15] And, in the style of a great modern counterrevolutionist, Hitler declared:

One must not think that the French Revolution would ever have come about by philosophical theories, if it had not found an army of instigators, led by demagogues of the grandest sort, who whipped up the passions of . . . the people, till finally that terrible volcanic eruption took place.[16]

In all social movements the masses are taken into consideration; both the ruling class and the attacking class appeal to the people. Yet the

---

[13]*Mein Kampf,* p. 223.

[14]Op. cit., p. 110.

[15]Ibid., p. 151. To the same effect Albert Mathies declares: "The great majority of men are unaware of injustice until it is pointed out to them. The denunciation of abuses is an essential preliminary to a demand for reform; a clearly formulated ideal, the prerequisite of a loyal following." See "French Revolution," *Encyclopedia of the Social Sciences.* On this point Lewis L. Lorwin also says: "The objective existence of class interests does not mean that these interests are always understood by the class itself. In fact for a number of reasons, a class may be devoid of class consciousness; the inherent contradictions between classes may not become clear at once because economic processes go through several stages of development. Ibid., "Class Struggle."

[16]Op. cit., p. 711. And already Danton and Delacroix had said: "Revolutions are not made on tea. . . . The principles of justice and humanity are well enough in theory and in the books of philosophers; but in practice it is necessary to employ other means; one must have cut-throats in one's pay." See Pierre Gaxotte, *The French Revolution,* trans. by Walter A. Phillips, p. 249.

outcome of the struggle may affect the interest of the people only indirectly. Some of the most violent class conflicts in history, fought in
the interest of one privileged class against another, have utilized the
exploited masses on both sides. Even though the real purpose of the
class is antagonistic to the interest of the common people, it will always
seek to convert them.[17] For instance, the Nazi leader, mindful of this,
says:

> If one had recognized the tremendous power which at all times is due
> to the masses as the bearer of revolutionary resistance, one would certainly
> have applied a different policy as regards social and propagandistic direc-
> tions. Then the center of weight of the movement would not have been
> removed to parliament, but stressed in the workshops and streets.[18]

Leadership

Ordinarily it is not possible to delimit definitely a political class by
observing actual personal characteristics such as occupation, wealth,
religious affiliation, or social-class position. The idealism of political
classes may override individual differences. Indeed the leadership of
the aggressor class may arise from the ruling class itself. Robert Michels
emphasizes this in concluding that "every great class movement in history has arisen upon the instigation, with the co-operation, and under
the leadership of men sprung from the very class against which the
movement was directed."[19]

Marx and Engels had already said: ". . . in times when the class-
struggle nears the decisive hour, the process of dissolution going on
within the ruling class, in fact, within the whole range of the old society,
assumes such a violent, glaring character that a small section of the ruling class cuts itself adrift and joins the revolutionary class . . ."[20] The
particular disadvantaged group, then, may not produce its own leadership. It is obvious, however, that no great part of one class will desert
and enter the ranks of the other; the desertion, though significant, occurs only in isolated cases.

---

[17]Louis Adamic quotes the financier, Jay Gould, as remarking symbolically: "I can
hire one half the working class to kill the other half." *Dynamite: The Story of Class
Violence in America,* p. 23.

[18]Adolf Hitler, op. cit., p. 138.

[19]*Political Parties,* trans. by Eden and Cedar Paul, pp. 238–39.

[20]*Communist Manifesto,* p. 26. Quite frequently in discussions of contemporary
political-class action charges are made that the aggressor class is planning an overthrow of democracy. This, however, is misleading. The attack is really against the
bourgeois economic system, and a supplanting of the latter need not necessarily
involve an abandonment of all possible forms of democratic method.

The Purpose and Composition of Classes

The political class is probably always motivated by some socio-economic interest. According to John Strachey: ". . . it is a change in economic conditions, a change in methods of production . . . which first shifts the balance of strength in the community, and so starts the whole movement."[21] The class aims primarily at controlling the policies of production and distribution of wealth. Sometimes this interest may be couched in a religious, racial, or even a nationalistic rationale, in which case some analysis will be necessary to determine the purpose of the class. A political-class movement will develop when, because of new methods of production or maturation of old methods, economic power has been shifted to some section of the population without at the same time shifting the political power. This is the basis of political-class discontent.

Of course, not all forms of social antagonism are political-class antagonism. As Pirenne points out:

Nothing was more tragic than the situation of the Flemish towns in which the social hatred raged with the frenzy of madness. In 1320–32 the "good people" of Ypres implored the King not to allow the inner bastion of the town, in which they lived and which protected them from the "common people," to be demolished. The history of this town, like that of Ghent and Bruges, abounds in bloody struggles, setting the cloth-workers at grips with "those who had something to lose." The struggle took on more and more the appearance of a class war between rich and poor. But it was this in appearance only. *There was no common understanding among the mass of workers in revolt.* The fullers, whose wages the weavers claimed to fix, or rather, to reduce, treated the latter as enemies and in order to escape from their exploitation, supported the "good people." As to the small-scale crafts, all detested the "odious weavers."[22]

There are many group skirmishes which result from local group friction. In their adjustments, however, the social order remains entirely out of view; furthermore, there may be international wars be-

---

[21]*The Coming Struggle for Power*, p. 21.

[22]Henri Pirenne, *Economic and Social History of Medieval Europe*, p. 206. (Italics added.) Eduard Heimann makes a similar observation: "The German Peasants' Revolts of 1524–25, which were choked in streams of blood by the nobles . . . had sprung only from the desire of the peasants to restore genuine feudal morality and responsibility by the nobles for their protection against abuse and exploitation." *Communism, Fascism or Democracy*, p. 39. So, too, other peasant revolts at about this period all over Europe, such as the *Jacquerie* uprising in France in 1358, were desperate movements mercilessly crushed by the nobles.

tween ruling classes which do not contemplate a rearrangement of the political-class alignment in any nation. A peasant revolt may be simply a defense of certain customary rights.

A gang, sect, denomination, social club, or lodge need not represent a political class. These are intraclass institutional groups, and they may have problems which they seek to solve politically; yet their end is ordinarily the fostering of their own limited interests rather than the controlling of the state for the purpose of reorganizing the economic order. Institutional groups of this kind may be called special-purpose groups; their outlook is circumscribed, specialized, and exclusive. They may, however, be altruistic. Within the ongoing social order they propose to work for their own welfare or for that of certain limited groups in the society.

Their limits of possible social activity are those of political and social reform; they are, at most, interested in a more propitious operation of the status quo. As an illustration, ordinary opportunistic labor unionism is not politically class-minded, though it is always interested in seeing its friends in office as an assurance of its own welfare. Labor unionism begins to have a political-class appeal when it becomes explicitly revolutionary—that is to say, with reference to a capitalistic society, when it becomes socialistic, syndicalistic, communistic, or anarchistic.[23]

Ordinarily only those persons who take the side of a political class will be included in that class, and this must be so because it is a conflict group. It is, therefore, practically impossible to define the membership of a political class in terms of objective criteria only. The correlation between the material position of a person and his social attitudes may not be perfect. Thus in attempting to delimit a political class, to differentiate proletariat from bourgeoisie, Goetz A. Briefs concludes:

A proletarian is a propertyless wage earner . . . who regards himself and his kind as constituting a distinct class, who lives and forms his ideas in the light of this class consciousness according to class ideals, and who on the basis of this class consciousness rejects the prevailing social and economic order. . . . To be a proletarian . . . is, therefore, not to have a certain occupation or a certain economic and social status, but to have a characteristic mental set, a predisposition to react to one's given environment in ways no better to be described than by the term proletarian.[24]

---

[23]The term "political class" in our meaning is not synonymous with Gaetano Mosca's ruling class, which seems to be limited to the administrative head of a government. See *The Ruling Class,* trans. by Hanna D. Khan.

[24]*The Proletariat,* pp. 50–51.

Recognizing this inevitable characteristic of the political class will enable us to explain what Professor Sorokin thinks is a contradiction. According to this writer, ". . . the theoretical conceptions of the Communists are vaguely different and contradictory, [because] in their practice . . . a proletarian has been regarded as anyone who has supported the Communists although he occupied the position of a capitalist or was a privileged and wealthy man. The non-proletarians have been regarded as all who have not supported the Communist government, though they were the common laboring men in factories."[25] This, obviously, is not an inconsistency of political-class action. One may put it briefly that a political-class member is one who believes in and is willing to follow the ideals of that class. This, at any rate, is a decisive characterization in open political-class conflict.

Relationship of Political and Social Classes

Sometimes a confusion of the meaning of social and political class has caused many writers to question the proposition that it is possible for an advanced society to be a "classless" society. They will argue that men are born unequal, both in physique and aptitude, that society will always contrive to distribute its favors among its members according to their contributions to the social welfare, and that this principle holds even though the range of social emoluments is narrower in some societies than in others. Clearly, however, this constitutes a social-class reference, which the advocates of a classless society could not have in mind. The latter are thinking about large groups with fundamentally divergent economic interests—about antagonistic groups—and not particularly of the co-operative status system. Observe, for example, the following argument of John Strachey:

Since there are, by definition, no classes in a communist society, there can be no class friction; there can be no necessity for the immense expenditures of social effort which are today necessary in order forcibly to adjust the relationship of inherently antagonistic classes.[26]

A political-classless society, then, need not imply a statusless society.[27] In other words, there seems to be no necessary functional relation-

---

[25]*Contemporary Sociological Theories*, p. 543, note.
[26]Op. cit., p. 349.
[27]It seems that R. H. Tawney has been forced to stretch his logic extremely in order to achieve some meaning of a classless society. He declares: "A society marked by sharp disparities of wealth and power might properly, nevertheless, be described as classless, since it was open to each man to become wealthy and powerful." Op. cit., p. 123.

ship between political and social classes. It may not be even true to
state that the greater the rigidity of the status system, the greater the
likelihood of the formation of political classes. The stable caste system
of India, for instance, has not been particularly disposed to political-
class conflict. At any rate, the absence of political classes does not imply
an absence of social classes.[28] But reference to one political class always
implies the existence of one or more counterclasses. If there is only one
unopposed political class, the society may be said to be politically classless.

Thus, in the days of rampant capitalism in the United States, there
was probably only one organized political class; there is probably only
one active political class in Russia today. Yet there have always been
social classes in these countries. There is always latent or open class
struggle in a society in which there is more than one political class; but
social classes, to reiterate, are not in conflict. They supplement and support each other.

The political class may become "class-conscious"; social classes, on
the other hand, cannot be. Class consciousness is a political-class attribute;[29] however, with reference to a social-class system, persons may
be status-conscious.[30] Although a significant number of persons in a
society may be characterized by some common economic or other
social interests, they do not become an active political class until they
develop class consciousness. Thus, the search for and conversion of
potential class members are major functions of political-class leaders.

---

[28]See on this point Sidney and Beatrice Webb, *Soviet Communism: A New
Civilisation?*, pp. 1021–24.

[29]It is to political-class consciousness which Robert Briffault refers when he says:
"There will . . . be a type of mind, an idealogy, corresponding to the economic
situation of a ruling land-owning aristocracy; another type determined by the economic situation of a trading middle class, or a bourgeoisie; another corresponding
to the situation of a servile proletarian class. The specific characters of those types
of mind and of their contents will vary according to their respective relations. Thus,
the character of the aristocrat mind will be modified according as its power is un-
challenged, or as it is involved in conflict with rival class interests. The middle class,
or bourgeois mind, will assume a slightly different form according as it is contending
for emancipation from feudal domination or its own power is challenged by the
proletarians. The proletarian mind will differ according as the servile class is completely crushed or is content and resigned, or acquires hopes of emancipation and
becomes 'class-conscious'. . . . The class mentality is thus not only determined by
a fixed tradition, but is constantly active and undergoing adjustment in relation to
changing conditions." *Reasons for Anger*, pp. 52–53.

[30]We are assuming here that social classes are conceptual entities. Persons of
given statuses occupying a certain span of the social-status continuum constitute
an entity only in the minds of individuals.

The Economic Man and the Class Struggle

Political classes have almost never been able to attain their ends without violence. This, of course, is due to the fact that the ruling class does not yield without it, and because this class holds its position by virtue of its monopoly of power. The Machiavellian postulate that a man's property—his economic interest—is as good and sometimes better than his life clearly obtains in interclass relationship. Political classes are never convinced merely by arguments at the round table. These groups match power, not wits. Adolf Hitler put it impressively:

Every negotiation which does not have power behind it would be ridiculous and fruitless. . . . Even the best negotiators can achieve slight success as long as the ground on which they stand and the chair on which they sit are not the shield arm of their nation.[31]

Ordinarily, the greater the apparent cogency of the logic of the one side, the greater the intransigence of the other. Conviction by argument and reasoning comes only when these are backed up by a show of overwhelming physical might. To put the matter otherwise, the ruling class knows well on which side its bread is buttered and it will not be hoodwinked, or argued, or cajoled out of its position. Moreover, the ascendant class cannot be eased down gently with a *Satyagraha* or a sit-down strike;[32] it will accept no substitute for an open matching of physical power.[33] "Attempts at persuasion fail miserably," says Robert Michels, "when they are addressed to the privileged classes, in order to induce these to abandon, to their own disadvantage, as a class and as individuals, the leading positions they occupy in society."[34] To expect

---

[31]Op. cit., p. 982. On this point the great William E. Gladstone remarked: "If no considerations in a political crisis had been addressed to the people of this country, except to remember to hate violence and love order and exercise patience, the liberties of this country would never have been obtained." Quoted in Emmeline Pethnick-Lawrence, *My Part in a Changing World*, p. 269.

[32]To be sure, "passive resistance" is ordinarily the only way to fight when one is empty-handed. Little children sometimes fight their parents in that way. Certain groups may make a virtue of this necessity and exploit it religiously. Even so, we should remember that not all fights are political-class struggles.

[33]Again Hitler is in point: ". . . in the last analysis, the decisive question is always this: what is to be done if passive resistance finally gets on the opponent's nerves and he launches a fight against it with brute force? Is one determined to offer further resistance? If so, bear, for better or worse, the most violent, bloodiest hounding. In that case one faces what one faces in active resistance, namely, struggle. Hence every so-called passive resistance has real significance only if backed up by a determination, if need be, to continue resistance by open struggle or by means of clandestine warfare." Op. cit., pp. 989–90.

[34]Op. cit., pp. 244–45. The author declares further: "A class considered as a whole never spontaneously surrenders its position of advantage. It never recognizes

a ruling class to commit suicide for the mere asking is clearly too colossal a presumption. As Leon Trotsky put it: "One can talk over petty details with an enemy, but not matters of life and death." Werner Sombart presents the common-sense logic of the position of the ruling class when he asserts:

> The utopists fail to see, in their optimism, that a part of the society looks upon the *status quo* as thoroughly satisfactory and desires no change, that this part also has an interest in sustaining it, and that a specific condition of society always obtains because those persons, who are interested in it, have the power to sustain it. . . . Now judge for yourself what a mistaken estimate of the true world, what boundless underestimate of opposing forces, lie in the belief that those who have power can be moved to surrender their position through preaching and promise.[35]

This discussion, to be sure, must rest partly upon historical proof, or at least the absence of it, for it cannot be shown that in the past any political class has yielded without a conflict. Indeed, the position has been taken that a major change in the social order necessarily involves drastic measures, because "no political system is so flexible as to be susceptible to fundamental change by 'legal' means; and illegality implies resort to force by the revolutionist as well as by the state which he attacks."[36]

As a matter of fact, the law itself is the instrument of the ruling class; hence it is a logical impossibility for another class to assume power legally. "It is no reproach to law," says Edward H. Carr, "to describe it as a bulwark of the existing order."[37] The political postulates of the opposing classes are inevitably antagonistic; as a consequence there can be no common judicial procedure. "The law is not an abstraction. It cannot be understood independently of the political foundation on which it rests and the political interest which it serves."[38]

The ideology of the ruling class and the established social order will be defended obstinately, not only because it ensures the interest of that

---

any moral reason sufficiently powerful to compel it to abdicate in favor of its 'poorer brethren.' Such action is prevented, if by nothing else, by class egoism. . . ." Thomas Jefferson realized this clearly when he wrote to John Quincy Adams in 1823 concerning the European class struggle between the bourgeoisie and the nobility, saying: "To obtain all this [liberty in European countries], rivers of blood must yet flow, and years of desolation pass over; yet the object is worth rivers of blood and years of desolation." *Democracy,* by Thomas Jefferson, ed. by Saul Padover, p. 239.

[35]Op. cit., p. 33.
[36]Alfred Meusel, op. cit.
[37]*The Twenty Years' Crisis,* p. 244.
[38]Ibid., p. 229.

class, but also because it will inevitably seem that its defense is "indispensable to the preservation of society."[39] The suppression of one political class by another, then, is seldom, if ever, a windfall. When the vested interests of the ruling class are threatened, its members will deal mercilessly with the challenging class, at the same time readily putting even their own lives in jeopardy. Thus, the exercise of violence is the constant and inevitable prerogative of the ruling class; the revolutionaries can assume power only after they have limited or relieved this class of its freedom to control the decisive instruments of violence.

The political class may strive to attain its ends through political machinery, as the Republicans of Spain attempted to do by elections in 1931 and 1936; or it may adopt counterrevolutionary methods,[40] as the Rebels of the same country did in 1936. But these initiating tactics merely illustrate further the foregoing principle that a ruling class will not allow itself to be displaced "peacefully." In this, probably the most spectacular recent contest between established political classes, the rich and powerful Church, the upper crust of the army, and the landed aristocracy mainly defied the attack of the leaders of labor, the middle-class intellectuals, civil servants, and peasants. The sanguinary nature of the ensuing struggle for power is well known.

It may seem appalling to those long used to living under the easy rule of one powerful political class that probably the only way of disposing of a strongly entrenched political class is by extirpating it; yet the exigencies of political-class struggle compel such a procedure. Ordinarily, obstruction or curtailment of the power of a political class merely infuriates it. "A radical revolution . . . exacts a heavy toll of human life and suffering; but the transformations it effects are more fundamental and permanent than those achieved at smaller cost under the leadership of moderates."[41] The supplanting of one class by another literally calls for the overturning of one class by another; and since the dominant political class always controls the State, the purpose of the attacking class must inevitably be the "overthrow of the Government," a terrible business at best. The signers of the American Declaration of Independence were under no illusions about this. Consider their

---

[39]See Henri Pirenne, op. cit., p. 51. Already Marx and Engels had said: "Just as, to the bourgeois, the disappearance of class property is the disappearance of production itself, so the disappearance of class culture is to him identical with the disappearance of all culture." *Communist Manifesto*, p. 35. For a naïve construction of this see W. H. V. Reade, *The Revolt of Labor against Civilization.*

[40]In so far as open violence is concerned, the methods of the revolutionary and the counterrevolutionary are essentially the same.

[41]Alfred Meusel, op. cit.

last words: "And for the support of this Declaration . . . we mutually
pledge to each other our Lives, our Fortunes and our sacred Honor."[42]

Violence, then, is a necessary consequence of political-class action,
and probably the swifter and more decisive the action, the more economical it will be in terms of human lives. The Spanish Republicans
attempted to temporize with the class in power instead of liquidating it,
and the result was the shedding of the blood and violent handling of
probably well-nigh half the population of Spain; furthermore, the
revolution still remains to be fought. It seems that in political-class
action especially it is foolhardy to try "leaping the abyss in two jumps."
When, therefore, the structure of a ruling class has become weakened
and decadent because of a new economic situation, its prompt destruction by the rising social class may be cheapest in terms of human
lives.[43] In the thick of the French Revolution, in 1790, when the King
and the aristocracy were plotting a counterrevolution with the aid of
foreign armies, Jean Paul Marat, "the friend of the people," exclaimed: "Five or six hundred executions would have assured you
repose, liberty and happiness; a false humanity has restrained your
hands and stopped your blows; this will cost the lives of millions of
your brothers; if your enemies triumph . . . they will cut your throats

---

[42]Both Thomas Jefferson and Benjamin Franklin were powerful alien subverters
of the French Government. With reference to the role which Franklin played in
prerevolutionary France, Pierre Gaxotte declares: "His house at Passy at once
became the headquarters of the agitators. He was the high priest of the philosophers,
the Messiah of the malcontents, the patron of the framers of systems. . . . People
wrote him from all quarters, begging him for advice. . . . A lawyer—Brissot—
asked him questions about the New World, where he was thinking of going to take
lessons in revolution. Another lawyer dedicated to him his first speech in court; and
this lawyer was Robespierre. . . . The United States had provided the revolutionary doctrine with something which it had hitherto lacked: namely, an example.
What was to happen in the future now depended wholly on the energy of the
Government." Op. cit., pp. 55–56. For his share in sapping the foundations of the
French Government, Thomas Paine was made a French citizen and elected deputy
for Pas-de-Calais. See also Samuel Bernstein, "Jefferson and the French Revolution," *Science and Society*, Vol. VII, Spring, 1943, pp. 115ff.

[43]In this discussion we should not be thought of as advocating violence or revolution. Peoples have revolted in the past and we expect them to continue to do so.
Our question then refers to how and when are revolutions successful. The situation
is ripe for revolution when some minority or majority of the population feels that it
is being unjustly "oppressed" and that it can command the *power* to bring the
government to terms. Indeed, Abraham Lincoln saw even a moral right in such
action: "Any people anywhere being inclined and having the power have the right
to rise up and shake off the existing government, and form a new one that suits
them better. This is a most valuable, a most sacred right—a right which we hope
and believe is to liberate the world. Nor is this right confined to cases in which the
whole people of an existing government may choose to exercise it. . . . A majority
of any portion of such people may revolutionize, putting down a minority, inter-
mingled with or near about them, who may oppose the movement. Such minority
was precisely the case of the Tories of our own revolution." John G. Nicolay and
John Hay, *Abraham Lincoln Complete Works*, Vol. I, p. 105.

without pity . . . to extinguish forever the love of liberty among you."
Ordinarily the social system must be literally purged, and the cathartic
is inevitably drastic.

Now that we have said this, however, we must hasten to add that
the potentialities of violence exercised by the different classes may not
be the same. In a real political-class struggle—that is to say, a struggle
for the recognition of a social system economically rooted in the society
itself—violence is particularly the effective instrument of the attacking
class. The leadership of the attacking class can seldom be killed off; it
is a sort of sporiferous social phenomenon, regenerating increasingly
under violence. Therefore, at a certain stage of intensity in the struggle,
the use of violence by the ruling class may serve only to crystallize anti-
tyrannical sentiment against itself, thus expediting its own doom. On
the other hand, the destruction of the leadership of the senescent ruling
class will necessarily mean its consumption, because with this event not
only is the old leadership supplanted, but also a new and more vigorous
social system emerges.

An example of a common type of fearful, hopeful thinking on this
subject, a position ordinarily taken by revisionist and Fabian socialists,
is the following argument by Professor John Dewey. This authority
advocates a "dependence upon socially organized intelligence" as a
humane substitute for class conflict:

> The curious fact is that while it is generally admitted . . . that a par-
> ticular social problem, say of the family, or railroads or banking must be
> solved, if at all, by the method of intelligence, yet there is supposed to be
> some one all-exclusive social problem which can be solved only by violence.
> This fact would be inexplicable were it not for a conclusion from dogma
> as its premise. . . . There is an undoubted objective clash of interests
> between finance capitalism . . . and idle workers and hungry customers.
> But what generates violent strife is failure to bring the conflict into the
> light of intelligence where the conflicting interests can be adjudicated in
> behalf of the interest of the great majority.[44]

It is evident that Professor Dewey, in his analogy between a "particular social problem" such as "banking" or the "family" and a
political-class-conflict situation, completely misunderstands his subject.

---

[44]*Liberalism and Social Action*, pp. 78–79. Sombart is outspoken in his analysis
of this attitude. "It is assumed," he says, "that it is only ignorance on the part of
the opponent that keeps him from accepting openly and freely this good, from
divesting himself of his possessions and exchanging the old order for the new. The
classic example of this childish way of viewing things is the well-known fact that
Charles Fourier daily waited at his home, between the hours of twelve and one,
to receive the millionaire who should bring him money for the erection of the first
phalanstery. No one came." Op. cit., pp. 33–34.

In other words, he has confused intraclass problems with interclass conflict. Ordinarily problems of banking, or the family, or education, or Coolidge versus Davis, are political-party, faction problems; they do not involve a challenge to the political order. In political-class struggle intelligence is used to maneuver the opponent for a destructive blow. Indeed, political-class antagonisms are too highly pitched to achieve solution at the round table.[45] The attacking class is treasonous and blasphemous from the beginning. It is un-American, un-German, or un-English, and ungodly. It is necessarily against "Law and Order," against "our form of Government," and against "our way of life"; consequently, it cannot be free to speak its mind.[45a]

The aim of the attacking class is not co-operation; it does not want law and order, since law and order means perpetuation of the old order. It does not want to discuss or to negotiate problems in a conciliatory manner with the old rulers, for such a procedure tends to continue the latter's prestige. Indeed, the two groups do not have the same but contrary problems. The end of the attacking class is the vanquishing not only of the old leaders but also of the old system itself—a problem which the ruling class cannot be expected to discuss. Therefore, the struggle for power tends to be involved with a succession of conspiracies, imprisonments, and summatory conflicts, while compromise and appeasement may postpone but not settle the basic antagonism. Moreover, very much of the sanctimonious abhorrence displayed by the ruling class and its apologists against the use of violence in the class

[45]Robert Briffault cites an incident in point: "At a meeting of the General Council of Trades Unions in 1925, Mr. F. Bramley, criticizing the attitude of the meeting, remarked: 'It appears to me you can discuss any other subject under the sun without getting into that panicky state of trembling fear and excitement and almost savage ferocity you get into when you are discussing Russian affairs. . . . You can discuss calmly and without excitement the operations of the Fascists in Italy; you can discuss with great calm the suppression of trade-unions organizations in other countries; you can discuss the activities of capitalist governments and their destruction of the trade-union movement in one country after another without this unnecessary epidemic of excitement. But when you begin to discuss Russia, you begin to suffer from some malignant disease.'" *The Decline and Fall of the British Empire*, p. 175.

In this connection Harold F. Laski observes: ". . . whenever privilege is in danger, it flies into that panic which is the mortal enemy of reason; and it is a waste of time to ask its consideration of arguments that, in another mental climate, it is capable of understanding." *Where Do We Go from Here?*, p. 164.

[45a]It is only by a recognition of this fact, for example, that we can explain the frantic efforts of the ruling class in the United States to silence Henry A. Wallace—to say nothing about thousands of lesser men. Thus, the Associated Press reported on June 11, 1947, that United States Representative Meyer (Rep. Kans.) declared before the House that the Attorney General should indict Mr. Wallace for treason. And he implicated President Roosevelt as he would a foreign enemy: "Let it not be forgotten that this Henry Wallace is one of the heritages left us by the late Franklin Roosevelt."

struggle is rooted in the desire to maintain the integrity of its class monopoly of violence.

Of course the significant fact is not violence per se but rather the conquest of power, and no two situations will be exactly alike. If the trained and disciplined forces in immediate control of the instruments of violence become involved in the temper of a class-divided people, then the chances of revolution become immediate. Then, too, violence need not accompany revolutions in satellite countries. If, for example, the United States and Great Britain were to become socialist—we do not assume that the Labor Government has established socialism in England—either by force or the threat of force, we should expect, say, Cuba or Canada to liquidate their capitalists "peacefully." Moreover, we should distinguish between the democratic trend in Western society and the complete yielding of the capitalists.

In political-class conflict the ruling class will always be intolerant. Speech is never free to be used as a threat to the reign of a political class. Jesus was quite conscious of this when He declared: "Behold, I send unto you prophets, and wise men, and scribes: and some of them ye shall kill and crucify; and some of them shall ye scourge in your synagogues, and persecute them from city to city." "The institutions which are democratic in form," says Rosa Luxemburg, "are in substance instruments of the dominant class interest. This is most obvious in the fact that so soon as democracy shows a disposition to deny its class character and to become an instrument of the real interest of the people, the democratic forms themselves are sacrificed."[46]

The irreconcilability of political-class antagonism is a consideration of primary significance for an understanding of the history of revolution. Those who believe in the possibility of peaceful settlement of all political problems will not understand, for instance, the passion which moved the royalist Convention Parliament to unearth the putrefied bodies of Cromwell, Bradshaw, and Ireton and hang them in public on the gallows of Tyburn; they will not be struck by the summatory, vitriolic clashes of interest groups which, before the Civil War, rendered the American Congress totally impotent as an institution for averting political violence; they could not explain the mission of the armies of

---

[46]*Gesammelte Werke,* III, pp. 59–60; quoted by Paul M. Sweezy, op. cit., p. 251. The ruling class organized for struggle must obviously be negative and defensive. It cannot develop a rational philosophy, for it has nothing new to offer. As a counterrevolutionary group it must seek its rationale in the ideals of the old order. With its back against the wall the ruling class desires only to be left alone with its power; it is fighting for life, not for growth. Hence, when attacked, the ruling class will rely on spirituality and tradition, and because it is rationally tongue-tied, its physical counterblows may be all the more vicious.

Great Britain, France, Japan, and the United States in Russia at the
end of World War I;[47] they will be unable to read meaning into the
action of the Dies Committee in prosecuting Americans who had fought
the Nazis and Fascists in Spain; they will not see why it is very necessary
that Harry Bridges be either deported from the United States or
silenced in jail; and they will not know that an assurance by the Allies
to "respect the right of all people to choose the form of government
under which they will live" is in fact an extremely involved political
matter.[48]

Today, since World War II, open political-class conflict is world-
wide, with the "great powers," on local battlegrounds, frantically feeling for each other's throat as they give support to the class antagonists
favoring their respective class interests. The class struggle goes on violently in China, Greece, India, Argentina, Yugoslavia, Italy, Rumania,
Hungary, Germany, Bulgaria, Poland, "the Levant"; in all these countries, and in others, such as France, where "free elections" are held, the
great powers are matching force, which is, in reality, a protraction of
their own domestic class conflict. In a very real sense, for instance, the
ruling class in the United States had been fighting its own proletarian
revolution by supplying Sherman tanks, military service, and food to
defeat the "communist" revolutionaries in China and in Greece.

Rosa Luxemburg has made a significant distinction between means
and ends and in so doing has pointed out the intent of the reformer
and the radical. Concerning the modern class struggle, she writes:
". . . people who pronounce themselves in favor of the method of
legislative reform in place of and in contradistinction to the conquest of
political power, a social revolution, do not really choose a more tranquil,
calmer and slower road to the same goal, but a different goal. Instead of
taking a stand for the establishment of a new society, they take a stand
for surface modifications of the old society."[49] They may be thought of
as "left fellow travelers" of the status quo.

---

[47]For a discussion of the nature of the "war of intervention" in Russia see Michael
Sayers and Albert E. Kahn, *The Great Conspiracy*, Chap. VI.

[48]On the diplomacy involved in the question of post-World War II political freedom for smaller nations one may read the story of its progress all over his daily
newspapers. The following news item is taken at random from this source. Says the
United Press, May 17, 1946: "The United States has served notice on Soviet Russia
it will fight developments of communism in Japan just as vigorously as it does at
home. It promised not to suppress communist parties in Japan, but left unsaid the
plain warning that it will do everything short of that to discourage them. This
political challenge to the only communist state in the world was first made by
George R. Atcheson, Jr., top American diplomat in Tokyo. . . . This conflict,
underlying all Big Three troubles for several years, has led many top Allied leaders
to ask: 'Are the two systems reconcilable?' "

[49]*Reform or Revolution*, p. 43. In this connection Leon Trotsky observes:
". . . the social democrats are ready to sanction—and that only *ex post facto*—

A political class cannot consider itself established until all effective, internal antagonisms are removed; hence the need for frequent purges during its infancy. Without suggesting an extenuation of the ruthless cruelty of the German Nazis, we may illustrate our point further by inquiring into the sufficiency of Dr. Frederick L. Schuman's conclusions. Says Schuman:

> Nazi terrorists tortured and killed literally for the subjective satisfaction, the inner release of tensions which these activities afford. . . . This thesis can be abundantly supported by a consideration of the personality structures of many of the Nazi leaders.[50]

It seems, however, that this approach seldom, if ever, leads to an appreciation of political-class action. To be sure, an examination of "personality structures" will help to inculpate the leadership of a political class, but it will not reveal the social imperatives which produce in such situations the desperate necessity to quiet every potential obstruction. One class is under the necessity of vanquishing the other, and, in Schuman's own words: "Those who cannot be liquidated by propaganda must be liquidated by force."[51]

In all significant social revolutions, organized religion will necessarily be involved. The Church and other forms of organized priestcraft thrive in harmony with and, on the whole, sanction the status quo; in other words, the Church is normally rightist; it is the most lethargic and inert of the institutions confronting the revolutionists, partly because it is essentially traditional.[52] In fact, the Church has a vested interest in the status quo and it will fight in the protection of this. Therefore, the social system cannot be changed radically unless the Church is either overthrown or forcibly brought into line with the

---

those overturns which hand the power to the bourgeoisie, but they implacably condemn those methods which might alone bring the power to the proletariat. Under this pretended objectivism they conceal a policy of defense of the capitalist society." *Op. cit.*, Vol. III, p. 169.

[50]*Op. cit.*, p. 290. Says R. P. Dutt on this point: "Behind the ranting megalomaniacs, bullies, drug-fiends and broken down bohemians who constitute the outer façade of Fascism, the business heads of finance-capital who pay the costs and pull the strings are perfectly cool, clear, and intelligent." *Fascism and Social Revolution*, p. 197.

[51]*Op. cit.*, p. 311. As Harold Laski puts it: ". . . where men differ profoundly upon matters of social constitution the procedure of democracy is at a discount until a new equilibrium of agreement has been found. If it cannot be found by consent, it must be imposed by force." *Op. cit.*, p. 164.

[52]Professor William Oscar Brown puts it in this way: "Religion, always and at all times, tends to sanction the current mores, values, ideals, practices, attitudes, and relationships—provided, of course, they have been established in a culture for a sufficient period of time." *Race Prejudice*, Ph.D. thesis, University of Chicago, 1930, p. 294.

movement. In discussing the modern class struggle, Werner Sombart says: "One of the conditions of the very existence of the proletariat lies in tearing asunder all of the old points of faith."[53]

Organized religion is never a private matter; it is inevitably political. In this regard, ever since the early Christians began to find their first converts among the slaves and common laborers of the Roman Empire, Christianity became an intensely political institution in the West. The established religion represents the ruling class, and it is "used in their interests." Frequently the State, God, and Society are associated in the minds of the people, and a blow at the State may be shifted, more or less, to either or both of the other two.

The ascendant political class will invariably take advantage of the coincident struggle to stigmatize the radicals as God-haters.[54] In actuality, however, religion as such need not be seriously involved. Historically the Christian Church has labored in the interests of feudalism; it has defended slavery; it is at the service of capitalism; and we should expect it to accommodate to any succeeding system. Again, Sombart, in discussing the adaptability of Christianity to a proletarian society, observes that Christianity "became the religion of Rome in its decadence and of the German tribes in the youthful freshness of their civilization, of feudalism as well as of those stages of civilization in which the free cities and later the bourgeoisie have had predominance. Then why may it not also be the religion of the proletariat?"[55] Religion evidently fills an

---

[53]Op. cit., p. 160.

[54]Probably Edmund Burke's stricture on the French Revolutionists illustrates this type of religio-political involvement as well as any. Instead of "the Religion and the Law," he declares, "by which they were in a great political communion with the Christian world, they have constructed their Republic on three bases. . . . Its foundation is laid in Regicide, in Jacobinism and in Atheism. . . . I call it Atheism by establishment when any State . . . shall not acknowledge the existence of God as a moral Governor of the world; when it shall offer to Him no religious or moral worship; when it shall abolish the Christian religion by a regular decree; when it shall persecute with a cold, unrelenting steady cruelty, by every mode of confiscation, imprisonment, exile, and death, all its ministers; when it shall generally shut up, or pull down, churches; when the few buildings which remain of this kind, shall be open only for the purpose of making an apotheosis of monsters whose vices and crimes have no parallel amongst men, and whom all other men consider as objects of general detestation, and the severest animadversion of law. When in the place of that religion of social benevolence, and of individual self-denial in mockery of all religion, they institute impious, blasphemous, indecent theatric rites, in honour of their vitiated, perverted reason, and erect altars to the personification of their own corrupted and bloody Republic; when schools and seminaries are founded at publick expense to poison mankind; from generation to generation with the horrible maxims of this impiety; when wearied out with incessant martyrdoms, and the cries of a people hungering and thirsting for religion, they permit it, only as a tolerated evil—I call this *atheism by establishment*. See *Burke Selected Works*, Vol. II, ed. by E. J. Payne, pp. 70–72.

[55]Op. cit., p. 163.

indispensable need of mankind, and society will always contrive to institutionalize it. The Church may be crushed beneath the grinding wheels of revolution, but there need be no fear that religion is likewise mangled in the process.

The dominant political class will also be disposed to take advantage of another basic confusion, that between the State and society. Society in this sense will seldom be defined, but as an amorphous concept it will be made to include especially many deep-seated loyalties of the group. Love of one's country, devotion to one's family as one has come to know it in its social setting, and a passion for "all the things one has learned to love and enjoy"—these are some of the values which may appeal for protection when "society" is threatened by an overthrow of the government. However, it need hardly be said that one may love his country and hate his government with equal intensity at the same time.

The political class in power, which is apprehensive of attack, will countenance only one political party and one political faction. Political classes that are firmly entrenched may encourage a system of parties and party factions, for the latter never bring the economic order seriously into question. Neither the Democrats in the Southern United States nor the Fascists in Spain, for example, could harbor two strong political parties; the same, of course, is true for Russia—Russia is still open to political-class conflict, especially that initiated from without. And their methods must necessarily be ruthless. The vanquished must be broken in spirit as well.

11. *Facets of the Modern Political-Class Struggle*

*I*N THE PRECEDING CHAPTER WE ATTEMPTED TO CHARACTERIZE political classes; there, however, we have made only sporadic reference to specific political-class situations. In this chapter our concern shall be to identify the modern political-class struggle in Western society, and in so doing we shall hope to be as simple as possible— perhaps too simple. At any rate, the majority of discussions on this subject are so involved that they tend to inhibit the ordinary reader.

Although the modern class struggle presents a problem of preeminent social significance, social scientists have given it very little attention—and evidently for good reason. John Strachey gives emphasis to the importance of the problem in saying:

The death of capitalism and the substitution of another economic system in its place will leave not a single side of life unaltered. Religion, literature, art, science, the whole of the human heritage of knowledge will be transformed. For no aspect of human life can remain unaffected by a change in the way in which human life itself is maintained.[1]

But the fact that most orthodox social scientists have avoided this subject is itself a social trait of political-class behavior. The mere recognition of the existence of political-class conflict tends to arouse the displeasure of the ruling class. "The position of the scientist in both endowed and state tax-supported institutions depends not only in the long but also in the short run on the existing social order. His membership-character is in the bourgeois region, and consequently he usually does not even so much as mention the class struggle."[2] Some writers who see the problem more or less clearly prefer to take the road of Erasmus, of whom it has been said: "". . . for no idea in the world, for

---

[1]Op. cit., p. 155.
[2]J. F. Brown, *Psychology and the Social Order*, p. 169.

no conviction, could he be induced to place his head upon the block, and suffer for what he at heart knew to be true and right."

It has been as serious as this, then, that the scholar's bread and butter ordinarily depends upon his avoiding the study of contemporary class conflict. To be sure, if he happens to be convinced that the status quo is right, he could speak freely.[3] At any rate, the social scientist is being constantly criticized for closing his eyes to the tremendous human drama unfolding before him. For instance, Robert S. Lynd says: "It is no accident that . . . a world of scientists who comb their fields for important problems for research have left the problem of the power organization and politics of big business so largely unexplored."[4] Even Hitler, that past master in the art of manipulating ideas for a purpose, warns the scholar:

One should guard . . . against refuting things which actually exist. The fact that the class question is not at all one of spiritual problems as one would like to make us believe, especially before elections, cannot be denied. The class pride of a great part of our people, just like the low esteem of the hand laborer, is, above all, a symptom which does not come from the imagination of one who is moon-struck.

But apart from this, it shows the inferior thinking ability of our so-called intelligentsia when just in those circles one does not understand that a condition which was not able to prevent the rise of . . . Marxism will far less be able to regain that which is lost.

The bourgeois parties . . . will never be able to draw the proletarian masses to their camp, as here two worlds face each other . . . and their attitude towards each other can only be a fighting one.[5]

---

[3]Cf. *In Fact*, October 29, 1945, where the whole issue is given over to a review of "U.S. College Professors in the Service of Fascism."

"It is often profitable," says Professor E. B. Reuter, "in terms of salary and security of tenure and academic honors and advancement, to defend exploitation and human exploiters and to justify class as well as racial discrimination and abuse. And in doing so, one has nothing to lose, except his self-respect and the respect of decent men." "Southern Scholars and Race Relations," *Phylon*, Vol. VII, third quarter, 1946, p. 234. And yet this is not quite so, for the scholar who challenges the exploitative system may lose not only his position but also "the respect of decent men."

[4]In Robert A. Brady, *Business as a System of Power*, p. xvi. For a discussion of the ways of the ruling class in America with social scientists who go against the grain of the status quo see Ferdinand Lundberg, *America's 60 Families*, pp. 388ff. Says Lundberg: "While the University presidents may meddle in public affairs to their trustees' content, and while the professors may also do likewise provided only that they support the *status quo*, especially in its more evil phases, it goes hard . . . with any faculty member who espouses an unorthodox point of view. . . . The instructors in the social sciences are taught circumspection by the mishaps of out-spoken colleagues. Those who remain often become, to all intents and purposes, social as well as academic eunuchs." Pp. 393–94.

[5]*Op. cit.*, p. 225. Pope Pius XI, in his plan for reconstruction of the social order, wrote in 1931: "Society today still remains in a strained and therefore unstable and uncertain state, being founded on classes with contradictory interests and hence

Probably not one in a hundred American college graduates majoring in the social sciences is equipped to understand the foregoing passage, far less to argue about it. To the ruling class such conditioning of the young is desirable; yet the powerful forces of social change move on.[6] And, as Werner Sombart well says: "We [need], above all, to see that the [social] movement springs not out of the whim, the choice, the malevolence of individuals; that it is not made, but becomes."[7] Our approach to this problem, then, is from the view that it is real and worthy of the best efforts of students of social problems. Moreover, the social determinism which seems to inhere in the social processes under consideration renders it fascinating. Thus Sombart declares impressively:

It seems to me that the first impression to be made upon anyone by quiet observation of the social movement must be that it is necessary and unavoidable. As a mountain torrent, after a thunder storm, must dash down into the valley according to "iron unchangeable law," so must the stream of social agitation pour itself onward. This is the first thing for us to understand, that something of great and historic importance is developing before our eyes. . . . Probably there are some who believe that the social movement is merely the malicious work of a few agitators . . . probably there are some who naturally are forced to the false idea that some medicine or charm can drive away this fatal poison out of the social body. What a delusion! What lack of intelligence and insight as to the nature of all social history![8]

---

opposed to each other, and consequently prone to enmity and strife. . . . The demand and supply of labor divides men on the labor market into two classes, as into two camps, and the bargaining between these parties transforms the labor market into an arena where the two armies are engaged in combat. . . . It is patent that in our days not alone is wealth accumulated, but immense power and despotic economic domination are concentrated in the hands of a few, and that those few are frequently found not the owners, but only the trustees and directors, of invested funds, who administer them at their good pleasure. . . . Free competition is dead, economic dictatorship has taken its place . . . the whole economic life has become hard, cruel and restless in a ghastly measure." See "Quadragesimo Anno Encyclical Letter of His Holiness Pius XI," quoted in Walter C. Langsam, *Documents and Readings in the History of Europe since 1918,* pp. 567–72.

[6]Even when young Americans are called upon to give their lives for a cause which fundamentally involves the class struggle, they must ordinarily do so without understanding its nature. Roy R. Grinker and John P. Spiegel, psychiatrists of considerable experience with the Army Air Forces, observe: "The average soldier is not well informed as to the final causes for the War or its ultimate necessity. . . . When the combat soldier overseas is asked what he is fighting for, the usual answer is short and pointed: 'So I can go home!' " *Men under Stress,* p. 181.

[7]Op. cit., p. 5.

[8]Ibid., pp. 169–70.

The Ruling Class

There are few social concepts more elusive than that of a ruling political class; and in capitalist society this is particularly so. The concept is likely to be identified with the idea of military power, with that of political office, or with that of mere wealth. Alexis de Tocqueville, in a sort of doctrinal echo of Aristotle, even thinks that in a "democracy" the government is controlled by the poor.[9] In locating the ruling class, however, it is necessary to rely upon two criteria: material interest and conscious political sympathy. The material interest of the individual in the system of production gives him his potential class affiliation, and his conscious sympathies born of class antagonism complete him as an active affiliate. In a capitalist society, the economic system, as is well known, is run by businessmen principally for their benefit; free workers are exploited for profit.

Roughly, then, businessmen constitute our ruling class.[10] Yet, obvious as it might seem, it is not ordinarily recognized that this ruling class has only recently achieved its power through bitter and bloody struggle with another ruling class. The present ruling class, which is so eager to identify its pattern of society with God, was at one time held in little respect by the landed ruling class. Members of our current ruling class were called "common," "ignoble," "ungentle," "bourgeois." Indeed, its members themselves had a low estimate of their position. The richest of them frequently married into the nobility and tried to forget their past in the city, and at one time the priests, at a price, listened to their dying confessions of mortal sin for their taking interest and making profits after the fashion of good businessmen. "No one would have dreamed in the Middle Ages that the despised creed of the trader and the money lender—a creed of selfishness and worship of the then lowest

---

[9]Thus he writes: "Whenever universal suffrage has been established, the majority of the community unquestionably exercises the legislative authority; and if it be proved that the poor always constitute a majority, it may be added with perfect truth, that in the countries in which they possess the elective franchise, they possess the sole power of making laws. But it is certain that in all the nations of the world the greater number has always consisted of those persons who hold no property, or of those whose property is insufficient to exempt them from the necessity of working. . . . Universal suffrage does therefore in point of fact invest the poor with the government of society." *Democracy in America,* 3d ed., Vol. II, p. 23. It is the same kind of conclusion which Aristotle draws for another democratic situation: ". . . in a democracy the poor ought to have more power than the rich, as being the greater number." *Politics,* trans. by William Ellis, p. 185.

[10]For a most convincing study of the determining role of big businessmen in the government and political life of the United States, see Ferdinand Lundberg, op. cit.

material values—should rise to be a compendium of everything most respectable in temporal affairs."[11]

However, economic power gradually shifted into the hands of the businessmen.[12] And as the dominant ways of trade and production continued to change, these capitalists began to recognize that they were being exploited or, more particularly, inhibited by the social system of the landlord ruling class. The laws were against them; the Church was against them; they had inferior social prestige; and yet they were becoming richer and more influential. To be sure, they realized the futility of merely asking the landed ruling class to reorganize the society so that businessmen in the city, who had come to control economic production, could take the helm and run the system in their own interest. Consequently, as a way out and sometimes unconsciously, they encouraged the development of a number of philosophers, writers, journalists, and propagandists, who undermined the morale of the people who supported the ruling class; and finally, in open battle, they chopped the leaders of the feudal order to pieces.

Then the business people, the bourgeoisie, freely fashioned laws and otherwise adjusted the society to suit their convenience. It would be a very great mistake to think that these revolutions, of which the French Revolution is the classic, were fought in the interest of the working people, either skilled or unskilled. As John Strachey puts it: "The liberty which had been established in eighteenth-century England was a liberty for the big merchants, the great land owners, and the trading aristocrats. They and they alone possessed the freedom of the market."[13]

---

[11]Thurman W. Arnold, *The Folklore of Capitalism,* p. 38.

[12]Speaking of the growth of classes in urban centers of the fifteenth century, Prosper Boissonnade concludes: "At the top appeared a growing minority of bourgeois capitalists; in the middle developed the small or medium bourgeoisie of masters, who formed the free crafts and corporations; below were the workmen, who were slowly becoming separated from the class of small masters; and at the bottom of all came the hired wage-earners of the great industry, reinforced by casual elements, who formed the new urban proletariat." Op. cit., p. 299.

[13]Op. cit., p. 26. Strachey continues: "The members of the middle class, having destroyed the feudal monopolists, became themselves the exclusive owners of the means of production: they became, in fact, the capitalist class as we know it today." Ibid., p. 49.

Sombart dilates upon this point: "Those historic occurrences in which the proletariat played a role, although they were not proletarian movements, are the well-known revolutions which we connect with the years 1789, 1793, 1839, 1832, 1842. . . . We have here movements which are essentially middle-class. In them political liberties are sought, and, so far as the proletarian elements are concerned, the masses fight the battles of the middle classes, like the common soldiers who fought in feudal armies. . . . The revolution of 1789 was purely a middle-class movement, and indeed carried on by the higher part of the middle class. It was a struggle of the upper middle class for the recognition of its rights, and for relief from the privileges of the ruling class of society—from the fetters in which it had

An illusion concerning the rule of this capitalist class lies in the fact that its laws are literally objective; power has been apparently given to things instead of to men. "The sacredness of private property" is the key concept. The bourgeois state is "first and foremost the protector of private property"; therefore, the owners of property, "accumulated on their own initiative," have power to set the machinery of the State in motion. The working class does not govern; it merely supports a form of government that has been already established in the interest of a ruling political class. The ultimate power in this system is in the hands of the great capitalist financiers.[14]

Capitalist Production and the Proletariat

Capitalism is a social system based upon free enterprise and upon production, by means of large quantities of capital goods, for private profit. The State is set up to administer and to defend this system.[15] The capitalist State is not a spiritual product; its function, from its inception in the medieval town, has always been primarily to secure the interest of a certain class. The intimate relationship of this interest and the State is not readily apparent, for the laws, the customs, the way of life of the society will ordinarily be thought of in its totality as a product of all members of society. Indeed, the individual is so much a part of

been held by feudal powers. It expressed this struggle in demands for equality and freedom, but it really meant from the very start a limited equality and freedom." Op. cit., pp. 38–39.

Henri Pirenne is also explicit on this point. "Everywhere," he writes, "it was the merchants who took the initiative and directed events. . . . They were the most active, the richest, the most influential element in the city population and they endured with so much the more impatience a situation which clashed with their interest and belittled their confidence in themselves. The role they then played . . . may fittingly be compared with that which the capitalistic middle class assumed after the end of the eighteenth century in the political revolution which put an end to the old order of things. In the one case as in the other, the social group which was the most directly interested in the change assumed the leadership of the opposition, and was followed by the masses. Democracy in the middle ages, as in modern times, got its start under the guidance of a select few who foisted their program upon the confused aspirations of the people." *Medieval Cities,* trans. by Frank D. Halsey, p. 178.

[14]For a good discussion of this, see Robert A. Brady, op. cit. We should guard against the illusion in which advocates of the status quo frequently become involved. In illustration William Graham Sumner declares: "Modern society is ruled by the middle class. In honor of the bourgeoisie it must be said that they . . . have not . . . made a state for themselves alone or chiefly, and their state is the only one in which no class has had to fear oppressive use of political power." *Folkways,* p. 169. Clearly, Sumner confuses the medieval idea of the bourgeoisie as a middle class in feudal society with the concept of the bourgeoisie as a ruling class in bourgeois society. Furthermore, the illusion of the social effects of overwhelming power has evidently blinded him to the means by which the bourgeoisie rule.

[15]Of course, the greater the advancement of democracy, the less will the system operate exclusively in the interest of the ruling capitalist class.

his society that he is seldom able to conceive of any other system in terms other than variants of his own. At any rate, capitalism is supported not only by the owners of capital goods, who produce for a profit, but also by a distinct class of free workers.

Before capitalism can take root workers must be proletarianized. The proletarianization of workers may be thought of as the "commoditization" of their capacity to labor; that is to say, the transformation of the major human element in production into a mass of persons mainly dependent for their means of subsistence upon the vicissitudes of a labor market. In this way labor is freed—indeed, as mercilessly freed as an inanimate commodity.

This working class should not be thought of simply as poor people or as miserable people; they are a class of people peculiar to a capitalist system of production. Their plane of living is, on the whole, very much higher than that of the hand workers under feudalism. To repeat, we must look for this class of workers only in a capitalist society. The proletariat does not exist in feudal societies; it is unknown in the caste system. The labor-market system, Charles Gide observes, "only becomes general with the modern capitalistic organization of industry, and may possibly disappear along with it."[16] The proletariat, to mention again the well-known fact, is a class of freed workers, freed from the land and freed from the ownership of the means of production. It sells its services in a "free" market to entrepreneurs, and its product becomes a commodity. The largest possible human interest which profit makers can have in workers is interest in their efficiency. As Alfred P. Sloan, Jr., Chairman of General Motors, says, "Increased efficiency means lower costs, lower selling prices, and expanded production";[17] and, we may add, especially greater profits.

The capitalist system "has as a necessary presumption the rending of all society into two classes: the owners of the means of production, and the personal factors in production. Thus the existence of capitalism is the necessary preliminary condition of the proletariat."[18] Capital-

---

[16]*Political Economy*, pp. 572–73.

[17]"Post-War Jobs," an address at the opening Fall Session of the Economic Club of Detroit, Oct. 11, 1943.

[18]Werner Sombart, op. cit., p. 9. On this point also Strachey says: "The very idea that it might be impossible to establish industry and commerce, not because of any technical reasons, but because no workers would respond to the offers of wages, does not occur to people. . . . Two essential conditions had to be secured before any such class of people, both able and ready to sell their power to labor, can exist. In the first place, all forms of slavery, serfdom, peonage, and villeinage must be abolished. For if the mass of the population belongs to certain overlords and landlords as their exclusive private property, it is no use for the enterprising entrepreneur to offer them wages in order to induce them to come and work for

ism tends to objectify the productive capacity of both the capitalists and the workers. The human element in production, as we have seen, is divided essentially into two camps: that of "entrepreneurship" and that of labor; and the divergence in interests of these two positions increases as labor refuses to be freely manipulated in the interests of "entrepreneurship."

On the surface it might seem that these two classes in modern society have been selected from a complex system of classes in order to gain a point. Certainly, one is likely to think, there are other possible groupings besides those of workers and capitalists. But here again one must distinguish carefully between functional classes and political classes.[19] There were many functional classes in western Europe in the middle of the eighteenth century, but only two significant political classes: the capitalists and the feudalists. Today the proletariat has become pivotal in the production system, but the latter functions mainly in the interest of the capitalists; and therein lies the source of dissatisfaction. The professional groups in the system do not form a political class; they tend to unite themselves by birth or position to one or another of the two primary political classes. The functional classes constitute a part of the "public" of the two political classes. It is in the latter sense that Professor A. N. Holcombe plans a program for "the middle class" that would serve to throw its weight as a "public" on the side of the ruling class.[20]

---

him. . . . Such condition of legal dependence must therefore be broken down. The establishment of the labor market . . . requires not only that the workers should be free—that they should not be possessed by any overlord or master—but also that they should neither possess nor have free access to the means of production. In other words, when the middle class freed the workers from the landlords they had to, and did, take very good care to free them from the land as well." Op. cit., pp. 40–41. See also Charles Gide, *Principles of Political Economy*, trans. by Edward P. Jacobsen, p. 146.

In discussing the ways of the capitalists as they operate today on the outer rim of Western society, Professor Mary E. Townsend says: "Most of the colonial powers have ruthlessly deprived the native of his land and then, ironically enough, forced him to work upon it by making it impossible for him to live otherwise." *European Colonial Expansion since 1871*, p. 194.

[19] Alfred M. Bingham evinces some misunderstanding of the nature of political classes. He says: "There are in fact many class struggles, for there are many classes. One may define classes arbitrarily as one will. One may classify as to sex, nationality, occupation, intelligence, or attitude. If, as the Marxists do, one chooses to classify as to general economic status in relation to means of production—that is, workers and owners—one must accept the limitations of such a classification. It is rough, vague, and bears no necessary relation to mental attitudes or political effectiveness. There may, under certain conditions, be as bitter conflict between groups of capitalists, over world markets, for instance, or between groups of workers . . . as ever between employers and workers." *Insurgent America*, p. 16. To Bingham, apparently, a political class is one item of a promiscuous social classification.

[20] *The New Party Politics.*

Causes of Proletarian Unrest

A very common approach to the study of modern class conflict is that, based on the assumption that since the masses are economically better off today than they ever were in history, class antagonism is mostly fictional. This approach inevitably leads to an argument centered about what has been called indelicately the "full-belly hypothesis" of socialism, and of course it can seldom attain the view that dissatisfaction with the social system itself may arise. The leaders of the proletariat look ahead to a better form of social organization, while the ruling class and its sympathizers tend to look backward and to compare instances of worse conditions of workers.[21] Professor Maynard Krueger's characterization of the capitalist system tends to put this view of the study of the social movement into perspective:

> The private profit system has not been able to provide either social security of a satisfactory sort or full employment of either men or resources. The private profit system produces the wrong kind of people. It conditions people; it teaches people to be predatory; it puts the emphasis on and it nurses and encourages the worst aspect of what is called "human nature" —the calculating kind of selfishness and acquisitiveness which gets in the way of the kind of life that we ought to be able to lead. It puts entirely too many people in a position where they are kicked around by private economic dictators. . . . It produces a few people with fantastic economic fortunes who exercise terrific political power and power over the agencies of public opinion. With all, it seems to me that it warps and corrupts the minds and souls of people and all their institutions.[22]

The relationship of the misery of a subordinate social class and revolution calls for a few words. We may state broadly that social misery of itself never breeds revolution; in fact, it is not improbable that the greater the misery of a social class the less the likelihood of its revolting. In Brahmanic India, for instance, we should expect that the outcastes will be the last to entertain revolutionary ideas. The serfs and slaves of feudalism never planned a revolution—a movement directed toward the institution of a new social system. "In reality," says Leon Trotsky with respect to proletarian revolutions, "the mere existence of priva-

---

[21] See a recent propagandistic work taking this position: Carl Snyder, *Capitalism the Creator,* p. 11.

[22] *The University of Chicago Round Table,* No. 228, September 26, 1943, p. 15. This does not mean to say, however, that socialism is simply a sentimental or moral movement. "What socialism really means," says John Strachey, "is giving nine-tenths of us a chance to get at least ten times as much individual, private property— ten times as much clothing, houses, gardens, motor-cars, supplies of food, furniture, and the like as we ever get today." *Socialism Looks Forward,* p. 102.

tions is not enough to cause an insurrection; if it were, the masses would be always in revolt. It is necessary that the bankruptcy of the social regime, being conclusively revealed, should make these privations intolerable, and that new conditions and new ideas should open the prospect of a revolutionary way out. Then in the cause of the great aims conceived by them, those same masses will prove capable of enduring doubled and tripled privations."[23] Thus it is only when a class comes to feel that it has power to insist upon superior rights that it thinks of revolt. De Tocqueville puts it interestingly:

As the noble never suspected that anyone would attempt to deprive him of the privilege which he believed to be legitimate, and as the serf looked upon his own inferiority as a consequence of the immutable order of nature, it is easy to imagine that mutual exchange of good will took place between two classes so differently gifted by fate. Inequality and wretchedness were then to be found in society; but the souls of neither rank of men were degraded.

Men are not corrupted by the exercise of power or debased by the habit of obedience; but by the exercise of a power which they believe to be illegal, and by obedience to a rule which they consider to be usurped and oppressive.[24]

The bourgeoisie who instigated and fought the capitalist revolutions were clearly not the most degraded and miserable part of the population; they were simply the most dissatisfied and the most powerful subordinate class. Their wails of misery, oppression, tyranny, and suffering were largely a function of their own inflated conception of themselves. Says Strachey: "The British middle class felt itself equal to the task. It was just because they were growing richer and stronger, and yet were given no increased share of power, that the English middle classes rebelled . . . classes do not rebel only because they are starving . . . yet it is such growing disproportions as these between the real strength of a class and the amount of political power which is allotted to it which cause those redistributions of power between sections of the community."[25]

---

[23]Op. cit., Vol. II, p. xi. It may not be inaccurate to assert that most of the desperate effort of Great Britain and the United States especially to "feed the hungry" in post-World War Europe is prompted not by merciful charity but rather by the frightful consciousness that the people, left to themselves, may rise, overthrow the capitalist ruling class, and establish a welfare economy. It is in this sense that American food has been used as a counterrevolutionary weapon. It is not so much the "feeding of the hungry millions" as it is a strategy of food distribution which serves the political purpose. For an indication of this as practiced after the World War I, see Sayers and Kahn, op. cit., pp. 86–87.

[24]Op. cit., Vol. I, p. xx.

[25]Op. cit., p. 21. To the same effect Hans Kohn observes: "The American colonies revolted not because they were oppressed, but because they were free and their

In some measure it is not the misery of poverty but rather the misery of invidious comparison which renders the workers dissatisfied. Werner Sombart recognizes this clearly:

It is much more characteristic that in the moment when great masses sink into misery, upon the other side shining like a fairy's creation, the millionaire arises. It is the contrast between the comfortable villa and elegant equipage of the rich, the magnificent stores, the luxurious restaurants which the workman passes as he goes on his way to his manufactory or workshop in the dreary part of the city; it is the contrast in conditions which develops hate in the masses. And that, again, is a peculiarity of the modern system, that it develops this hate and permits hate to become envy. It seems to me that this happens for the reason that those who display this grandeur are no longer the churches or the princes; but that they are those very persons on whom the masses feel themselves dependent, in whose direct economic control they see themselves, in whom they recognize their so-called "exploiters." This definite modern contrast is that which principally excites the intensity of this feeling of hate in the masses.[26]

A more tangible source of proletariat discontent, however, is the economic uncertainty of the profit system—its anarchy. Basically, the system has little regard for human beings as such; it is practical and mechanistic. So far as the proletariat is concerned, the system is interested in the productivity of its labor and not in its welfare. In capitalistic production labor is included in the same impersonal accounting as natural resources and capital, a fact which ordinarily brings home to the worker a fearful sense of being cut adrift in a sea of anonymity to eat and especially to be eaten as opportunity arises. Moreover, in the very nature of good business practice the profit maker cannot be satisfied.

Unemployment has become endemic in the capitalist system. Yet it is not so much the fact of unemployment as a recognition that unemployment is a function of the profit motive, which has the potentiality of

---

freedom carried the promise of still greater freedom, one unrealizable in the more settled and static conditions of the old society." *The Idea of Nationalism,* p. 272. But see Frederick L. Nussbaum, op. cit., pp. 248–54, for some "limiting conditions of early capitalism."

[20]Op. cit., pp. 10–11. And that great advocate of democracy, De Tocqueville, admits: "It cannot be denied that democratic institutions have a very strong tendency to promote the feeling of envy in the human heart; not so much because they afford to every one the means of rising to the level of any of his fellow-citizens, as because those means perpetually disappoint the persons who employ them. Democratic institutions awaken and foster a passion for equality which they can never entirely satisfy. This complete equality eludes the grasp of the people at the very moment at which it thinks to hold fast. . . . The lower orders are agitated by the chance of success, they are irritated by its uncertainty; and they pass from the enthusiasm of pursuit to the exhaustion of ill-success, and lastly to the acrimony of disappointment." Op. cit., Vol. II, pp. 4–5.

galling the worker. This is especially true in times of business-cycle troughs. The hard times of old, the famines, were recognized to be acts of God. Beyond a probable magical interpretation no one could be held blamable for them. But the great modern economic debacles, the business depressions, are recognized as inevitable consequences of capitalism. These cannot be prevented while private profit remains the supreme goal of the economic order. Lewis Corey expresses a common attitude on this major failing of capitalism:

These recurrent breakdowns of prosperity are a typical, damnable spectacle of capitalist civilization. Men, women, and children starve or agonizingly approach starvation while wheat and corn rot, vegetables perish, milk and coffee are destroyed. The wheels of industry slow down while millions of workers eager to work are condemned to unemployment. Wants go unsatisfied on an enormous and oppressive scale, although all the means exist to satisfy the wants. . . . This monstrous state of affairs was unknown to the people of pre-capitalist civilizations: they knew want as a result of scarcity, natural calamity, or war, and the torment of labor lay in its severity. Capitalist civilization introduced a new form of want, want in the midst of abundance; a new torment of labor, torment of workers deprived of work while there is an abundance of the means and objectives of working. Our ancestors would have considered the situation idiotic; it is considered idiotic today by the non-capitalist, developing socialist civilization of the Soviet Union.[27]

Thus there is a double cause for irritation among the workers. They suffer privation and degeneracy at a time when the markets are glutted with goods. A depression is the opposite of a famine. During a famine there are practically no goods, but during a depression there is a plethora of goods. It is the abundance of goods which jams the profit system and causes the entrepreneur to shut down his machinery and turn out the workers to starve. "There must be something fundamentally wrong with our economic system," says Lloyd George, "because abundance produces scarcity."[28] Indeed, capitalism has a limited capacity for prosperity. For instance, a foreign country which sends a capitalist country very much cheap or even free goods merely "dumps" them upon the latter with probable disastrous results.

The system, of course, having been organized in the interest of profit makers, cannot be particularly concerned with the workers' plight. The workers must wait until the large stocks of goods work themselves down either by gradual consumption, decay, and waste, or by their purpose-

---

[27]Op. cit., pp. 12–13.
[28]Report of speech at Cambridge in *Manchester Guardian Weekly,* April 7, 1933; quoted by R. P. Dutt, op. cit., p. 34.

ful destruction. Then and only then can the owners of the means of production again give the word to rehire labor and start producing. Thus the process of building up stocks to another glut is on its way. Under capitalism, the more economic goods we have, the greater the likelihood of a famine among the masses.

But discontent with the periodic crises of the profit system becomes increasingly aggravated as it becomes more and more obvious that capitalism offers only war as a solution. During the last century depressions frequently corrected themselves; since about 1914, however, capitalism has lost its power to shake off the malady; "it only passes from one state of crisis to another." As Fenner Brockway puts it typically, "Capitalism offers us two futures, both disastrous to the human race—either war or economic collapse. It holds out no other hope."[29] Therefore, the conviction is not only that the system has reached its stage of continuing morbidity, but also that it is a vicious diseconomy for modern society to entrust its machinery and technology to capitalism. At the heart of the system a comparatively few rich businessmen in fierce financial maneuvering among themselves run the society and the lives of the people, utilizing with equal abandon both natural and human resources, according to the dictates of their own private interest and profit.

One point of confusion to the worker is the inevitable definition which capitalism gives to his services—that of a commodity. "When once a labor market has been established, the ability of men to work is also turned into a commodity. For it is the distinguishing characteristic of a labor market that in it people's power to work is bought and sold by the hour, day, or week."[30] Paul M. Sweezy points out the likelihood of workers' misunderstanding freedom of the market for personal freedom: "The world of commodities appears as a world of equals.

---

[29] *Workers' Front,* p. 11. And in an explanation of data on social trends, Sir William H. Beveridge says: "The figures cited are only a statistical presentation of what has now become a commonplace: that the only sovereign remedy yet discovered by the democracies for unemployment is total war." *Full Employment in a Free Society,* p. 112. One palliative is the making of international loans as a sort of pretext for gifts, which tend to have somewhat of the same effect on the capitalist economy as investment in war materials.

J. A. Hobson puts it thus: "Capitalism no doubt favors expenditure on armaments as a profitable business proposition. But it needs armaments because it needs war. War is a profitable business policy. Its distructiveness is the other way out of the plethora of peaceful productivity. If foreign markets do not expand fast enough to take off the surplus of capitalist production, an era of destructive waste is the only acceptable alternative. . . . In other words, a periodic blood-letting seems required as a treatment for an economic plethora." *Democracy and a Changing Civilization,* p. 54.

[30] John Strachey, op. cit., p. 39.

The labor power of the worker is alienated from the worker and stands opposed to him as any commodity to its owner."[31]

But the shortcomings of capitalism are only one aspect of the development of proletariat discontent. The other two are the proletariat's acquisition of increasing power and its increasing recognition that an economic order which admits of planning in the interest of the people is an immediate possibility. Capitalism abhors planning; to attempt to introduce it is to precipitate conflict.

Never before in history has a cultural situation developed wherein the burden of producing a social revolution devolves upon the base of the population. In overthrowing feudalism, for instance, the bourgeoisie, a rival ruling class, fought for themselves in the name of the masses, but until capitalism created the opportunity the masses had never fought for themselves in their own interest.[32]

The current class struggle is an inherent attribute of capitalism;[33] and this makes it characteristically different from all previous class conflicts. In Brahmanic India the priests wrested power from the military class, but there is no necessary conflict between priests and warriors in society. Whenever a bourgeois people gain a foothold in a feudalistic or prefeudalistic society, there will be class conflict; yet feudalism of itself does not produce a bourgeois class. On the other hand, the proletariat is not only a potential or active political class; it is also an inevitable product of capitalism. Indeed, the capitalists and the proletariat are twin-born of the same economic matrix, capitalism; therefore, the challenging proletariat is not the offspring of a distinct change in the mode of production as was the case with the rise of the European "middle class."

To put it in other words, feudal systems do not evolve "naturally"

---

[31]Op. cit., p. 39. For a broad discussion of similar sources of discontent, see Erich Fromm, *Escape from Freedom*, pp. 123–35.

[32]See P. Boissonnade, op. cit., pp. 299–315, for a review of early proletarian unrest. A slave uprising, of course, should not be thought of as a revolutionary struggle.

[33]On this point what N. S. B. Gras has to say seems to be pertinent: "So long as the handicraftsman was free to sell to any merchant, and so long as he was the owner of his raw materials and tools and commanded a profit (rather than a wage) from his enterprise, little could be said against the new system. But when in the early modern period industrial entrepreneurs arose who reduced the handicraftman to economic dependence, the new system stood condemned first by the sufferers and later by the general public. For industry, the change from retail to wholesale handicraft meant specialization in function, the separation of industrial from commercial capital, a larger supply of goods, and greater skill. It also was the beginning of the subordination of the workers and their exploitation. Revolts and civic turmoil in the larger industrial towns of the Middle Ages were signs of the slowly developing system of wholesale handicraft." "The Economic Activity of Towns," in *The Legacy of the Middle Ages*, p. 438, C. G. Crump and E. F. Jacob, eds.

into capitalism; feudalism contains no necessary internal social antagonisms; it may persist indefinitely without necessarily transforming itself into anything else. But capitalism, especially industrial capitalism, because of its inevitable dialectical development, its internal contradictions, is unstable and will sooner or later resolve itself into a more permanent system. The bourgeois class had a sort of exterior, parasitic growth which finally strangled feudalism, but the proletariat has developed within the very heart of capitalism, which it now threatens, at least in its ideological leadership, to slough off.

Moreover, the greater the advancement of capitalism, the greater the relative potential power of the proletariat. Hence capitalist society nurtures the very political class that is necessarily devoted to the destruction of capitalism. This is the idea of social determinism in modern political-class conflict.

Fascism

There is considerable difference of opinion among even scholars concerning the characteristics of the fascists as the organization of a political class. Sometimes the conflict of views is purposely induced by the ruling class itself. Ordinarily, in the capitalist democracies, the people are made to believe that the fascists are a foreign tribe, while in the fascist countries the people are taught to believe that fascism is developed in the interest of the masses. At any rate, the first error to guard against appears to be that of thinking of fascists and potential fascists as unsocial, degenerate people—gangsters; indeed, the very opposite of this is nearer the truth.

Those persons in a capitalist society who finally organize in an active fascist party are mainly the most respectable and respected people. They are the undeniably 100-per-cent German, or English, or American, or Spanish citizens. The fascist party and its sympathizers would ordinarily include the majority of men who have achieved great business success, of politicians of upper chambers, professional men of the highest order, distinguished scholars, eminent bishops and cardinals, the most powerful newspaper owners and editors, learned judges, the valiant upper crust of the military forces, and so on.[34] And this is quite

---

[34]Robert A. Brady lists the following as the principal groups constituting the European fascists: "The die-hard landed aristocracy; the industrial, commercial, and financial barony; the old privileged and caste-like military hierarchy; the professional and imperial-minded upper reaches of the civil service bureaucracy, and the ruling cliques of the fanatical and cynical party demagoguery which has been ambidextrous enough to conjure—out of the witless frustrations of the still leaderless unemployed and growing ranks of the declassed rural and urban lumpen-

natural since fascism is a rightist, conservative, capitalist reaction. The fascists constitute essentially the cream of a capitalist society. Adolf Hitler,[35] the great leader and spokesman of the fascists in all capitalist countries, expressed their conviction: "A view of life which, by rejecting the democratic mass idea, endeavors to give the world to the best people . . . to the most superior men, has logically to obey the same aristocratic principle also within this people."[36] Therefore, to locate this group that is now attempting to stabilize its inheritance of the earth we must look about the pinnacle of capitalism.

The fascists are the capitalists and their sympathizers who have achieved political-class consciousness; they have become organized for action against the proletariat, and especially for defense against the normal disintegration of the capitalist system. They despise the masses, conceding them neither capacity to think nor to develop their own leadership. Fascism, according to Hitler, "has to start from the principle that for humanity blessing has never lain in the masses, but in its creative heads who therefore . . . have to be looked upon as the benefactors of mankind. . . . Certainly, this interest is not satisfied and is not served by the rule of the masses who are either unable to think or are inefficient, in any case not inspired."[37]

Nothing arouses the antagonism of the organized capitalists so completely as visions of progress in the Russian proletarian society.

> We must never forget [Hitler warns again] that the regents of present-day Russia are common bloodstained criminals; that here is the scum of humanity which, favored by conditions in a tragic hour, overran a great state, butchered and rooted out millions of its leading intellects with savage bloodthirstiness and for nearly ten years has exercised the most frightful regime of tyranny of all time.[38]

---

bourgeoisie—a mass following." See his book review in *Science and Society*, Vol. VII, No. 2, Spring, 1943, p. 175. See also George Seldes, *Facts and Fascism,* New York, 1943.

In the modern class struggle, as we have alluded to in a previous section, the fascists always seek the allegiance of the "middle class." This is the "public" for whose well-being the capitalists always seem to have an inordinate solicitude. In *The New Party Politics,* A. N. Holcombe develops the thesis that the bourgeoisie can stabilize their position by winning and maintaining the good will of these adjuvant functionaries of capitalism. In practice fascism has been able to appeal with considerable success to the "middle class."

[35] For a discussion of the use of demagogues by the ruling class, see Daniel Guerin, op. cit., Chap. VI, "The Rise and Fall of the Fascist Plebeians."

[36] Op. cit., p. 661.

[37] Ibid., p. 665.

[38] Ibid., p. 959. In 1790, during the great bourgeois revolution, Edmund Burke, more responsible but similarly motivated, declared in the British House of Commons: "The French have shown themselves to be the ablest architects of ruin that have hitherto existed in the world. In that very short space of time they have com-

This is the nature of the political-class conflict between the fascists and the proletariat. And the former have shown both at home and abroad that they themselves are no novices at butchery. With respect to the German proletariat, the Leader vowed: "On the day when Marxism is smashed in Germany, its chains will really be broken forever";[39] and then he proceeded to smash it with an iron fist, only, however, to find the pieces still menacingly animated.

Fascism is outspokenly anti-democratic; its reactionary nature makes this inevitable. Although capitalist democracy never meant that the masses should run the government, the idea of political democracy itself increasingly opened the way for some obstruction to the dominant purpose of the capitalists. Business may endure political democracy but not economic democracy. Robert S. Lynd has this to say on the point:

> Liberal democracy has never dared face the fact that industrial capitalism is an intensely coercive form of organization of society that cumulatively constrains men and all of their institutions to work the will of the minority who hold and wield economic power; and that this relentless warping of men's lives and forms of association becomes less and less the result of voluntary decisions by "bad" or "good" men and more and more an impersonal web of coercions dictated by the need to keep "the system" running.[40]

The purpose of capitalist democracy is to provide a favorable situation for the exercise of free enterprise and not for the planning of a society that will make business a social service. If the commonality attempts to take the latter view of democracy and to implement it, the capitalist will quickly scrap the institution. As John Strachey observes:

> The retention of power by the capitalist class by means of the success of a fascist party necessarily implies the scrapping of all democratic institu-

---

pletely pulled down to the ground their monarch, their church, their nobility, their law, their revenue, their army, their navy, their commerce, their arts and their manufactures. . . . Were we absolute conquerors, and France to lie prostrate at our feet, we should be ashamed to send a commission to settle their affairs, which could impose so hard a law upon the French, and so destructive of all their consequences as a nation, as that they had imposed upon themselves. . . .

"Our present danger from the example of a people whose character knows no medium, is, with regard to government, a danger from anarchy; a danger from being led through an admiration of successful fraud and violence, to an imitation of the excesses of an irrational, unprincipled, proscribing, confiscating, plundering, ferocious, bloody, and tyrannical democracy. On the side of religion, the danger of their example is no longer from intolerance, but from atheism; a foul, unnatural vice, foe to all the dignity and consolation of mankind; which seems in France . . . to have been embodied into a faction, accredited and almost avowed." See *The Parliamentary History of England,* 1789–91, Vol. XXVIII, pp. 354–55.

[39]Adolf Hitler, op. cit., p. 987.

[40]In Robert A. Brady, op. cit., p. xii.

tions. It involves revelation, without any attempt at a democratic disguise, of capitalist dictatorship. And a wise capitalist class will certainly not dispense with the serviceable mask of democracy, which has stood it in good stead, until no other course is open to it.[41]

Hitler himself indicates the powerful undercurrent of capitalist government, shorn of its superstructure and fanfare of political democracy:

The movement is anti-parliamentarian; that means . . . it rejects a principle of a decision by the majority, by which the leader is degraded to the position of the executive of the will and opinion of others.[42]

It should be emphasized that the distinguishing fact about fascist governments is not that they are dictatorships. There is a popular belief, sometimes purposely indoctrinated, that all dictatorships subsume an identity of economic organization.[43] Nothing, however, is farther from the truth. When a people is at war, a degree of dictatorship becomes imperative, and the greater the intensity of the conflict, the more complete the dictatorship is likely to become. "Fighting groups cannot be tolerant, nor can they harbor cynics."[44] Hence the presence of a dictatorship does not necessarily indicate the form of social organization. The proletarian government of Russia, for instance, is a dictatorship; all fascist governments are also dictatorships, but these two types of economic organization lie at opposite extremes of modern social systems.

Furthermore, they differ even in the durability of their dictatorships. The proletarian dictatorship has no basis for continuance after capitalist aggression, especially from without, has ceased; but since the fascist

---

[41]Op. cit., p. 262. To the same effect Robert S. Lynd states further: "Organized business enterprise is less and less willing to tolerate checks on its activities by the state; more and more it needs the state as an active ally; and the national state, in turn, having delivered itself over by accepting the definition of its welfare as synonymous with the welfare of its business system, needs increasingly the utmost of agressive efficiency from its businessmen. Business is in politics and the state is in business." Op. cit., p. x.

[42]Op. cit., p. 478.

[43]This kind of thinking recurs in similar social situations. On February 9, 1790, Charles J. Fox, in an attempt to clear himself from a charge by Edmund Burke of sympathy with the French Revolution, declared before the British House of Commons that what he had said should not be taken to mean that he was a friend of democracy. "He declared himself equally the enemy of all absolute forms of government, whether an absolute monarchy, an absolute aristocracy, or an absolute democracy." See *The Parliamentary History of England,* 1789–91, Vol. XXVIII, p. 363.

By attempting a timeless, universalistic analysis of dictatorship, J. A. Hobson falls into this error. See his *Democracy and a Changing Civilization.*

[44]George E. Vincent, "The Rivalry of Social Groups," *American Journal of Sociology,* XVI, 1910–11, pp. 471ff.

dictatorship can never expect a cessation of either internal or external aggression, it must endure. The social condition which produced fascism is not removed by fascism itself. Fascism is born of and perpetuated by irreducible conflict; hence its dictatorship must be permanent. It is an attempt to halt and to turn back a democratic trend. Dwight Macdonald makes the observation that, "since fascism merely suppresses without solving the contradictions of capitalism, the class struggle goes on as violently as ever underneath the frozen surface."[45] With respect to internal conflict it should be made crystal-clear that the capitalists cannot conceivably eliminate the proletariat as a class; it could at most only temporarily destroy or drive its leadership underground. On the other hand, the proletariat can eliminate the capitalists completely; it must do this if socialism is to be achieved. In a word, there can be no pure bourgeois society because the antagonistic proletariat can never be fully purged. Normally, therefore, communism is a peaceful form of social organization, but normally fascism is a reactionary form of conflict organization which may temporarily quiet though never eliminate its antagonists.

The Ways of Fascism

The fascists, as we have observed, are the organization of a political class in action; hence they are geared for violent struggle. To be sure, they cannot themselves fight their counterrevolution; they must have even the masses, their potential antagonists, to support them. Says Strachey:

The fascist method implies essentially the attempt to create a popular mass movement for the protection of monopoly capitalism. Its adoption means that the directing capitalist groups consider that the regular state forces at their disposal are inadequate or unsuitable for repressing the workers. Thus, an attempt is made to create, by the employment of skilled demagogues, the expenditure of large sums of money, and the reckless dissemination of propaganda designed to play on every prejudice, a mass party composed of a petty bourgeois nucleus, combined with such backward workers and peasants as can be successfully deceived. The party is then used for the destruction by terror of working-class organizations of struggle, the workers' defense organizations, clubs, trade unions, newspapers and party "machines."[46]

---

[45]In Daniel Guerin, op. cit., pp. xii–xiii.
[46]Op. cit., p. 262. Hitler shows that he clearly understands the procedure. "The great masses of a nation," he writes, "will always and only succumb to the force of the spoken word. But all great movements of the people are volcanic eruptions of human passions and spiritual sensations, stirred either by the cruel Goddess of Misery or by the torch of the word thrown into the masses, and not by the lemonade-

It is this high-powered appeal to the masses, then, which brings about confusion in some and conviction in others. Indeed the people may be consciously prepared for the fascist counterrevolution. Thus Lynd points out: "Organized business is extending this anti-democratic web of power in the name of the people's own values, with billboards proclaiming 'What's Good for Industry Is Good for Your Family,' and deftly selling itself to a harassed people as 'trustees,' 'guardians,' 'the people's managers' of public interest."[47]

In any fascist movement emphasis upon race superiority and racial antagonism or intolerance helps to confuse the masses and to develop a degree of racial egocentrism. As an example of this technique, consider Hitler's artistry in the following: "In Russian bolshevism we must see Jewry's twentieth-century effort to take world domination to itself."[48]

Fascism and the established religion, or rather the modern Church, are on the whole closely associated, and naturally so. The Church as a whole, as we have seen, is always reactionary; it upholds and stabilizes the social norms and values of the status quo, hence its natural sympathy must be with the counterrevolutionary class.[49] In their revolutions the capitalists had to reckon with the Church, and today, in like manner, the Church confronts the proletariat. Concerning the capitalist struggle with the Church, De Tocqueville declares: "By a singular concourse of events, religion is entangled in those institutions which democracy assails and it is not infrequently brought to reject the equality it loves, and to curse the cause of liberty as a foe. . . . The religionists are the enemies of liberty and the friends of liberty attack religion."[50] Thomas Jefferson himself took notice of the fact that the

---

like outpourings of aestheticizing *literate* and drawing-room heroes. Only a storm of burning passion can turn the people's destinies, but only he who harbors passion in himself can arouse passion. Passion alone will give to him . . . the words that, like beats of a hammer, are able to open the doors to the heart of a people." Op. cit., pp. 136–37.

[47]Op. cit., pp. xiii–xiv.

[48]Op. cit., p. 960. See also Robert A. Brady, *The Spirit and Structure of German Fascism*, pp. 53–63.

[49]E. T. Krueger and W. C. Reckless make a similar observation: "The church . . . regards itself as the protector and conservator of the social sentiments. It affirms the 'inherent' rightness of the mores, and through its pronouncements and teachings it formulates a moral philosophy and fixes the body of sentiments into an inviolable code of conduct." *Social Psychology*, p. 273.

Friedrich Engels had already observed: ". . . the people must be kept in order by moral means and the first and foremost of all moral means of action upon the masses is and remains—religion." *Socialism Utopian and Scientific*, Fortieth Anniversary Ed., p. 27.

[50]*Democracy in America*, Vol. I, pp. xxv–xxvi. With respect to the integration of the Church and politics in the United States, this writer states further: "Religion

priest has always been "in alliance with the despot, abetting his abuses in return for protection of his own."[51]

Indeed the function of the Church as a prime deflator of social movements has been repeatedly recognized. After the Napoleonic revolutions in Europe the reactionary nobility entrenched themselves with the support of a reinvigorated Catholic Church. Professor Geoffrey Bruun, in describing the backwash of a later upsurge of liberalism and democracy, asserts: "The propertied classes had . . . been so gravely alarmed by the socialist and communist menace in 1848 and 1849 that they cast about for measures to combat it, and in several states (France, Austria, Prussia) the government and the middle class repented the curbs which they had imposed upon the Roman Catholic Church and welcomed it again as a useful ally in combating socialist heresies."[52] It should also be recalled that the "infallible" leadership of the Catholic Church has consistently defined practically every revolutionary development in science or social ideology as a direct attack upon its vested interests. The involvement of the fifteenth-century astronomers with the selfish policies of the Church was no less serious than that of the nineteenth-century biologists and paleontologists.

However, the Church has now been accommodated to capitalism; hence it is, as we should expect, up in arms on its own initiative against any threat to the status quo. In an editorial in the English *Catholic Times,* the duty of the Catholic Church is thus clarified: "Our mission of salvation to Europe is to establish a united anti-communist Front. We must restore friendly relations with Italy and Germany, even at a great sacrifice, and then induce France, which will not be difficult, to fall into line with us on grounds of political safety."[53]

---

in America takes no direct part in the government . . . but it must nevertheless be regarded as the foremost of the political institutions of that country; for if it does not impart a taste for freedom, it facilitates the use of free institutions." Op. cit., Vol. II, p. 146. Putting it another way, Robert Briffault concludes: "Religion as a whole is but a form of loyalty to the interests of English property." *The Decline and Fall of the British Empire,* p. 116. See also on this point Henri Pirenne, *Medieval Cities,* pp. 128ff. and pp. 179–80. Moreover, it was quite obvious to the philosophers of the French Revolution that organized religion stabilized the worst traits of the *ancien régime;* the system was shaken to its foundations when the National Assembly liquidated the great feudal estates of the Church.

[51]Quoted by Samuel Bernstein, op. cit., p. 118. The same conclusion is reached by a modern observer. Says Nikolai Bukharin: "The Church, in addition to serving as a pacifier of the masses, restraining them from violations of the established order of things, itself was and still is a portion of the exploiting machinery, constructed according to the same general plan as the larger exploiting society." Op. cit., p. 177.

[52]Wallace K. Ferguson and Geoffrey Bruun, *A Survey of European Civilization,* p. 870.

[53]Quoted by F. A. Ridley, *The Papacy and Fascism,* p. 208. Some of the most militant fascist movements in the United States—to say nothing of Europe—such

Probably no sect of the Christian religion is so thoroughly opposed to the proletarian movement as the Roman Catholics. The established authority of tradition in the Catholic Church makes it fundamentally antipathetic to social change. "The papal court," says Briffault, "viewed England in Elizabethan days in much the same manner as it views Bolshevik Russia today."[54] The Roman Catholic Church has never wholly given up its medievalism; and proletarianism is even farther removed from its hierarchical formalism than capitalism. Moreover, it has been well recognized that "the Roman Catholic Church is the richest single land and property-owning 'corporation' in Europe. Its policies were and are always in defense of its metaphysical and physical property."[55]

Recently the Pope reached a rather complete accord with the aims and methods of fascism. The papacy evidently lent financial support to the fascist venture in Abyssinia, and "in the Spanish Civil War it allied itself openly with Il Duce." Says Robert A. Brady in his revealing study of the development of solidarity between the Roman Catholic Church and fascism: "In the Lateran Accord of 1929 Fascism adopted the papacy on condition that the papacy concede popular allegiance to the objectives of Fascism and the State and Empire in which those objectives were embodied."[56]

In America the Catholic Church is steeped in the class conflict. One of its leading organs, *Our Sunday Visitor,* is a potent source of fascist propaganda. The way in which the issue is being joined may be illustrated by the following commentary from an anti-fascist weekly newsletter. The latter comments upon the propagandistic technique adopted

---

as the Youth for Christ and the Christian Youth of America are disguised as religious organizations.

[54]*Op. cit.,* p. 147. Pope Pius XI sets up clearly the opposition of the Catholic Church to the social movement. Thus he declares: " 'Religious Socialism' or 'Christian Socialism' are expressions implying a contradiction in terms. No one can be at the same time a sincere Catholic and a true socialist." See Walter C. Langsam, op. cit., p. 572. For a discussion of the place of the Catholic Church in the modern class struggle, see George Seldes, *The Catholic Crisis,* especially Chap. X, "The Vatican and the World." See also William Howard Melish, "Religious Developments in the Soviet Union," *American Sociological Review,* June, 1944, pp. 279–86; "The Western Catholiç Bloc," *The Nation,* Vol. 162, June 29, 1946, pp. 775–77; J. Milton Yinger, *Religion in the Struggle for Power,* pp. 142–52.

[55]See Robert Bek-Gran, "5 Keys to Europe," *Politics,* November 1944, p. 317. The medieval Church, of course, was a very much more formidable political institution; it owned probably more than one third of all the land in western Europe.

[56]*Business as a System of Power,* p. 64. See also, for a discussion of democracy and the masses, Pope Pius XII, "The Dignity of Liberty of Man," Christmas address, Vatican City, December 24, 1944, reported in *Vital Speeches,* Vol. II, January 1, 1945. According to Pope Pius, "Democracy . . . can be realized in monarchies as well as in republics. . . . The masses are the capital enemy of true democracy and of its ideal of liberty and equality."

by *Our Sunday Visitor* (April 26–28) in offering a prize for the best answer to this multiple-choice question:

QUESTION: Why should all Christians favor the Nationalist [*Franco-fascist*] cause in Spain?

1. Because the so-called Loyalists persecute all religion. [*This is 100 per cent false.*]

2. Because the Loyalists killed more than 14,000 priests and religious. [*This is totally false; the Loyalists did not kill anyone not armed and fighting them.*]

3. Because Franco is fighting against communism to preserve democracy. [*This is false because Franco has publicly denounced democracy and adopted fascism.*]

4. Because all non-Christians favor the Loyalists. [*This is false because among those favoring the Loyalists 99 per cent were Christians.*]

5. Because to favor the Loyalists is to fail to distinguish between good and evil. [*The Loyalists were anti-fascist.*]

6. Because the Nationalists permit full religious freedom. [*This was false when it was written, and is still false to an extent.*]

7. Because Franco favors fascism, which is an ally of Christianity. [*The first part of this statement is the only true statement in this section.*]

8. Because, if the Loyalists win, communism will soon rule Western Civilization. [*It is now generally admitted that a Loyalist victory would have stopped the fascist axis from starting the present war.*][57]

But, as we have attempted to show in the preceding chapter, this is to be expected. It may be pointed out again that religion in a capitalist society must be revolutionized if the economic order is to be revolutionized. The religion of capitalism is not the religion of feudalism. Capitalism could not reach maturity before medieval Catholicism had been revamped and brought into working consistency with the ends of capitalism; therefore, modern institutionalized religion is to a very large extent bourgeois-made. Indeed, Max Weber even thinks that the Protestant religion embodies the vital spirit of capitalism, the essence which made capitalism possible, so that the distinguishing social fact of bourgeois society is its characteristic religious ethics. A radical capitalist revolution, then, must inevitably involve a radical reformation of its religious basis. Proletarian society can be built only upon a funda-

---

[57]*In Fact,* May 8, 1944. The comments in brackets are by *In Fact.*

mentally different system of ethics—that is to say, proletarian ethics. Thus, as anti-proletarian reaction sets in, we should expect the ruling class in both England and the United States especially to develop an increasingly intimate diplomatic and propagandistic affiliation with the Vatican, the time-honored hotbed of world-wide reaction.[58]

Another significant feature of fascism is nationalism. Nationalism is essential to fascism because mature capitalism is not only concerned with internal political-class struggle but also with international struggle for world markets. Again Brady is in point; says he:

> If we can draw any certain lesson from events in the recent past it is surely this, that organized business in one national system will show no mercy to organized business in another national system, once conflicts of interest have forced matters to the arbitrament of war.[59]

Extreme nationalism makes it possible for the capitalist state to muster its full strength in international conflict. Hitler expresses the temper of fascist nationalism in the following declaration: "Not with the call, 'Long live universal suffrage and the secret ballot,' had the young regiments once marched towards death in Flanders, but with the cry, '*Deutschland über alles in der Welt.*' "[60] But nationalism breeds counternationalism; hence fascism merely clears the way for unending struggle "between mighty antagonists each of whom can enlist the power of whole states." Sweezy puts it thus: "Capitalism, by its very nature, cannot settle down but must keep expanding, and since the various sectors of the world capitalist economy expand at different rates, it follows that the balance of forces is bound to upset in such a way that one or more countries will find it both possible and advantageous to challenge the *status quo* with respect to territorial boundaries."[61]

No one can give a meaningful interpretation to certain paradoxes in World War II without understanding the internal and external conflict necessity of capitalism. In so far as the aim of the fascists is the destruction of the proletarian movement, they are the allies of the ruling class in all the capitalist countries; but in so far as their aim is

---

[58]On June 6, 1946, a number of Protestant church leaders urged President Truman to sever "all diplomatic relations with the Vatican." These leaders expressed solicitude for the increasing political involvement between the government of the United States and the reactionary politics of the Vatican, and through their representative, Dr. Samuel Cavert, general secretary of the Federal Council of Churches of Christ in America, asked that Myron C. Taylor be recalled from the Vatican.

[59]Op. cit., pp. 4–5.

[60]Op. cit., p. 260.

[61]Paul M. Sweezy, *The Theory of Capitalist Development,* p. 320.

the redivision of world markets and territories, they face head-on col-
lision and war with the capitalists of other states. Thus the basis of
many of the seeming inconsistencies in the politics of World War II
lies in the fact that the capitalist alliance was interested in destroying
the fascists as competitors for world markets and natural resources but
in saving them as bulwarks against the proletariat.[62]

Although it has been frequently asserted by such authorities as the
former Secretary of State of the United States, the Honorable Cordell
Hull, that the purpose of World War II was to destroy fascism wherever
it was found, the fact remains that fascism cannot be destroyed by war
between capitalist nations. Since a fascist state is a capitalist state in a
certain stage of degeneration, the most that brother capitalist nations
can hope to accomplish for a defeated fascist nation is the artificial setting up of a "capitalist democracy" which, if left to itself, will move
rapidly back to its former position. Fascism, as a political-class phenomenon, can apparently be liquidated only by intranational action,
revolutionary action, of the opposite political class. However, an international imperialist war may so weaken the military power of a fascist
government as to present the opportunity for its overthrow. But since
capitalism itself is an international system, any attempt by the common
people to liquidate fascism in favor of economic democracy will tend
to arouse the violent reactions of the great capitalist nations. It is the
latter situation which, after the fall of Adolf Hitler, produced Winston
Churchill as the outstanding champion of fascist governments all over
Europe.[63]

Nature of the Revolution

In modern political-class antagonism nothing needs to be more
clearly realized than that the proletariat will never supplant the capitalists peacefully. Sombart puts it well: "Combat is the solution of the
difficulty for this hard and unlovely proletarian generation . . . not
peace, not reconciliation, not a general brotherhood, but battle. . . .
Out of this is to come a generation of men qualified to live and to work

---

[62]The following is an Associated Press report of Dec. 3, 1944: "The Left Wing
Commonwealth National Committee, meeting in London today, issued a statement
condemning British policy in Europe as reactionary. 'In Belgium,' the statement
said, 'an unpopular government has been maintained by British bayonets, and in
Italy and Greece British influence and British armored forces are used on the side
of reaction. Those who fought against the Nazis are disarmed, and those who
collaborated with the Nazis are often protected.' "

[63]See Michael Sayers and Albert E. Kahn, op. cit., for a discussion of Churchill's
attitude toward socialism before Nazi Germany became a threat to the British
Empire.

in an order of society higher than the present capitalistic order."[64] This fact of inevitable conflict becomes clearly apparent when it is realized that the aim of the proletariat is a new order. "If the proletariat sets an aim clearly before itself, this goal can only be, from the class standpoint, the overthrow of the capitalistic order."[65]

A revolutionary group, a political class, cannot become a political party—in fact, a political faction—of the existing government without defeating its purpose. Political party factions tend to feel responsibility for the existing government. Labor "parties" tend to be reformist, whereas a true proletarian movement never loses sight of the fact that it can never adopt the fundamental political assumptions of the government; it does not, moreover, expect the capitalist state to die merely of inanition.[66]

Although the fascists are in fact a counterrevolutionary group, their methods must nevertheless be revolutionary.[67] Hitler himself describes the fate of revolutionists who deal in the political values of the existing government:

From the moment the Pan-German movement sold itself to parliament, it gained "parliamentarians" instead of leaders and fighters.

Thus it deteriorated to the level of ordinary political parties of the day and lost the force to oppose a catastrophic destiny with the defiance of martyrdom. Instead of fighting, it now learned to "speak" and to "negotiate." The new parliamentarian considered it, within a short time, a nicer duty, because it involved less risk to fight for a new view of life with the "intellectual" weapons of parliamentary eloquence than to throw himself into a fight, and possibly risk his own life.[68]

And decades before Hitler, Werner Sombart had written with reference to the proletariat: "This franchise that had fallen into the lap of the working man inclined the leaders of the proletariat to purely parliamentary agitation, and for a long time hindered them from a right

---

[64] Werner Sombart, op. cit., pp. 112–13.

[65] Ibid., p. 104. For a discussion of the question of violence in modern political-class conflict, see John Strachey, *Socialism Looks Forward,* pp. 45–48.

[66] In illustration, see Clifford Allen, "Has Britain Turned Socialist?" *The Western Socialist,* Vol. XII, September 1945, pp. 103–04; and Harold Laski, *Parliamentary Government in England,* pp. 153–54. Cf. N. Lenin, *Left-Wing Communism.*

[67] On this point Strachey writes: "Fascism is a 'revolutionary'—actually counterrevolutionary, of course—force in but a very limited sense of the word. It does not seek to substitute the rule of one class for that of another, which is the only genuinely revolutionary act: on the contrary, its whole purpose is to preserve the rule of the capitalist class. . . . The fascists became 'revolutionary,' not in order to destroy the rule of the capitalist class, but in order to destroy weak capitalist governments which supinely allow the strength of the workers to grow to unmanageable proportions." *The Coming Struggle for Power,* p. 263.

[68] Op. cit., p. 135.

understanding of the non-political aims of the proletariat."[69] As a matter of fact, the larger the number of seats the Social Democrats held in the *Reichstag,* the less revolutionary they became.

It appears that capitalism cannot be transformed into socialism by means of the institutions and values of capitalism; the socialist state may arise only upon the ashes of these institutions. The proletariat cannot vote for socialism in a bourgeois parliament because the capitalists will not permit themselves to be destroyed by their own instrument. The machinery of the capitalist state has been fashioned by the bourgeoisie to suit the needs of their class; therefore, in the achievement of its ends, the working class must contrive its own institutions. Indeed, even though it were possible to take over the capitalist state ready-made, this state organization will not be adapted to the new proletarian society.

As we have already intimated, socialism cannot be instituted on the system of ethics developed by capitalism; consequently, a labor party seeking to gain the power must be prepared to ignore bourgeois concepts of right and wrong and to *force* the bourgeoisie to accept a new system of ethics as a mandate of the people. We may illustrate this: Suppose a labor government decides to "socialize" industry—i.e., the means of production—by a "just and fair compensation" to the private owners of them—a sort of extension of the idea of eminent domain; very little may probably be thereby accomplished. In fact, such a procedure may be not only highly uneconomical but also disastrous to the government itself.

In the first place, it must at least tacitly accept capitalism, and there is no reason to believe that a labor government will be a better capitalist entrepreneur than the bought-out businessmen: the likelihood is that it will be worse. Then, too, it will not make sense to have the people pay for the industries of their country. They clearly could not do so completely. We need no Keynesian equation to show that if the government taxes the people to pay gradually for the industries, businessmen will first seek other industries at home for their investments; and, when opportunity for home investments becomes scarce, they will export their capital, thus leaving the country and the people heavily obligated to foreigners. The great capitalists may even follow their investments, since the home country will continue to become less and less favorable to "free enterprise."[70]

Socialism, it seems, begins with the conviction that capitalism is pres-

---

[69]Op. cit., p. 86. For a discussion of this subject, see Harold J. Laski, op. cit.

[70]Cf. John Strachey, op. cit., pp. 132–33; and A. C. Pigou, *Socialism versus Capitalism,* pp. 25–30.

ently wrong; it begins with the realization that between itself and capitalism two mortally incompatible systems of ethics are involved. The capitalists believe that, in accordance with their sacred principle of freedom of contract, they have the right to exploit human beings in their own private interest. On the contrary, the socialists believe that production and the income of industry belong to the workers, to be disposed of by them in the interest of their own welfare. These two views are unalterably opposed; they involve two distinct forms of social organization.

Therefore, the function of a labor party which is in "control of the government" would seem to be (a) to get control of the military power by making sure that it is in the hands of convinced socialist officers, and (b) to dispossess without compensation the bourgeois masters of industry. This will clearly be justice in a democracy, for in a democracy the great mass of people must inevitably believe that none of their members should have the private right of control over the livelihood of others. In this situation, moreover, the very act of capitalist exploitation naturally becomes criminal. The leaders of the workers, then, are concerned with educating the workers to the point where they come to realize the nature of the opposition which confronts them and the probable human cost of reducing it.

We may illustrate the trend of modern political-class action by the following scheme. Here the movement from feudalism to socialism is illustrated. At the side of the landlords the bourgeoisie arose, and the standard-bearers of each class developed political organizations for conflict. Out of this conflict came a new system, capitalism, and a new ruling class. Capitalism also brought forth the proletariat, the potential antagonists of the bourgeoisie. The militant members of each of these classes are now organizing for conflict, and the new system, socialism, is evidently in the offing.

This illustration is rather simplified—possibly too much so. It does not take into consideration peculiar national variations or cultural lags. Moreover, as Leon Trotsky remarks pointedly, "Capitalism is not a national but a world-wide system." It has developed on a world scale, and its manifestation in different nations and colonies may be thought of as many weaker or stronger pillars culminating in a pinnacle, its finest expression. "The revolution in Russia was a breaking of the weakest link in the system of world-wide capitalism."[71] In this connection Karl Marx also observes:

The form of this relation between rulers and ruled naturally corresponds always with a definite stage in the development of the methods of labor

---

[71]Leon Trotsky, op. cit., Vol. III, p. 176.

and its productive social power. This does not prevent the same economic basis from showing infinite variations and gradations in its appearance, even though its practical conditions are everywhere the same. This is due to innumerable outside circumstances, natural environment, race peculiarities, outside historical influence, and so forth, all of which must be ascertained by careful analysis.[72]

Since capitalism necessarily harbors two political classes, the bourgeoisie are likely to feel the tremors of proletarian unrest during the very crisis created by their bid for power. The French Revolution had its communistic upthrust, while the Russian proletariat overthrew their bourgeoisie before the latter could consolidate their position. Indeed, even the Cromwellian revolution had its Diggers.[73]

Then, too, fascism may be skipped. As Dutt remarks concerning this: "Fascism is not inevitable. Fascism is not a necessary stage of capitalist development through which all countries must pass. The social revolution can forestall fascism, as it has done in Russia. But if the social revolution is delayed, then fascism becomes inevitable."[74] Indeed, since capitalism exerts its power and force beyond national boundaries, all the stages in its development and decay need not be repeated, without exception, in every country.

Thus our schematized illustration of the social movement represents only a social tendency toward which Western civilization is moving. In some European countries feudalism has not yet been completely vanquished, while other groups such as anarchists and syndicalists help to complicate the free movement of the capitalist dialectic.

We should be very much misled if we were to lose sight of the fact that the struggle between political classes is basically a struggle between social systems. The *tiers état* represented the modern urban way of life. It included not only the bourgeoisie but also the workers, the artisans, petty traders, intellectuals, and so on. What is significant, however, is that a victory for this way of life was a victory for a specific ruling class, the bourgeoisie, who finally fashioned the society upon an ideal of free competition and profit making. The struggle between the proletariat and the bourgeoisie is basically a conflict between a profit system and a planned welfare economy. A victory for the proletariat will affect the institutional structure of the society so fundamentally that the whole society will necessarily assume a new configuration.

The class organization for struggle is constituted by the militant ele-

---

[72]*Capital*, Vol. III, p. 910.
[73]See *The Works of Gerard Winstanley*, ed. by George H. Sabine.
[74]R. P. Dutt, op. cit., p. 18.

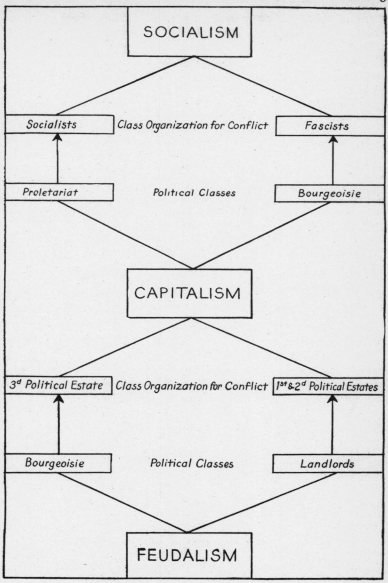

Trend of Modern Political-Class Action

ments of the class. For example, the communists or socialists of any country are not the whole political class. They are, properly speaking, the organizational and ideological standard-bearers of the proletariat who are the true rank and file of the political class. As part of the modern class struggle itself, the bourgeoisie, in their propagandistic attacks upon Russia, have insisted that the Russian Communist party rules the rest of the proletariat antagonistically. Bukharin seems clear on this point. Says he:

The struggle of the working class is inevitable; this struggle must be guided; this guidance is the more necessary since the opponent is powerful and cunning, and fighting him is a serious matter. We naturally expect to find the entire class led by that section of it that is most advanced, best schooled, most united: the party.

The party is not the class; in fact, it may be but a small portion of the class, as the head is but a small part of the body. But it will be absurd to attempt to find an opposition between the party and the class. The party is simply the thing that best expresses the interest of the class.[75]

The Struggle in the United States

The explanation usually suggested for the quietude of the workers in the United States is that their solidarity is constantly disrupted by the relatively easy movement of individuals into upper social classes. On this question Ogburn and Nimkoff are at hand.

American social conditions . . . have given to the masses a psychology unlike that possessed by the English people. The son of an English laborer has considerably more expectation of following in his father's footsteps than does the son of an American worker. . . . Thus the sympathies of the American workers have not been tied up so definitely with those of their own economic group; evidence of this is the relative weakness of trade unions in the United States as compared with those in England.[76]

[75]Nikolai Bukharin, op. cit., p. 305. In the following statement by Harold Laski a distinction may be made between the political faction and the party in England where the increasing power of workers in the Labor party now presents a double party situation: ". . . until our own day we have been governed in all fundamental matters by a single party in the state since 1689. For though that party has given the appearance, by its technique of division into two main wings, of bifurcation, the fact always has been until now that both wings did define in common the ends of parliamentary government. . . . The electorate . . . was . . . choosing between two wings of the same party rather than between different parties. The line of demarcation between them was . . . quantitative rather than qualitative in character." *Parliamentary Government in England,* pp. 83, 145. See Arthur Rosenberg, *A History of Bolshevism,* trans. by Ian F. D. Morrow, pp. 27ff. for a discussion of fundamental difference between Lenin and Trotsky on party organization.

[76]*Sociology,* pp. 330–31.

However, this explanation does not appear to be the whole reason; it may not even be the principal reason. Since about the latter part of the last century, labor in the United States has become increasingly conservative. Does this mean that there is a concomitant increase in social mobility? Does it mean that opportunities for workers to become capitalists are increasing? Evidently not.[77]

The principal reason for the weak proletarian movement in the United States seems to lie in the strategy of a small but powerful group of workers themselves. Before the achievement of dominance of business unionism in American labor, the workers were repeatedly coming into conflict with the ruling class. Their natural condition of struggle was everywhere evident. In commenting upon the temper of organized workers in this period, Selig Perlman writes:

The movement bore in every way the aspect of a social war. A frenzied hatred of labor for capital was shown in every important strike. . . . Extreme bitterness towards capital manifested itself in all the actions of the Knights of Labor, and wherever the leaders undertook to hold it within bounds they were generally discarded by their followers, and others who would lead as directed were placed in charge. The feeling of "give no quarter" is illustrated in the refusal to submit grievances to arbitration when the employes felt that they had the upper hand over their employers. . . . No warning from a leader, however high, was capable of restraining the combative rank and file.[78]

In a similar vein Corey sums up the militance of the labor movement of the period:

The great strikes of 1877 assumed the character of mass insurrections, and were followed by strikes of an equally militant character, culminating in the 8-hour strikes of 1886 and ending with the great Pullman strike of 1894 (the Debs Rebellion). The militancy of American labor in this stage is indisputable, comparable with the militance of any labor movement anywhere.[79]

The battle songs of the workers also indicate clearly their consciousness of class antagonism. Says Louis Adamic: "On the streets of

---

[77]It is interesting to observe how our practice looks when viewed from Europe. Thus J. Ramsay MacDonald said in 1912: "The brutal force which money exerts in America in the workshop, the corrupt force it can exert on the bench and in the capital of every state, make it the most natural thing imaginable for labor to contemplate a resort to such force as it can command—dynamite, sabotage, bad work, the revolutionary strike." In the London *Daily Chronicle,* quoted by Louis Adamic, *Dynamite: The Story of Class Violence in America,* p. 99.

[78]John R. Commons and Associates, *History of Labor in the United States,* Vol. II, pp. 374–75. See also John Swinton, *A Momentous Question: The Respective Attitudes of Labor and Capital,* and Samuel Yellen, *American Labor Struggles.*

[79]Lewis Corey, op. cit., p. 556.

Chicago, in saloons, wherever else workers gathered, one could hear
early in 1886 such songs as:

> *Toiling millions now are waking—*
> *See them marching on;*
> *All the tyrants now are shaking,*
> *Ere their power's gone.*

Chorus

> *Storm the fort, ye Knights of Labor*
> *Battle for your cause;*
> *Equal rights for every neighbor*
> *Down with tyrant laws."*[80]

And in the agitation leading to the Haymarket Riot, workers read
from their newspapers such violent passages as the following:

Bravely forward! The conflict has begun. . . . Workers, let your watchword be: No compromise! Cowards to the rear! Men to the front! The
die is cast! The first of May is here. . . . Clean your guns, complete
your ammunition. The hired murderers of the capitalists, the police and
militia are ready to murder. No workers should leave their houses in these
days with empty pockets.[81]

Gradually, however, labor was to be tamed by some of its own leaders into a highly individualistic form of organization. The great revolutionary labor struggles of the last quarter of the nineteenth century
tended to degenerate into the sporadic, individualistic racketeering and
petty violence of interbusiness rivalry. In 1886 the American Federation of Labor defeated a true workers' organization, the Knights of
Labor, in a jurisdictional strife and began a policy which clearly bears
a greater share of the responsibility for the peaceful exploitation of the
masses of workers than the activities of the employers themselves. This
policy has also been adopted by the great railroad brotherhoods; and
its apparent success has been a source of envy among unorganized
workers.

We call the Knights of Labor a true workers' organization because it
was interested in all workers. Business unionism is not interested in all
workers, but only in those whose organization pays. The guiding principle of Samuel Gompers, who held the presidency of the AFL and its
parent organization almost continuously from 1882 to 1924, centered

---

[80]Op. cit., p. 62.
[81]Ibid., p. 69.

about the watchword: "If it doesn't square with your due book, have none of it."[82]

The AFL organizes those workers in positions of greatest strategy in the labor market, the skilled workers, the so-called labor aristocrats. Its federated nationals charge high dues, pay good benefits, and depend for their strength on the consciousness of a brotherhood of skill and of mutual if exclusive interests. They act as a monopoly of labor to the degree that it is possible.[83]

At this point we should mention that the unorganized worker is practically helpless as a bargaining or political force. Outside of a labor union he could hardly become conscious of his proletarian interests; therefore, other things being equal, the smaller the organization of the workers, the less the likelihood of radicalism among the proletariat. The business unionism of the AFL cannot and does not have an interest in the organization of all workers; on the other hand, an organizing policy which includes and has for its end the incorporation of the great mass of workers must inevitably be radical.

Every indiscriminate organization of workers will be revolutionary. Conservative unionism is the inevitable result of discrimination among workers on the basis of their capacity for organization co-operatively with business. But the great mass of unskilled and semiskilled proletariat cannot be thus organized, for it is upon the opportunity for coincident exploitation of this mass by the selected workers that the conservatism of the latter mainly depends.

Almost without exception the capitalist labor-economists who write textbooks divide labor unionism into conservative and revolutionary, with the expressed or implied conclusion that revolutionary unionism is pathological. The social determinism involved in the nature of union membership itself is seldom if ever recognized. However, businessmen are by no means unaware of this fundamental characteristic of labor. Dutt cites the following statement circulated by letter among German business leaders. Says the writer of the letters: "Any united workers' movement springing up from below must be revolutionary, and this rule would not be able to hold out against it for long, not even with the means of military power."[84]

Labor leaders, who do not understand the ultimate antagonism be-

---

[82]*Seventy Years of Life and Labor,* Vol. I, p. 287.

[83]See J. Raymond Walsh, *C.I.O.,* p. 19.

[84]R. P. Dutt, op. cit., p. 171; from the *Deutsche Führerbriefe.* These "Führerbriefe," or "Letters to Leaders," constitute a "political-economic private correspondence" originally issued in 1932 for confidential circulation to the heads of finance-capital, organized in the Federation of German Industry. Ibid., p. 170.

tween the working class and the bourgeoisie, are always frightened by the extremes to which worker-conscious unions go when they clash with the employers. These leaders ordinarily mistake immediate demands for higher wages and better conditions of work for the real destiny of the working class. At any rate, it took years of selection of workers and ruthless suppression of rank-and-file organization by capitalistically minded labor leaders before conservative unionism came to character-ize the American labor scene.

The remarkable fact of the role assumed by the AFL is not that it does not organize the masses of workers but that it stands directly in opposition to the organization of these workers. The AFL stands as an impregnable barrier, a formidable wall of ice, against the development of a working-class consciousness in the United States. Though its mem-bership ordinarily amounts to only about one tenth or less of the or-ganizable workers, it always speaks in the name of the underprivileged masses in its own interest. It collaborates whenever possible with em-ployers, because, to put it in Gompers's rationalization: "I knew that the cause of labor was so just and our methods *so practical* that a hear-ing before employers must necessarily result in better relations."[85]

This, of course, is business diplomacy adopted by a privileged clique of workers. As a business they pit themselves against other businesses, and their greatest enemy is not infrequently the out-group workers, organized or unorganized, which they conceive to be their immediate competitors. What they are really asking for is a share of the lucre which, when obtained by a "hearing," ordinarily means collaboration in the further exploitation of the mass of unorganized workers—a sec-ondary exploitation of weak workers by the leadership of workers in strategic positions. This trait of business unionism may justly be called labor cannibalism. In characterizing the opportunism of the British trade unions (1850–80), from which the infant AFL took a pattern, Werner Sombart observes:

This *practical* tendency finds its true incorporation in the old English trade-union, which . . . is the shrewdest scheme for the protection of personal interests that has ever been conceived; diplomatic, adroit, smooth towards that which is above—towards the employer; exclusive, narrow, brutal towards that which is underneath—towards four-fifths of the "out-siders," the poorer classes of workmen. The trade unions are capitalistic and businesslike organizations.[86]

---

[85]Op. cit., p. 400. (Italics added.)

[86]Op. cit., pp. 68–69. "The constitution [of the AFL] was copied almost verbatim from that of the British Trade Unions Congress and its Parliamentary Committee." See Lewis L. Lorwin, *The American Federation of Labor*, pp. 10–13 *passim*.

Louis Adamic states pointedly the present position of the AFL: "The attitude

The most effective and consistent method used by the AFL to keep the masses of workers unorganized and docilely exploitable is the refusal to organize the strong with the weak workers. The insistence upon picking out the skilled workers in an industry and disregarding all others has destroyed many opportunities for wider labor organization. On this score Gompers states in smooth diplomatic language:

> The Federation having no power of compulsion, could not enforce practices contrary to the wishes or rules of affiliated unions. The Federation does not instruct unions as to the structure of their organization. Unions may select the industrial form if they so desire.[87]

As an illustration of what this means, when in 1935 the auto workers offered themselves to the AFL as an industrial union, the "affiliated unions" in convention assembled rejected them. "The auto workers could not vote for what they wanted; the votes were in the hands of the national crafts. The cards were stacked in advance."[88] As practical business people the crafts wanted to siphon off the skilled workers at a "hearing" with the employers and to leave the masses totally unprotected and helplessly exploitable. It would then be perfectly good business practice of the few organized skilled workers to have their wage increase offset by a reduction in the wages of the unorganized masses.

Because of the structure and business aims of the AFL it is practically impossible for it to favor a policy which seeks the unlimited organization of workers. Indeed, an essential element in the strength of craft unionism rests upon a definite selection of workers for organization. As Dr. Louis S. Reed points out:

> The great majority of unions in the Federation being craft unions, to ask these unions to endorse the principle of industrial unionism was, accordingly, almost like asking them to commit harikari. For, it is evident, craft unionism and industrialism are mutually exclusive and conflicting.

---

of the AFL toward society at large was, in most vital respects, not unlike that of the capitalists. The trade-union leaders were bent upon getting for themselves and their members everything that could be had under the circumstances, whenever possible, by any means—dynamite included—that involved no great risks to themselves or the future of their organization. It did not concern them whether those benefits were attained at the expense of the capitalist, the unorganized proletariat, the organized labor outside the AFL, or the country as a whole. Politically, they 'played the game' as it was played by the capitalists, that is, to gain immediate economic advantages or benefits. They were not antagonistic to the wage system. . . . They accepted the capitalist system and proposed to make the best of it." Op. cit., pp. 90–91. For a description of the British trade-union movement, which is similar to that of American business unionism, see Fenner Brockway, op. cit., p. 21.

It is true that the AFL has had industrial internationals affiliated with it, but these were never permitted to limit its craft control.

[87]Op. cit., pp. 406–07.

[88]J. Raymond Walsh, op. cit., p. 36.

. . . The establishment and spread of industrial unions . . . could only mean the loss by craft unions of members, influence, and strength.[89]

Nothing shows up the character of business unionism so well as the history of the AFL's struggle with the CIO. The eight international unions which separated from the AFL constituted the original CIO and organized a number of major industries. One would think that the AFL, having this great job of organization finished, would consider it a windfall to give charters to the great new unions. Not so, however. The condition of accepting these workers into the Federation is that they allow their unions to be raided and shattered by the international craft unions according as the latter's business profits indicate.

The AFL and other business unions, therefore, have been a real barrier to the formation of a true proletarian movement in the United States. Their methods of struggle with the workers' movement have been exactly that of the businessman. "Already the AFL," says J. Raymond Walsh, "has begun waving the red shirt and yelling 'Bolshevik!' and in a few localities the less responsible representatives have tried Jew-baiting to stop the CIO."[90]

Decades ago business unionism in the United States established its plan of action against the proletarian movement. At the close of the last century, in an AFL convention, Gompers declared: "I want to tell you, Socialists, that I have studied your philosophy. . . . I declare it to you, I am not only at variance with your doctrines, but with your philosophy. Economically, you are unsound; socially you are wrong; industrially you are an impossibility."[91]

And up to the time of his death in 1924 he was still of the same opinion. Expressing himself on the new civilization that was being built in Russia, he said: "After five years the Soviets have demonstrated beyond question that socialism is economically unsound, socially wrong, and industrially impossible."[92] Estimating the proletariat leadership in implicit terms of profits and success, the values of the businessman, he declared further: "The conspicuous socialists have uniformly been men whose minds have been warped by a great failure, or who

[89] *The Labor Philosophy of Samuel Gompers*, p. 132.

[90] Op. cit., p. 274. Walsh observes further: The AFL "have even entered into collusive contracts with employers to close out their rivals. . . . They have attacked their recent associates as communists, as racketeers, as members of an alien race." Ibid., p. 280. Consider also the extremely reactionary attitude of the AFL in its refusal to attend the 1945 World Trade Union Conference called in London by the British Trade Union Congress, because, it argued, the CIO and the workers of the Soviet Union were represented.

[91] Op. cit., p. 397.

[92] Ibid., p. 398.

found it absolutely impossible to understand fundamentals necessary to developing practical plans for industrial betterment."[93]

Thus business unionism[94] not only collaborates with the capitalists in the exploitation of the masses for a part of the profits, but also stands as the great bulwark against the development of a significant workers' movement. It is for this reason business unionists have been denounced as "betrayers of the workers." Indeed, the business unions, in their pre-occupation with problems of splitting profits with employers, have literally sacrificed the masses of workers who most need organization. The strongest section of the American proletariat has made a succession of opportunistic deals with the businessmen; these deals have resulted temporarily in some substantial increases in wages and in big salaries for its leadership besides the effective exploitation, disorganization, and demoralization of the great mass of American workers. The interest of the leadership in this kind of unionism is graphically indicated by Louis Adamic. Says he:

Today the AFL is utterly spiritless. Its leaders are pompous, high-toned Babbitts, some of them with stock-exchange tickers in their offices. Its conventions compare with those of the Elks, the Rotarians, and the National Association of Soap Manufacturers. They invite army generals to address them. William Green . . . goes to West Point to review the cadet corps and receive honors such as are ordinarily rendered only to visiting royalty.[95]

But the peaceful exploitative tactics of the AFL have not really stopped the movement of social forces. Its alliance with the employers against the masses of underprivileged workers is quite fictitious. As Walsh correctly says: "The forces that attack the CIO today with its unskilled workers will tomorrow attack the AFL with its skilled, whenever the tensions in our society drive property to defend its profits at the expense of democracy."[96] This prediction was published in 1937. Ten years later, on June 23, 1947, an anti-labor Congress passed the Taft-Hartley bill, one of the most crippling attacks on all organized labor in the history of the United States. And this, we may be sure, is

---

[93]Ibid., p. 383. See also Lewis L. Lorwin, op. cit., pp. 30, 73–75.

[94]The policy and practices of the AFL may be taken as representative of all business unions in the United States; indeed, the great railroad brotherhoods are even more opportunistic and exploitative than many of the AFL internationals.

[95]Op. cit., pp. 251–52. Speaking of the post-World War I period of the history of the AFL, Carroll R. Daugherty says: "For every union official with a vision and aggressiveness, there were many who appeared entirely willing to live mild, undisturbed lives of white-collar, middle-class ease, supported comfortably by the dues of existing members." *Labor Problems in American Industry,* p. 339.

[96]J. Raymond Walsh, op. cit., p. 280. We should mention, however, that already it seems the militant CIO is being tamed.

but the first unmistakable expression of ruling-class displeasure over the democratic advancement of the workers during the last decade. Moreover, the essential antagonism between the worker and the capitalist becomes readily apparent when labor refuses to organize individualistically. As soon as the superior workers identify their interest with all workers and thus abandon their opportunity for temporary gain at the expense of their fellows, labor tends to become revolutionary.

The leaders of such unions as constitute the railway brotherhoods and the AFL typically dread the idea of ultimate responsibility for entrepreneurial control of industry by the workers. Their utopian dream is that of perpetually whittling away the total income, using their position of great bargaining strategy to obtain for themselves a relatively large share of the sum which goes to labor. The end must be to have industry run by private enterprise in the interest of labor, particularly organized skilled labor with strategic bargaining power. There is in the ideology of this faction of labor a basic distrust of the masses of workers, a distrust of economic democracy. And yet it could never be honestly encouraged by businessmen because its immediate function and ideals are parasitic. As the lesser of two evils, however, businessmen prefer it to that faction of labor which recognizes that in modern society private business enterprise is dispensable and that businessmen are a principal source of social waste.

Business unionism, nevertheless, is not entirely without accomplishment in securing the ends of the proletariat. The mere fact of its organization in industry is a notable achievement. Thus says Dr. Reed aptly:

> The very attainment of organization and the securing of a collective agreement constitute a veritable revolution in status, both for workers and employers. By that single step, the workers have enormously increased their own power at the cost of the employers'. . . . The effect of their ever-expanding demands is to shift more power to themselves, to absorb the power of the employer, and to restrict his control of industry. A union, therefore, is not anti-capitalistic merely because it prefaces its constitution with a preamble stating that it aims to overthrow the existing order. Nor does the union accept capitalism in saying that it does. Rather by the very logic of its nature and function, a strong union is anti-capitalistic, and changes the existing order in its day to day activity.[97]

Whether they realize it or not, then, all industrial workers—from the ultra-individualistic railway brotherhoods to the group-conscious maritime unions—are fundamentally "communistic."

---

[97]Louis S. Reed, op. cit., p. 24.

The State and the Class Struggle

Probably one of the most difficult aspects of socialist thought to digest, even among socialists themselves, has been the idea of the vanishing proletariat state;[98] and yet it is based upon a simple truism. By definition, according to the socialists, the state is an instrument of class exploitation. If, in a proletarian society, there will be no political classes, then there will necessarily be no state. In commenting upon the taking over of power by the proletariat, Engels says:

> As soon as there is no longer any social class to be held in subjection, as soon as class rule . . . [is] removed, nothing more remains to be repressed, and a special repressive force, a State, is no longer necessary. The first act by virtue of which the State really constitutes itself the representative of the whole of society—the taking possession of the means of production in the name of society—this is, at the same time, its last independent act as a State. State interference in *social relations* (relations between classes) becomes in one domain after another, superfluous, and then *dies out of itself;* the government of persons is replaced by the administration of things, and by the conduct of processes of production. The State is not "abolished." It withers away.[99]

This is the central idea of the vanishing socialist State. It is clear that the socialists intend to do nothing to "abolish" the State. Their preoccupation is with the abolishment of political classes; this end achieved, the State merely atrophies from disuse. "The proletariat seizes political power and turns the means of production into state property. But, in doing this, it abolishes itself as proletariat."[100] Herein lies the crucial difference between the design of the anarchists and that of the socialists. The anarchists see the State rather than the social forces which produce the State as their primary concern.

The anarchists have no clear idea as to what the proletariat will put in place of the State, nor how it will use its revolutionary power.[101] This is utopianism. The socialists, however, do not seek to destroy the State directly. Their end, to repeat, is the liquidation of the exploiting capitalist class and consequently of all political classes. They insist on using the machinery of a state to accomplish this. Having eliminated the exploiters from within and from without, the State naturally be-

---

[98]Friedrich Engels and Nikolai Lenin are the leading exponents of the socialist theory of the state; see Lenin, *The State and Revolution,* and Sherman H. M. Chang, *The Marxian Theory of the State.*

[99]Op. cit., pp. 129–30.

[100]Engels, op. cit., p. 69.

[101]See Lenin, op. cit., p. 216.

comes obsolete. It should be observed that, of the known types of advanced societies, only a socialist system can hope to achieve state-lessness.

The socialists do not confuse the idea of a state as a power organization serving the exploitative purpose of a ruling class with administrative institutions devoted only to the accomplishment of increasing well-being among the whole people. Indeed, Engels's statement, "The government of persons is replaced by the administration of things," may be paraphrased: The exploitation of persons is replaced by the exploitation of things.

Moreover, it is likely that, with a hasty consideration of the idea of the vanishing socialist State, one may think of the socialist community as being finally in chaos. However, planning and social control are particularly the business of the proletariat. Clearly, a stateless society need not be a planless society. Whereas in the capitalist society the social scientist is likely to be looked upon with suspicion, in the socialist society his function will be most desirable. In the latter system the un-limited application of science to the problem of human welfare will not constantly run afoul of the businessman's profits.

The whole sphere [says Engels] of the conditions of life which environs man, and which have hitherto ruled man, now comes under the domination and control of man, who for the first time becomes the real, conscious lord of Nature, because he has now become *master of his own social organization.* The laws of his own social action hitherto standing face to face with man as laws of Nature, foreign to and dominating him, will then be used with full understanding. . . . Only from that time will man himself, more and more consciously, make his own history—only from that time will the social causes set in movement by him have . . . the results intended by him.[102]

Views of the Social Movement

Finally, a word should be said about certain popular views of the social movement. A common practice of capitalist economists is to criticize mercilessly some one or a number of points in Karl Marx's theory of value, price, and distribution. Having ripped through the Marxian conclusion, they dust off their hands and retire in the assurance that they have disposed of the social movement. This perform-

---

[102]Friedrich Engels, op. cit., 1902, pp. 134–35.
    On this point, and in reference to Soviet Russia, Maurice Parmelee observes: "All cultures of the past have found their ideological basis in religion, theology, and metaphysics. For the first time in the history of mankind a culture is based upon science. This is one of the most momentous events in human annals. . . ." *Bolshevism, Fascism, and the Liberal-Democratic State,* p. 59.

ance may be likened to that of a socialist economist who successfully refutes some arguments of David Ricardo's and on that ground concludes that capitalism has only a mythical existence.

Marx's writings have value only in so far as they help us to understand the actualities of the social movement; detailed negative criticism of them does not appear to have value per se.[103] As Eduard Heimann puts it:

What [Marx] did was to study the newly formed proletarian men to comprehend their blind instincts, and to express them in a coherent objective program of society that the workers could recognize for themselves. . . . He revealed to them the goal to be attained at the end of the road along which they were being driven by the inner necessity of their communal work; he showed them the meaning of their existence.[104]

Another rather vulgar view of the movement is that evinced in the argument that "the personal expenditures of the rich amount to very little, and [that] if their 'wealth' and incomes were evenly distributed, this would materially affect only the large body of incapables, derelicts, and mentally deficient survivals of neolithic population out of which modern civilization has arisen."[105] Some intelligent social scientists have actually computed the number of dollars each person in the United States would receive if the wealth of the rich were divided among them and, finding this amount to be only a small sum, come to the conclusion that socialism is a fallacy. Of course this is ridiculous, for it must be clear that the new social order contemplated by the proletariat —by democracy—does not mean a mere sharing of dollars while still retaining capitalism. "The distinguishing fact," says John Strachey, "is that in a communist society no incomes shall be derived by virtue of the possession of the instruments of production."[106] Moreover, production by use of large quantities of capital goods is a primary motive of socialism; that is to say, capitalistic production without capitalism.

"The distinguishing feature of Communism is not the abolition of

---

[103]A remarkable illustration of the uses of Marxian criticism is that presented in one of Werner Sombart's later publications. Under the influence of the rise of Nazism, this distinguished author who had written realistically as a social scientist has, in his convenient criticism of Marx and laudation of the "divine" plan of National Socialism, speedily degenerated into a puerile scholastic dialecticism. One is literally astonished to observe the former scholar weaving his way into compatibility with "German Socialism," and this all in "the spirit which finds its expression in the words: 'all for our country.' " See *A New Social Philosophy,* trans. by Karl F. Geiser. Cf. Talcott Parsons, "Capitalism in Recent German Literature: Sombart and Weber," *The Journal of Political Economy,* Vol. 36, pp. 658–61.

[104]*Communism, Fascism or Democracy,* p. 95.

[105]Carl Snyder, op. cit., p. 411.

[106]Op. cit., p. 344.

property generally, but the abolition of bourgeois property." Any view
of socialism which does not assume a logical social order developing out
of a senescent capitalism is utopian. Such vacuous statements as "There
will be no family under socialism," or "God will be abolished under
socialism," or "Socialism means dictatorship" are typical of utopian
thinking. We can know what will necessarily characterize a socialist
society only by reasoning within the frame of reference of a capitalistic
economic order without capitalists, an order determined by and devoted
to the welfare of the whole people. The detailed features of such a
system will depend upon the degree of resistance of capitalists during
the period of "transvaluation of values" and the social history peculiar
to the people.

A variant of what may be called the share-the-wealth view of socialism is the argument that, with the rise of the modern corporation, so
large a number of persons have come to own shares of stock that it may
be said profits have become socialized. To the great majority of small
stockholders, however, dividends are of the nature of interest; these
small stockholders have none of the functions of entrepreneurship.
Here, too, the significance of capitalism as a social system based upon a
peculiar method of production is reduced to the simple idea of distribution of profits. The question of class conflict inherent in the system
is translated into a question of status relationship between the rich and
the poor. It is assumed that the only aim of the proletariat is to have
more money regardless of the system in which it is produced. Suppose,
for instance, the activities of gangsters were to be judged anti-social;
would their decision to share their income among certain interest groups
be sufficient to liquidate the source of antagonism against them? The
difficulty with capitalism inheres not so much in the way profits are
distributed as in the social pathology developing out of the system of
profit making per se.

Probably no fact is more difficult for the capitalistically oriented person to grasp than that the origin of human initiative may not have been
coeval with capitalism.[107] The following statement by the former
United States Ambassador to Russia, Joseph E. Davies, is typical of
this difficulty. In communications with the Secretary of State he explains the absence of pure communism in Russia:

> The idea of a "classless" society has been and is being destroyed in
> practice. The government itself is a bureaucracy with all the indicia of
> class, to wit: special privileges, higher standards of living, and the like.

---

[107]For a classic statement of the nature of motivation in capitalist society, see Sir
Henry S. Maine, *Popular Government*, p. 50.

. . . Writers, artists, even leaders of jazz bands, receive high compensation and have the class privileges which money provides in luxuries and the like. . . .

In industry, classes have been established and are being rapidly intensified and developed through the system of offering greater pay for greater work. This in turn has induced higher standards of living among certain of the workers, and class consciousness is evinced in differences in housing and living conditions and indications of style consciousness on the part of women and wives of the workers. . . . "Class," after all, is only a word to define an idea; the basis of which is that there are different groups of men which are differentiated, as among themselves. . . . The only insistent and constant stimulus to the workers was found to be the profit motive.

Based on the idea of a selfless society, the state here is constantly threatened with the fact that it cannot destroy the instincts of human nature toward self-interest. These are imbedded in the glandular, nervous, and physical organism of men and are the resultant of atavistic forces of centuries. If these instincts cannot be eradicated in a generation or two, this experiment must fail.[108]

We have quoted at length from Davies not only because his ideas are untouched by sociological sophistication but also because they are politically authoritative and popular. Although it is the prime reason for his going astray, we shall not dwell upon the author's basic confusion of social and political class.[109] However, we should mention that workers do not have a "profit motive"; more wages are not the same thing as more profits. Furthermore, a proletarian society does not propose to abolish "self-interest." One may insist that it does only if one assumes that "self-interest" is an exclusive trait of capitalism.[110] This belief that men cannot live co-operatively as well as exploitatively is only about three hundred years old, hence it is sheer nonsense to speak of it as having a biological residue. In order to encourage superior personal initiative it is sufficient that society compensates it with superior social recognition, and clearly the means of such compensation have not all been pre-empted by capitalism. In a socialist society, "to be 'somebody' means doing something, not having something."

---

[108]*Mission to Moscow*, Pocket-book Ed., pp. 110–11, 341, 349.

[109]Cf. Mildred Fairchild, "Social-Economic Classes in Soviet Russia," *American Sociological Review*, June 1944, pp. 236–41.

[110]On this point Harold J. Laski is outspoken. Says he: "When [capitalism] broke down the principle of birth as the foundation of privilege and replaced it with the principle of wealth, it secreted a fatal poison in the very roots of its soil. That poison was the establishment of the idea that the acquisition of property as the main source of power was the true end of man. Not holiness, not culture, not fellowship, were vital articles of faith. Social life was . . . a 'beneficent private war' in which, because the fittest survived, the fate of the individual was a matter of indifference to the cosmos." *Reflections on the Revolution of Our Time*, p. 356.

Indeed, there may be a real question whether that elfish glee experienced by the "hardheaded businessman" over the sight of the compounding growth of his profits, in total disregard of their human basis, is a greater source of inspiration than the genuine elation derived from the applause and appreciation of one's fellows for services contributed to the welfare of the group as a whole.

The capitalist argument that human beings will not exert themselves unless they are at least potentially able to take off some small fraction of the things which they produce in the form of profits to enjoy selfishly and individually in isolation is, to say the least, a degenerate commentary on the possibilities of human nature. Socialism abolishes private property in the means of production but not in consumers' goods. In his explanation of the phenomenal growth of industry in the pre-World War II Soviet Union, Albert Rhys Williams observes: "Among their incentives to exert themselves to the utmost is the knowledge that the profit from their labors does not go into private pockets but into the public pool for the benefit of all. Others are the awards and decorations bestowed for signal and faithful service. . . . There is, also, assurance that no barriers of caste or race will keep them from the highest posts, with manifold opportunities to fit themselves therefor."[111]

We should remember also that not so long ago it was generally believed that the workers had to be kept poor or they would have no initiative. Arthur Young said with assurance: ". . . every one but an idiot knows that the lower classes must be kept poor, or they will never be industrious. . . . They must be, like all mankind, in poverty, or they will not work."[112] In fact, this argument still remains at the pith of the belief that profits are the greatest stimulus to human endeavor and, consequently, most beneficial to human society. It may be shown,

[111]"Meet the Russian People," *Survey*, February 1944, p. 44.

[112]*The Farmer's Tour through the East of England*, Vol. IV, p. 361. For a background of the development of this attitude, see Eli F. Heckscher, *Mercantilism*, Vol. II, pp. 145–72.

Laski seems to be again in point; thus he asserts: "Given reasonable remuneration, there is not, historically, an atom of evidence to suggest that men work less eagerly in public, than in private, employment, granted that the work interests them and that an equal esteem is attached to its performance. If, in a given society, the man who can acquire most is most highly regarded, it is very probable that ambitious and able men will drift into the most lucrative occupations. And if, as with ourselves, the defense of the power and privilege which attach to wealth is an urgent preoccupation of the ruling class in society, they will, of course, see to it that everything possible is done to cry down principles of social action which threatens their power and privilege. . . . But where the standard of public judgment is not set by the power to acquire wealth merely, there is not an iota of serious evidence to support this argument. Here, at least, the experience of the Soviet Union is conclusive." Op. cit., p. 379.

however, that if men are inspired they may summon initiative to serve and to produce in an intensity limited only by their physical powers.

Sometimes liberal thinkers charge that "the radicals," "the communists," shift their policy in the most unpredictable ways. They sometimes find the radicals feverishly advocating some domestic or foreign policy and praising the statesman who champions it, and later, without giving any apparent reason, switching to an opposite policy and denouncing the same statesman for his position on the question. This has been called derisively, "the communist line"—an erratic, untrustworthy political philosophy.

At any rate, the reason for these shifts appears to be that socialists, whether they be Americans, or Englishmen, or Spaniards, must work through the existing administration of capitalist states in seeking to foster their own disparate ends. The ends of the capitalist statesman and those of the socialist leader are never the same. But it may so happen that the immediate policy of the capitalist statesman may serve the ends of the socialists, and, to the extent that this is so, the latter will support that policy and the statesman who advocates it.

For instance, Winston Churchill is fundamentally anti-democratic and reactionary. But when for imperialistic motives he championed the cause of Russia against the great fascist powers led by Germany, he endeared himself to the socialists all over the world. A victory for fascism would have been a much greater reverse for socialism than the threat of British imperialism. The ends of the two were different, but the immediate policy served the purpose of both.

In like manner, when the reformer, Franklin D. Roosevelt, took office as President of the United States, attacked the "economic royalists," and sponsored Section 7A of the National Recovery Act, he was praised as the great liberator of the workers; he took a step in the direction of democracy and socialism. When he refused effectively to aid Loyalist Spain against fascist Italy and Germany, the socialists denounced him; when during the first stage of World War II he sought to take the United States into the war on the side of Britain and France, they denounced him again and seemed to take sides with Senator Burton K. Wheeler and Charles Lindbergh. The motive here was to have the great European capitalists destroy themselves by the very plans which they had concocted for the destruction of communism. But when Germany attacked Russia, the war became mainly a class war between socialism all over the world and the developed fascism of Europe. The socialists now found it expedient to urge America and England to fight a religious war against fascism. The policy of the radicals, in being consistent with ends antagonistic to capitalism, may be inconsistent with the immediate policies of capitalist nations.[113]

Moreover, part of the seeming inconsistency of socialist policy is due to the inevitable inconsistency between the supposed ideals and practices of the capitalist ruling class all over the world. For instance, after some public pressure upon the State Department of the United States for a statement on the purpose and aims of the United States in World War II, Secretary of State Cordell Hull declared in a world-wide radio address on April 9, 1944:

> There can be no compromise with Fascism and Nazism. It must go everywhere. Its leaders, its institutions, the power which supports it must go. . . . There cannot be any compromise with fascism—whether in Italy or in any other country. It must always be the enemy, and it must be our determined policy to do all in our power to end it.

This, indeed, was an objective worthy of the tremendous sacrifice which the American people were making; it was a good answer to their question: What are we fighting for? But when on April 17, 1946, the question of the United Nations severing diplomatic relations with Franco Spain came up in the Security Council, the Department of State of the United States, supported by the British representative, led the fight against such action on the pretext that it might result in civil strife in Spain, and in the meantime the United States proceeded to sell Franco surplus American Army supplies. All these seeming inconsistencies, however, may be explained by an understanding of the modern class struggle.

Even as Hull was speaking, one understood that he was putting himself on the spot—that he could not really mean what he was saying. He was saying, in effect, that the United States was fighting a class war on the side of socialism. We should expect no inconsistency between the policy of the United States as Hull enunciated it here and the "communist line," and there is none; this capitalist, political switch is quickly forgotten, yet it is pivotal. It is today the primary source of conflict

---

[113]The experienced Lenin had already discussed the problems of struggle which confronted the weaker political class: "To carry on a war for the overthrow of the international bourgeoisie, a war a hundred times more difficult, prolonged and complicated than the most stubborn of ordinary wars between countries, and to refuse beforehand to maneuver, to utilize the conflict (even though temporary) of interests between one's enemies; to refuse co-operation and compromise with possible (even though transient, unstable, vacillating, and conditional) allies—is not this an infinitely laughable thing? Is it not as though . . . we were to renounce beforehand the idea that we might have to go sometimes . . . in zig-zags, sometimes retracing our steps, sometimes giving up the course once selected and trying various others?" *Left-Wing Communism,* authorized trans., pp. 66–67.

among the great powers. In reality the ruling class in Britain and the United States never intended to fight such a war; it did not, and probably will never, go to war merely to defeat fascism in other countries. However, it cannot say so to the people; as usual, it must use the values of the people to achieve its own ends. Mr. Hull's statement was undoubtedly made to allay and placate the inordinate upsurge of democratic feeling during the war. After the war the capitalists began forthwith to reorganize their forces for reaction, and European fascism, with the open assistance of the American ruling class, again tended to recover its function in the international class struggle with Russia and with the workers of every country.[114]

[114]See Edgar Snow, *Stalin Must Have Peace*, Pt. II, pp. 156ff., for a review of paradoxes in United States-Russian diplomacy.

12. Modern Democracy and the Class Struggle —

*I*N PRESENT-DAY WESTERN CIVILIZATION "DEMOCRACY" HAS BE-
come a war cry—a war cry of both the capitalists and the proletariat
in their struggle for power. And yet quite frequently the public is at a
loss about the meaning of democracy. It has been often said, for instance, that democracy has different meanings: neither the British, the
Americans, nor the Russians mean the same thing when they refer to
democracy. In reality, however, they do mean the same thing; they
only conceive of it in different stages of development. If we view the
phenomenon in its historical context we shall be able easily to observe
that modern democracy has not yet fully emerged in any part of the
world.[1]

Ordinarily the British and the Americans, among others, call their
form of government and social system democracy, but, strictly speaking, this is a misnomer. The fact is that these social systems have been
continually becoming something else; modern democracy is still in its
fetal stage.[2] In the United States, Thomas Jefferson, Andrew Jackson,
Abraham Lincoln, and Franklin Roosevelt are all symbols of democratic progress. In England the Cromwellian revolution and the Level-
ers, the Reform Bill of 1832 and the Chartist movement, and the rise to
political ascendancy of labor mark great episodes in the development of
democracy. Ever since the rise of towns in the later Middle Ages,

---

[1] Cf. C. Delisle Burns, *Political Ideals*, p. 276.

[2] The fundamental error of William E. H. Lecky in his critique of democracy appears to be the belief that democracy has been already achieved in modern Western
society. Says he: "Democracy has completely triumphed in two forms—the American and the French—and we see it fully working before us. Men may like it or
dislike it, but only rare and very peculiarly moulded minds can find in the government of either republic a subject for real enthusiasm." *Democracy and Liberty*,
p. 43. For an earlier discussion with a similar assumption, see Sir Henry Sumner
Maine, op. cit., p. 337; and for a review, Benjamin Evans Lippincott, *Victorian
Critics of Democracy*, Minneapolis, 1938.

Western society has been moving away from a definable, non-democratic society toward a still unattained democracy.

To be accurate, then, the British and American systems should be called governments with democratic tendencies. They are oligarchic-democratic or capitalist democratic hybrids.[3] Therefore, the question of crucial significance must logically be: How far has the particular system advanced toward its apparent goal of an accomplished democracy? Moreover, the criteria here involved will be obviously based upon the extent to which capitalist practices and ideals give way to those of democracy. It is in this sense that it has been said democracy should be "respected rather more for its potentialities than for its achievements." As Arthur Rosenberg points out:

> The medieval state was a clear, unequivocal type, just as a socialist state would also be a definite form. In addition to other manifestations of the bourgeois state, the decisive, important, basic fact of bourgeois private property is common to modern democratic states. Therefore within states based upon the same fundamental economic fact it is not very easy to determine the exact point where democracy ceases and oligarchy begins. . . . Social forces change incessantly even though the constitutions remain intact. Thus, except for a few changes, the Constitution of the United States is still the same as in the days of Washington, and yet what immense changes have occurred in American society and consequently also in the real American constitution since then![4]

From the standpoint of degrees of development of democracy in the three great nations of the world—the United States, England, and Russia—the United States is probably most backward and Russia farthest advanced.[5] England (disregarding her colonial imperialism for

---

[3] Cf. Henry J. Ford, *The Rise and Growth of American Politics,* pp. 61ff.

It may be mentioned, incidentally, that for this very reason it becomes very difficult for either England or the United States to impose their oligarchic-democratic systems upon conquered nations. The hybrid systems not only limit specific definition but also present a major problem to the British and American mentors in determining where to establish the balance of power. The tacit assumption appears to be that the balance existing at home will be transferred to the foreign country, but even at home it is always under a potential threat of disruption.

It should be expected also that these very promoters of "democracy" abroad, because of their origin in the hybrid states, may have quite different conceptions of their mission according as they lean toward the oligarchic or the democratic side of the parent system. In this enterprise of indoctrinating foreign peoples in the theory and practice of democracy, Russia may be the most decided and specific, because, although that country has not yet fully achieved democracy, it is very much less divided by the ideologies of two major conflicting systems.

[4] *Democracy and Socialism,* p. 357; see also pp. 3–10.

[5] Concerning the democratic movement, Professor Carl L. Becker remarks: "It will be said that in Russia the ideals of Communism are not in fact lived up to. That is true. It is also true that the ideals of democracy are not lived up to in the United States, England, or any other democratic country. . . . But the ideal

the moment) is far more worker-conscious than the United States, while Russia has already successfully fought her proletarian revolution. As fear of internal and external counterrevolution diminishes, the problem of abolishing the Russian proletarian dictatorship should be a relatively simple matter. In that country a clear democratic foundation has been established. On this point Dr. Frederick L. Schuman makes the following lively assertion:

> Only those observers who are invincibly ignorant, or blinded by irrational fear and hatred, will deny that the Soviet system of business and power has, for all its abuses and crudities, promoted the liberation of men from impoverishment, exploitation, illiteracy, and prejudice and served the cause of human dignity and self-respect on an immense scale. These purposes are of the essence of the democratic dream. In this sense the USSR is a democratic polity.[6]

Meaning and Significance of Modern Democracy

If we are to be consistent in the use of the concept democracy, it is necessary to define it. Democracy may be thought of either as a form of government or as a social system including the government. As a form of government—a political system in which "the people" participate in deciding matters of public interest—democracy has been common among primitive peoples and in ancient Greece and Rome. In this sense the Hindu village panchayat is a democracy.[7] In modern democracy,

---

forms are not to be despised or lost sight of for all that. . . . The worst thing that can be said about the Americans or the English or the Russians is that they do not live up to their ideal aims." *Freedom and Responsibility*, p. 105. See also Woodrow Wilson, *Constitutional Government of the United States*, p. 203.

The United States may be thought of as the "last great stronghold of capitalism." But for the financial and military aid of the United States, to say nothing of moral approbation, British imperialism would speedily come to an end. It is likely that there is greater antagonism in the United States to the democratic reforms in England than there is in England itself. Of some significance is the appearance of the British Prime Minister, Clement Attlee, in the winter of 1945, before the Congress of the United States in order to explain by various arts of oratory that the reforms of the British Labor Government are not really anti-capitalist. It should also be noted that this government was elected by vote of the British people.

[6]*Soviet Politics*, pp. 585–86. C. D. Burns observes: "This ideal of democracy, which has set Russia ablaze, burns as well if less fiercely in other lands." Op. cit., p. 284. See also E. H. Carr, *The Soviet Impact on the Western World*, p. 11.

[7]It was possible, by conceiving of "the word democracy" as a "formula and practice of suffrage—a mechanism of rule," for James Burnham (*The Machiavellians*, pp. 236–54) to show that almost any form of social system can exist under democracy; or indeed to show, to his own satisfaction at any rate, that democracy is not possible at all. This kind of thinking, however, tends to be a sort of historical game played with abstract definitions. It led Burnham to say that Henry A. Wallace's election "was not a voluntary expression of the will of the people at large" because Wallace is a "Bonapartist *mystique*" who tells the people particularly that "the new democracy, the democracy of the common man," included "economic

however, the form of government is not the crucial fact; it is rather the dependent instrument of a determinable democratic system.

Democracy as a social system is a modern phenomenon; it is significantly different from the ancient or primitive social systems. Moreover, it did not grow out of or develop as a higher *stage* of ancient democracy. In other words, modern democracy does not have its origin in Grecian democracy any more than does the modern factory system. Above all, we should be misled by thinking of the democratic movement as primarily a developing system of ideologies or, as it is sometimes believed, a system of "foreign ideologies." The democratic movement is the most practical and insistent social force in Western society. Democracy as a social system is the direct outcome of the rise of capitalism, and it is essentially a system of economic and social organization; the form of government is being fashioned to facilitate this system. Within this context it has had three well-recognized periods of growth: that of "(1) the elimination of the vestiges of the old régime—the heritage of the middle ages; (2) the establishment of the liberal regime of the 'benevolent bourgeoisie'; and (3) the attack upon the supremacy of the bourgeoisie by the proletariat, beginning about the middle of the 19th century."[8]

Democracy, then, was made possible of achievement by the bourgeoisie, but it cannot be achieved by the bourgeoisie. In fact, the bourgeoisie is unalterably opposed to democracy.[9] The task of establishing a democracy necessarily devolves upon the proletariat, and its final accomplishment must inevitably mean its supersession of capitalism. We may put it in still another way: capitalism not only destroyed the old land economy but also gave birth to a new type of society which gains

---

democracy, ethnic democracy, educational democracy, and democracy in the treatment of the sexes."

In a play with the logic of a definition of the word Jean-Jacques Rousseau wrote: "To use the term in its rigorous acceptation, a true democracy has never existed, and will never exist. It is against the natural order of things that the majority should govern and the minority be governed. . . . If there were a people of gods its government would be democratic. So perfect a government is not suitable for men." *The Social Contract,* trans. by Rose M. Harrington, 2d ed., pp. 102, 104.

[8]Harry E. Barnes, "Democracy," *The Encyclopedia Americana,* 1940; see also by the same author, *The History of Western Civilization,* Vol. II, p. 489.

[9]Lord Acton makes this observation: "The deepest cause which made the French Revolution so disastrous *to liberty* was *the theory of equality.* Liberty was the watchword of the middle class [the bourgeoisie], equality of the lower [the proletariat]. It was the lower class that won the battles of the third estate; that took the Bastille, and made France a constitutional monarchy; that took the Tuileries, and made France a Republic. They claimed their reward. The middle class, having cast down the upper orders with the aid of the lower, instituted a new inequality and a privilege for itself." *The History of Freedom and Other Essays,* p. 88.

in relative strength and influence with the advancement of capitalism.

Modern democracy, therefore, is antagonistic to capitalism; the greater the development of democracy, the greater the limitations upon capitalist freedom and the stronger the proletariat. Thus, as history shows clearly, whatever fraction of democracy we possess today has been achieved in increments by and for the masses against the more or less violent opposition of bourgeois and even of remnant feudal classes. The great source of strength of the proletariat inheres not only in its indispensability to capitalist production, but also in its inevitable improvement in strategic position as capitalism develops. Moreover, the proletariat has been able to make certain periodic, democratic gains as a consequence of the military involvement of the bourgeoisie. Usually the bourgeoisie has had to make democratic concessions as a reward for the services of the proletariat both in the former's conflict with feudalism and among themselves internationally.

In its struggle for democracy, the first great aim of the proletariat everywhere has been the extension of the suffrage. Ordinarily, when a capitalist nation has conceded universal manhood suffrage, it is said to be a "political democracy."[10] The mere fact of universal suffrage and representative institutions, however, need not indicate the exact extent to which democracy has attained maturity. To the extent that the questions put to the people concern the welfare of capitalism, to that extent also the ballot is not in the service of the proletariat. For here "the people are a sovereign whose vocabulary is limited to two words, 'Yes' and 'No.' This sovereign, moreover, can speak only when spoken to."[10a] The focus of interest of democracy is in the well-being of the masses, and this interest cannot be made dependent upon the success or pleasure of businessmen.[10b] As Harold Laski observes: ". . . capitalist democracy was a compromise . . . approved by the capitalist so long as its democratic aspect did not threaten the foundations of capitalism."[11]

---

[10]"The British constitution . . . is the expression of a politically democratic government; it is not the expression of a democratic society. . . . Our society is, overwhelmingly, what Mr. Tawney has called an acquisitive society, and its main governmental apparatus is in the hands of those who have been themselves successful in acquisition." Harold J. Laski, *Parliamentary Government in England*, pp. 24–25, 27.

[10a]E. E. Schattsneider, *Party Government*, p. 52. See also William B. Munro, *The Government of European Cities*, p. 258.

[10b]President Calvin Coolidge put the capitalist conception of the people's welfare as follows: "We justify the greater and greater accumulation of capital because we believe that therefrom flows the support of all science, art, learning, and the charities which minister to the humanities of life, all carrying their beneficent effects to the people as a whole." Speech at Amherst College alumni dinner, New York, November 27, 1920.

[11]*Where Do We Go from Here?*, p. 30.

In a political democracy, such as that of the Northern states of the United States, political concessions give essentially every normal, adult individual the privilege of supporting a social system in which every individual has the theoretical right and opportunity to remain or to become bourgeois.

But the situation is dynamic. The masses and their leaders have been constantly seeking to take hold of this popular support of capitalism and to use it for the purpose of transferring economic power to themselves. In the words of Lewis Corey: "Bourgeois democracy, in the 'rights' it 'grants' the workers, now undermines capitalist rule where once it was sustenance and support."[12]

Clearly, then, accomplished democracy—democracy with its substance residing in the people—will be finally attained only when the democratic form has been fully impregnated with power to control the State and its economic resources. When the economic power of the State has been completely won from the bourgeois plutocracy by the great mass of people, the bourgeoisie will have, of course, been liquidated and capitalism will have come to an end. It is a realization such as this which prompted Rosa Luxemburg to say: "He who would strengthen democracy should want to strengthen and not weaken the socialist movement."[13]

In reality the essential fear of socialism is a fear of democracy, for socialism merely puts the government of the people into their own hands. To argue against socialism is not to argue against any known practice, existing or contemplated, but it is, rather, to argue against the capacity of a people to devise a system of practices most suitable to the utilization of their human and natural resources. The fear of socialism is a fear of the postulated ideals of the so-called democracies; it is a fear based upon the belief that the people cannot in fact run their society according to their best interest—in fine, the struggle for and against democracy is the struggle between the two great social systems of modern civilization.[14]

As we have previously observed, ever since about the time of the Cromwellian revolution an increasingly large proportion of the common

---

[12]Op. cit., p. 522.

[13]Op. cit., p. 41. Cf. Hans Kohn, op. cit., pp. 345–63.

[14]In his discussion of the economic basis of the Constitution of the United States, Charles A. Beard observes: "In turning over the hundreds of pages of writings left by eighteenth century thinkers one cannot help being impressed with the fact that the existence of a special problem of a working-class, then already sufficiently numerous to form a considerable portion of society, were outside the realm of politics, except in so far as the future power of the proletariat was foreseen and feared." *An Economic Interpretation of the Constitution of the United States,* p. 25.

people in Europe and in America has inched its way toward democracy. But it should be emphasized that the struggle for democracy is not a struggle against evil spirits or against "the wickedness of human nature"; it is in fact a struggle against an identifiable ruling class—against the form of government and social organization which the ruling vestigial-feudal or capitalist class constitutes and defends.

When, for instance, we hear it said that the British take their reforms by evolutionary and not by revolutionary methods, the meaning is that the British proletariat is confronted by one of the most powerfully entrenched ruling classes of modern times. The Whig-Tory combination, according to its political-class interest, has set its face against democracy, and only by virtually imperceptible degrees have the workers been able to nibble away certain democratic concessions. They have found their Nemesis principally in British "middle-class" liberalism—Manchester liberalism. As R. W. Postgate puts it: ". . . the history of the English working class reminds one of a helpless prisoner, knocking uselessly at one door, turning to the other, returning again to the first, and all in vain. The alternations of political radicalism, industrial Owenism, political Chartism, 'old' trade unionism, etc., succeed each other monotonously, and by neither door can the workers find an exit from their prison."[15]

Probably nothing illustrates so well the nature of the struggle for democracy against the capitalist oligarchy—in this case the British oligarchy—as the Chartist movement during the two decades preceding 1850. When the Chartists, the common working people, petitioned the liberal-conservative Parliament, among other things, for such "radical" reforms as universal manhood suffrage and the secret ballot, they were rejected and their bid for a degree of democracy violently put down. Moreover, what is of especial significance is the fact that the workers were clearly conscious of the extent and source of the physical might which opposed their democratic movement. Today, after long struggle, the British people have achieved these rights, but they do not yet have a democracy, and it is patently clear that they will not have a government of the people and by the people as a gift of the ruling class

Freedom and Democracy

One of the most persistent arguments of the capitalists and their apologists against democracy is that it destroys "freedom." Indeed, for

[15]*Revolution from 1789 to 1906,* p. 104.

most people in Western society the word "freedom" has acquired a certain rapturous stereotype on which the advocates of the status quo seldom fail to capitalize. This, of course, is not surprising, for the social trait is as old as capitalism itself—it is elemental in bourgeois civilization. And long before the rise of capitalism Christianity had associated freedom, spiritual freedom, with earthly peace and bliss—witness the power of the Gospels: "Ye shall know the truth, and the truth shall make you free." Occasionally even the proletariat may be so conditioned by this pervasive idea of "freedom" that it will yield to many an anti-democratic contention when confronted with the suggested possibility of interference with the integrity of "freedom."[16] Sometimes the public is designedly made to think of "freedom" as the opposite of confinement, as the opposite of imprisonment—a glad state of liberation. As a matter of fact, everybody wants "freedom"; and yet, no society will ever be able to secure unlimited, abstract freedom for its members. Every social system has definite potentialities for social freedom, and we can know what these are only by a study of the social system itself. Professor Harry D. Gideonse points out that "freedom always meant 'freedom' within a given framework of social institutions, legal standards and regulatory practices."[17]

Sometimes it is argued that capitalism has abolished the "slavery" of feudalism and has given the individual his freedom, the end toward which all civilization has been tending. To be sure, the fact that no one wanted individualism in a feudal society is seldom if ever brought out. As Erich Fromm observes: "Medieval society did not deprive the individual of his freedom, because the 'individual' did not yet exist."[18] Sometimes, indeed, there is a further implication that the modern trend toward democracy is a return to feudalism—"the road to serfdom," "the assault upon freedom," "the return to slavery."

As a form of social organization, however, socialism is the very antithesis of feudalism. If we can conceive of any similitude in the development of these two systems, it is this: Just as at the dawn of feudalism the smaller landowners gave up their holdings to tne great landlords and became his men in lieu of his protecting them against the lawless, raiding gangs who roamed over the country, so also the common people

---

[16]For a discussion of the meaning of bourgeois liberty, see John Strachey, op. cit., pp. 58–64; and for a summary of definitions of liberty see Arthur N. Holcomb, *The Foundations of the Modern Commonwealth*, pp. 253–94.

[17]"Freedom and Planning in International Economic Relations," in Findlay Mackenzie, ed., *Planned Society*, p. 679.

[18]*Escape from Freedom*, p. 43.

of modern times have increasingly become willing to give up their empty individualism in favor of concerted action against the powerful financial lords who exploit them and the resources of their country objectively, that is to say, in their own individual interest, without mercy.[19] In liquidating the feudal ruling class the bourgeoisie substituted themselves as masters of the common people.

But is it really true that freedom is lost in a democracy—that we cannot have democracy and freedom too? Is bourgeois freedom the only human freedom? As a matter of fact, it may be shown that the social history of Western society from feudalism to socialism has been the history of a continually widening base of freedom—movement from a social situation in which the masses were totally non-political objects to one in which they may become full-fledged determiners of their social destiny. Feudalism, to be sure, had its freedom and its power. The nobility, which possessed freedom and power, was quite willing to die for their perpetuation. Under feudalism the possession of land gave the individual power and freedom, just as under capitalism the possession of great wealth gives the individual power and freedom. Now, for the first time in history, the masses have become ready to capture the source of freedom. Democracy will turn power and freedom over to the people. The bourgeoisie destroyed the freedom of the feudal nobility so that they themselves might be free, and the common people, the proletariat, are now seeking to destroy bourgeois freedom so that they themselves may be free. The latter is a struggle for the positive freedom

---

[19]In discussing the development of individualism Erich Fromm concludes: ". . . the individual became more alone, isolated, became an instrument in the hands of overwhelmingly strong forces outside of himself; he became an 'individual,' but a bewildered and insecure individual." Op. cit., p. 120.

Freedom, as a social trait of capitalist society, means individualism; in caste or feudal societies there is neither necessity nor desire for individualism. In the caste system the nearest approach to individualism is that social condition of isolation achieved by outcastes, a state which has been termed "living death." Freedom, in the sense of absence of restraint upon the individual, is a rather non-significant concept for the study of social systems. Only God is free from and independent of physical and social restraints. But for this very reason the discussion of freedom in the latter sense is valuable for propaganda purposes. There is surely an elemental human desire for freedom in the sense of absence of "restraints." An infant of tender age could be put into violent rage by simply pinning down his legs and arms. This, however, is not the idea of bourgeois freedom. Once upon a time a Northern banker stopped to joke with a janitor of his bank. Said he, "I am disgusted with all these wartime bureaus and red tape; they show just what one will have to go through in a communist system. Here it is almost a week since my doctor advised me to go to Florida for my health, and I still haven't my allowance of gas for the trip. Give me a free society any time." To this the janitor replied: "Well, sir, ever since I was born I have never been free nor ever shall be free to go to Florida for my health. Your freedom has been restrained for a week—mine for a lifetime." As Sidney and Beatrice Webb point out: "There is no freedom where there is no opportunity of taking advantage of it." *Soviet Communism: A New Civilization,* p. 1034.

of all the people.[20] In addition, the proletariat will gain a negative freedom: *freedom from exploitation.*

The nature of capitalist freedom was recognized long ago. For instance, in his criticism of the French Declaration of the Rights of Man (April 24, 1793), Maximilien Robespierre declared: "You have multiplied articles to ensure the *greatest freedom in the exercise of property,* and have not said a single word to define its legitimate character; so that your Declaration seems made not for men, but for the wealthy, the monopolists, the stockjobbers and the tyrants."[20a] And Charles A. Beard declares: "The [United States] Constitution was essentially an economic document based upon the concept that the fundamental private rights of property are anterior to government and morally beyond the reach of popular majorities."[21] Indeed, the basis of all bourgeois freedom is freedom of the market and of exploitation, and the correlative freedom of the common people is very largely freedom to be exploited.[22]

In reality, it is not "freedom" which is in question but rather two distinct brands of freedom struggling for ascendancy: freedom of the few as over against freedom of the masses. These two kinds of freedom, capitalist and democratic, are inversely correlated. Again Charles A. Beard observes in his study of early bourgeois tendencies in the United States: ". . . the crowning counterweight to 'an interested and overbearing majority,' as Madison phrased it, was secured in the peculiar position assigned to the judiciary, and the use of the sanctity and mystery of the law as a foil to democratic attacks."[23] Capitalism constricts

---

[20]Speaking of the rise of capitalism, J. L. Hammond and Barbara Hammond observe: "For the working classes the most important fact about that wealth was that it was wealth in dangerous disorder, for unless these new forces could be brought under control of the common will, the power that was flooding the world with its lavish gifts was destined to become a fresh menace to the freedom and happiness of men." *The Town Labourer, 1760–1832,* p. 16.

[20a]See R. W. Postgate, *Revolutions from 1789 to 1906,* p. 44.

[21]Op. cit., p. 324.

[22]In their *Communist Manifesto* Marx and Engels put it in this way: "[The bourgeois system] has resolved personal worth into exchange value, and in place of numberless indefeasible chartered freedoms, has set up that single, unconscionable freedom—Free Trade. In one word, for exploitation, veiled by religious and political illusions, it has substituted naked, shameless, direct, brutal exploitation." P. 15. And Carl L. Becker illustrates the point further: "For the owners of the English cotton mills in the 1830's freedom of contract was a cherished liberty, but for the anemic women and children who contracted to work in the mills because the alternative was starvation, it was a species of wage slavery." Op. cit., p. 3. To the same effect see John Strachey, op. cit., pp. 63–64. It is to this idea of liberty which Abraham Lincoln referred in saying: "Plainly, the sheep and the wolf are not agreed upon a definition of the word 'liberty.' "

[23]Op. cit., p. 161. Sometimes even political thinkers of the stature of former Vice-President Henry A. Wallace may confuse hopelessly the meaning of freedom and democracy as they developed and function in modern society. Says Wallace in his

the freedom of the people, so that they are more or less impotent to act in accordance with their own welfare. The people are not free when a relatively few masters of industry could deny them the control of their resources. Under capitalist freedom the people may not eat or shelter themselves unless, in the production of food and shelter, some individual makes a profit. On the contrary, democratic freedom aims to put power—economic power—into the hands of the people themselves. With the achievement of democracy they will, as never before, be able to decide how and when their resources should be spent.

It is interesting to observe the way in which Professor Friedrich A. Hayek states the conditions of capitalist freedom:

It is only because the control of the means of production is divided among many people acting independently that nobody has complete power over us, that we as individuals can decide what to do with ourselves. If all the means of production were vested in a single hand, whether it be nominally that of "society" as a whole or that of a dictator, whoever exercises this control has complete power over us.[24]

In this passage Hayek does not put the question fairly; yet it indicates very clearly the great fear: the fear of democracy. If the resources, the means of production, are vested in "society," the people will not have "complete power over us," but rather *complete power over themselves*.[25] In a "democracy the State will be the political organization of

great speech, "The Price of Free World Victory," May 8, 1942: "The idea of freedom—the freedom that we in the United States know and love so well—is derived from the Bible with its extraordinary emphasis on the dignity of the individual. Democracy is the only true political expression of Christianity."

[24]*The Road to Serfdom*, p. 104. We shall quote rather extensively from this work because it expresses the anti-democratic attitude of the capitalist class quite effectively. On the question in point Hayek repeatedly makes a spurious analogy between a monopolist, as we have come to know this fearful creature, and a democratic society: "Our freedom of choice in a competitive society rests on the fact that, if one person refuses to satisfy our wishes, we can turn to another. But if we face a monopolist we are at his mercy. And an authority directing the whole economic system would be the most powerful monopolist conceivable." Ibid., p. 93. Here the purpose appears to be to frighten the people with the prospect that they will create a Frankenstein if they were permitted to control their resources.

For a rather normative discussion of freedom with an obvious inclination to identify capitalist individualism with social freedom, see Frank H. Knight, "The Meaning of Freedom" and "The Ideal of Freedom," in Charner M. Perry, ed., *The Philosophy of American Democracy*. With a similar purpose but more artificial approach, see Gerard de Gre, "Freedom and Social Structure," *American Sociological Review*, Vol. XI, October 1946, pp. 529–36.

[25]Sidney and Beatrice Webb, in their discussion of attempts to establish a democracy in the USSR, observe: ". . . what is being built up in the USSR is not a government apart from the mass of the people, exercising authority over them. What they believe themselves to be constructing is a new type of social organization in which the people themselves, in their threefold capacity of citizens, producers and consumers, unite to realize the good life. This is in fact not a state in the old sense

all citizens, who are subjects only as instruments of or as obedient to the regulations made by themselves."[26] Under capitalism the people cannot have complete power over themselves for, in their attempts to achieve this, they are continually frustrated by private masters. To get this power they must first get it over the capitalists and their private officials. Moreover, compared with the total population, the individuals who control the means of production are not "many" but few.[27] In the United States in 1944, 60 per cent of the industrial workers were employed by 2 per cent of the manufacturing concerns. In regard to this fact and with reference to certain abstract freedoms of British citizens, Sir William H. Beveridge concludes:

> This list of essential liberties . . . does not include liberty of a private citizen to own means of production and to employ other citizens in operating them at a wage. Whether private ownership of means of production to be operated by others is a good economic device or not, it must be judged as a device. It is not an essential citizen liberty in Britain, because it is not and never has been enjoyed by more than a very small proportion of the British people. It cannot even be suggested that any considerable proportion of the people have any lively hope of gaining such ownership later.[28]

And, indeed, to the extent that these "independent" few control the national resources they control our lives—literally our very existence. Here a major freedom is sacrificed in the interest of individualism. But the unmistakable tendency of the masses is toward the recapture of that major freedom which will give them the right to control themselves through the purposeful control of their resources. Even so, however, the crux of the matter is not merely the fact of numbers in control; it is rather the question of social motivation and economic interests. J. L.

---

of the word, but an organized plan of living which the people as a whole adopt." *Soviet Communism: A New Civilization*, p. 1072. For a time, no doubt, that political class—numerically a small minority of the total population—in whose interest Professor Hayek is speaking, will surely feel that it is being ruled over. But as other vanquished classes have accommodated themselves to new systems, so also we should expect this one to become reconciled to democracy.

[26]C. D. Burns, op. cit., p. 283.

[27]"If democracy was to live," as Professor Avery Craven sees it historically, "the emphasis had to shift from [bourgeois] freedom to equality. If men were to be equal, however, they could no longer achieve equality for themselves. Government would have to become more active. Democracy would be a choice from then on. It would have to be planned if it were to continue to exist. And all this in the face of strong men . . . who had no interest or desire for either freedom or equality for anyone except themselves." *Democracy in American Life*, p. 143.

[28]Op. cit., p. 23. It should be mentioned, however, that this argument is not entirely consistent with capitalism, for a fundamental assumption of capitalism is that the means of production should be accumulated by competition in the open market as private property—this is capitalist freedom.

and Barbara Hammond, in their discussion of the beginnings of modern industrialism, point out:

> The new industry increased human power to a remarkable degree, and it seemed to this oligarchy the most natural thing in the world that the economic should resemble the political structure, and that in the mill, as in the State, all this power should be concentrated in the hands of a few men, who were to act and think for the rest. Economic science seemed to add a sanction to the law of inequality for it showed that the sovereign authority of capital was the condition of success in the world trade. In industrial as in political life, the mass of men must be content with an obedience that asks no questions. Thus the new industry, instead of guiding mankind to a new experience of freedom, common to all classes, confirmed the power of the few, and made the mass of men still less their own masters.[29]

The capitalist minority who contends that the minor freedom, individualism, is the better and more precious one is anti-democratic. It should be recognized, however, that on this very ground the modern class struggle is joined, and the final test is ordinarily revolution. In this way the people will be called upon to demonstrate conclusively "that the mass of mankind has not been born with saddles on their backs, nor a favored few booted and spurred, ready to ride them legitimately, by the grace of God." To paraphrase one writer: Democracy gives the people a chance; what they make of that chance is still their affair.[29a]

It is significant that although the reactionary, capitalist economists can assure the high bourgeoisie tremendous material values in the continuance of capitalism, they have virtually nothing except "freedom" to offer the great masses of people. They contend that a hungry man with bourgeois freedom is better off than an economically secure worker with democratic freedom. Consider in illustration the reasoning of Professor Walter E. Spahr as he opposes a bill to assure employment to the workers of the United States:

> Continuing full employment cannot be assured in a *free* society [that is to say, under capitalism]. If this bill should become law, the probable effect would be to discourage rather than to encourage private enterprise. . . . The Federal Government will have assumed an explicit responsibility for "full" employment, and for unemployment in this country. . . . A basic question presented to the people of the United States by the Full Employment Bill is whether their thinking and activities are to continue in the direction of *preserving and enlarging the freedom of the individual*

---

[29]Op. cit., p. 324.
[29a]John Strachey, *Socialism Looks Forward*, p. 121.

or whether they are to follow those of Socialist-Communist-Authoritarian Europe.[30]

The name calling at the end of the last sentence is a common propagandistic device. At any rate, the Full Employment Bill is simply another attempt of the workers and their leaders to push democracy another step forward, and, to be sure, it runs head on into a clash with the interests behind "free enterprise." It is, indeed, a bold and tragic irony that the most determined antagonist of the common people should submit to them the very essence of its privilege and power, bourgeois freedom, as a basis of arguments intended to confuse and distract them.

Professor Hayek does the same thing in this way. Says he:

> Even though some workmen will perhaps be better fed, and all will no doubt be more uniformly dressed in that new order, it is permissible to doubt whether the majority of English workmen will in the end thank the intellectuals among their leaders who have presented them with a socialist doctrine which endangers their personal freedom.[31]

Here the worker is asked to look upon democracy with apprehension. The people themselves, it is intimated, will be unable to fashion anything better than this demi-paradise of bourgeois freedom; they will regiment themselves, to their own dissatisfaction and disgust. Thus the trend toward democracy becomes "the road to serfdom." In fact, one corroding fear of modern democracy is that it will reduce all persons in the society to the level of the "degenerate masses."[32] This, however, could never be an end of democracy, for it does not drag down but lifts

---

[30]"Full Employment in Exchange for What?" *The Commercial and Financial Chronicle,* September 27, 1945. (Italics added.) In a two-volume work written in collaboration by twenty-one "top-flight economists and businessmen" as a commission of the National Association of Manufacturers, the conclusion is reached "that the authors and contributors base their whole approach on the dignity, indeed on the sanctity of the individual as individual." *The American Individual Enterprise System,* by Commission of National Association of Manufacturers, New York and London, 1946, p. xi. It is not, it seems, that we do not like socialism, for we have been inevitably going in its direction. Strachey agrees with Spahr in this way: ". . . it is perfectly possible to do away with mass unemployment, even before the present economic system has been fully abolished; but it can only be done by measures which will seriously modify the system, and take an appreciable step toward socialism." Op. cit., p. 99.

[31]Op. cit., pp. 199–200. For a just, though merciless criticism of Hayek, see Herman Finer, *Road to Reaction.* Finer's own position, however, is weak; he seems to have no sense of the economic potentialities of social systems and of social movements.

[32]Lecky put this argument characteristically: "One of the great divisions of politics in our day is coming to be whether . . . the world should be governed by its ignorance or by its intelligence. According to one party, the preponderating power should be with education and property. According to the other, the ultimate source of power, the supreme right of appeal and control, belongs legitimately to the

up the civilization. In a democracy there will be no need for a "multitude of ignorant poor." Here progress can have but one meaning: continual advancement in enlightenment and physical welfare of all the people.[33]

The argument, however, is almost beside the point, for it is not particularly that the ruling class fears that the masses lack the ability to govern themselves, since it has never taken the initiative in the preparation of the people for self-government. Rather it is a self-interested objection to any relinquishment of its power to control the social system, power which this class conceives to be naturally beyond the constitutional right of the people. Democracy is thus thought of as an unjust, irrational usurpation—an unconscionable dishonesty—which the leaders of the people seek to impose upon the rightful and traditional owners of the business system. From this point of view democracy is wrong, disorderly, and larcenous—a movement which should be and ordinarily is put down by the organized might of the capitalist state.

Individualism and Democracy Incompatible

Quite frequently, even among persons who call themselves socialists, it is not clearly seen that, the greater the advancement of democracy, the greater also will be the limitations upon individualism.[34] Yet the

---

majority of the nation—or, in other words, to the poorest, the most ignorant, the most incapable, who are necessarily the most numerous.

"It is a theory which assuredly reverses all the past experience of mankind. In every field of human enterprise, in all the competitions of life, by the inexorable law of Nature, superiority lies with the few and not with the many, and success can only be attained by placing the guiding and controlling power mainly in their hands. . . . Surely nothing in ancient alchemy was more irrational than the notion that increased ignorance in the elective body will be converted into increased capacity for good government in the representative body. . . . The day will come when it will appear one of the strangest facts . . . that such a theory was regarded as liberal and progressive." Op. cit., pp. 25–26.

Guido de Ruggiero puts the same idea in this way: "The evil of democracy is not the triumph of quantity, but the triumph of *bad quality*, which is revealed by numbers no less clearly than by every other manifestation of the democratic spirit." *The History of European Liberalism*, p. 376. (Italics Ruggiero's.)

[33]"Some people think," says Joseph Stalin, "that socialism can be consolidated by a certain equalization of people's material conditions, based on a poor man's standard of living. This is not true. . . . In point of fact, socialism can succeed only on the basis of a high productivity of labor, higher than under capitalism, on the basis of an abundance of products and of articles of consumption of all kinds, on the basis of a prosperous and cultured life for all members of the society." *Leninism,* p. 367.

[34]On this score Max Eastman apparently makes a questionable reference to Karl Marx: "Marx was the first to see . . . that the evolution of private capitalism with its free market had been a precondition for the evolution of all democratic freedoms. It never occurred to him . . . that if this was so, these other freedoms might disappear with the abolition of the free market." Quoted by Carl L. Becker, op. cit., p. 89.

process of democratic development may be defined as a continually increasing limitation of individual freedom (i.e., individualism) in favor of greater social equality and freedom for the masses. Although his purpose is to condemn democracy, Hayek is essentially right in saying:

There can be no doubt that most socialists . . . still believe profoundly in the liberal ideal of freedom and that they would recoil if they became convinced that the realization of their program would mean the destruction of freedom.[35]

It must be admitted that the opportunities which bourgeois freedom presents, the remote chances of the worker's becoming economically powerful and of his ruling over the lives of others privately and individualistically, are precious values of capitalism. Yet nothing should be clearer than that we cannot have "freedom," as Professor Hayek conceives of it—i.e., the *laissez faire* individualism of capitalism—and have democracy also.[36] In this regard J. A. Hobson states, ". . . excessive stress on individual liberty becomes an obstacle to the true growth of democracy."[37] Thus, democracy and competitive individualism are incompatible; and the trend of modern civilization is inevitably against this sort of freedom. As Henry Pratt Fairchild observes: "What is of importance to the modern man is not freedom to do as he likes as an individual, but freedom to decide the kind of society he wishes to live in. Social liberty is the twentieth-century desideratum. . . . Only through social liberty can there be attained that form of personal freedom which is harmonious with the conditions of modern life."[38]

If the resources of a people are to be controlled by that people in the interest of its own welfare, the economic interest of the individual cannot be allowed to stand in the way. And, conversely, if the profit-

---

[35]Op. cit., p. 31.

[36]Lord Acton is responsible for some considerable part of the abstract thinking about freedom. He conceives of freedom as a supra-social phenomenon instinctively sought after in all times and places as "the highest political end" by men of good will, but frequently withheld or defeated by the wicked. Thus, without much regard to the social origin of beliefs, Acton asserts: "By liberty I mean the assurance that every man shall be protected in doing what he believes his duty against the influence of authority and majorities, custom and opinion." Op. cit., p. 3.

The following is an argument by James Burnham based upon "human nature" as a static, instinctual phenomenon out of which "freedom" or "despotism" unfolds: "A considerable degree of liberty is not usual in human society. If we review the history of humanity, so far as we know it, it is apparent that despotic regimes are far more frequent than free regimes, and it would therefore seem that despotism is more nearly than freedom in accord with human nature." Op. cit., p. 250.

[37]Op. cit., p. 13.

[38]*Profits or Prosperity*, p. 199.

making interest of the entrepreneur is to be served, the welfare of the people cannot be allowed to stand in the way, here the people's welfare could never become a primary purpose of production.

Under capitalism a profit maker is free to exploit the human and natural resources of the people in his own interest; a slum dweller is free to live and die in filth. The new freedom of democracy is the freedom of the people so to govern themselves that they may be able to make judgments which can limit these minor freedoms. The people in a democracy may decide without hindrance both that slums should be cleared and that the individual who makes a profit from slums should give up that right. There is a loss of one kind of freedom and a gain of another; we cannot have them both. A labor union, the core of proletarian action, tends to destroy the freedom of the employer to develop and to patronize the cheapest labor market; it also destroys the freedom of the worker to sell his labor in such a market. If "freedom from want" is not just another euphonious cliché of "the democracies," it must necessarily mean some substitution of proletarian freedom for capitalist freedom. Sir William H. Beveridge is in point when, in consideration of employment specifically, he declares: "To ask for full employment while objecting to these extensions of State activity is to will the end and refuse the means."[39] It is both a practical and an ideological contradiction to desire bourgeois freedom and social equality at the same time.[40] In the words of Professor Fritz Fleiner, *"Demokratie und individuelle Freiheit sind Gegensätze."*[40a]

Sometimes it is intimated that capitalism is basically interested in "the fundamental value and dignity" of the individual. This conclusion is seldom if ever demonstrated, but it is ordinarily associated with individualism. As a matter of fact, however, democracy is the supreme champion of individual worth and personal value because it reaches down irresistibly and facilitates the political upthrust of that major group of persons known as the masses; it concerns itself with the personalization of the least privileged individuals. Democracy tends to con-

---

[39] Op. cit., p. 36. But the significant fact is the inevitability of this trend. As Carl Becker points out: ". . . there is really no use in saying we do not want any form of collectivism or managed economy . . . no use, that is, in saying we do not want any sort of governmental regulation of private economic enterprise. We already have a good deal of it; and it is about as certain as anything can be that we shall have more." Op. cit., p. 106.

This does not mean to say, however, that every economic activity of a socialist state will be finally centralized. In a democracy the people will be the arbiter of any question concerning the degree of centralization of production.

[40] Cf. Karl Mannheim, *Ideology and Utopia*, pp. 183–84.

[40a] *Schweizerisches Bundesstaatsrecht*, p. 25.

fer upon every individual a priceless sense of wantedness in the society —a sense of being a recognized part of a supremely vital organization. By this means alone the individual is able to form a positive conception of himself as a responsible social object. On the other hand, individualism champions the cause of the successful few and of the ablest; it despises the weak and jealously withholds its privileges and recognition from the common people.

As we have seen, the social system in which individualism functions typically is deaf and icy toward the welfare of individuals who cannot compel the attention of the oligarchy. In this system the individual is ordinarily presumed to be worthless until he is able to prove his worth. Therefore, paradoxically, the greater the measure of capitalist individual liberty, the greater the tendency to define the individual as having no intrinsic social worth. Capitalism seeks to atomize and segregate the individuals who constitute the masses of common people, not because of an inherent solicitude and respect for the rights and political influence of these individuals but because by means of their atomization their political influence and economic power may be nullified. Thus, the same ideal of individualism, which augments the dignity and power of the members of the ruling class, serves, when applied to the masses, as a powerful weapon of oppression and abasement. The value which individualism recognizes in the common people is a "use value."

There seems to be no theoretical reason for believing that in a society which abhors individualism the people will feel any need for it. Socialism, the system of democracy, is not simply capitalism without individualism; it is rather a distinct social system in which bourgeois individualism does not function. In a democracy one cannot "spend" his individualism because it is not one of the values of democracy. In a democracy one derives his life satisfactions through the welfare of his fellows and not by "objectively" seeking to wring as much as he can out of them for his private enjoyment. Democracy will probably give social reality to Christianity, a perennial desideratum of Western society. Those highly atomized conflicts and rivalries among individuals under capitalism will be quieted, so that the power of the group will be pooled and augmented for the task of mastering its environment expeditiously and economically. When individualism has lost its claim to indispensability in the social system, it may be viewed critically; and the likelihood is that it will then seem so absurd that only its disadvantages, which certainly are many, will be emphasized. For it cannot be gainsaid that individualism, in its negative aspects, is a separative, indifferent, unbrotherly, selfish, gloating, antagonistic, predatory, asocial attitude.[40b] Those who desire individualism with the abolishment of capitalism are not socialists but anarchists, and consequently unpredictable utopians.[41]

Capitalism and the Fear of Democracy

Bourgeois society tends increasingly to become *amoral,* and consequently more fearful and militaristic. The morality to which the present-day capitalists ordinarily pay lip service is the morality of democracy; notwithstanding this, however, their practice and interest must be sternly anti-democratic. Thus it becomes exceedingly urgent for capitalist social scientists to attack the social structure of democracy.

Sometimes it is argued that democratic institutions themselves will not work; a democracy may be ruled by the ignorant. Accordingly, Hayek stresses the ineffectiveness of democratic assemblies: "The inability of democratic assemblies to carry out what seems to be a clear mandate of the people will inevitably cause dissatisfaction with democratic institutions."[42] And he points out further that a people organized democratically will have no means of controlling their own resources: "For such a task [direction of the resources of the nation] the system of majority decision is . . . not suited. . . . A democratic assembly voting and amending a comprehensive economic plan clause by clause . . . makes nonsense. . . . Even if a parliament could, proceeding step by step, agree on some scheme, it would certainly in the end satisfy nobody."[43]

[40b]So, indeed, for example, J. Ellis Baker, historian of the Netherlands, has already done in his criticism of the Dutch burgher politicians of the seventeenth century: ". . . all sense of national cohesion, of community of interest, of responsibility, of duty and of self-sacrifice, had been killed, by an anti-national and immoral policy pursued by [the burghers], which, in the name of individualism and of utilitarianism, had elevated the part above the whole, had created universal anarchy, and had inculcated deliberate and sordid selfishness in all by teaching that each individual should work for his own profit, thus increasing to the utmost the vice of selfishness . . ." *The Rise and Decline of the Netherlands,* p. 391.

[41]Not even Henry A. Wallace, who wrote a book to emphasize the trend toward human welfare in modern society, has been able to abandon one of the horns of this dilemma. "Can economic mechanisms be found," he inquires, "which will enable all of us over a great continent to work not only for our own ends but for the general welfare? . . . Can this be done without losing the personal privileges and liberties which we prize as the essence of democracy?" And he answers: "The philosophy of the future will endeavour to reconcile the good which is in the competitive, individualistic, and libertarian concept of the nineteenth century and the co-operative concepts which . . . seem destined to dominate the late twentieth century." *Whose Constitution,* pp. 308, 311.

[42]Op. cit., p. 62.

[43]Ibid., p. 64.

In fact, according to Hayek, a democracy will destroy itself in the very act of attempting to make plans for the utilization of its resources:

. . . agreement that planning is necessary, together with the inability of democratic assemblies to produce a plan, will evoke stronger and stronger demands that the government or some single individual should be given powers to act on their own responsibility. The belief is becoming more and more widespread that, if things are to get done, the responsible authorities must be freed from the fetters of democratic procedure.[44]

Probably as good an illustration as any of the place of democracy, or socialism, in the class struggle is the subtle way in which it is sometimes identified even with fascism. It should be remembered that it has been convenient, during and after World War II, for certain fascists who live in "the democracies" to criticize fascism. This practice may have a double value: (a) it is likely to divert the attention of the reader from the fascist character of the arguments, and (b) it may give the advocate an opportunity to transfer any developed antagonism against fascism to socialism by identifying socialism with fascism and then directing public hate against both of them under some such dissimulative caption as "totalitarianism." Observe, for instance, the way in which Professor Hayek accomplishes the latter end. First he cites Peter Drucker as "justly" expressive of his views:

The complete collapse of the belief in the attainability of freedom and equality through Marxism has forced Russia to travel the same road toward totalitarianism, purely negative non-economic society of unfreedom and inequality, which Germany has been following. Not that communism and fascism are essentially the same. Fascism is the stage reached after communism has proved an illusion and it has proved as much an illusion in Stalinist Russia as in pre-Hitler Germany.[45]

To be sure, it cannot be shown that Hitler overthrew a communist society in Germany; it is true, however, that he was instrumental in overthrowing the democratic efforts of the Spanish people in favor of fascism. This is not a "stage"; it is a counterrevolution. Indeed, but for the wisdom of the Russian leadership, Germany, with the help of the capitalist nations, would have done to Russia what she did to Spain. The conflict situation here is consistent with the theory of the class struggle.[46] At any rate, after preparing his readers with the stereotyped

---

[44]Ibid., p. 67.

[45]Ibid., p. 29; cited from Peter Drucker, *The End of Economic Man*, 1939, p. 230.

[46]Since this device of Hayek and his authority seems to be part of a system of anti-Russian antagonism, we shall cite John Strachey's summary of persistent capitalist aggression as a means of setting it in its proper perspective: "It is largely we [the

concept, "totalitarianism," Hayek proceeds to show "how closely related" communism and fascism are:

It is true that in Germany before 1933, and in Italy before 1922, communists and Nazis or Fascists clashed more frequently with each other than with other parties. They competed for the support of the same type of mind and reserved for each other the hatred of the heretic. But their practice shows how closely they are related. To both, the real enemy, the man with whom they had nothing in common and whom they could not hope to convince, is *the liberal of the old type*. While to the Nazi the communist, and to the communist the Nazi, and to both the socialist, are potential recruits . . . they both know that there can be no compromise between them and *those who really believe in individual freedom*.[47]

The counterrevolutionary practices of the fascists, the defenders of a decadent capitalist society, and the revolutionary practices of the democratic forces within capitalism may evince certain traits which are common to them as conflict groups; it would be sheer nonsense, however, to assume that these revolutionary traits identify them as social systems. We should emphasize that capitalist reactionaries ordinarily do not admire fascism; they accept it only as a last resort in the face of a serious threat from democracy. Yet they do not always see clearly that fascism is the only retrogressive system available to them at this stage in the transformation of capitalism.

British] and the other capitalist States of the world who have made Russia tough. First we made war on her; then we subsidized all the Russian landowners and capital owners who had been turned out, to make war on her; then we drew what we called a 'sanitary cordon' round her; then we boycotted her; then we refused her all credits; then we refused to make common cause with her against the Nazis, hoping they would attack her. And now people are surprised because she is very tough, pretty rough, depends on nobody but herself, and trusts nobody but herself.

"Russia has been through unspeakable difficulties and sufferings, of which the German invasion was only the last: but she has been through them, and has come out one of the strongest nations on earth. This giant strength of Russia is built on the concrete foundations of a socialist economic system." Op. cit., p. 129.

[47]Op. cit., pp. 29–30. (Italics added.) But observe how Professor Carl L. Becker compares the two systems: "Communism is democratic—that is, the dictatorship is regarded as temporary, a necessary device for carrying through the revolution, to be replaced ultimately by a government of, by, and for the people; Fascism is anti-democratic—the dictatorship and the suppression of individual liberties are regarded as permanent. Communism is international—it preaches the brotherhood of man and the equality of nations; Fascism is anti-international—it denies the equality of nations as well as the equality of individuals, and preaches the supremacy of the nation or of the master-race. Communism is pro-intellectual—it declares that social progress rests on knowledge, and that knowledge can be attained only by the disinterested search for truth; Fascism is anti-intellectual—it regards science and the search for truth as of no importance except in so far as they can be used for the attainment of immediate political ends." Op. cit., p. 104.

This, then, is what the modern social revolution amounts to. It involves the taking over of the businessman's society, fashioned by him in his own interest, by the masses of the people who at one time lived in that society only by suffrance—lived in it and had value only in so far as the traders and manufacturers were able to use them in the furtherance of business interests. From one point of view it may seem presumptuous that the masses of people should now declare that "democracy" demands that the material and productive wealth of the nation should be taken out of the hands of its traditional heirs, the business oligarchs, and utilized in the interest and welfare of all the people —that within the same urban, capitalist milieu the descendants of the totally non-political common people should today ask that their voice be given equal weight in the control of available economic resources. This, however, is exactly what modern democracy means; and it is with reference to its achievement that we logically use the phrase, "the coming new world."

Democracy, therefore, is the great social movement against which the bourgeoisie have been constantly struggling, and in doing so they have sought alliance even with the anachronistic feudal ruling class and the medieval Church. The achievement of the goal of this movement, as we have attempted to show, must necessarily mean the end of capitalism. But with the coming of democracy the people of the world will, for the first time, possess a social morality sufficient to cope with their advancement in technology. They will then not find it necessary, as they now do, to pervert their social scientists in the interest of human exploitation; but rather there will be every reason for encouraging the development of a science of human welfare with normal potentialities to make contributions to human happiness equal or even greater than those of the physical sciences. It is to this end which the distinguished British social scientists, Sidney and Beatrice Webb, referred, when they wrote:

The principle of universalism, on which . . . the provision for health, schooling, training for life and choice of occupation is based in the USSR, with its drastic ousting of all disqualifications of sex or race, inferiority of social position or lack of means, necessarily implies a vast unloosing of human energy, a great increase in available capacity, and, at least, a not inconsiderable development of genius that would otherwise not have been able to fructify. . . . It looks as if nowhere in the world—not even in the United States—is there so much variety and diversity in the choice of employments effectively open to every member of the population as in the USSR. And this diversity and multiplicity of occupation and employment is continuously increasing with the growth and extension, throughout the vast area, of an ever more nearly complete social equality. . . .[48]

---

[48]Op. cit., pp. 1023–24.

In corroboration Schuman writes: "The Russian adventure makes a long forward stride toward human mastery of man's fate through the deliberate mobilization of collective intelligence for the definition of community goals and the planned application, on a vast scale, of scientific knowledge for social betterment. The blind, plant-like growth of folk cultures, and the dynamic but uncontrollable automatism of the laissez-faire economies of the early machine age, here give way to the purposeful guidance of all activities of production and distribution." Op. cit., p. 582.

13. *A Close-up of the Class Struggle*

*I*F THE THEORETICAL DISCUSSION OF THE CLASS STRUGGLE IN THE preceding three chapters has any value, it is to be found primarily in its usefulness as a means of understanding the contemporary maneuvers of the two great political classes. Every day in the newspapers the story of the class struggle is being told; ordinarily—since the end of World War II especially—some fifty to one hundred per cent of the front-page news of the metropolitan dailies is concerned with it. To be sure, the news is not always unbiased; yet it emphasizes the increasing tempo and excitement in a colossal struggle for power. In the United States this crystallization of class antagonism goes back to the depression of 1929 and the administration of President Roosevelt. To study Franklin D. Roosevelt and his administration, therefore, is to have an opportunity to observe the deep forces of the class struggle from a particularly advantageous point of view.

Because of his ideology and practice, in part, Roosevelt gave definition to the diffused class antagonism and brought the ruling class into a desperate consciousness for reaction. As he himself pointed out: "The program of the New Deal involved the most controversial social questions in the last seventy-five years of our history. Tremendous interests were at stake—interests which would hesitate at nothing to gain their ends."[1] Indeed, not simply individual interests but the very place of the capitalist class in the system came immediately into question.[2]

The coincidence of the personality of Roosevelt with that period in

---

[1] Samuel I. Rosenman, ed., *The Public Papers and Addresses of Franklin D. Roosevelt*, Vol. 6, p. lxii.

[2] Gerald W. Johnson puts it pointedly: "Popular uprisings are familiar enough in our political history. It is part of the techniques of every campaign to assert the existence of an uprising, and the party out of power makes every effort to create one. But these uprisings are directed against men, or groups, or organizations that are supposed to have evaded the law or perverted it to their own use. These upris-

the history of American capitalism was an unusual concourse of events. He was probably the only man in the United States capable of carrying democracy thus far without open violence. He deserted the ruling class to become a leader of the social movement. On this John Franklin Carter comments: "One of the 'haves' [Roosevelt] has always sided with the 'have nots,' and the fact that his college and business associates damn him as 'a traitor to his class' simply reinforces the moral strength of his position as a man who is willing to sacrifice his own privileges for the general good."[3]

Roosevelt fought under the banner of liberalism, a respectable stereotype, yet most of what he said and did was really democratic and consequently socialistic or communistic. Although he was not fully consistent in his democratic ideology and practice, it was for these that he was loved and supported by the masses and hated by the bourgeoisie; he was neither particularly loved nor hated for his periodic lapses into liberalism and capitalist motivations. Hence, of primary significance to us is an analysis of his place in the movement for democracy.

The Problem and Meaning of Democracy

Although Roosevelt never saw clearly that the achievement of democracy must necessarily involve the liquidation of capitalism, he realized that democracy was on its way. "Democracy is not a static thing. It is an everlasting march."[4] "The task which this generation had to do," he asserted, "has been begun. The forward march of democracy

---

ings, therefore, have . . . a limited objective—to eject the rascals and to restore the law to its purity. These affairs are usually annoying to the party in power and they may inflict serious damage upon it; but they are thoroughly understood and so are the methods of dealing with them. Therefore the emotional reaction against them is confined to irritation with, perhaps, some degree of apprehension, when they seem likely to succeed; but they do not arouse bewilderment and wild terror. In 1932, however, when it became clear that the blind fury of the dispossessed was striking, not at individuals, but at the very system of law itself, panic swept through those classes that found the existing system tolerable, if not perfect. It was a new experience to this generation." *Roosevelt, Dictator or Democrat?*, pp. 14–15.

[3]*The New Dealers*, p. 15. (Published anonymously.)

"Franklin D. Roosevelt," observes Ernest K. Lindley, "was the first American with any practical chances of reaching the presidency to grasp the essentials of the distributing mechanism of capitalism and at the same time to see that the processes which had begun with the industrial revolution had at last brought the United States to the point where it was doubtful that this distributing mechanism could automatically operate. He had already challenged the laissez-faire system because it had concentrated dangerous economic powers in the hands of a comparatively few men and made it impossible for millions of other men to rise above poverty or, at least, to attain security by their own endeavours." *The Roosevelt Revolution,* p. 17.

[4]Address at Los Angeles, October 1, 1935. These citations are mainly from Samuel I. Rosenman, ed., op. cit., 9 vols.

is under way. Its advance must not and will not stop. . . . We shall
. . . make available the good things of life created by the genius of
science and technology . . . not for the enjoyment of the few but for
the welfare of all. For there lies the road to democracy that is strong."⁵

To Roosevelt, then, democracy did not mean mass voting for capitalist devices, but rather the utilization of the economic resources by the
social group for the welfare of all. Thus he pointed out further:

> For too many of us the political equality we had won was meaningless
> in the face of economic inequality. A small group had concentrated into
> their own hands an almost complete control over other people's property,
> other people's money, other people's labor—other people's lives. . . .
> The royalists of the economic order have conceded that political free-
> dom was the business of the government, but they have maintained that
> economic slavery was nobody's business. . . . Today we stand committed
> to the proposition that freedom is no half-and-half affair. If the average
> citizen is guaranteed equal opportunity in the polling place, he must have
> equal opportunity in the market place.⁶

Moreover, Roosevelt brought out clearly the nature of the negative
struggle between bourgeois and proletarian freedom in modern civilization. "In the hands of a people's Government this power [economic
power] is wholesome and proper. But in the hands of political puppets
of an economic autocracy such power would provide shackles for the
liberties of the people. Give them their way and they will take the
course of every autocracy of the past—power for themselves, enslavement for the public."⁷

Democracy, as we have seen, puts the resources of a people into their
own hands. It assumes that the people have finally grown up and that
they and their leaders can assume responsibility for their social destiny.
Probably the most momentous and courageous decision in modern
times, a decision taken by a people who were apparently not afraid to
assume their own social destiny, was that made by the first Congress of
the Soviet Dictatorship as Lenin announced to it: "We shall now pro-

---

⁵Campaign address at Cleveland, November 2, 1940.

⁶Acceptance of the renomination for the presidency, Philadelphia, June 27, 1936.

⁷Annual message to Congress, January 3, 1936. And he said further: "Unhappy
events abroad have retaught us two simple truths about the liberty of a democratic
people. The first truth is that the liberty of a democracy is not safe if the people
tolerate the growth of private power to a point where it becomes stronger than their
democratic state itself. That, in its essence, is Fascism. . . .

"The second truth is that the liberty of a democracy is not safe if its business system does not provide employment and produce and distribute goods in such a way
as to sustain an acceptable standard of living. . . . Among us today a concentration
of private power without equal in history is growing." Recommendations to the
Congress to curb monopolies and the concentration of economic power, April 29,
1938.

ceed to construct the socialist order." At this stage democracy approaches the limit of its consummation. President Roosevelt probably sensed such a responsibility when he said: "It is a sobering thing . . . to be a servant in this great cause. We try in our daily work to remember that the cause belongs not to us, but to the people."[8] And he seemed dimly to indicate what, in part, will be expected of a people living in a modern democracy:

It is time to provide a smashing answer to those cynical men who say that Democracy cannot be honest and efficient. If you will help, this can be done. I, therefore, hope you will watch the work in every corner of this Nation. Feel free to criticize. Tell me of instances where work can be done better, or where improper practices prevail. Neither you nor I want criticism conceived in a purely fault-finding or partisan spirit, but I am jealous of the right of every citizen to call to the attention of his or her Government examples of how the public money can be more effectively spent for the benefit of the American people.[9]

This intolerance of criticism against democracy itself becomes exceedingly intensified in countries such as Soviet Russia where the proletarian revolution has been accomplished. The enemies of democracy usually take this to mean that all criticism is prohibited in a democracy and that all "freedom" of speech is lost.

Capitalism Prostrate

But capitalism itself must endure criticism, because it is devoted principally to the interest of the few; hence, it must always argue that it is superior to a system devoted to the general welfare. A mistake in a democracy can only result in self-criticism by the people, but a breakdown of capitalism involves the responsibility of the dominant political class in the system. Moreover, as Roosevelt recognized, from the point of view of the people's welfare, the system is leaderless: "We know that a leaderless system of economy had produced and would again produce economic and social disaster. Private leadership has been non-existent from the point of view of seeking the objectives of national welfare."[10] And he constantly described the far-reaching consequences of the collapse.

Four years of continuing fear of losing capital, of losing savings, of losing jobs, had developed under the deadening hand of the depression

---

[8]Acceptance of the renomination for the presidency, Philadelphia, June 27, 1936.
[9]"Fireside Chat," April 28, 1935.
[10]In introduction to *Public Papers, etc.*, op. cit., Vol. 2, p. 9.

into fear of eviction from homes and farms, and fear of actual starvation. Millions of people, gripped by this greater fear, had begun to feel that the machinery of modern American economics and government had broken down so completely . . . that an entirely new type of mechanics for existence would have to be invented.[11]

The social problem involves not so much the fact of social misery as it does some consciousness among the people that there is no need for its existence. In a similar discussion the President declared: "It is not in despair that I paint you that picture . . . because the Nation, seeing and understanding the injustice of it, proposes to paint it out."[12]

The New Order

Thus Roosevelt set out to "find practical controls over blind economic forces and blindly selfish men."[13] In this he found the masses of the people very much in accord with him; they wanted not only escape from the depression but also a new order of things.

The American people responded to the call for action with eager enlistment—enlistment in the struggle against ruthless, self-seeking, reckless greed and economic anarchy. . . . It is very certain that the American people understood that the purpose of the reorganization was not only to bring back prosperity. It was far deeper than that. The reorganization must be permanent for all the rest of our lives in that never again will we permit the social conditions which allowed the sections of our population to exist in an un-American way, which allowed the maldistribution of wealth and power.[14]

---

[11]Ibid.

[12]Second inaugural address, January 20, 1937.

[13]Ibid. "We believe," he said, "that people are even more important than machines. We believe that the material resources of America should serve the human resources of America." Campaign address at Providence, October 21, 1936.

J. A. Hobson, the British economist, comments on this attempt of Roosevelt to subordinate profits to social welfare as follows: "It is an attempt to put capitalism on a low or no-profit basis. If capitalists were alive to the full implications of the policy, they might accept it as the sole alternative to industrial collapse. Or, if they were capable of a sustained sacrifice of profit to national recovery and in the spirit of chivalrous leadership which idealists have sometimes envisaged, they might accept. But the success of the appeal either to reason or to patriotism is exceedingly unlikely. For it implies a change in thought and in heart so big and so rapid as to constitute a spiritual miracle. And miracles do not happen . . . the whole trend of thought and sentiment during the past century of capitalism has been closed to such a revolution. To cut profits out of the capitalist system would be to the great majority of businessmen to remove the lynch-pin from the chariot of economic progress. . . . A voluntary surrender of profits in order to retain the empty form of capitalist control must be dismissed as a psychological impossibility." Op. cit., pp. 59–60.

[14]Extemporaneous address before the code authorities of six hundred industries, March 5, 1934.

As he saw it, the new order should be devoted to the people's welfare and not to the enhancement of profits. In a "fireside chat" on October 22, 1933, he put the question to the nation in this way: "How are we constructing the edifice of recovery—the temple which, when completed, will no longer be a temple of money-changers or of beggars, but rather a temple dedicated to and maintained for a greater social justice, a greater welfare for America—the habitation of a sound economic life?"[15] Thus, he decided "to use the instrumentalities and powers of Government" to achieve the new order and outspokenly disavowed any intention of leaving the social system to be regulated by "economic laws." "I have no sympathy" said he, "with the professional economists who insist that things must run their course and that human agencies can have no influence on economic ills."[16]

The Ruling Class

However, Roosevelt was not so naïve as to assume that he could reconstruct the society according to the ideals of democracy without the fierce antagonism and opposition of the capitalist ruling class. His addresses to the people were fighting words, and he described the traits of the bourgeoisie as effectively as Karl Marx ever did:

Plenty is at our doorstep, but the generous use of it languishes in the very sight of the supply. Primarily this is because rulers of the exchange of mankind's goods have failed through their own stubbornness and their own incompetence, have admitted their failure, and have abdicated. Practices of unscrupulous money-changers stand indicted in the court of public opinion, rejected by the hearts and minds of men.

True, they have tried, but their efforts have been cast in the pattern of an outworn tradition. . . . Stripped of the lure of profits by which to induce our people to follow their false leadership, they have resorted to exhortations, pleading tearfully for restored confidence. They know only the rules of a generation of self-seekers. They have no vision, and when there is no vision the people perish. The money-changers have fled from their high seats. . . . The measure of restoration lies in the extent that we apply social values more noble than mere monetary profits.[17]

---

[15]Moreover, he asserted: "We have . . . a clear mandate from the people, that Americans must forswear that conception of the acquisition of wealth which, through excessive profits, creates undue private power over private affairs and, to our misfortune, over public affairs as well." Annual message to Congress, January 4, 1935.

[16]"Fireside Chat," July 24, 1933.

[17]Inaugural address, March 4, 1933.

It should be observed that frequently the reactionary power of capitalist pressure groups has forced even President Truman, a man not known particularly for his concern with democracy as a fighting cause, to point out to the people of the United States the anti-social motives of big businessmen. In one of his speeches, his radio address on the meat shortage, October 14, 1946, he said: "The responsibility rests

The way in which Roosevelt recognized the increasing concentration
of wealth in the hands of a few is of significance; it is a sort of fruition
of the predictions of certain social scientists of the latter half of the
nineteenth century. Thus he declared:

. . . out of this modern civilization economic royalists carved new dynasties.
New kingdoms were built upon concentration and control over material
things. Through new uses of corporations, banks and securities, new
machinery of industry and agriculture, of labor and capital . . . the whole
structure of modern life was impressed into the royal service.
    There was no place among the royalty for the many thousands of small
businessmen and merchants. . . . It was natural and perhaps human that
the privileged princes of these new economic dynasties, thirsting for power,
reached out for control of the Government itself. They created a new
despotism and wrapped it in the robes of legal sanction. In its service
new mercenaries sought to regiment the people, their labor and their
property. . . .
    The hours men and women worked, the wages they received, the con-
ditions of their labor—these had passed beyond the control of the people,
and were imposed by the new industrial dictatorship. . . . Private enterprise, indeed, became too private. It became privileged enterprise.[18]

Furthermore, Roosevelt perceived clearly the conflict between the
ambitions of the great businessmen and democracy: "They seek to
substitute their own will for that of the majority, for they will serve their
own interest above the general welfare. They reject the greater principle of the greater good for the greater number, which is the corner-
stone of democratic government."[19]

It should be remembered that Roosevelt was speaking from experience and that his convictions were immediately determining his policy;
he was not a "Marxian dealing in foreign ideologies." As he said, his

---

squarely on a few men in the Congress who, in the service of selfish interests, have
been determined for some time to wreck price controls no matter what the cost might
be to our people . . . the same few men in the Congress again debated how they
could do lip service to an anti-inflation program and still scuttle price controls—
how they could pass a so-called price-control law and, at the same time, take care
of the interests they wanted to enrich. . . .
    "This group, today as in the past, is thinking in terms of millions of dollars in-
stead of millions of people. This same group has opposed every effort of this administration to raise the standard of living and increase the opportunity for the
common man. This same group hated Franklin D. Roosevelt and fought everything
he stood for. This same group did its best to discredit his efforts to achieve a better
life for our people."
    [18]Acceptance of the renomination for the presidency, Philadelphia, June 27, 1936.
    [19]Address at Roanoke Island, August 18, 1937. Again: ". . . much of our troubles
today and in the past few years has been due to a lack of understanding of the elementary principles of justice and fairness by those in whom leadership in business
and finance was placed." "Fireside Chat," June 28, 1934.

conclusions were "the result of observations of what the country had gone through during the days of false prosperity after the World War and the days of darkness after the panic of 1929; and it was the result especially of [his] experience as governor during four difficult years."[20] Furthermore, these conclusions are consistent with the historical position and characteristics of the capitalist ruling class. He challenged the power of big business frontally, something which no other president has been able to do. John Franklin Carter put the situation graphically:

> The railways, the coal and oil men, the iron and steel industries, and their bankers formed a Hindenburg line which had wrecked previous offensives. They had forced Theodore Roosevelt to back down and take the round-about and ineffective route of Trust-busting. They had smashed Woodrow Wilson's efforts at control. They had for bloody generations ruled themselves, shooting down strikers, circumventing laws, buying Governors and State Legislators, dictating to the Federal Government, secure in the knowledge that American life could not go on without steel, fuel and transportation, and that in any showdown Washington would have to "come to Poppa"![21]

The Lines of Battle

Roosevelt joined the bourgeoisie in a bloodless conflict, always, however, recognizing the tremendous power of the latter. Accordingly he exclaimed: ". . . here in America we are waging a great and successful war. It is not alone a war against want and destitution and economic demoralization. It is more than that; it is a war for the survival of democracy."[22] This is, to interject, the only war between the two great political classes—in fact, this is the very basis of the class struggle. The great capitalists are bent upon the strangulation of democracy, which they like to call communism, while the masses of the people, the

---

[20]Samuel I. Rosenman, ed., op. cit., Vol. 2, p. 4.

[21]Op. cit., pp. 30–31.

In a further characterization of the ruling class Roosevelt said: ". . . the most vociferous opponents of reform in this small minority were actuated not by any conscientious apprehension about further recovery, but by a realization that their own economic control and power, which they had enjoyed during the so-called boom era, were being destroyed. Through speculative use of other people's money, through the exploitation of labor which could not bargain on equal terms, through unrestrained power to manipulate corporate securities, finances and devices, this handful of men had been able to build up economic empires for themselves, which not only controlled the labor, property and lives of thousands of their fellow citizens, but in some cases dominated the process of Government itself. . . . To promote their own advantage, they began a vast, expensive campaign of propaganda to appeal to the electorate of the nation to stop the whole program of reform." Samuel I. Rosenman, ed., op. cit., Vol. 3, p. 5.

[22]Acceptance of the renomination, Philadelphia, June 27, 1936.

proletariat, are determined that democracy should be attained. Therefore, the President felt keenly the counterblows. Said he:

Never before in all our history have these forces [business and financial monopoly, speculation, reckless banking, class antagonism, war profiteering] been so united against one candidate as they stand today. They are unanimous in their hate for me—and I welcome their hatred. I should like to have it said of my first Administration that in it the forces of selfishness and of lust for power met their match: I should like to have it said of my second Administration that in it these forces met their master.[23]

However, Roosevelt took confidence in the fact that his position was not unique, but that he was merely part of a continuing process of struggle against the ruling class for democracy. "Andrew Jackson," he observed, "was compelled to fight every inch of the way for the ideals and the policies of the Democratic Republic. . . . An overwhelming proportion of the material power of the Nation was arrayed against him. The great media for the dissemination of information and the moulding of public opinion fought him. Haughty and sterile intellectualism opposed him. . . . It seems sometimes that all were against him—all but the people of the United States."[24]

It is significant that Roosevelt touched upon the pith of the morality of the class struggle—the intolerance of the masses for a system which cannot concern itself primarily with social well-being. "We are beginning to abandon our tolerance of the abuse of power by those who betray for profit the elementary decencies of life."[25]

Sometimes he almost seemed to believe that he had conquered capitalist power in the United States, for he said in his second inaugural address, January 20, 1937: ". . . we have begun to bring private autocratic powers into their proper subordination to the public's government. The legend that they were invincible—above and beyond the processes of democracy—has been shattered. They have been challenged and beaten." However, capitalist power has many more lives; it is not vanquished so easily. Reviewing his struggle at a later date, he saw that the leaders of big business were merely regrouping and closing ranks for more fanatical resistance.

Although few in number, they had the resources which enabled them to make the most noise, and to become the most vociferous in the press,

---

[23]Campaign address at Madison Square Garden, New York City, October 31, 1936.

[24]Address at the Jackson Day dinner, Washington, D.C., January 8, 1936. On this same occasion the President remarked: "We are at peace with the world; but the fight goes on. Our frontiers today are economic, not geographic. Our enemies of today are the forces of privilege and greed within our own borders."

[25]Second inaugural address, January 20, 1937.

over the radio, through the newspapers and outdoor advertising, by floods of telegrams and letters to the Congress, by employment of professional lobbyists, by all the many means of propaganda and public pressure which have been developed in recent years.

In 1938 the efforts of this minority, consistent in its opposition since 1933, rose to new heights. They had tried stubbornly at the polls in 1936 to stop the program of reform. They had failed. They had tried in 1937 to stop it in the courts, where they had been so successful during 1935 and 1936. Here, too, they had failed. Therefore, through the years of 1937 and 1938, their activities to impede progress and to bring about a repeal or emasculation of the New Deal measures of reform were redoubled.[26]

Probably the most irritable aspect of Roosevelt's struggle with the ruling class was his attempt to counter its deceptive propaganda—its reliance upon the theory that if a lie is big enough and it is told frequently enough the people will believe it. The capitalists do not have a morality, hence they must use the moral values of the masses themselves in their propaganda against the masses. "It is the old strategy of tyrants," the President observed, "to delude their victims into fighting their battles for them."[27]

Their principal device was, and still is, to identify themselves with the United States and every conceivable thing that is worth while in it —indeed, to identify themselves with God Himself—so that an attack against them and their system becomes *ipso facto* an attack against God and Society. In their propaganda they take it for granted that their interests must be the interests of all good Americans; therefore, only the "un-American" would be so treasonous as to question the basis of those interests. "These economic royalists complain that we seek to overthrow the institutions of America. What they really complain of is that we seek to take away their power."[28] It is a fact, however, that, since the institutions of capitalism are mainly built about capitalists, the overthrow of the capitalists will, in a sense, overthrow the institutions also. In their place, democratic institutions will necessarily be substituted.

---

[26]Samuel I. Rosenman, ed., op. cit., Vol. 7, pp. xxi–xxii.

[27]Campaign address at Madison Square Garden, New York City, October 31, 1936.

[28]Acceptance of the renomination for the presidency, Philadelphia, June 27, 1936. This, it should be observed, is the crucial intent of communism, the taking over of the economic power of the State by "the people" and the purposeful direction of urban civilization in the interest of all the people. Violence is not communism; yet it is historically certain that at a given stage of discontent of the people any immediate decision to accomplish this democratic purpose will be met by the unrestrained violence of the ruling class. The apparent advocacy of violence by the communists is essentially a warning that the violence of the ruling class will have to be reckoned with.

Today the ruling class almost never attacks democracy frontally; it attacks "communism" instead. It has built up a horror stereotype about communism which it easily transfers to the democratic efforts of the people. The propaganda carefully guards the people against a realization that democracy is in fact communism—that the struggle against democracy is identical with the struggle against communism. In this use, communism is the principal negative stereotype under which the capitalists wage war against democracy. "The attack used [by those who mistrusted democratic government] was a name-calling barrage of propaganda, charging that whatever the duly elected executive and legislative representatives tried to do was 'regimentation' or 'communism' or 'dictatorship.' "[29]

Since the ruling class cannot safely attack democracy itself, it frequently accepts the term and seeks to identify it with capitalism, so that the people are confused in the belief that this class, in championing its own cause, is in fact supporting democracy. Roosevelt was exasperated by these tactics of the bourgeoisie, and he said to the people: "They profess adherence to the form, but, at the same time, their every act shows their opposition to the very fundamentals of democracy. They love to intone praise of liberty, to mouth praises about the sanctity of our Constitution—but in their hearts they distrust majority rule because

---

[29]Samuel I. Rosenman, ed., op. cit., Vol. 6, p. lxi.

Dictatorship, as we have already noted, is not a form of social organization. In so far as the modern class struggle is concerned, it may arise spontaneously at a certain stage and as a part of the conflict. The following remarks by Roosevelt indicate the temper of the social situation which produces a proletarian dictatorship: "I am prepared under my constitutional duty to recommend the measures that a stricken nation in the midst of a stricken world may require. These measures, or such other measures as the Congress may build out of its experience and wisdom, I shall seek, within my constitutional authority, to bring to speedy adoption.

"But in the event that the Congress shall fail to take one of these two courses, and in the event that the national emergency is still critical, I shall not evade the clear course of duty that will then confront me. I shall ask Congress for the one remaining instrument to meet the crisis—broad Executive power to wage a war against the emergency, as great as the power that would be given me if we were in fact invaded by a foreign foe. . . .

"We do not distrust the future of essential democracy. The people of the United States . . . have registered a mandate that they want direct, vigorous action. They have asked for discipline and direction under leadership. They have made me the present instrument of their wishes. . . . May [God] guide me in the days to come." Inaugural address, March 4, 1933.

Had the situation continued to develop so that Roosevelt had assumed "war powers" against the ruling class—"the emergency," as he called it—and had he been convinced about the destiny of democracy, there would have been a dictatorship of the proletariat in the United States. A successful counteraction of the ruling class would have undoubtedly resulted in a fascist dictatorship.

On this J. A. Hobson's observation is interesting. Says he: ". . . the emergency will not pass. For it is an expression, not of a passing disturbance in the business system, but a permanent vice in that system, concealed in its earlier stages but now openly manifest." Op. cit., p. 39.

an enlightened majority will not tolerate the abuses which a privileged minority would seek to foist upon the people as a whole."[30] A common practice is to identify the democratic state with the struggle for democracy, and this ordinarily leads to confusion—in the anti-democratic propaganda the confusion is intentional.[31]

Then, too, finding that Roosevelt had become a symbol of the cause of democracy, a champion of the common people, this class sought to set up its politicians as Roosevelt men. On being elected to office, they fought the President from within. Roosevelt had to take to the field in congressional elections in order to warn the people of these "traitors of democracy." As he pointed out:

> The blunt fact is that these men were deliberately repudiating the very principles of progress which they had espoused in order to be elected— and which were, in some cases, the only reason that they had been elected. ... It is a comparatively simple thing for a nation to determine, by its votes, whether it chooses the liberal or the conservative form of government. On the other hand, a nation can never intelligently determine its policy, if it has to go through the confusion of voting for candidates who pretend to be one thing but who act the other.[32]

Another old and deceptive trait of the bourgeoisie is their conscious and deliberate production of intergroup prejudice among exploited peoples; it is, as we shall attempt to show in a later chapter, the key to an understanding of race prejudice and antagonism. In the struggle against democracy, heavy reliance is put upon these tactics. Success in it results in almost complete distraction of the proletariat from its fundamental democratic efforts. In a Labor Day address at Denton, Maryland, in 1938, the President had to deal with one instance of this:

> ... the strategy of the cold-blooded few to divide and conquer, to make common men blind to their common interests, becomes more active. Class conscious itself ... that small minority is deliberately trying to create prejudice between this and that group of the common people of America. You ... have in recent weeks been treated to a number of examples of

---

[30]Address at Roanoke Island, August 18, 1937.

[31]William Randolph Hearst, perhaps the most insistent crusader against democracy in the United States, has reached some sort of perfection in this duplicity with his expression "red fascism." Under this banner he attacks the people's struggle for democracy in this way: "[The proletariat of ancient Rome] was without property of any kind, and without the constructive or executive ability to acquire any. ... The truth is that government by the proletariat, government by the least capable and the least conscientious element of the community—government by the mob, government by ignorance and avarice ... is the fearful failure that it needs must be and definitely deserves to be." See his full-page article in the Chicago *Tribune,* November 29, 1946. Readers familiar with *Mein Kampf* will observe how closely this echoes the Nazi doctrines.

[32]Samuel I. Rosenman, ed., op. cit., Vol. 7, pp. xxvii, xxxi.

this deliberate attempt to create prejudice and class feeling which can be charitably explained only as political hysteria. But it does not help the cause of . . . effective democracy anywhere to laugh off such things in campaign time on the general theory that anything is fair in love and politics.

Today above all else that minority is trying to drive a wedge between the farmers on the one hand and their relatives and logical partners in the cities on the other. It is trying to narrow the broad definition of "labor" in the mind of the farmer, who above all people has always known what it means to have to labor from sun-up to sun-down. It is trying to make the farmer forget that the people in the cities who, like him, labor for their daily bread are his own people.

Roosevelt, a Reformer

And yet this great advocate of democracy never seemed to have visualized the end of the road over which he was traveling. He sought the subjugation of the power of big business in the interest of democracy, but he apparently did not recognize the insatiable demands of democracy for the final liquidation of private business enterprise—for the complete conquest of power by the people. Thus he remarked characteristically:

No one in the United States believes more firmly than I in the system of private business, private property and private profit. . . . If the Administration had the slightest inclination to change that system, all that it would have had to do was to fold up its hands and wait—let the system continue to default to itself and to the public.[33]

Again:

Because we cherished our system of private property and free enterprise and were determined to preserve it as the foundation of our traditional American system, we recalled the warning of Thomas Jefferson that "widespread poverty and concentrated wealth cannot long endure side by side in a democracy." Our job was to preserve the American ideal of economic as well as political democracy against the abuse of concentration of economic power.[34]

Sometimes Roosevelt seemed to think that he was merely adjusting the old system so that it might function better: "What we seek is balance in our economic system—balance between agriculture and industry, and balance between the wage earner, the employer and the consumer. We seek also balance that our internal markets be kept rich

---

[33]Radio campaign address to dinners of businessmen held throughout the nation, October 23, 1936.

[34]Campaign address at Chicago, October 14, 1936.

and large, and that our trade with other nations be increased on both sides."[35]

Sometimes, also, in his reformist mood, he seemed to become utopian: "The task of reconstruction which we undertook in 1933 did not call for the creation of strange values. It was rather finding the way again to old, but somewhat forgotten, ideals and values. Though the methods and means and details may have been in some instances new, the objectives were as permanent and as old as human nature itself."[36]

It is this fact of limited insight in Roosevelt which, in a sense, makes him a part of the historical data in the great world transformation of capitalist Western society to democracy. He himself quotes John Stuart Mill on socioeconomic determinism:

History shows that great economic and social forces flow like a tide over communities only half conscious of that which is befalling them. Wise statesmen foresee what time is thus bringing and try to shape institutions and mould men's thoughts and purposes in accordance with the change that is silently coming on.[37]

Yet the "tide of social forces" seemed to have flowed even past Roosevelt and left him grappling with straws on the shores of time. Years before the slow-up in Roosevelt's democratic militancy, in 1934, John Franklin Carter observed: ". . . the revolution will get ahead of current revolutionaries and either leave them behind as embarrassed conservatives or rush them headlong into real radicalism."[38]

Roosevelt, at any rate, was not to be rushed into "real radicalism." Here and there the impatience of the people irked him, and he seemed constrained to deal with them in almost the same terms as those used by the business interests to stop him. "In some quarters," he said, "labor had gone too far in its demands and in its conduct, especially with respect to sit-down strikes."[39]

However, it is in his address to the American Youth Congress on February 10, 1940, that Roosevelt showed most clearly his concern for

---

[35] Extemporaneous address before the code authorities of six hundred industries, March 5, 1934.

[36] Samuel I. Rosenman, ed., op. cit., Vol. 2, pp. 9–10.

[37] Address delivered at Savannah, November 18, 1933.

[38] Op. cit.; p. ix.
Concerning Martin Luther's antagonism to the radical movement of the German peasantry, Stefan Zweig observes similarly: "The fate of every revolutionary is that he who wishes to replace the old order by the new has to let loose the forces of chaos, and he risks being outstripped by others yet more radical than he, who will make confusion worse confounded." *Triumph und Tragik des Erasmus von Rotterdam,* trans. by Eden and Cedar Paul, *Erasmus,* p. 190.

[39] Samuel I. Rosenman, ed., op. cit., Vol. 7, p. xxiii.

the spreading radical temper of the youth of the nation and his absorption of the capitalist propaganda on "communism." He addressed the
group in Washington on the White House lawn—conscious of its sympathies. His remarks should be quoted at length, for they are significant
in understanding certain complications of the class struggle in the
United States.

I think [he said] that some of us realize that if we had a different form
of Government this kind of a meeting on the White House lawn could
not take place. . . .
Do not seek or expect Utopia overnight. Do not seek or expect a
panacea—some wonderful new law that will give to everybody who needs
it a handout—or a guarantee of permanent remunerative occupation of
your own choosing. . . . Take, for example, the question of the employment
of old people and the employment of young people. . . .
. . . let me make it very clear in the beginning that it is not at all certain
that your opportunities for employment are any worse today than they
were for young people ten years or twenty years or thirty years ago.
I suggest . . . that on social and economic matters you and I are substantially in agreement as to the objective, but that there are some of you
who think that objective can be gained overnight. I do not.
. . . do not as a group pass resolutions on subjects which you have not
thought through and on which you cannot possibly have complete knowledge . . . in the field, for example, of national defense or international
economics. . . . Such a decision ought not to be influenced by any gathering of old people or young people, or anybody else, local or national, who
get a smattering of the subject from two or three speakers. . . .
One of the big local American Youth Congress Councils . . . took a
decisive stand against the granting of American loans to Finland . . . on
the ground that such action was "an attempt to force America into the
imperialist war." My friends, that reasoning was unadulterated twaddle
based . . . on ninety per cent ignorance of what they are talking about.
I can say this to you with a smile. . . . Here is a small Republic in northern Europe, which, without any question whatsoever, wishes solely to
maintain its own territorial and governmental integrity. Nobody with any
pretense at common sense believes that Finland had any ulterior designs
on . . . the Soviet Union. . . . Please do not pass resolutions of this
kind. . . .
I disliked the regimentation under Communism. I abhorred the indiscriminate killings of thousands of innocent victims. I heartily deprecated
the banishment of religion. . . . The Soviet Union . . . is run by a dictatorship as absolute as any other dictatorship in the world. It has allied itself
with another dictatorship, and it has invaded a neighbor so infinitesimally
small that it could do no conceivably possible harm to the Soviet
Union. . . .
It has been said that some of you are Communists. . . . As Americans
you have a legal and constitutional right to call yourselves Communists. . . . You have a right peacefully and openly to advocate certain

ideals of theoretical Communism; but as Americans you have not only a right but a sacred duty to confine your advocacy of changes in law to the methods prescribed by the Constitution of the United States—and you have no American right, by act or deed of any kind, to subvert the Government and the Constitution of this Nation.

Although it has been very much a part of the class struggle in the United States, we shall not discuss the President's views about Finland. Later developments must certainly have given the American Youth Congress the last "smile."[40] "Democracy is on the march," Roosevelt recognized clearly, but it should not be allowed to march too quickly. His statement that he did not expect it to be achieved "overnight" is obviously an extreme, rationalizing concession to his own reformist temper, for no one had insisted on an "overnight" transformation of the system. The point of significance is, however, that he gave the protectors of the status quo a moral opportunity to defend the system. If the capitalist system cannot be changed "overnight," then it should not be changed at all, for the forces which are now limiting change have an "admitted" right to continue to do so. Indeed, Roosevelt's admission was interpreted to mean that these forces had a moral right to order an about turn, to have democracy march in the opposite direction, and to silence by law all those who think they "have a right peacefully and openly to advocate certain ideals of theoretical Communism."

Nature of the Reaction

There are two points which identified Roosevelt, even though remotely, with the reactionaries against whom he struggled. They robbed him of consistent resoluteness and left his most confirmed supporters the easy prey of the watchdogs of capitalism. He conceived of the Constitution as something more sacred than the consummate will of the people, and he did not clearly realize that democracy is always "subversive" of capitalism—of the status quo.

These indecisions made it possible for the capitalists to challenge him from the beginning and frequently caused him to deny the very democracy for which he was struggling. Apparently Roosevelt subconsciously feared the consequences of an achieved democracy. What he said and did contributed greatly to the final winding up of capitalism; but, like a true reformer, he sincerely believed that his mission was only to make the existing system work more felicitously.

To be sure, he had little opportunity to become a proletarian dic-

---

[40] For a discussion of the role of Finland in the international struggle against the Soviet Union, see Michael Sayers and Albert E. Kahn, op. cit.

tator in the United States. He was probably more advanced in his thinking than any controlling member of his party or Cabinet, and the people as a whole had too little political education to support him effectively. Indeed, the great tragedy of Roosevelt's time is that it found him with a nation badly prepared intellectually for his plans of action in the interest of a democratic society. There was difficulty even in finding "socially minded" personnel for the New Deal. He had to lead a people who emotionally and physically wanted economic democracy but who, at the same time, had only a confused understanding of it. They were ideologically enslaved by a worshipful reliance upon the idea of the social indispensability of "free business enterprise," and conditioned by capitalist propaganda to a mortal dread of "communism."[41] Thus, in the very act of reducing the power of the bourgeoisie, Roosevelt had to pay lip service to his allegiance to the welfare of capitalism. And now that Roosevelt is gone it is as if the people do not know what he really stood for; they wish for him, for leadership of his type, but they have, on the whole, no ideological foundation sufficient to create a clear-cut demand.

This confusion of the people did not simply happen by chance; it was planned. From the time Roosevelt took office a determined effort was made by certain members of Congress—who steadily increased in number as the depression receded[42]—business organizations and individuals, and a host of public agencies to smell out, warn, hold up to public censure, or discharge from employment any person or group who had "communistic" tendencies—that is to say, anyone who dared to back the New Deal in Rooseveltian terms. The process was to build up in the minds of the people a diffused, horror stereotype of communism —utterly false—then to identify the individual or group with it, and finally, before the very eyes of the people and sometimes even with their approbation, to put his head upon the block. In this way, then, the reactionaries fairly completely took every support from under Roosevelt; they rooted it out all the way from the members of his

---

[41]As John Franklin Carter observes: ". . . one of the amazing and disheartening effects of the old economic order was its success in breeding generation after generation of young conformists and juvenile reactionaries. The private schools and better universities of America—far from being the hot-bed of revolution or even the cradle of intellectual curiosity concerning the social order—were part and parcel of the industrial plant. They turned out unimaginative and unquestioning business men stamped in the mould most suited to operate the business machinery as it existed and to dread economic radicalism as they would dread the plague." Op. cit., pp. 41–42.

[42]Roosevelt felt the power of reaction more, with increasing recovery: "To hold to progress today is more difficult. Dulled conscience, irresponsibility, and ruthless self-interest already reappear. Such symptoms of prosperity may become portents of disaster! Prosperity already tests the persistence of our progressive purpose." Second inaugural address, January 20, 1937.

Cabinet to the least of government employees. In order to maintain the sacredness of the status quo the reactionaries forced many persons in strategic positions to swear allegiance to the flag and to take oaths of loyalty.

A remarkable instance of how the charge of communism has been used by persons in different stages of advancement in their tolerance of democracy is indicated by Roosevelt's letter (April 17, 1939) to Thomas R. Amlie, nominated for a place on the Interstate Commerce Commission but withdrawn because of intense opposition to him as a communist in a Senate committee.

> Those who have called you a Communist do not perhaps realize that such name-calling ill serves the democratic form of Government which this Nation as a whole wishes to continue.
> A quarter of a century ago I, too, was called a Communist and a wild-eyed radical because I fought for factory inspection, for a fifty-four-hour-a-week bill for women and children in industry and similar measures.[43]

However, the charge of the capitalist politicians that Roosevelt was a communist is in its essence correct. His policies and actions had the potentialities of taking the economy step by step, inch by inch, out of the hands of the bourgeoisie and of turning it over to the people as a whole; and this is exactly what is meant by communistic activities. The logical conclusion of such a trend must necessarily result in the overthrow of the capitalist order. There has probably been no individual in the history of the United States who has done so much to bring about democracy and therefore communism in the United States as President Roosevelt; and there has been no individual so much beloved by the people and so much hated by the bourgeoisie as he.[43a]

---

[43] It is interesting to note that Roosevelt does about the same thing to those of more advanced democratic thinking than he: "Be it clearly understood . . . that when I use the word 'liberal,' I mean the believer in progressive principles of democratic, representative government, and not the wild man who, in effect, leans in the direction of Communism." "Fireside Chat," June 24, 1938.

[43a] A sociologist, a colleague of the writer, has criticized him for referring to Mr. Roosevelt as a communist. It seems, however, that the social scientist cannot be too much concerned about dictionary definitions for his identification of social phenomena. In so far as the social process involves the democratic tendency, Roosevelt may be thought of as the arch-American communist of his age; and there is probably no question but that the ruling class conceives of him in this way. To be sure, the House committee on un-American activities does not make this charge directly, but this is only because the committee fears that to do so may lead the public to a realization of the identity of its struggle for democracy and communism.

Consider in illustration the following procedure. In May 1947 the committee gave out to the press its sensational findings "that flagrant Communist propaganda films were produced in Hollywood 'as a result of White House pressure.' " The report left no doubt that "White House" meant the former President Roosevelt. The great newspapers played this up as stage setting for a proposed Hollywood

To be sure, the businessmen drew their own picture of communism—a picture which they themselves did not believe—and made it everywhere easily available to the public. Communism, they said, was godless, massacred the people in cold blood for the sport of it, developed self-interested dictatorship, and established a society productive only of increasing social retardation. By various devices the New Deal was identified with this picture and Roosevelt was constantly pressed to join the issue on open political class grounds. The opposition, feeling sure that it had the "mind" of the public strongly conditioned against communism, sought to make him the ideal un-American citizen. In defense the President charged:

> ... there are subversive forces in this country ... the easiest term to apply is to call them the Fascist element in the United States, who are able to get very large sums of money quickly into their possession and sweep the country off its feet with some kind of a great publicity move before the country has an opportunity to think about it one way or the other. The people get this tremendous mass of stuff thrown at them. . . .[44]

And yet so effective was this strategy that not even Roosevelt seemed to be able to take time to think about its stereotype; it apparently led him to reject communism and, in so doing, contributed to the con-

---

witch hunt; and, among these, the Chicago *Tribune* carried, on June 2, 1947, an editorial entitled "Roosevelt's Red Propaganda." Said the editor in part: "Jack Warner, head of a motion-picture company, told the congressional committee on un-American activities that coercion originating with President Roosevelt forced him to produce the film, *Mission to Moscow*. . . . These latest disclosures are enlightening as to Mr. Roosevelt's method but certainly add nothing to what the public already knows about his purpose. His purpose, disclosed by a thousand acts, was to establish a totalitarian state in America and make himself an American Stalin." This, then, is what a communist is. The American people know of Mr. Roosevelt's interest in the welfare of the masses, but it would be sheer blindness not to recognize that such a direction of purpose involves today the very substance of political-class antagonism—the struggle for power between the people and the ruling class. It is possible to make this apparently derogatory identification of Mr. Roosevelt and Stalin only because it can be assumed that the public does not understand the nature of the democratic movement.

[44]Special press conference with members of the Associated Church Press, Washington, D.C., April 20, 1938.

In this regard J. A. Hobson remarks: "Experience has taught [the conservatives] that the working-class movement in politics is innocuous, so long as the mind it expresses is the mind of a mob. Their party machinery, their Press, their handling of political and social events have, therefore, been continually directed to making and preserving a mob-mind, sensational, fluid, indeterminate, short sighted, credulous, disunited. In such a mentality there is no will of the people, no effective common sense. Under such conditions it is easy for the ruling and possessing classes to confuse the electorate by dangling before their eyes specious unsubstantial benefits, to divide them by conflicting appeals to trade and locality, to subject to undetected mutilation any really inconvenient or dangerous reform, and in the last resort to draw across the path of policy some great inflammatory national appeal to passion. Until the people evolve an intelligent will able to resist those influences, a real democracy will continue to be impossible." Op. cit., pp. 105–06.

fusion which his antagonists sought to establish. In a sense they compelled him to deny his cause. Thus he declared:

> Desperate in mood, angry at failure, cunning in purpose, individuals and groups are seeking to make Communism an issue in an election where Communism is not a controversy between the two major parties.
>
> Here and now, once and for all, let us bury that red herring, and destroy that false issue. . . . I repudiate the support of any advocate of Communism or of any other alien "ism" which would by fair means or foul change our American democracy.[45]

This, then, was a positive victory for the bourgeoisie. These tactics were—and still are—a very important part of the strategy of the ruling class. To have achieved a public denial and expression of contempt for communism by the very persons in whom the people, in their quest for light on democracy, put their unreserved trust as leaders of great courage, prescience, and integrity was to suggest a confirmation of the horror propaganda about communism. The fact is that it was communism which was in question as it still is today. What Roosevelt did not see was the way in which communism was identified with everything significant that he conceived to be democracy; and his denying that it was simply played into the hands of the reactionaries.[46]

Involvement of the Schools

Probably in no other institution is the communist stereotype so carefully guarded as in the schools of the nation; and the principal method of conditioning the faculties is that of investigation and public "exposure." "The defense of capitalism and nationalism requires that the whole system of secondary education and of the universities shall be subjected to the emotional bias of patriotism, and that the teaching of history, economics, and civics shall be directed to provide intellectual defences against the inroads of the new economic and political democracy."[47]

When in the middle of the thirties Roosevelt began to settle his grasp on the vitals of the old order, the witch hunt in the schools rose to a

---

[45]Address delivered at Democratic State Convention, Syracuse, September 29, 1936.

[46]Similar tactics are constantly used, and with some considerable success, to disrupt the solidarity and blunt the aggressive edge of the CIO. Some of the great newspapers and skilled radio commentators play up the conservative, business faction of the CIO as respectable American citizens. The democratic faction, which centers its attention on the welfare of the masses of workers, is called communist. The top leaders of the CIO have developed no decisive answer to this, but ordinarily allow themselves to be put on the defensive in answering questions as to the unions' plans for "getting rid of the communists" within their ranks.

[47]J. A. Hobson, op. cit., p. 109.

feverish pitch. Its methods may be illustrated by an "inquisition" at the University of Chicago.

A multimillionaire chain-drugstore owner, Charles Walgreen, found the incident which justified an investigation by an Illinois State Senate committee into the charge that "subversive communistic teachings and ideas advocating violent overthrow" of the government were being "instilled in the minds of many students of certain tax-exempt colleges and universities in the state." Walgreen's niece, Lucille Norton, eighteen years of age, entered the University of Chicago in the fall of 1934; and through her he made the following discovery, which he gave in testimony at the Senate committee's investigation in Chicago, May 13, 1935:

After attending the University of Chicage for a time her thoughts as disclosed by her conversation centered on communism and its various tendencies. During her first quarter at the University, Social Science was a compulsory subject. Among the selected readings, it required in the syllabus of it the *Communist Manifesto* by Karl Marx and F. Engels, in which the institution of the family, as we know it, is belittled and criticized and its alleged sacredness ridiculed. She took the course and the required reading, and it was during this period that she told me that the family as an institution was disappearing. . . .

We were discussing communism and capitalism and lightly I said to Lucille: "You are getting to be a communist," and she said, "I am not the only one—there are lots more on the campus."

I said to Lucille, "Do you realize that this means the abolition of the family, the abolition of the church, and especially do you realize it means the overthrow of our government?" And she said, "Yes, I think I do, but doesn't the end ever justify the means?"

"Don't you realize this means bloodshed?" I said. Again she said, "Yes, but how did we get our independence—wasn't it by revolution?"

"Well, Lucille, are they really teaching you these things over at the University?" I asked. And she said, "No, I don't think they are teaching it to us."

"Are they advocating these things?" and she said, "No, not exactly."

"Well," I said, "where do you get all these radical ideas?"

"Well," she said, "we have a lot of reading on communism."

Walgreen withdrew his niece from the university and the newspapers took up his cause, intimating in various ways that the communists had captured the University of Chicago. The sensation led to the investigation.

At the hearing the president of the university, Robert M. Hutchins, said in part:

I have the complete outlines of 161 of these courses [on social, political, and economic problems]. There is nothing subversive in them. . . . I call your attention particularly to the syllabus in Social Science I, the general course taken by Freshmen and Sophomores. The references to Communism are entirely to books; these books discuss different views of the subject. . . . The members of the Faculty are law-abiding, patriotic citizens. Some of them, of course, are dissatisfied with the current economic, social, and political conditions in this country. But they all believe in orderly change under the law.

None of them advocates or has advocated the violent overthrow of the government. . . . The University . . . would dismiss any professor who . . . was found to have advocated the overthrow of the government by violence. Anybody who thinks that any of our faculty is doing so should inform the State's attorney so that a prosecution may be instituted.

Charles E. Merriam, chairman of the Department of Political Science, defended his position in this wise:

I am Chairman of the Department of Political Science, and am chiefly responsible for the type of civic education in the University of Chicago. . . . When did I become subversive or begin the overthrow of the American Government? . . . I am responsible for the selection and retention of Dr. Schuman [charged by Walgreen with advocating "free love"]. . . . He is not a Communist or a Socialist. There are doubtless some who think badly of him for voting for Roosevelt in the last election, but I am unable to regard that as subversive or unconstitutional. He once allowed his name to be used on a document he had not read, but many better men have made worse mistakes. . . .

If there is unrest in the land, and there is, and if many men in the bitterness and discontent reach out blindly in a feverish struggle to find a way out, then seek out the causes of discontent and cure them.[48]

No specific recommendation for dismissal was made by the committee, but it is obvious that the university remained on probation. At the "trial" Albert Durand, a representative of the American Legion, exclaimed: ". . . a red flag floats on the University of Chicago." All this the president and the faculty had to deny. No one dared to say that the American people had a right to revolt if they wanted to; no one explained what the overthrow of the government really meant. The value of these witch hunts is to elicit a public denial of any communistic tendencies on the part of the faculty and to condition it to shy away from any investigation of vital social problems unless it is apparent that its conclusions will be in glorification or in resigned acceptance of the status quo.

It is fairly certain that the social sciences, having experienced such panic and warning, will thereafter tend toward scholastic ruminations and statistical refinements of inconsequential details. To the public,

---

[48]*The Daily Maroon*, May 14, 1935, published at the University of Chicago, carried a fairly complete report of the hearing.

communism, a form of social organization, had been identified with "criminal revolution" and, since it could not be defended by even "the greatest social scientists in the world," it must be "something" that is very bad indeed. With this type of achievement the opportunity for understanding the democratic process is partly struck down at its roots.[49]

The struggle against democracy in the schools is also carried on by a careful reading of the books. The War Department's suspension, in October 1946, of the use of the economics text prepared from *Economics: Principles and Problems,* by Professors Paul F. Gemmill and Ralph H. Blodgett of the University of Pennsylvania and the University of Illinois, respectively, may be taken in illustration. The objectionable communist material in this book was a suggestion that "equality of opportunity" should be instituted by heavy inheritance and income taxes and "the extension of social services." The National Small Business Men's Association was a leader of the attack against the text. On November 18, 1946, it sent the following letter to its members:

DEAR MR. MANUFACTURER:

Our President—DeWitt Emery—speaking in Washington recently, accused the War Department of teaching communism.

The basis for Mr. Emery's statement is the War Dept. Manual EM 763—Economics: Principles and Problems. Shortly after Mr. Emery brought this to the attention of the country, the War Dept. withdrew the manual temporarily, pending further study of the matter. However, we will insist upon a thorough investigation immediately after the 80th Congress convenes in January. We shall want to know why our War Dept. adopted these textbooks, and, even though Manual EM 763 has been withdrawn, we want to know how many other manuals are still in use which are just as bad or worse.

The War Dept. may not be altogether to blame in this case, since we now learn that the book was selected for the War Dept. to be used in the Armed Forces Institute, by a committee of 100 civilian educators. We have a list of 106 colleges and universities which have adopted the textbook on economics. We are writing each of these schools to determine whether or not the book is actually being used. . . .

We need your support and active participation in this campaign, and urge you to join with us in the other important work we are doing. The cost is insignificant—$18—and it will be the best investment you ever made.

Sincerely yours,
D. H. HOLLOWAY, *Treasurer*[50]

---

[49]In order to perpetuate his idea of democracy Charles Walgreen later established a five-hundred-thousand-dollar foundation at the University of Chicago for the study and indoctrination of "American Institutions."

[50]Reprinted in *In Fact,* Vol. XIV, No. 11, December 16, 1946.

The protest for suppression of the book was actually made by Senator C. Wayland Brooks of Illinois. After having killed the text in some of its vital uses, its antagonists went for the scalps of the professors themselves. Among them, the Chicago *Tribune,* an outstanding private committee for the investigation of un-American activities, practically coerced Professor Blodgett to make a public denial of any sympathy with communism. In answer to the fearful charge, Blodgett, in evident desperation, wrote the newspaper:

> In trying to make me out a communist, you are decidedly barking up the wrong tree. I am of good Vermont Republican stock, and have been a Republican myself since I reached the appropriate age. . . . I am known to the faculty and students of the University of Illinois as a conservative, and these good people will register only amusement or indignation in the face of your accusations. . . .

Then Mr. Blodgett went on to extricate himself:

> Your article suggests that Gemmill and I have "an economic philosophy embracing a cradle to the grave security financed largely by oppressive taxation of large estates and personal incomes." Actually, we favor some broadening of the social security program as it existed before the war, but I am greatly opposed to proposals for a system of cradle to the grave social security. . . .

The author proceeded to explain to the anti-democratic editor of the *Tribune* that the text will be revised and the following good word in the interest of capitalism will be inserted:

> In suggesting means for bringing about an increase in economic equality, we have limited ourselves to recommendations which we are convinced could be worked out within the framework of a capitalistic economy. Indeed, we hold that the proposals we have outlined, so far from weakening the present economic order, would do much to strengthen it. . . .

The *Tribune* in full possession of its authority, answered him in disciplinary fashion:

> Mr. Blodgett . . . protests that the *Tribune* is "trying to make me out a communist." In none of the three stories which the *Tribune* published concerning the textbook was there more than incidental mention of Blodgett as coauthor. The communist inclinations of Gemmill were set forth as described by the house committee. Blodgett chose his company and if he finds himself sleeping in the same bed with a fellow traveler, that is his responsibility.[51]

---

[51]For Professor Blodgett's letter and the *Tribune's* editorial in answer to it, see Chicago *Tribune,* October 13, 1946.

To be sure, the question here is not one of the right of Colonel Robert R. McCormick to argue the validity of any statement made in university textbooks, but it is rather his power and that of his class to pervert and frighten into silence the social scientists of the nation which is in question. Even the most feeble excursions of these scholars into the field of vital social problems is readily stifled and, instead of being able to think freely over the whole area of social possibilities, they are turned back upon themselves to be limited "to recommendations which . . . could be worked out within the framework of a capitalistic economy."[52]

The Committee on Un-American Activities

The ideological battle against Roosevelt reached some sort of climax in 1938 with the appointment of the Dies Committee by the House of Representatives to investigate un-American activities. Probably the Dies Committee has been more responsible for the void in democratic enthusiasm following the death of the President than any other antidemocratic force in the country. As William Gellermann observes: "Dies has been effective in reducing the limits of American tolerance toward individuals and organizations in America whose opinions and social ideals are out of harmony with the intellectual folkways and economic interests of the dominant group in American society, which Dies labeled 'American.' "[53] It is significant, then, to observe the techniques of this instrument of political-class antagonism.

The major problem of the Dies Committee was that of undermining the New Deal by identifying it with the negative stereotype of communism and then giving "merciless publicity" to this identification. As Congressman Martin Dies himself declared: "Stalin baited his hook with a 'progressive' worm, and New-Deal suckers swallowed bait, hook, line, and sinker."[54] Mrs. Franklin D. Roosevelt, Harold L. Ickes, Henry A. Wallace, Robert H. Jackson, Mrs. Mary McLeod Bethune, and almost every other conceivable individual and group with progressive democratic ideas were sought out and stigmatized before the public.

---

[52]For a discussion of this, see James Harvey Robinson, *The Mind in the Making,* especially pp. 173, 121, 202.

[53]*Martin Dies,* p. 3.

The term "un-American" is a political-class concept; the ruling class and its interests are American. When Roosevelt wanted to infer that the bourgeoisie had been deposed, he said: ". . . the resolute enemy within our gates is ever ready to beat down our words unless in greater courage we will fight for them." Acceptance of the renomination for the presidency, Philadelphia, Pennsylvania, June 27, 1936.

[54]*The Trojan Horse in America,* p. 285.

The Dies Committee could do this because the social force behind it was and still is the ruling class of the nation.

> In one of its important aspects [says Professor Gellermann] the Dies committee was virtually a Republican anti-New Deal campaign committee, supported in its activities by the taxpayers of the United States. The fact that there were so-called Democrats on the committee only added to its effectiveness. While ostensibly investigating un-American activities the Dies group was actually seeking to discredit a popularly elected administration.[55]

The Dies Committee, indeed, was simply "the spearhead of American reaction." Roosevelt was constantly irritated by its tactics. He was particularly concerned about the way Dies disposed of Governor Frank Murphy in the investigation of the Detroit sit-down strike in the fall of 1938.[56]

However, the focus of the committee's attack was the Communist party of the United States, the most outspoken group in the struggle against capitalism. Its propagandistic connections with Soviet Russia gave Dies an excellent opportunity to identify communism itself as un-American. Thus he concluded: "Communism is nothing more nor less than organized treason."[57] Dies never made a distinction between the

---

[55] Op. cit., pp. 68–69. And he points out further: "[The Dies committee] is a common front of conservatives of both old parties against the New Deal and all those who believe in industrial democracy." Ibid., p. 104.

[56] "I was very much disturbed," the President remarked. "I was disturbed not because of the absurdly false charges made by a coterie of disgruntled Republican officeholders against a profoundly religious, able and law-abiding Governor; but because a Congressional Committee charged with the responsibility of investigating un-American activities should have permitted itself to be used in a flagrantly unfair and un-American attempt to influence an election.

"At this hearing the Dies Committee made no effort to get at the truth, either by calling for facts to support mere personal opinion or by allowing facts and personal opinion on the other side. On the threshold of a vitally important gubernatorial election, they permitted a disgruntled Republican judge, a discharged Republican City Manager and a couple of officious police officers to make lurid charges against Governor Frank Murphy, without attempting to elicit from them facts as to their undeniable bias and their charges, and without attempting to obtain from the Governor or, for that matter, from any responsible motor manufacturer, his version of the events." A statement on the Dies Committee investigation of un-American activities during the sit-down strikes in Michigan, October 25, 1938.

All the hearings of the Dies Committee were characterized by this procedure. See William Gellermann, op. cit., p. 14, for a corroboration of this. The American Civil Liberties Union found that ". . . the Committee has persisted in spreading baseless or prejudiced testimony of a sensational and irresponsible character all over the record and the press without giving those charged a fair chance to reply. It has seen un-Americanism almost wholly as Communism, with occasional excursions into anti-democratic forces of reaction, evidently to offset criticism of bias. It has charged Communist connections to a host of agencies and individuals whose only loyalty was to a liberal democracy." Editorial, "On Un-Americanism," *Civil Liberties Quarterly*, March 1947, No. 64.

[57] Op. cit., p. 236.

propagandistic and underground activities of the struggle for communism and communism itself.

From the point of view of the ruling class, however, the struggle for communism or democracy must necessarily be treasonous. Consciously or unconsciously its end must be the overthrow of the legitimate heirs of capitalist culture. "Our allegiance to American institutions," Roosevelt declared, "requires the overthrow of this power."[58]

In the modern class struggle the term "un-American" refers to all those persons or groups who oppose the ideology and practices of the ruling class, the class in whose peculiar interests the economic order functions. The unmistakable un-Americans are those who advocate and struggle for a consummate democracy in the United States. However, the process of social change in capitalist society tends to be irreversible. A successful reactionary movement by the "true Americans" does not return the system to its previous condition but rather to some heightened state of social dysphoria characteristic of fascism. As Professor Gellermann points out: "Anything which tends to destroy democracy in the United States is a step in the direction of fascism."[59]

Democracy, then, as Roosevelt observed, is and has been always on the march; it is never satisfied until achieved. It must, therefore, be a sort of "fifth column" undermining capitalism—a fifth column which the capitalist ruling class could never hope to liquidate and with which it must evidently continue to fight a losing battle. Democracy is by its very nature subversive of the status quo; thus it seems apparent that any ardent advocate of democracy must inevitably be subversive, radical, and "un-American."

Probably a distinction should be made between the terms "fifth column" and "pro-foreign nation." When two nations are at war, that person who, through words or actions, evinces some deep sympathy for the foreign nation is a "pro-foreign national." The fifth column, however, may be thought of as a group of political-class affiliates within a nation that accepts or is willing to accept the aid of members of the same class in another nation in order to overthrow or limit the power of the domestic ruling class. For instance, during World War I, which was essentially an imperialist war, the Britisher who took the side of the Germans was a pro-German. However, in World War II, where the class struggle sometimes overshadowed the imperialist interests, the fifth columns were either the fascists or the communists of the different nations, depending on the possibility of an alliance with an invading power against the opposite domestic political class.

---

[58]See Samuel I. Rosenman, ed., op. cit., Vol. 5, p. 234.
[59]Op. cit., p. 7.

The Dies hearings on un-American activities run into many thousands of printed pages, yet there is no startling revelation in them. Its purpose was—and still is—to put on infamous public display that which had already been known. One sample may serve to illustrate the involvement of domestic and foreign political-class antagonisms. Milton Wolff was born in Brooklyn in 1915. In 1940 he was brought before the Dies Committee to testify to his un-American activities. The questioning, in part, follows:

Mr. Matthews: Are you a member of the Communist party?
Mr. Wolff: I am not.
Mr. Matthews: Have you ever been a member of the Young Communist League?
Mr. Wolff: I have not.
Mr. Matthews: When you went to Spain did you travel on a passport issued in your own name?
Mr. Wolff: I did.
Mr. Matthews: American passport?
Mr. Wolff: Yes, sir.
Mr. Matthews: Was there a notation stamped on it that it was not good for travel in Spain?
Mr. Wolff: There was.
Mr. Matthews: When you applied for that passport what reason did you give for traveling abroad?
Mr. Wolff: I don't remember the reason.
Mr. Matthews: But you did not state that you were going to Spain?
Mr. Wolff: I did not.
Mr. Matthews: When you applied for the passport was it your intention to go to Spain?
Mr. Wolff: It was. . . .
Mr. Matthews: When you arrived in France did you go directly to Spain?
Mr. Wolff: I did.
Mr. Matthews: What did you do with your passport when you arrived in Spain?
Mr. Wolff: I turned it over to some people there for safekeeping, because I did not want to have it on me while I was in action, because I was aware of the fact that there was a very real possibility of losing it. Later events proved the correctness of my reasoning because I lost all of my other personal belongings that I came to Spain with.
Mr. Matthews: What was your position in the Spanish Loyalist Army?
Mr. Wolff: When I first got there, it was that of a soldier. When I left, I was commander of the Lincoln Battalion.
Mr. Matthews: When were you appointed to the position of commander of the Lincoln Battalion?
Mr. Wolff: After a year and a half of fighting on the front line. I don't know the exact date.
Mr. Matthews: Who appointed you to that position?

Mr. Wolff: I was recommended by Colonel Valledor, who was the commander of the Fifteenth Brigade. I was recommended by him to the Minister of Defense, and the Minister of Defense appointed me commander of the battalion.

Mr. Matthews: How long did you hold the position of commander of the Lincoln Battalion?

Mr. Wolff: For a half year.

Mr. Matthews: And what types of work had you done before you went to Spain?

Mr. Wolff: I was an art student. I was in a CCC camp and I worked in —as a shipping clerk at one time.

Mr. Matthews: And you had been in Spain approximately a year and a half when you say you were made commander of the Lincoln Battalion? (No answer.)

Mr. Matthews: Now how did you happen to join the Loyalist Army?

Mr. Wolff: When the war broke out in Spain, I recognized it, or it was my opinion at least, that it was a war of democracy against fascism. I understood that the regularly elected republican government of Spain was under attack by a rebellious army, much the same as the Southern Army attacked the regularly elected Government of the North during the Civil War.

I also realized that Italy and Germany had a very strong hand on the fascist side as against that of republican Spain.

At that time in America we were already beginning to feel and see the actions of our democratic breed of fascism—I am Jewish, and knowing that as a Jew we are the first to suffer when fascism does come, I went to Spain to fight against it. There was a chance to fight on the front——

Chairman Dies: Isn't it true that you also suffer under communism?

Mr. Wolff: I have no idea of that at all. As far as my knowledge goes, I know of no instances where Jews have suffered under communism.

The Chairman: Didn't you know that the Government of Soviet Russia was under a communist dictatorship just as bad as a fascist dictatorship?

Mr. Wolff: I knew the Government of the Soviet Union, as far as I know, was elected by the people. I knew that there was a strong Communist party in the Soviet Union. I was not aware of the existence of any dictatorship in the Soviet Union.

The Chairman: Didn't you regard Stalin as a dictator just like Mussolini and Hitler?

Mr. Wolff: No, I did not.

The Chairman: You do now?

Mr. Wolff: I do not.

The Chairman: You don't think he is a dictator?

Mr. Wolff: I do not.

The Chairman: Do you think that is a democracy?

Mr. Wolff: I don't know what type of government it is, but I do know it is my opinion that it is not a dictatorship.

The Chairman: Do you think it is a democracy?

Mr. Wolff: No, I don't think it is a democracy—I don't think it is a democracy, for instance, similar to—I imagine that you are referring to

and your standard is based on American democracy. I don't think it is
that type of democracy.

The Chairman: Is it any type of democracy?

Mr. Wolff: I don't know.

Mr. Voorhis: What do you think of the support of Germany by Russia?

Mr. Wolff: What is that?

Mr. Voorhis: What do you think of the support of Germany by Russia?

Mr. Wolff: At this time I would like to ask the committee a question.
I received a subpoena in court last week asking me to appear before the
House Committee Investigating Un-American Activities, headed by
Martin Dies of Texas. I would like to know what my opinion of Soviet sup-
port of Germany or alleged support of Germany has to do with the sub-
poena that was served on me.

The Chairman: Well, you gave your opinion with reference to the
democracy in Spain. I was trying to get your idea of what you meant by
democracy.

Mr. Wolff: I was more familiar with democracy in Spain than I was
either in the Soviet Union, since I had never been there.

The Chairman: You had never been in Spain either.

Mr. Wolff: When I got to Spain I was aware of it.

The Chairman: But at the time you joined——

Mr. Wolff: There was no need for me to go to the Soviet Union to defend anything there. There was no struggle. All I knew there was in Spain
a regularly elected government.

The Chairman: Let us proceed.

Mr. Matthews: In the event of a war between the United States and
the Soviet Union, which side would you support?

Mr. Wolff: Is there such a war today?

The Chairman: You certainly would know. You went over and fought
in Spain.

Mr. Wolff: Is there such a war today?

The Chairman: If there were such a war.

Mr. Wolff: Is there a war today between the United States and Soviet
Russia?

The Chairman: If war should break out between the United States and
the Soviet Union, would you support this Government?

Mr. Wolff: If war should break out between the United States and the
Soviet Government, I would be glad to give my answer.[60]

This last was the trump question of the committee; it ordinarily
caused witnesses considerable embarrassment. Advocates of democracy
are naturally eager to fight against fascism, especially against fascist
nations. They are not ordinarily enthusiastic about fighting imperialist
wars, but they will be put to the severest tests if they were compelled to
fight a political-class war on the side of reaction against democracy.
The master question of the committee was tantamount to this: "Sup-

---

[60] *Hearings before Special Committee on Un-American Activities,* House of Representatives, 76th, 3rd, pp. 7785–88.

pose the ruling class in the United States were to begin a counterrevolution against the democratic gains of the American people, would you support the ruling class?" Dies knew all this, but he was depending upon public misinformation and inability to distinguish between the old nationalistic wars and the modern class struggle in order to brand contenders for democracy with the stigma of un-Americanism.

World War I began and practically ended as a pure imperialist war; World War II was partly imperialist and partly political-class, with the imperialist interests distorting the alignment of the political classes; the agitation for World War III is purely political-class and it is to the advantage of the capitalists and fascists to begin the violent phase of this war as early as possible, because the longer it is delayed, the stronger will become the democratic forces of the world. However, this is not to say that later some advanced democratic nation, say the USSR, will attack the capitalist ruling classes, say, in the United States. Rapid gains of democracy have been and will continue for some time to be achieved through internal revolution—not directly through international war. In the class struggle international war is primarily an instrument of apparent value to the anti-democratic powers of the world.

It is obvious from these and other questions that the committee was interested in bringing out its point that the Spanish Loyalist government was not worth fighting for, since it was as bad as that of the fascists who helped to destroy it. To the committee, Soviet Russia was the standard of infamy, so that if it could be shown that a witness had some sympathy for the socialist system of Russia, the conclusion was clear that the latter inculpated himself as un-American. Moreover, one of the principal interests of the committee was to identify Hitler and Stalin, out of the very mouths of "communists," as identical dictators. This done, it could reason that since Stalin is like Hitler, and since Roosevelt "swallowed Stalin's bait," then Roosevelt and the New Deal were like Hitler and fascism. The propaganda would thus reach the negative sanctions of practically everyone in the United States.

Involvement of the Church

As we should expect, religion holds a central place in every stage of the class struggle. In the first report of the committee, communism is defined in part as "a world-wide political organization advocating the abolition of all forms of religion."[61] Throughout the investigation "re-

---

[61]*House Report of the Special Committee on Un-American Activities*, 76th Congress, Report No. 2, January 3, 1939, p. 12. And Martin Dies in his *Trojan Horse* says: "Communists aim not only to destroy the Church and to train a whole genera-

ligion" was relied upon, in a characteristic way, to stigmatize persons suspected of communist sympathies as un-American. It should be noted, however, that Dies and the political class for which he was speaking need not have any particular religious interest—neither a personal interest such as that of the ordinary believer, nor a vested economic interest such as that which the priests ordinarily have. His interest may be only in the use of the people's religiosity as an anti-democratic, propagandistic weapon. It is in the latter sense that religion may be thought of as a "social opiate." In such a case the deep religious conviction of the people is exploited for the purpose of confusing and befogging their thinking on the vital socioeconomic interests in question.

It should be pointed out what attitude the Roman Catholic Church, through its great leaders, assumes in the vanguard of organized, religious reaction to the movement for democracy in the United States. Soon after His Eminence Francis Cardinal Spellman returned to the United States from the Vatican he wrote an article which summarized the position of his Church with respect to communism.[62] His argument follows the typical pattern: (a) that the boys who died in World War II gave their lives not to the cause of destroying fascism all over the world but to protect the United States against communism; (b) that communism will destroy "freedom" in the United States; (c) that his objective "is to help save America from the godless governings of totalitarianism, for [he] believes that every 'ism' based on bloodshed, barbarism, suppression, and slavery is un-American"; (d) that "there is no middle course between Democracy and Communism . . . [for] wherever Communism appears, slavery appears"; and (e) "that the first loyalty of every American is vigilantly to weed out and counteract Communism." There could be no question about the "vigilance" of organized Catholicism in the United States; it has taken on the full panoply of propagandistic war, and, in this, there seems to be no limit to the level of probity to which it may descend. For instance, in a three-column anti-communist advertisement by the Knights of Columbus in a number of metropolitan dailies the public is told:

Whether you call them Communists or Nazis is of little consequence; the objectives, the methods and the ideologies of both are almost identical. . . . There is no real difference between the *Red Fascists* with head-

tion in atheism; they aim also to put aside all that the human race has developed in the way of high ethical or moral standards since man emerged from the jungle. Communism is the restoration of the jungle code." P. 240. Again: "Religion cannot survive the triumph of Communism." P. 247.

[62]"Communism is Un-American," *The American Magazine,* July 1946, pp. 26ff.

quarters in Moscow and the Brown Fascists who came like pestilence out of Berlin.[63]

Organized Labor

The fact of continuing significance in recent developments in the class struggle, however, is the new status of labor in the industrial system of the nation. The focus of progressive action is the Congress of Industrial Organizations; and it was Franklin D. Roosevelt who opened the way to this progress. Almost like a labor leader, he demanded of the Congress in 1933 "that Congress provide the machinery necessary for a great co-operative movement throughout all industry in order to obtain wide re-employment, to shorten the working week, to pay a decent wage for the shorter week."[64] And, in a review of accomplishments under the NRA, he said:

In our progress under the Act the age-long curse of child labor has been lifted, the sweatshop outlawed, and millions of wage earners released from starvation wages and excessive hours of labor. Under it a great advance has been made in the opportunities and assurances of collective bargaining between employers and employees. Under it the patterns of a new order of industrial relations are definitely taking shape.[65]

It is this "new order of industrial relations" later guaranteed by the National Labor Relations Act with which we are here concerned. This act finally made collective bargaining in the United States respectable. In the midst of the depression it reversed the ordinary cycle of labor-union membership from an expected "low" to an all-time "high." As we have pointed out elsewhere, the CIO has taken the initiative in this movement; consequently it has been made the center of anti-labor antagonism.[66]

---

[63]The New York *Times,* August 18, 1946. (Italics added.)

[64]Recommendation to the Congress to enact the National Industrial Recovery Act to put people to work, May 17, 1933.

[65]Recommendation to the Congress that NRA be extended, February 20, 1935.

[66]Ordinarily, when attacks are made against the CIO, the AFL, which has only a very limited objective in the organization of workers, is praised for its good behavior. The way in which this is done may be indicated by the following account from Martin Dies, op. cit. (pp. 145–46) : "From the evidence presented before the Special Committee on Un-American Activities, it is very clear that Communists played an important role in bringing about the withdrawal of the CIO unions from the AFL and the formation of the CIO.

"When Lewis and his followers established the CIO, they were immediately confronted with a problem growing out of the scarcity of trained experienced organizers. Their immediate task was to organize the workers in the heavy industries . . . in line with the wishes of the Administration.

"There is no question but that the President regarded it as a necessary part of his program to have the workers organized for collective bargaining. The President felt

Briefly, the facts of significance in this movement seem to be these:
Workers today have a legal right to organize for purposes of collective
bargaining, and they cannot be legally discriminated against by employers for such union activities;[67] the labor movement is now directed
toward the organization of all organizable workers; in bargaining labor
has begun to insist upon an examination of the profit-making activities
of the employer; the price structure of the system has become an immediate concern of the workers; and "political action" has become an
increasingly effective device in support of the labor movement.

The USSR and the Class Struggle

Even this very limited view of the class struggle will obviously be in-
complete without a glance into its international involvements. Today
the international, political-class issue has become clear-cut and demon-
strable: it has resolved itself virtually to a struggle between the ruling
class in the United States and the upthrust of democracy all over the
world. In areas of major consequence the ammunition and various
details of the armed forces of the United States are sent directly against
the people, but in minor areas such as the East Indies, the West Indies,
and South America the ruling classes—especially that of Great Britain
—are subsidized to carry on the business of laying waste the democratic
efforts of the people. The issue has been constantly befogged by its
definition as a drive against "Russian expansion" by "freedom-loving
peoples." Thus a curtain of obscurity has been drawn across the class
struggle, while it has been made to appear as the old issue of capitalist
imperialism and land grabbing. In a very real sense, however, the ruling
class in the United States is already fighting its own proletarian revolution abroad, and it is only by an understanding of this that we could
explain the apparently reckless expenditure of funds in a negative international program. The cost can hardly be counted since it involves the

---

that no recovery could be brought about until this was accomplished. There was reliable information that the President sent for William Green and asked him to
organize the heavy industries on a mass scale, but that Mr. Green informed the
President it was impossible to do this as quickly as the President wanted it done.
After Green had rejected his proposal, the President sent for John L. Lewis and
made the same request of him.

"Lewis was quick to seize upon this opportunity, and with the approval of the
Administration and the valuable aid given him by the National Labor Relations
Board, he set about to organize the workers in the mass-production industries. There
was one thing lacking—trained organizers and leaders. But the Communist party
was ready to meet this need."

[67]National Labor Relations Board vs. Jones & Laughlin Steel Corporation, 301
U.S. 1. However, the Taft-Hartley Labor Act (June 23, 1947) was especially
designed to limit the advance of unionism.

very existence of that class which has always controlled the resources of the people.

Since the death of President Roosevelt anti-democratic reaction has become increasingly apparent. In international relations the war cry of this reaction has been: "Stop Russia now." Time, as never before, seems to have definitely taken the side of world-wide democracy, hence the reason for almost hysterical suggestions by the capitalist classes to stop it now at its core of incitement with World War III. From the point of view of the interests of the capitalist, ruling class it is very much more necessary to have war with Russia today than it was during the twenties and thirties. This is the last effective way of demonstrating to the world that democracy is a social system inferior to that of capitalism. Although the Soviet Union has carried the major part of the burden of the Allies in the European war, the capitalist nations have been deeply frustrated by its consequences.

If reactionaries are chosen to determine the international policies of the United States, diplomatic conflict with Russia is assured. The problem of the capitalist reactionaries is to carry the world back to its pre-World War II condition of capitalist power and to close all doors opened to democratic gains during the war. When Senator Tom Connally and former Secretary of State James Byrnes, both from the Deep South and with no tradition of democratic zeal, came together with Senator Arthur Vandenberg, a leader of reactionary Republicanism, as a team to devise the policies for the United States in the reconstruction of the world, diplomatic deadlocks with the Soviet Union could have been safely predicted. Such men, as Franklin Roosevelt was wont to say, have the interests of the ruling few at heart and not that of the great masses of people of the world. However, these limited interests are couched in an intense nationalism which defines the Soviet Union as opposed to all the people of the United States.

It seems fairly certain that diplomatic leadership with democratic proclivities would have been much more disposed to compromise with Russia on world problems. This prediction may be supported indirectly by the fact of the relative ease with which Roosevelt and his missionaries reached decisions with Russia and the intense criticism of him by the present reactionaries for his having worked thus smoothly with that nation.

Undoubtedly the post-World War II peace negotiations between Great Britain and the United States on the one hand and Russia on the other turn pivotally upon the question whether reactionary or democratic interests will assume the dominant power in the different coun-

tries of Europe and Asia. As we have seen, the content of the fundamental struggle is ordinarily expressed in such terms as "spheres of
influence," "Russian expansion," "veto power," "atomic power," and
so on. In one of his important radio addresses expressing his inability
to "understand Russia" (October 18, 1946), Byrnes told the people of
the United States:

> America stands for social and economic democracy at home and abroad.
> . . . It would be strange indeed if in this imperfect world our social and
> economic democracy were perfect, but it might help our Soviet friends to
> understand us better if they realized that today our social and economic
> democracy is farther away from the devil-take-the-hindmost philosophy
> of bygone days than Soviet Russia is from Czarist Russia.

Since the national fate of the American people is being determined
largely by this kind of thinking, nothing should be of greater consequence in this matter than to ask the question: Is that so? Moreover,
since race relations are vitally enmeshed in the progress of world
democracy, Mr. Byrnes's admonition to the Soviet Union on the same
occasion should certainly be brought into question. "We in America
know," said he, "that people of different races and stocks can live together in peace in the United States. They should be able to live together in peace in Europe." Seeing that Byrnes is a political leader from
South Carolina and knowing of Russia's racial policies, it is somewhat
difficult to conceive of a stable peace built upon this sort of diplomacy.[68]
It should be recognized, moreover, that the United States is the only
major nation of the world without an effective political party whose
primary objective is the achievement of democracy, and this may suggest the reason why both in its domestic politics and international
diplomacy its ruling class tends to be democratically irresponsible.

Then again it should be remembered that in political-class conflict it
is class interest and not "abstract morality" which determines behavior. Therefore, if in any international council an overwhelming
number of the nations are represented by the capitalist interests within
those nations, the democratic representatives will be automatically
outvoted on every vital international question, while almost the only
function of the presence of these democratic advocates of proletarian
rights will be to lend moral sanction to the imperialist, exploitative

---

[68]It should be remarked that fear and suspicion of the USSR are primarily fear
and suspicion of the common people at home; and since we do not expect the people
at home to give up their struggle for democracy, we could never hope to find a solution for the antagonism between Soviet Russia and capitalist United States. The
principal danger of the USSR to the ruling class in the United States is the former's
alarming prospects for economic and social success.

intent of the capitalist powers. It is this overbalance of capitalist nations which the United States and Great Britain have at their disposal
and which they have converted into a moral question of solicitude for
the opinions of "smaller nations" in international deliberations. The
foreign policy of the United States, like that of all capitalist nations, is
largely predetermined by the economic interests of businessmen; and
the difficulty of achieving consistency in this policy is that of reconciling
a profit-making purpose with the overwhelming desire among most
peoples to reconstruct their social order on the basis of production for
group welfare. The problem of foreign diplomacy, therefore, is that of
describing the interests of businessmen as identical with those of the
masses of disconsolate peoples all over the world.

Probably there is no single material fact so determinative of the
trend of diplomatic relationship between the United States and Russia
as the use of atomic energy as a weapon. In the United States the ruling
class and its military organization have developed about this phenomenon a system of terror propaganda calculated to instill so much
fear in the people that they will lose sight of the fact that they have all
the power that is necessary easily to put the bomb out of existence. So
far as world public opinion is concerned—and that is stronger than any
weapon that any nation can produce—the bomb is a weapon of
desperation.

It is worse than the poisonous gases which have been outlawed by
international agreements and which not even the unprincipled Nazis
attempted to use in the last war. Even if the bomb had no explosive
power at all but only its processual, toxic aftereffects, it already stands
outlawed as a weapon in the public opinion of the civilized world. As
the Japanese radio broadcast said soon after August 6, 1945, when the
atomic bomb was dropped on Hiroshima: "International law lays
down the principle that belligerent nations are not entitled to unlimited
choice in the means by which to destroy their opponents."[69]

As a sort of moral justification, it may be argued that Japan would
have used it upon the United States if she had discovered it first. Today, however, the continued perfection of the weapon with the admitted purpose of a possible need to use it in war evinces some sort of
hysteria on the diplomatic level and introduces an exceedingly distracting element in the settlement of international affairs. Nor is the argument that the use of the bomb shortened the war and, on the whole,
was less costly in human lives a sound one. The same reasoning might

---

[69]The New York *Times,* August 9, 1945.

have been employed in justification of the use of any of the poisonous or asphyxiating liquids and gases just as soon as it was made clear that Japan could not retaliate against the United States in kind.

The reactionaries who call for war against Russia now—"the atom-bomb diplomats"—usually conceive of their class as bearers of the standard of world morality. Thus, according to William C. Bullitt, former United States Ambassador to Russia and France:

> In the task of lifting mankind to the moral level made vital by the atomic bomb, religion and statesmanship can labor shoulder to shoulder. We, as individuals and as a nation, can ask God to make us the instruments of His justice and peace, and try to be worthy instruments.[70]

To outlaw the atomic bomb is not to give up any part of the monopoly which the United States now has on that knowledge, developed in different parts of the world, about the splitting of the atom, but it is to take out of the hands of the ruling, capitalist class the basis for considerable intrigue and propaganda about Russia's desire to obtain "the secret" so that she might manufacture bombs for possible immediate use against the United States. A tremendous amount of reactionary politics may succeed under the ensuing wave of nationalism, for to fear the Soviet Union is to hate it. One way, though dangerous, of achieving domestic unity is to develop a common fear for a foreign power.

Moreover, the creation of an artificial panic about Russia's intent to attack the United States with atomic bombs—although of all the nations in the world only the United States is actually manufacturing atomic bombs—may also be intended to put at rest militant democracy at home. It gives the ruling class an opportunity to make public display of the overwhelming destructive power available in support of the status quo.

---

[70]*The Great Globe Itself,* pp. 214–15. For a similar thesis, though rather within the lunatic fringe of such thinking, see James Burnham, *The Struggle for the World.*

14. *The Literature on Class*

*I*N THE FOREGOING CHAPTERS ON CLASS WE HAVE CONSTANTLY alluded to the possibility of confusion in discussions of this subject. At this point a few references to some leading authorities in the field may help us to appreciate the different approaches to the phenomena of class. It must be admitted, however, that the brevity of some of these excerpts may not do justice to the work of these authors. Some of them will probably only indicate sources of material for further reading. We shall hope that the selection is representative. Of the many articles on class in the *Encyclopedia of the Social Sciences*, none makes a distinction between political and social classes. Estates, as social-status phenomena, are not considered at all. Some contributors discuss the phenomena of social classes and others those of political classes, sometimes even mixing the characteristics of both, yet always under the caption *class*. Although Karl Marx and Friedrich Engels are the great pioneers in descriptions of the behavior of political classes, they seem never to have presented a clear picture of the distinction between status groups, occupational groups, and political classes. Let us look again at the views of these authors.[1]

Karl Marx and Friedrich Engels

At the beginning of our chapter on "The Political Class" we cited the celebrated passage from the *Communist Manifesto* on "class struggle." So far as we know, Marx and Engels never revised their conception of the class groups mentioned there; and this has apparently been responsible not only for considerable misunderstanding of their theory of class struggle but also for a number of rejections of the entire

---

[1]For a recent discussion of various definitions of class, see Pitirim A. Sorokin, *Society, Culture, and Personality*, pp. 263ff.

Marxian approach. The classes that have carried on an uninterrupted fight, according to these writers, are: "freeman and slave, patrician and plebeian, lord and serf, guild-master and journeyman, oppressor and oppressed, bourgeoisie and proletariat."

Of this selection, however, the only true political classes are bourgeoisie and proletariat; and practically all of the writings of Marx and Engels on the class struggle have been concerned with the behavior of these two political classes. In feudal and pre-feudal days freeman and slave, patrician and plebeian, lord and serf were all social-estate groups. On the other hand, guild-master and journeyman are occupational groups. The sporadic conflicts between the latter groups were personal; they never had the potentialities of revolution. Journeymen never wanted to overthrow "society" in order to set up a new system. The terms "oppressor" and "oppressed" are too generalized to have meaning for definitions of political classes. In fact, it might not be entirely incorrect to say that the greater the seeming oppression of one group by another, the less the likelihood of political-class action on the part of the oppressed group.

Othmar Spann

In the *Handwörterbuch der Staatswissenschaften,* Othmar Spann, in his article "Klasse und Stand," attempts a distinction between these two concepts. Unfortunately, however, Spann seems to be more interested in what should be than in what is. He criticizes the "Marxistic, individualistic idea" of class formation because it conceives of society as being pathological; whereas society should be thought of as a healthy organism with class supplementing class. "The basic social fact, the basic law of all estates [*Ständewesens*]," he writes, "is the stratification of society into higher and lower orders according to rank. Even if the phenomena of *Stand* are considered in the individualistic sense as 'class' this law holds true." Spann denies the class-struggle writers further in holding that "the *Stand* (or more exactly, that which according to the individualistic conception of society is called class and according to the universalistic conception *Stand*) does not arise from the way of production and division of labor, but rather it is the spirit and direction of life which lead to a certain kind of economy and kind of labor." Among the Marxian writers, Spann includes Max Weber, calling him "a friend of the socialists," and, quoting from *Wirtschaft und Gesellschaft,* he concludes that "Weber's conception is therefore typical of the entire science of today."

At one point in this article one would think that the author had reached a clear differentiation of these concepts. He says, for instance: "The group in action, if seen isolatedly, is called class—class in an individualistic, Marxist sense; but the group in action, if seen organically, that is to say, as an integral part of the totality of the activities of a society and of the totality of culture [*das Gesamtgeistige*] from which activities are derived, is called estate *(Stand)*." However, from this Spann does not follow and develop a consistent analysis. Instead, he lapses into such confusions as the following: "He who wants to recognize the constructive element, in fact, the real element in historical society, must see class as *Stand,* as an acting aggregate. He must understand the spiritual aggregates of which they are the expression."

Werner Sombart

Werner Sombart[1a] is clearer. He distinguishes between estates *(Stände)* and classes. His conception of "social class" or "class" is that which we have called political class above. To him: "Estates are large unions based upon a community of living, and organically integrated in a community; classes, on the other hand, are large individualistic unions held together externally by common interests in an economic system and mechanically integrated in a community."[2] Estates develop naturally as a factor in community life, but they are essentially legal entities. "To this inner nature the estate owes its political significance: it becomes almost everywhere a *legal community* and is integrated as such, with certain tasks, in the whole of the state. . . . The estate feels itself as being a part of a great organism, to whose aims it subordinates its own aims."[3]

Quite different from the estate is the social class (political class in our meaning).

The class does not arise in a natural way, but is created artificially. To be sure, certain communities of destinies of life are present, but not that easy living together in a natural community. The class presents a consciously developed conviction of belonging together; therefore, class cohesion is brought in from the outside, so to speak, by way of a reflective process of consciousness. So long as a community of interest has not been impressed on the consciousness of the individuals, the class will not come into being. Therefore, a class has class consciousness, but we consider it to be nonsense to talk of *class-honor,* to which some conscious process of class-solidarity corresponds.[4]

[1a]"Stände und Klassen," *Der Moderne Kapitalismus,* II, 2.
[2]Ibid., p. 1091.
[3]Ibid., p. 1092.
[4]Ibid., p. 1093.

Sombart definitely recognizes "class" as a conflict group, but he thinks "the social class is an entirely modern formation. Antiquity knows only germs of social classes. The latter emerged as an offspring of capitalism in recent European history."[5] Thus he conceives of "class action" as essentially a bourgeoisie-proletariat struggle;[6] in our sense this constitutes only one situation of political-class struggle.

Sombart also sees a distinction between "class," estate, and "social strata"; that is, the status order we have called social class above. Thus he says, and we shall quote him fully:

> Besides these fairly clearly definable large groups, estate and class, we distinguish in addition a social structure, whose limits, however, disappear in a fog. We designate these also in German by the expression "Stand," or "ordre" in French, and "class" in English, but only with some prefix such as "middle"—e.g., the *Mittelstand*, the *moyen ordre,* or the middle class. These groups obviously have nothing to do with an estate or a class in the previously designated meaning, for they really exist as a unity only in the conception [*in der Vorstellung*] of statisticians, social theoreticians, social pedagogues and other third persons. This social structure is conceived of by dividing the members of a community into [mostly] three parts or strata according to their income: an upper, a middle, and a lower stratum.[7]

The author goes on to discuss the origin of estates from professional interests.

Max Weber

Max Weber is not so clear as Sombart. One part of his discussion[8] is too much in outline form and another[9] is almost an economic philosophy of class (political class). Class is here conceived of as a function of the market. Indeed, the author speaks of "class position" as "market position."

Weber recognizes many types of class: "possessing or property class," "earning or income class," "social class," and subdivisions of these, but here class becomes a classification rather than a sociological concept. At any rate, such leading passages as the following are confusing:

> The organization of classes purely on the basis of property is not dynamic, i.e., it does not necessarily lead to class struggle and class revolution. The decidedly positively privileged property class of slave owners often

[5]Ibid., p. 1094.
[6]Ibid., p. 1094.
[7]Ibid., p. 1094.
[8]*Wirtschaft und Gesellschaft,* Vol. I, Chap. II, "Stände und Klassen."
[9]Ibid., "Klasse, Stand, Parteien," Vol. II, pp. 631–40, *passim.*

exists side by side with the much less positively privileged class of peasants, even with the "déclassé," frequently without any feeling of class antagonism. . . . A classical example of the lack of class antagonism was the relation of the "poor white trash" to the planters in the Southern States. The "poor white trash" was far more hostile to the Negroes.[10]

This leads us to think that political classes may be organized on a property basis; however, when such is the case, they evidently are "not dynamic," which reasoning seems to involve a mixture of the idea of status and of political-class action. By accepting the illusion of basic antagonism between "poor white trash" and Negroes, Weber seems to evince some misunderstanding of the nature of political-class action. Moreover, his discussion of "status segregation" developing into caste, with "ethnic" or blood relationships as the basis of caste, is very misleading.

Neither are we at all sure of ourselves, after reading Weber's typological discussion of class, on being presented with the following:

A society may be called estatelike [*Ständisch*] where social differentiations are made mainly according to estates, classlike [*Klassenmässig*], if they are made primarily according to classes. Of the "classes," the "social class" is nearest to the estate, the "income class" is furthest. Estates are often formed, in terms of their center of gravity, by "property classes."[11]

---

[10]Ibid., Vol. I, p. 178.

[11]Ibid., p. 180.

Recently C. Wright Mills in his detailed review of Warner and Lunt's book, *The Social Life of a Modern Community*, seems to have employed Max Weber's categories of class criteria with some enthusiasm. To Mills *class* "includes the sheerly economic and nothing else," *rentier*, salaried, wage earner, et al.; status refers to the "distribution of 'prestige,' 'deference,' 'esteem,' 'honor' "; and *power* refers to the influencing attributes of individuals: "Who can be expected to obey whom." (See *American Sociological Review*, April 1942, Vol. VII, p. 262.) He assumes that these three are "analytically separable dimensions," and that it is possible to make "distinctions between class and status, between class and class-awareness, and between status and status awareness." He evidently feels also that Weber's concept of "negatively privileged income classes" and "positively privileged income classes" might have been employed to advantage in that study.

But of all Mills's excellent criticism of those results, the least convincing is his attempt to suggest possibilities for these references. Weber's "class" is only one possible functional classification of economic groups. It is rather meaningless in a study of social classes because its divisions ordinarily have homogeneity neither in wealth, interest, nor "class awareness." Therefore, the suggestion that these divisions of his class are associated with a determinable and separable status remains to be demonstrated. Prestige, deference, esteem, honor can have no existence apart from the social facts which confer them; indeed they are inconceivable apart from such facts.

The second bipartite classification into negatively and positively privileged income groups is not recognized as such by members of American communities. Furthermore, although Weber does give examples of functional groups belonging to each of the latter divisions, the problem of separating all persons in the society on the basis of this criterion of privilege is quite another matter. Moreover, granting for the moment that this is done, what, really, do we have finally? Two income groups in opposition? See also H. H. Gerth and C. Wright Mills, "Class, Status, Party," a translation of Max Weber in *Politics*, October 1944, pp. 271–78.

R. M. MacIver

In discussing the work of Professor MacIver[12] we have an opportunity to observe the characteristic approach of the English and American sociological literature. This approach may be described as a disdain for careful study of the political class, a frank denial that there is any such class, or a confusion of the concept of social and political classes. The analysis in most textbooks stands approximately at parity with the following.

In his definition MacIver says: "We shall . . . mean by a social class any portion of a community which is marked off from the rest . . . primarily by social status. . . . It is the sense of status, sustained by economic, political, or ecclesiastical power and by the distinctive modes of life and cultural expressions corresponding to them, which draws class apart from class, gives cohesion to each, and stratifies the whole society."[13] In this definition we probably have as significant an error as any in the various conceptualizations of social classes. A social class is not "marked off from the rest"; neither is it "drawn apart" from other classes; furthermore, it has no "cohesion" as an entity.

In seeking actual social classes by way of such a definition, the author goes clearly astray. Thus he asserts:

The owner-farmer and the tenant-farmer [in North America] . . . form a social class as we have defined it, for the factor of status is bound up with their mode of living, their sense of proprietorship, their relatively low and inelastic income, *their economic solidarity set over against that of other groups,* and their relative, though diminishing, segregation from the cultural influences which play upon urban populations.[14]

The false lead continues to gyrate even to the extent of including ethnic relations. Thus the author writes:

A broader class distinction may be asserted in the name of the pride of race, such as that between the West European stocks and the "new immigrant," between Gentile and the Jew. But these barriers do not create clearly defined social classes, and some of them seem to be transitional lines, becoming less determinative in the degree in which cultural differences between groups are merged in the new environment. Only the racial barrier of color completely resists the triumphant claim of wealth to be at length the chief determinant of class, and this defeat is less decisive because of the general poverty of the colored people.[15]

---

[12]*Society,* Chap. IX, "Class and Caste."

[13]Ibid., p. 167. Further, "Class distinctions rest in the last resort . . . on status." P. 167.

[14]Ibid., pp. 169–70. (Italics added.)

[15]Ibid., pp. 170–71.

Professor MacIver also questions the position of the class-struggle writers in a way not uncommon among American sociologists. "It should be observed," he emphasizes, "that we have not defined social class in purely economic terms. This alternative mode of definition, generally maintained by the followers of Karl Marx, stresses a very important factor that commonly underlies class distinctions, but it is inadequate sociologically."[16] Continuing, the author brings the three concepts of political class, social class, and estate into one wad as a contradiction of the Marxists. Thus he declares: "Certainly in countries of western civilization the Marxist dichotomy is too sweeping to fit the facts of the class system. So broad a division and so sharp a cleavage are more applicable to a feudal order, such as that of pre-revolutionary Russia, than a complex industrialized society."[17]

In judging the Russian system, the concepts of political class and status are entangled; in other words, a political-classless society is understood to mean a statusless society. Accordingly, he observes: ". . . the communist ideal of a 'classless society' is by no means fully realized in communist Russia, where there remain different degrees of prestige attaching to occupation, party membership, and political position."[18]

Furthermore, MacIver thinks that class struggle emerges when tradition weakens and classes cease to be complementary. "If . . . tradition weakens and class struggle emerges, the attitudes of the opposing classes—one conservative and striving to maintain, the other radical and striving to overthrow an order—cease to be complementary and become as different as the social values for which they respectively strive."[19] And class sentiment unites those who feel alike; more specifically, it unites the upper against the lower class. "[Class sentiment] does . . . unite those who feel distinct from other classes, but it unites them primarily because they feel distinct. Above all, it unites the 'superior' against the 'inferior.' It emanates from the belief in superi-

---

[16]Ibid., p. 167.

[17]Ibid., p. 177.

[18]Ibid., p. 174. The following passage illustrates still further MacIver's confusion of status and political class: "It is unjustifiable to think of them all as belonging to the large capitalists and financiers. If they are united, it is only in a negative position, as being generally anti-socialistic; but this is hardly enough to constitute them a social class. They differ widely in their social stations and ambitions." Ibid., p. 178.

[19]Ibid., p. 173.

In a question presented for discussion, John Lewis Gillin, et al., epitomize a similar confusion: "Explain why in the Middle Ages inferiority and superiority in social status did not create class conflict, while today the ostentatious assumption of superiority by any class results in resentment by those who, by inference, are inferior." *Social Problems,* 3d ed., p. 65.

ority; so that class division is really imposed on the lower by the higher classes."[20] Thus the latter brings us back to the original misconception.[21]

A. W. Kornhauser

In a study of certain statistics[22] intended to throw light on class relationships in the United States, Professor Kornhauser begins by asking the following questions: "Is our contemporary American Society composed of 'classes'? Does the population fall into several broad social groups holding opposed viewpoints and values? Or is it rather true, as so often is dogmatically declared, that in America there are no classes, there are only the artificial antagonisms stirred up by alien agitators and political demagogues?"[23] Evidently Kornhauser is about to initiate a study of political-class struggle in the United States. But one wonders as he reads that "problems of 'class' are concerned essentially with the social orientation presumed to grow out of people's contrasting objective conditions. A social class consists of those sections of the population which feel similarly concerning their position and interests, which have a common outlook and distinctive common attitudes."[24] And as the author reaches a conclusion, one is almost convinced that he is now talking about social classes; that is to say, social status. Thus he says: "Whatever gaps remain in the evidence . . . the conclusion is definite that income and occupational classes do differ in scholastic background and in intellectual ability as measured by tests. The upper classes are, in this sense, 'superior.' All the studies, however, show a great amount of overlapping of groups."[25]

Notwithstanding, the argument switches again to a political-class discussion. Without warning the author writes: "That large differences do exist between income and occupational groups in their opinion on important issues of the day can no longer be denied even by those least willing to admit the fact. The split of opinion on various New Deal measures and other current issues has become increasingly apparent."[26]

---

[20] MacIver, op. cit., p. 173.

[21] MacIver does say that "the system is no longer tier above tier, but a continuous incline" (ibid., p. 175); and that "in feudal times it was a series of disconnected stages." Ibid., p. 171. However, these statements only add to the confusion, for they are made sporadically, without apparent relevance.

[22] "Analysis of Class Structure of Contemporary American Society," in *Industrial Conflict,* ed. by George W. Hartmann and Theodore Newcomb.

[23] Ibid., p. 199.

[24] Ibid., p. 200.

[25] Ibid., p. 209.

[26] Ibid., p. 232.

At length, however, the purpose of the researcher dawns upon us: it is to show that differences in social status go hand in hand with "differences in contentment"; and differences in contentment will result in differences in desirability of the status quo. In other words, "the figures tend to support the hypothesis . . . that the differences among socio-economic classes are largely differences in contentment, life-satisfactions, personal adjustments. These variations in feeling can be expected naturally to manifest themselves in opposed views concerning the present social order and the desirability of change in a 'radical direction.' "[27]

At any rate, whatever Professor Kornhauser's figures show, his expectation that lower-status (class) people are "naturally" more radical is open to question. Indeed, we may state that the proposition is erroneous and follows, in fact, from a confusion of the status and the political-class idea. It is not the misery of status but the "misery of comparison" which breeds discontent. Status groups are "naturally" harmonious; social discontent is a political-class attitude which must be studied as such. We may venture to state that "radicalism" is most likely to develop in situations of general cultural or industrial change. We should expect the outcastes of India, for instance, to live from generation to generation without developing radicals; but with the increasing urbanization of India, the educating of untouchables, and a larger and larger number of renegade Brahmans becoming their leaders, social unrest will be inevitable.

Other Authorities

In the following paragraphs we shall make briefer reference to the works of other students of social stratification.

William F. Ogburn and Delvin Peterson analyzed the votes cast on a number of social questions by "the upper- middle- laboring- and rural-class" together with the city dwellers in Oregon and came to the conclusion that "the figures show little indication of class conflict, nor do they point to a revolution. They rather point toward harmony and show a considerable ability on the part of the social classes to get along together."[28] It seems to us, however, that neither social classes nor political classes were isolated; and for that reason one could hardly be certain about the meaning of the results.

---

[27] Ibid., p. 243.

[28] "Political Thought of Social Classes," *Political Science Quarterly,* Vol. 31, 1916, p. 317.

Paul Mombert, in his discussion of class, attempts to achieve a monistic explanation of class. He finds that other writers have had quite different conceptions of class and concludes that the fact "that various theorists should have found the essential nature of class in such different attributes is to a great extent due to their having in mind different historical periods, for in the historical development of classes essential changes have taken place in their nature."[29] Apparently Mombert thinks that the phenomenon of class has changed essentially in its evolution. It seems that the author does not realize that he is saying that the social class has become a political class. For what else could the following statement mean: "The determining forces in class formation have been in early times social and in recent times mainly economic"?[30] And probably estates, social classes, and political classes find themselves easily combined in the assertion that "in the course of historical development new criteria for the essential nature of classes have arisen to supplant the old."[31]

Raymond B. Cattell agrees that there are no gaps in the status structure of most Western societies. "But in relation to other variables and other societies, e.g., that of India, it is obvious that discontinuities exist, and that the term 'social stratum' is accurate as a metaphor in its full geological sense."[32] Cattell evidently thinks that castes are discrete social classes.

Sorokin, Zimmerman, and Galpin have developed a whole system of skewed and off-color hypotheses and conclusions as a result of their basic confusion of the phenomena of social stratification. Here is the essential position of these authors:

The agricultural population . . . is stratified economically from the standpoints of wealth, income, and economic standard of living; occupationally from the standpoint of domination and control on the one hand and subjection and execution on the other; and politically from the standpoint of social and political privileges and prestige. Although the rural pyramid is much less stratified than the urban . . . stratification has always existed to some extent among the agricultural population.
. . . it is possible to discriminate the following principal strata of the agricultural population:

    1. Proprietors of large, latifundia-type, agricultural enterprises.
    2. Proprietors of smaller capitalist agricultural enterprises.

---

[29]"Class," *Encyclopedia of the Social Sciences.*
[30]Ibid.
[31]Ibid.
[32]"The Concept of Social Status," *The Journal of Social Psychology,* Vol. 15, May 1942, p. 296.

3. Managers and tenants of large capitalist enterprises.
4. Proprietors of farmer-capitalist agricultural enterprises.
5. Proprietors of farmer agricultural enterprises.
6. Tenants of capitalist agricultural enterprises.
7. Tenants of farmer-capitalist agricultural enterprises.
8. Tenants of farmer agricultural enterprises.
9. Higher employees of capitalist and farmer-capitalist enterprises.
10. Proprietors of the peasant-consumptive agricultural enterprises.
11. Tenants of peasant-consumptive agricultural enterprises.
12. Proprietors of proletarianizing or small decaying agricultural enterprises.
13. Hired laborers of various types.

. . . in essentials their hierarchial sequence is practically that given above, and, what is more important, all these strata actually exist, within the total agricultural population of various countries. Each of these strata is divided further into a series of substrata according to the amount of income, prestige, and occupational function. Thus the whole agricultural population gives a rather high pyramid of social stratification.
. . . the existence of different social strata with their differences in economic, occupational, and social-political fields, always leads to greater or lesser conflicts of interests and to psycho-social and *economic antagonism between these strata.* The greater the stratification, the greater become these conflicts and antagonisms. In the city, where stratification is greater than in the country, the antagonisms of class struggles are also greater. But since stratification exists in the rural aggregate also, it follows that such an aggregate is not entirely free from clash, conflict, and *antagonisms in the relationships of the strata that constitute the aggregate.* As the social distance between the very top of the rural pyramid and its lowest stratum of hired laborers or poor peasants is particularly great, the antagonisms between these strata are particularly conspicuous. In a latent form it always exists. *From time to time it takes the form of an overt explosion in a revolutionary movement of the poorest rural classes against the large landlords and landholders.* History is filled with the records of such movements.[33]

Professor Sorokin and his collaborators assert very much more than they demonstrate. At any rate, we may state briefly that they appear to be in error because they assume: (a) that their classification of types of agricultural functions applies universally to agricultural peoples, (b) that it is a description of natural social strata, (c) that modern urban populations are socially stratified into discrete strata, (d) that the so-called social strata are political classes and therefore conflict groups, and (e) that class conflict is a function of social distance. As

[33]Pitirim A. Sorokin, Carle C. Zimmerman, and Charles J. Galpin, *A Systematic Source Book in Rural Sociology*, Vol. I, pp. 362–68. (Italics added.)

we have attempted to show from previous discussions, all these assumptions are highly questionable.[33a]

Statements like the following by Alfred Meusel are unsuspectingly confusing: "The transition from capitalism to a classless socialist society involves more radical and far reaching changes than suppression of the feudal order by the bourgeois system, both of which are marked by internal antagonism between an upper and a lower class."[34] The terms "upper" and "lower classes" have been ordinarily used to designate status groups in a social-class system; and the use of them in this reference to political-class antagonism tends to lump the concepts.

Morris Ginsberg offers the following definition of social classes; however, it seems better as a description of social estates.

Classes in modern society [he writes] may be described as groups of individuals who, through common consent, similarity of occupation, wealth and education, have come to have a similar mode of life, a similar stock of ideas, feelings, attitudes and forms of behavior and who, on any or all these grounds, meet one another on equal terms and regard themselves, although with varying degrees of explicitness, as belonging to one group.[35]

W. Lloyd Warner and Paul S. Lunt have published two volumes[36] representing studies based mainly on a mistaken conception of the social-class structure of a contemporary American city. They are the most pretentious works on social class in recent literature; and at the same time a monumental illustration of what is likely to occur when a researcher goes into the field with a conviction which must be satisfied. In this case the conviction was that the status system of a modern urban center in the United States is divided into ascertainable, segregable, social classes.

The two volumes, of course, do not show this; yet somehow "six classes and seven different kinds of social structure" are made to appear.[37] The persons, themselves, in the community investigated were not conscious of the full determinants of their status, for the authors say: "It must not be thought that all people in Yankee City are aware of all the minute distinctions made in this book."[38] At any rate, the fact

---

[33a]For a different statement but equally faulty approach, see Pitirim A. Sorokin, *Society, Culture, and Personality*, pp. 256–95.

[34]"Revolution and Counter-Revolution," *Encyclopedia of the Social Sciences.*

[35]"Class Consciousness," *Encyclopedia of the Social Sciences.*

[36]*The Social Life of a Modern Community* and *The Status System of a Modern Community*, Vols. I and II, respectively, of Yankee City Series.

[37]Op. cit., Vol. II, p. 15; see also Vol. I, p. 28.

[38]Op. cit., Vol. I, p. 91.

that "the six social classes" set "apart from" one another are not in "Yankee City" but rather in the books is brought out most clearly in Volume II. There it is possible to move classes or parts of them about like men on a checkerboard without even so much as a thought of an on-going society. The authors have achieved an artificiality which is progressively dissociated from reality because their basic assumption is unreal.[39]

A. M. Carr-Saunders and D. Caradog Jones, after a fairly exhaustive demographic study of "the social structure of England and Wales,"[40] confessed that they had been able to find no social classes—they were unable to find segregable social strata. However, although these authors might be able to force such investigators as Warner and his associates to admit that they, too, did not find social classes in the United States, the English students are themselves identifying social and political classes.

Thus they inquire: "Do social classes exist? We hear less than formerly of the 'upper,' 'middle,' and 'lower' social classes. We do, however, hear much about 'class consciousness' and 'class warfare.' If class warfare is a fact, it should be possible for the statistician to estimate the strength of the battalions ranged against each other."

From the outset, then, the authors seem to have mixed the concepts of social class and political class. Status groups do not have "battalions." And the battalions of political classes may permit themselves to be entirely known only after or during a revolution.

"Social classes," they continue, "may . . . be a sheer figment of the imagination. . . . At one time many factors conspired together to produce an 'upper' class. . . . There is no longer any recognizable 'upper' class, and as to the 'middle' class, it never was anything more

---

[39]More specifically this study of a social-class system seems to have gone astray because:

(a) The researchers had no workable definition of social class; consequently they were never able to organize their data according to a precise and consistent set of class criteria. This deficiency renders even their display of crude data untrustworthy.

(b) They believed that the "veterinary" techniques and methods developed to meet the exigencies of the study of simple, preliterate societies could be adopted with little, if any, modification to the study of complex, enlightened urban centers. The blank-mind or exploratory procedure has apparently been effectively employed in many anthropological projects; but as an approach to the study of social phenomena in modern society, it may involve a degree of rambling effort which amounts to utter wastefulness.

(c) Of little concern with the community studied as a functional entity, and inordinate preoccupation with static ideas about social structure.

(d) Of inadequate statistical preparation for the handling and interpretation of mass social data, and of their not developing out of the exigencies of the problem itself a sufficient statistical methodology.

[40]*A Survey of the Social Structure of England and Wales.*

than a heterogeneous assemblage of very diverse and non-cohesive elements."

Here the idea of the old estate system seems to be associated with that of the modern conceptual social class. The authors go on to think of workers as a status group and, in the same breath, to identify them as a political class. At length they arrive at the inevitable confusion in their criticism of the proletarian leadership for having read bad books. Thus they write:

At the present day the wage-earning element of the employed group does, it is true, exhibit a certain degree of cohesion. The specific characteristics of wage-earning are well marked. . . . Many factors do thus combine to produce one moderately cohesive and self-conscious group. But it is misleading to speak of class divisions and class distinctions today, because no other similar groups exist. . . . When . . . it comes to practical issues there is seldom or never to be found a sharp dividing line between wage-earners and the rest. The line sometimes falls in one place and sometimes in another.[41] Persuasive appeals are made to workers by hand and brain. . . . Strident orders are issued to embark upon class warfare. But who is on one side and where is the enemy? The belief in the existence of social classes, or even of one social class . . . is the result of studying social theory of doubtful value and of neglecting social facts.[42]

Finally we present some contributions from Kimball Young.[43]

Within the caste or class itself [the author generalizes] there is a distinct sense of co-operation, common interest, and awareness of status. That is, there are common habits, attitudes, sentiments, ideas and values upon which the members agree and upon which they may and do act in har-

[41]The authors' difficulty here may be simply a non-recognition of the difference between "practical issues" and political-class questions.

[42]All quotations from the work cited, pp. 70–73.

A similar position is taken by a Mexican writer, Lucio Mendieta y Nuñez. Says Nuñez: "What role do social classes perform in the organization and functioning of society? For a long time there has been talk of 'class struggle' as a result of the division of the human groups in society; as a consequence whereof it would seem that in this struggle is summed up the sociological importance of the classes. A careful observation of the facts, however, leads us to the conviction that no such struggle is going on, that in this case we have to deal with a phrase become indestructible thanks to the political dynamism with which it is weighted.

"For a class struggle properly conceived to exist, it would be necessary for each class to be organized and to oppose, as an organization, the others, at the same time seeking to gain a more or less well-defined objective. We have already noted, however, that the social classes are complexes of a cultural and economic character, put together or formed in the social realities as such, not as artificially constituted for struggle. . . .

"Those talking of class struggle would find it hard to explain against whom the middle class is fighting. . . . The existence—ignored by the Marxist classification— of the three classes: higher, middle, and lower is evident." *American Sociological Review*, Vol. 11, April 1946, pp. 175–76.

[43]*An Introductory Sociology*, rev. ed.

mony. . . . Unity as well as a sense of difference from others is supported by all sorts of external marks of privilege and prestige, such as costumes, badges, and distinctive duties and rights.[44]

To be sure, there were no illustrations of this. However, after criticizing the class-struggle writers evidently without recognizing their meaning, Young concludes:

> The class struggle implies the break-down of a particular equilibrium which has grown up among the classes. Where one class—military, political, ecclesiastical, or economic—has come to dominate a society, the whole societal structure may be ordered in reference to this. But a crisis, like the Industrial Revolution, a new religion, or a war, may bring about tensions and unrest leading to an attempt by other classes to overthrow the dominance of the elite at the top.[45]

The following selection illustrates clearly the amorphous nature of these ideas:

> Intra-class conflict is a form of struggle between those who are members of a large group and who accept some common premises of behavior. It is never so violent or destructive as inter-class conflict. Within the wide class of aristocracy, for example, there is always rivalry and conflict for status, jealousy for honors and privileges. Within the working classes there is struggle for jobs, status and advancement. . . . So-called native American laborers have periodically opposed the demands of immigrant workers for a larger share of the jobs and the pay. Within the races themselves there is often an intense struggle. . . . The mulatto is opposed by the pure black, who is jealous of the former's achievements. Within the sect or denomination the members may carry on an intense campaign for power. In short, intra-class conflict is but another term for factional fights within any we-group. . . .[46]

In this chapter we have not attempted to cite exhaustively from the literature on social stratification.[47] Our purpose has been to present a representative sample of the thinking on this subject; and for this we selected from the more recent works.

---

[44]Ibid., p. 811.

[45]Ibid., p. 680.

[46]Ibid., pp. 681–82.

[47]For very recent distortions of this subject, see Raymond B. Cattell, "The Concept of Social Status," *The Journal of Social Psychology*, Vol. XV, May 1942, pp. 293–308; "The Cultural Functions of Social Stratification I" and "The Cultural Functions of Social Stratification II," *The Journal of Social Psychology*, Vol. XXI, February 1945, pp. 3–55. Also B. Moore, Jr., "A Comparative Analysis of Class Struggle," *American Sociological Review*, Vol. X, February 1945, pp. 31–37.

15. Class and Caste

*I*N THIS CHAPTER WE SHALL ATTEMPT A SPECIFIC COMPARISON
and differentiation of some of the characteristics of the caste and
the social-class system. Some repetition may be necessary in the interest
of clarity.

Castes as Rigid Classes

Recently writers on aspects of social stratification have been thinking
of social status in terms of a continuum of societies. At one end are
societies in which the status of the individual tends to remain fixed for
life; at the other are societies in which the opportunity for advancement
of status of the individual is recognized and even encouraged. In other
words, at the one end are caste systems, at the other the so-called "open
class systems."

In 1498 the Portuguese adventurers who landed at Calicut with
Vasco da Gama observed that in India society was organized in a number of endogamous groups with inferior and superior social positions
held in perpetuity. They compared this with the social mobility familiar
to them in the West and finally called it *casta*. Since then (about the
middle of the sixteenth century) almost numberless writers have made
the same observations. A recognition of relative rigidity of social status
among different status systems, then, is no contribution of modern
sociologists.

What is new, however, is an insistent attempt by many students of
social stratification to identify rigidity of social status, in whatever
social context it is found, with caste; and to conceive of castes as mere
petrified, rigid, or endogamous social classes. For instance, A. L.
Kroeber says:

Castes . . . are a special form of social classes which in tendency at
least are present in every society. Castes differ from social classes, how-

ever, in that they have emerged into social consciousness to the point that custom and law attempt their rigid and permanent separation from one another.[1]

However, if we examine these situations more closely we should recognize that the structure of a social class is categorically different from that of the caste. If we think, for the moment, of a social class as a status stratum consisting of individuals with heterogeneous economic, political, and religious interests, then, so far as we know, there has been no instance in which a class became increasingly stable until at length it crystallized into a caste. Apparently the factor which is supposed to produce the rigidity or inertia in the transformation of a class into a caste is endogamy. But, historically speaking, endogamy has had the function of securing the segregation of class membership rather than that of solidifying classes. At this point we should mention that a class, one conceptual segment of a classification, does not move; only status-bearing entities may have social mobility.

The belief that the caste system consists of four castes constituting a status gradient has led to very much confusion. As a matter of fact, there has never been any support for this belief.[2] Indeed, so far as the caste system is concerned, an endogamous social class is anomalous. The conception of the social class may include castes, while the caste consists of individuals. The social class may be conceived as a form of social stratification and differentiation; the caste may be a form of social differentiation only. Castes may have collateral social status; social classes must of necessity be hierarchically superposed. Thus two different castes may be socially equal—that is to say, they may be of the same social level just as, for instance, stationary engineers and elec-

---

[1]"Caste," *Encyclopedia of the Social Sciences.* Shridhar V. Ketkar concludes: "Classes are converted into castes by becoming endogamous." *The History of Caste in India,* Vol. I, p. 28. According to Ogburn and Nimkoff: "Class societies may be represented as extending all the way from those like the above [castes], which are relatively rigid or closed, to those which are flexible and open." *Sociology,* p. 317. And Davis and Dollard say: "Caste in the [American] South is nothing more nor less . . . than a system of limiting social participation between color groups, and thus differentiating between these groups with regard to the most fundamental opportunities in human society. *In this latter respect it is quite like our system of social classes. It differs from the class system in its arbitrary and final definition of the individual's status.*" *Children of Bondage,* pp. 19–20. To the same effect, see Talcott Parsons, "An Analytical Approach to the Theory of Social Stratification," *American Journal of Sociology,* Vol. XLV, May 1940, p. 855. E. A. Ross is explicit: "Class hardens into caste when the jealous upper class resists or retards the admission of commoners, however great their merit or wealth." *Principles of Sociology,* p. 341.

[2]On this point E. A. Gait agrees: "It has . . . been shown by Senart and others that the division into castes has no direct relation with the division into classes. The castes came into existence independently, without any regard to the classes. The individual castes no doubt claimed to belong to one or other of the classes, but this they still do." *Census of India, 1911,* Vol. I, Part 1, p. 365.

tricians may be of the same social class. Frequently in class systems lateral status extends beyond the immediate society, so that an American, a Greek, an Englishman, and an Italian of the upper social class in their respective countries will tend to recognize each other in free association on common ground. In other words, an Englishman may go to France and marry within his class with impunity. The caste, however, is socially bounded on every side.

We may illustrate further. There is in some of these caste-class analogies the spurious historical implication either that existing castes have been at some time social classes or that existing social classes might be expected to "harden" into castes. It need hardly be said, however, that neither of these propositions has been demonstrated. Social classes are not founded upon occupational limitations in the sense that castes are. One of the principal features of castes is that they identify themselves functionally. Thus, if it were possible to conceive of the "middle class" in the United States as becoming endogamous, the resulting social entity would be very much different from any group that we have ever known as a caste in India. It would contain priests, racketeers, dancers, nurses, tanners, doctors, butchers, teachers, sewerage workers, undertakers, farmers, mechanics, Protestants, Mohammedans, Catholics, Jews, whites, reds, and blacks, and so on. Clearly, no one could fit this social agglomeration into the concept of caste.[3] "Class and caste stand to each other in relation, not of parent and child, but of family and species. The general classification is by classes, the detailed one by castes. The former represent the external, the latter the internal view of social organization."[4]

The greater the disparity in position between social class and social class, the less frequent are interclass marriages and the stronger are the sanctions against them. Indeed, the two extremes of most class hierarchies may be thought of as endogamous with respect to each other. Yet obviously classes are not transformed into castes directly as difference in social position increases.

---

[3]Of course reasoning would be seriously inverted if we were to assume that should the class become endogamous it would soon cease to be so diverse. The group must first cease to be diverse before it can achieve caste endogamy, and not vice versa.

[4]E. A. Gait, op. cit., p. 366.

Structure of Class and Caste "Hierarchy"

Since in a social-class society status attributes are achieved competitively, the shape of the status gradient must of necessity be pyramidal.[5] In other words, the greater the desirability of the status, the greater the difficulty of achieving it. The higher one rises, the keener is the rivalry and the fewer the rivals. Thus the size of the class tends to vary inversely with superiority of status. The shape of the caste hierarchy is, however, unpredictable, for caste membership is principally a function of the birth rate of caste populations. Although we have no data on caste membership by "natural districts" in India, figures for the country as a whole show that some of the higher castes, such as Brahmans and Shaikhs, have the largest membership. Indeed, the Brahmans have a larger membership than any other.[6] We may venture the speculation that since the lowest castes are usually recruited from those primitive tribes on the periphery of the caste system it is probable that the shape of the caste hierarchy may appear like an inverted truncated pyramid.

The social-class gradient is a status continuum. We think of it as including discrete strata only for purposes of analysis and comprehension. Castes, however, are distinct segregable social groupings. While conceptual, class strata—if they are to be meaningful—must be few, the numbers of castes may be practically unlimited. Castes may be classified, but classes are already social classifications. As we have indicated elsewhere, there may be social classes within castes,[7] but it is obvious that there can be no sense in speaking of social classes within social classes. A *crucial* difference between a social class and a caste is that, with reference to the social order, the caste is a status-bearing entity, while the social class is a conceptual stratum of status-bearing entities.

Therefore, the class is not a form of social organization; that is to say, it is not organized in the sense that a caste is. To illustrate, we may think of segregating all the castes in Brahmanic India according to some scheme of classification and then pigeonholing them under the following headings: high, low-high, middle, low, and lowest. Here,

---

[5]In most modern communities there are probably a smaller number of persons in the lowest status groups—those who have fallen out of the competitive stream, the dross of the society, those who live on charity—hence a beehive structure may more nearly represent the fact.

[6]See *Imperial Gazetteer of India*, new ed., Vol. I, Table XII, p. 498. Cf. J. C. Kumarappa, "Handicrafts and Cottage Industries in India," *The Annals*, May 1944, p. 107.

[7]See also Abbé Dubois, *Hindu Manners, Customs, and Ceremonies*, 3d ed., pp. 82–92.

then, will be a hierarchy of classes of castes. We may be able to describe these classes and even show that some vague sense of their approximate status tends to determine differential behavior attitudes of persons within them. But what finally is the nature of these two structures: our classes and the castes? Clearly the classes are not forms of social organization and, as such, we should expect them to have little if anything in common with the castes constituting them. Moreover, it would seem obvious that other taxonomists, according to their criteria of classification, may arrive at quite different distributions of castes.

In a class system it is the family or person who is the bearer of social status; in the caste system it is the caste. The caste system emphasizes group status and morality; the individual without a caste is a meaningless social entity. He is an object naturally ignored by the rest of society. In the process of subjectively classifying persons for consistent behavior relationships, the individual's rank may be determined only through a knowledge of his caste. On the other hand, it would be ridiculous to say that we know an individual's rank through a knowledge of his social class.[8] We do not define an individual's status by first determining his class position, but rather we determine his class position by ascertaining his status.[9]

If we were thinking of status hierarchies only, it is not class and caste which we should compare, but rather individuals and families in the class system, and subcastes or castes (endogamous units) in the caste system. In both cases the number of statuses would be large beyond comprehensible limits. To make the hierarchy wieldy, then, some scheme of classification with reference to the purpose in hand must be consciously or unconsciously devised. We may illustrate the position of the person in the social class system and in the caste system by the following diagram.

The Problem of Classification

Because class is collective rank, each social class must inevitably have a hierarchical position. Quite obviously, then, there can never be a dispute concerning the place of a class. A caste, on the other hand, may have no determined place in the caste hierarchy; it will thus be able

---

[8] Cf. Kingsley Davis, "A Conceptual Analysis of Stratification," *American Sociological Review,* Vol. 7, June 1942, p. 312.

[9] It is recognized, however, that the ability of a person of lower status to associate with persons of higher status (social climbing) tends to advance the status of that person. Cf. H. H. Gerth and C. Wright Mills, *From Max Weber: Essays in Sociology,* p. 405.

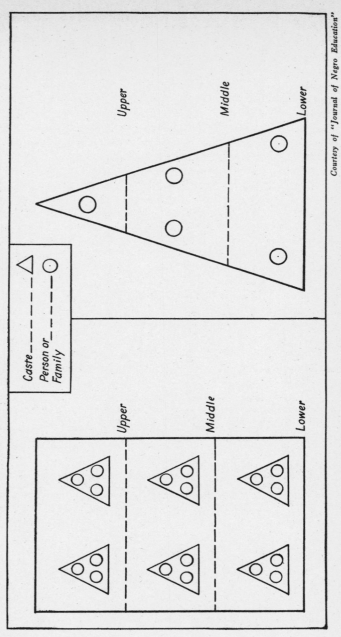

Caste

Person or
Family

Upper

Middle

Lower

Social Status in Caste and Social-Class Systems

to claim distinction only. In other words, castes sometimes find themselves in the position of the individual whose precise class rank is either undetermined or undeterminable. Yet the individual lives on, and so does the caste. Hierarchical organization is essential to the caste system but not to the individual caste. It is this fact which is responsible for considerable intercaste conflict. Each caste is supposed to have an immemorial right to a definite niche in the caste hierarchy, but the integrity of this sanctum rests finally upon custom and public opinion.[10] And it is in these capricious areas that impregnable caste positions must be maintained.

The social class has objective reference to social position; it implies two co-ordinates: one the composite of status criteria, and the other the number of persons capable of meriting the judgment. It is a more or less arbitrary ordinal segment of the social-status continuum with incomprehensive margins.

Indeed, from the point of view of the individual, the class system may be thought of as a hierarchy of conceptual, social-status frontiers; and since normally every person in our class system vies for superior status, he may be said to be marginal in whatever position he finds himself. Social classes, then, may be thought of as somewhat nebulous social strata varying in meaning and position with the status of the persons seeking to estimate them. This, of course, is not intended to detract from the social significance of classes. Reciprocal status classification of persons in society is an intuitive procedure necessary in organizing attitudes for consistent behavior. Even within the caste system, ranking

---

[10]"As to the particular subdivision of each caste, it is difficult to decide the order of the hierarchy observed amongst them. Sub-castes which are despised in one district are often greatly esteemed in another, according as they conduct themselves with greater propriety or follow more important callings. Thus the caste to which the ruler of a country belongs, however low it may be considered elsewhere, ranks among the highest in the ruler's own dominions, and every member of it derives some reflection of dignity from its chief.

"After all, public opinion is the surest guide of caste superiority amongst the Sudras, and very slight acquaintance with the customs of a province and with the private life of its inhabitants will suffice for fixing the position which each caste has acquired by common consent." Abbé Dubois, op. cit., p. 23.

The following discussion by the Hindu writer, J. H. Bhattacharya, indicates further the indecision which questions of caste status sometimes involve: "There is very considerable difference of opinion as to the exact position of the Kshettris in the Hindu caste system. Some authorities take them to be the same as the bastard caste *Kshatri,* spoken of by Manu as the offspring of a Sudra father by a Kshatriya mother. The people of this country include the Kshettris among the Baniya castes, and do not admit that they have the same position as the military Rajputs. The Kshettris themselves claim to be Kshatriyas, and observe the religious rites and duties prescribed by the Shastras for the military caste. But the majority of them live either by trade or service as clerks and accountants, and their caste status ought, it seems, to be intermediate between that of the Rajputs on the one hand, and the Baniyas and the Kayasthas on the other." *Hindu Castes and Sects,* p. 138.

tends to follow some generally accepted system of classification. The concept of "the four castes" is one of these generally accepted ideal types of classification.

There is, in fact, no such thing as an objective social class amenable to physical circumscription; neither is there a recognizable social-class hierarchy in class systems of advanced Western societies. In other words, the class system is not stratified; stratification is an idea only.[11]

It seems necessary now to state the meaning which we have accepted in this study for the concept "social stratification," since the term itself is not clearly defined in the literature. Sometimes it has been used to indicate status differentiation in any social context. Thus, according to Kingsley Davis and Wilbert E. Moore: "If the rights and perquisites of different positions in a society must be unequal, then the society must be stratified, because that is precisely what stratification means."[12] In this sense, therefore, all societies are socially stratified: "Every society, no matter how simple or complex, must differentiate persons in terms of both prestige and esteem, and must therefore possess a certain amount of institutionalized inequality."[12a] If this meaning were consistently held by social scientists—that social-status differentiation, atomized or otherwise, means social stratification—then it would be sheer logomachy or worse to say that modern urban society is not stratified. In such a situation we should have to find some other concept to distinguish internally grouped and ungrouped social-status structures.

But this is not the case. Professor Kimball Young, for instance, conceives of social stratification more literally as "the process of forming caste, class, or other status-giving groups, or of determining level or plane of status for the individual within a group, community, or society."[13] Therefore, like the dictionary definition of stratification—the segregation into layers or strata, especially horizontal layers differentiated from their neighbors—Young probably limits the concept. Yet it

---

[11]A fairly misleading definition of class is the following: "Classes are inclusive, loosely organized groupings whose members behave toward each other as social equals and toward outsiders as social superiors or inferiors, and who as individuals either stay in the group to which they are born, or rise or fall to different levels depending upon the way their social attributes correspond to the values around which the particular class system is organized." Robert L. Sutherland and Julian L. Woodward, *Introductory Sociology*, pp. 363–64. And an ideally incomprehensible definition is the following: "A social class . . . is the largest group of people whose members have intimate access to one another." Davis, Gardner, and Gardner, *Deep South*, p. 59. One might as well set himself the task of determining where the sky begins as to go out with such a definition, say, in Chicago, to locate social classes.

[12]"Some Principles of Stratification," *American Sociological Review*, Vol. 10, April 1945, p. 243.

[12a]Ibid.

[13]*An Introductory Sociology*, rev. ed., p. 599.

seems to have been applied in other ways. In a study of a small artificial community one author criticizes certain other studies as follows:

. . . they confuse general stratification with other types of stratification, or they concentrate on general "social" stratification without regarding the elements that make it up . . . the factors underlying status or general stratification are usually inferred from a "class" analysis. Such a practice arises from a failure to distinguish conceptually and empirically the types of stratification. "Class" analysis of social settlements bury economic, status, power, and other types of stratification under general labels of "social," "status," or "class" stratification. As a result, it is impossible to discern the principles underlying each type of stratification, or the inter-relationships of the individual stratification structures.[14]

It is not our purpose here to settle disputes about the meaning of this term but rather to decide upon the way in which we shall use it so that our central idea, that the social-status continuum of a social-class system is not objectively segregated into layers, may be clarified. It is this mistake, as we see it, that has led many researchers into the field look-ing for social classes and sometimes actually supposing that they have isolated social classes. Therefore, we accept a somewhat literal use of the term connoting a condition of objectively recognizable, discrete strata. We think of each social estate as a social stratum because it is a broad social-status level recognized in custom and sometimes in law; in like manner the so-called "four castes" of ancient India appear to have been in reality four estates. In the modern social-class system where there is a status pyramid of a heterogeneity of atomized status-bearing objects we shall not speak of social stratification. If we were allowed we should prefer to say social-status "particulation" or "pyramida-tion"; yet it has seemed more meaningful to think of stratified and non-stratified social-status systems.

A social class is a heuristic concept significant mainly to the person conceiving of it. As A. C. Mace well says: "Awareness of one's class as a whole must be purely conceptual. The inter-familial links of any member of a class supply connections with only an insignificant portion of the class."[15] The researcher who goes into the field looking for a social class is hunting for something that is not there; he will find it only in his own mind as figments of the intellect. To be sure, if he insists, he is likely to think that he has indeed isolated social classes in the homo-

[14]William H. Form, "Status Stratification in a Planned Community," *American Sociological Review*, Vol. 10, October 1945, p. 605. H. P. Fairchild, in his *Diction-ary of Sociology*, defines stratification as "the horizontal division of society into fairly definite identifiable layers, such as class, caste, and status," p. 309. And: "The ar-rangement of societal elements into groups on different horizontal levels," p. 293.

[15]In *Class Conflict and Social Stratification*, ed. by T. H. Marshall, p. 160.

geneous web of social interaction. His Procrustean arrays may even seem natural to him.[16]

Social classes are "held apart," not by "institutional arrangements," but by the segregating criteria which the researcher has devised. Strictly speaking, a class does not have members because it is not an organization. When we speak of the "middle class," for example, it must be understood that persons in the middle of the middle class are no more in a class than are persons on the conceptual borders of that class. A still more serious limitation is the problem of determining how much of the middle is the middle class. In other words, the qualitative status continuum can be divided only arbitrarily, for we can hardly imagine a status hiatus between our selection of classes.

Thus, no definition of social class which conceives of class as a segregated reality can be acceptable.[17] Simpson's complaint that we have not "an objective measure of class" is a suggestion that we should fashion a tangible yardstick to measure a largely intangible construct. This writer also desires a definition of class which will show the objective "differentiation of population in terms of fundamental material characteristics."[18] The difficulty with this is simply that the population is not objectively differentiated into classes.

A remarkable misdirection of view has evidently been responsible for sterile conceptions of status systems. Most definitions have concentrated not upon the society itself, but upon an ideal construct developed for the purpose of aiding in understanding the nature of status differentiation in our society. In other words, most definitions have described not an on-going status system, but some taxonomic concept devised for easy comprehension of such a system. There may be also an influencing carry-over from the medieval feeling for estates, which, in fact, constituted social-status groups highly isolable.

The class system, in reality, has no inherently verifiable social classes.

---

[16]Observe, for instance, with what leisurely assurance Davis, Gardner, and Gardner speak of themselves: "The researchers concluded that the three main class divisions *recognized by the society* could be objectively described.

"Because of the limitations of time, it was impossible to *stratify every individual in the society* by the interview-observation technique; but once the characteristics of the known individuals had been determined, *criteria were available for placing any individual* about whom some important facts were available." Op. cit., p. 63. (Italics added.)

[17]Classes are not organizational aggregates. According to Nikolai Bukharin: "It is we who make the aggregation—that is a mental aggregate, a paper aggregate, not a real living aggregate. Such artificial groupings may be called imaginary or logical aggregates." *Historical Materialism,* p. 84.

[18]George Simpson, "Class Analysis: What Class is Not," *American Sociological Review,* Vol. 4, December 1939, pp. 830, 831.

When we say, for instance, that difficulty besets a person's rising from one social class into another, we do not mean that that person is ever conscious of the exact location of a class barrier. Obstacles to status advancement are myriad and diffused. His problem is of the same kind every step of the way up; only it tends to become gradually more difficult as he advances toward the vertex of the status system.

Persons behave toward other persons and not toward social classes,[19] for a class is merely a segregating concept; it cannot have a status as a person does. A social class is, in fact, what people think it is; and the criteria of status may vary from society to society, or from community to community—indeed, from status circle to status circle. Wealth, education, health, family record, talent, and so on, may be status values. But since these may vary by infinitesimally small increments; since they are generally interdependent variables, so that, for example, wealth without education may not mean the same thing as wealth with education; and since they may not always be precisely known[20]—the margin of discretion may be very great.

The following analogy may be helpful: We all know the difference between daylight and darkness. But could we speak of a hierarchy of light or of definitely distinguishable shades of light between noon and midnight? There are some valleys and hills, and even spots in shadow and in reflected light, all affecting the imperceptible gradations of light; and, although this illustration is much simpler than the problem in hand, we may expect real differences of opinion as to minute degrees of light. However, persons will readily understand what illumination is meant by noon, twilight, and nightfall. So, too, in our own society we have a broad, workable idea of what is meant by the upper, middle, and lower class.[21]

---

[19]Persons in the caste system behave toward persons also but principally as *members* of a subcaste organization. One, for instance, could not challenge a caste-man without arousing more or less serious reactions from his fellows; in other words, to challenge a caste-man is, at least in principle, to challenge the caste itself. In the caste system the individual as a social-status entity has not emerged.

[20]Note, for instance, with what care individuals guard the facts concerning their financial worth. To ask a man what his salary is or how much money he has in the bank is to enter into his most private affairs. Furthermore, it will evidently be of no particular advantage to the researcher to try to discover such social facts as are not generally known in the community, for then he himself is likely to become the arbiter of social status. He should rather allow himself to be guided by the beliefs which people hold about one another's status. Social status in a social-class system is the product of an interplay of personal estimates of status-bearing objects in the community; and a man may so live as to keep the community fooled or guessing about him.

[21]In this study we have used the terms "class hierarchy" and "class stratum" conceptually.
There is, undoubtedly, considerable sociological insight to be gained from a study

Since the criteria of classification in both class and caste systems are more or less subjective, and since a class is not an organized entity, we should expect a tendency in persons of the class system and of the caste system to represent themselves as belonging to that class which is their immediate aspiration. In other words, persons like to claim membership in certain classes and will do so if their claim can be at all supported. As a consequence, not infrequently that class to which they assign themselves will differ from the class to which they are assigned by their neighbors. Census commissioners in India have discovered an inclination and willingness among castes to give themselves a dignified class status instead of stating their position with respect to other castes in the district. Ordinarily the *varna* class terms are resorted to. Confronted with this problem, Commissioner J. H. Hutton insisted: "The use of *varna* . . . is quite impossible, since practically every Hindu who claims to be a Hindu at all would claim to be either Brahman or Kshatriya. Even castes of Chamars in the United Provinces have dropped their characteristic nomenclature, and at this census returned themselves as Sun- or Moon-descended Rajputs. This, of course, does not imply any correspondingly respectful treatment of them by their neighbors."[22] In like manner we should expect many persons in Amer-

---

of the way of life of persons of different social status in modern society. Such studies as Harvey W. Zorbaugh, *The Gold Coast and the Slum;* Robert S. and Helen M. Lynd, *Middletown;* E. Franklin Frazier, *The Negro Family in Chicago;* St. Clair Drake and Horace R. Cayton, *Black Metropolis;* and even literary works such as J. Saunders Redding, *No Day of Triumph,* and John Steinbeck, *Grapes of Wrath,* are contributions to our knowledge of the behavior and condition of the low and of the high. In these there could be no question about the utility of a rough-and-ready reference to the lower, the middle, and the upper class.

However, we should guard against straining the concept as Drake and Cayton do in *Black Metropolis.* In their discussion of "the system of social classes" the authors say: "Everybody in Bronzeville recognizes the existence of social classes, whether called that or not. People with slight education and small incomes . . . are always referring to the more affluent . . . as 'dicties' . . ." etc. Then, using census data for education, rental, and occupation, they conclude: "At the top of the social pyramid [the upper class] is a scant 5 per cent of the population." A block diagram shows that there are 30 and 65 per cent in the middle and in the lower class respectively. The third step is the presenting of a number of selected verbalizations and characterizations of persons assumed to be representative of their class, with the implication that classes as social entities have been isolated. This procedure has been popularized by Professor W. Lloyd Warner.

Probably the fallacy of the implication may be made apparent simply by asking the question: Why is there not 3 per cent or 10 per cent instead of "a scant 5 per cent at the top of the social pyramid"? The answer seems to be clear that exactly 5 per cent are on the top because the researchers themselves decided to pigeonhole or lop off that part of the population which receives an income above an arbitrarily selected figure, and so on with other status criteria. These fictitious groupings, if taken for what they really are, may have some valuable purpose; but they become mystical entities when attempts are made to describe them functionally.

[22]*Census of India, 1931,* Vol. I, Pt. 1, p. 432. See also *Census of India, 1921,* Vol. I, Pt. 1, p. 223. Hutton's observation indicates also that it is a man's "neigh-

ica, for instance, who might be objectively classified as lower class, to claim status in the popular middle class.

Social status is largely an imputed social attribute; it cannot be carried as one might carry his weight.[23] The difference between the estimation of position by the status bearer and the outside observer is probably due to difference in point of view. The observer sees the probable social indices of position, while the person or caste tends to concentrate upon the meaning of these. For instance, differences in wealth may be taken objectively as a significant factor determining status; but many lower-class persons may argue that being "a good Christian" puts them in a higher class than having more money merits the non-religious individual. And this notwithstanding obvious deferences which they may yield to the wealthier. It should also be remembered that the personal estimate of so tangible a thing as a dollar tends to vary with the income of the estimator. It follows, therefore, that statuses will tend to vary with the value systems of the persons judging them.

Furthermore, the great class strata in which a person or caste claims membership are not the only determinants of behavior. Among others, very much smaller differences—status differentials—are recognized; and the more rigid the class system, the greater the social significance of small differences in status. What a person really has is not class but status; social class is a conceptual status pigeonhole. Moreover, in any society a person tends to be what he does; and the social estimation of what he does tends to be his social status. Women and children usually derive their status from that of the family.[24]

Class and Caste Mobility

A man's caste is a personal matter; it is primary and possesses him traditionally. "To a Hindu his caste is the determining factor in his life, and beside it his age, civil condition, birth-place, and even his occupa-

---

bors" and not his anonymous class that is of continual concern to him as a status-bearing entity. The individual is treated categorically—that is to say, as a class member—only by persons far away from him in status.

[23]"A person's status in a group has a double aspect. On the one hand, it rests in the minds of his associates, since it is the way they treat him and consider him. On the other hand, status is registered in the mind of the individual himself, as a sort of reflection of how he stands in the eyes of others. Thus he may accept or submit to the place assigned to him and be content, in which case the accommodation between him and his fellows is complete as a functional relationship. Or he may resent the place given him and desire a different position. In this case, his status is unsettled and he finds himself in conflict with others." E. T. Krueger and Walter C. Reckless, *Social Psychology,* p. 83.

[24]Cf. Elin L. Anderson, *We Americans,* p. 53.

tion are matters of comparative indifference."[25] A man's social class, on the other hand, is impersonal, secondary, and to him only vaguely circumscribed; he cannot perceive it unless through cliques or "gangs," and its imputed members as a whole are strangers to one another. The caste is a sympathetic unity; the social class, once again, is a conceptualized social-status segment of society. The class is internally competitive, with family set against family in ceaseless emulation; the caste is internally co-operative, with families fraternally interested in each other. Members of a class are constantly striving upward and away from their fellows, a situation which leads to their individuation; the interest of caste members, on the other hand, is bound up with the fortune of the caste in a sort of fatalistic fraternal solidarity.

An individual may leave his class behind him and forget it with impunity; a man's caste status, however, cannot be so easily sloughed off. The following is an illustration of sentimental attachment of individual and caste:

> The Bengal Talis . . . have largely deserted their traditional occupation of oil-pressing in favor of trade, and are a fairly prosperous community. Under Warren Hastings, a high official who belonged to their community, having amassed a great fortune, offered a munificent gift to the temple of Puri, in the hope of raising the status of his caste. The local priests refused to accept the gift from a member of a caste which was then regarded as unclean. The would-be donor appealed to the pandits of Hooghly and Nabadwip, and persuaded them to decide that the Bengal Teli is a trading caste, deriving its name not from *tel,* "oil," but from *tula* or "balance," used by traders in their business. In consequence of their ruling, the Telis of Bengal proper are now regarded as a clean Sudra caste.[26]

There is no rivalry—to say nothing about social antagonism—between social classes, for classes are not functional entities. Rivalry is a characteristic function of status bearers, such as persons in the class system and castes in the caste system. The greater the stability of the class system, the greater the social distance between persons of the different putative classes, and, naturally, the greater the difficulty of upward movement. The extremes of social distance between person and person on this earth is probably attained in southern India between certain castes of Brahmans and the "unsightables." In the United States, "interclass" social distance is "short" and comparatively easily bridged.

---

[25] *Census of India, 1921,* Vol. I, Pt. 1, p. 223.
[26] "Caste," *Encyclopedia of Religion and Ethics.*

When we say that a person born in a certain caste cannot aspire to rise out of it, we do not mean that he is hopelessly barred from advancement. He may not rise, leaving his caste behind him; yet, though difficult, it is not impossible for him to move up with his entire caste. Of course the caste does not rotate upward in the way illustrated by W. Lloyd Warner;[27] it moves up in its entirety as a person or family might. Therefore, a person's status might change while his caste affiliation remains intact.

So far as the individual is concerned, in the caste system the limits of ambition are definitely narrowed; his caste competitors are identified; hence rivalry may sometimes flare into conflict,[28] and failure is not so heavily penalized as in the class system. In class societies ambition is theoretically limitless; competition tends to be individuated and anonymous; hence rivals are not ordinarily openly identified, and failure is more tragic because responsibility is atomized and personalized. A person may be declassed, may fall in class position, but he cannot be outclassed in the sense that he may be outcasted. A social class cannot expel an individual for the simple reason that it is not organized for such a function. The declassed individual is still within some class, but the outcaste has no caste whatever.

Finally we may differentiate briefly between social class, caste, and race so far as status is concerned. The idea of degrees of rigidity of social status of the family or individual as belonging to a caste or class is not similar to the idea of status of the individual as belonging to a race. In other words, whether a man is a Kayasth or a Kumbar does not imply the same type of reference as if we were thinking of him as a Hindu or an Englishman. The caste is a status bearer in the caste system; the person or family is a status bearer in the class system; the social class refers to the classification of statuses, while racial subordination and superordination refer to an intergroup power relationship. The biological fact that the Britisher in India, for example, cannot become a Hindu does not of itself make him a white-caste member. The whites hold their position as a conquering race, not as a part of the caste system.[29]

---

[27] See "American Caste and Class," *The American Journal of Sociology,* Vol. XLII, September 1936, p. 225.

[28] G. S. Ghurye, for instance, observes: "Contemporary caste-society presents the spectacle of self-centered groups more or less in conflict with one another." *Caste and Race in India,* p. 181.

[29] Raymond L. Buell recognizes the nature of this antagonism. Thus he says: "In a community where inter-racial feeling develops as a result of white settlement, there is a feeling, subconscious at least, that the natives will revolt against the whites and that in this revolt they will be joined by the native soldiers. In order to

To make this point clear, let us consider a hypothetical social-status continuum which is intended to represent societies whose social structure permits different degrees of freedom of movement from one status position to another. Let us say that the United States is free, England is midway, and Brahmanic India is least free. Now think of inserting into this same continuum the status relationship between, say, whites and Hindus, Mohammedans and Hindus, and Negroes and whites in South Africa. Clearly the two social phenomena are incommensurable. We may put it thus: Social classes segregate a people conceptually by grade or rank, while race or nationality differentiates peoples in their aggregate.[30]

In India that man who refers to himself as a *high-class white* man means, first, that he is socially better than men below him in social-class status, and, secondly, that he is racially different from the Indians about him. The idea, *white man,* may mean also that he is racially *superior to* all Indians; but this attitude tends to organize all East Indians, regardless of caste status, against all white men of all classes; it tends to dichotomize them definitely into power groups. There is no social gradation in this relationship.

In his autobiography Jawaharlal Nehru refers to personal relationships between his high-status family and Englishmen: "As individuals we had usually met with courtesy from the Englishman, and we got on well with him, though like all Indians, we were, no doubt, racially conscious of subjection, and resented it bitterly."[31] Here we have a fairly clear distinction between class and race relations. As high-class Hindus, the Nehrus meet white men on a satisfactory level; as persons belonging to a colored race, however, their relationship with whites is insufferable. In the latter area of social interaction they show and feel the deepest antagonism against the Europeans.

It is not necessary for social classes or castes to defend their position by building forts and trenches about them; yet white men in both India and South Africa, for instance, never lose sight of the fact that they must retain control of the trigger.

---

protect Europeans against this possibility, the governments of white settlement colonies believe that a European military organization should be established." *The Native Problem in Africa,* Vol. I, p. 378.

[30]The following use of these concepts by Donald R. Young is highly questionable: "The American Indian, once constituting an inferior caste in the social hierarchy, now constitutes little more than a social class, since today his inferior status may be sloughed off by the process of cultural assimilation." *Research Memorandum on Minority Peoples in a Depression,* Social Science Research Council, Bulletin No. 31, 1937, pp.18–19.

[31]*Toward Freedom,* p. 93. See also p. 264.

Part Three

RACE

Introduction

*T*HE TERM "ETHNIC" MAY BE EMPLOYED GENERICALLY TO REFER to social relations among distinct peoples. Accordingly, an ethnic may be defined as a people living competitively in relationship of superordination or subordination with respect to some other people or peoples within one state, country, or economic area. Two or more ethnics constitute an ethnic system or regime; and, naturally, one ethnic must always imply another. In other words, we may think of one ethnic as always forming part of a system.

Ethnic systems may be classified:

1. According to the culture of the ethnics:
   a. Degrees of cultural advancement (simple or complex).
   b. Type variation, e.g., Occidental or Oriental.
   c. Pattern, e.g., variation in language, religion, nationality, or other ways of living.
2. According to physical distinguishability:
   a. Race, e.g., black, brown, red, white, etc.
   b. Mixed bloods.

Thus, difference among ethnics may center about variations in culture, such as those claimed by British, Afrikander, and Jews of South Africa; or it may rest upon distinguishability, such as that of whites, East Indians, Bantu, and Cape Colored of the same area. When the ethnics are of the same race—that is to say, when there is no significant physical characteristics accepted by the ethnics as marks of distinction—their process of adjustment is usually designated nationality or "minority-group" problems. When, on the other hand, the ethnics recognize each other physically and use their physical distinction as a basis for the rationale of their interrelationships, their process of adjustment is usually termed race relations or race problems.

Cultural or national ethnics and racial ethnics are alike in that they are both power groups. They stand culturally or racially as potential or actual antagonists. The degree of the interethnic conflict can be explained only by the social history of the given relationship; and neither race nor culture seems in itself to be an index of the stability of the antagonism. The status relationship of both cultural and racial ethnics may persist with great rigidity for long periods of time or it may be short-lived. The opposition between the English and the Irish and between the Jews and Catholics in Spain are instances of rather long-time cultural antagonisms. The Mohammedans and the Hindus in India present a situation in which the formerly subordinated Hindus are apparently about to take the place of their old Mohammedan masters, but the centuries-old hostility persists. Both culture and race prejudices are dynamic group attitudes varying in intensity according to the specific historical situation of the peoples involved.[1]

Ethnic, political class, social class, estate, and caste may be compared. Castes, estates, and social classes belong to or comprise status systems of socially superior and inferior persons. These systems are peaceful, and degrees of superiority are taken for granted according to the normal expectations of the system. Lower-status persons are not preoccupied with ways and means of demoting their superiors. When these systems are functioning at their best, social acts recognizing degrees of superiority in the status hierarchy are yielded with the same kind of alacrity as that which college boys lavish upon their athletic heroes.

On the other hand, political-class and ethnic relations do not constitute ordered systems but rather antagonistic regimes. Political classes tend to break up the orderly working of a status system and struggle toward or against revolutionizing it. The aggressive political class aims at social disorder for the purpose of instituting a new order.[2] Ethnics

---

[1] It appears that the principle of racial and nationality assimilation laid down by Lloyd Warner and Leo Srole is too simple. As they see it: ". . . the greater the difference between the host and the immigrant cultures, the greater will be the subordination, the greater the strength of ethnic social systems, and the longer the period necessary for assimilation of the ethnic groups. . . . The greater the racial difference . . . the greater the subordination of the immigrant group . . . and the longer the period necessary for assimilation." The process of assimilation is further delayed if the immigrant is divergent in both cultural and physical traits. There is probably some truth in this birds-of-a-feather hypothesis, yet it seems that it may be too truistic and crude for significant analysis of internationality and racial assimilation. See *The Social Systems of American Ethnic Groups*, pp. 285–86.

[2] Abraham Lincoln was pertinent when in 1848 he said in Congress: "It is a quality of revolutions not to go by old lines and old laws; but to break up both, and make new ones." J. G. Nicolay and John Hay, *Abraham Lincoln, Complete Works*, Vol. I, p. 105.

are peoples living in some state of antagonism, and their ambitions tend to vary with the situation. Some ethnics are intransigent; others seek or oppose assimilation; still others struggle for positions as ruling peoples. In political-class action not only status groups but also ethnics may be split to take sides on the basis of their economic rather than their ethnic interests or status position. On the contrary, ethnic antagonism may so suffuse other interests that political-class differences are constantly held in abeyance.[3]

We shall discuss further the problems of national ethnics in a following chapter, and we shall use the popular expression "race relations" to refer to the problems of adjustment between racial ethnics.

The Concept—Race Relations

It is evident that the term "race relations" may include all situations of contact between peoples of different races, and for all time. One objection to the use of this term is that there is no universally accepted definition of race. The biologist and the physical anthropologist may indeed have considerable difficulty with this, but for the sociologist a race may be thought of as simply any group of people that is generally believed to be, and generally accepted as, a race in any given area of ethnic competition. Here is detail enough, since the sociologist is interested in social interaction. Thus, if a man looks white, although, say in America, he is everywhere called a Negro, he is, then, a Negro American. If, on the other hand, a man of identical physical appearance is recognized everywhere in Cuba as a white man, then he is a white Cuban. The sociologist is interested in what meanings and definitions a society gives to certain social phenomena and situations. It would probably be as revealing of interracial attitudes to deliberate upon the variations in the skeletal remains of some people as it would be to question an on-going society's definition of a race because, anthropometrically speaking, the assumed race is not a *real* race. What we are interested in

---

[3]Edgar H. Brookes describes the situation in South Africa which illustrates this: "Economically the Poor White, the Coloured man and the detribalized, urban Native are in the same category. Yet no political party in South Africa, with the exception of the Communists, has made any serious or sustained attempt to draw them all together in opposition to capitalism. It is most significant that the Poor White proletariat of the towns does not in general vote for Communist or even for Labor candidates; but for some Party—whether the main National Party or not—which claims to be 'nationalist.' They are not class-conscious. They prefer to join with their fellow-white men, even if capitalists, than with their non-white fellow-workers. . . . As was long the case in the Southern States of America, as indeed still is the case there, the Poor White has sacrificed his economic to his sentimental interests, and the immediate economic protection offered him on colour lines." *The Colour Problems of South Africa*, p. 29.

is the social definition of the term "race." To call that which a group has been pleased to designate a race by some other name does not affect the nature of the social problem to be investigated.[4]

We may think of race relations, therefore, as that behavior which develops among peoples who are aware of each other's actual or imputed physical differences. Moreover, by race relations we do not mean all social contacts between persons of different "races," but only those contacts the social characteristics of which are determined by a consciousness of "racial" difference. If, for example, two persons of different racial strains were to meet and deal with each other on their own devices—that is to say, without preoccupation with a social definition of each other's race—then it might be said that race here is of no sociological significance. But if their behavior tended to be fashioned by ethnic attitudes toward each other's actual or purported physical differences, then the situation may be called a social contact between ethnics, and it may be also referred to as race relations. However, these ethnic attitudes are based upon other and more fundamental social phenomena.

---

[4]Cf. William Oscar Brown, "Race Prejudice," Ph.D. thesis, University of Chicago, 1930, pp. 4–5. It should be made patently clear that the laboratory classification of races, which began among anthropologists about a hundred years ago, has no necessary relationship with the problem of race relations as sociological phenomena. Race relations developed independently of anthropological tests and measurements.

16. *Race Relations—Its Meaning, Beginning, and Progress*

A Definition

*I*N A DISCUSSION OF "THE ORIGIN" OF RACE RELATIONS IT SHOULD be well to determine at the outset exactly what we are looking for. We shall proceed, therefore, by first eliminating certain concepts that are commonly confused with that of race relations. These are: ethnocentrism, intolerance, and "racism."

Ethnocentrism, as the sociologists conceive of it, is a social attitude which expresses a community of feeling in any group—the "we" feeling as over against the "others." This attitude seems to be a function of group solidarity, which is not necessarily a racial phenomenon. Neither is social intolerance (which we shall consider in more detail in a subsequent chapter) racial antagonism, for social intolerance is social displeasure or resentment against that group which refuses to conform to the established practices and beliefs of the society. Finally, the term "racism" as it has been recently employed in the literature seems to refer to a philosophy of racial antipathy. Studies on the origin of racism involve the study of the development of an ideology, an approach which usually results in the substitution of the history of a system of rationalization for that of a material social fact.[1] Indeed, it is likely to be an accumulation of an erratic pattern of verbalizations cut free from any on-going social system.

What then is the phenomenon, the beginnings of which we seek to determine? It is the phenomenon of the capitalist exploitation of peoples and its complementary social attitude. Again, one should miss the point entirely if one were to think of racial antagonism as having

---

[1]See Hannah Arendt, "Race-Thinking Before Racism," *The Review of Politics,* Vol. 6, January 1944, pp. 36–73; and Fredrick G. Detweiler, "The Rise of Modern Race Antagonisms," *The American Journal of Sociology,* Vol. 37, March 1932, pp. 738–47.

its genesis in some "social instinct" of antipathy between peoples. Such an approach ordinarily leads to no end of confusion.[2]

The Beginning of Racial Antagonism

Probably a realization of no single fact is of such crucial significance for an understanding of racial antagonism as that the phenomenon had its rise only in modern times.[3] In a previous chapter on "the origin of caste" we have attempted to show that race conflict did not exist among the early Aryans in India, and we do not find it in other ancient civilizations. Our hypothesis is that racial exploitation and race prejudice developed among Europeans with the rise of capitalism and nationalism, and that because of the world-wide ramifications of capitalism, all racial antagonisms can be traced to the policies and attitudes of the leading capitalist people, the white people of Europe and North America.

By way of demonstrating this hypothesis we shall review briefly some well-known historical situations. In tracing the rise of the Anglo-Saxons to their position as the master race of the world[4] we shall omit consideration of the great Eastern civilizations from which Greece took a significant cultural heritage. There seems to be no basis for imputing racial antagonism to the Egyptians, Babylonians, or Persians. At any

---

[2]Consider, for instance, the following definitive statement by Professor Robert E. Park: "This [prejudice against the Japanese] is due to the existence in the human mind of a mechanism by which we inevitably and automatically classify every individual human being we meet. When a race bears an external mark by which every individual member of it can infallibly be identified, that race is by that fact set apart and segregated. Japanese, Chinese, and Negroes cannot move among us with the same freedom as members of other races because they bear marks which identify them as members of their race. This fact isolates them. . . . Isolation is at once a cause and an effect of race prejudice. It is a vicious circle—isolation, prejudice; prejudice, isolation." In Jesse F. Steiner, *The Japanese Invasion*, p. xvi.

Since, however, we may assume that all races "bear marks which identify them as members of their race," it must follow, according to Park, that a certain human capacity for classification makes it impossible for races to come together without racial antagonism and prejudice. We shall attempt to show that this instinct hypothesis is too simple.

[3]Cf. Ina Corine Brown, *National Survey of the Higher Education of Negroes,* U.S. Office of Education, Misc. No. 6, Vol. I, pp. 4–8.

[4]Professor G. A. Borgese makes an observation pertinent to this remark: "The English-speaking mind is not fully alive to the gravity of this issue. Unlike their German cousins and foes, the Anglo-Saxon stocks did not strive to *become* the master race or *Herrenvolk* holding sway over the world and mankind. . . . Yet, unlike their German cousins and rivals, they have succeeded in *being* a *Herrenvolk,* a race of masters." "Europe Wants Freedom from Shame," *Life,* March 12, 1945, pp. 41–42. (Italics Borgese's.)

"The Germans needed all of Hitler's ranting and daily doses from the Goebbels propaganda machine to persuade them that they were better than other people. Englishmen simply take it for granted and rarely waste a syllable discussing it." See John Scott, *Europe in Revolution*, p. 216.

rate, the Greeks were the first European people to enter the stream of eastern Mediterranean civilization, and the possibility of racial exploitation did not really occur until the Macedonian conquest. Our point here is, however, that we do not find race prejudice even in the great Hellenistic empire which extended deeper into the territories of colored people than any other European empire up to the end of the fifteenth century.

The Hellenic Greeks had a cultural, not a racial, standard of belonging, so that their basic division of the peoples of the world were Greeks and barbarians—the barbarians having been all those persons who did not possess the Greek culture, especially its language. This is not surprising, for the culture of peoples is always a matter of great moment to them. But the people of the Greek city-states, who founded colonies among the barbarians on the shores of the Black Sea and of the Mediterranean, welcomed those barbarians to the extent that they were able to participate in Greek culture, and intermarried freely with them. The Greeks knew that they had a superior culture to those of the barbarians, but they included Europeans, Africans, and Asiatics in the concept Hellas as these peoples acquired a working knowledge of the Greek culture.

The experience of the later Hellenistic empire of Alexander tended to be the direct contrary of modern racial antagonism. The narrow patriotism of the city-states was given up for a new cosmopolitanism. Every effort was made to assimilate the barbarians to Greek culture, and in the process a new Greco-Oriental culture with a Greco-Oriental ruling class came into being. Alexander himself took a Persian princess for his wife and encouraged his men to intermarry with the native population.[5] In this empire there was an estate, not a racial, distinction between the rulers and the un-Hellenized natives.

Moreover, the inclination of Alexander to disregard even cultural differences in his policy toward the peoples of his empire seemed to have stimulated one of the most remarkable philosophies of all time: that of the fundamental equality of all human beings. In Athens, in about 300 B.C., Zeno developed a system of thought called stoicism

[5]In describing the composition of Alexander's army invading India, E. R. Bevan says: ". . . mingled with Europeans were men of many nations. Here were troops of horsemen, representing the chivalry of Iran, which had followed Alexander from Bactria and beyond, Pashtus and men of the Hindu Kush with their highland-bred horses, Central-Asiatics who ride and shoot at the same time; and among the camp-followers one could find groups representing the older civilizations of the world, Phoenicians inheriting an immemorial tradition of shipcraft and trade, bronzed Egyptians able to confront the Indians with an antiquity still longer than their own." *The Cambridge History of India,* Vol. I, p. 351.

which held in part that "all men should be fellow citizens; and there should be one life and order, as of a flock pasturing together, which feeds together by a common law." This doctrine was not a reaction to race prejudice but rather to certain invidious cultural distinctions among the peoples of the time; and the idea has come down to us by way of the Roman law, the preaching of St. Paul, and the writings of the philosophers of the Enlightenment. It has been given a democratic emphasis in the American Declaration of Independence and in amendments to the Constitution of the United States.

The next great organization of peoples about the Mediterranean Sea —and in so far as European civilization is concerned this may be thought of as constituting the whole world—was the Roman Empire. In this civilization also we do not find racial antagonism, for the norm of superiority in the Roman system remained a cultural-class attribute. The basic distinction was Roman citizenship, and gradually this was extended to all freeborn persons in the municipalities of the empire. Slaves came from every province, and there was no racial distinction among them. Sometimes the slaves, especially the Greeks, were the teachers of their masters; indeed, very much of the cultural enlightenment of the Romans came through slaves from the East. Because slavery was not a racial stigma, educated freedmen, who were granted citizenship upon emancipation, might rise to high positions in government or industry. There were no interracial laws governing the relationship of the great mass of obscure common people of different origin. Moreover, the aristocracy of the empire, the senators and *equites,* was constituted largely from responsible provincials in the imperial administration.

One should not mistake the social relationship among the various social estates of the Greek and Roman world for race relations. The Spartiates, *Perioikoi,* and Helots of Laconia, for instance, were not races but social estates; neither did the *Metics,*[6] the alien residents of Periclean Athens, constitute a race. In early republican Rome intermarriage was forbidden between the privileged patrician class and the plebeian mass, but this was a social-estate partition rather than a racial accommodation.

If we have not discovered interracial antagonism in ancient Greece

---

[6]The Metics may probably be better thought of as presenting a multinationality situation. On this point Gustave Glotz, referring to the Metics of various national origins, concludes: ". . . there was formed in Greece in the fifth and sixth centuries a kind of international nation which was preparing, chiefly in economic interests but also in the domain of ideas and in the very framework of society, for the cosmopolitanism of the Hellenistic period." *Ancient Greece at Work,* p. 191.

and Rome, the chances of discovering it in the system which succeeded the fall of the Roman Empire are even more remote. With the rise of the politico-religious system of Christianity, Western culture may be thought of as having entered its long period of gestation. Its first signs of parturition were the Crusades. But during all this time and even after the Renaissance the nature of the movement and of the social contact of peoples in this area precluded the possibility of the development of race prejudice.

The general pattern of barbarian invasions was that of a succession of peoples of increasing cultural inferiority moving into areas of higher culture. Thus, the German nations which invaded the Roman Empire had a smaller capacity for maintaining a complex culture than the Romans had when they conquered the Greeks; and probably the Celtic people of Britain had still fewer resources to continue their Roman cultural heritage. In the movement of barbarian peoples from the East and North toward the general area of the Mediterranean no nationalistic sentiments stood in the way to limit their amalgamation with the native populations.

One aspect of this era of barbarian invasion, the movement of Asiatics into Europe, is of especial significance. The Asiatics were better warriors than rulers. We may say rather conclusively that the white man's rise to superiority over the colored peoples of the other continents is based pivotally on his superiority as a fighter. This is, however, a rather recent achievement. In the Middle Ages the Asiatics outfought him. The Huns, Saracens, Moors, Seljuk Turks, Ottoman Turks, Tartars—all went deep into Europe, subjugated and sometimes enslaved white peoples who today are highly race-prejudiced. At any rate, we shall not find racial antagonism among these invaders. The most powerful of them were Moslems, and both the economic base and religious sanctions of Mohammedanism are opposed to race prejudice. Under Mohammedanism—at least in so far as it has not been recently corrupted by capitalist ideals—the criterion of belonging is a cultural one; furthermore, Islam is a proselyting culture.

In Europe itself the policies of the Roman Catholic Church presented a bar to the development of racial antagonism. The Church, which gradually attained more or less religious, economic, and ideological dominance, had a folk and personal—not a territorial or racial—norm of belonging. The fundamental division of human beings was Christian and non-Christian. Among the non-Christians the heathen, the infidel, and the heretic were recognized by differential negative attitudes; however, as a means of entering the Christian community, conversion or recantation was freely allowed and even sought after. There was in medieval Europe—indeed in the Christian world—an effective basis for the brotherhood of peoples. Although a man's economic, contractual relationship in his community determined his livelihood, to be excommunicated by the Church almost had the effect of putting him beyond the purview of society itself. In the Middle Ages, then, we find no racial antagonism in Europe; in fact, Europeans were, at this time, more isolated and ignorant about foreign peoples and world geography than the Romans and Greeks were.

But gradually, under a commercial and religious impulse, Europe began to awaken and to journey toward strange lands. The First Crusade may be taken as the starting point which finally led to world dominance by Europeans. When after their travels in the last quarter of the thirteenth century the Polos returned from the court of the great Kublai Khan in China to tell Europeans a story of fabulous wealth and luxury, the astonished people could hardly believe what they heard. Yet Marco Polo's memoirs were a great stimulant to traders. It was not until the discovery of America and the circumnavigation of the globe, however, that the movement assumed a decidedly irreversible trend. The period between the First Crusade and the discovery of America continued to be characterized by the religious view of world order; but it set a pattern of dealing with non-Christian peoples which was to be continued, minus only its religious characteristics, to this day. To the extent that the religious controls remained effective, racial antagonism did not develop; what really developed was a Jew-heathen-infidel antagonistic complex which was to color European thought for some centuries.

Up to the eleventh century Christian Europe was hemmed in from the North, East, and South by heathens and infidels; the Mediterranean was almost encircled by the Arabian Mohammedans, a people whose culture was superior to that of the northern Europeans. In the eleventh century, however, under the organizing influence of the popes, the holy warriors of Christendom began to carry conquering crusades into the territory of the heathen Slavic and infidel Asiatic peoples. As a general rule the Church made the lands and even the peoples of the non-Christian world the property of the Crusaders, and the trader ordinarily followed the cross.

In fact, it was this need for trade with the East, especially by the Italian, Spanish, and Portuguese merchants, and its obstruction by the Mohammedans whose country lay across their path in the Near East, which induced the Portuguese, in the fifteenth century, to feel their way down the African coast in the hope of sailing around this continent to the East Indies. Here began the great drama that was, in a few hundred years, to turn over the destiny of the world to the decisions of businessmen. But our concern at this point is to indicate that racial antagonism had not yet developed among the Europeans.

In the first place, the geography of the world was still a mystery, and some of the most fantastic tales about its peoples were believed. Stories of the splendor, luxury, and wisdom of the peoples of the East held all Europe in constant wonderment. No one would have been surprised if some traveler had returned from the heart of Africa to break the news that he had found a black monarch ruling over a kingdom surpassing in grandeur and power any that had then existed in Europe. In short, the white man had no conception of himself as a being capable of developing *the* superior culture of the world—the concept "white man" had not yet its significant social definition—the Anglo-Saxon, the modern master race, was then not even in the picture.

But when the Portuguese began to inch their way down the African coast they knew that the Moors and heathens whom they encountered were inferior to them both as fighters and as culture builders.[7] This, however, led to no conclusions about racial superiority. Henry the Navigator, himself, sought in those parts a Christian prince, Prester John, with whom he planned to form an alliance "against the enemies of the faith." All through the latter half of the fifteenth century the Portuguese sailors and explorers kept up this search for the kingdom of the lost black prince.

Of more significance still is the fact that there was as yet no belief in any cultural incapacity of these colored people. Their conversion to Christianity was sought with enthusiasm, and this transformation was supposed to make the Africans the human equals of all other Christians. The Portuguese historian, Gomes Eannes de Azurara, writing in the middle of the fifteenth century, gives us some idea of the religious motives for Prince Henry's exploits among the peoples on the West African coast. One reason for the Navigator's slave raids:

. . . was his great desire to make increase in the faith of our lord Jesus Christ and to bring to him all souls that should be saved,—understanding

---

[7] It should be noted that the Portuguese felt they were superior because they were Christians, not because they were white. In an address to his men just before they attacked an unsuspecting west-coast community, the captain of a caravel declared: ". . . although they are more in number than we by a third yet they are but Moors, and we are Christians one of whom ought to suffice for two of them. For God is He in whose power lieth victory, and He knoweth our good wills in His holy service." Azurara, *The Discovery and Conquest of Guinea*, p. 138.

that all the mystery of the Incarnation, Death, and Passion of our Lord Jesus Christ was for this sole end—namely the salvation of lost souls, whom the said Lord Infant [Henry] by his travail and spending would fain bring into the true faith. For he perceived that no better offering could be made unto the Lord than this. For if God promised to return one hundred goods for one, we may justly believe that for such great benefits, that is to say, for so many souls as were saved by the efforts of this Lord, he will have so many hundreds of guerdons in the Kingdom of God, by which his spirit may be glorified after this life in the celestial realm. For I that wrote this history saw so many men and women of those parts turned to the holy faith, that even if the Infant had been a heathen, their prayers would have been enough to have obtained his salvation. And not only did I see the first captives, but their children and grandchildren as true Christians as if the Divine grace breathed in them and imparted to them a clear knowledge of itself.[8]

This matter of cultural conversion is crucial for our understanding of the development of racial antagonism. For the full profitable exploitation of a people, the dominant group must devise ways and means of limiting that people's cultural assimilation. So long as the Portuguese and Spaniards continued to accept the religious definition of human equality, so long also the development of race prejudice was inhibited. Although it is true that the forays on the African coast were exceedingly ruthless, the Portuguese did not rationalize the fact with a racial argument. To kill or to take into slavery the heathen or infidel was to serve the highest purpose of God. As Azurara pointed out: ". . . though their bodies were now brought into subjection, that was a small matter in comparison to their souls, which would now possess true freedom for evermore."[8a] In granting to Prince Henry a "plenary indulgence," Pope Eugenius IV gave "to each and all those who shall be engaged in the said war [slave raids], complete forgiveness of all their sins."[8b]

The Portuguese people themselves had developed no racial hatred for the captives. Azurara relates how the townspeople at Lagos wept in sympathy for the suffering of the Moors as families were broken to be distributed among different masters. And, it seems, the captives were quite readily assimilated into the population.

. . . from this time forth [after their partition] they began to acquire some knowledge of our country, in which they found great abundance; and our men began to treat them with great favour. For as our people did not find them hardened in the belief [i.e., Islam] of the Moors, and saw how they came unto the law of Christ with a good will, they made no

---

[8]Op. cit., p. 29. See also C. Raymond Beazley, *Prince Henry the Navigator.*
[8a]Op. cit., p. 51.
[8b]Ibid., p. 53.

difference between them and their free [Portuguese] servants, born in our own country. But those whom they took [captured] while still young, they caused to be instructed in mechanical arts. And those whom they saw fitted for managing property, they set free and married to women who were natives of the land [of Portugal], making with them a division of their property as if it had been bestowed on those who married them by the will of their own fathers. . . . Yea, and some widows of good family who bought some of these female slaves, either adopted them or left them a portion of their estate by will, so that in the future they married right well, treating them as entirely free. Suffice it that I never saw one of these slaves put in irons like other captives, and scarcely any one who did not turn Christian and was not gently treated.

And I have been asked by their lords to the baptisms and marriages of such; at which they, whose slaves they were before, made no less solemnity than if they had been their children or relations.[9]

The Portuguese had no clear sense of racial antagonism, because its economic and rationalistic basis had not yet developed among them. Indeed the Portuguese and Spaniards never became fully freed of the crusading spirit, which constantly held in check their attainment of a clear appreciation of the values of competitive labor exploitation.[10] The Church received its share of African servants; as yet, however, it had no idea of the economic uses of segregation and "cultural parallelism"—of the techniques for perpetuating the servile status of the black workers. It had developed no rationalizations of inborn human inferiority in support of a basic need for labor exploitation. On the contrary, its obsession with the spiritual values of conversion left the Negroes free to be integrated into the general population. It is reported that before the returning captains of one commission of caravels "did anything else [in the distribution of captured Moors] they took as an offering the best of those Moors to the Church of that place; and another little Moor, who afterwards became a friar of St. Francis, they sent to St. Vincent do Cabo, where he lived ever after as a Catholic Christian, without having understanding or perception of any other law than that true and holy law in which all the Christians hope for salvation."[11]

---

[9]Op. cit., p. 84.

[10]Speaking of the activities of the Portuguese at Goa, India, soon after 1498, L. S. S. O'Malley says: "The Portuguese territories were intended to be outposts of their empire and their religion. . . . Colonization was effected not so much by immigration as by marriage with Indian women. There was no color bar, and the children of mixed marriages were under no stigma of inferiority. . . . Proselytization began soon after the capture of Goa. . . . At the same time the spread of Christianity was assisted by an appeal to material interests. Converts were to be provided with posts in the customs, exempted from impressment in the navy, and supported by the distribution of rice." *Modern India and the West*, pp. 44–45.

[11]Azurara, op. cit., p. 80.

The next era in the history of race relations commenced with the discovery of America. If we see that race prejudice is an attitudinal instrument of modern human, economic exploitation, the question as to whether race prejudice was found among the primitive peoples of the world will not arise. It would be, for instance, a ridiculous inversion of thought to expect the native peoples of America to have had race prejudice for the white invaders.[12] But modern society—Western civilization—began to take on its characteristic attributes when Columbus turned the eyes and interests of the world away from the Mediterranean toward the Atlantic. The mysticism of the East soon lost its grip on human thought, and the bourgeois world got under way. The socioeconomic matrix of racial antagonism involved the commercialization of human labor in the West Indies, the East Indies, and in America, the intense competition among businessmen of different western European cities for the capitalist exploitation of the resources of this area, the development of nationalism and the consolidation of European nations, and the decline of the influence of the Roman Catholic Church with its mystical inhibitions to the free exploitation of economic resources. Racial antagonism attained full maturity during the latter half of the nineteenth century, when the sun no longer set on British soil and the great nationalistic powers of Europe began to justify their economic designs upon weaker European peoples with subtle theories of racial superiority and masterhood.

It should be observed that this view is not generally agreed upon. A popular belief among writers on modern race relations is that the phenomenon has always been known among most, if not all, peoples. This approach apparently tends to give theories of race relations a "scientific" aspect, but it contributes little to an understanding of the problem.

For instance, Jacques Barzun may be misleading in his saying that "if anyone deserves burning in effigy for starting the powerful race-dogma of Nordic superiority" it is Tacitus. This is supposed to be so

---

[12]Although Columbus participated in the enslavement of the Indians of the West Indies, which finally led to their extermination, his first impression of them is well known: "They are a loving uncovitous people, so docile in all things that I do assure your Highness I believe in all the world there is not a better people or a better country; they love their neighbours as themselves, and they have the sweetest and gentlest way of speaking in the world and always with a smile." Again, "As they showed us such friendship and as I recognized they were people who would yield themselves better to the Christian faith and be converted more through love than by force, I gave them some coloured buttons and some glass beads . . . and [they] became so attached to us that it was a marvel to behold." See Francis A. MacNutt, *Bartholomew De Las Casas,* pp. 18, 19.

because Tacitus, in his admiration of the primitive "Germans," made assertions "embodying the germ of present-day Nordicism."[13] Yet it seems evident that neither Tacitus, St. Paul, Noah, nor the Rig-Vedic Aryans are responsible for the racial practices and ideologies developed among modern Europeans. Moreover, the use of the metaphor "germ" is likely to convey the idea that this excursus of Tacitus, his "noble-savage" description of the virtues of the tribal Germans, was continually built upon by them over the centuries, until at last it blossomed into nazism.

We might just as well rely upon that notable charge of Cicero to Atticus in the first century B.C., "Do not obtain your slaves from Britain because they are so stupid and so utterly incapable of being taught that they are not fit to form a part of the household of Athens," as a basis for the explanation of modern race prejudice against the British— the only difficulty being that there has never been any such prejudice.

When white scholars began their almost desperate search of the ancient archives for good reasons to explain the wonderful cultural accomplishments among the whites, European economic and military world dominance was already an actuality. Most of the discoveries which explain the racial superiority of the tall, long-headed blond may be called Hamite rationalizations; they are drawn from bits of isolated verbalizations or deductions from cultural situations which cannot be identified with those of modern race relations. Probably the most widely accepted of these has been the biblical story of the descendants of Ham as a people cursed forever to do the menial work of others.

When English, French, and German scholars discovered the Aryans in the Sanskrit literature of the Hindus, the Hindus themselves were unaware of the Aryans' racial potentialities. The concept "Arya" meant practically nothing to them. It remained for the nationalistic Germans to recognize that the term "Aryan" designated Germans particularly and that, because of this, the right of Germans to exploit all other peoples of the world, not excluding the Hindus, was confirmed.

In the study of race relations it is of major importance to realize that their significant manifestations could not possibly have been known among the ancients. If we had to put our finger upon the year which marked the beginning of modern race relations we should select 1493–94. This is the time when total disregard for the human rights and physical power of the non-Christian peoples of the world, the colored peoples, was officially assumed by the first two great colonizing

---

[13]*Race, A Study of Modern Superstition*, pp. 11, 28.

European nations. Pope Alexander VI's bull of demarcation issued under Spanish pressure on May 3, 1493, and its revision by the Treaty of Tordesillas (June 7, 1494), arrived at through diplomatic negotiations between Spain and Portugal, put all the heathen peoples and their resources—that is to say, especially the colored peoples of the world—at the disposal of Spain and Portugal.[14]

Sometimes, probably because of its very obviousness, it is not realized that the slave trade was simply a way of recruiting labor for the purpose of exploiting the great natural resources of America.[15] This trade did not develop because Indians and Negroes were red and black, or because their cranial capacity averaged a certain number of cubic centimeters; but simply because they were the best workers to be found for the heavy labor in the mines and plantations across the Atlantic.[16] If white workers were available in sufficient numbers they would have been substituted. As a matter of fact, part of the early demand for labor in the West Indies and on the mainland was filled by white servants, who were sometimes defined in exactly the same terms as those used to characterize the Africans. Although the recruitment of involuntary labor finally settled down to the African coasts, the earlier kidnapers did a brisk business in some of the most enlightened European cities. Moreover, in the process of exploiting the natural resources of the West Indies, the Spanish conquistadors literally consumed the native Indian population.

This, then, is the beginning of modern race relations. It was not an abstract, natural, immemorial feeling of mutual antipathy between groups, but rather a practical exploitative relationship with its socio-attitudinal facilitation—at that time only nascent race prejudice. Although this peculiar kind of exploitation was then in its incipiency, it

---

[14]As early as 1455 Pope Nicholas V had granted the Portuguese exclusive right to their discoveries on the African coast, but the commercial purpose here was still very much involved with the crusading spirit.

[15]In a discussion of the arguments over slavery during the Constitutional Convention, Charles A. Beard observes: "South Carolina was particularly determined, and gave northern representatives to understand that if they wished to secure their commercial privileges, they must make concessions to the slave trade. And they were met half way. Ellsworth said: 'As slaves multiply so fast in Virginia and Maryland that it is cheaper to raise than import them, whilst in the sickly rice swamps foreign supplies are necessary, if we go no farther than is urged, we shall be unjust towards South Carolina and Georgia. Let us not intermeddle. As population increases, poor laborers will be so plenty as to render slaves useless.' " *An Economic Interpretation of the Constitution,* p. 177. Quote from Max Farrand, *Records,* Vol. II, p. 371.

[16]In a discussion of the labor situation among the early Spanish colonists in America, Professor Bailey W. Diffie observes: "One Negro was reckoned as worth two, four, or even more Indians at work production." *Latin American Civilization,* p. 206.

had already achieved its significant characteristics.[17] As it developed and took definite capitalistic form, we could follow the white man around the world and see him repeat the process among practically every people of color. Earl Grey was directly in point when he described, in 1880, the motives and purpose of the British in one racial situation:

> Throughout this part of the British Dominions the colored people are generally looked upon by the whites as an inferior race, whose interest ought to be systematically disregarded when they come into competition with their own, and who ought to be governed mainly with a view to the advantage of the superior race. And for this advantage two things are considered to be especially necessary: first, that facilities should be afforded to the white colonists for obtaining possession of land heretofore occupied by the native tribes; and secondly, that the Kaffir population should be made to furnish as large and as cheap a supply of labor as possible.[18]

But the fact of crucial significance is that racial exploitation is merely one aspect of the problem of the proletarianization of labor, regardless of the color of the laborer. Hence racial antagonism is essentially political-class conflict. The capitalist exploiter, being opportunistic and practical, will utilize any convenience to keep his labor and other resources freely exploitable. He will devise and employ race prejudice when that becomes convenient.[19] As a matter of fact, the white proletariat of early capitalism had to endure burdens of exploitation quite similar to those which many colored peoples must bear today.

However, the capitalist spirit, the profit-making motive, among the sixteenth-century Spaniards and Portuguese, was constantly inhibited by the philosophy and purpose of the Roman Catholic Church. A social

---

[17]Francis Augustus MacNutt describes the relationship in Hispaniola: "Columbus laid tribute upon the entire population of the island which required that each Indian above fourteen years of age who lived in the mining provinces was to pay a little bell filled with gold every three months; the natives of all other provinces were to pay one *arroba* of cotton. These amounts were so excessive that in 1496 it was found necessary to change the nature of the payments, and, instead of the gold and cotton required from the villages, labour was substituted, the Indians being required to lay out and work the plantations of the colonists in their vicinity." *Bartholomew De Las Casas,* p. 25.

[18]Quoted by E. D. Morel, *The Black Man's Burden,* p. 30.

[19]In our description of the uses of race prejudice in this essay we are likely to give the impression that race prejudice was always "manufactured" in full awareness by individuals or groups of entrepreneurs. This, however, is not quite the case. Race prejudice, from its inception, became part of the social heritage, and as such both exploiters and exploited for the most part are born heirs to it. It is possible that most of those who propagate and defend race prejudice are not conscious of its fundamental motivation. To paraphrase Adam Smith: They who teach and finance race prejudice are by no means such fools as the majority of those who believe and practice it.

theory supporting the capitalist drive for the impersonal exploitation of the workers never completely emerged. Conversion to Christianity and slavery among the Indians stood at cross-purposes; therefore, the vital problem presented to the exploiters of labor was that of circumventing the assimilative effects of conversion to Christianity. In the West Indies the celebrated priest, Las Casas, was touched by the destructive consequences of the ruthless enslavement of the Indians, and he opposed it on religious grounds. But work had to be done, and if not voluntarily, then some ideology had to be found to justify involuntary servitude. "The Indians were represented as lazy, filthy pagans, of bestial morals, no better than dogs, and fit only for slavery, in which state alone there might be some hope of instructing and converting them to Christianity."[20]

The capitalist exploitation of the colored workers, it should be observed, consigns them to employments and treatment that is humanly degrading. In order to justify this treatment the exploiters must argue that the workers are innately degraded and degenerate, consequently they naturally merit their condition. It may be mentioned incidentally that the ruling-class conception of degradation will tend to be that of all persons in the society, even that of the exploited person himself; and the work done by degraded persons will tend to degrade superior persons who attempt to do it.

In 1550, finally, the great capitalist interests produced a champion, Gaines de Sepulveda, brilliant theologian and debater, to confront Las Casas in open debate at Valladolid on the right of Spaniards to wage wars of conquest against the Indians. Sepulveda held that it was lawful to make war against (enslave) the Indians:

1. Because of the gravity of their sins. . . .
2. Because of the rudeness of their heathen and barbarous natures, which oblige them to serve those of more elevated natures, such as the Spaniards possess.
3. For the spread of the faith; for their subjection renders its preaching easier and more persuasive [and so on].[21]

It is not surprising that Sepulveda won the debate. His approach was consistent with the exploitative rationalizations of the time. He con-

---

[20]Francis Augustus MacNutt, op. cit., p. 83.
    It should be kept clearly in view that this colonial movement was not a transference of the feudal manorial economy to America. It was the beginning of an entirely different economic enterprise—the dawn of colonial capitalism, the moving out of "white" capital into the lands of colored peoples who had to be exploited unsentimentally and with any degree of ruthlessness in the interest of profits.

[21]MacNutt, op. cit., p. 288.

trived a reasonably logical justification for the irrepressibly exploitative situation. This clearly was in answer to an urgent necessity for such an authoritative explanation; the whole world, so to speak, was calling for it. As a characteristic, it should be observed that no explanation at all need have been made to the exploited people themselves. The group sentiment and feeling of the exploited peoples were disregarded entirely.

Sepulveda, then, may be thought of as among the first great racists;[22] his argument was, in effect, that the Indians were inferior to the Spaniards, therefore they should be exploited. Yet the powerful religious interest among the Spaniards limited the establishment of a clear philosophy of racial exploitation. Some years earlier an attempt was made to show "that the Indians were incapable of conversion," but this was finally squelched by a threat to bring the advocate before the tribunal of the Inquisition.[23] It remained for later thinkers, mainly from northern European countries, to produce the evidence that "native peoples" have an inferior, animal-like capacity for culture.[24]

In the years to follow there will be unnumbered sermons preached and "scientific" books written to prove the incapacity for cultural conversion of exploitable peoples, and always with the implied or expressed presumption that this incapacity should stand as a bar to movements for the cultural assimilation of such peoples. (The ultimate purpose of all theories of white superiority is not a demonstration that whites are in fact superior to all other human beings but rather to insist that whites must be supreme. It involves primarily a power rather than

---

[22]Among the Spanish writers of the time (about 1535 onward) who were in rather complete accord with the drastic methods of human exploitation in the New World was Gonzolo Fernandez de Oviedo, whose prolific works have been collected in the commentary, *Historia General y Natural de las Indias,* 4 vols. It was Oviedo's opinion, even after visiting America on a royal commission, that the Indians were not far removed from the state of wild animals, and that coercive measures were necessary if they were to be Christianized and taught the uses of systematic labor.

[23]MacNutt, op. cit., pp. 94–95.

[24]"Beasts of burden do not have rights which human beings are bound to respect; they may be exploited at will. The latter convenience is a desideratum in the capitalist exploitation of labor, regardless of the color of the laborer. However, the fact of difference in color and culture makes available to the exploiters of colored workers a valuable means of securing their dehumanization in the eyes of a certain public, that is to say, the public of the exploiting class. When a philosophy for the dehumanizing of the exploited people has been developed with sufficient cogency, the ruling class is ready to make its grand statement, sometimes implicitly, and to act in accordance with it: The colored people have no rights which the master race is bound to respect. The exploiting class has an economic investment in this conviction and it will defend it with the same vigor as it would an attack upon private property in land and capital.

a social-status relationship.) Assimilation diminishes the exploitative possibilities. This social situation is not especially a derivative of human idiosyncrasy or wickedness, but rather it is a function of a peculiar type of economc order which, to repeat, has been developed in the West among Europeans. The exploitation of native peoples, imperialism, is not a sin, not essentially a problem of morals or of vice; it is a problem of production and of competition for markets.[25] Here, then, are race relations; they are definitely not caste relations. They are labor-capital-profits relationships; therefore, race relations are proletarian bourgeois relations and hence political-class relations.

The commercial activities of the merchant adventurers from the northern European cities were much less involved with the universal interests of the Church. The Anglo-Saxon and Germanic merchants came later to the great area of capitalist opportunities, and their profit-making purpose was much more clearly defined. Here, too, the bitter economic competition between different groups of raiders and traders cradled the nationalism which was to become a characteristic political trait of modern peoples. Out of this early economic war of shifting national fortunes England soon emerged as the "great slave trader of the world" and at the head of the most powerful economic empire.

It may be well to emphasize that the white people who went out from Europe to "civilize" and exploit the resources of the colored peoples were mainly capitalists, urban dwellers, business people from the beginning. Their way of life was basically antagonistic to the feudal and prefeudal agricultural systems which they encountered everywhere; therefore, the colored people had to be suppressed if the urgent purpose

---

[25]Of course one should not be particularly disturbed about the fact that, although one never had the necessity or even the thought of exploiting colored people, yet an almost irresistible bitterness seems to well up as one finds himself in certain social situations with colored people. It is this very reaction which derogatory racial propaganda sets out to achieve and, knowing that even human nature itself is a social product, it would be surprising if the people did not hate whichever group the ruling class convinced them should be hated. Moreover, we naturally tend to dislike people who are degraded or brutalized. A degraded person is a contemptible person who should be despised and kept at a distance—the Christian Gospels notwithstanding.

Such ambivalent conclusions as the following by Dr. Louis Wirth may be misleading: "Ethnic, linguistic, and religious differences will continue to divide people, and the prejudices that go with them cannot suddenly be wiped out by fiat. But whereas personal prejudices and antipathies can probably be expected to yield only to the tedious process of education and assimilation, collective programs and policies can be altered considerably in advance of the time when they have unanimous group consent. Law and public policy can go far toward minimizing the adverse effect even of personal prejudices." In Ralph Linton, ed., *The Science of Man in the World Crisis*, p. 368.

of the white opportunists was not to go unanswered.[26] In this connection Max Weber asserts:

A man does not "by nature" wish to earn more and more money, but simply to live as he is accustomed to live and to earn as much as is necessary for that purpose. Wherever modern capitalism has begun its work of increasing the productivity of human labor by increasing its intensity, it has encountered an immensely stubborn resistance of this leading trait of pre-capitalistic labor. And today it encounters it the more, the more backward (from a capitalistic point of view) the laboring forces are with which it has to deal.[27]

The system of chartered companies, adopted by the colonizing European countries, ordinarily put the welfare and destiny of whole peoples directly into the hands of profit makers. What E. D. Morel says of the British South African Company for the exploitation of Southern Rhodesia is characteristic of the system:

In such a fashion were the powers of government and administration, involving the establishment of a police force, the making of laws, the raising of revenue, the administration of justice, the construction of public works, the grant of mining and forestry concessions, and so on, in an African country three times the size of England, eventually conferred upon

[26]Leonard Woolf makes a pertinent observation on this point: "The manufacturers and traders who were the harbingers of imperialism in the hills and plains of Asia and the forests of Africa went there with certain definite economic objects: they wanted to sell cotton or calico, to obtain tin or iron or rubber or tea or coffee. But to do this under the complicated economic system of Western Civilization, it was necessary that the whole economic system of the Asiatic and African should be adjusted to and assimilated with that of Europe. . . . In the process the lives of the subject peoples have been revolutionized and the bases of their own civilization often destroyed. . . . Nothing like this and upon this scale has ever happened in the world before." *Imperialism and Civilization*, pp. 48–49.
See also James Mill, *The History of British India,* Vol. I, pp. 22–23, for an interesting account of a taboo against the employment of "gentlemen" by the early seventeenth-century "adventurers" in their East India trade; also Henry Stevens, *The Dawn of British Trade to the East Indies, as Recorded in the Court Minutes of the East India Company 1599–1603,* p. 28.

[27]*Protestant Ethic and the Spirit of Capitalism,* p. 60. Concerning England itself, Paul Mantoux writes about this process of the proletarianization of labor: "Once the problem of capital and plant had been solved, that of labour arose. How was it to be recruited and governed? Men used to working at home were generally not inclined to go to the factory. In the early days factory labour consisted of the most ill-assorted elements. . . . All these unskilled men, unused to collective work had to be taught, trained, and above all disciplined, by the manufacturer. He had, so to speak, to be turned into a human machine, as regular in its working, as accurate in its movements, and as exactly combined for a single purpose as the mechanism of wood and metal to which they became accessory. Hard-and-fast rules replaced the freedom of the small workshop. Work started, meals were eaten and work stopped at fixed hours, notified by the ringing of a bell. . . . Everyone had to work steadily . . . under the vigilant eye of a foreman, who secured obedience by means of fines or dismissals, and sometimes by more brutal forms of coercion." *The Industrial Revolution in the Eighteenth Century,* p. 384. See also J. L. and Barbara Hammond, *The Town Labourer, 1760–1832,* Chap. II.

a corporation, whose interest in that country was to make money out of it.[28]

Probably it is unnecessary for us to restate the history of the planter class in the West and its problems of exploitation, or the drama of white colonization in other parts of the world. Yet it may be in place to indicate further the relationship of race antagonism to the broader bourgeois-proletariat conflict. As we mentioned previously, the relationship of producers to white workers has been frequently such as to demonstrate the common status of workers as a factor of production, regardless of color. In some of the early experiments with labor in the West Indies both white and black workers were used in the field and their treatment and value were ordinarily determined by their relative economic productivity.[29] But it is the early mercantilist labor theory and practice which show naïvely the fundamental exploitative drive; and we may illustrate this from the situation in England, the leading capitalist nation.

Mercantilism may be thought of as that system of economic philosophy, trading practice, and direction of production which has for its purpose the securing of advantages to a nation in international economic competition. It is the state capitalism which the postfeudal capitalists developed.[30] Nationalism is the emotional matrix of this state, economic competition. Although mercantilism reached some sort of high point in overt expression in the late eighteenth century, its essential ideology continues in what has been sometimes called neo-mercantilism. Roughly speaking, the early mercantilist defined the "wealth of the nation" in terms of the monetary payments which other nations were compelled to pay in order to offset their unfavorable balance of trade; today more emphasis is put upon the success of the heavy industries of a nation. The worker's place in the system has been primarily related to production, and he has been regarded as an item of cost—that is to say, as both a necessary and important factor of pro-

---

[28]Op. cit., p. 36.

[29]See Frank Wesley Pitman, *Development of the British West Indies, 1700–1763*, p. 45; Eric Williams, *Capitalism and Slavery*, pp. 3–29; and Lowell Joseph Ragatz, *The Fall of the Planter Class, passim.*

[30]Gustav Schmoller gives a significant definition: ". . . in its innermost kernel [mercantilism] is nothing but state making—not state making in a narrow sense, but state making and national-economy making at the same time; state making in the modern sense, which creates out of the political community an economic community, and so gives it a heightened meaning. The essence of the system lies not in some doctrine of money, or the balance of trade; but in something far greater:— namely, in the total transformation of society and its organization, as well as of the state and its institutions, in replacing of a local [town] and territorial economic policy by that of the national state." *The Mercantile System*, pp. 50–51. Cf. Carl Bucher, *Industrial Evolution*, p. 136.

duction and as an impediment to the entrepreneur in his basic urge to undersell his competitors. The worker, then, was indispensable, but he should be paid only so much as would be sufficient to keep him alive and able to labor—a subsistence wage. Thus, as Eli F. Heckscher concludes: "With practically insignificant exceptions, all official wage-fixing . . . prescribed maximum wages. Out of every ten interferences with the relationship between employers and employed, at least nine were in the interest of the employers."[31] And, says Rees, "The desideratum was a population as large as possible, as fully occupied as possible, and living as near as possible to the margin of subsistence."[32]

But low wages were supposed to have other values besides those of limiting cost of production. They tended to keep the worker in a constant state of necessity, which disposed him to labor. In this respect the mercantilists' characterization of the English workers is very much like that continually addressed to colored workers and native peoples. A man will not work seven days a week if he could live by the earnings of one; therefore, if the employer is to have a sufficient supply of labor, a day's wage should be no more than that which the worker must spend in that day. Edgar S. Furniss calls this "the doctrine of the utility of poverty." According to Arthur Young, writing in 1770, "[Great earnings] have a strong effect on all who remain the least inclined to idleness or other ill courses, by causing them to work but four or five days to maintain themselves the seven; this is a fact so well known in every manufacturing town that it would be idle to think of proving it by argument."[33] There were riches, then, in the poverty and necessitous state of the masses: "in a free nation where slaves are not allowed of, the surest wealth consists in a multitude of laborious poor."[34]

If, however, low wages did not produce the desired results, it was felt that the law should compel idle workers to find employment. As one writer suggested in a series of questions:

Whether if human industry be the source of wealth, it doth not follow that idleness should of all things be discouraged in a wise state? Whether

---

[31]*Mercantilism,* Vol. II, p. 167.

[32]J. F. Rees, "Mercantilism and the Colonies," *Cambridge History of the British Empire,* Vol. I, p. 563. To the same effect Heckscher observes: "By forcing down wages . . . the export of such products as contained relatively more human labor could be increased; and such a policy could at the same time restrict the import of the same group of products. . . . The corollary was that efforts had to be made to maintain as abundant supply of labour as possible at as low a price as possible." Op. cit., Vol. II, p. 153.

[33]Quoted by Edgar S. Furniss, *The Position of Labor in a System of Nationalism,* pp. 119–20.

[34]B. Mandeville, *Britannia Lenguens,* p. 153, quoted by Eli F. Heckscher, op. cit., Vol. II, p. 164.

temporary servitude would not be the best cure for idleness and beggary? Whether the public hath not the right to employ those who cannot or will not find employment for themselves? Whether sturdy beggars may not be seized and made slaves to the public for a certain term of years?[35]

To be sure, no producer will express himself so bluntly in England today, but this attitude and practice of forced labor is still common among Europeans in their dealings with native peoples. Vagrancy laws are still posted in courthouses and city halls in the Southern states of the United States. The technique of "keeping books" and making commodity advances to workers also tends to secure the planter's labor supply.

Moreover, the mercantilist feared the prospects of the laborer's getting out of his place. It was felt that some class of people should be depended upon to do the common work, and that the status of this class as common workers should remain permanent. It was some tendency in the working class to be independent which called forth reactions akin to racial antagonism. Says William Temple in 1770: "Our manufacturing populace have adopted a notion that as Englishmen they enjoy a birth right privilege of being more free and independent than any country in Europe. . . . The less the manufacturing poor have of it, the better for themselves and for the estate. The laboring people should never think of themselves independent of their superiors for, if a proper subordination is not kept up, riot and confusion will take the place of sobriety and good order."[36] This is, let us interpose, precisely the idea of "the Negroes' place" in the United States.

Undoubtedly the most persistent menace to the peace and good order of the classes was the rise of popular education. For, as Mandeville said in 1723: "To make the society happy and people easy under the meanest circumstances, it is requisite that great numbers of them should be ignorant as well as poor."[37] Therefore, it became the immediate busi-

---

[35]George Berkeley (1750), quoted by Edgar S. Furniss, op. cit., p. 80. Furniss also cites an anonymous author on the duties of the laboring classes: "Such journeymen, day laborers, or others, who shall refuse to work the usual hours, for the price hereby stipulated, shall immediately, by the peace officer of the parish, be carried before a neighboring Justice of the Peace, and be by him committed to Bridewell, there to be kept to hard labor till they shall think proper to obey the laws of their country." Ibid., p. 84.

[36]Ibid., p. 56.

[37]See Heckscher, op. cit., Vol. II, p. 167. And in 1763 an anonymous author of *Considerations of the Fatal Effects to a Trading Nation of the Excess of Public Charity* declared: "The charity school is another universal nursery of idleness; nor is it easy to conceive or invent anything more destructive to the interest and very foundation principles of a nation entirely dependent on its trade and manufactures than the giving an education to the children of the lowest class of her people that will make them contemn those drudgeries for which they were born." Quoted by Furniss, op. cit., p. 148.

ness of the ruling class to obstruct or at least to direct the education of the common people. If the workers had to be educated, they should receive vocational and industrial education; they should be turned back to their natural duty and not away from it, since "few that have once learnt to write and read, but either their parents or themselves are apt to think that they are fit for some preferment, and in order to it, despise all laboring employments."[38] And Thomas Ruggles made the typical statement: "There must be in society hewers of wood and drawers of water. If all are good penmen, where are those who will contentedly live through a life of toil?"[39] Thus, the training advocated for the workhouse children, the children of the poor, was intended to keep them within the occupational level of their parents; and intellectual pursuits were ruled out.[40] Professor Furniss describes the position of the eighteenth-century white workers in England as a class, which is virtually a description of the position of colored people in certain modern racial situations:

The proponents of the workhouse in both of its forms evidently conceived of the laboring population as a class united to the social body by bonds of duty and drawing from their connection with the nation certain rights. The fact that the laboring population was viewed as a *class* and dealt with as a class shows that individualistic concepts of society did not embrace them. As a class they were to be patronized by the government; as a class, coerced, disciplined, punished, when patronage failed to awaken the expected response. Much was said of their duties and their station in life, little or nothing of their opportunities for advancement in the social scale; few were the proposals to throw them upon their own resources as individuals, many those which advocated comprehensive government action to control their conduct as a group.[41]

---

[38]J. Prollexfen, *A Discourse of Trade, Coyn, and Paper Credit,* quoted by Heckscher, op. cit., pp. 166–67.

[39]*History of the Poor.* Although Ruggles was making a plea for the just treatment of the common people, he did not go beyond the following demand: "By this expression [the claims of the poor on society] no abstract ideas of a claim to equality, either in legislation or property, have been canvassed; but simply that claim to a fair retribution for their strength and ability to labor, which is their only birthright." Ibid., 1797 ed., p. ix.

[40]It is to this characteristic of capitalist society Harold Laski refers when he says: "There is a vested interest in the perpetuation of ignorance which is endemic in our civilization. We cannot get rid of ignorance save as we are willing to attack that vested interest; and the signs are clear that it will bitterly defend itself if we move to the attack." *Reflections on the Revolution of Our Time,* p. 3. See also J. A. Hobson, op. cit., pp. 105–06.

[41]Op. cit., p. 87. The Hammonds quote the president of the Royal Society, Giddy (1767–1839), as developing the following logic: "[Giving education to the laboring classes] would teach them to despise their lot in life, instead of making them good servants in agriculture, and other laborious employments to which their rank in society had destined them; instead of teaching them subordination, it would render them factious and refractory . . . it would enable them to read seditious pamphlets,

The white common people, after continual struggle along the way to democracy, have gained more or less right to be educated freely. But colored people, in South Africa and the Southern United States typically, are still suffering from the crude pressures of exploitation. The argument still holds that the Negro should be taught "labor, not learning." The desperate resistance to the giving of Negroes an equal opportunity for education is well known. It is necessary, so to speak, that their educable potentialities remain as nearly as possible undiscovered.

Sometimes, in studies of education in the South, the backward state of the system is attributed to the economic poverty of the region. This, however, does not seem to be the primary reason. The South does not want its poor white people and its Negroes particularly to be educated away from "those drudgeries for which they were born." If, for instance, some jinnee were to appear before the assembled governors, senators, and bankers of the South and present them a little hill of gold bricks to be used for educational purposes, they would probably begin to discuss among themselves what effect it might have on the stability of the social system; but if the jinnee interrupts with the condition that every time a gold brick is taken for the education of a white child another should also be taken for that of a Negro child, then we should expect the council to say without hesitation, "Gather up your bricks as fast as you can and betake yourself to Hades." Today it is almost as easy to get Federal funds for education in the South, but little general enthusiasm and certain possibilities of Negroes participating equally result in rejection of the aid.

It is, moreover, on this principle of vocational and industrial education—"teaching black workers to work"—that Booker T. Washington felt sure of himself. He knew that on this ground the ruling class had to listen to him; and, indeed, it accepted him as leader of the Negroes and watched carefully the program of the school which he established. However exalted his motives might have been, yet he enunciated one of the deepest intents of the exploiters of labor—of black labor especially —when in giving utterance to an essentially mercantilist labor philosophy he declared: "We shall prosper in proportion as we learn to dignify and glorify common labor and put brains and skill into the common occupations of life. . . . No race can prosper till it learns

---

vicious books, and publications against Christianity; it would render them insolent to their superiors; and in a few years the result would be that the legislature would find it necessary to direct the strong arm of power toward them, and to furnish the executive magistrate with much more vigorous laws than were now in force." Op. cit., p. 57.

that there is as much dignity in tilling a field as in writing a poem."
And, turning to the white exploiting class, he said confidently: "You
are in debt to the black man for furnishing you with labor that is almost
a stranger to strikes, lock-outs, and labor wars; labor that is law-abiding,
peaceful, teachable . . . labor that has never been tempted to follow
the red flag of anarchy, but always the safe flag of his country and the
spotless banner of the Cross."[42]

Thus the white ruling class tended to agree with Washington when
he advocated dignity in common labor—the doing of manual occupations efficiently and dignifiedly; that is to say, in essence, the doing of
menial occupations contentedly. This very class would have brought
him to his knees had he advocated *superior education* on the grounds
of its enhanced productivity and inevitably inherent dignity. A superior
education tends to make the individual superior, because it puts him in
a position to accept occupations that the society has defined as superior;
whereas there is no assurance that the ordinary, efficient worker would
be able to arrogate to himself an artificial dignity that the social system
itself does not generally recognize. One reason why there is in fact little
dignity in manual labor is that the laborer himself is ordinarily not
dignified.[43] To dignify a person is to refine and educate him far beyond

---

[42]*Selected Speeches of Booker T. Washington,* E. D. Washington, ed., pp. 33, 82.
In Washington's own words: ". . . the bulk of opinion in the South had little
faith in the efficacy of the 'higher' or any other kind of education for the Negro.
. . . While the education which we proposed to give at the Tuskegee Institute was
not spontaneously welcomed by the white South, it was this training of the hands
that furnished the first basis for anything like united and sympathetic interest and
action between the two races. . . .
"Many white people of the South saw in the movement to teach young Negroes
the necessity and honour of work with the hands a means of leading them gradually
and sensibly into their new life of freedom. . . . They perceived, too, that the
Negroes [the slaves] who were master carpenters and contractors under the guidance
of their owners could greatly further the development of the South if their children
were not too suddenly removed from the atmosphere and occupation of their fathers.
. . . The individual and community interest of the white people was directly appealed to by industrial education. . . . Almost every white man in the South was
directly interested in agricultural, mechanical, or other manual labor; in cooking
and serving of food, laundering and dairying, poultry raising, and everything related to housekeeping in general. . . .
"Therefore there came to be a growing appreciation of the fact that industrial
education of the black people had a practical and vital bearing on the life of every
white family in the South. There was little opportunity for such appreciation of the
results of mere literary education." *Working with the Hands,* pp. 13-14.
[43]As a matter of fact, the white planters were accustomed to see their skilled
black workers as slaves. On this point Richard B. Morris observes: "Failing to maintain an adequate number of white artisans, the Southern colonies then trained
Negro slaves for the skilled trades. The files of the *South Carolina Gazette* revealed
that Negroes were trained and practicing virtually all the crafts needed for maintaining the plantation economy. In addition to those engaged in husbandry, the
well-organized plantation employed carpenters, coopers, stone-masons, a miller, a
black-smith, shoemakers, spinners, and weavers. The wealthier planters often car-

the training necessary for the successful performance of a manual skill; and when this is done in a capitalist society, manual labor usually loses such a person.

This, of course, is not a criticism of Washington; it may be indeed a commendation of his intuition in sensing the basis of race relations. It makes no reference to his widely recognized contribution to the advancement of Negroes among skilled workers. Yet, so long as Washington accepted the morality of capitalism, he had to conceive of the labor power of colored people in this fashion. "Washington was in some respects a greater leader of white opinion than he was of Negro opinion,"[44] and "white opinion" was inevitably against the best interest of Negroes, as it still is to this day. There are many sincere Southern white people who believe that the success of the Negroes depends upon their adopting the industrial philosophy of the English eighteenth-century workhouses.

Although both race relations and the struggle of the white proletariat with the bourgeoisie are parts of a single social phenomenon, race relations involve a significant variation. In the case of race relations the tendency of the bourgeoisie is to proletarianize a whole people—that is to say, the whole people is looked upon as a class—whereas white proletarianization involves only a section of the white people. The concept "bourgeois" and "white people" sometimes seems to mean the same thing for, with respect to the colored peoples of the world, it is almost always through a white bourgeoisie that capitalism has been introduced. The early capitalist settlers among the colored peoples were disposed to look upon the latter and their natural resources as factors of production to be manipulated impersonally with "white capital" in the interest of profits. It is this need to impersonalize whole peoples which introduces into the class struggle the complicating factors known as race problems. If the colored people themselves are able to develop a significant bourgeoisie, as among the Japanese and East Indians, race relations are further complicated by the rise of conscious nationalism. As we shall attempt to show in a later chapter, situations of race rela-

---

ried on industrial enterprises on a considerable scale, necessitating the employment of a sizable number of skilled workmen. . . . Some white artificers were generally needed to start such enterprises, but they were in the main carried on almost exclusively by negro slaves who were often hired out by their masters to others in need of skilled help." *Government and Labor in Early America*, p. 31.

Vocational education as a technique of exploitation was practiced with ferver and zeal among the sixteenth-century Latin-American colonists. See Bailey W. Diffie, *Latin American Civilization*, p. 359, *passim*.

[44] Guy B. Johnson, "Negro Racial Movements and Leadership in the United States," *American Journal of Sociology*, July 1937, Vol. 43, p. 63.

tions may be distinguished according to the exploitative convenience of the white bourgeoisie.

The Progress of Racial Antagonism

This, then, is the nature of racial antagonism; developing in Europe, it has been carried to all parts of the world. In almost fateful terms Kipling's celebrated poem written in 1899 describes a desperate conflict, "the white man's burden," a like obligation, incidentally, never assumed by any other race in all the history of the world:

> *Take up the White Man's burden—*
> *Send forth the best ye breed—*
> *Go bind your sons to exile*
> *To serve your captives' need;*
> *To wait in heavy harness,*
> *On fluttered folk and wild—*
> *Your new-caught, sullen peoples,*
> *Half-devil and half-child.*[44a]

The Europeans have overthrown more or less completely the social system among every colored people with whom they have come into contact. The dynamism and efficiency of capitalistic culture concluded this. The stability of color and inertness of culture, together with effective control over firearms, subsequently made it possible for whites to achieve a more or less separate and dominant position even in the homeland of colored peoples. "The white man's conception of himself as the aristocrat of the earth came gradually through the discovery, as surprising to himself as to anyone else, that he had weapons and organization which made opposition to his ambition futile."[45]

It should be made clear that we do not mean to say that the white race is the only one *capable* of race prejudice. It is probable that without capitalism, a cultural chance occurrence among whites, the world might never have experienced race prejudice. Indeed, we should expect that under another form of economic organization, say socialism,

[44a]*Rudyard Kipling's Verse, 1885–1926*, p. 320.
[45]Josef W. Hall (Upton Close), *The Revolt of Asia*, p. 4. In this early period there was a more or less conscious development of the exploitative system. In later years, however, the infants that were born into the developed society had, of course, to take it as they found it. The social system determined their behavior *naturally;* that is to say, the racial exploitation and racial antagonisms seemed natural and the *conscious* element frequently did not exist. In other words, the racial fate of the individual was determined before he was born.

the relationship between whites and peoples of color would be significantly modified.[46]

The depreciation of the white man's color as a social gift goes hand in hand with the westernization of the conquered peoples of color. The Hindus, for example, are the same color today as they were in 1750, but now the white man no longer appears to them to be the cultural magician of other days. His secret of domination has been exposed, and the Hindus are now able to distinguish between his white skin and that secret. Therefore, he is now left with only his nationalism and superior might, for should he pull a cultural rabbit out of his hat, some Hindu would promptly pull another, which might even overmatch the first. Krishnalal Shridharani puts it thus: "[The Saxon] has been accustomed to regarding himself as a supreme being for centuries. Now he faces a world which refuses to recognize him as such. With all his civilized values, he will have to go on the role of military tyrant."[47] There is no assumption, then, that race prejudice is a biological heritage of the white race.

But we should not lose sight of the fact that whites have pre-empted this attitude.[48] Since the belief in white superiority—that is to say, white nationalism—began to move over the world, no people of color has been able to develop race prejudice independent of whites. It may be, however, that the Japanese have now reached that stage of industrial

---

[46]See a popular discussion relative to this by Hewlett Johnson, *The Soviet Power,* Book V; Bernhard J. Stern, "Soviet Policy on National Minorities," *American Sociological Review,* June 1944, pp. 229–35, and particularly Joseph Stalin, *Marxism and the National Question.*

[47]*Warning to the West,* p. 274.

[48]Pearl S. Buck likes to repeat the fact that "we differ in one important regard from the peoples of Asia. Race has never been a cause for any division among those people. But race prejudice divides us deeply." "The Spirit Behind the Weapon," *Survey Graphic,* Vol. XXXI, No. 11, November 1942, p. 540.

In a broad historical description of this process Leonard Woolf says: "In no other period of world's history has there been such a vast revolution as the conquest of Asia and Africa by Europe. . . . Until very nearly the end of the nineteenth century, Europeans themselves regarded it with complacent pride as one of the chief blessings and glories of Western Civilization. The white race of Europe, they held, was physically, mentally, and morally superior to all other races; and God, with infinite wisdom and goodness, had created it and developed it so that it might be ready, during the reign of Queen Victoria in England, to take over and manage the affairs of all other people on earth and teach them to be, in so far as that was possible for natives and heathens, good Europeans and good Christians. Indeed, until the very end of the century, the natives and heathens themselves seemed to acquiesce in this view of the designs of providence and the blessings of being ruled by Europeans. It is true that in almost every case originally a considerable number of Africans and Asiatics had to be killed before the survivors were prepared to accept the domination or, as it was called, protection of the European State; but once the domination was established there were few revolts against European rule which could not be met with a punitive expedition." Op. cit., pp. 15–16.

development, nationalistic ambition, and military power sufficient to question their assignment to inferior racial rank; no other colored race has ever dared to do this.[49] Indeed, since 1905 the Japanese have known how it felt to overcome the white man and make him like it.

Furthermore, the Japanese are culturally ripe for a belief of their own in yellow superiority. But the problem now confronting them is not similar to that which lay before the Europeans when they began to take on the burden of exploiting the colored peoples of the world. The white opportunists had then come upon no race able to fathom thei cultural superiority and power. Today, however, the Japanese are no only blocked at every point by powerfully entrenched whites but also relatively limited in their possible area of dominance.

A still more crucial question is whether this world is large enough to accommodate more than one superior race. Barring the apparent illogic of the superlative, we should bear in mind that color prejudice is more than ethnocentrism; race prejudice must be actually backed up by a show of racial excellence, secured finally by military might.[50] No race

---

[49]And we should expect that all peoples of color will be gratified and inspired by this kind of accomplishment. It tends to restore their self-respect as nothing else can. "When the white man began his series of retreats before the yellow hordes," Shridharani writes, "it was soothing balm to the ancient wounds of Asia. More than any Japanese words the Japanese deeds made propaganda. The white man, the most hated creature in Asia, was put to flight at Hong Kong, in Malaya, in Burma, and above all at Singapore." Op. cit., p. 196.

Dr. Sun Yat-sen finds inspiration for all the colored peoples in Asia in the exploits of Japan. "Japan," he says, "is a good model for us, if we wish for prosperity of China. . . . Formerly it was thought that of all the people in the world only the whites were intelligent and gifted"; but today Japan has shown all this to be false and hope has returned to the peoples of Asia. *Le Triple Demisme,* French trans. by Pascal M. d'Elia, pp. 20–21.

One fairly widely read East Indian, P. S. Joshi, puts it in this way: "The whiteism steps an insane dance in all the continents of the world. There are in Asia only a handful of whites. . . . Still they have, by reason of their political might, introduced the colour bar in India, China, the Philippines, and other countries. Had not Japan been triumphant over Russia, had not white prestige suffered a severe blow, the same colour bar would have spread . . . throughout the continent of Asia." *The Tyranny of Colour,* p. 4.

[50]Raymond Kennedy emphasizes the point that in the belief of racial superiority the confidence in superior might is elemental. Thus he writes: "The European peoples were enabled, some four hundred years ago, to extend conquest over the entire 'native' world. The 'natives,' who were just as good, man for man, as the Europeans, lacked the superior material equipment of the latter, and were either slaughtered or subjugated. The possessors of guns came to believe that they were also possessors of superior racial endowments, and attributed their success not to material advantages, but to innate mental and physical superiority. They were white and the beaten peoples mostly black, brown, yellow, and red; consequently inferiority must be linked with color and race." *The Ageless Indies,* pp. 185–86. To the same effect see Leonard Woolf, op. cit., p. 12.

Lin Yutang puts the idea in his own way: "How did nineteenth century imperialism begin, and how did the white man go about conquering the world, and what made him think he was superior to other peoples? Because the white

can develop color prejudice merely by wishing to do so. It would be ridiculous for the Chinese to say that they are prejudiced against whites when Europeans segregate the Chinese even in China.[51]

Of course one should not mistake reactionary racial attitudes for prime movers. One has only to imagine a situation developing in Asia in which whites come to recognize themselves as inferior to, say, Japanese—in which whites come to look upon Japanese as a master race in the same sense in which Europeans have been looked upon—to realize what a tremendous revolution in nationalistic feeling and power relationship must transpire. It would involve an exchange in the exploitative position of the races, which could not be fully established until the yellow and brown people actually subdued the Europeans in their homes and there, in Europe, directed the economy in the interest of great capitalists living in the East. Josef W. Hall (Upton Close) states graphically the nature of white superiority in the East:

> The white man walked as a god, above the law . . . secure in exploitation. In his "sacred cities" there were parks, into which no native was allowed to come. His clubs excluded the native, however high born or well educated. His person was sacrosanct. . . . He could pass through contending armies—carrying any information he might wish. He could shelter any native political criminal and assist in any plot and remain inviolate. He could exert himself at will to tear down native custom, religion and industry, and still be protected according to treaty stipulations.[52]

Then, too, it is even more difficult to conceive of a race becoming superior in the East without being so also in the West.

Still another primary consideration serves to indicate the insuperable difficulties in the way of any other race aspiring either to duplicate the racial record of Europeans or to dominate them. Today communication is so far advanced that no people of color, however ingenious, could hope to put a cultural distance between them and whites comparable

---

man had guns and the Asiatics had none. The matter was as simple as that." And he brings the argument up to date: "China will never . . . be accorded true equality until she is like Japan, twenty years from now, when she can build her own tanks and guns and battleships. When that time comes, there will be no need to argue about equality, such being the standards of the modern age." *Between Tears and Laughter,* pp. 21, 4.

[51]In reporting on social conditions in China, Theodore H. White says: "No one can understand China today . . . who does not understand the hatred and bitterness of the intelligent Chinese for the foreign businessman who treated him like a coolie in his own land. In some cities this foreigner closed the public parks to Chinese; on some boats Chinese were not allowed to ride first-class." See "Life Looks at China," *Life,* May 1, 1944, p. 100. See also Nathaniel Peffer, *The White Man's Dilemma,* Chap. IX.

[52]Op. cit., pp. 109–10.

to that which the Europeans of the commercial and industrial revolution attained in practical isolation over the colored peoples of the world. And such a relationship is crucial for the development of that complex belief in biological superiority and consequent color prejudice which Europeans have been able to attain. Therefore, we must conclude that race prejudice[53] is not only a cultural trait developed among Europeans, but also that no other race could reasonably hope to duplicate the phenomenon. Like the discovery of the world, it seems evident that this racial achievement could occur only once.

The color prejudice of whites has other potentialities; it functions as a regulator of minor racial prejudices. Whenever there are two or more races in the same racial situation with whites, the whites will implicitly or explicitly influence the relationship between these subordinate races. In other words, the whole racial atmosphere tends to be determined by the superior race. This is a consideration of highest significance in understanding race relations. In the more or less tacit admission of white superiority and in competition among subordinate races for white favor, the situation is set for channelization.

The race against whom the whites are least prejudiced tends to become second in rank, while the race that they despise most will ordinarily be at the bottom. Thus more or less directly the superior race controls the pattern of all dependent race prejudices.[54] However, the

---

[53]It should be borne in mind that race prejudice is not simply dislike for the physical appearance or the attitudes of one person by another; it rests basically upon a calculated and concerted determination of a white ruling class to keep some people or peoples of color and their resources exploitable. If we think of race prejudice as merely an expression of dislike by whites for some people of color, our conception of the attitude will be voided of its substance.

[54]The noted Southern writer, David L. Cohn, gives an illustration of this process. "The Anglo-Saxon," he writes, "bitterly hates, and prevents wherever possible, the marriage of his kind with black or yellow peoples. There are separate schools for Chinese in Mississippi, because by statute they are not permitted to attend white schools. . . . There are many Chinese in the [Mississippi] Delta. They are successful merchants. Some of them live with their Chinese wives; others have Negro mistresses and families of half-breed children. To the casual eye these children are often indistinguishable from full-blooded Chinese. The fear arose in the white community that if Chinese children were permitted to attend the public schools, these Chinese-Negro half-breeds would go along. The result was that separate schools for the Chinese, at the expense of the community, were provided for by law. Theoretically, these schools are of the same quality as the white schools. Actually, it is impossible to make them of the same quality without prohibitive expense. Chinese children, therefore, do not enjoy the same facilities for education that are open to white children.

"The leaders of the Chinese, knowing the real reason for the exclusion of their children from the public schools, hope, one day, to have the barriers removed. To this end, they are insisting that their men shall refrain from having Negro mistresses, and no half-breed children. When they feel that they can prove to the satisfaction of the white community that the children whom they present for ad-

whites are not entirely free in the exercise of their prejudice. The actual cultural advancement or national power of the subordinate races may not be without some reciprocal effect in the final adjustment of the races. Referring to the South African situation, P. S. Joshi declares: "The whites estimate all non-whites as inferior to themselves. The natives are the 'untouchables' of their country. The Asiatics rank lower than whites, and claim to be higher than the coloured or natives. This caste-phobia is a derivation of the colour bar."[55]

Europeans have mixed their blood with that of practically every colored people in the world. In no situation, however, where whites have interbred with colored races have they accepted the mixed-bloods without discrimination.[56] The tendency has been to accept the mixed-bloods according to their lightness of color, and this notwithstanding interracial laws socially proscribing all persons of colored blood. The anti-color codes merely limit acceptability.

Caste prejudice is an aspect of culture prejudice; while race prejudice —as distinguished from culture prejudice—is color-and-physique prejudice. The latter is prejudice marked by visibility, physical distinguishability; it is not, however, caused by physical differences. We may repeat that precise anthropometrical definitions of race are not of crucial significance.[57] Racial attitudes are based upon simple obvious criteria, and the findings of anthropometry, whether genuine or spurious, may simply provide a basis for their rationalization. Color prejudice, as a psychological phenomenon, is a complex emotion manifested by a positive attitude of distance and a reaction; specifically it is an

---

mittance to the white schools are racially pure Chinese, they may attempt to have the statute repealed." *God Shakes Creation,* pp. 219–20.

Should the Chinese make the necessary response, we should expect them to show an even greater hatred for Negroes than that of the whites, but the view of this racial situation would be very much distorted if one attempts to understand Chinese-Negro relationship independently of the controlling white prejudice.

See also Krishnalal Shridharani, "Minorities and the Autonomy of India," *Group Relations and Group Antagonisms,* R. M. MacIver, ed., pp. 200–06.

[55]Op. cit., p. 28.

[56]The writer is not unmindful of the situation in some parts of Brazil.

[57]We may illustrate this point. After delivering an invective against the assumed racial superiority of the whites in India, Krishnalal Shridharani declares: "An overwhelming majority of the Indian people belongs to the so-called white race, according to all anthropological and ethnological data. The tropical sun may have imparted pigmentation to the skin of the Indo-Aryan . . . but the ethnologist knows that the Indo-Aryan is of Caucasian origin." *Warning to the West,* p. 191. The ethnologist may be equally convinced about the race of white American Negroes, but just as the British in India pays him no attention, so also white Americans turn to him a deaf ear. Says Robert Briffault, in his incisive review of the ways of the white sahibs in India, "The Hindus were treated, as they have been ever since, as 'niggers.'" *The Decline and Fall of the British Empire,* p. 78.

insistent attitude of white superiority and dominance and an accommodating reaction of persons of color. It is a cultural trait of Western society which took form during the era of explorations.

To achieve a simple understanding of the concept, it may be well for us to observe the problem from the point of view of the initiating factor; that is to say, the white factor in the relationship. As stated above, in the contact of color groups, whites have set the stage for the pattern which the racial adjustment will assume. It varies according to their needs and aspirations, while the colored groups attempt to meet the aggressor on whatever seem to them the most favorable grounds. Therefore, an understanding of modern race relations will be achieved only if we look at the situation from the point of view of the desires and methods of Europeans in their dealings with peoples of color. The caste hypothesis of race relations will hardly help us to understand why the white ruling classes in the West Indies contend with most exacting logic that the contact of East Indians and Negroes there is socially advantageous, while in Kenya they reason with equal verve that the contact of Indians and Negroes is socially insalubrious.[58] It would hardly give us a hint to the reason for the Portuguese's remarkable freedom from race prejudice in Brazil as compared with their scrupulousness about color in Hawaii. We should have no clue at all concerning the irreconcilable ways of the Dutch—their anti-color attitudes in South Africa as against their comparative liberality in Java.

What the white dominant group will do depends upon the nature of the color situation—the exploitative situation. The Australians are

[58]See *Report of the Committee on Emigration from India to the Crown Colonies and Protectorates,* London, 1910.

Warren S. Thompson comments upon the situation in Africa: "When all is said that can truly be said about the nefarious practices of the Indians in their dealings with the Negroes in East Africa, it seems more than probable that the chief objection to their economic relations with the natives is to be found in the fact that they render the white man's exploitation of the Negroes more difficult and less profitable than it would otherwise be. Naturally this is resented, and it certainly sounds better to object to the nefarious exploitation of the Negro by the Indian than to say that the Indian is not wanted because he makes white people work harder to maintain their profits, and renders their lives less pleasant than they would be if they did not have to compete with him. This is too frank an avowal of their own exploitative purposes." *Danger Spots in World Population,* p. 169. See also India, Central Bureau of Information, *India in 1930–31,* pp. 49ff., and Maurice S. Evans, *Black and White in South East Africa,* p. 291.

In 1919 the Kenya Economic Commission reported: "Physically the Indian is not a wholesome influence because of his repugnance to sanitation and hygiene. In this respect the African is more civilized than the Indian, being naturally cleanly in his ways. . . . The moral depravity of the Indian is equally damaging to the African. . . . The presence of the Indian in this country is quite obviously inimical to the moral and physical welfare and the economic advancement of the native." Quoted by Raymond Leslie Buell, *The Native Problem in Africa,* Vol. I, p. 291.

too white-conscious to permit "olive-skinned" Italian immigration;[59] and recently white Americans who risked very much to introduce Africans into the United States and who mixed their blood rather freely with them have become too white-conscious to allow southern Europeans and Levantines to immigrate to the United States. In the following chapter we shall discuss some typical racial situations.

[59]Warren S. Thompson, op. cit., pp. 223ff.

17. *Situations of Race Relations*

*L*ET US NOW EXAMINE SOME *modern* SITUATIONS OF FREE RELA-tionship between whites and persons of color; situations, to re-peat, in which the aggressive whites have sought most conveniently and efficiently to exploit the human and natural resources of the colored peoples.

1. Situations in which the colored person is a stranger in a white society, such as a Hindu in the United States or a Negro in many parts of Canada and in Argentina—we shall call this the stranger situation.

2. Situations of original white contact where the culture of the col-ored group is very simple, such as the conquistadors and Indians in the West Indies, and the Dutch and Hottentots in South Africa—the original-contact situation.

3. Situations of colored enslavement in which a small aristocracy of whites exploits large quantities of natural resources, mainly agricultural, with forced colored labor, raised or purchased like capital in a slave market, such as that in the pre-Civil War South and in Jamaica before 1834—the slavery situation.

4. Situations in which a small minority of whites in a colored society is bent upon maintaining a ruling-class status, such as the British in the West Indies or the Dutch in the East Indies—the ruling-class situation.

5. Situations in which there are large proportions of both colored and white persons seeking to live in the same area, with whites insisting that the society is a "white man's country," as in the United States and South Africa—the bipartite situation.

6. Situations in which colored-and-white amalgamation is far ad-vanced and in which a white ruling class is not established, as in Brazil —the amalgamative situation.

7. Situations in which a minority of whites has been subdued by a dominantly colored population, as that which occurred in Haiti during the turn of the eighteenth century, or the expulsion of whites from Japan in 1638—the nationalistic situation.

A little more detail should help to elucidate these situations.[1]

The Stranger Situation

In cases where colored persons in the total population are so few that they can neither be expected to compete with whites nor serve any considerable purpose as a labor force there is usually little racial antagonism against them—until, perhaps, they attempt to enter the higher rungs of society where participants are fewer and competition keener. In certain parts of Canada, for example, Negroes have relatively wide social opportunities, and Negro-white intermarriage goes on with a freedom that is wholly unknown in the United States.[2] Although in the United States Hindus suffer far greater legal disabilities than Negroes, no Hindu will willingly exchange his status for that of a Negro. He falls within a general Asiatic ban which is a sort of official prophylaxis against his coming into the country in numbers large enough to make him a significant competitor; but socially he is a stranger.

There have been cases of West Indian Hindus in the United States who had long since given up the turban and the sari; as they came to understand the nature of Negro-white relationship, however, they returned to the Oriental dress and marked well their distance from American colored people. As Hindus, they are conceded certain privileges and opportunities which are denied Negroes even of much lighter complexion. But not so in Natal. In the United States the Hindu is still a romantic figure; in South Africa he is a "damn coolie."

Yet fewness in number is not necessarily the prime factor in the situation. If the individual goes into a community where a negative attitude has been indirectly nurtured, he will not then really be a stranger. He will be singled out for differential treatment on the basis of prepared racial sentiments. An individual Negro is not a stranger in

---

[1]There may be other situations of race contacts, but it does not seem advisable to attempt a permutation of those cited. To do this may not only result in situations which do not exist in fact but also in some that are totally fanciful. In a following chapter we shall discuss the racial situation on the Pacific Coast, which presents a different pattern.

[2]It should be pointed out that Canadians are by no means unmindful of the destiny of whites in their relationship with peoples of color. In British Columbia no Chinese, or Japanese, or East Indian can vote; these are discriminated against; and whether the person of color is or is not a British subject is of no moment.

all-white communities of the South. Furthermore, developed attitudes may be transferred to new communities.

If a man with African ancestry known as a Porto Rican goes to a certain barber shop in Honolulu—one that seeks to attract tourist patronage —he can get his hair cut. But if a man with African blood is identified as a Negro of mainland origin, he, when he seeks the service of this shop is told that he has come to the wrong place.[3]

Probably the extreme of this situation was that of the American Indian in Europe during the age of discovery. The relatively few American Indians who either went or were carried to European countries were known to be "savages," but everywhere the reaction toward them was that of mass curiosity and wonderment. They encountered no socially established ethnic definition; sometimes they were entertained and honored by royalty and sometimes they were pitied for their cultural backwardness. In so far as their exploitation was concerned, however, they were frequently made to review the military might of certain nations so that on their return home they might recount their experience to overawe their tribal fellows. On the brighter side of their living abroad Carolyn T. Foreman writes:

The Indians proved a source of great interest to scientists; the portraits of many of them were painted by famous artists in Europe; kings and queens received them as fellow sovereigns, showering them with gifts of money, jewels, and clothing while entertaining them in royal style; philosophers, poets, and historians wrote of them; gala performances were staged at the theatres and operas of European cities for their entertainment.[3a]

During the world wars Negro American soldiers in Europe were largely racial strangers. In every country the cordiality of the people was in remarkable contrast to the normal racial antagonism of their white American comrades. It has been reported that the restrictions and difficulties set up in the way of intermarriage by the United States Army have left hundreds of World War II Negro babies in England with anomalous status, a striking example of a positive racial attitude impinging upon a social situation of diffused racial norms.

The Original-Contact Situation

The original-contact situation is not so much a type as a stage in the process of developing a more or less stable pattern of race relations. It

[3]Romanzo Adams, *Interracial Marriage in Hawaii*, p. 24.
[3a]*Indians Abroad. 1493–1938*, p. xix.

may precede others which we are considering. When the native colored groups have a very simple culture, they are almost completely at the disposal and mercy of the whites. They are subordinated and awed by the latter's sophistication and calculations. In some cases the preliterates are looked upon practically as game to be exploited and dispossessed at will. Civilized ethics are abandoned, and the law of the frontier is justice.

"Forced trading" soon creates an economic vacuum in their old way of life. Native women are ordinarily considered booty, hence miscegenation is common but intermarriage rare. Indeed, there is ordinarily such great disparity between the cultures that the common understanding necessary for intermarriage is seldom attained. From a cultural point of view the natives are thought of as little children or savages.

If there is great exploitative zeal among the whites and the native population is comparatively small, it may be exterminated, as was the case of the Indians in the West Indies and the Tasmanians of Australasia;[4] or, in case there is sufficient hinterland, it may be pushed back, as were the Indians of the United States and the Negroes of East Africa.[5] Here they may be able to endure the pains of acculturation more easily. In time, however, they may become more or less adapted

[4]For instances of native extermination on contact with whites, see James Bryce, *The Relations of the Advanced and Backward Races of Mankind,* 2d ed., pp. 10–11. Sometimes the physical durability and resistance of the people are so great that they may survive even the cruelest atrocities and pressures. A classic example of this is the survival of the peoples of the Belgian Congo under Leopold II.

[5]The authority and decision with which native peoples may be dispatched are illustrated by the method used in Kenya and described by Warren Thompson: "In Kenya there are highland areas in which the white man can live in reasonable comfort even though they are under the equator. This was called by the British a 'white man's country' and it was desired to reserve it for future white settlement. In order to so reserve considerable parts of it, it was necessary to clear out some of the native tribes, and this was done with what looks to the outsider like complete indifference to their right and with much unnecessary suffering. It so happened that one of the peoples whose lands were coveted was a particularly friendly group of Negroes which had been of great assistance to the British in actually bringing the country under their control. They thus merited special consideration at the hands of their masters, but instead of receiving it, they were compelled to leave their native lands for much poorer lands in a less favorable situation. Moreover, the migration was not well planned and resulted in great hardship both in direct suffering on the road and through the loss of a very considerable part of their cattle, on which they depended for a living. . . .

"When this land became available, the British found that they needed laborers to develop it. For a 'white man's land' in east Africa does not mean land in which the white man expects to do his own work as a settler in Canada or Australia would, but a climate in which he can live in moderate comfort and ease, provided he can get cheap labor to do the actual field work. It being necessary to have labor now that the land was available, it was decided that the natives should work for the white man whether they cared to do so or not. It would be for their good to be kept busy and would prevent their getting into mischief and having so much time to 'plot against the whites.' " Op. cit., pp. 165–66.

to Western culture, in the process of which race problems develop and multiply.

The Slavery Situation

The slavery situation is probably the purest form of established race relations. Without disguise it defines the slaves, the colored people, as chattel, and exploits them in production virtually on the same economic principle as that employed in the exploitation of beasts of burden. It is in this situation that the capitalist, exploitative basis of race relations with its powerful drive toward dehumanizing the worker is most clearly observed. The master may consciously decide to use up his slaves because their replacement is cheaper than their conservation.

Modern slavery necessarily demands that the social system define the colored bondmen as irredeemably subsocial; it is upon this basis only that the ideological superstructure of the exploitative interest of the master class may be contrived. The pith of this ideology is not so much that the colored people are inferior as that they must remain inferior. Slaves can have no social organization of their own, no rights independent of their master's personal wishes; they can have neither status, function, nor social and geographical mobility like a caste; they cannot be permitted to contradict or dispute any question with the master. They are immediately and perpetually manipulable as instruments of production and must remain completely below the level of conscious organization and direction of community life.

Modern slavery may be thought of as developing out of a need for the rapid proletarianization of workers. In this situation white common laborers, already highly proletarianized, are scarce or non-existent, and therefore the colored people, as slaves, ordinarily constitute "the masses." The experienced white worker is ordinarily employed in such administrative positions as overseers, drivers, or gang foremen. Labor unions of any kind are generally unknown. The master class, having more or less complete freedom to employ its labor force at any function, is able to use its slaves in competition with any plethoric, white, manual workers until the latter, in desperation, are driven to some extremity of existence as poor whites.

The situation is usually dangerous, unstable, and apprehensive. Teachers, preachers, free-colored people, humanitarians, all tend to become threats to the peace and order of the community. A system of etiquette, which has to be sensitive enough to detect any tendency in the slave toward insubordination, is developed. Moreover, since slave uprisings are constant social expectations, this etiquette conveniently contrives to involve and implicate the poor whites, so that, even though the latter are economically disadvantaged in competition with slave labor, they tend to become, nevertheless, morally obligated and bound up in a common fate with the white master class. Then, too, since the system never gets into the "mores" of the people, considerable reliance is put upon physical coercion and exemplary cruelty in its maintenance.

Here the colored people do not have social status in the sense that whites do. The slave derives his social status not particularly from any attribute of his own, but from the social status and power of his master. In other words, a slave who has ingratiated himself with a powerful master is likely to be treated with circumspection even by whites of the community. An ill-treatment of such a slave may be construed as disrespect for the master. On the whole, however, slaves are not respected as persons; among the slaves themselves there is no self-respect independent of the master. Indeed, the slave can have no personality capable of responsible, self-assertive behavior. His individuality remains submerged beneath the overwhelming authority of the master.

The sexual and familial life of the slaves are determined by the master. Slaves may be bred and raised like animal stock, with one or a few males functioning as sires to a community of breeding females. Children, of course, are the property of the master. In some slavery situations, mainly among Latin peoples, masters have been known to marry slave women. This relationship, however, has been usually forbidden by law; concubinage has been somewhat more common.

Ordinarily the sexual relations between master and slave have been promiscuous and, in the South at any rate, even this never gained social sanction. In fact, the primary social definition of the slave as a subsocial, working animal leads to the corollary definition of sex relations between white men and slave women as sodomy; the white man "defiles his body by lying with a Negro." Quite frequently, however, the powerful sexual urge confronted by the easy sexual opportunities of the bondwomen overrides the social fiction and many mulatto children are born. The latter, in turn, tend to become socially restless and consequently more or less serious threats to the system.

In this situation sex relations between slave men and white women are very rare. Marriage, of course, could not be sanctioned; the social disadvantages to the white woman of even a clandestine relationship are so great that she tends to be effectively inhibited. A pregnancy of this kind is a social calamity of the first order. To bear a child for a "beast of the field," a slave, is to "dishonor God" and abuse one's self most shamefully. Such a white woman always expects to be scorned and ridiculed as a sexual pervert by the community; her colored child presents her with an insoluble social problem. Public authorities must find a way either to relieve her of it or to institutionalize her with it.

Since the colored man, the slave, tends to be a social non-entity, slave women who have become concubines of white men gain in social status. Such women tend to rise in the estimation of other slaves and may even be envied by interested white women. The relationship, however, is always more or less surreptitious. It is probably most convenient among great plantation owners who practically dominate the community.

There are tremendous natural urges and social compulsives in the slavery situation determining the behavior pattern of the slaves. The purposeful, independent slave is ordinarily "sold down the river"; the runaway or insurrectionist, "the lover of freedom," is ordinarily "broken on the wheel" or "quartered." The obsequious, ingratiating, and resigned slave ordinarily reaches the best adjustment in the system. The Bush Negroes of the Guianas, the Maroons of Jamaica, and the runaways in the North are examples of slaves breaking away to freedom; yet slaves as a whole tend to achieve some workable degree of accommodation.

The finally accommodated slave, a rather exceptional individual in modern slavery, conceives of himself as inconsequential and worthless except as he is able to satisfy his master by his work; he also tends to define the members of his group as having no other reason for existence. This supine devotion of the accommodated slave and the tremendous power of the master over his life fate may occasionally affect the master so deeply that in sympathy the relationship becomes personalized and much of the cruel necessities of exploitation may be tempered with condescension. Matthew G. Lewis, an absentee Jamaican planter, presents, in his *Journal of a West Indian Proprietor,* a classic illustration of accommodated slaves:

Whether the pleasure of the Negroes was sincere may be doubted; but certainly it was the loudest that I ever witnessed: they all talked together, sang, danced, shouted, and, in the violence of their gesticulations, tumbled over each other, and rolled upon the ground. . . .
The shouts, the gaiety, the wild laughter, their strange and sudden bursts of singing and dancing, and several old women, wrapped up in large cloaks, their heads bound round with different-colored handkerchiefs, leaning on a staff, and standing motionless in the middle of the hubbub, with their eyes fixed upon the portico which I occupied, formed an exact

counterpart of the festivity of the witches in Macbeth. Nothing could be more odd or more novel than the whole scene; and yet there was something in it by which I could not help being affected. Perhaps it was the consciousness that all these human beings were my slaves. . . .

Soon after reaching the lodging house at Savannah la Mar, a remarkably clean-looking Negro lad presented himself with some water and a towel—I concluded he belonged to the inn—and, on my returning the towel, as he found that I took no notice of him, he at length ventured to introduce himself by saying, "Massa not know me; me your slave!"—and really the sound made me feel a pang at the heart. The lad appeared all gaiety and good humor, and his whole countenance expressed anxiety to recommend himself to my notice, but the word "slave" seemed to imply that, although he did feel pleasure then in serving me, if he had detested me, *he must have served me still.* [Italics added.]

The Ruling-Class Situation

Where whites are mainly sojourning rulers, their numbers are usually relatively small. Ordinarily "home" is in Europe or America, and they seldom set their roots in the area. Here there is little hope of developing a significant white population. The white man's principal need is not a home but a satisfied and exploitable people to develop the resources of the country. This ruling class adopts a policy of "cooperation"; and, other things being equal, favors are distributed to the mixed-bloods on the basis of their apparent degrees of admixture. In other words, a premium is put upon degrees of whiteness among the people of color. Degrees of color tend to become a determinant of status in a continuous social-class gradient, with whites at its upper reaches. Thus, assuming cultural parity among the group, the lighter the complexion, the greater the economic and social opportunities. In this situation, then, there are significant color distinctions among the colored people themselves. Usually a color scheme is established, with generally recognized names for the different shades; and color problems of a more or less momentous nature come into being.

The system tends to generate among even those of light complexion a painfully morbid bitterness against fate, a diffused attitude of hatred and despair, the basis of which appears to be without social definition.[6] The colored people as a whole tend to become perennially preoccupied

---

[6]Many students of race relations have resorted to a biological interpretation of this attitude and with rather sterile results. The conclusion of Olive Schreiner is at hand: " 'I could bite my own arm,' a coloured girl once said in our presence, 'when I see how black it is. My father was a white man!' The half-caste alone of all created things is at war within his own individuality. The white man loves the white man incarnate in him, and the black man loves the black." *Thoughts on South Africa,* quoted with approval by Everett V. Stonequist, *The Marginal Man,* p. 21.

with the problem of degrees of pigmentation and lament the luck of their dusky progenitors. Brothers of different color may become estranged, and dark parents may keep themselves out of the way of their lighter children. Indeed, children may implicitly disavow their darker parents, while lighter persons who have been awarded in social status for their lightness may become rigid and even fierce at any attempt of darker persons to recognize them publicly and familiarly.[7] This constricting sense of color shame tends to be heightened when the relationship is under the surveillance of white people. Lighter persons seek to group themselves and to clique darker aspirants into oblivion. In fact, true friendship between lighter and darker young people is scarcely possible, for even schoolboys evaluate the color of their pals.

In business and official positions, darker colors are particularly penalized. These may go farthest in those occupations which call for unusual talent. In this situation, therefore, colored people cannot be asked to recognize all white persons as superior to themselves; yet the color obsession has its existence in that very fact. Coveted goals are made to appear available to all men alike, and the occasional attainment of high position by a darker colored person is all the more tantalizing. The color question is seldom, if ever, discussed in the press or on the platform, but it has extensive currency in esoteric discussion. Among the colored people there may be pride in lightness of color; pride of race, however, is a meaningless imponderability.

Ordinarily the basis of the system is only vaguely recognized. In an ideal situation the position of the white ruling class is impregnable. Its members are envied, admired, and imitated religiously, but they are

---

[7]At the basis of this attitude there is a powerful implicit play of racial sentiment. The prejudice of the mixed-blood is derived from the dominant prejudice of the whites; and it waxes or wanes directly as the situation gives the white man an opportunity to hold the mixed-blood responsible for the blackness of his aspiring associate. The mixed-blood, in his association with whites, strives to identify his racial sentiments with those of the whites; in fact, one criterion of complete achievement of whiteness by the native is the complete identification of his racial sentiments with those of the European. Now, the black man who attempts a familiarity with the mixed-blood in the presence of whites or other mixed-bloods of comparative whiteness puts the mixed-blood in a difficult situation. In the eyes of the whites he is caught red-handed in a debasing revelation; he thus stands accused until he can clear himself. If he can make it obvious to the whites that he has put a supercilious distance between himself and the darker person, very little or no explanation may be necessary. But if the darker person be a relative, say his mother, he is likely to suffer the deepest kind of emotional disturbance. He may hate her for her untimely appearance, which, she ought to have known, could have only a degrading effect upon him, and proceed to estrange himself from her for the occasion. He may decide to recognize her and thus reveal the true extent of his pollution, with its consequent penalty of demotion in social status; or he may take some middle ground in the hope that he will be able subsequently to talk himself out of guilt.

never questioned. The rest of the population is too absorbed with the immediate business of achieving increments of whiteness or their equivalent to give much attention to the inciting social force in the system. The system tends to be self-regulating. The colored people as a whole do not look upon whites as a people particularly prone to race prejudice, but rather each aspiring color stratum grapples with the problem of holding its own and of whittling away the distance attitudes from the stratum above. Therefore, to any given color group, the persons who are most exasperatingly color-prejudiced are not necessarily white people, but rather the cold-shouldering, snubbing, lighter-color group immediately above.

The ambitious individual who has been rebuffed is particularly disconsolate, for he must usually bear his ill fortune alone. He cannot appeal to color groups below him, since to do so might induce familiarity; neither could he allow the latter groups to observe his misfortune, for they might take the situation as an opportunity for gloating. He cannot disclose the whole truth even among his own group without revealing that he had planned to steal a march on them. He is left finally to reconstruct his self-respect and to devise new methods of approach. To many the struggle is exceedingly exhausting, for ground gained is seldom secure. The goal is apparently attained when the mixed-blood has become so light in complexion that he is generally accepted as a *native white*.

The white ruling class seldom contests the claim of such a person. It merely assigns him a different and more insidious social task, that of the social climber. This is usually sufficient to maintain the desired distance, for the social life of the white upper class is ordinarily carefully organized on a "private-club" basis, and it is a past master of the blackball. The native whites are the real bulwark of the status quo. To the colored people of darker shades they are serious, sensitive, and meticulous in their demands that the full etiquette of class distinction be observed; on the other hand, the European whites, free from any suspicion, are able to relax in the easy assurance that deference comes to them *naturally*.

In this situation there is never a lynching; interracial conflicts are practically unknown and, though they are in the majority, colored men are never stigmatized with a propensity, say, to rape white women. Furthermore, the poor-white problem never develops. Colored men may marry white women with impunity, and laws are never openly biased in favor of whites. When the colored population consists of many colored races, the situation becomes particularly favorable for amalgamation. The small white ruling class, already limited in its power to segregate, now finds it practically impossible to identify any one group for racial discrimination. "Equality among all peoples" tends to become the social philosophy. Instances of this are found in the island of Trinidad, and in Hawaii especially.[8]

The Bipartite Situation

Where whites are in numbers large enough to fill all preferred occupations or where there is possible competition with a large colored population along the whole cultural hierarchy, definite racial attitudes are developed. Here the tendency is to dichotomize the society into color groups, for any system of increasing acceptability according to degrees of lightness of color will quickly threaten white dominance. We do not have, in this case, merely a white ruling class, but a white population; therefore, anything short of dichotomy will leave masses of white persons subordinated to numbers of enterprising colored persons, a situation extremely favorable for rapid amalgamation and consequent depreciation of color per se as a social value.

Then, too, the social definition of the dominant place of husbands in the family tends to put a white wife of a man of color in a situation embarrassing to the whites. She is the embodiment of their pretensions; hence their sympathies must follow her in her yielding and subordination to the "inferior" colored man. In a most realistic way this tends to abrogate the theoretical claims of all whites to dominance. And for this reason, in the United States, for instance, even Negro women are not fundamentally displeased over the marriage of Negro men and white women.

In the ruling-class situation there are colored "ladies" in the upper social classes; but in this, the bipartite situation, the whites ordinarily define all colored females as "Negresses" or "nigger women." This is necessary because, should it appear that colored womanhood possesses some remarkable degree of refinement and elegance, it would be inconsistent to characterize all white men who marry colored women as depraved. There must be some tacit, if not expressed, suggestion that all colored women are prostitutes, polluted, and carnal, so that only the

---

[8]The assimilation policy of the French in West Africa falls into this category. Here a cultured black elite serves as the control group. Jealous of its privileges and sensitive to its importance, this elite has no sense of solidarity with the uneducated black masses. See Raymond Buell, op. cit., Vol. II, pp. 81–86.

For a discussion of this situation of race relations, see Everett V. Stonequist, "Comparison of Race Relations in Hawaii and Jamaica," *The West Indian Review,* September 1935.

most disreputable white men may reach moral depths sufficiently low to marry them.

Accordingly, among many whites, it has become second nature to say that "only low-class white men have anything to do with colored women." This attitude—legal restrictions aside—has made most colored women in the South particularly opposed to the idea of marrying white men. Indeed, other things being equal, even Negro men who look white are no ideal of colored women. They abhor the suggestion that they are concubines.

But this technique of racial defamation is not so effective in the case of Negro men. Ordinarily a man's character is not nearly so delicate as that of a woman. Once it has been established that all Negro women are wenches, the white man who marries one automatically identifies himself as degenerate. In the case of the Negro-man-white-woman marriage, however, the principal attack is shifted not to all white women but to those particular white women who marry Negroes.

These are supposed to be women with ungovernable sexual passions who may find satisfaction only in the assumed animal appetites of Negro men. It follows that a "white lady" with refined sensibilities will never marry a Negro man, and of course the white policy makers must inevitably insist that all white women should be white ladies. But this defense does not cause Negro men to recoil from the relationship as Negro women tend to do. The accusation of animal virility is not necessarily a derogatory one; furthermore, the man brings his white spouse among Negroes, where the white stereotypes are largely impotent. It is to Negro society that he looks for approbation, and the character of his wife tends to be measured by his own social stature.

Therefore, those white persons who conceive of themselves as being charged with the maintenance of continued white dominance will contrive segregation barriers and rationalizations to secure a bipartite racial system. Here the term "social equality" is taboo, racial laws are always partial, and cultural merit among people of color is given minimal recognition.

In this situation, lightness of color within the colored group is not nearly so highly prized as in the preceding illustration. In fact, it appears that a certain shade of brownness[9] (at least in men), rather than increasing whiteness, may become an ideal among the colored people. Here the lighter person is hardly rewarded with wider opportunities,

---

[9] See Charles S. Johnson, *Growing Up in the Black Belt,* and Charles Henry Parrish, *The Significance of Color in the Negro Community* (i.e., in Louisville, Kentucky), Ph.D. thesis, University of Chicago, 1944.

and the possession of a darker complexion is hardly so unfortunate an attribute.

Moreover, the tendency of whites is to be less discriminating about color values within the colored group, a fact which naturally tends to make degrees of color a social factor of less moment to colored people themselves. The social distance between shades of color is narrowed. Some colored people, especially those who are definitely dark, may even welcome the definition of the whites: "If you are not white, you are black." However, the vulgarism that all Negroes or all Hindus look alike may be particularly poignant to an accomplished light-complexioned person. None the less colored persons who try in a way that would be acceptable in the preceding situation to capitalize their light color are, in this situation, marked men within their race.

Thus, we may conclude that, the greater the insistence of the dominant whites upon a bipartite system of social segregation of the races, the less the social advantage of lightness of color within the colored group. Because marriage is ordinarily more important in the life of women than in that of men, and because the tendency of colored men to marry lighter is scarcely abated in this situation, we should expect the foregoing principle to be truer for colored men than for colored women. Incidentally, it may be mentioned also that, the greater the insistence upon, and accomplishment of, a bipartite racial system, the greater the relative cultural advantage of being white.

When there are more than one significant colored group in the population, it becomes the interest of the whites to prevent their coalescence. In the United States, for example, laws are enacted prohibiting intermarriage between Negroes and Indians or Negroes and Malays, and so on, while in South Africa the Negro-East Indian mixed-blood is particularly detested.[10] Dominance can always be more easily maintained

---

[10] Arthur F. Raper cites an interesting case in Bolivar County, Mississippi: "The small Chinese element in Bolivar and other delta counties is racially significant, because it occupies a position midway between the Negroes and the whites, thereby giving rise to unique situations. One of the best grocery stores in Rosedale is owned and operated by a Chinese. They are permitted limited social privileges with the whites in proportion as they do not mingle socially with the Negroes.

"Recently in Greenville, thirty miles south, a Chinese boy who married a white girl was forced to leave. This marriage would probably have been permitted to pass, except for the fact that the boy's brother had previously married a Negro. Since that time the white people have held several anti-Chinese meetings, to which Negroes were invited. The Negroes, however, did not attend, and subsequently a white committee waited upon them to ascertain their attitude toward the Chinese. The immediate purpose of the movement was to establish a boycott against Chinese business, in which the co-operation of the Negroes was essential." *The Tragedy of Lynching*, p. 106.

The 1926 Native Policy Bill of General Hertzog separates the natives from every other racial group, whites, colored, or Indian. The "bill grants the franchise

by keeping these people apart; and the dissemination of ingenious pure-blood myths facilitates this purpose. Whereas in our third situation the white-colored mixed-bloods are generally welcomed as a racial liaison group, in the present one they are usually branded inferior mongrels.

In the ruling-class situation the white ruling class encourages cultural refinement among the colored people. So long as the colored person eschews antagonistic political ideas, he is complimented, at least ostensibly, for striving to acquire all the amenities of the upper class. To speak well, to dress fashionably, to live in an attractively appointed home, to assume a dignified bearing, to develop family pride is to merit the favor of the ruling class. Here, then, colored people may brush off their lower-class fellows with impunity. The cultural *rapprochement* of the ruling-class whites and the upper-class colored people facilitates the use of the latter as a cultural cushion and an instrument of exploitation of the masses.

In the situation under discussion, however, the whites carefully suppress such attitudes; here colored persons may acquire marks of cultural distinction only by sufferance. Moreover, the cultural degradation of the colored people as a whole is believed to be an asset to the whites, and they strive to achieve it.[11] In the South, for example, the Negro who speaks good English to a typical Southern white man insults him; such a person is characterized a "cocky nigger" and merits reduction. The colored person is most acceptable in the clothes of the manual worker, and he who perchance acquires material goods of some worth must be careful not to make it appear that his conception of himself as a citizen has advanced commensurably, for this would be the surest indication that he is getting out of place. The cry that Negroes are inferior is an illusion; what is real is the fierce insistence by the white

---

to the *existing* colored population." But "persons born of mixed unions in future shall be regarded as natives," inheriting all the latter's social disadvantages. And Hertzog said in his Smithfield speech supporting the bill: "The result of this policy has been that an alliance of [the colored people] and the native population has been stopped. Luckily they [the Cape Colored] felt that their interests were more closely allied to those of the Europeans than that of the Native. It is their wish just as much as it is ours that they should stand by themselves with regard to the franchise." Quoted by Raymond Leslie Buell, op. cit., Vol. I, p. 142.

Of course it would be as undesirable for the native tribes to come together. Says Edgar H. Brookes, "We may . . . rule out the association of the Bantu with other Africans in a great movement of pan Africanism. Such a movement would be regarded by most nationalist thinkers as highly dangerous to White supremacy." *The Colour Problems of South Africa,* p. 30; see also p. 34.

[11]With reference to an earlier age of race relations in the United States, De Tocqueville makes a similar observation. Since the whites, he says, "will not raise the Negroes to their own level, they sink them as nearly as possible to the brutes." Op. cit., Vol. II, pp. 246–47.

ruling class that Negroes do nothing which might lead either themselves or other people to believe that they are equal or superior to whites.

In this situation, even severe states of social pathology among the colored people may serve the implicit purpose of the whites. Since cultural *rapprochement* is fatal to this purpose, the whites in South Africa, for example, advocate cultural parallelism; while those in the Southern United States practice cultural repression among the colored people. Actually, the latter policy is also intended to achieve cultural parallelism.[12] In the United States a relatively illiterate, criminal, diseased, base, poor, and prostituted colored people serves by comparison as proof to the world that Negroes do not deserve the social opportunities available to whites. This state of degradation tends to characterize the cultural life of the Negroes and to make it distinct from that of whites. It is, of course, in the interest of the ruling-class whites to keep it thus distinct. They seek, through myriad and powerful devices, to make the colored person, as a human being, ashamed of his very existence; indeed, the accomplishment of racial shame is a psychological goal of the Southern oligarchs. In the South Negroes have been lynched for "trying to act like white men."[13] As Myrdal observes: "The South did not want —and to a great extent, still does not want—the Negro to be successful as a freedman. White southerners are prepared to abstain from many liberties and to sacrifice many advantages for the purpose of withholding them from the Negroes."[14]

For this reason emphasis is never put upon improvement of the colored people; in fact, the idea of "improvement" or "progress" is looked upon with apprehension by whites. Hence jails are always more tolerable than schools and Old Testament preachers more acceptable than social-service workers.[15] However, the ruling-class whites never intend

---

[12]Observe, for instance, the intent of the Honorable Chauncey Sparks, governor of Alabama, in his declaration: "There is no need for racial jealousies, no need for racial conflicts, but there is a great field for racial pride. This pride cannot be maintained unless each race is developed along its own lines." Founder's Day address delivered at Tuskegee Institute, April 4, 1943. This, obviously, is a plea to Negroes that they should co-operate with their exploiters in isolating themselves. Naturally, if Negroes in the South can be made to believe that they have "lines" of development distinct from those of whites, segregation may be more easily imposed upon them.

[13]See Arthur F. Raper, op. cit., p. 36.

[14]Gunnar Myrdal, *An American Dilemma,* Vol. I, p. 223.

[15]Without recognizing the inciting force in the situation Dr. Gunnar Myrdal says: "The low plane of living . . . and all the resulting bodily, intellectual, and moral disabilities and distortions of the average Negro make it natural for the ordinary white man not only to see that the Negro is inferior but also to believe honestly that the Negro's inferiority is inborn. This belief means . . . that all

that the disease and crime perpetuated among the colored people should overflow among them. The spread of disease is limited by segregation, and for crime by colored people against whites the criminal is punished mercilessly. Excessive criminality and social disorder within the colored group tend to keep its members occupied with self-criticism, recrimination, individual expressions of hatred for the colored group as a whole, and with desperate social devices contrived by individuals or families in their attempts to develop, more or less isolatedly, decent living conditions. Among the masses it has been said, "Their cares are brutish because they are treated as brutes."

A social fact of major significance in this situation is the insistence upon a suppression of civic pride among colored people. Although in the ruling-class situation the colored people are ruled by whites, the masses are never deprived of the sense of having a country. Here the colored people know that they have a permanent home and, if pressed, they will readily become conscious of the fact that the whites are foreigners. Therefore, these people can develop a genuine patriotism; and, in spite of their exploitation, their lives are more frequently planned; they are securely anchored in the social system. It is not uncommon to hear an East Indian or a West Indian, with head erect and confident, say of himself: "I am a British subject!" Out of these attitudes defensive nationalism among the colored people tends to have a comparatively easy growth.

But civic pride is denied colored people in the bipartite situation, and this fact is in no small measure responsible for their social instability. It keeps them spiritually on the move; it denies them the right to call their country home; it limits patriotism severely, thus making a genuine love of one's country virtually impossible. Implicitly or explicitly the white ruling class has insisted upon Negro dependence, upon gearing the existence of Negroes to its interest, and as a consequence Negroes tend to be irresponsible and uninspired for civic pride and initiative. Restrictions upon co-operative efforts of colored people in communal life tend to determine their pattern of community organization. Here their effort becomes tentative, they establish impermanently, and their impaired sense of ownership in their country tends to be reflected in their comparatively disreputable communal life. In America especially,

---

attempts to improve the Negro by education, health reforms, or merely by giving him his rights as a worker and a citizen must seem to be less promising of success than they otherwise would be. The Negro is judged to be fundamentally incorrigible and he is, therefore, kept in a slum existence which, in its turn, leaves the imprint upon his body and soul which makes it natural for the white man to believe in his inferiority." Ibid., p. 101.

fanatical gambling and the emergence of wealthy messiahs register somewhat the mental atmosphere of the colored community.[16]

Few, if any, colored persons in the Southern United States, for example, are able to assume the full bearing of Americans, with all its privileges and responsibilities; and their inelegant material appointments are ordinarily symptomatic of the absence of this vital social drive. This condition, of course, is a desirable end of the white ruling class; indeed, its purpose is epitomized in its boast: "This is a white man's country." Spiritual and physical instability among the colored people perpetuate their dependence and render them the more easily exploitable. It is in this sense that George W. Cable says caustically: ". . . the master-caste [in the South] tolerates, with unsurpassed supineness and unconsciousness, a more indolent, indifferent, slovenly, unclean, untrustworthy, ill-mannered, noisy, disrespectful, disputatious, and yet servile domestic and public menial servant than is tolerated by any other enlightened people."[17]

Civic pride among the colored people, then, if permitted at all, must be limited to some tentative racial pride, which in turn must be carefully voided of nationalism, the very pith of such an attitude.

Although both the United States and South Africa are "white men's countries," they differ somewhat in the potentialities of their racial dichotomy. In the United States the great majority of the population is white; in South Africa it is black. There is comparatively little fear in the United States that Negroes will use force in asserting themselves. Hence segregation and discrimination practices may be adopted with a high degree of finality. In South Africa, however, the whites are concerned about the mixed-bloods. In a sense, the latter occupy a position similar to that of the *gens de couleur* in pre-revolutionary San Domingo; and the whites are not unmindful of the possibility that they may assume a similar role in a racial crisis. They are, therefore, allowed only so much social privilege as will keep them apart from the natives, yet not enough to close the social breach between them and the whites.

The planned racial dichotomization of South Africa is revealing. Here the policy-making whites have sought to utilize even more basic

---

[16]In this connection Alexis de Tocqueville makes a point that still has a modicum of validity: "The Negro, who is plunged in this abyss of evils, scarcely feels his own calamitous situation. Violence made him a slave, and the habit of servitude gives him the thoughts and desires of a slave; he admires his tyrants more than he hates them, and finds his joy and his pride in the servile imitation of those who oppress him: his understanding is degraded to the level of his soul." Op. cit., Vol. II, p. 183.

[17]*The Negro Question,* p. 23; see also pp. 67–68.

means of keeping the races socially isolated. Their policy is to prevent the acculturation of the natives, a plan which is obviously expected to accomplish both the territorial and cultural segregation of the natives and thus ensure their continued exploitation. The policy is conducted under the anthropological euphemism "that the natives should be allowed to develop along their own lines." W. O. Brown's generalization that "dominant races have a vested interest in the perpetuity of the cultures of weaker races[18] fits this situation. "Many English speaking colonists," Maurice S. Evans observes, "seem to have a repugnance to hearing the natives using the English language, and go so far as to decline to carry on a conversation in it; and so Kitchen-Kaffir is invariably the medium used in the towns and is the rule even in the country districts."[19] But this cultural antagonism is readily translatable into economic terms:

In South East Africa, the white man draws a distinction between what he considers the work of a white man and Kaffir work, and is very jealous of any infringement of what he thinks are his labor rights; all clerical work, practically all handicrafts, all skilled work in connection with machinery, all supervision are regarded as the prerogative of the European. If a firm employed native clerks, they would probably be boycotted; if a native was seen doing the skilled work in connection with the erection of a building, the press would teem with indignant letters. To plough, to dig, to hoe, to fetch and carry, to cook—all laborious and menial toil is the duty of the black man.[20]

Even more than in the Southern states it is thought that parallel development is possible. The native must be educated so that he will be able to govern himself according to the principles of his African institutions,[21] the object being a planned cultural isolation. Thus Edgar H.

---

[18]"Culture Contact and Race Conflict," *Race and Culture Contacts,* E. B. Reuter, ed., pp. 43–44. See also Jawaharlal Nehru, op. cit., p. 276.

[19]Maurice S. Evans, op. cit., p. 51. In commenting upon the use of "Bazaar Malay" by the Dutch as an interracial language in Indonesia, G. H. Bousquet asserts: "The real truth is that the Dutch desired and still desire to establish their superiority on the basis of native ignorance. The use of Dutch diminishes the gap between inferior and superior—and this must be avoided at all cost. *A French View of the Netherlands Indies,* trans. by Philip E. Lilenthal, p. 88. How the ruling-class whites may profit by the continuance of certain parts of the native culture is illustrated by an incident which took place when the Prince of Wales visited India in 1921. A number of leaflets were issued in the vernacular by the Government of the Central Provinces explaining that, "according to Hindu Scriptures, the King's Son was a part of God, therefore all Hindu boys should fulfil their religion by assembling to cheer the Prince of Wales." See Reginald Reynolds, *The White Sahibs in India,* p. 277.

[20]Maurice S. Evans, op. cit., pp. 154–55.

[21]It should be observed that no native custom which contravenes the exploitative purpose of the white man will be allowed to stand.

Brookes declares that "we are driven to define the Nationalist programme for the future of the Natives . . . as the building up side by side with the [White] South African nation of a parallel nation. . . . The Bantu nation will embrace all the Natives of the Union of South Africa, and it will be kept clear by sharp lines of distinction both from Europeans in South Africa and also from Natives outside the Union borders."[22] It must be obvious, of course, that no such thing as the development of an independent nation is really intended, for it is well known that long before this the Bantu would have tested their strength against the whites.[23]

The Amalgamative Situation

Where there is no white ruling class answerable to a foreign white power, and where amalgamation between the white and black population is far advanced, it becomes practically impossible to make lightness of complexion a definite mark of status. The color scheme is confused, and attempts to arrange it involve delicate and socially distasteful issues. Even though a preponderance of dark-colored people are in the lower economic strata, the population is necessarily marbled with color. Therefore, the group cannot attain a white "universe of discourse" and consensus sufficiently strong to achieve clear-cut white dominance. In the interest of social peace, therefore, an official policy of non-interference with color relationships must be followed. Intermarriage becomes a matter of personal tastes, and there arises no organized sentiment for or against it. Individual cultural achievements tend to be estimated on their merits; and unless some powerful foreign white economic clique, such as American tourists and businessmen in Brazil, initiates opposite racial tendencies, such a population is well on its way to complete amalgamation.

It is interesting to inquire into the reasons for these highly amalgamated populations. Europeans of Mediterranean stock settled Latin America and they have mixed quite readily with the colored peoples. The Anglo-Saxons have also mixed their blood in the north. But there

[22]Op. cit., p. 31.

[23]Brookes puts it in this way: "Here then would be a subject race, which was at the same time proletariat, asked in a shrinking world to keep clear of both pan-Africanism and Bolshevism, and be contented with a permanently inferior position in its own land. It would have become by education and experience group-conscious. It would have constantly dinned into its ears theories of nationalism and before its eyes examples of nationalism in practice. It would organize in self-defense. And it would not be otherwise than that that organization should be of an anti-white character." Ibid., p. 32. See also Lord Olivier, *The Anatomy of African Misery.* pp. 68–84.

are no intermarriage prohibition laws in Latin America. We have suggested that in race relations the desires of the whites are controlling and that these will manifest themselves differently in different situations. These desires are affected, however, by still other social determinants. Among these the intensity of nationalistic and imperialistic social attitudes of the European nation from which the whites came seems most significant.[24]

Directed nationalism gives the individual his group conception of himself; his personal ego tends to be raised to the level of his national pretensions. Therefore, the greater the nationalism, the more inflated will be the individual's conception of himself, and the greater his unwillingness to intermarry with other peoples. Nationalism emphasizes to the individual the vital necessity of retaining and enhancing group identity. It propagates the feeling that the individual is an altogether superior being even among persons of his own color though of another nation. It stimulates "group conceit." While the sex urge may overcome nationalistic sentiments, the latter may be strong enough to retard intermarriage significantly. Among the Japanese (a people of color) intense nationalism and exploitative zeal have evidently limited the possibility of their amalgamating with their conquered peoples. It should be stated also that nationalism had its beginnings and achieved its highest perfection among white peoples, Europeans. "Nationalism is unthinkable before the emergence of the modern state in the period from the sixteenth to the eighteenth century." Like the racial antagonism which it inspires, then, "nationalism is not a natural phenomenon, not a product of 'eternal' or 'natural' laws; it is a product of the growth of social and intellectual factors at a certain stage of history."[25]

Intense nationalism such as that developed among the northern industrial European states tends to transform the subjects of a nation into a sect with national prayers and national hymns. These appeals strive to be mandatory upon the Deity, aggressive, and symbolic of national destiny in a context of assumed aspirations of other peoples and nations. The religious loyalties of the Middle Ages were "transmuted into the political loyalties" of the rising state. "European nationalism," says

[24]Parker T. Moon associates these concepts: "Nationalism means that people considering themselves similar in language, 'race,' culture, or historical traditions should constitute a separate sovereign state; imperialism, on the contrary, means domination of non-European native races by totally dissimilar European nations. Antithetical as these two principles may seem, the latter is derived from the former through economic-nationalism or neo-mercantilism." *Imperialism and World Politics*, p. 33.

[25]Hans Kohn, op. cit., pp. 4, 6. See also *Nationalism, A Report by a Study Group of Members of the Royal Institute of International Affairs*, Chap. III.

Leonard Woolf, "became a religion with the state as the object of worship. The idea of an empire became closely connected with the idea of patriotism in the minds of nationalists."[26] This state religion, nationalism, may be as effective in limiting intermarriage between, say, Englishmen and some people of color as Mohammedanism is in restricting the marriage of Moslems with, say, Christians.

Groups, even within single states, who are bent upon racial aggression always carry the flag and sing the national hymn. Moreover, it should be observed as a fact of prime significance that bourgeois nationalism is anti-democratic and consequently anti-proletarian. In saying that nationalism is the emotional basis of race prejudice we are not presenting the question one step removed from solution. Nationalism is an integral part of the non-material cultural imperatives of capitalism, and it has developed as a function of the rise of capitalism.[27] It provides the collective attitude for capitalist aggression and exploitation of other peoples. Says Carlton J. H. Hayes:

. . . prior to the advent of modern nationalism obvious physical differences were generally viewed as interesting results of climate or curious freaks of nature, and the popular prejudice was not so great as to prevent the New World from a very considerable fusion of white emigrants, especially those from traditionally Catholic countries of Portugal, Spain, and France with red Indians, and even with blacks. . . . It was only in the nineteenth century—the century of rising, raging nationalism—which universally magnified racial prejudices and racial intolerances.[28]

Of course love for one's country, the desire to be among one's own people, is not nationalism. This is the more passive emotion, which may be called patriotism. Says Sombart: "Patriotism . . . is that indefinable power exercised upon the soul by the sound of the mother tongue, by the harmony of the [folk] song, by many peculiar customs and usages, by the whole history and poetry of the home land."[29]

But nationalism is more than the emotional set of a people in international competitive struggle; it is particularly an exploitative, sociopsychological instrument of actual or potential ruling classes; and it seeks its principal support and effective expression in an organized

---

[20]Op. cit., p. 44. "The violent racialism to be found in Europe today," says Julian Huxley, "is a symptom of Europe's exaggerated nationalism: it is an attempt to justify nationalism on a non-nationalist basis, to find a basis in science for ideas and policies which are generated internally by a particular economic and political system." *Race in Europe*, Oxford Pamphlets on World Affairs, No. 5, p. 31.

[27]See Carlton J. H. Hayes, *Essays on Nationalism*, Chap. II.

[28]Ibid., pp. 235–36.

[29]*Socialism and the Social Movement in the Nineteenth Century*.

capitalist state. The more nationalistic a people, the more secure the State, which is always at the service of the ruling class especially. Therefore, the propagation and intensification of nationalism becomes the indispensable duty of the ruling class; and when, as a ruling people, whites find themselves among a people of color, their nationalism tends to be exclusive. Should counternationalism arise, there will be conflict on the spot.

In the past offensive nationalism has been most thoroughly developed among the British, who have been fairly consistent in maintaining their identity among peoples of color. The British and Americans take their nationalism for granted. On the other hand, one has simply to glance at the teachings of modern Germany and Italy to perceive the relationship between nationalism and ethnic relations.[30]

Besides the foregoing explanation we may observe the difference in colonizing policy of the Latin and Anglo-Saxon peoples. Spain and Portugal, in their early contact with colored peoples, were influenced by the medieval idea of Christianizing the heathen and of commercial exploitation of native resources. In pursuance of this end, therefore, amalgamation with the colored peoples was advocated as a salutary colonial policy; the white population grew imperceptibly upon this

---

[30]"In no way conceived as an anti-Black movement, South African nationalism has become so, as a result of the psychological impossibility of including the Bantu in a program appealing inevitably so largely to sentiment and emotion." Edgar H. Brookes, op. cit., pp. 26–27.

Recently both Dr. Robert E. Park and Dr. Donald Pierson attempted to explain the ethnic situation in Brazil. Both, however, seem unconvincing. "Brazil," says Park, "is a vast country and has been colonized . . . by a wide variety of peoples. . . . With the exception of the Italians, these different peoples have settled in more or less closed communities in widely separated parts of a vast territory. Dependent upon water transportation rather than upon rail to maintain economic and political unity, Brazil has been haunted by the fear that the country would some day fall apart. Under these circumstances, it has seemed that the security and solidarity of the nation depended upon its ability to assimilate and ultimately to amalgamate its different immigrant populations. From this point of view, the Negro has not constituted a problem." *Negroes in Brazil,* by Donald Pierson, pp. xix–xx.

From this statement we do not know whether Park means that Brazil adopted a formal policy of white integration and national solidarity; and certainly it does not follow that Negroes must necessarily have been included in any assimilation policy among Brazilian whites.

Pierson's explanation is truistic. "It may be," he hypothesizes, "that the Portuguese, like the Moors and other Mohammedans, were . . . a 'color blind' people; that is, awareness of color and other racial differences were not so pronounced with them as with us." Ibid., p. 327. Probably this does not say much more than that the Portuguese are not a color-conscious people because they were not color-conscious. Furthermore, the statement has a biological ring. Reference to retinal capacity or any other such implication of innate conditioning ordinarily leads through sociological blind alleys. It will not help us very much in an explanation of the relationship of the Portuguese and the natives in, say, Angola, East Africa.

basic social attitude. Where, however, as in North America, the whites came later as settlers with the avowed purpose of taking over and of making the country their home, amalgamation has not been accepted as a policy. Thus, in addition to nationalism, the purpose of the whites, whether exploitation or settlement, tends to determine the type of race relationship which will develop.

Moreover, the Protestant religion of the northern European whites, whose early colonization was mainly private enterprise,[31] and the Roman Catholic faith of the Latins, whose early colonization was under the aegis of a monarch, are important considerations in explaining the difference in these racial situations.[32] Among the Latins there was a strong tradition in favor of a continuation of the old religious criterion of equality, while among the Anglo-Saxons an objective, capitalistic orientation facilitated the maneuvering of the colored people into positions which seemed most suitable to their continued segregation. In this discussion it has been taken as understood that neither Spain nor Portugal ever attained the industrial development of northern Europe.

The Nationalistic Situation

In reaction to white dominance, a large colored population may possibly become restless and revolt against the system. Usually, for a short period of time, whiteness becomes exceedingly depreciated, while persons of color assume the prestige of former white rulers. There is such a budding reaction in India today; the Indian Mutiny of 1857 almost succeeded in turning the color scheme. "In Haiti, discrimination runs against the white man rather than against the Negro. A public career for a person of purely Caucasian origin would be rarely, if ever, possible."[33]

Such a country, however, cannot be isolated from the rest of the world; hence, in spite of possible local desires, its world policies must be couched in terms of world opinion, and with this goes an ever-present insistence upon white supremacy.[34] Thus all the local variants

---

[31]For a brief discussion of this, see Edward Potts Cheyney, *European Background of American History,* pp. 123–46.

[32]In describing the place of religion in the colonization of Latin America, Professor Bailey W. Diffie concludes: "It is doubtful whether there is an example of an institution in any country, in any epoch, whose responsibility for the type of civilization was as great as that of the colonial Catholic Church." Op. cit., p. 269.

[33]Chester Lloyd Jones, *Caribbean Backgrounds and Prospects,* p. 28.

[34]Jacques Barzun expresses this idea: "Equally important, though generally overlooked, is the fact that articulate minorities in other countries than Germany are fully as much engaged in thinking and talking about race. The only difference

of race relations are more or less conditioned by this international belief. The idea of white superiority hangs over the world like a great mist, and former attempts to lift it have resulted only in its condensation over the intractable area. In this Great Britain has set the ultimate pattern of intrigue, subtlety, and force in dealings with peoples of color; she is the great modern stabilizer of world white dominance. As Briffault puts it: "There is indeed no parallel in history, ancient or modern, to the dominance which, in the nineteenth century, England came to wield over the world."[35] And the source of this domination is undoubtedly England's imperialistic achievements among colored peoples.

A Special Case?

We have presented here some typical patterns of race relations; some of their features, however, may vary from case to case. Cuba and the Dominican Republic are countries with highly mixed populations; they should be like Brazil in racial adjustment, but they are smaller and too dependent upon the United States and Great Britain. Thus they are more like those countries where there is a small white ruling class. Haiti and Liberia ought to be free from "color consciousness"; if they were, however, they would be further atrophied in isolation. For instance, in establishing personal contacts with the English and Americans especially, Haiti understands that it is expedient to send forward her lighter colored persons. Our whole analysis, of course, rests upon the basic idea of a white-colored relationship. Indeed we now have a conceptual basis for a world study of race relations. By following Europeans in their contacts with peoples of color a world map of types of race prejudice and discrimination may be made.

But it may not be easy to retire the belief that race prejudice and racial domination are inherent social attitudes among all races. A friendly critic expostulated with the writer on the score that he has not

---

is that no other government has yet gone so far as the Nazi regime in adopting race as a popular slogan. . . . But read attentively the press and political literature, not only of England, France, Italy, and the United States, but also Mexico, Turkey, Rumania, and Scandinavia: you will not read very far before you are told or left to infer that whites are unquestionably superior to the colored races; that Asiatic Peril is a race-peril; that the Japanese of late seem to have become very yellow indeed . . . that the great American problem is to keep the Anglo-Saxon race pure from the contamination of Negro (or southern European, or Jewish) 'blood.' The quarrel about race and blood is often carried even closer home, as when we are informed that among the whites the tall blond Nordics are a superior breed, destined to rule the world, and that brown-eyed, round-headed Latins, whether in Europe or in South America, are a degenerate, revolutionary lot." *Race, A Study of Modern Superstition,* pp. 6–7.

[35]*Decline and Fall of the British Empire,* p. 9.

accounted for the prejudices obtaining between non-white races. That he has not shown, for instance, what kind of race prejudice exists between Chinese and Japanese or between Japanese and Filipinos in Hawaii, and that Hawaii itself should not have been included in the typical ruling-class situation described above.

The racial situation in Hawaii seems so complex and even unique that it may be well to inquire whether, indeed, it should be excluded from our generalization. In the first place, the history of early contact between whites and Hawaiians has not been exceptional. The effects of early white contact were the liquidation of Hawaiian culture, the decimation of the population, and the control of economic life in the country by whites. The Beards summarize it in this way: "Though [the Hawaiians] were converted to Christianity and taught to read and write, economic competition, whisky, and disease cut them down like grain before a sickle. And in the process the whites got control of nearly all the land in the kingdom, overcoming the cupidity and resistance of the dusky proprietors by the lure of money and pressures of various kinds."[36]

The Hawaiians were humanely subdued, but the purpose of the white man was as determined as ever; and in the end, Queen Liliuokalani, in the hands of the sugar planters, was as pathetic and helpless a figure as the great Inca, Atahualpa of Peru, before Friar Valverde and Pizarro. Only the conquistadors had a less understanding world with which to rationalize and, consequently, could work upon the "primitives" with greater expedition and acclaim. At any rate, there was no trace of race prejudice among the Hawaiians on first contact with whites.

Hawaii is not a white man's country; white men constitute a small ruling class. And typical of this situation, there are no Anglo-Saxon laborers or field workers. What the Beards say about conditions even before the fall of royalty in Hawaii is essentially true today. "In spite of the royal government maintained in the 'palace' at Honolulu, approximately five thousand whites, mainly Americans, were the real masters of eighty thousand natives, Chinese, and Japanese. In short, the fate of the Hawaiian Islands was already sealed. They were to become an imperial province inhabited by Orientals and directed by white capitalists."[37]

---

[36]Charles A. and Mary R. Beard, *The Rise of American Civilization,* p. 357.

[37]Op. cit., p. 358. For a discussion of later population figures, see *The American Empire,* William H. Haas, ed., pp. 228–35; and William C. Smith, "Minority Groups in Hawaii," *The Annals,* Vol. 223, September 1942, pp. 38–39.

We should expect in Hawaii that, the more individuals of mixed-blood approach the physical appearance of whites, the more, other things being equal, they would be favored by the ruling class. And such is in fact the case. Here the mixed-bloods form a liaison group, and a man's light color has economic value. Says Romanzo Adams, "White employers and executives, who tend to favor the lighter complexioned part-Hawaiians for the positions of greater dignity and income, would say that they are more capable."[38] It must follow, then, that lightness of color would be an asset in the marriage bargain and that the birth of a light-complexioned child would be a blessing.[39] In explanation Adams says: "At first the light complexion was associated with superiority of status, then it became a sign of superiority, and now tends to be regarded as superior in itself."[40]

Furthermore, we should not expect the whites to raise a racial issue publicly in Hawaii, and consequently not to have it so raised at all. But this, of course, does not preclude their playing one race against the other in their own interest. When during the last quarter of the nineteenth century the Chinese began to leave the plantations to seek opportunities about the cities, the white planters conducted a bitter campaign against them; but it was relatively weak because it lacked anti-racial content. On the West Coast it would have had different results. The few thousand whites in Hawaii had to appeal to other colored races, and an anti-racial campaign would surely have rebounded. "Had a white man coined a color slogan to fling at the Chinese, it would have hit the Hawaiians, whose friendly co-operation was necessary, with even greater offense."[41]

Sometime later the sugar and pineapple growers leveled the same kind of attack against the Japanese. Now they said that the Chinese made good laborers but that the Japanese were "cocky, quarrelsome, independent, and altogether too numerous."[42] The Japanese, of course, were brought in to take the place of the formerly unmanageable Chinese. One thing, however, they did not dare to call the Japanese yellow, a fact which deprived them of their keenest weapon of exploitation.

In Hawaii there is considerable intraracial organization, especially among first-generation immigrants; but this fact is not crucial in the

---

[38] Op. cit., p. 106.

[39] Ibid., pp. 104, 106, 107.

[40] Ibid., p. 107. Cf. William C. Smith, "The Hybrid in Hawaii as a Marginal Man," *The American Journal of Sociology*, XXXIX, pp. 462ff.

[41] Romanzo Adams, op. cit., pp. 59, 61.

[42] See Louis R. Sullivan, "The Labor Crisis in Hawaii," *Asia*, Vol. XXIII, No. 7, July 1923, p. 511ff.

situation. Naturally, if there are unassimilated colored races in the population, they will not be struggling against their color for position in the culture. The first-generation East Indians in Trinidad, for example, are plantation workers; they live like Hindus. They must first be ensnared by the capitalist compulsives of European culture before their striving for advancement comes face to face with the purpose of the white ruling class. The new immigrants continue to live more or less in the cultural haven of their fellow immigrants.[43]

William C. Smith indicates clearly the spirit of the racial situation in Hawaii:

> It is a matter of tradition and principle that there is or should be no prejudice. That is a doctrine to which the leading spokesmen for the Territory subscribe, and practically all members of the community feel bound to maintain it. . . . Beneath this apparently calm surface, however, are found inequality discrimination, prejudice, cynicism, and bitterness. The plantation system . . . has manipulated the importation of laborers . . . so that a small group of white Americans are in control not only of the sugar industry but of all aspects of life in the Territory.
>
> Much is said about the educational opportunities in the islands, and the young people are urged to use them in order to become good Americans. They are told about the "room at the top" that is open to all on an equal basis. The children go through the schools and even through the university looking forward to the days when they will play important roles in the further unfolding of the great American epic. . . . Many, however, are awakened quite rudely from their dreams when, with diplomas in hand, they seek employment. Then they find barriers, some of them very subtle, to be sure, while their Caucasian classmates . . . move unopposed into the preferred positions.[44]

In Hawaii, then, a man's color is a matter of no little concern to him. Officially all persons, white or colored, are equal; but in practice the color of the Anglo-Saxon is economically most valuable and, to be sure, socially most satisfying. Among the mixed-bloods, superiority

---

[43]Jitsuichi Masuoka has studied race preference among Japanese in Hawaii, the most solidly organized and least assimilated racial group in the islands. Briefly, he finds that the first- and second-generation Japanese together prefer to have, as playmates of their children: first Japanese, second the ruling-class whites, then Chinese, and lastly—the tenth and eleventh racial choice—the Filipinos and Puerto Ricans. They show a decided preference for white-Hawaiian mixed-bloods over the Asiatic-Hawaiian. Barring the influence of certain cultural sympathies developed in the Orient, such as those toward the Koreans, the Japanese follow in their preference the racial status pattern dominated by the ruling-class whites in Hawaii. Masuoka explains variations from this pattern in terms of reaction. "Not infrequently," he says, "[members of the second-generation Japanese] resent the superior status of the whites, their tendency to maintain an obvious air of superiority, and their disposition to patronize other races." "Race Preference in Hawaii," *The American Journal of Sociology*, Vol. XLI, March 1936, pp. 635-41.

[44]Op. cit., p. 43.

ranks from this norm. In this situation, to study color prejudice from the point of view of the subordinated races would be to see the tail as wagging the dog.

Personality Factors

Two recognizable attitudes of superiority seem to develop in the ruling-class and bipartite situations. In the ruling-class situation colored people are not hopelessly depressed; for them the ceiling of opportunity is high, but attainable. Although the color ranks are practically checkmated by color cliques, color is never explicitly accepted by the group as a whole as a consideration limiting success. There are ordinarily sufficient instances of brilliant victories over color barriers to warrant sanguine illusions that they do not exist. Exemplifying cases of colored persons holding positions of enviable dignity are always available. As a consequence, colored people assume the bearing of freemen; indeed, not infrequently, success is accompanied by a show of exaggerated importance. The successful are impatient with the "degenerate masses," and they tend to remain aloof from any idea which seeks to identify them with the problems of colored people as a whole. The Negro leader, Marcus Garvey, on returning to Jamaica from the United States, realized the latter fact more vividly than he had expected.

Not so, however, in the bipartite situation. Here people of color tend to be humbled, not only by the engrossing importance of their color but also by the fact that the color interest is inevitably common to them all. Here the colored person of lowest class has an intuitive way of quickly establishing rapport with the most advanced colored gentleman, for the basis of their sympathy is elemental. It tends to keep the social-class hierarchy among them quite obtuse.

It is interesting to observe the pattern of behavior which develops when colored persons from these two cultures meet on common ground. In the United States, West Indian Negroes are likely to be first admired by American Negroes for their intractability to color restrictions and for their relative absence of a sense of inferiority in their dealings with white people as such. Later, however, the West Indian who has been accustomed to picking his friends and who puts emphasis upon family status is likely to arouse resentment among Americans. The West Indian frequently finds the American wanting in dignity and class refinement; Americans, on the other hand, are likely to find him conceited and boring. The pattern of relationship is by no means thus limited, but we shall not dilate upon it.

In the case of whites, attitudes of superiority are more likely to arise in the bipartite situation. Here white gentlemen and aristocrats, who despise all forms of menial work, are developed. The upper classes assume a condescending, paternal attitude to all lower-class persons, and their sense of power tends to be fully supported by the obsequiousness of the colored masses. In the ruling-class situation, on the other hand, the white man is generally compromising. He is living in a colored man's country and his attitude toward white people "from home" tends to be apologetic. The latter usually have great prestige among them, and the need for explaining their position usually puts whites in such a situation on the defensive. Usually they are working toward the end that they shall be able to merit retirement and a comfortable life "back home."

Probably the most significant difference between the ruling-class and the bipartite situations is to be found in their segregation practices. In the ruling-class situation there is ostensively no segregation; in the bipartite situation, however, the races are segregated both in custom and in written law. There is what might be called white exclusiveness in the ruling-class situation; that is to say, the whites segregate themselves[45] in residential areas and in their social activities. Overtly the practice is made to rest on the presumption that every man has a right to choose his own associates and to live exclusively if he so desires. Yet the occasional acquisition of residential property by a colored family in a white community never results in a public disturbance; it never results even in a public discussion. Such notices as FOR WHITES ONLY or COLORED and WHITE do not appear in this situation, while both colored people and whites ordinarily attend schools and churches without overt segregation.

In the bipartite situation, on the other hand, explicit segregation is at the foundation of all the racial discrimination and exploitative practices of the whites. In fact, segregation is here absolutely necessary to maintain white ruling-class dominance. The colored zones, belts, and camps are fundamental restrictions upon the colored people. They restrict the latter's freedom of physical movement, the *sine qua non* of a normal life under capitalism.

It would be an egregious error to think of imposed racial segregation as a mutually desirable spatial limitation between the races. What segregation really amounts to is a sort of perennial imprisonment of the

---

[45]Self-imposed segregation need not be degrading. It is of the nature of privacy, and the whites resort to it primarily for the purpose of conserving and augmenting their powers of dominance and control.

colored people by the whites. Moreover, this imprisonment provides the proper milieu for the planned cultural retardation of the colored people. Here they may mill and fester in social degeneracy with relatively minimal opportunity for even the most ambitious of them to extricate themselves.

In this situation, also, the concrete evidence of what is known as white racial superiority is at hand. Gobinesque contrasts between whites and colored people can now be easily supported by even mensurative data. In the ruling-class situation there is the stark fact that the lighter the color of the individual the greater, other things being equal, his economic and cultural advantage. Ordinarily the colored people take this fatalistically; that is to say, they attribute it implicitly to some inherent misfortune of being born colored. But they will not understand an ideology built about the assumption of mental inferiority of colored people as a whole, for the evidence developed in this situation is ordinarily opposed to it.

In the bipartite situation, on the other hand, the cultural limitations achieved by segregation are so pervasive that color inferiority could be pointed out on almost any count. The ocular proof of this inferiority, of course, serves to justify the continued exploitation and discrimination of the colored people; it never serves to support a conclusion that, the greater the social handicap of a people, the greater the need for social assistance.

Crisis and Panic in Race Relations

Although in the foregoing discussion we have referred to the personality problems of individuals, it may be well to deal a little more specifically with this subject. In both the ruling-class and bipartite situations persons of color are likely to be confronted with a series of racial crises and panics due to discrimination. They may be called upon, even as children, to adjust and accommodate themselves to reactions ranging all the way from the simple snub to the baying of dogs and the lynchers' rope. This is part of the process by which the individual achieves a conception of himself as a colored person.

The slighting and snubbing which ordinarily crisscross the lower levels of intensity in race relations are sometimes identified with similar phenomena in social-class relationships. But they are not really identical. The social climber is better prepared to understand the pretensions to exclusiveness of upper-class persons; the poor man with resignation usually leaves the ways of the rich to God. At any rate, the social-class system is at relative peace with the techniques for maintaining social distance among status groups. Discrimination based upon color, on the other hand, may involve severe mental anguish and panic. The social norms do not allow a lower-class person the right to "rub elbows" with upper-class persons, but these norms do impell the colored person to rise in status individually as if the paradoxical restraints of color were non-existent. In other words, the system judges the colored person as if he were under no social handicaps of color; he is, therefore, frequently confounded and irked in the realization that his color is to him the decisive social fact of his life.

A rebuff due to one's color puts him in very much the situation of the very ugly person or one suffering from a loathsome disease who is made to feel suspected or exposed. The suffering which this is likely to engender may be aggravated by a consciousness of incurability and even blameworthiness, a self-reproaching which tends to leave the individual still more aware of his loneliness and unwantedness. The extreme situation of terror in racial antagonism is probably the man hunt of the lynching mob. Here the colored person becomes the baited beast frantically alone before the fully uncovered teeth of race prejudice.

There seem to be two principal situations in which the colored person may be distressed or tormented for his color: (a) among other persons of lighter color and (b) among whites. In the ruling-class situation discrimination is based upon smaller differences in shades of color, but it does not culminate in serious violence as in the bipartite situations. As a means of color control there is more overt teasing, laughing, and ridicule in the ruling-class situation than in the bipartite situation, but in both these situations the colored person who finds himself among whites—in school, at a hotel, or in semi-public social gatherings, such as dances and picnics—may be made to experience the same paroxysms of shifting emotions.

The dominant socio-psychological pressure of color prejudice seems to produce a collapsing effect upon the individual's self-respect—to render him ashamed of his existence. It is intended to reduce him to a condition of no social consequence, and to a lesser or greater extent he commonly accepts the definition. The achievement of a degree of enforced isolation by the various methods of overshadowing, excluding, and estranging the colored person regulates the color system and gives each individual a fairly accurate racial conception of himself.

In this section we have attempted only to characterize the situation in which the individual may be tortured by race prejudice. The conditions for specific cases may vary tremendously. Moreover, the range of possible incidents is probably unlimited. In the United States, for instance, the discriminatory attitude may produce results ranging all the way from a slight nettling of the colored person to a full-blown lynching for "trying to act like a white man."

The Eurasians

The ruling-class situation describes the relationship which characterizes the race problem of the Eurasians. The case of the Eurasians of India is particularly revealing, however, for they stand at the junction between caste and race relations. The Eurasians of India are a white-Indian mixed-blood people, and mainly a British-Indian mixture. Before the Portuguese, who came earlier than the British, fully understood the temper of the Hindus, they actually planned a mixed-blood intermediary. At Goa they encouraged the marriage of Portuguese men to Indian women. "No less than 450 of [Albuquerque's] men were thus married, and others who desired to follow their example were so numerous that [the navigator] had great difficulty in granting their requests."[46] These mixed-bloods, however, never assumed the role designed for them. Their status and identity dwindled with the failing fortunes of the Portuguese. Therefore, the significant group of Eurasians today are mainly of British descent.[47]

The problem of the Eurasians is different from that of any other mixed-blood group because the colored masses from which this class came belong to a caste system. Inadequate recognition of this fact has resulted in very much spurious thinking, not only about the status of the Eurasians themselves, but also about that of mixed-bloods in all other parts of the world.[48]

[46]Edgar Thurston, *Castes and Tribes of Southern India,* Vol. II, pp. 233–34. See also Frederick Charles Danvers, *The Portuguese in India,* Vol. I, p. 217.

[47]"The descendants of the British in India have sorted out into three distinct groups. *The first* comprises those who were sent to England for their education and never returned to India, or who on retirement from service settled down in England. These have gradually been absorbed into the native population of England, and are no longer distinguished from the Britisher. The second continues in India as a distinct race. The third is being, or has been, absorbed into the Indian Christian population." Herbert A. Stark, *Hostages to India,* p. 36.

[48]The authors who have mistaken this situation are numerous indeed. The following may be taken as a type of reference: "The stigma which all countries attach to half-breeds is perhaps nowhere felt more keenly than in India, where the Eurasian is rejected both by the pure European whom he imitates and the natives of the country whom he affects to despise." *Bengal Census Report, 1881.* Quoted by William Crooke, *Things Indian,* p. 192. See also, to this effect, E. B. Reuter, *The Mulatto in the United States,* p. 19; Ogburn and Nimkoff, *Sociology,* p. 387; and Paul Fredrick Cressey, "The Anglo-Indians: A Disorganized Marginal Group," *Social Forces,* December 1935, Vol. 14, p. 267.

The Eurasians are naturally conditioned to seek assimilation with the British, but the caste system puts the British in a unique position of opposing strategy. Ordinarily this small white ruling class in India should have been constrained to yield many social privileges to the Eurasians, but the former has sensed its strategic position and is thus able to make almost unlimited demands upon these mixed-bloods without necessarily making any concessions to them.

As a characteristic of this situation, we observe Eurasian girls preferring to marry lighter men—even white men—while Eurasian men seek desperately the color status of native whites. As Kenneth E. Wallace, himself a Eurasian, says: "The light-hued Eurasian is often tempted to pose as a domiciled European."[49] The status of the Eurasians with respect to the caste system, be it remembered, is that of outcastes. The British are also outcastes, but they have a society of their own in India. The mixed-bloods are dependent upon this society not only because they were nurtured in it, but also because practically no other means of livelihood are open to them. No wonder they are preoccupied with their color. "A peculiar snobbishness . . . might be noted, the fairer looking down on the darker, all despising the Indian and affecting the European. . . . It might also be observed that as a community they do not cohere, that they lack unity, pride of race, and initiative."[50] "Pride of race" is, of course, a sentiment which can hardly be achieved by these people. Their social pride can have no meaning in India unless they become a caste; on the other hand, bred to British culture, they have the alternative of pride in European civilization.

The Eurasians, then, unlike, say, the Jamaican mixed-bloods, are caught between caste prejudice and race prejudice. And indeed, although their cultural sophistication is generally above that of the darker colored masses, the repulsion of caste is probably more decisive than that of race. Thus the mixed-bloods in India cannot become the leaders of the Indian masses, for Brahmanism has already provided for non-intercourse with them. Their ostracism comes natural with the Hindus, since, unless the people are conquerors, their social system has no way of respecting persons outside of a caste. They cannot expect sympathy from the Hindu masses. Individually they may have social entree only by way of the lower strata of castes, and this at the dreadful expense of regressing toward an inferior cultural level. The British are conscious of the Indians' apathy toward the Eurasians; hence they can exploit them with impunity. Eurasians are inevitably dependent

---

[49]*The Eurasian Problem,* p. 30.
[50]Ibid., pp. 5–6.

upon the British; they are Christian and Western in culture; their mothers were outcasted and their fathers insisted upon their westernization.

Here, then, is a mixed-blood group with a unique social problem. It is interesting to observe some verbal manifestations of the clash of social interests in this situation. The British call the Eurasians "half-castes." This term is inaccurate, but it serves well the former's derogatory purpose. The caste system has made no provision for half-castes. A person is either incaste or outcaste. Of course his caste status may be questionable, but then his living will ordinarily be precarious. The offspring of parents from two different castes are not half-castes; they are full members of some caste. What the whites in India really mean is that Eurasians are half-race or rather mixed-race. They are literally thinking of blood. On the other hand, the East Indians call the Eurasians "outcastes." In the sense that all people in the world who do not belong to the caste system are outcastes, the term is applicable. It is not so well used when it implies that Eurasians have either been expelled from some other caste or that they constitute part of the community of depressed castes. Finally, the mass of Eurasians look upon themselves as a true mixed-blood people who seek assimilation to the dominant culture. They exploit their lightness of color as a technique of achieving freedom of cultural participation[51] and call themselves Anglo-Indians or Eur-Asians.

The White Woman

We have mentioned the fact that in the ruling-class situation there are no coercive sanctions against men of color marrying white women; but in all color situations, with possible exception to caste members in India and nationalistic Japanese, there is a social urge among colored men to marry white women. This urge, of course, is not an "ungovernable sexual craving" for white flesh, as some rationalists would have us believe, for women of any color are totally sufficient for the satisfaction of any such simple desire. In fact, under such passion, white men have found colored women of every race fully adequate. Thus it must not be supposed that it is the white woman as a mere sexual object which is the preoccupation of colored men; it is rather her importance to him as a vehicle in his struggle for economic and cultural position.

---

[51]The Chinese Eurasians are evidently confronted with a similar situation. They are hedged between the powerful self-sufficient Chinese culture and the declining influence of the race-conscious Europeans. The irresponsibility of most of their white fathers is also against them. See Herbert Day Lamson, "The Eurasian in Shanghai," *The American Journal of Sociology,* Vol. XLI, 1936, pp. 642–48.

The particular advantage of a man's white skin is not that he has a supreme privilege of claiming a white woman in marriage; indeed, many do not choose to marry at all. His color, however, is a symbol of relatively unlimited cultural opportunity. So far as the sexual opportunity of marrying a white woman is concerned, some white men would gladly be colored; but so far as cultural opportunity is concerned, none would rather be colored.

The value of a white skin tends to depreciate directly with cultural advantage. When the Portuguese were forced to leave Goa, their proud light-skinned mixed-bloods stood face to face with the cold caste system. "Confronted with lack of patrons, lack of friends, lack of agricultural facilities, and lack of every resource, they sank rapidly in the social scale, and in the space of two centuries the majority of them have reverted to Indian stocks."[52]

In situations where Negroes may not marry white women the principal fear is not that if they did it would become more difficult for a white man to obtain a white wife, for the hostility is not diminished when Negroes come into the area with white women from abroad. The size of the white sex ratio is not ordinarily a factor. Neither are white Southerners, for example, particularly disturbed over the fact that in other countries there is considerable interracial marriage. We should miss the point entirely if we take as literally describing the situation the defense that white men must protect their sisters and daughters from the lust of black men. The status quo would be as effectively damaged if colored men went to Mars, married Martian white women, and brought them into the South as wives.

Therefore, it is not intermarriage, per se, which is determining, but rather the cultural advantage which restriction secures to the white group. Protecting the "honor and sanctity of white womanhood" constitutes a most convincing war cry and an excellent covering for the basic purpose that colored people must never be given the opportunity to become the cultural peers of whites. Incidentally, the greater the insistence upon the purity of white womanhood, the greater is the tendency of whites to conceive of colored women as undespoilable wenches. A Natal resident, Negro or Indian, may go to England and marry a white woman, but this would be practically out of the question in Natal. To return to South Africa with her would be to threaten white dominance in that area.

It is interesting to observe that the Bantu leader, D. D. T. Jabavu,

---

[52]Herbert Alick Stark, op. cit., pp. 6–7.

in listing some of the grievances of his people, never once intimated that they were handicapped by a limitation of the opportunity to marry white women. What seems important to him are such things as the extortionate poll tax on Bantu males only, the crowding of South African natives on restricted land areas, unfair wages and definite limitation of opportunity to rise occupationally, police brutality and the curfew, partiality of the laws and their unjust administration, grossly unequal provisions for education, and denial of suffrage.[53] Yet, even so, there is a close association between cultural parity and intermarriage. As we have already intimated, amalgamation is the final solution of race problems. To grant cultural parity is to eliminate the basis of intermarriage restrictions; and to permit intermarriage is to make cultural discrimination on the basis of race impossible. Since the Negro man is ordinarily the cultural aggressor, he may proceed both to whittle away the cultural advantage of whites and to marry white women, so that the physical basis of color discrimination may be finally obscured. In this strategy the white man who aims to preserve his cultural advantage is particularly his foe. The role which the Negro woman will take depends upon the situation. Furthermore, there is no support either in fact or reason for the belief that it is only the dross of colored men who desire intermarriage with white women; on the contrary, we should expect this desire to be experienced particularly among the most ambitious and aspiring colored men.

Intermarriage between whites and people of color has never taken place principally among the dregs of society. That this is a current belief is evidence of the effectiveness of the propaganda of white ex-

---

[53]"It is the little things," says Jabavu, "that tell most in our social relationship with the whites. If I am stranded in the rural areas, I dare not go to a Boer farm speaking English and wearing boots and a collar without inviting expulsion and execration; but if I go barefooted and collarless and in rags I shall enjoy the warmest hospitality. . . . Once when I quietly boarded a train at Middledrift, I was unexpectedly hailed by a white lady: 'Heigh, where are you going to, you black devil?' . . . In seaside resorts, we blacks can bathe . . . only in an absurdly small section of the beach where the edge is least desirable, elbowed out by miles of excellent frontage available for the happy white race, there being no resting seats for us although we pay town rates.

"In public hospitals, where there are no Bantu nurses, our lot is not always a happy one, and I can confirm this from the experience of one of my children at the hands of an unsympathetic white nurse. . . . In the Civil Service we are confined to junior clerkships, even in our native areas. . . . Positions as interpreters in the Supreme Court and many lower courts are a preserve for whites who, at least, can never be as proficient as the Bantu in the vernacular languages. . . . In many cases salesmen in shops delight in keeping us waiting while they gossip with their European friends, and flare out in anger, hurling vituperative epithets, if you dare humbly to interrupt and ask to be served." "Bantu Grievances," in I. Shapera, *Western Civilization and the Natives of South Africa*, pp. 285–99. See also Raymond Leslie Buell, op. cit., pp. 58–70, 118ff.

ploiting classes, propaganda which goes to make up the substance of race prejudice. When it was convenient for white men to marry Hottentot, or East Indian, or Hawaiian, or any other women of color, they ordinarily obtained women from the upper class. And they themselves were not degenerate. Now that men of color—African, East Indian, West Indian, Chinese—are occasionally marrying white women, it may be shown that on the whole these men are from the upper or middle classes of the population. Of course we are not here speaking of prostitution, which is pathological intraracially as well.

Our hypothesis, then, is that to conceive of the mere presence or absence of intermarriage—that is to say, the idea of "keeping blood pure" —as a postulate in studies of race relations will almost always lead to sterile results. In race relations, solicitude about purity of blood has been a means, not an end. "Pure blood" has value only when in preserving it a calculable social advantage can be maintained.

The social situation will be determined by racial expediency rather than by supposed basic attitudes of racial integrity. In fact, Europeans are particularly lacking in endogamous attitudes. So far as readiness to mix their blood with others is concerned, they are probably as willing as any people in the world. The black, caste-conscious Hindu of southern India would be far more reluctant to intermarry than any white people. In Hawaii, where there are many ethnics, it is not white people but the Japanese who intermarry with other groups least. "Why, of all the white peoples of the world," says Romanzo Adams, "have the race-conscious Americans and British played the leading role in amalgamation with the Hawaiians? . . . The civilian [white] men have been much less numerous since 1878 than the Chinese, and they have been better provided with women of their own race, but they have, nevertheless, intermarried with the Hawaiian and part-Hawaiian women more than the Chinese have."[54]

Western civilization and Christianity in particular have developed no definite sanction against race mixture. In fact, romantic love, the antithesis of endogamy, is a social trait of Western culture. Depending upon the social situation, however, endogamy among whites may or may not have practical value. In some situations it has proved a most effective instrument for maintaining white dominance over peoples of color. When this is the case, whole philosophies and schools of anthropology are developed to give it natural justification and explana-

---

[54] *Op. cit.*, pp. 121–22. As a cause of the high white intermarriage rate, Adams thinks: "The most important thing is just the being away from home—away from his parents, relatives, and neighbors." But distance away from home should hardly be a factor, since these same whites in India or South Africa would hardly intermarry with colored people.

tion; they are constrained to define it as an instinct. As a theme, "the powerful biological urge to maintain the purity of the white race" has been most satisfying. What could be more natural, then, than to believe that intermarriage is the key to all problems of race relations? In racially dichotomized societies the status quo cannot be maintained without drastic sanctions against white-woman-colored-man marriage. In other words, the white woman is here in a critical position; defending her "purity" becomes a sacred duty. We may assume that the race problem is solved when the white woman becomes free to follow her sentiments in choosing either white man or colored man in marriage.

The Church and Race Relations

Elsewhere we have discussed the incompatibility of Christianity and caste and its freedom from anti-racial doctrines. The established Church, however, is far more flexible. All denominations of the Christian Church in whatever part of the world tend to follow the locally established pattern of race relations. Unlike applied Mohammedanism, for example, the Christian Church has no consistent ethical philosophy of race relations. Indeed, the Church has usually been the leader of the white purpose in the particular situation, and this is not entirely surprising. We do not expect the Church, as stabilizer of the morality of the social system, to counter the nationalism of the ruling class. Indeed, paradoxical as it may seem, race prejudice is in fact a decent and respectable attribute; it is a mark of refinement and a characteristic of aristocrats. Therefore, since the Church is ordinarily expected to be the author of social refinement, it has not only made terms with segregation and other discriminatory practices but also tends to perpetuate them in situations where even the popular social sanctions are relatively indifferent. One may expect, for example, to find frequent instances of Roman Catholics and Protestants segregating or excluding colored people from their schools and churches, not only in the South but also in the Northern United States where secular institutions may not segregate.

In color-class countries like Barbados, Jamaica, and Trinidad, the Church could be depended upon to perfect all the subtleties of color distinction. In short, the Church, being naturally conservative, sanctions and stabilizes the mundane interests of the ruling class.

Plan for Resolving a Racial Situation

We have already mentioned what seems to us to be the inevitable resolution of interracial conflict. Many conscientious students, however, believe that co-operation and good will between white and colored races will surely come if the whites are assured that the colored race has given up all designs upon race mixture. "For the fear of race-mixture," concludes R. F. Alfred Hoernle in reference to South Africa, "has poisoned in the past, and is still poisoning at present, all other relations between the two groups."[55] And this writer continues:

The most we can aim at and hope is to reduce such relations to small proportions, by establishing the firmest possible will in both groups to maintain the rule that white shall marry white and black shall marry black, and that extramarital relations between white and black, with the resulting additions to the coloured population, are . . . to be avoided. It is a principle which has been established as one of the defining elements in group pride and group identity of the whites, and it is becoming similarly a defining element in the group pride and group identity of the Bantu. To ask whether it is right or wrong that both groups should build themselves upon this principle seems to me irrelevant and futile. . . .[56]

In these racially dichotomized societies the immediate problem tends to obscure long-run values, and they confuse symptoms with disease. The Bantu can give up neither the aim of amalgamation nor the desire for cultural equality without crystallizing his position of inferiority. The white man has made color a constituent element in economic competition; and to peoples of color, in immediate contact with whites, who cannot now or never become nationalistic, it is economically imperative that they accept this challenge and seek to liquidate the color impediment by amalgamation. The white man has set up the competitive norm; it seems, therefore, clearly preposterous to ask the colored people to remain unresponsive to it.

The Bantu, like other peoples of color, will certainly adopt the idea of progress with other traits of Western culture, and modern racial ideology goes with these. To follow a plan of racial segregation is to play completely into the hands of the white ruling class. Moreover, the apparent development of group pride among the Bantu can have but one meaning. It is a reaction; hence, the stronger it becomes, the greater the need for the expression of physical might among whites; in time we should expect this situation to be highly productive of Bantu nationalism.

---

[55]"Race Mixture and Native Policy in South Africa," in I. Shapera, op. cit., pp. 278–79.
[56]Ibid.

18. Race Prejudice, Intolerance, and Nationalism

R ACE PREJUDICE AND INTOLERANCE ARE SOCIAL ATTITUDES THAT
have not been clearly defined in discussions of intergroup antagonism. These attitudes have been confused particularly in descriptions and comparisons of Jews and Negroes as "minority groups," and
the result has been an accumulation of many spurious conclusions. In
this attempt to distinguish these attitudes we shall also consider in
illustration the social situations of Negroes and Jews; then, by a somewhat different approach, we shall essay a definition of the social position of modern subordinate nationality groups and that of the Asiatics
on the Pacific coast.

Intolerance

The common practice, in analyses of race relations, is to assume that
race prejudice and intolerance are identical social facts. For instance,
Dr. Ruth Benedict says:

Traditional Anglo-Saxon intolerance is a local and temporal culture-
trait like any other. . . . In this country it is obviously not an intolerance
directed against a mixture of blood of biologically far-separated races, for
upon occasion excitement mounts as high against the Irish Catholic in
Boston, or the Italian in New England mill towns, as against the Oriental
in California.[1]

We may illustrate this point further. According to Ellsworth Faris:

The conflict between Jews everywhere and those among whom they live
is a racial conflict. That the Jews belong to a separate biological race is

---

[1] *Patterns of Culture*, p. 11. To the same effect Carlton Hayes asserts: "Intolerance toward Negroes in the United States is perhaps the acme of racial intolerance in modern nationalism . . . a nationalism which has been communicated
from the West to the Far East may carry in its train to the Far East the racial
intolerance as well as the international war which has characterized the West."
Essays on Nationalism, pp. 237–38.

doubtful and perhaps not true. Nevertheless the conflict is sociologically racial, for they are regarded as a separate race, are treated as a separate race, and hold themselves together as if they were a separate race.[2]

The conclusion here is explicit: there is no difference between anti-Semitism and race prejudice—and this is the question before us.

Anti-Semitism, to begin with, is clearly a form of social intolerance, which attitude may be defined as an unwillingness on the part of a dominant group to tolerate the beliefs or practices of a subordinate group because it considers these beliefs and practices to be either inimical to group solidarity or a threat to the continuity of the status quo. Race prejudice, on the other hand, is a social attitude propagated among the public by an exploiting class for the purpose of stigmatizing some group as inferior so that the exploitation of either the group itself or its resources or both may be justified. Persecution and exploitation are the behavior aspects of intolerance and race prejudice respectively. In other words, race prejudice is the socio-attitudinal facilitation of a particular type of labor exploitation, while social intolerance is a reactionary attitude supporting the action of a society in purging itself of contrary cultural groups.

Position of Jews and Negroes

We may think of intolerance as a suppressive attitude and of race prejudice as a limiting attitude. Anti-Semitism is an attitude directed against the Jews because they are Jews, while race prejudice is an attitude directed against Negroes because they want to be something other than Negroes. The Jew, to the intolerant, is an enemy within the society; but the Negro, to the race-prejudiced, is a friend in his place. As Joshua Trachtenberg points out, the Jew "is alien, not to this or that land, but to all Western society, alien in his habits, his pursuits, his interests, his character, his very blood. Wherever he lives he is a creature apart. He is the archdegenerate of the world, infecting its literature, its art, its music, its politics and economics with the subtle poison of his insidious influence, ripping out its moral foundation stone by stone until it will collapse in his hands."[3] Thus to the intolerant domi-

---

[2]*The Nature of Human Nature,* p. 341. See also *Jews in a Gentile World,* Graeber and Britt, eds., p. 78, where J. O. Hertzler argues in support of Faris's conclusion that the Jews are a race "from the standpoint of sociology."

[3]*The Devil and the Jews,* p. 3. In the same vein Adolf Hitler attacked the Jew: "His blood-sucking tyranny becomes so great that riots against him occur. Now one begins to look more and more closely at the stranger and one discovers more and more new repellent features and characteristics in him, till the chasm becomes an unsurmountable one. In times of most bitter distress the wrath against him finally breaks out, and the exploited and ruined masses take up self-defense in order

nant group the Jew is not only an alien but also an aggressor against the society itself. "The Jew was the adversary without peer of Christendom, and *ipso facto* he was to be classed with all who sought destruction of the Church and of Christian society, whether they attacked from within or from without."[4]

This conception of the Jews as a guest-folk perverting and even damning the hospitality of their host has been turned to violent hostility against them.[5] Indeed, intolerance seems to contain an element of reciprocation, since the persecutor, irritated by the intractability or even the assumed destructive potentialities of the persecuted, tends also to feel tormented and persecuted. One anti-Semite has been quoted as saying: "While we pray for the Jews, they persecute and curse us!"[6] The Jews are thus conceived to be more than passively divisive; they are also charged with hating and betraying the society in which they live.

The Problem of Assimilation

Probably the clearest distinction between intolerance and race prejudice is that the intolerant group welcomes conversion and assimilation, while the race-prejudiced group is antagonized by attempts to assimilate. The Jews are a people who refuse to assimilate; that is to say, to give up their culture and lose their identity in the larger society. They conceive of the values of their culture as so significant or superior that they are willing to suffer considerable persecution rather than give them up. "[The Jews] have had a different faith, have refused intermarriage even when it was desired on the other side, have at times seemed to be impolite in refusing the Gentile's hospitality, and have regarded themselves as a special chosen people in a way which must often seem irritating to people who did not share the Jewish faith."[7] Thus, when the Jews are regarded as being stubborn, "as men who know the truth and deliberately reject it," violent emotions are ordinarily stirred up against them.

---

to ward off the scourge of God. They have got to know him in the course of several centuries and they experience his mere existence as the same distress as the plague." Op. cit., p. 426.

[4] Joshua Trachtenberg, op. cit., p. 81.

[5] In an inverted expression of anti-Semitic aggression Hitler develops this passion for Jewish extermination: "[The Jew] pursues his course, the course of sneaking in among the nations and of gouging them internally, and he fights with his weapons, with lies and slanders, poison and destruction, intensifying the struggle to the point of bloodily exterminating his hated opponents." Op. cit., p. 960.

[6] Trachtenberg, op. cit., p. 182.

[7] Talcott Parsons in *Jews in a Gentile World*, p. 115.

Probably most of the stability of the religio-cultural pertinacity of the Jews is due to the nature of their historical conflict with Christianity. After all, it is a Jew whom the Christians worship—a religious radical who causes the Jewish hierarchy so much embarrassment that they seem never to be able to accept him as their God. Jesus might have been able to organize His popular support for the forceful overthrow of the corrupt priesthood, the "serpents [who] devoured widows' houses," but the Romans would not have permitted such a show of physical power. The revolution was abortive, and the Jews encysted themselves with their traditional persecution ideology against all such future attacks.

Assuming the continuance of the present social order, the one condition of peace between Jews and Gentiles is that the Jews cease to be Jews. And they are apparently given extraordinary encouragement to do so. "If I were a Jew," Faris declares, "I should marry for love but I should try to marry a non-Jewish girl. There are excellent eugenic arguments for crossings of this sort and, if fate should work out this way, the gesture and example would count for much."[8] One has only to substitute the word "Negro" for "Jew" in the foregoing passage in order to appreciate the distinction between race prejudice and intolerance.

This fact of seeming to reward the object of intolerance for its conversion or contribution to social peace and harmony seems to be elemental in the phenomenon. Jesus had to ponder the implicit offer of the ruling elite—"All this power will I give thee, and the glory of them"—as a price of His selling out in the interest of the status quo. And, among many other instances, the purple of the Church was constantly held up before Erasmus of Rotterdam as a means of channeling his ideas. Indeed, some of the best-paid, anti-socialist propagandists today are former "dangerous" radicals.[9] The intermarriage of Jews

---

[8] Ellsworth Faris, op. cit., p. 352. Probably no one will dream that it is possible for all Jews, say, in the United States to call a conference and thereupon decide to give up Judaism, after which anti-Semitism will have come to an end. The problem is infinitely more complicated. But this certainly is true: Almost any Jew, with comparatively little difficulty, may decide to marry a Gentile and bring up his children in the Christian tradition. As Edward A. Ross points out: "You may elude religious persecution by changing your creed, but you cannot dodge racial aggression by changing your race." "The Post-War Intellectual Climate," *The American Sociological Review,* Vol. 10, October 1945, p. 648.

[9] J. O. Hertzler, with some doubts about its ever occurring, reaches a similar conclusion. Says he: "To cease to be a cultural irritant the Jew must be completely assimilated . . . he must deliberately mould himself and his life on Gentile patterns. . . . He will have to be completely absorbed ethnically. That means he will have to marry non-Jews, generation after generation, until he has no grandparents who were considered as Jews and no children who by any chance might

with Gentiles and of Negroes with whites are both infrequent occurrences, but the inhibiting social forces in each situation are essentially distinct.

Negroes and Jews as Allies

The question has been frequently raised as to the possibility of Negroes and Jews, as "minority groups," collaborating for the purpose of advancing their social position. Recently Dr. Werner Cahnman put it in this way: "Both Jews and Negroes are threatened by the same hatred and the same hostility. Upon the strength of this they could unite in action. But their reaction to the situation is different: the Jews are cautiously defending where the Negroes are militantly attacking."[10] Yet it is doubtful whether Jews and Negroes have a common basis for continuing action against the dominant group. In reality they are not "threatened by the same hostility," and there is some probability that there is as much reason for antagonism between them.[11]

In so far as Jews are bourgeois-minded businessmen and manufacturers, they are likely to be, at least implicitly, race-prejudiced. They will sooner understand the limiting racial policies of the ruling class than the ambition of Negroes for social equality. Because the Negroes are almost entirely a proletarian group, while the Jews tend to be professional and businessmen,[12] there is particular opportunity for the development of a disparity of interest between them. As Negroes become increasingly assimilated in the larger society, the likelihood is that they, too, will become intolerant.

---

have any distinguishing 'Jewish' characteristics. . . . In general, he will have to disappear entirely as a Jew, be dissolved in the life and being of the larger world." In *Jews in a Gentile World,* p. 98.

[10]"An American Dilemma," *The Chicago Jewish Forum,* Vol. 3, No. 2, Winter, 1944–45, p. 94.

[11]For a discussion of Jewish and Negro relations in the United States, see Roi Ottley, *New World A-Coming,* pp. 122–36; Lunabelle Wedlock, *The Reactions of Negro Publications and Organizations to German Anti-Semitism;* Harold Orlansky, "A Note on Anti-Semitism among Negroes," *Politics,* Vol. 2, August 1945, pp. 250–52; and Kenneth B. Clark, "Candor about Negro-Jewish Relations," *Commentary: A Jewish Review,* Vol. I, February 1946, pp. 8–14.

[12]Gunnar Myrdal generalizes the situation this way: "Jews are the leading retail merchants in many Negro neighborhoods and are the leading employers of Negro servants in Northern cities. The natural dislike of the dominant person by the subordinate person in an unequal economic bargain thus seems to be the cause of any striking anti-Semitism that appears in certain Negro groups." Op. cit., p. 1143.

However, this observation is impressionistic. Jews are not the "leading employers of Negro servants in Northern cities," but it is probably true that there is some overt reasons for Negroes accepting the national stereotype of Jews as hard-bargaining employers. Nor is it necessary to assume that Jews are in numbers mainly businessmen.

There is a sense in which we may conceive of racial antagonism as contributing to the amelioration of anti-Semitism. The potentialities against which the present-day dominant whites struggle in their racial aggression are more dangerous than the possible disorganizing presence of the Jews. The threat to the entire social system is definitely increased if the black and the white proletariat are permitted to become unified and class-conscious—ruling-class Jews and all may be marked for liquidation. If the Jewish bourgeoisie can keep the fear of this threat before the minds of the dominant white Gentiles, it is likely that they will be able to establish a Jew-Gentile, bourgeois solidarity against the colored people and, of course, against the white proletariat also. This will tend to allay the intensity of anti-Semitism. To the extent, however, that the proletariat gains solidarity and power, to that extent also the Jewish bourgeoisie may come in for its full share of proletarian hatred, and probably more so from the most exploited group, the colored people.

Since the Jews are a traditionally persecuted group, they should not be expected to make a spectacle of their race prejudice. A South African Indian writer indicates the ground for antagonistic feeling between his race and the Jews:

> The Jews attempt to oust the Indians out of the commercial fields. . . . In general [they] may be termed inimical to the Indians. A certain writer has pointed out that the Jews never fight openly; they make a gentle rush. This has been true in South Africa. The Jews have never openly come out against the Indians. They have been playing a back-alley game.[13]

It would seem then that there is some real reason for the separate struggle of Negroes and Jews, for their social disabilities are rooted in different and apparently disparate social situations. And yet it may happen that the motives for both anti-Semitism and race prejudice call for heightened expression at the same time, a fact which may lead to the identification of a common enemy and thus drive the Jews and Negroes together in sympathy. When in 1934, for instance, the Nazi party declared that "the continuation of marriages with bearers of colored or Jewish blood is incompatible with the aims of the National Socialist party," the colored people and the Jews had to come together in opposition to a common danger.[14]

---

[13]P. S. Joshi, op. cit., p. 37.

[14]In America, on the other hand, where the colored population is significant, the fascists may adopt a different strategy. In a crisis they will most likely set Negroes against Jews or vice versa, so that the major proletarian struggle may be subordinated to an augmented and intensified minor cultural conflict.

Naturalness of Race Prejudice and Intolerance

It is possible to conceive of any social fact as a natural phenomenon without implying that it is an inseparable function of social organization. Probably intolerance is as old as human society, but race prejudice has developed only recently in Western society, and this is a consideration of prime importance. An insufficient analysis of race prejudice and intolerance may lead one to conclude that "prejudice toward a racial or a religious group is a collective phenomenon with roots in the distant past."[15] The phenomena, however, do not have the same root.

If we assume that social solidarity is a desideratum in all societies, then leaders of the dominant intrasocietal group will always be intolerant of culturally divergent groups which threaten the stability of the social order. The presence of a different race need not be of itself a disorganizing factor, but a group which will not or cannot be assimilated ordinarily produces "social indigestion."[16] Moreover, there is probably no society so loosely organized as to permit subordinate groups to threaten its existence. As an insignificant Oriental cult, the followers of Jesus might have been tolerated or even disregarded. But when Jesus began to preach "to the multitude, and to his disciples, saying: 'Woe unto you, scribes and Pharisees, hypocrites! for ye are like unto whited sepulchres, which indeed appear beautiful outward, but are within full of dead men's bones, and of all uncleanness. . . . Ye generation of vipers, how can ye escape the damnation of hell?' " the time had come for the leaders of the Jews to be intolerant and to persecute Him and His followers. No society would bear such a threat to "law and order"—to the status quo.[17]

So also it might have been possible for medieval religious leaders and modern nationalists to disregard the Jews as of no consequence; just as, for instance, the gypsies are ordinarily tolerated, if not encouraged. But Jews are seldom social non-entities; they enter effectively into the eco-

---

[15]Ellsworth Faris, op. cit., p. 348.

[16]Concerning the Jews, J. O. Hertzler observes: " . . . the Jewish culture is always a foreign culture—an undigested element—within the larger areal culture." In *Jews in a Gentile World,* p. 74.

[17]To this end, therefore, "assembled together the chief priests, and the scribes, and the elders of the people, unto the palace of the high priest . . . and consulted that they might take Jesus by subtlety and kill him." Indeed the final effects of counterpropaganda are pathetically illustrated as Jesus pleaded "to the multitudes: 'Are ye come out as against a thief with swords and staves for to take me? I sat daily with you teaching in the temple, and ye laid no hold on me.' " However, "they that laid hold on Jesus led him away to . . . the high priest, where the scribes and the elders were assembled." Intolerance does not argue or debate; it simply bares its teeth.

nomic and political life of the community. Therefore, the anti-Semitic leader is never at a loss for spectacular instances of Jewish wealth, power, and prestige to vitalize his theme of Jewish cultural hostility.

There is apparently no reason to believe that with increasing democratic organization of society there will be a correlative decrease in social intolerance. The focus of intolerance may change—that is to say, Jews may be tolerated—but, since we may expect that even in an advanced democracy social values will be jealously defended, no group regarded as alien and disruptive of social harmony and solidarity could be assured a peaceful, tolerated existence. As Lord Acton observes: "The true democratic principle, that the people shall not be made to do what it does not like, is taken to mean that it shall never tolerate what it does not like."[18] Obviously, this does not mean to say that in a democracy Jews will be regarded as alien; it is not unlikely, however, that, say, anarchists might be. Moreover, anyone who challenges the status quo, whether he be a Socrates, Galileo, Hus, or Marx, must expect intolerance. Certain types of societies are able to tolerate a relatively large variety of beliefs and practices, but none will tolerate beliefs and practices which seem to threaten its existence.

To be sure, it is only necessary that the dominant group believes in the menace of the cultural tenets and practices of the other group; whether they are actually harmful or not is not the crucial circumstance. From the point of view of modern urban civilization, for instance, very much of the earlier persecution of Protestants by the Roman Catholic states of Europe was clearly ill advised; yet we still think that it was very fortunate that Catholic Europe did not allow itself to be swamped by Islam.

It is this awareness, therefore, in a threat to the social order or the status quo, either by unassimilability or religio-political intractability, which constitutes the basis of intolerance and persecution.[19] The early Christians in Rome could not escape persecution, and when they finally dominated Western society they themselves gave to the world its classic lessons in persecution. We may think of intolerance, then, as the means by which the group through its ruling class seeks to protect or to enhance its social solidarity.

Race prejudice, on the other hand, developed gradually in Western society as capitalism and nationalism developed. It is a divisive attitude

---

[18]*History of Freedom and Other Essays,* pp. 93–94.

[19]For a discussion of anti-Semitism from the point of view of ethnocentric or "unconscious nationalism" conflict, see Gustav Ichheiser, "The Jews and Anti-semitism," *Sociometry,* Vol. IX, February 1946, pp. 92–108.

seeking to alienate dominant group sympathy from an "inferior" race, a whole people, for the purpose of facilitating its exploitation. In a previous chapter we have attempted to show that race prejudice is peculiar to the system of capitalist exploitation.[20]

The assertion that Jews have everywhere suffered very much injustice and persecution among other peoples may be a negative plea in a situation of rising anti-Semitic feeling, since the remedy for the devil is more, not less, persecution. Those who will not be converted and are supposed to have explicitly rejected the morality and social norms of the group may be thought of as willingly putting themselves beyond the purview of the social conscience. On the other hand, where race prejudice is mounting it may be idle or even aggravating to argue that the Negro seeks only social equality; that is to say, only the right to live as other men in the larger society. For it is against this very urge among Negroes to identify themselves with the dominant group that the hostility is aroused.

A Restatement

The dominant group is intolerant of those whom it can define as anti-social, while it holds race prejudice against those whom it can define as subsocial.[21] Persecution and capitalist exploitation are the respective behavior aspects of these two social attitudes. Thus we are ordinarily intolerant of Jews but prejudiced against Negroes. In other words, the dominant group or ruling class does not like the Jew at all, but it likes the Negro in his place. To put it in still another way, the

---

[20]It should be recognized, however, that with the rise of extreme racial antagonism in Europe an attempt has been made to reduce the Jews along with certain white nationalities to the status of exploitable racial groups. As Salo Baron observes: "Modern anti-Semitism led to another highly important consequence: for the first time it peremptorily refused assimilation of the Semitic Jews to the Aryan ruling majority. The view of former generations, that the difference between Jew and Gentile consisted chiefly in a difference of creed or culture, was abandoned. The new anti-Semites maintained that no matter how strong an effort was made by the individual, no matter how favorable the external circumstances, the attempt to assimilate was utterly futile." "Nationalism and Intolerance," *The Menorah Journal*, Vol. XVII, November 1929, p. 153. Having developed race prejudice, with its powerful conviction of immutable, human inferiority, a condition far more debasing than that of the "ostracized ideologists," it may become convenient to use the weapon of race prejudice in addition to that of intolerance against the persecuted group. And so, too, in order to make race prejudice more effective, it may be bolstered up by certain appeals to intolerance.

[21]Professor J. F. Brown makes this observation: "Those whom we consider below us we may despise or pity, but we neither love nor hate them as we do our equals. . . . Negroes are discriminated against everywhere in the United States, but we do not have a wholesale anti-Negroism with the personalized virulence of anti-Semitism." In *Jews in a Gentile World*, p. 140.

condition of its liking the Jew is that he cease being a Jew and voluntarily become like the generality of society, while the condition of its liking the Negro is that he cease trying to become like the generality of society and remain contentedly a Negro.

From the point of view of the dominant group, the Jew is our irreconcilable enemy within the gates, the antithesis of our God, the disturber of our way of life and of our social aspirations; the Negro as our servant, on the other hand, is our indispensable friend. Therefore, it is conceivable that Negro Americans may become anti-Semitic; and Jews, in so far as they are businessmen, may learn to loathe forward and ambitious Negroes. Intolerance is probably as old as social organization, while race prejudice came into being only recently with the rise of a particular form of social organization. Intolerance demands recantation and conversion;[22] race prejudice loathes the idea of conversion.

When our social organization is threatened with internal disruption, as during the Black Death in Europe or the frantic attempt of the Germans to throw off the "shame of Versailles," we may become desperate and massacre the Jews.[23] They are the most stubbornly separative group that we can find. This negative attitude includes the phenomenon of scapegoating. But when we are under economic pressure, as during a depression, or made enraged by having to do our own menial labor while Negroes "idle," we pounce upon some of them, beat them into understanding, and command our police to pick them up as vagrants. A Jewish pogrom is not exactly similar to a Negro lynching. In a pogrom the fundamental motive is the extermination of the Jew; in a lynching, however, the motive is that of giving the Negro a lesson in good behavior.

We want to assimilate the Jews, but they, on the whole, refuse with probable justification to be assimilated; the Negroes want to be assimilated, but we refuse to let them assimilate.

Nationalism

Elsewhere in this study we have considered nationalism in its relation to racial antagonism; at this point we shall attempt to describe briefly

---

[22]Conversion for the Jews, however, is not a simple matter. In Spain from the fourteenth century onward, the Jews who became converted, the *conversos,* continued in their economic prosperity and aroused thereby the suspicion and jealousy of the ruling class. The new Christians, having been converted under pressure, were always suspected of insincerity.

[23]See *Jews in a Gentile World,* pp. 94ff., for many classic instances of frenzied uprisings against Jews when the social order seemed to be threatened.

the phenomenon as a factor determining the relationship among national ethnics. It is necessary first for us to differentiate the concepts "race" and "nation." A race, in so far as social interaction is concerned, may be thought of as any people who are distinguished, or consider themselves distinguished, in social relations with other peoples, by their physical characteristics. On the other hand, a nation or national ethnic may be thought of as a tribal group conscious of cultural unity; in addition we may think of modern nations as being nationalistic. The problems which develop when more than one of these nationalistic groups find themselves living under the same political state have been called national minority problems. We may repeat, these problems are of recent origin; before the rise of nationalism in Europe "nations" were landed estates. There was cultural difference without political unity and consciousness among peoples.

Probably the term "national minority" may best be thought of as meaning "subordinate nation"; thus we may speak of subordinate nationality problems.[24] This may be more cumbersome, yet more meaningful. As the term "minority group" has been used, it may refer to a nationalistic group which exceeds in number of individuals the "majority" group. In fact, the idea of the position of the opposing group is not conveyed by the antonym "majority" but rather by such words as "dominant" or "superordinate."[25] The struggle among national groups, then, is a struggle for power.

---

[24]A word should be said about the use of the term "minority group." Under this heading is ordinarily included any "group of people who, because of their physical or cultural characteristics, are singled out from the others in the society in which they live for differential and unequal treatment, and who therefore regard themselves as objects of collective discrimination." See Louis Wirth, "The Problem of Minority Groups," in *The Science of Man in the World Crisis,* Ralph Linton, ed., p. 347. This definition, which probably had to be as inclusive as it is because of the tremendous scope of the non-significantly modified concept "group," promises and frequently accomplishes a confusing discussion. Indeed, it is practically unlimited, for under it we may discuss political-class problems, problems of religious sects, problems of particular economic interest groups, race problems, nationality problems, and so on. Wirth even speaks of "where the minority occupies the position of a caste"! Ibid., p. 354.
Very much of the responsibility for the medley of incongruous ideas about race relation and nationality groups frequently encountered in Donald Young's *American Minority Peoples* is no doubt due to the false lead of the ill-defined concept "minority peoples." For a definitive attempt to derive some meaning of this amorphous concept, see "The Meaning of Minorities," by Francis J. Brown, in *Our Racial and National Minorities,* Francis J. Brown and Joseph S. Roucek, eds., Chap. I.

[25]The concept may lead to such word play as the following: "When the American speaks of problems of minorities, he is seldom conscious that he is actually speaking about himself and his own problems. Yet, both in size and in performance, the Caucasian rates a position as the world's number one minority problem. The Caucasian minority has a majority psychology." Buell G. Gallagher, *Color and Conscience,* p. 6.

But although the struggle between national ethnics is political, it is not exactly similar to political-class conflict. The principal concern of political classes is with the form of government; the revolutionists seek to reorganize the State in the interest of its class ideals—economic and political. Moreover, an open class struggle is ordinarily an intrasocietal conflict, and it may take place among members of the same nationality, as, for instance, the French Revolution. On the other hand, the subordinate ethnic struggles for national independence or national recognition. Independence, of course, may mean the right to secede either for the purpose of establishing a separate state or of uniting with another state. In seeking to achieve greater political recognition the subordinate nationality may strive either for increased participation in the affairs of a state or for the attainment of a dominant position within it.

An exploited race tends to become a subordinate nationality when it has gained a degree of political unity and consequently makes appeals to national importance and rights as a basis for achieving political recognition. Most of the colonial native peoples are actual or potential subordinate nationalities. The Filipinos, East Indians, and Javanese are probably at the same stage of national development; the Trinidadians and Jamaicans are only slightly nationalistic, while Haiti might be taken as the classic illustration of an exploited racial group which has achieved nationhood. Negro Americans will probably never become nationalistic; the numerical balance of the races will not allow the development of nationalistic antagonism on the part of the colored people. To say, as Robert E. Park does, that Negroes in the United States are a "national minority" may be misleading. Yet it is fairly certain that African Negroes in every continental colony will in time develop nationalism.

Subordinate nationalities are seldom, if ever, "assimilationist," for the nationalism itself which produces them is a separative social attitude; group integrity is the emotional core of nationalism. On the other hand, an exploited racial group may be assimilationist. Ordinarily, subordinate-nationality antagonisms are less divisive than racial antagonisms. In a bipartite racial situation, probably the most effective type of exploitative relationship, the white nationalities tend to act as a unit in dominating the colored people. This is especially true in South Africa.

In the United States we may consider the white Southerners and the Northerners as two nationalities of the same race, the Southerners being the subordinate group. The cultural difference in the South, with its peculiar economic pattern, gives it a sufficient basis for the development of nationalism. Although its attempts to form a separate and independent nation have been frustrated, its nationalistic fires still smolder. The Civil War, of course, was not an interracial strife; Negro slavery merely constituted a part of the essential circumstances about which the two nationalities struggled. We should have expected the white people of the North to take sides with the Southern whites, had the conflict been a nationalistic conflict between blacks and whites of the area.

The reason for this should probably not be sought in some "consciousness of kind" instinct, but rather in the political-class situation of the colored people. In our secular, exploitative system few, if any, economic conflicts between ruling political classes can be as dangerous as a conflict between one of these classes and a proletarian group. The white nationalities of South Africa, for instance, are implacably decided on their common purpose of exploiting the natives; this is their basic interest, and their internationality problems must not so divide them as to defeat it. It is a similar passion, which on little agitation wells up in the capitalist ruling classes, regardless of nationality, against organized proletarian movements. Adolf Hitler, with some considerable success, attempted to exploit it even in the very heat of his worldwide international conflict.

The Jews in the United States and probably in most parts of Europe do not constitute a subordinate nationality; neither do Roman Catholics. But in Palestine the Jews are a nationality group which cultivates Zionism, its nationalism, apparently with the intent of achieving national dominance in that country.[26] The positive behavior aspect of nationalism, it should be remembered, is international and imperialistic aggression.

Since nationalism developed recently mainly under the stimulation of international economic rivalry, we should seek the basis for the status relationship of different national ethnics in the pattern of conflict relationship among the nations involved. There seem to be two principal situations in which subordinate nationalities may be related to the dominant state: (a) that in which the entire national group is included within the dominant state, such as the many nationalities in-

---

[26]For a discussion of Jewish nationalism and the Zionist movement, see Louis E. Levinthal, "The Case for a Jewish Commonwealth in Palestine," *The Annals,* Vol. 240, July 1945, pp. 89–98. Says Levinthal: ". . . the Jewish people, as a people, has been homeless since A.D. 70. This national homelessness has prevented the free, normal, and creative development of Jewish cultural, spiritual, and religious values . . . a publicly recognized and legally secured national home will serve as a cultural, spiritual, and religious center, enriching Jewish life wherever Jews live." Ibid., p. 96.

cluded within the Russian and the Austro-Hungarian states before 1917; and (b) that in which only a fraction of an independent nation is included within the dominant state, such as the Italians in France or the Germans in Poland. In these situations the pattern of inter-nationality relationship will tend to be determined by the fortune of the nations in world politics and diplomacy.

To be sure, the immediate historical causes of the development of nationalism in a subordinate national group which is wholly included in a superordinate state will vary with the peculiarities of the inter-national history and of the culture of the peoples involved. But we should expect such peoples to be intensely stirred by great wars and by the waves of idealism which ordinarily accompany them. After World War I many subordinate nationalities, mainly in the Baltic and Balkan areas, organized sovereign states.

Where the subordinate nationality is only a comparatively small fraction of a dominant nation, its behavior and fate will be determined principally by the power relationship existing between its parent nation and other great nations. This relationship, of course, may be exceed-ingly involved—indeed, no less so than the story of international wars and diplomacy. To illustrate—the Germans in Poland, Denmark, the Netherlands, Belgium, Luxemburg, France, Switzerland, Italy, Austria, Czechoslovakia, Hungary, Rumania, and so on, will present quite different problems for these states as Germany moves through its cycle of frightful power to defeat. If we could imagine the United States being defeated by, say, Japan, we could also imagine a quite different problem presented to the South American countries by various Euro-pean and Asiatic subordinate nationalities.

Probably the reason why the United States does not have so serious a subordinate-nationality problem as most continental European coun-tries is that it did not develop in a similar matrix of international con-flict. To be sure, its peculiar institutions and economic base—especially the relative fluidity of its social-status system—are contributing influ-ences. The United States, like most American countries, is a nation of immigrants. It is English-speaking without being British. The French in Louisiana have less reason to be nationalistic than the French in Canada; in Canada the British and the French tend to be subnationali-ties reflecting the nationalistic rivalries of their parent countries.

Just as the subordinate nationalities of a single parent nation experi-ence different fortunes in different dominant states, so also we should expect a variety of subordinate nationalities in one state to have more or less favorable status as power groups. Among the subnationalities of

European origin in the United States, the English probably have the highest status, while some one or more of the Balkan nationalities, probably the Turks, have the lowest status. The status of the Asiatic and African nationalities is complicated by racial stereotypes. However, we should probably not say that differences in language are the bases of conflict among nationalities. The bases are nationalism and the existing pattern of power relationship. Yet we should expect that, other things being equal, the greater the disparity of culture between nationalities, the greater the opportunity for the development of national antagonism.

In the United States the prestige of Americanism and the economic and political advantages available to the assimilated "foreigner" tend to lead to assimilation. In fact, in this situation of persons of different nationality we may think of them as the "foreign-born," for assimilation rather than nationalism tends to be the controlling social attitude. The different nationality groups are seldom regarded as subnations. Some of them, like the English and the French, rapidly lose themselves in the general population, and such groups as the Italians and Poles seek particularly shelter and sympathetic contact in national communities, so that the pains of assimilation may be more easily endured.

Unlike certain situations in Europe, no nationality group in the United States can reasonably hope to become independent and secede, while the disadvantages of gaining political recognition as a subordinate nation are apparently so great that no national group seems to desire it. In the United States, then, aggressive nationalism among minor nationalities is rather unknown. Consequently the group life of the various nationalities may be thought of as tribal rather than nationalistic, and the problem becomes more nearly one of assimilation than of nationalistic conflict. As we have seen, however, in the case of such groups as the Chinese, Japanese, and Mexicans, nationality problems are complicated by racial antagonisms.

Nationalism and Intolerance

Professor Salo Baron submits a "law of anti-Semitism," which may be stated briefly as follows: The larger the number of nationalities within one state, the less the likelihood of the development of anti-Semitism within that state. He defines three types of state-nationality situations: (a) those in which the purview of political power of the State coincides with the nationality, *the national State,* such as France and Italy, "because the slight minorities within their territories do not

change effectively their national complexion"; (b) those in which the
State includes many nationalities, *the State of nationalities,* such as
Poland, Czechoslovakia, and Russia; and (c) those in which the State
includes only part of a nationality, the whole being divided among two
or more states, *the part-of-a-nationality-state,* such as "the German
nationality, which is divided between two independent and separate
States, Germany and Austria, with important sections in" other countries. "These . . . are the three types of States under which the Jewish people have lived in the Diaspora. If we . . . consider the treatment of Jewry under these various types of States, we shall . . . be
able to formulate our law as follows: *The status of the Jew is most
favorable in pure states of nationalities, most unfavorable in national
states, and somewhat between the two extremes in states which include
part of a nationality only.*"[27] And in support of this hypothesis Baron
continues:

The reason is self-evident. The national state, feeling strongly the
strangeness of the Jew in its otherwise homogeneous body national, has
always tried to eliminate it by full assimilation, which often took the
shape of enforced conversion, or of full exclusion, which generally meant
expulsion. The state of nationalities, being composed of many different
groups, [is] less concerned about the existence of another distinct element,
and could see more clearly the meritorious qualities of a group different
from all the others. . . . In the [part-of-a-nationality state] the pyscho-
logical situation [is] somewhat similar to that of the national state, but
the lack of complete unity often precludes a uniform policy and expul-
sions from one section are nullified by admissions into other regions.[28]

In other words, the greater the national solidarity within any given
state, the greater the likelihood of anti-Semitism. Putting it still otherwise, anti-Semitism is an inverse function of national solidarity within
independent states. But this hypothesis is hardly a complete explanation
of anti-Semitism; moreover, Baron's presentation of historical support
is not always convincing. There may be a high correlation between the
incidence of multinationality states and tolerance; the correlation of itself, however, may not explain anti-Semitism. If the multinationality
State happens to be an empire, the subjects may be a congeries of
mutually alien peoples.

It does not seem to be the mere objective existence of a larger number of nationalities within the State which produces favorable treatment of the Jews but rather the extent to which the State finds a policy

[27]Op. cit., p. 506. (Italics are Baron's.)
[28]Ibid., p. 506.

of "nationality" *laissez faire* most suitable to the continuance of its rule. When the State becomes militant in its attempt to achieve solidarity among its nationalities on some basis of common culture, such as a common religion or a common destiny, anti-Semitism may arise.

To be sure, it should be easier for a state that has already achieved a high degree of national solidarity to become anti-Semitic. But a state with a nationally homogeneous population is likely to recognize foreign groups of any kind more easily and become antagonistic to them also. Apparently a social group becomes intolerant not merely because it recognizes an alien group in its midst but rather because it is able successfully to blame that alien group for some frustration to social aspiration or for instrumenting social dysphoria. Anti-Semitism, it seems, could be explained only in consideration of the peculiar unassimilability of the Jews and the social situation developing about them in relation to other peoples.

Race Prejudice, Class Conflict, and Nationalism

The United States has set the pattern of Oriental exclusion for such countries as Canada and Australia. On the Pacific Coast, and in California especially, a distinct and rather involved racial situation has developed; perhaps it may be thought of as the completion of a "race-relations cycle." Here, because of the rapid cultural advancement of these colored people, the natural history of race relations has been greatly expedited. Like all racial situations, we approach this one also from the point of view of the white man's initiative—he is the actor in chief; the Asiatics react to their best advantage.

The Asiatics came into California because there was a great demand there for their labor; they came because the relatively high wages in California enticed them. But the "pull" was far more significant than the "push." No matter how great the lure of higher wages, they could by no means have "invaded" the Coast if the encouragement and inducement of certain hard-pressed white employers did not facilitate it. The great wave of Asiatic common labor began to move upon the Western Hemisphere after the decline of the Negro slave trade—after 1845 especially. The West Indies, the Pacific Coast of America, and even South and East Africa received their quotas. The Asiatics came not as slaves but mainly as coolies; and gradually, among others, California and other Pacific states had their Chinese and Japanese problem; Trinidad and South Africa, their East Indian problem; and Cuba, its Chinese problem.

These "coolies" came mostly as contract laborers, some form of indentured-servant relationship; and "Wherever they were imported, they were used as substitutes for slave labor in plantation areas."[28a] The Japanese, however, came later and probably with somewhat more personal initiative. Carey McWilliams summarizes the process of their coming:

With the conclusion of the Reciprocity Treaty of 1876 between Hawaii and the United States—which opened the islands for American capital—the sugar interests of Hawaii began to clamor for Japanese labor. As early as 1868 these interests had "practically stolen" 147 Japanese for plantation labor in the islands. Most of these initial immigrants, however, were returned to Japan in response to a sharp note of protest. The execution of the Reciprocity Treaty was followed, in 1886, by the adoption of the Hawaiian-Japanese Labor Convention. It was this agreement that, for the first time, "officially opened the doors for the immigration of Japanese laborers to the outside world." Under the terms of the agreement approximately 180,000 Japanese were sent to Hawaii—the largest single body of workers that Japan sent to any land.[29]

Following the Chinese Exclusion Act of 1882, Chinese workers on the Pacific Coast became less available and employers began to look to the Japanese for the supply of their labor deficiency. As H. A. Millis observes with respect to the agricultural interest: "Many farmers faced the practical problem of finding substitutes for the disappearing Chinese, who had shaped their investments and methods."[30] A large fraction of the immigrants came by way of Hawaii. Thus in 1910 the United States Immigration Commission reported:

With the strong demand for common labor prevailing in the west, the Japanese contractors on the Coast, and especially those doing business in San Francisco and Seattle, induced many to come to the United States. Some of these contractors were for a time regularly represented by the agents sent to Honolulu; recourse was made to advertising in the Japanese papers published there, cheap rates were secured, and in some instances assistance was given in other ways to those desiring to reach the mainland.[31]

The Chinese, the Japanese, and a much smaller number of East Indians, then, came to the Coast as workers—mainly as common

---

[28a]Cary McWilliams, *Brothers under the Skin,* p. 85.

[29]*Prejudice,* p. 304.

[30]*The Japanese Problem in the United States,* p. 109.

[31]*Reports of the U.S. Immigration Commission: Immigrants in Industries,* Vol. 23, p. 14.

laborers.[32] And this is probably the principal source of antagonism in this racial situation—a conflict between workers of different races. Before discussing this, however, it may be well to observe the numerical relationship among the races involved. The Asiatics were always a smaller minority in California than Negroes have been in the South. In 1920, at the height of the anti-Japanese agitation in California, the Japanese constituted about two per cent of the population, and in 1940 about one and one half per cent. The Chinese population fell from about nine per cent in 1860 to six tenths of one per cent in 1940.

A remarkable fact about the California anti-Oriental movements is that they have been mainly initiated by white workers instead of exploiters of labor, the class which we have attempted to show is responsible for all modern racial antagonism. In this respect the California situation appears to be the very opposite of the Negro-white relationship in the South. But first let us review briefly the role of labor in the anti-Orientalism on the Coast.

According to Lucile Eaves, ". . . from the early fifties to the present time, there have been organizations in which all classes of wage-workers joined to promote the exclusion of Asiatic labor. It is the one subject upon which there has never been the slightest difference of opinion, the one measure on which it has always been possible to obtain concerted action."[33] And further: "By the persistent efforts of the working people of California first the state and then the nation have been converted to the policy of Oriental exclusion."[34] Ever since the middle of the nineteenth century, then, when California was indeed a very young state, white workers reached consensus against the Asiatic worker.

The history of white-worker-Asiatic antagonism in California is one of considerable agitation and periodic violence against Chinese and Japanese. The influence of organized labor in politics has been stronger in California than in any other state of the United States, and apparently no small part of this influence is due to the solidarity which labor has been able to develop about a continuing menace to its welfare—the threat of competition from Asiatic labor.

---

[32]Concerning the Japanese, Dr. Millis concludes: "Most of those who immigrated directly or indirectly to the Pacific Coast previous to 1908 came to begin as wage earners on the lowest rung of the industrial ladder. They came to Japanese boarding houses and from there most of them secured their first employment as section hands on the railway, as agricultural laborers in the field and orchard, or as domestic servants and house cleaners in the large cities." Op. cit., p. 31.

[33]*A History of California Labor Legislation,* p. 6.

[34]Ibid., p. 105.

This reaction of labor, however, is not peculiarly a racial phenomenon; the conflict is essentially between employer and worker. Indeed, workers will react to inanimate objects, to machinery, in a characteristic way if the latter is introduced suddenly as a significant substitute for labor. Workers have been known to riot and attack machines in a way not unlike their attacks upon other workers who, because of lower standards, are favored by employers. In 1844 the leader of a British trade union wrote:

Machinery has done the work. Machinery has left them in rags and without any wages at all. Machinery has crowded them in cellars, has immured them in prisons worse than Parisian bastilles, has forced them from their country to seek in other lands the bread denied to them here. I look upon all improvements which tend to lessen the demand for human labor as the deadliest curse that could possibly fall on the heads of our working classes, and I hold it to be the duty of every working potter—the highest duty—to obstruct by all legal means the introduction of the scourge into any branch of his trade.[35]

Although today trade unionists do not express themselves in this way, the attitude is not lost; workers merely approach the problem differently. They insist upon sharing the profits which accrue to the employer because of the increased productivity of the machine. But competition with substandard workers puts standard workers in an even more disadvantageous position in their struggle with capitalists. As one anti-Oriental puts it:

Our grievance is against the humble, tireless, mean-living, unalterably alien, field and factory hand, who cuts wages, works for a pittance and lives on less, dwells in tenements which would nauseate the American pig, and presents the American workman the alternative of committing suicide or coming down to John Chinaman's standard of wages and living. . . . Self-protection is sufficient ground on which to base exclusion."[36]

[35]Edmund Potter, head of the Potters' Trade Union, quoted by Sidney and Beatrice Webb, *Industrial Democracy*, 1920 ed., pp. 392–93; see also W. Cunningham, *The Growth of English Industry and Commerce*, 5th ed., Vol. I, pp. 444–45.

[36]San Francisco *Bulletin*, November 18, 1901, quoted by Elmer Clarence Sandmeyer, *The Anti-Chinese Movement in California*, p. 106. That this attitude is not essentially racial may be indicated by a similar expression of feeling against white immigrants on the East Coast of the United States: "This unlimited and unrestricted admission of foreign emigrants is a serious injury to the native laboring population, socially, morally, religiously, and politically; socially, by overstocking the labor market and thus keeping wages down; morally and religiously, by unavoidable contact and intercourse; and politically, by consequence of want of employment and low wages, making them needy and dependent, whereby they become the easy prey or willing tools of designing and unprincipled politicians. And in this way the native population is deteriorated and made poor, needy and subservient: and these realities produce want of self-respect, hopelessness, laxity in morals, recklessness, delinquencies, and crimes." From *Emigration, Emigrants, and Know-Nothings*, by a Foreigner, quoted by Lawrence Guy Brown, *Immigration*, p. 94.

It should be noted that this attitude is not an exploitative attitude; it is a conflict between two exploited groups generated by the desire of one group of workers to keep up the value of its labor power by maintaining its scarcity. In Trinidad, British West Indies, Negro workers, in almost identical terms, fought against the continued introduction of indentured East Indian laborers;[37] and between 1930 and 1932 Negroes on the South Side of Chicago demonstrated against the employment of white "foreigners" by certain public utilities.[38] However, there is no racial antagonism between Negroes and East Indians in Trinidad, and it would be somewhat of an inversion of reason to expect Negro Chicagoans to have race prejudice toward white "foreigners." We may cite, of course, many illustrations of this attitude among whites in the United States—beginning, perhaps, with the early anti-Irish attitude in the East. Every conflict between strikers and "scabs" produces similar attitudes among the strikers. In 1910 the platform of the Socialist party of California contained this plank:

We favor all legislative measures tending to prevent the immigration of strike breakers and contract laborers and the mass immigration and importation of Mongolian or East Indian labor, caused or stimulated by the employing classes for the purpose of weakening the organization of American labor and of lowering the standard of life of the American workers.[39]

Professor H. A. Millis presents a case of labor displacements in Florin, a small town southeast of Sacramento, which has been called "the best locality in the United States for the study of Japanese agricultural life":

The basket factory [in Florin] was established ten years ago. At first most of the employees were white women and girls of the community. They were found to be unsatisfactory in certain respects and were rapidly displaced by Japanese. . . . It is said that the white women were difficult to manage, could not be depended upon to report for work regularly and, though paid by the piece, did not wish to work more than ten hours per day, or work overtime, or on Sundays, as it was thought the interest of the business required. In all these matters the Japanese were more acceptable to their employers, who are white men prominently connected with shipping firms in Sacramento. Paid by the piece, they formerly worked twelve to fourteen hours per day, and on Sunday, when the demand was such as

---

[37]See *Report of the Committee on Emigration from India to the Crown Colonies and Protectorates,* London, 1910.

[38]For newspaper stories of this movement, see the Chicago *Whip* from September 30, 1930, onward.

[39]Quoted in *Reports of the U. S. Immigration Commission,* Vol. 23, p. 173.

to make long hours profitable. At present all the employees, except a representative of the non-resident manager, are Japanese.[40]

This apparently racial conflict, then, is in fact an extension of the modern political-class conflict. The employer needs labor, cheap labor; he finds this in Asiatic workers and displaces white, more expensive labor with them. White workers then react violently against the Asiatics, indeed, not unlike the way in which early handicraft workers reacted against the machine. On this point Eliot Grinnell Mears observes: "The organized-labor attitude . . . while strenuously opposed in its public utterances to Oriental immigration, is actually interested in racial questions only in so far as they affect competitive conditions in industry. . . . The issue is capital and labor, not race and labor."[41]

On the Coast the Oriental may be thought of as one significant aspect of the subject matter in the conflict between capital and labor. "The Chinaman," says the Sacramento *Record Union* (January 10, 1879), "is here because his presence pays, and he will remain and continue to increase so long as there is money in him. When the time comes that he is no longer profitable *that* generation will take care of him and will send him back."[42] And Sandmeyer observes:

The Chinese were charged with contributing to monopoly in connection with the great landlords and the railroads. . . . Since these landed interests were among the most ardent advocates of continued Chinese immigration the charge was frequently voiced that California was in danger of

[40]Op. cit., p. 155. And Millis continues: "Laborers reacted most strongly . . . because they thought their standards were imperiled. The Chinese acquired a firm position in the manufacture of cigars, shoes, and garments in San Francisco. They were used to defeat the ends of organized labor, and labor unionists reacted strongly against them as they do against other 'scabs' and cheap workmen. In other parts of the country, for example in the manufacture of shoes in Massachusetts, there was talk of hiring the Chinese to take the places of striking union men and to control the labor situation. They were a menace—as workingmen saw them. Were not the Japanese also? Did they not begin very much as the Chinese? . . . Were they not employed as strike breakers in the manufacture of shoes in San Francisco? White laborers reacted against the Japanese because they competed on a different level. It does not matter so much that their competition never extended far when their immigration was not greatly restricted. It was potential in any case. . . . The labor unions stand for the setting of progressive standards and offer strong resistance when any group of men or set of circumstances threaten or seem to threaten these standards. Without organization, workingmen react in very much the same way in the face of new competition." Ibid., pp. 242–43.

[41]*Resident Orientals on the American Pacific Coast*, pp. 93–94.

[42]Quoted by Elmer Clarence Sandmeyer, op. cit., pp. 31–32. The author continues: ". . . employers and those seeking employment differed widely concerning the effect of the Chinese in the State. With few exceptions employers considered them beneficial as a flexible supply of labor, cheap, submissive, and efficient; but those whose only capital was their ability to work were almost unanimous in the opinion that the Chinese were highly detrimental to the best interests of the state." Ibid., p. 33.

having a "caste system of lords and serfs" foisted upon it. . . . The anti-Chinese element in California looked upon these "monopolists" as among the chief mainstays of the Chinese. . . . These great landowners were regarded as worse than the plantation owners of slave days.[43]

The famous California Workingmen's Party organized in 1877 was a radical, outspokenly anti-capitalist assemblage. The leaders "called upon the workmen and their friends in every county, town, city, and hamlet to organize branches of the Party at once, and prepare for a campaign that would enable them to draft a constitution which should place the government in the hands of the working people."[44] In fact, the Workingmen's Party in 1878 practically succeeded in controlling the California Constitutional Convention and got into the new constitution a considerable part of its "radical" platform.[45]

The workers were able in large measure to defeat the exploitative purpose of the ruling class in California partly by the help of that class itself. Capitalist exploiters of labor have some necessity to keep their labor freely exploitable, and one means of accomplishing this end is to keep it degraded. In California both Chinese and Japanese proved to be exceedingly intractable as a permanent labor force, and this tended to bring the primary elements of racial antagonism into play. Concerning the situation after the Chinese had been fairly well subdued, Carey McWilliams (quoting the San Francisco *Chronicle*) says: "By 1905 the fight had been narrowed down to the Japanese. 'The Chinese,' the *Chronicle* observed, 'are faithful laborers and do not buy lands. The Japanese are unfaithful laborers and do buy lands.' "[46] In this connection the United States Immigration Commission also observes:

The representatives of several . . . boards of trade, even while opposed to the immigration of Japanese, stated that their communities would gladly make use of more Chinese if they were available. The reasons advanced for the favorable opinion of the Chinese as against the Japanese were their superiority as workmen, their faithfulness to employer, a less general desire to acquire possessions of land or to engage in business, and the absence of a desire on their part to associate with others on equal terms.[47]

On the farm these extraordinarily temporary laborers economized their earnings in wages and aspired forthwith to become independent farmers. To be sure, the Asiatics were not brought to California to be-

[43]Ibid., pp. 32–33. See also p. 85, and Eliot Grinnell Mears, op. cit., p. 56.
[44]Lucile Eaves, op. cit., p. 31.
[45]Ibid., p. 36.
[46]Op. cit., p. 19.
[47]*Reports of the U.S. Immigration Commission,* Vol. 23, p. 174.

come farmers; they were brought or encouraged to come as wage workers. Therefore, when a government survey reported: "There are probably more white laborers working for Oriental farmers than there are Oriental laborers working for American farmers,"[48] the anti-Oriental antagonism of the farmer became aggravated. In California a number of laws were enacted which more or less effectively excluded the Oriental from the privilege of farming.

As businessmen, also, Chinese and Japanese are out of their place. They are looked upon by other businessmen as foreign competitors, with the characteristic relationship of a struggle for markets. As H. A. Millis points out with reference to both the businessman and farmer:

Laundrymen in San Francisco and elsewhere, barbers, proprietors of small tailor shops, and others have protested when the Japanese have entered the circle of competition and cut prices or brought about a loss of patronage. The cry of "race problem" has been employed to accomplish economic ends. The growers of vegetables about Tacoma and Seattle, and the growers of berries about Los Angeles have protested ineffectively when the acreage has been increased by Japanese growers and prices have fallen. The newcomers "ruined the market," it was said.[49]

As business competitors the Asiatics meet their most powerful white antagonists. Confronted with the negative sanctions of the latter group, they are indeed friendless. But, as we have seen, employers have been on the whole more in favor of than against them. Yet the masterly attitude of the employer group may be indicated by a suggestion to Governor William D. Stephens by a California businessman: ". . . the Mexicans are employed to do practically all the common labor in the Imperial Irrigation District. . . . If this Mexican labor could be extended up through the entire state, 'the white farmers could do the managing and superintending of the farms, as the Japanese and

[48]*California and the Oriental: Report of State Board of Control of California, to Gov. Wm. D. Stephens,* rev. ed., January 1, 1922, p. 115. This report continues: "The Japanese farmers and every member in the family, physically able to do so, including the wife and little children, work in the field for long hours, practically from daylight to dark, on Sundays and holidays, and in the majority of cases, live in shacks or under conditions far below the standards required and desired by Americans. . . . American farmers cannot successfully compete with the Japanese farmers if the Americans adhere to the American principles so universally approved in America." Pp. 116–17.

[49]*Op. cit.,* p. 243. On this point Raymond Leslie Buell makes the following comment: ". . . if the anti-Japanese laws [prohibiting the purchasing or leasing of land] are religiously enforced, they will not solve America's Japanese problem. They merely transfer the Japanese from the farms to the cities. . . . Japanese competition in industry is likely to prove more harmful to American labor than if Japanese remain on farms where white labor is scarce." "Again the Yellow Peril," in Julia E. Johnsen, ed., *Japanese Exclusion,* p. 43.

Hindus do now, and we could get along very well without our Japanese . . . in the agricultural pursuits of the state."[50]

Although the sporadic aggression of the employers gave considerable encouragement and stimulation to the anti-Asiatic movement among white workers, the latter may not have achieved the purpose of Asiatic exclusion so completely had it not been for their favorable alliance with Southern politics. It may seem strange that the politicians of the South, who advocate the interest of a ruling class that has fairly well subdued white labor through the widespread exploitation of black workers, should deem it advisable to take the side of the workingmen of California in their struggle against their employers' desire to exploit cheap Oriental labor. And yet it was probably the weight of the Southern vote in Congress which made it possible for California to put over its national policy of anti-Orientalism.

In the South organized labor is weaker than in any other section of the country; on the Pacific Coast it is stronger. The South has been powerfully dominated by a white exploiting class, so much so, indeed, that white labor has never been able effectively to organize against it. White labor had no voice at all against the immigration of black workers into the South; as a consequence white labor was considerably degraded.[51] In fact, the white common people of the South were so thoroughly propagandized that they actually helped the master class to fight the Civil War in the interest of the continued exploitation of black labor on an extremely low level.[52] In the South there is a biracial system; and since the Negroes are degraded, the work which Negroes ordinarily do also tends to be degraded. The prospects on the Coast after 1850 were very favorable for the development of a biracial system, with Asiatic coolies taking a place similar to that of Negroes in the South and part of the white common people assuming the status of poor whites.

---

[50]*California and the Oriental,* etc., p. 136.

[51]For a discussion of faint antagonism of white workers against the competition of free Negro workers and slaves, see Richard B. Morris, *Government and Labor in Early America,* pp. 182–88.

[52]In this connection Carey McWilliams observes: "With the narrow construction placed on the Fourteenth Amendment in the famous Slaughter House decision in 1873 and the decision in 1875 which held the Civil Rights Statute unconstitutional, the Supreme Court had, so to speak, let the bars down so far as the Negro problem was concerned. Prior to this time the South had shown a lively interest in the possibility of substituting Chinese coolie labor for Negro slave labor. It had been suggested in Memphis in 1869 that such a substitution might be in order; and on several occasions about this time Southern planters had visited California with this purpose in mind. Once they realized, however, that they had again regained control of the Negro, their interest in Chinese labor swiftly abated." *Brothers under the Skin,* p. 83.

But certain historical events, one of them the discovery of gold in California, brought a great wave of highly independent white workers into violent competition with the Asiatics, thus frustrating the tendency toward a bipartite racial system. All the whites could not take the position of a small ruling class because they always outnumbered the Asiatics. The alternative was to organize and stop the tendency toward the situation which developed in the South.

Immigration, of course, is a problem of the Federal Government; and the influencing of national policies may not be easy, especially when it is in the interest of workingmen mainly in one state.[53] However, the South came to the rescue of California not because of an interest in the white workers or dislike for the exploiters of Oriental labor but because it wanted to develop a national tradition to the effect that when the interests of a colored people come into conflict with those of white people the former must always give way. The problem was defined as a conflict between the whites and the Asiatics in California. If this were admitted, then white people in the South should be conceded the right to control "their" Negroes without interference from the national government. This logic was possible in spite of the fact that the articulate white people in the South were masters, while those on the Coast were organized workers. Carey McWilliams puts it in this way:

This correlation between the Negro problem and the Chinese question is clearly indicated in the vote in Congress on the important measures introduced after 1876 affecting the Chinese. Without exception, these measures were passed by the vote of representatives from the Pacific Coast and the Deep South. Again and again, Southern Senators and Congressmen lined up with representatives of the Pacific Coast to railroad through Congress measures aimed at driving out the Chinese.[54]

But did the white workers of California have no other alternative? Suppose a very significant number of Asiatic workers had actually established residence on the Coast, could they not have been organized also? They probably could and would have been organized—even though with considerably more difficulty than if they had been white workers. The cultural bar between the European and the Asiatic

---

[53]As we have seen, organized labor had considerable influence in the politics of California. "The labor vote had attained such proportions in numbers and solidarity as to make elections to public office almost impossible without its support, and it was generally understood that in order to secure the labor vote a candidate must declare himself against the Chinese." Elmer Clarence Sandmeyer, op. cit., p. 57; see also Lucile Eaves, op. cit., p. 23.

[54]Op. cit., p. 83; see also Lucile Eaves, op. cit., p. 176.

makes it difficult and at certain stages practically impossible for the two groups to reach that common understanding necessary for concerted action against the employer. Moreover, the first generation of Asiatic workers is ordinarily very much under the control of labor contractors and employers, hence it is easier for the employer to frustrate any plans for their organization. Clearly this cultural bar helped to antagonize white workers against the Asiatics. The latter were conceived of as being in alliance with the employer. It would probably have taken two or three generations before, say, the East Indian low-caste worker on the Coast became sufficiently Americanized to adjust easily to the policies and aims of organized labor. Eventually, however, they would have been organized just as Negroes are being gradually organized.

But since the Asiatic was not yet a very considerable element in the population, the white workers decided not to listen to arguments from other interest groups concerning the possibility of assimilating him. Although it must be quite obvious that Orientals have been, are being, and can be assimilated to Western culture, there has been very much argument on this very question. Ordinarily their assimilation is to the advantage of white workers, for the assimilated Asiatic either ceases to be a laborer or becomes more easily organizable. Nevertheless, workers may become frantic when it is argued that since the Asiatics are assimilable they should be allowed to immigrate in unlimited numbers. They will naturally use every means, including those developed by the employer class, to demonstrate the "impossibility" of assimilating the Asiatic.

On the other hand, the assimilation of colored workers is ordinarily against the primary interest of labor exploiters. The assimilated colored worker is either lost for exploitation or becomes intractable; therefore, it is in the interest of employers to convince a certain public that the Asiatics are unassimilable. Success in this conviction will tend seriously to retard assimilation. Here again a basic conflict of interest seems to converge in an identical argument, and in this situation it is sometimes difficult to discover the interest behind the rationalization. In fact, an employer having an immediate need for more labor may even contend that the Asiatic is readily assimilated. The following illustrates the nature of the arguments against assimilation:

Granting equality, the standards of the races are almost as opposite as the poles, and there is no possibility of a common trend ever being evolved. Assimilation is impossible. True, there are a few marriages here and there, but they are the exceptions that prove the rule. . . . The two peoples run along different lines physically. As they differ in color so do they in tradition, habits and aspirations.[55]

We should recognize, however, that many arguments in favor of the impossibility of Oriental assimilation are in reality arguments in favor of the prohibition of Oriental assimilation. By legal enactment the anti-assimilationists prohibit intermarriage between whites and "Mongolians," provide for separate schools and for residential segregation. In illustration, K. K. Kawakami tells us: "A number of Japanese farmers and business men asked the leading Americans of the city [i.e., Lodi, a farming town] to be their guests at a dinner. . . . Upon the heels of this meeting came a resolution of the Lodi post of the American Legion, condemning the American participation in the banquet and declaring: '. . . that we look with disfavor and disapproval on any gathering intended to promote good fellowship and social affiliation between the Japanese and our own people.' "[56] And without apparently recognizing the intent of the anti-assimilationists, Kiichi Kanzaki declares:

Instead of agitation, America should meet the problem with an attitude predicated on the policy of how to Americanize and assimilate the Japanese that are here, so that they may not be left as a foreign and isolated group in America.[57]

Notwithstanding this, however, we cannot assume that the Chinese and Japanese culture fell off like water on a duck's back. Consider, for instance, the simple pigtail, the queue, of the Chinese. To cut it off the Chinaman may have to go through a terrific personality disturbance, and to keep it may forever limit the possibility of Americans being at ease in his company. As Millis observes: "With a different language, with queue and different dress, with no family life, with different customs and steeled against change as they were, the reaction against them was strong and immediate when they ceased to be objects of curiosity."[58]

In the end the Chinese on the Coast have been practically gypsyfied.[59] "The Chinaman was a good loser." He has withdrawn from the

---

[55]John S. Chambers, "The Japanese Invasion," *The Annals,* Vol. XCIII, January 1921, pp. 24–25.

[56]"The Japanese Question," *The Annals,* Vol. XCIII, January 1921, p. 82.

[57]"Is the Japanese Menace in America a Reality?", *The Annals,* Vol. XCIII, January 1921, p. 97.

[58]Op. cit., pp. 240–41. To be sure, a master race need not suffer in this way. According to Jesse F. Steiner: "The American in Japan never intends to become a Japanese—he is not laughed at because of his customs. He feels that his customs have prestige. But the Japanese must conform in America." Op. cit., pp. 93–94.

[59]On this point see R. D. McKenzie, "The Oriental Invasion," *Journal of Applied Sociology,* Vol. 10, 1925, pp. 125–26.

struggle; he is no longer a significant threat to the standards of white labor. He may now be treated with a high degree of indifference or even amiability. "Except for a few large agricultural corporations, the Chinese are generally engaged in small commercial enterprises supplying the needs of their countrymen. Owing to the effectiveness of the Chinese Exclusion Act, the Chinese can not be considered a menace for the future."[60]

But the Japanese have never given up; their youthful nationalism prevents them from becoming an inconsequential people on the Coast. As one observer puts it: "The Chinese and the Hindoo may have intelligence; may have industry, but they are not aggressive, they do not seek to dominate, nor are they backed by powerful nations intent upon the domination of the Pacific Ocean, if not the world."[61]

In some respects, race relations on the Coast are internationality relations; therefore, the relationship of whites to Hindus, Chinese, or Japanese have depended to some extent upon the power relationship of the parent nations of these peoples. The local attitude toward the Asiatics has been constantly involved with international treaties and diplomacy, and Japan has been the most determined nation with which the United States has had to deal. It is not, of course, that Japanese are more nationalistic than Americans, but rather that the Japanese have had to be aggressive in their struggle for position among the actually superior white nations. Discrimination against Japanese on the Coast naturally has been taken as insults to Japan. Moreover, as H. A. Millis observes: "[Japanese] emigrants have been treated . . . almost as colonists."[62]

---

[60]*California and the Oriental*, etc., p. 115. And according to the *Tentative Findings of the Survey of Race Relations*, 1925, ". . . there has been a clear tendency on the part of the Chinese to withdraw from competitive forms of labor and business and to enter less productive urban callings. In some cities, notably in border and sea-coast communities, there is a pronounced tendency for an increasing number of Chinese to engage in lotteries and other disorganizing callings." Quoted by Eliot Grinnell Mears, op. cit., p. 197.

[61]John S. Chambers, op. cit., p. 25. And Carey McWilliams explains: "All first-generation immigrant groups in America are inclined to be nationalistic. Until 1924, the Issei [or first-generation Japanese] were probably no more inclined in this direction than any other immigrant group; but afterwards they did develop, in some cases, what has been termed a 'suppressed nationality psychosis.' Nationalistic tendencies increased. They fought to retain the language schools despite the fact that the schools themselves were an admitted failure. They thought that the schools would be one means of instilling in their children a sense of pride in their background. They thought they might assist in bridging the chasm that had begun to separate the two generations. Their children, they said, were in danger of developing an inferiority complex and of sinking 'to the level of Indians.'" *Prejudice*, pp. 95–96.

[62]Op. cit., p. 249.

The more nationalistic a people, the less will be its tendency to assimilate, the more it will tend to value its culture, especially its non-material culture, its religion. Moreover, when two highly nationalistic groups come into contact, there will be mutual fear, distrust, and intolerance. On the Coast intolerance for the Japanese has been partly due to nationalistic conflicts. As one anti-Japanese saw it: "The irrigated part of Placer County is practically a little Japan. . . . Controlling the land, they can perpetuate the ideas, habits, religion and loyalties of the mother country and do this indefinitely."[63] Difference in religion may be one basic reason for intolerance for the Chinese and Japanese. A different god implies a different system of morality. "Brotherhood," says Marshall De Motte, an anti-Asiatic, "implies one father and cannot exist between peoples holding entirely different ideas as to the Fatherhood of God and man's responsibility to man."[64]

That racial antagonism is not determined by biological, innate cultural incapacity or inferiority of the subordinate group is demonstrated by this racial situation. Sometimes it is openly admitted that the Japanese are a culturally superior people. On this very account, however, it is most difficult to exploit them and consequently they are most undesirable. "We admire their industry and cleverness, but for that very reason, being a masterful people, they are more dangerous. They are not content to work for wages as do the Chinese . . . but are always seeking control of the farm and of the crop."[65] David Warren Ryder puts it paradoxically: "Because they are orderly and not in jail, because they are thrifty and energetic, because they marry, set up homes and raise families, they are 'dangerous,' they are a 'menace,' they 'threaten white supremacy.' "[66] In fact, within limits, the greater the tendency of

---

[63]Elwood Mead, "The Japanese Land Problem in California," *The Annals,* Vol. XCIII, January 1921, p. 51. Carey McWilliams also observes: ". . . witnesses before the Tolan Committee advanced the usual stock arguments against the Japanese. . . . Particular emphasis was placed on the language schools, the charge of dual citizenship, and the influence of Buddhism and Shintoism upon the resident Japanese." Op. cit., p. 121.

[64]"California—White or Yellow." *The Annals,* Vol. XCIII, January 1921, p. 23.

[65]Hon. James D. Phelan, "Why California Objects to the Japanese Invasion," *The Annals,* Vol. XCIII, January 1921, p. 17. On this point Col. John P. Irish says: "As the Chinese had been condemned for their imputed vices, so the Japanese are condemned for their imputed virtues, for their sobriety, their industry, their intelligence and skill, for their respect for law and for their honesty. Dr. Benjamin Ide Wheeler, President emeritus of the State University of California, in a speech against them said: 'Their good taste, persistent industry, their excellent qualities and their virtues render their presence amongst us a pitiful danger.' " "The Japanese Issue in California," *The Annals,* Vol. XCIII, January 1921, p. 75.

[66]"The Japanese Bugaboo," *The Annals,* Vol. XCIII, January 1921, p. 51. See also H. A. Millis, op. cit., p. 139.

an exploited people to overthrow the harness of exploitation, the greater the opposition from their exploiters.

We may conclude, then, that the Asiatics came to the Pacific Coast as an exploitable labor force. There they encountered the violent opposition of white workers. The white workingman's antagonism against the Asiatics was essentially a class conflict between labor and capital. The ruling class never had the opportunity to develop and maintain strong racial antagonism against the Chinese; therefore, when the latter ceased to be a threat to labor they were treated with a high degree of indifference. However, the aggressive nationalism and imperialism of the Japanese excited counternationalism, intolerance, and counterimperialism among American capitalists especially. Since both race prejudice and nationalism are based upon a potential power relationship between groups, we should expect Japanese in the long run to be most respected by the white ruling races because of their remarkable facility in modern warfare. Race relations in the Pacific—in the world, for that matter—have been revolutionized mainly because of the physical might of Japan.

19. *Race and Caste*[1]

Race Relations Physical, Caste Cultural

JUST AS A SUDRA BEGETS ON A BRAHMAN FEMALE A BEING EX-
cluded from the Aryan community, even so a person himself
excluded procreates, with females of the four castes, sons more worthy
of being excluded than himself."[2] This postulate from Manu reveals
graphically a pattern of caste stratification that is the opposite of every
known system of race relations. Thus, if we consider only the two castes
mentioned, Brahman and Sudra,[3] it is obvious that the lawgiver maintains that successive crosses between lower-caste men and pureblood
Brahman women result in offspring of increasing inferiority. In other
words, the mixed progeny of a Sudra and a Brahman woman is very
much superior to the man whose father is, say, one sixty-fourth Sudra
along the male line, while his mother is pure Brahman. Yet so far as
physical difference is concerned, it is clear that the latter must be considered virtually pure Brahman. We are not, of course, assuming here
that there was originally a recognized physical difference between the
two castes; the point is that the meaning of "blood" in caste relationships is not the same as in racial situations.

The crucial symbol of race relations is physical identifiability. When
we speak of Chinese, Indians, Europeans, Negroes, or Filipinos, we
expect responses indicating consciousness of ocular evidence of physical
differentiation. But when we refer to such groups as Chamars, Banyas,
Telis, Doms, Brahmans, Kayasthas, or Jolahas, no sense of physical
distinction need be aroused. We see rather only East Indians. If we are

---

[1] In this chapter we shall refer to conditions of race relations in the United States
almost exclusively. In the succeeding chapter, the problems of race relations will be
discussed analytically.

[2] Manu, X, 30.

[3] We have discussed above some factors concerning the probability that Sudras
constituted a single caste. Unless confusion results, we shall continue to use the
term to represent the lower castes.

familiar with these castes, one name might suggest filth and human degradation, while another might call to mind scrupulous cleanliness and superciliousness, or very likely a certain occupation, or any one of a composite of cultural traits.

To come upon a new caste in the caste system is a matter of no particular moment, but the appearance of a new race is always startling. No Hindu in Brahmanic India is ever expected to know all the castes any more than an American family is expected to know individually all other families in the United States. It is sufficient, for caste characterization, to apply certain established norms to the stranger. A new caste may be consciously organized, yet it is beyond the power of human beings to establish a new race. The caste has almost no capacity for assimilating outsiders; its membership is theoretically closed. On the other hand, there is a natural attraction between races in contact, and sooner or later they amalgamate. The concept of amalgamation is not applicable to castes, for physical *rapprochement* does not affect the distinction or stability of castes. Indeed, historically, caste rigidity in India has proceeded hand in hand with physical amalgamation. It cannot be assumed, however, that the one caused the other. Obviously, when two or more races have amalgamated, all possible "race questions" will have been answered.

It is impossible for a person to become a member of any given race other than by birth; but, although the membership of castes ordinarily is limited by birth, it is quite possible for two or more castes to merge if they so will it—consequences notwithstanding.[4] As we have mentioned above, an individual may be initiated into a caste. In the caste system the heritage which gives him distinction is cultural, hence he might be dispossessed of it; the individual born of a given race, however, inherits physical marks which are not only inalienable but also beyond the discretion of the race itself. It is manifest, then, that to be born within a given race, there is no alternative but to die within it;[5] in the

---

[4] "There is . . . apparently a tendency toward the consolidation of groups at present separated by caste rules. The best instance of such a tendency to consolidate a number of castes into one group is to be found in the grazier castes which aim at combining under the term 'Yadava' Ahirs, Goalas, Gopis, Idaiyans, and perhaps some other castes of milkmen, a movement already effective in 1921. . . . There is little evidence as yet that marriage is being practiced within these consolidating groups, but it is a development the possibility of which may not be overlooked. The Census Superintendent of the Central Provinces quotes 'specific instances' . . . of marriage between members of different sub-castes of Brahmans, and between members of different sub-castes of Kalars, where the union would formerly have been condemned." *Census of India, 1931,* Vol. I, Pt. 1, p. 431.

[5] We are not unmindful here of the phenomenon of passing. However, only physically marginal men pass; hence, they may be said to have been born with the necessary physical characteristics.

case of caste no such obdurate rule obtains. In fact, the individual might abandon his caste at will, while he cannot possibly give up his race.

Race problems, then, are social problems which have reference to groups physically identifiable. Therefore, we should expect two races in contact and having some basic racial antagonism to develop different problems for persons with different degrees of admixture. And such is, in fact, the case. For instance, in the United States a white person with very little Negro blood is confronted with different problems from those which either the pure white or black person must meet. Ordinarily the disinterested public treats this white Negro like a white man and insists that he behave like one. Thus he may be forcibly prevented from sitting among Negroes in public conveyances, while a dark-complexioned Negro may be assaulted on the highway because his Negro wife looks white.

These are but crude indices of the mental conflicts of these people. And so, too, for the various grades of physical distinguishability, the racial problems tend to vary. In the caste system we should not expect to find any such group of marginal persons because the criteria of belonging are not physical marks. A man either belongs to a caste or he does not. There are no half-caste persons in the sense that there are half-race men. The problem which a caste has of knowing its members is of the same order as that of a family's knowing its constituents.

A caste, should it desire to affiliate outsiders, must *admit* them as new members. On the other hand, if a person has the physical marks of another race, he may without any formality whatever assume that race. A white Negro, for example, may decide to "pass," and he will if his appearance does not betray him. But a person may not "pass" into a caste; he can get into it only by formal admission.[6]

After a certain pattern of race relations has been developed, official or even scientific classification of the races has little, if any, effect upon their social relationship. In the caste system, however, an official scale of caste precedence is of considerable importance to the castes concerned. Whether we call all Hindus Caucasians or not, for instance, a light- and a black-complexioned Hindu in the United States must not expect to receive similar social treatment. But in the caste system it is of tremendous difference whether the census labels a caste clean or unclean Sudra. A man in the caste system is known for what he is; in a race system he is known primarily by how he looks.

---

[6] We should mention that reference is here made to the primary endogamous circle and not to the wider class group, such as Brahmans, Chamars, and so on.

When a Hindu girl marries into a higher caste her success is not reckoned in terms of physical criteria, for, according to Western ideas of race superiority, her caste may be physically superior. She marries, so to speak, into a higher culture; into a caste, say, of merchants, priests, or landowners. Interracial marriage, however, always involves problems of amalgamation; and the more pronounced the physical distinction, the more insistent the problems. Race prejudice rests upon physical identifiability; caste prejudice is preoccupied with cultural distinction.

A recognition of this fact may be of significance as a basis of social prediction. For instance, if we assume that both types of prejudice are inimical to social well-being, then we may ask what the factors involved in their dissolution are. We have no basis for believing that time alone will dissolve the caste society, but time has probably settled most race problems. The caste system in India will yield only to the impact of a culture more powerful than itself, while amalgamation of races will be postponed only so long as the dominant race is able to retard it.

Thus in America, Negroes are not allowed freedom of opportunity to participate in the culture principally because of an apprehension of amalgamation and its meaning in Western society. Negroes and whites are constantly approaching the race problem from different points of view, yet the end must be the same. Assuming the standpoint of fundamental rights of citizens, Negroes ask only that they be permitted to participate freely in the public life of the community. On the other hand, the articulate conservative whites hold that freedom of participation in public life must inevitably lead to "social equality" and thence to unrestrained amalgamation. Thus the outstanding freedom of democracy must be denied Negroes in the interest of racial purity and dominance. There is an inherent dilemma in American race adjustment which must remain unstable until democracy has been fully achieved. In Brahmanic India, however, amalgamation is far advanced, democracy is unknown, and the society is highly integrated and at peace with its system.

In its milieu, Brahmanism is the dominant culture, and thus far only Western culture has been able to challenge its stability. Caste disorganization will proceed with the advance of Western culture; indeed, we should expect that with the incursion of Western culture caste will disintegrate, while ideas of racial distinction and social seriation will be augmented.

Structure of Caste and Race Relations

It is sometimes said that the British form a ruling caste in India. This view, however, seems to be inaccurate. The British are, in fact, a ruling race. A caste is an assimilated dependent segment of a system; consequently, it cannot be set off against the system. If the British were, indeed, a caste, they would not be known as a people, but rather as some such group as Rajanya, or Baniya, or Brahman. One of the sources of conflict in India is that the white rulers refuse to be so recognized. The British distinguish themselves by their color and they dominate the Indians. The probability that their rule has been far more humanitarian than the crude pressure of upper castes is irrelevant.

Racial antagonism tends to divide the society vertically. Although all colored people in the racial situation may be considered subordinate to whites, with the latter horizontally superposed, from the point of view of a power relationship the races tend to be diametrically opposed. The caste system, on the other hand, tends to stratify it in a status hierarchy.[7] In the latter sense there is no status-hierarchical relationship between the white ruling class in India and the dark-skinned natives. It is not a common social-status relationship at all; one group dominates while the other is dominated, and a we-feeling is virtually absent among them. The British are not the highest caste; they stand face to face with the whole caste system. In other words, they have no position in the caste system; their sympathies follow a color line.

Both racial and caste separation tend to inhibit social mobility, but this common factor should not be conceived of as identifying them. The mobility which racial antagonism abhors is movement across a color fence which surrounds each race regardless of social position of the individuals. The mobility which the caste system limits is movement from one corporate group to another within an "assimilated" society.

The situation may be further illustrated by considering the relationship between Mohammedans and Hindus. For centuries before British rule the Mohammedans had been a ruling power in India. Since they were not race-conscious, however, they amalgamated with the Hindus. But the Mohammedans stand in religion opposed to the Hindus, a situation which tends to divide these two groups sharply. In time the Mohammedans yielded to the social structure of the Hindus, so that

---

[7]It would be inaccurate, however, to say that a caste forms a "definite stratum" of the caste hierarchy.

today there are castes on both sides of the line. Thus there are three systems of social restriction. The castes on either side do not intermarry among themselves, while Hindus and Mohammedans stand aloof. There is a power relationship between the latter and a status relationship among their castes. The two social phenomena are distinct, for while we may speak of two sets of caste hierarchies, the relationship between Hindus and Mohammedans does not suggest a *hierarchy* at all. Neither is there any hierarchy between the East Indians as a whole and the British.[8]

The structure of race and of caste relationship is incommensurable. Caste has reference to the internal social order of a society; race suggests a whole people, wherever found about the globe, and a people in actual world dispersion will not conceive of themselves as members of a caste. While there may be rivalry for position among castes, between races in opposition there will be struggle for power. A caste—that is to say the endogamous group—is an organization; a race is not ordinarily an organization.

Race and Caste Consciousness

Race sentiment and interest tend to be universal, while caste sentiment and interest tend to be circumscribed and localized. If a part of the membership of a caste were to migrate to some area beyond easy reach of the other, the likelihood is that it will become a new caste. Not so, however, with a race. The Indian people are very much concerned about the relationship of Hindus and other races over the whole world. Thus the East Indians in Africa and in the West Indies may be outcastes because of their migration from India, but they are by no means given up by the race. Caste pride is based upon internal group invidiousness, while race pride cuts across caste lines and reaches out to a whole people, commanding their loyalty in a body.

Whether caste discrimination is crueler than race discrimination is beside the point. Thus it is a common practice to throw into the laps of Indian nationalists the fact that white people are not nearly so inhuman to East Indians as the upper-caste Indians are to the outcastes, the conclusion being that the nationalists are but "sounding brass" when

---

[8]We use the term "hierarchy" here to mean a social gradient of persons in a social-status system. Thus we do not think of conquered and conqueror as forming a hierarchy. The Germans, for instance, subdued the French, but, for that period, we do not think of the Germans and French as forming a "power hierarchy." In short, we prefer not to think of power groups as forming hierarchies.

they oppose the British on the grounds of race prejudice. Consider, for example, the following challenge of Sir Michael O'Dwyer to the Hindus:

What a volume of protest would be raised throughout the Empire if the Indian settlers in South Africa or Kenya were debarred the use of the public water supply or the right to use a public highway or entry to a public building or admission to state schools on grounds of social inferiority. And yet these injustices are perpetrated today everywhere in India under the sacred name of caste on some fifty millions of Indians.[9]

That the lot of the outcastes is an unhappy one is undeniable, yet we may be sure that the Indians will never see eye to eye with O'Dwyer. Indeed, it is possible for Hindu leaders to be outspokenly self-critical and still maintain a consummate hate for the dominant race. Thus Mahatma Gandhi says of his people:

The laws of Cochin State are in a way much worse than those of South Africa. The common law of South Africa refuses to admit equality between white and coloured races. The common law of Cochin bases inequality on birth in a particular group. But the incidence of inequality in Cochin is infinitely more inhuman than in South Africa; for an untouchable in Cochin is deprived of more human rights than the coloured man in South Africa. There is no such thing as unapproachability or invisibility in South Africa. I have no desire to single out Cochin for its disgraceful treatment of untouchables; for it is still unfortunately common to Hindus all over India, more or less.[10]

This statement of Gandhi was not, of course, calculated to rouse the Hindus against anyone; it is a sort of self-criticism looking to the support of some reform movement. But those laws against people of color in South Africa have the effect of bringing every Hindu together in mortal opposition to practically every white man. Confusion of this distinction has been a source of most egregious errors in recent sociological writings, which have assumed that "whenever rights, privileges, and duties" are unequally divided between two in-marrying groups there is established a "caste system." In the caste system there is a gradient of increments of superiority and inferiority from the depths of human degradation to the exalted guru; and unless we can conceive

---

[9]Quoted from O'Dwyer's article in *The Royal Colonial Institute Journal* by Albert James Saunders, "Nationalism in India," Ph.D. thesis, University of Chicago, 1925, p. 126. It should be mentioned that the attempt of the Indian Constituent Assembly to legislate against untouchability (April 1947), which indicates further weakening of the caste system, does not invalidate this discussion of basic traits of the system.

[10]*Young India, 1924–1926*, p. 726.

of a society's committing suicide, we should not expect Hindus as a whole to revolt against the system.

It is so, too, for instance, with Negroes. In their relationship with whites, Negroes in America are solicitous about the fate of Negroes all over the world. The feeling arises from a consciousness of identity of interest in opposing white mastery of their race. Stories of Nazi Germans stripping France of its monuments to Negro heroes or of Jim Crow laws in South Africa concern American Negroes as a whole probably as vitally as stories of attempts to delete the Constitution from the textbooks of Negro children in Mississippi. This is race consciousness, not caste consciousness. With race the feeling of fellowship is universal; with caste it is localized within some society. The same acute sense of gratification which the defeat of Jim Jeffries by Jack Johnson brought to the hearts of American Negroes spread forthwith even among the Negroes of Central Africa. The purview of caste feeling, however, does not extend beyond the sea. Should he migrate, the caste-man is readily abandoned by his caste. Slight cultural variations in religion, custom, or occupation tend to estrange or split castes. Yet these are of practically no effect when one race is opposed to the other. It may be well to discuss briefly at this point one rather covert aspect of race and caste loyalty, the phenomenon known as "passing."

Passing

Given a common culture, passing may be thought of as a procedure by which a mixed-blood person—having the physical characteristics of the dominant race—assumes full membership in that race so that he may participate in the social advantages which it has reserved to itself. One form of passing may be called *shuttling*. Here the mixed-blood moves back and forth between the two races, leading a primary, familial life in the one, and a secondary, industrial life in the other. Almost always the familial group is of the subordinate race. Of course the shuttler is open to greater risk of detection than the passer who has decided once and for all to make a complete break with one race.

A caste-man does not pass; neither is he preoccupied with passing into another caste. However, the foolhardy may shuttle in pursuit of some transient gain, such as sitting in at the feasts and celebrations of other castes. On the other hand, we should expect most, if not all, subjugated peoples to desire to pass. Obviously it is possible only for marginal men to pass, yet the general attitude is socially significant. If, for instance, the following question were put to American Negroes:

"Would you wish that you were white?" the answer would be obvious.[11]
It would not be so obvious, however, if the same question were put to
Negroes who had not yet felt the full pressure of white exploitation.[12]
But if one were to ask all East Indians whether they would like to
become Brahmans, the question would elicit the same sort of response
as if Americans were asked whether they would all like to become
priests, or judges, or congressmen.

We should expect that the greater the cultural advantages reserved
by the dominant race, the greater will be the desire to pass. That passing is particularly a device for widening the individual's economic and
social opportunities might be substantiated by the fact that it occurs
most frequently during early adulthood. So far as personal initiation is
concerned, it may not occur in childhood or in old age. Indeed, those
unsuccessful and unencumbered colored persons who have passed often
return with advancing age to their colored family tree.

Race Conflict Addressed to the System Itself

Race conflict is directed either against or toward the maintenance of
the entire order of the races. On the other hand, caste rivalry never
brings the caste system into question; its purview of opposition is circumscribed by identified castes. As a matter of fact, races are not status-
bearing entities in the sense that castes are. For instance, Negroes and
whites in the United States stand toward each other in the relationship
of subordination and superordination, a relationship implying suspended conflict. Conversely, castes stand toward each other in the relationship of superiority and inferiority, a relationship implying *natural,*
socially accepted, peaceful status ordering of the society. In the first
case we have a power relationship in which definite aims and ends of
each group are opposed; the second is a situation of mutual emulous-
ness among little status-bearing groups.

---

[11]A few sympathetic critics of the writer inform him that this apparently obvious
expectation is really one of major social complications. Negroes, they maintain, will
be horrified by the idea of becoming white. And, indeed, this is probably true. It is a
remarkable psychological fact that individuals tend to like themselves, and few
would voluntarily prefer to live in other bodies. But the question is: Given the existing social advantages and disadvantages of color differences in the United States,
would one prefer to be born white or colored? The writer is not unmindful of the
rationalization that it is fortunate to be a Negro because the Negro race has a
"cause." This, it has been said, makes life dramatic, and even tragedy is better than
no drama at all. Cf. E. Franklin Frazier, *Negro Youth at the Crossways,* pp. 51–53.

[12]The Bantu "feels himself an integral part of a great people, up to whose standard he is bound to live, and in whose eyes, as in his own, he is one of the goodliest
and completest creatures of God's earth." Olive Schreiner, *Thoughts on South
Africa,* quoted by Everett V. Stonequist, *The Marginal Man,* p. 22.

Intercaste jealousy and invidiousness tend to strengthen the fabric of the caste system; interracial conflict, on the other hand, is usually a challenge to the pattern of interracial adjustments.[13] Thus we might say that the greater the rivalry between caste and caste, the more stable the caste system; while the greater the conflict between race and race in one society, the greater the opportunity for settling interracial differences. It is only when the subordinate race has obtained a relatively advanced conception of itself that it will make a bid for increased "social equality." Of course failure or a definite achievement of further suppression by the superordinate race will obviously widen the breach between them.

Such Indian outbreaks as the Mutiny of 1857 and the Amritsar Affair were conflicts which cut across caste barriers on the side of the Hindus, and across class strata on the side of the British whites. They pitted each group vertically against the other, and latent race attitudes came vividly into view.

The world position of a race tends, moreover, to determine the attitude of its members in their relationships with other races. Thus Englishmen in India derive all their dominant attitude not only from the might of the nation which they represent but also from the position which white people occupy over the whole world. Mohammedans in India are humiliated by a military reverse of the Turks, and East Indians attained a new gratifying conception of themselves in the 1904–05 defeat of Russia by Japan (a colored people), while Marcus Garvey saw the hope of black men in great ships of war manned by Negroes. This principle of power and force which seems to underlie race adjustments gives it a peculiarly eruptive and unstable character.

Race Attitudes Dynamic

"What, then, is this dark world thinking? It is thinking that as wild and awful as this shameful war [World War I] was, it is nothing to compare with that fight for freedom which black and brown and yellow men must and will make unless their oppression and humiliation and insult at the hands of the White World cease. The Dark

---

[13]The following conclusion by P. S. Joshi may illustrate the point: "The South African white . . . has been and will ever be striving to perpetuate the colour bar. The South African non-white too will . . . struggle to have it effaced. If no way of a satisfactory compromise is found at this juncture, the conflict will . . . create such a havoc in South Africa that the entire white civilization will be dislocated, and an unparalleled internecine war will flare up." Op. cit., p. 7.

To the same effect Joshi quotes Professor Edgar Brookes: "To keep the [colour bar] would mean in a century's time such a state of tension as to bring the whole civilization of the sub-continent to a state of chaos and civil war." Ibid., p. 302.

World is going to submit to its present treatment just as long as it must and not one moment longer."[14] This "rising tide of color" which is the expressed hope of some colored leaders and the fear of some whites may be rather farfetched; at any rate, it illustrates an attitude which ever strives toward realization.

While the caste system may be thought of as a social order in stable equilibrium, the domination of one race by another is always an unstable situation. In a situation characterized by race prejudice, individuals in the subordinate group are always seeking to destroy the social barrier; and at points of sympathetic contact between the races, members of the superordinate group are constantly devaluating racial pretensions. As an illustration, consider the following, a fairly common reaction in the Deep South:

Stop this "lily-white" nonsense. Quit being sidetracked by this Bourbon wail of Negro. Recognize this vital force of the immovable truth that an injustice to one American citizen will react upon all. You can't have one law for the white man and another for the Negro in our form of government. You know that those who have most talked of suppressing blacks have really suppressed you . . . and most of all Southern whites.[15]

These attitudes tend to be summatory, and a day of reckoning usually becomes the goal of the dominated race. The instability of the situation produces what are known as race problems, phenomena unknown to the caste system.

Race Relations Pathological

We may call any system of group adjustment pathological which harbors latent conflict attitudes directed toward its destruction. No form of seeming oppression of one group by another is of itself conclusive. In some cultures slavery is normal, in others extreme class subordination, and in still others outcasting. A stable social adjustment may be thought of as one in which the beliefs of a people are in harmony with their practices and in which the social system itself never comes up for critical public discussion. The occasion for a defense of the social order does not arise, and this notwithstanding the possible adverse judgment of persons residing in other societies. Ordinarily the beginning of social disorganization is heralded by critical discussion and cynical appraisal of the social system by members of the society.

---

[14]W. E. B. DuBois, *Darkwater*, p. 49.

[15]Joseph C. Manning in the newspaper, *Southern American,* quoted by Ray Stannard Baker, *Following the Colour Line,* p. 264.

We may illustrate the pathological nature of modern race relations with a consideration of Negro-white opposition in the United States.

Struggle of the "social conscience" with itself has characterized the mental state of whites throughout its history of dominance over Negroes. The following rationalization by the Reverend J. C. Postell of South Carolina in 1836 is not only typical of the period but also illustrates a necessary striving to synchronize beliefs and practices.

It [slavery] is not a moral evil. The fact that slavery is of Divine appointment, would be proof enough with the Christians that it could not be a moral evil. . . . If slavery was either the invention of man or a moral evil, it is logical to conclude that the power to create has the power to destroy. Why then has it existed? And why does it now exist amidst all the power of legislation in State and Church, and the clamor of the abolitionists? It is the Lord's doings and marvelous in our eyes; and had it not been for the best, God alone, who is able, long since would have overruled it.[16]

The basic ideological problem of whites in their relationship with Negroes, then, is that of reconciling two standards of morality. The powerful democratic Christian beliefs developed in Western society are on the side of the Negro; the racially articulate whites must shoulder the task of demonstrating that these beliefs do not include colored people.[17] Thus they strive to see democracy as implying equal opportunity among whites in their exploitation of Negroes. But such an interpretation must be constantly reinforced, for it rests insecurely on a broader world view. Not infrequently it is attacked from within the ranks of whites themselves, while practically all Negroes have been opposed to it. There are probably more words spent upon the race problem in the South than on all other social problems combined.

We may think of the racial adjustment in the South as being in a state of great instability. The cultural pattern is unsatisfactory to both races, a serious problem to each, and it is antipathetic to the fundamental social norms of the country. Respect for law in a representative form of government must be relied upon for the preservation of social institutions. But in America respect for the white race takes precedence, a condition which has resulted, especially in the South, in endemic social dysphoria. Thus we may conceive of the interracial accommodation as a persistent, malignant system which remains ominous of violent

---

[16]Parker Pillsbury, *The Church as It Is,* quoted by Trevor Bowen, *Divine White Right,* p. 107.

[17]To be sure, these beliefs are not in themselves social determinants; they merely evince the basic ideological conflict between two social systems—those of the democratic proletariat and the oligarchic capitalists.

interracial strife. Anxiety, fear, mutual mistrust, and social stricture are typical mental states.

In the South the most powerful means of control and of maintaining the status quo are surreptitious and indeed criminal in the light of constituted law. The established institutions of the country do not function in support of the system; they must be suspended when white dominance is threatened. The mob, night riders, gangs, and ruling-class organizations such as the Ku Klux Klan; slugging, kidnaping, incendiarism, bombing, lynching, and blackmailing are the principal reliance of the racially articulate whites for securing their position. The instability of this accommodation may be indicated by the fact that many whites are ashamed of it. The following passage by William H. Skaggs speaks for a minority of whites:

> In the romances of mythology, ancient and medieval history, the knights-errant who were the champions of women fought in the open. Neither in the Iliad, nor the Aeneid, nor in the narratives of Plutarch, or the Chronicles of Froissart, do we find the record of a gallant knight prowling around after dark and unmercifully beating some poor, unfortunate serf.[18]

It should be emphasized that although in Western society these acts of racial aggression are defined as pathological, in Brahmanic India intercaste violence may be consistent with the fundamental beliefs of the society. A Brahman need not resort to clandestine terrorization of lower-caste men in order to establish his superiority, for undisputed public opinion gives him the right overtly to subdue disrespectful inferiors. Therefore, as a constituted form of punishment, a Brahman may direct the flogging of a low-caste man. The position of high-caste Hindus is guaranteed to them in Hindu society, but in America there is no such fundamental guarantee for whites. Its establishment must be maintained from day to day.[19]

There is here, then, an irreconcilable antithesis which must inevitably remain a constant source of social unrest. The "lawlessness of judges" in deciding the law and the "unlawful enforcement of the law" by policemen are common perversions of American institutions, but they are pivotal in the racial system. The social anomaly is inherent.

There is, of course, no unlimited freedom of participation in the culture for Negroes, and freedom of speech for both races is limited by the interest of the white ruling class. Whole systems of pseudo-

---

[18]*The Southern Oligarchy,* p. 332.

[19]This does not mean to say that the South considers its treatment of Negroes criminal.

scientific teachings are fostered, while sympathetic knowledge of the social life of colored people is practically kept out of reach of white persons. In a democracy these obstacles to communication must necessarily result in pathological social strictures.

We have attempted to show in this section that racial antagonism necessitates constant vigilance and social preoccupation, and that while attitudes of white dominance are generally recognized by Negroes, they are seldom, if ever, accepted. In the caste system, on the other hand, there is social tranquillity. In attempting to explain their social systems, most peoples will seek some sort of justification in religious terms; it is a way of achieving divine sanction for the social fact. The Hindus, more than any other people of comparable magnitude, have been able to couch their social behavior in a religious frame of reference. The following is a brief view of the success which racially articulate whites have had in bending Christianity to this task.

The Church, a Factor

It was during the days of slavery that the most insistent attempts were made to develop a religious rationale for white, ruling-class policy. The Church in the South exploited every vestige of class differentiation in the Bible. God—seldom Jesus—gave his approval.[20] With the close of the Civil War, however, the arguments became more subtle. Discriminatory practices against the colored people were either condoned by some of the churches or justified on the grounds that they contributed to the welfare of Negroes.

The struggle for consistency in the basic social beliefs continues. Segregation in or exclusion from the churches and church schools is inimical to the dominant theme of Christianity. Indeed, it has been said that the Church must choose between race prejudice and Christianity, for it cannot have both.[21] While it is in the process of making this choice, the white Church, in the South especially, like the courthouses, will continue to be ominous symbols of white dominance. The dominant group must compromise with Christianity. We need hardly mention again that the Church as an instrument of the dominant interest has never been able to achieve anything approaching the consensus of Hinduism in the caste system.

---

[20] See Harper and Others, *The Pro-Slavery Argument,* and John H. Hopkins, "Bible View of Slavery," *Papers from the Society for the Diffusion of Political Knowledge,* No. 6.

[21] See Trevor Bowen, op. cit., p. 148; and Buell G. Gallagher, *Color and Conscience.*

Education, a Factor

We have alluded above to the fact that one of the principal sources of prestige controlled by Brahmans is learning. What the Brahmans realized so clearly some three thousand years ago has been also repeatedly adopted by other groups interested in maintaining social ascendancy. Obviously the fact of educational discrimination is not per se an index of caste relationship. There is a good deal of truth in Ray Stannard Baker's point that "every aristocracy that has survived has had to monopolize education more or less completely—else it went to the wall."[22] In the South before the Civil War the poor whites were effectively excluded from educational opportunities, and ordinarily it was criminal to teach a Negro to read. Equal educational opportunity means opportunity for inferior classes to acquire the sophistication of dominant groups, the instrument of attack upon the philosophy and pretensions of the latter. "What the North is sending the South is not money," said James K. Vardaman, a post-Civil War Southern governor, "but dynamite; this education is ruining our Negroes. They're demanding equality."[23]

Education enhances the power of communication of the subordinate group and puts it in possession of the technique of social organization. It tends, therefore, to develop a degree of social unrest among the subordinate group, a condition which cannot fail to disturb the status quo. Thus, in characteristic fashion, a leading Southern politician, Senator B. R. Tillman of South Carolina, predicted ominously:

Every man . . . who can look before his nose can see that with Negroes constantly going to school, the increasing number who can read and write among the colored race . . . will in time encroach upon our white men.[24]

The white ruling class has not been able to keep the printed page entirely away from the Negro; it has, however, severely limited his access to it and has succeeded somewhat in channeling his thinking.

One means of limiting the effectiveness of education is the strategy of making education itself seem useless to Negroes. They are barred, by force if necessary, from opportunities which call for initiative in thinking, so that relatively their education tends to become a costly luxury deteriorating rapidly from non-use. A truncated educational career be-

---

[22]Op. cit., p. 247. Indeed, every ruling class is interested in education which preserves, not in that which disturbs, the status quo.

[23]Quoted, ibid.

[24]Ibid., p. 246.

comes the disillusioning lot of many. In the caste system, an individual is naturally limited by his caste dharma, and the idea of education serving as a means of broadening the functional scope of the individual is anomalous. The British, in their limited attempts to put in practice Western principles of popular education, have sometimes felt the compelling resistance of the caste society.[25] In the caste system there is no universal right to an education, and even members of one's own caste would not appreciate his claim to a right of freedom to use his attainments. In race situations, however, whites are on the defensive in setting up barriers to free exploitation of one's ability.

Occupation

Factors influencing the choice of occupation for both races in the United States are fundamentally different from those which operate in the caste system. The questions asked by caste members in viewing the field of labor are different from those which confront whites and blacks. In estimating the possibilities of an occupation, the caste-man wants to know primarily the attitude of his caste and the degree of "purity" of the occupation. When the system is functioning normally,

---

[25]J. C. Nesfield, inspector of schools in the North-Western Provinces, relates his experiences: "In one school there was a boy of the Kurmi caste, which is one of the most industrious agricultural castes in Upper India. He had passed a very good examination in the highest standard of the village schools; after telling him that he had now completed all that a village school could give him, I inquired what occupation he intended to follow. His answer at once was—'Service; what else?' I advised him to revert to agriculture, as there was scarcely any chance of his getting literary employment; but at this piece of advice he seemed surprised and even angry.

"At another school I met a Pasi, a semi-hunting caste, much lower in every respect than that of the Kurmi. He was a boy of quick understanding and had completed the village school course in Nagari as well as Urdu, and could read and write both characters with equal facility. He asked me what he was to do next. I could hardly tell him to go back to pig-raising, trapping birds, and digging vermin out of the earth for food; and yet I scarcely saw what other opening was in store for him. At another school there was the son of a Chuhar, or village sweeper, a caste the lowest of all the castes properly so called. He was asked with others to write an original composition on the comparative advantages of trade and service as a career. He expressed a decided preference for trade. Yet, who would enter into mercantile transactions with a sweeper even if a man of that caste could be started in such a calling? Everything that he touches would be considered as polluted; and no one would buy grain or cloth from his shop, if he could buy them from any other. There seems to be no opening in store for this very intelligent youth but that of scavengering, mat-making, trapping, etc., all of which are far below the more cultivated tastes he has acquired by attending school. And in such pursuits he is not likely to evince the same degree of skill or enjoy the same contentment as one who has grown up wholly illiterate.

"In these and such like ways, the attempts made by the government to raise the condition of the masses and place new facilities of self-advancement within their reach, are thwarted by the absence of opportunities and by the caste prejudices of the country." Quoted in *Cambridge History of India*, Vol. VI, p. 343.

however, individual choice of occupation is ruled out; the individual inherits his vocation. To both whites and Negroes, on the other hand, income and personal adaptability to the occupation are primary considerations; the nature of competition, fair or unfair, in the field is another important factor.

At the basis of these situations lies the difference between the economic order of the two societies. The theory of production which obtains in the caste system is founded upon hereditary group specialization and co-operation. It maintains that the most satisfactory economic system is one in which each group has a specified occupation rendering service on a sort of intergroup barter basis. It holds further that, since each group must consequently be dependent upon others for more or less of its goods and services, the general welfare demands that castes do their work properly and without failure or suffer the consequences of social displeasure. No group has a right to change its work; yet in the event that some occupation becomes plethoric or unproductive, the caste may assume another *less respectable* occupation. The latter provision is necessary to make it as distasteful as possible for castes to change their occupations. Thus a man's work becomes a social duty, and to wish for change is to shirk a grave responsibility.

Here the determinism of price and equilibrium economics operate only feebly, for the system is conceived in static terms; furthermore, the state of the market is an extremely sluggish determinant of occupational structure. There is, in fact, no "labor market" in the caste system. So far as production is concerned, the caste system is not unlike, in functional conceptualization, a colony of ants or bees, with each class of insects doing its work naturally and harmoniously. Human beings may put varying estimates on the work of each class of insects; yet, for the continuance of the insect society, the work of each may be indispensable. And so, too, it is a postulate of the caste system that the occupation of the lowest caste, though relatively inferior, is none the less important to the system. We may take our analogy a little farther in observing that castes are supposed to work with the same sort of symbiotic harmony as the insects, neither envying nor usurping each other's functions.

Production in the caste economy, then, is carried out by hereditarily specialized producers' associations which have not only a social right to peaceful enjoyment of their specialty but also a sacred duty to execute it faithfully and contentedly.[26] Profits or differential income are

---

[26]Caste specialization, as distinguished from modern industrial specialization, is specialization according to product. That is to say, each caste claims the production

not controlling, for the producers of goods do not measure the value of their services by what they might earn in the production of other goods. In other words, castes do not have the alternative opportunity of working in those industries which yield the largest returns. Hence, accommodation rather than opportunism is the social basis of production. Moreover, the productive activities of castes are not mere jobs or positions; they are ways of living. The individual in the caste system never thinks of occupation as a means of advancing his social status, which is so closely bound up with that of his caste.[27] We may recall also that the system is not forced, as in slavery, where the master may use his slave in a variety of occupations; but rather it is a type of social order calling for voluntary group production and exchange.

On the other hand, economic competition in America precludes dependence of one race upon the other for its material existence. In the South, Negroes are practically excluded from such occupations as the practice of law, military service in peacetime, and the holding of political office. It is necessary that the white ruling class monopolize these occupations, for they are indispensable to the strategy of white dominance. Competition of different varieties and even open exploitation tend to keep Negroes out of many employments; so far as constitutional and religious *right* to any given occupation is concerned, however, both Negroes and whites are on equal footing. Even though the probability of its materialization now seems little indeed, there is nothing in our social system which condemns a Negro for aspiring, say, to the presidency of the nation. In fact, he, like all others, is theoretically encouraged to "hitch his wagon to a star." Thus, not only are the races not identified with any particular occupation, but there is also no accepted plan for the sharing of occupations.

The most that we can say is that Negroes, because of their subordination, will be found mainly on the lower rungs of the occupational ladder; as workers they are ordinarily exploited, but striving to enhance their economic participation is characteristic. In an unpublished study of the buying power movement among Negroes in Chicago the present writer discovered from an investigation of the files of the *Chicago Whip* that Negroes had applied in large numbers for a variety of jobs that were seldom if ever open to them. Many had been trained for

of a certain commodity or service. Castes do not come together for the purpose of producing in concert a single commodity. In fact, the assembly-line idea is not conducive to caste stability.

[27]With the incursion of Western culture, there is in urban India today some modification of the limitations of occupational choice.

occupations from which they were ordinarily barred.[28] We may conclude, then, that although on the surface it might appear that the occupational limitations of the caste system are comparable to those developed under a system of racial exploitation they are, in fact, two definitely distinguishable social phenomena.

Aspiration, a Factor

In practically every instance of white-colored race contacts there has been a remarkable stimulation of ambition among the colored group.[29] In most instances the white dominant group has observed this attitude with apprehension. It is, however, exceedingly pertinacious, for it goes hand in hand with acculturation.

Unlike castes in India, Negroes in America have been seeking to increase their participation and integration in the dominant culture. Cessation of such striving is an inseparable feature of the caste system. Indeed, culturally speaking, the castes in India have arrived. If, for instance, the Negro-white relationship were a caste relationship, Negroes would not be aspiring toward the upper social position occupied by whites; their concern, rather, would be almost entirely with the development of a socially sufficient internal organization. It is this centrifugal cultural drive among Negroes which produces fear and antagonism among the white ruling class. Thus the scheme of race relationship in America centers about attempts of Negroes to reach new levels of participation and opposition to these attempts by whites.

Even as far back as the days of slavery Negro aspiration was everywhere evident. We could not conceive of an institution of hope, such as the Negro spirituals, developing among the lower castes of India; nor of the latter's producing such masters of compromise and appeasement as the early Negro preacher personality type. The slaves sang:

> *Bye and bye*
> *Ah'm gonna lay down dis heavy load*

and

> *Walk together chillen,*
> *Don'tcha get weary!*

Probably no one who has seen the Negro preacher in his cabin church of the Deep South, marching triumphantly over the king's Eng-

---

[28]See also Charles S. Johnson, *Growing Up in the Black Belt*, Table 9, p. 195, for a study of the deviations of choice of occupation of Negro children from the occupations of parents.

[29]In rare instances, as in Australia, where the black and white cultures differ very greatly, there has been only feeble effort among the colored to emulate the whites.

lish amid great surges of "Amen! Amen!!" and "Yes, Lord!" lifting his congregation in repeated affirmations of faith and hope, could fail to realize that these people are far from being resigned in spirit. Their spontaneous songs of freedom and courage in the face of great trial, their incessant call at the "gates of heaven," these are not unlike in emotion the spirit of liberty which has everywhere in Christendom moved men to action. Hinduism provides no such powerful escape from the claims to superiority of dominant castes. Ray Stannard Baker tells a story of hope among post-Civil War Negroes:

Just at the close of the war [President R. R. Wright of the Georgia State Industrial College] was a boy in a freedman's school at Atlanta. One Sunday, General O. O. Howard came to address the pupils. When he was finished, he expressed a desire to take a message back to the people of the North. "What shall I tell them for you?" he asked. A little black boy in front stood up quickly and said: "Tell 'em, Massa, we is rising."[30]

In the South, Negroes have been effectively excluded from politics, but they are by no means apathetic to the fact that they have heavy stakes in this field. In his farewell address, one of the last remaining Civil War Negro congressmen, George H. White, said:

This, Mr. Chairman, is perhaps the Negroes' temporary farewell to the American Congress; but let me say, Phoenix-like he will rise up some day and come again. These parting words are in behalf of an outraged, heart-broken, bruised, and bleeding, but God-fearing people, faithful, industrious, loyal people—rising people, full of potential force. . . . The only apology that I have to make for the earnestness with which I have spoken is that I am pleading for the life, the liberty, the future happiness, and manhood suffrage of one-eighth of the entire population of the United States.[31]

Langston Hughes has given a sympathetic interpretation of the encouragement and sacrifices of the many colored mothers who welcome drudgery that their children may have wider social opportunities. Thus a mother counsels in the last lines of the poem, *Mother to Son:*

> *So boy, don't you turn back.*
> *Don't you sit down on the steps*
> *'Cause you finds it's kinder hard.*
> *Don't you fall now—*
> *For I'se still goin', honey,*
> *I'se still climbin'*
> *And life for me ain't been no crystal stair.*

---

[30] Op. cit., p. 92.
[31] Congressional Record, 56th Congress, 2d Sess., January 29, 1901, p. 1638.

Sometimes, of course, the going is very difficult, and even strong men rail against the unyielding barriers. Again Hughes seems to symbolize this attitude:

> *My hands!*
> *My dark hands!*
> *Break through the wall!*
> *Find my dream!*
> *Help me to shatter this darkness,*
> *To smash this night,*
> *To break this shadow*
> *Into a thousand lights of sun,*
> *Into a thousand whirling dreams*
> *Of sun!*[32]

Among the most revealing aspects of the relationship, however, is the open criticism of whites by a minority of whites. This phenomenon seems to be present in virtually all types of race relations, but it is practically unknown in the caste system. Furthermore, its absence is not a mere chance occurrence; it is rather the peculiar social view of castes which precludes it. The following is a typical expression of the former kind of sentiment:

We southern whites are more the victims of slavery than the Negroes because, possessing a little economic advantage, we have nourished the constant inclination toward unfairness. The Negro, with notable patience, has nevertheless not failed through the long years to be aspiring; above all in the present juncture, he demands justice, and here he is our master.[33]

In a previous section we have attempted to examine the function of marriage in the caste system. We shall now look into the role of marriage in race relations and its meaning as an identifying criterion of caste.

Race, Caste, and Intermarriage

It is common knowledge that in the United States the crucial problem of race relations is that of Negro-white intermarriage. This is ap-

---

[32]Excerpt from *As I Grew Older*. See James Weldon Johnson, *The Book of American Negro Poetry*, 1931.

[33]Broadus Mitchell, *Black Justice*, American Civil Liberties Union pamphlet, May 1931, pp. 6–7. See also René Maunier, *Sociologie coloniale*, pp. 77–83, for a discussion of progressive and regressive cultural tendencies among different races in contact with Western culture. In his speech of March 15, 1941, at the dinner of the White House correspondents' association, President Roosevelt said: "There never has been, and there isn't now, and there never will be any race of people fit to serve as masters over their fellow men."

parently the crowning fear of white men. Very few, indeed, even of those who would criticize their white brothers for discrimination against Negroes, have had the courage to face the fierce opposition to any principle of free marital preference between the races. The articulate whites have held generally that, the larger the number of light-complexioned Negroes, the greater the difficulty of segregating them; hence neither intermarriage nor miscegenation can be permitted. Moreover, it is not of the essence of importance whether the father of the mixed-blood is white or black.

We think that some authors put too much emphasis upon the "sexual gains" of whites in the South. It is true that Negro men do not have the white man's opportunity to select women from either race, but there is reason to believe that sometimes Negroes conceive of this disparity of opportunity as an investment. That the ruling-class whites so understand it is manifest from the equal application of the marriage restriction laws. On this score Baker cites a typical attitude. "Our people," says a district attorney in Mississippi, "our white men with their black concubines, are destroying the integrity of the Negro race, raising up a menace to the white race, lowering the standard of both races, and preparing the way for riot, mob, criminal assaults, and finally, a death struggle for racial supremacy."[34]

Had the Southern situation been a caste system, the sexual "loss" to Negroes might have been absolute. In America, however, regardless of which race takes the initiative in bringing it about, amalgamation is one sure way of solving race problems. The white guardians of race purity are never so bitter, never so condemnatory, as when they deal with white men's consorting with Negro women. To these guardians of the status quo it is treason against one's own race. Even though such laws were not unconstitutional, we could hardly conceive of a rule which bars the marriage of Negro men and white women and at the same time sanctions sexual relationship between white men and Negro women. It is apparent that either situation will bring about the same end.

Although in the caste system there is no particular social impulsion, other than possible physical desire, for low-caste men to covet women of higher castes, there is a definite social advantage to colored men in their marrying white women. In a racial system which puts a cultural premium upon lightness of color, a Negro man can give his children considerable advantage by such a marriage. And as a matter of fact, in

---

[34]Ray Stannard Baker, op. cit., p. 167.

those states in which intermarraige is not prohibited, it appears that some four out of every five mixed marriages are of Negro men and white women.[35] Because of the racial antagonism on this question, the couple may be embarrassed in either group. Other things being equal, however, their children should fare better than the father because of their lighter complexion. Assuming that the sex ratios are similar for the races, we should expect that, should the cultural advantage of whites decrease relatively, the number of intermarriages will increase and the ratios of men intermarrying will tend to approximate each other. It has been reported that intermarriage has increased in Soviet Russia with the extension of economic and political equality to all racial groups.[36]

Marriage Restriction Laws

Since only somewhat more than half of the states prohibit intermarriage between different races, the question arises as to the meaning of these laws[37] with respect to the race-caste hypothesis. All the states which prohibit intermarriage between whites and some other race also prohibit it between whites and Negroes. Some states which once had miscegenation laws have repealed them, while the laws which now exist have been individually enacted over a period of years. Furthermore, the laws apply only from the date of enactment, so that all prior interracial marriages are legal.

Now if we are to examine the question whether marriage prohibition is a criterion of caste in America, we should like to ask whether it is statutory or customary prohibition which is determining. It would be contrary to reason to hold that a caste system in a given state is

---

[35] See Robert E. T. Roberts, "Negro-White Intermarriage," unpublished master's thesis, University of Chicago, 1940, p. 10.

[36] Bernhard J. Stern, "Intermarriage," *Encyclopedia of the Social Sciences.*

[37] Twenty-seven states forbid marriage between whites and Negroes: Oregon, California, Nevada, Idaho, Utah, Arizona, Colorado, North Dakota, Nebraska, Missouri, Indiana, Kentucky, Tennessee, West Virginia, Virginia, Maryland, Delaware, Oklahoma, Texas, Arkansas, Louisiana, Mississippi, Alabama, Florida, Georgia, South Carolina, and North Carolina.
Some fifteen states expressly or impliedly forbid marriage between whites and Mongolians: Arizona, California, Georgia, Idaho, Mississippi, Missouri, Montana, Nebraska, Nevada, South Carolina, Oregon, Utah, South Dakota, Wyoming, and Virginia.
Ten states impliedly or expressly forbid Malay-and-white marriage: Arizona, California, Georgia, Maryland, Nevada, Oregon, South Carolina, South Dakota, Virginia, and Wyoming.
Five bar unions with Indians: Arizona, Georgia, North Carolina, Oregon, and South Carolina. Two bar unions with Asiatic Indians: Arizona (Hindus), and Virginia (Asiatic Indians).
See Charles S. Mangum, Jr., *The Legal Status of the Negro,* p. 253.

instituted or abolished with the enactment or abrogation of an inter-marriage law. Clearly, then, the statute does not establish the caste. But American Indians and Negroes are forbidden to intermarry in Louisiana and Oklahoma, while in Maryland, Negroes may not marry Malays. Could it be that these different groups are castes? In Idaho a white person may marry a Mongolian but not a Negro; shall we assume that Chinese and whites form a caste in opposition to Negroes? "Persons of different races" are prohibited from intermarrying in South Dakota; is this state most truly representative of a racial caste system in America? The mere posing of these questions seems to make it evident that the operation of the statutes provide no support to the race-caste hypothesis.

The alternative is that custom and not law provides the negative sanctions, from which fact we must conclude that custom may operate with different degrees of rigidity in contiguous states, those with and those without an intermarriage law. In the United States there is undoubtedly a definite opposition to intermarriage between whites and peoples of color, yet this attitude tends to become very much confused when we attempt to explain it in terms of caste. The possibility of hypergamous marriage among castes in India is a factor contributing to a further elucidation of these social situations.

Hypergamy

Although Herbert Risley wrote extensively on hypergamous marriage in India, he never saw hypergamy as a social phenomenon distinguishing caste and race relations. In India superior-caste males may marry inferior-caste women, and this does not result in consolidation of castes. It is declared in the laws of Manu that:

> For the first marriage of twice-born men, wives of equal caste are recommended; but for those who through desire proceed to marry again the following females, chosen according to the direct order of the castes, are most approved. . . . A Sudra woman alone can be the wife of a Sudra, she and one of his own caste, the wives of a Vaisya, those two and one of his own caste, the wives of a Kshatriya, those three and one of his own caste, the wives of a Brahmana.[38]

Thus the higher the caste, the greater the opportunity for "mixture of blood." Yet hypergamy has not resulted in a lessening of caste consciousness. "If caste was based on distinction of race," says R. V. Russell, "then apparently the practice of hypergamy would be objec-

---

[38] Manu, III, 12–13. See also Vishnu, XXIV, 1–4.

tionable, because it would destroy the different racial classes."[39] In the Punjab outcaste women, Chamars, are sold to Jats, Gujars, and Rajputs as wives.[40]

The taking of colored women by white men, at least in their early contact with a people of color, is also considered a form of hypergamy; in fact, some writers have found it possible to identify caste and race relations on this very point. But the significant difference between these two forms of hypergamy is that in the case of castes the identity of the groups is not affected by it; while in the case of race relations, the more frequent the intermarriages, the less clear the racial distinctions. Women taken from lower castes may be a total loss to the latter— unless it be that the lower caste gains some spiritual gratification from a sense of one of its members participating in a higher dharma—but the gain to the people of color varies all the way from complete amalgamation to the establishment of a restless mixed-blood people, who tend to become a challenge to the pretensions of their fathers' race. Hypergamy can never become a law in a biracial system, for the system will be doomed from the moment of its enactment. Here again, then, we have a social fact which seems common to two different situations, yet whose social meanings are distinct.

Endogamy

Endogamy is self-imposed restriction upon outmarriage by a social group. Any group which explicitly limits marriage of its members to persons within the group may be called endogamous. In Western society there are negative sanctions against upper-class persons marrying lower-class persons, yet we do not ordinarily think of the upper class as being endogamous. In fact, a social class cannot be endogamous because it has no consciousness of its limits.

With the exception of hypergamy, endogamy among castes in India is a basic trait. A group cannot function within the Brahmanic system if its social area of choice of partners in marriage is undefined. The caste is a truly endogamous social entity. The prohibitions against outmarriage are not a reaction to similar actions of some other castes; they are the most reliable means available to the caste for protecting its heritage. Furthermore, the social heritage of low castes is to them as important as that of high castes is to the latter.

Some students of the caste system have concluded that endogamy

---

[39] *The Tribes and Castes of the Central Provinces of India,* Vol. II, pp. 363–64.
[40] George W. Briggs, *The Chamars,* p. 42.

among castes is similar to endogamy as they observe it between race and race in Western society. But if we return to our situation in the United States we shall see that neither Negroes nor whites belong to groups that are endogamous in the caste sense. Their choice of partners in marriage is limited only by matters of cultural compatibility or localized racial antagonisms. A caste is organized as a caste not particularly with respect to some specified group but rather with reference to every conceivable group or individual. White people in the United States, on the contrary, may marry whites from any other part of the world. Generally they are opposed to intermarriage with peoples of color, but unless racial antagonism becomes directed, a marriage here and there is not particularly objectionable. When the social situation is favorable, as in Hawaii, whites may intermarry more readily than some other races.

Being themselves a colored people, Negroes have only a cultural inhibition. They will intermarry comparatively freely with every other race in the United States. Indeed, as we have mentioned above, in some state whites have found it contrary to their interest to permit marriage between Negroes and other peoples of color within the state. The opposition of Negroes to intermarriage with whites is a rather complex reaction. It varies in response to the attitude of whites in different parts of the country. It may be possible to illustrate three significant types of endogamy: caste, race, and estate endogamy.

In Figure A the marriage system of castes is represented by an outer circle enclosing castes, with an inner circle marking off the exogamous parts of the castes. An individual born within a section of the small circle—sapinda, gotra, clan, sept, pravara—must look outside of it for a mate, though not beyond the limits of his caste.[41] Thus, within the system, each caste is closed to the other. Even marriage among castes of collateral status is avoided.

Figure B illustrates the pattern of race endogamy obtaining in the United States between whites and Negroes or Chinese or Indians or Japanese. The inner circle represents the familial or exogamous group, and the middle bar indicates a negative intermarriage sanction among whites against some specific race or races. Thus, with the exception of near relatives and some identified race, each race is free to marry among any of the other peoples of the world. Therefore, the race is not a closed endogamous unit. While the caste sanction declares that the individual may not marry out of his caste, the racial sanction stipu-

---

[41] For a discussion of this, see S. V. Karandikar, *Hindu Exogamy*.

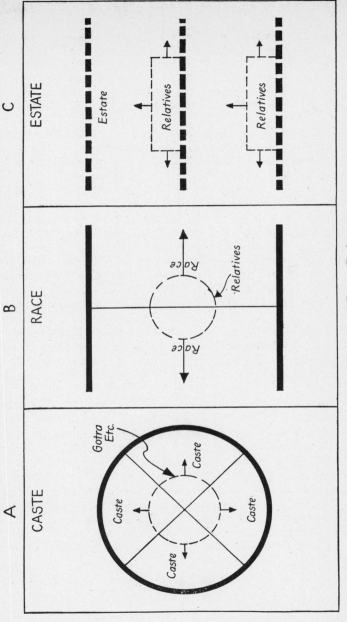

Caste, Race, and Estate Endogamy

lates Negroes, or Chinese, or Indians as races with which its members may not intermarry. The endogamous attitude of the proscribed colored race is ordinarily founded in resentment, a counterattitude. Some such feeling as the following is apparent: "If they do not care to intermarry with us, we shall hate the very thought of seeming to crave the opportunity of intermarrying with them." And so the color bar gains a negative support.[42]

Figure C illustrates the process of endogamy in an estate system. The inner rectangle represents the familial exogamous group, while the horizontal lines indicate more or less distinct estate barriers or strata. Within a given estate which may extend beyond national boundaries, marriage is freely sanctioned—differences in culture, of course, are limiting factors. Although lateral unions are normal, persons within the estate may seek to "marry up," a tendency which is resisted. Thus the social estate tends to be endogamous with respect to lower estates, but exogamous with respect to upper ones. Furthermore, the wider the disparity in social-estate position, the more rigid the sanctions against estate intermarriage. Practically all that we have said about estate endogamy may also be said about social classes, with the exception that it is the individual or family or clique which defends or strives after status.

We may conclude, then, that endogamy is of different significance in caste and race relations. The caste is locked within its immediate marital circle; the race, on the other hand, is opportunistic and will intermarry or refuse to do so as its interest or cultural strategy demands.

Race and Caste Stability

Rigid social sanctions are developed in both the caste system and among races in opposition. But contrary to the belief of some writers, rigidity in itself is not the distinguishing social fact. We have no definite measure of rigidity of social distance; therefore, to speak of "the *rigidity* which the *caste system* has attained in the South" may be misleading. Here, too, the meaning of the social phenomenon as it functions in given social situations involves the significant problem.

In the caste system each caste knows or assumes that it knows its place. The very nature of racial opposition, however, precludes attain-

---

[42]According to Ray Stannard Baker, "The prejudice of white people has forced all colored people, light or dark, together, and has awakened in many ostracised men and women who are nearly white, a spirit which expresses itself in a passionate defense of everything that is Negro." Op. cit., p. 156.

ment of such a degree of adjustment. The poet pictures some of this indecision thus:

> *My old man's a white old man,*
> *And my old mother's black;*
>
> . . . .
>
> *My old man died in a fine big house,*
> *My ma died in a shack.*
> *I wonder where I'm gonna die,*
> *Being neither white nor black?*[43]

The desire for interracial peace is certainly a desideratum among the white ruling class of the South, but in this respect Negroes are on the defensive. Observe, for example, the purpose of Hoke Smith, a typical Southern politician:

Those Negroes who are contented to occupy the natural status of their race, the position of inferiority, all competition being eliminated between the whites and the blacks, will be treated with greater kindness.[44]

It is, notwithstanding, the Negroes' unalterable attitude against acceptance of a place of natural inferiority—that is to say, a condition of certain exploitability—which keeps race problems very much alive. There is no peace; evidently there shall never be social complacency while whites continue to maintain such a position.

When I first went to the South [says Baker] I expected to find people talking about the Negro, but I was not at all prepared to find the subject occupying such an overshadowing place in southern affairs. In the North we have nothing at all like it; no question which so touches every act of life, in which everyone, white or black, is so profoundly interested.[45]

One factor which contributes to the flux of race relations in America is the irregularity of interracial practices and discrimination. It provides an opportunity not only for countless attacks upon the color line, but also for a minority of whites to disregard rules favored by the articulate ruling class. Segregation and "Jim Crow" are tangible symbols of white dominance, yet these practices are sufficiently inconsistent to make their application frequently unexpected. In some cities in the Deep South white taxicabs compete for Negro passengers; in others they refuse Negro trade. In some cities Negroes must enter and leave the streetcar from the rear; in others they may enter at the

---

[43]Langston Hughes, *Cross.*
[44]Quoted by Ray Stannard Baker, op. cit., p. 249.
[45]Ibid., p. 26.

center. The effect of "Jim Crow" laws as a stereotyping factor in race discrimination is graphically illustrated by Stephenson:

> Suppose, for instance, a colored passenger were to board a train at Philadelphia for Evansville, Indiana, and go through Maryland, West Virginia, and Kentucky. Pennsylvania and West Virginia have no "Jim Crow" laws, Maryland and Kentucky have. When the colored passenger reaches the Maryland line, must he enter a car set apart for colored people? When he reaches the West Virginia line, may he go back into the coach with white passengers? When, again, he reaches the Kentucky line, will he be forced to return to the car set apart for his race? And, finally, when he comes to Indiana, may he once more return to the car for white passengers?[46]

These apparently minor variations in the laws, customs, and etiquette contribute vitally to the instability of the whole system.[47] Moreover, the very dynamic character of our capitalist society precludes the attainment of that final racial adjustment so much desired by the exploiting class.

We may conclude, therefore, that race adjustment is not a static accommodation. Years ago Booker T. Washington recognized this very clearly. There have always been backward-circling currents, but the direction of the stream has been unmistakable. "The story of the American Negro has been one of progress from the first."[48] The race problems assume different aspects from decade to decade, and the issues tend to become more and more challenging.

Dynamics of Race Relations

The fundamental social force operating among Negroes is social assimilation and amalgamation. In America there has been a strain toward assimilation among most unassimilated groups. This is particularly powerful among Negroes because their parent culture was not only designedly extirpated, but it also lost virtually all prestige on the American scene. Colored people, then, are oriented toward the broader culture of the country; only through social rebuffs are they turned back upon themselves. In this the attitude of whites and Negroes is not similar but opposed. The racially articulate whites feel that they must guard their exploitative advantage (not specifically

---

[46] Gilbert T. Stephenson, *Race Distinction in American Law,* p. 217.

[47] For a discussion of legal variations in Jim Crow laws, see Charles S. Mangum, Jr., op. cit., Chap. VIII; and C. S. Johnson, *Growing Up in the Black Belt,* pp. 276–80, for variations in race etiquette in the rural South.

[48] Booker T. Washington, *The Story of the Negro,* Vol. 2, pp. 397–98; see also James Weldon Johnson, "The Negro and Racial Conflict," *Our Racial and National Minorities,* ed. by Francis J. Brown and Joseph S. Roucek, p. 350.

their occupation) for exclusive enjoyment, while Negroes are seeking increasing cultural participation. The difference between the racial attitude of whites and caste attitude is that whites *wrongfully* take the position of excluding groups from participating freely in the common culture, while castes *rightfully* exclude others from participating in their dharma.

The world view of the caste is turned inward, and its force is centripetal; that of Negroes is turned outward, and its force is centrifugal. Negroes, in America at least, are working toward the end that Negroes as a social symbol would become non-existent. However, the caste of Brahmanic India of either low or high status is devoted toward the perpetuation of itself.[49] The solidarity of Negroes is admittedly temporary; it is a defense-offense technique. The ideal of Negroes is that they should not be identified; they evidently want to be workers, ministers, doctors, or teachers without the distinction "Negro workers," "Negro ministers," and so on. In short, they want to be known unqualifiedly as American citizens, which desire, in our capitalist society, means assimilation and amalgamation.

It may not be out of place to say in conclusion that this question about whether race relations are caste relations is not simply an argument about words. In this essay we have attempted to show that they are political-class relations. To accept one view or the other is virtually to redefine one's approach to the study of the subject. One great disappointment about the procedure of those students who have conceived of race relations as caste relations is that they have not employed the caste concept as a hypothesis or a theory, but rather they have used it mainly as a substitute title or name for "race." It is likely that if they had attempted to use caste as an instrument of analysis, they should have discovered that, thus applied, it is decidedly worthless.

---

[49]According to James Weldon Johnson, "We should by all means make our schools and institutions as excellent as we can possibly make them; and by that very act we reduce the certainty that they will forever remain schools and institutions for 'Negroes only'. . . . We should gather all the strength and experience we can from imposed segregation. But any good we are able to derive from the system we should consider as a means, not an end. The strength and experience we gain from it should be applied to the objective of *entering into,* not *staying out of,* the body politic." *Negro Americans, What Now?,* p. 17. To the same effect Frederick D. Patterson writes: "If the most is made of segregated opportunities now, those who develop thereby will do much . . . to break down segregation and other barriers to normal participation." *What the Negro Wants,* Rayford W. Logan, ed., p. 274.

20. The Meaning of Heredity and Outcasting in Caste and Race Relations

The Problem

*T*HERE ARE FEW CHARACTERISTICS OF THE CASTE SYSTEM WHICH are so generally recognized as heredity, and yet the function of heredity in the system has been commonly misunderstood. Almost without exception those authorities who have identified caste and race relations have been prone to mistake the meaning of heredity among castes. Consider, in illustration, the following typical conclusion:

> In essence the caste idea seems to be a barrier to legitimate descent. A union of members of the two castes may not have a legitimate child. All such children are members of the lower caste and cannot be legitimated into the upper caste by the fact that they have an upper caste father or mother.[1]

The orientation here, as usual, is biological and evidently deduced from an observation of the obdurate dichotomized type of interracial adjustment in the South. Thus an insidious truism concerning American race relations has served to skew fundamentally thinking about caste. It runs somewhat as follows: "No colored child can become white; in some colored-white societies whites have decided to ostracize all peoples of color; hence no intermarriage can result in offspring of equal status with whites. Since heredity is the 'essence' of caste, it must follow that socially bipartite race systems are caste systems." To those who think that castes are anti-color devices, this reasoning seems irrefragable. It may be shown, however, that this very idea of heredity helps us further to distinguish between caste and race relations.

In the first place, it may be well to emphasize that two or more castes may have the same general status in the caste system. Therefore, when we speak of the offspring of an intercaste marriage, higher and lower status need not be necessarily implied. One might ask,

---

[1]John Dollard, *Caste and Class in a Southern Town*, p. 63.

then: What is the problem of legitimizing children born to members of different castes with equal status? Further: What do castes really inherit? How does this differ from the inheritance of races? Before attempting to examine the latter question, we shall discuss broadly the nature of heredity among castes.

Nature of Heredity among Castes

Of all things which children of mixed-caste marriages might inherit, the physical possibilities are of the least significance. Of primary importance seems to be an imputed character. Manu declares that from "blamable marriages spring sons who are cruel and speakers of untruth, who hate the Veda and the sacred law."[2] As a rule, the lower the caste of the man and the higher that of the woman, the more vicious the children.[3] The early Hindu law books are not always consistent on the question of the status of children of hypergamous marriages. According to John D. Mayne, "They give no conclusive evidence that the sons of all inter-caste marriages were ostracized from the upper caste."[4] One of the early law books declares: "On women of lower caste than their husbands sons are begotten who follow the caste of their mothers."[5] While Manu assures us that "he who was begotten by an Aryan on a non-Aryan female may become like to an Aryan by his virtues. . . ."[6] The estate of the father of sons born to wives of decreasing caste status goes to these sons in proportions decreasing directly with the status of their mothers.[7]

But variations in the possibilities of inheritance in the system seem to be even more widespread. The principal reason for this seems to be the absence of a physical basis of inheritance. The child of an inter-caste marriage may become a legitimate member of the upper caste; it may descend to the lower caste; it may go into a caste of intermediate

---

[2] Manu, III, 41.

[3] Vishnu, XVI, 3, 6, 14.

[4] John D. Mayne, *A Treatise on Hindu Law and Usage*, 8th ed., Sec. 88.

[5] Vishnu, XVI, 2.

[6] Manu, X, 67.

[7] "If there are four sons of a Brahmana springing from four different wives of the four castes, they shall divide the whole estate of their father into ten parts. Of these, let the son of the Brahmana wife take four parts; the son of a Kshatriya wife, three parts; the son of a Vaisya wife, two parts; the son of a Sudra wife, a single part." Vishnu, XVIII, 1–5. See also Manu, IX, 149, 151, and VIII, 416.

"This relationship subsisting between husband and wife of two different, not to say widely separated castes, was not held to be disgraceful or worthy of denunciation. On the contrary, while it was less dignified for a Brahman to marry a woman of a lower caste than a woman of his own, yet marriage in the one caste was just as legal as marriage in the other." M. A. Sherring, *Hindu Tribes and Castes*, Vol. I, p. xvi.

status, or it may fall to a position beneath that of either caste. The Chandala, a Sudra-man-Brahman-woman cross, occupies a status beneath that of either parent, while the children of Brahman men and Sudra women ordinarily have a status above Sudras, "for through the power of the seed sons are born . . . who are honored and praised."[8] Of especial interest to us is the rather frequent identification of the children of hypergamous marriages with the caste members of the father. On this point Sherring observes:

> The infanticide practiced by Rajpoots has been a fruitful cause of the intermingling of low caste blood with their own. Failing to secure wives for their sons, on account of the great paucity of girls in their own tribes, they have, for many generations, contracted alliances with girls of low castes, especially the Raj Bhars, who having been purchased or carried off from their families, have been transformed into Rajputanis, or wives of Rajpoots.[9]

One device for maintaining exclusiveness among castes is that of taking the women of a given caste but refusing to return the favor by giving daughters in marriage. "Thus, Kurils will take Dohar girls in marriage, but will not give their daughters to Dohars."[10] And the off-spring of such marriages follow the caste of their fathers. "In the Kangra Hills the son of a Brahman father and a Rajput mother is reckoned a Brahman."[11]

Racial Differences

In race relations it is almost always sufficient merely to look at a man to identify him; in caste relations his status must be inquired into. A man's child by a woman of lower caste, according to the pleasure of his caste, may be initiated and accepted into his caste. In the case of a racially dichotomized society it is not possible to legitimize the children of mixed marriages by their unreserved inclusion into the dominant race. This is so because nothing short of making the colored child of an interracial marriage white will be sufficient. The

---

[8]Manu, X, 72.

[9]Op. cit.

[10]George W. Briggs, op. cit., p. 35.

[11]*Census of India, 1911,* Vol. I, Pt. 1, p. 378. "Throughout the Panjab the Jats and Gujars and certain classes of Rajputs who have not enough women of their own, sometimes buy as wives Chamar and other low caste women, accepting without inquiry the allegation that they belong to their own caste. So long as they themselves are satisfied, no one else seems to mind." Ibid. See also R. V. Russell, *The Tribes and Castes of the Central Provinces of India,* Vol. I, p. 365.

1901 *Census of India* explains further certain possibilities of inheritance based upon deficiences of the sex ratio. Thus:

Where females are in marked defect, a relaxation of the restrictions on marriage inevitably follows. Sometimes it takes the form of expressly permitting males of a higher caste to marry females of a lower one. Thus in the Panjab, Khatris will marry Arora women and the Aroras in their turn take as their wives women of lower castes. But, more often, it leads to laxity in inquiring into the status and antecedents of the proposed bride, and to a willingness to accept the statements that may be made regarding her by her guardians or vendors. In this way there is in some parts a regular traffic in young females. Girls are often enticed from their homes in the Panjab and sold either in some other part of that province or in Sind. The purchasers of women in the Panjab are mainly Jats, Aroras, and Kirars, but the practice is also known among the Kombohs and Khatris.[12]

A race inherits, then, physical marks, real or imputed; the caste inherits intangible cultural or personality attributes. It is true that a person's caste ordinarily comes to him as a cultural heritage, but we may emphasize that descent within the meaning of the Brahmanical system does not have the same application as can be given it in discussions of race relationships in, say, the Southern states of the United States. To use the term at all in describing race relationships in the South, we must mean racial identity, for a person of Negro blood born in England or France or the West Indies, who happens to be in the South, must expect to assume the racial status of all other Negroes. It should be gross, indeed, to hold that all Negroes in the world belong to the same caste by descent.

If we look beyond the misguiding truth that a colored child cannot become white, then we may examine the meaning of legitimacy in racially dichotomized societies. In the first place, it appears that the mixed-blood offspring may be legitimate according to statutory law. Consequently, although mixed-blood children may not be accepted as white in any part of the United States, in all states where mixed marriages are not declared illegal the child may inherit property as though his parents were of one race.[13] In one state, Indiana, the child is legitimate, even though there is an intermarriage prohibition law.[14] In the eyes of the law, then, the mixed-blood child may be legitimate. We know of no case in Hindu law where a child who is able to inherit

---

[12]Vol. I, Pt. 1, Sec. 227. See also J. J. Meyer, *Sexual Life of Ancient India,* Vol. I, p. 57; N. K. Dutt, *Origin and Growth of Caste in India,* Vol. I, p. 587.

[13]Kennington vs. Catoe, 68 S. C. 470, 47 S. E. 791 (1904).

[14]Indiana Statutes Annotated (Burns, 1933), Sec. 44–107.

without discrimination the estate of his father remains debarred from inheriting his father's caste.

In the second place, the child may be unreservedly accepted by both mother and father as a natural member of their family. In Haiti, before the revolution, white planters married colored women, and their children ordinarily inherited normal parental affections. These children, however, were not regarded by the white public as its equal. The criterion of acceptance depended not upon superiority of caste but upon superiority of race; in other words, their color alone determined their acceptability. If the colored woman happened to be light enough in complexion, the children were likely to be considered white as a matter of course. And finally the child may be legally defined as a member of its colored-parent group, as in the United States; or it may enter a new group, such as the Cape Coloreds of South Africa or the Eurasians of India. However, by the very definition and purpose of a dichotomized racial situation, the children of mixed marriages can never be given social opportunities identical with the dominant whites. To be legitimized in the white group, of course, can mean only that the mixed-blood child has equal economic, juridical, and social opportunities with the whites.

All Hindus inherit not only a caste status with respect to other caste-men, but also the physical marks of Hindus. Because of the latter heritage they may be considered social subordinates of white men. But the latter assumption develops a power relationship of white dominance and not a caste position of inferiority. The Hindu's racial heritage identifies him with all other Hindus, while his caste heritage differentiates him from all other-caste Hindus. All caste members must of necessity inherit some racial affiliation, but obviously racial affiliation does not presuppose caste membership.

When reference is being made to relationships between races, it becomes rather cumbersome to think of the legitimizing of children as a determining factor. If the colored parent is accepted among the whites, then the child will also be accepted; but if the parents are not accepted, the children may be. In America both parties to a mixed Negro-white marriage can belong legitimately to neither group; yet, according to the lightness of color of the colored partner, their children may become a part of either the white or the Negro group.

Outcasting

The term "outcasting" employed as a factor in discussions of race relations ordinarily refers to racial ostracism socially imposed as a penalty for intermarriage. However, the phenomenon of outcasting is far more involved than this. Restricted to the meaning presented here, the term may be suggestive in popular use. But in the hands of the student seeking an understanding of race relations, it is likely to be misleading. As a substantive, the term "outcaste" may be used in two ways to indicate: (1) a person belonging to one of the menial, depressed tribes or castes who are generally considered impure, such as the Chamar, Dom, or Bhangi; or (2) that person who has been expelled from a caste as a punishment for breach of caste rules. It is with the latter meaning that we shall now be concerned.

Outcasting, in the latter sense, is a well-recognized, dependable form of punishment in a caste system. It has the effect of not merely lowering an individual in the estimation of his fellows, but also of putting him beyond the bounds of his caste. An outcasted person does not continue to be a member of his caste. Barring the death penalty, a caste can inflict no greater punishment upon one of its members. Thus, the Abbé Dubois tells us:

The expulsion from caste, which follows either an infringement of caste usage or some public offense calculated, if left unpunished, to bring dishonor to the whole community, is a kind of social excommunication, which deprives that unhappy person who suffers it, of all intercourse with his fellow creatures. It renders him, as it were, dead to the world, and leaves him nothing in common with the rest of society. In losing his caste he loses not only his relatives and friends, but often his wife and children, who would rather leave him to his fate than share his disgrace with him. Nobody dares eat with him or even give him a drop of water. If he has marriageable daughters, nobody asks them in marriage, and in like manner his sons are refused wives. He has to take it for granted that wherever he goes he will be avoided, pointed at with scorn, and regarded as an outcaste.

If after losing caste a Hindu could obtain admission to an inferior caste, his punishment would in some degree be tolerable; but even this humiliating compensation is denied him. A simple Sudra with any notion of honour and propriety would never associate or even speak with a Brahmin degraded in that manner. It is necessary, therefore, for an out-caste to seek asylum in the lowest caste of Pariahs if he fails to obtain restoration in his own; or else, he is obliged to associate with persons of doubtful caste.[15]

---

[15]*Hindu Manners, Customs, and Ceremonies,* 3d ed., p. 38.

A person once outcasted can seldom regain admission to his caste. For some offenses, however, principally those against one's relatives, the offender may be pardoned by his caste. He usually prostrates himself before the assembled caste-men, "listens without complaint to the rebukes which are showered upon him, receives the blows to which he is oftentimes condemned, and pays a fine. . . ."[16] There are many wrongs which may merit the penalty of outcasting. Among some castes the eating of beef stands as an unpardonable enormity; "people have been outcasted because they had *smelt* beef."[17] Whole families may be outcasted for becoming involved in the marriage of a widow; while refusal to attend the funeral of a relative or failure to invite certain caste-men to one's feast is to court the judgment. Prohibited intercaste marriages hold a secure place among capital offenses, but these are rare, for in India marriage is a major business of castes. Relatives and leaders of the caste assume too pivotal a role in weddings to make unsanctioned marriages a frequent occurrence. It should be remembered, of course, that the significance of caste rules ordinarily varies with the caste.

Now let us consider the possibilities of outcasting among races. It has been frequently said, in support of the race-caste hypothesis, that in the United States white persons are outcasted for marrying colored persons and vice versa. We propose to examine the accuracy of this conclusion. When we speak of a white or Negro person's losing caste for breach of caste rules, what really do we mean has been lost? In this society only the state can punish, and outcasting is no constituted form of punishment. It is not even recognized by the state. Outcasting must mean, then, that the white or Negro race shuns one or a group of its members, though the latter may stand unblemished before the law. It seems too indefinite, however, to hold that a race can shun a person, for a race is ordinarily too socially heterogeneous. Only some persons of certain social-class levels may laugh at or ridicule the individual for breach of social-class convention. In fact, the likelihood is that social-class demotion may be mistaken for outcasting.

For the breach of many types of social sanctions, or even misfortunes, such as loss of employment, going to prison, intermarriage with Indians, Jews, or Negroes, white persons may suffer more or less serious loss of class status, yet they can never "lose caste" in the sense of becoming anything other than white persons. Far less is it possible to conceive of the "white caste" as a whole, or any significant part of

---

[16]Ibid., p. 41.

[17]J. N. Farquhar, *Modern Religious Movements in India*, p. 419.

it, as falling or rising into some other caste. This seems to be a vital distinction between caste and race relations.[18]

Moreover, neither a Negro nor a white person can be outcasted in the sense that a Hindu caste-man can be, for the simple reason that neither belongs to a caste as the Hindu does. Death alone can remove an individual from his race.[19] Although the latter fact seems clearly evident, much confusion has resulted from letting it out of view. A man could be expelled from his caste and forgotten; he cannot be expelled from his race. A white man in the United States who has committed the cardinal sin against his race, let us say by intermarrying, will continue to represent his race. In spite of sentiment against him, he remains a major concern of interracial policy makers.

Therefore, the racially articulate whites are interested, as all the interracial laws indicate, in disrupting his mixed marriage and not in outcasting him. In fact, the instrumentality of outcasting is not available in the American social order. In the caste system the outcaste is dead so far as his former caste is concerned, but a race cannot thus easily give up its members. Should the white woman or man find sanctuary among colored persons, he will remain even as threatening to white dominance as if there were no white sentiment against him.

The crux of the matter lies in the fact that no race by vote or sporadic agreement can determine who shall be included within its ranks. Sociologically speaking, races are defined by intergroup conflict and not by internal selection. A caste, however, is the sole arbiter of questions concerning its membership. It may exclude or include persons at will, and birth presents no bar to this prerogative. The destiny of a caste is consciously in the hands of its members.

---

[18]In India it seems quite possible for entire castes to change their status and identity. "The Sahnsars of Hushyarpur were admittedly Rajputs till only a few generations ago, when they took to growing vegetables, and now rank with Arains. Some of the Tarkhars, Lohars, and Nais of Siras are known to have been Jats or Rajputs who within quite recent times have taken to the hereditary occupation of these castes; and some of the Chubans of Karnal, whose fathers were born Rajputs, have taken to weaving and become Shekhs," Danzil Ibbetson, *Panjab Castes,* p. 8.

[19]The caste system presumes life membership in the caste, but the biological fact of race ensures inevitable affiliation.

21. *The New Orthodoxy in Theories of Race Relations*

*I*N THIS CHAPTER WE SHALL DISCUSS THE RACIAL THEORY OF TWO reputable scholars, Robert E. Park and Ruth Benedict, and elaborate somewhat our own point of view.[1] We shall not, of course, give any consideration to the views of the political biologists who continue to be interested in developing somatic theories of race relations. Trying to deal scientifically with these theories is exceedingly depressing, for almost invariably their apparent objectivity is only a mask for an ulterior purpose.

We cannot defeat race prejudice by proving that it is wrong. The reason for this is that race prejudice is only a symptom of a materialistic social fact. If, for instance, we should discover by "scientific" method that Negroes and Chinese are "superior" to tall, long-skulled blonds—and this is not farfetched, since libraries have been written to prove the opposite—then, to the powers that be, so much the worse for Negroes and Chinese. Our proof accomplishes nothing. The articulate white man's ideas about his racial superiority are rooted deeply in the social system, and it can be corrected only by changing the system itself.

Race prejudice is supported by a peculiar socioeconomic need which guarantees force in its protection; and, as a consequence, it is likely that at its centers of initiation force alone will defeat it. By stepping clear of the whole unnumbered productions of intellectual apologists for Nordic racial pretensions, Adolf Hitler has come into the open and has shown quite clearly the real process by which "Aryans" are made and

---

[1]In our selection of a noted sociologist and an anthropologist who have shown considerable interest in race relations, we are not primarily interested in equating theories. We shall hope only that a critical review of their position may throw light upon significant currents of thought in the field. Moreover, it does not seem necessary to refer to certain statements by these writers merely because they appear correct but have no bearing upon the thesis developed in this study. Social theories gain in meaning and significance if their authors are known; and this fact, we shall hope, is the justification for our personal approach.

unmade. Those people are "Aryans" who have the physical might to support their claim.

The study of race relations, then, is fundamentally a sociological study. In the past, however, the sociologists have not been sufficiently convincing in their analysis to command general recognition. We turn now to a consideration of the character of their thinking.

Robert E. Park

Professor Robert E. Park needs no introduction to American social scientists. His position as a major sociologist and outstanding teacher is well known; his continued interest in the study of race relations is equally well known. He was one of the most consistent opponents of that host of pseudo scientists who take it upon themselves to explain why peoples of color are inferior to white people and how they became that way.

Dr. Park wrote no book on race relations, but he was very much concerned with the theory of race relations in his *Introduction to the Science of Sociology* done in collaboration with E. W. Burgess. His theory will be found mainly in his numerous articles, and evidently the most significant of these is that contributed to the volume, *Race Relations and the Race Problem,* edited by Edgar T. Thompson.

A critical examination of Park's ideas on race relations is valuable not only because it may throw some light upon the state of conservative thinking in this field, but also because it may bring into small focus theories that have gained considerable currency in the social sciences.

The Meaning of Race Relations

In attempting to gain insight into modern race relations Professor Park goes into the life of Ancient Greece and Rome and then concludes: "It is obvious that race relations and all that they imply are . . . the products of migration and conquest. This was true in the ancient world and it is equally true of the modern."[2] This apparently truistic conclusion can have meaning only when we know that "all . . . relations of cultural or racial minorities with a dominant people may be described . . . as types of race relationship, even though no evidences exist either of race conflict, on the one hand, or of obvious racial diversity on the other."[3]

To Park, then, the mere cultural difference of a dominant and a

---

[2] "The Nature of Race Relations," in *Race Relations and the Race Problem,* Edgar T. Thompson, ed., p. 7.
[3] Ibid.

subordinate people is sufficient to produce the phenomenon which we have come to know as "race relationship." Is it necessary to specify "dominant people"? What if the "cultural relations" take place between peoples of collateral cultural status within the same geographical area? With such a definition it becomes quite easy for Dr. Park to find race problems among the ancient Greeks. He does not differentiate significantly between the types of social systems which may or may not produce the variation in human nature necessary for an expression of racial antagonism. On this score Ruth Benedict observes interestingly:

The principal objective of early imperialism was to secure tribute and to bind the subjugated areas to the capital, not, as in later forms, to exploit a new labor market in working mines or plantations. Therefore, it was economical to honor the most able of the conquered peoples and to depute authority to them. In regard to the folkways and cultural life of the provinces, Roman policy was one of *laissez faire*.[4]

Professor Park asserts further: "The struggles of minor nationalities for self-determination is a phase of race conflict; a phase . . . in which language rather than color is the basis of division and conflict."[5] The question here is whether either color or language has ever been *the basis* of race conflict. We shall revert to this in a later section.

It seems quite obvious that this definition is entirely too broad to be of service in analyzing race relations as they are commonly understood; and, as we shall see, Park uses it mainly as a stumbling block. It may be suggested that Dr. Park intends to refer here to something quite vital, that such contacts as take place between a dominant culture group and a "minority people" present all the characteristic relations and mechanisms that we are familiar with in the case of racial conflict. But this is the very question under consideration. Park states neither the characteristics of racial conflicts nor those of culture-group conflicts; hence, if it is necessary, we shall have to accept this identity upon his arbitrary opinion.

Race Prejudice

Race prejudice, Dr. Park admits, has been a very difficult social attitude to define; "no one has yet succeeded in making it wholly intelligible."[6] But our author proceeds to identify the phenomenon:

Race prejudice is like class and caste prejudice—merely one variety of a species . . . as far as race relations are concerned, racial minorities

---

[4]Ruth Benedict, *Race: Science and Politics,* pp. 160–61.

[5]Robert E. Park and Ernest W. Burgess, *Introduction to the Science of Sociology,* p. 646.

[6]Ibid., p. 578.

are merely social classes . . . race prejudice in the southern states is caste prejudice.[7]

The omnibus scope of the concept of race relations is here continued until it becomes clear that there is confusion. If, so far as race relations are concerned, racial minorities are social classes, is class conflict race conflict? Is there antagonism between social classes? What, at any rate, is a social class? If race prejudice is like caste prejudice, what is caste prejudice? These queries remain unanswered.

The following definition also goes beyond mental grasp: "Race prejudice may be regarded as a spontaneous, more or less instinctive, defense-reaction, the practical effect of which is to restrict free competition between the races."[8] Could one say, for instance, that the race that is prejudiced is merely suffering from an inferiority complex? This definition seems to allow such a deduction.

Park does not even settle upon a working definition of *a race,* "since ethnologists themselves are not agreed upon any classification of the human family along racial lines."[9] But he says, "The closest approach we shall ever make to a satisfactory classification of races as a basis of antipathy will be that of grouping men according to color. . . . This would give us substantially the white . . . the yellow . . . and the dark . . . races. The antipathies between these general groups . . . will be found to be essentially fundamental."[10] What now becomes of our all-inclusive definitions of race relations and race prejudice? If this is in fact the author's[10a] classification of races, then race prejudice must exist only between peoples of different color. If not, he should have included in it the social phenomena of classes, castes, minority groups, and nationalities.

Moreover, Dr. Park has here made a significant assumption, the clarification of which is vital for an understanding of race relations. He assumes that there are fundamental color antipathies between whites, yellows, and blacks. Of course Park does not demonstrate this, and we might ask the question: What historical evidence is there to show that before the white man made his contact with the peoples of color there existed race prejudice among these peoples?

---

[7]"The Basis of Race Prejudice," *The Annals,* Vol. CXXXX, November 1928, p. 11ff.

[8]Park and Burgess, op. cit., p. 623; see also Park's repetition of this definition in J. F. Steiner, *The Japanese Invasion,* p. xiii.

[9]Park and Burgess, op. cit., p. 634.

[10]Ibid., p. 636.

[10a]For simplification of reference we shall assume that the citations from Park and Burgess, *Introduction to the Science of Sociology,* are by Park.

Caste and Race

The major part of Professor Park's racial theory is involved with his ideas of caste, and this very fact constitutes his major failing. On the origin of caste in India, he writes:

A permanent caste system in India seems to have had its origin in the obvious diversity of racial types in the Indian population. It is a well-recognized fact that visibility is an important factor in maintaining social distance and incidentally making class distinction hereditary.[11]

This statement covers considerable ground, but it is typical of all the racial theories of "the origin" of caste. As we have attempted to show in a previous chapter, there is available no historical evidence that caste in India had a racial origin. To repeat, the deductive procedure behind this belief is that of imputing the writer's own racial conditioning to an age which could not possibly have known it. Why should "visibility" produce thousands of castes in India? The naked Indian eye has never been so delicate a color detector. But what really is Park's meaning of caste? Although he presents no clear description of it, he declares:

The sect is a spontaneous association; the caste is, in many ways, a *forced* association. After having chosen a profession—let it be priest, soldier, magistrate—a man belongs necessarily to a caste. . . . In India the caste is determined by birth, and it is distinguished by a characteristic trait: the persons of one caste can live with, eat with, and marry only individuals of the same caste.

In Europe it is not only birth, but circumstances and education which determine the entrance of an individual into a caste; to marry, to frequent, to invite to the same table only people of the same caste, exist practically in Europe as in India. . . . We all live in a confined circle, where we find our friends, our guests, our sons- and daughters-in-law.[12]

Therefore, we might say in conclusion to this passage, everyone in the world belongs to a caste. Clearly the author has reached an almost unlimited expansion of the concept of caste. Indeed, he says: "Every religious society tends to assume the character of a caste . . . in so far at least as it prohibits or discourages marriage outside the church or the sect."[13] And "the prostitute, in America, until recently constituted a caste."[14]

We may also observe the contradiction that in India, after a man

---

[11] In Edgar T. Thompson, ed., op. cit., p. 16.
[12] Park and Burgess, op. cit., pp. 205–06.
[13] In Edgar T. Thompson, ed., op. cit., p. 44.
[14] Park and Burgess, op. cit., p. 722.

has chosen his profession, he belongs to a caste, yet his caste is determined by birth. Moreover, it should be interesting to know in what ways the caste is a forced association.

With this frame of reference Park proceeds to interpret race relations in the United States. First, however, there are some traits of caste which are particularly important in this analysis. "Etiquette," he writes, "is the very essence of caste, since the prestige of a superior always involves the respect of an inferior."[15] But why should etiquette be the essence of caste and not that of class or the family or any other little-dog-big-dog relationship?

At any rate, in an earlier statement, Park seemed to have favored a different "essence." Thus he observes:

Sighele points out that the prohibition of intermarriage observed in the most rigid and absolute form is a fundamental distinction of the caste. If this be regarded as the fundamental criterion, the Negro in the United States occupies the position of a caste.[16]

Therefore, we arrive at the conclusion that race relations in the United States are in fact caste relations. "The 'color line' is . . . a local variety of what students of society and human nature call caste."[17] This was not always so, but we are not at all certain when it came about.

The social order which emerged with the abolition of slavery was a system of caste—caste based on race and color. . . . So firmly was the system of caste fixed in the habits and customs . . . of both races in the South that all the social disorganization incident to the Civil War and Reconstruction were not sufficient wholly to . . . destroy it.[18]

The question here is: Was slavery the caste system or did the caste system arise after slavery? Dr. Park does not answer this clearly. In the passage above he seems to say that slavery was caste. And to the same effect he asserts: "It was when, after the abolition of slavery, the caste system broke down that the discords and racial animosities that we ordinarily identify with the race problem began."[19]

With this confusion we pass to another stage in the evolution of race

[15]In Bertram W. Doyle, *The Etiquette of Race Relations,* p. xx.
[16]Park and Burgess, op. cit., p. 722.
[17]Park, in Bertram W. Doyle, op. cit., p. xvii.
[18]Ibid., p. xvi.
[19]Ibid., p. xxi. Again: "The caste system as it had existed was maintained not by law but by a body of customs that was more or less self-enforcing. One evidence of the change in race relations, as a result of emancipation, was the efforts of the southern communities to enforce by statute racial distinctions and discriminations which were difficult or impossible to maintain by custom and tradition." Ibid., p. xx.

relations: "The Negro group has gradually ceased to exhibit the characteristic of a caste and has assumed rather the character of a racial or national minority."[20] However, this appears to be contradicted forthwith. In referring to the Jim Crow experience of Congressman Mitchell on a train, the author declares: "This is an *instance of caste* a little less innocent and amiable than the casual mistake of addressing a bishop as 'boy.' "[21]

At this point we may consider Park's explanation of endogamy among Negroes. He reaches this position: ". . . restrictions on intermarriage . . . make the Negro an endogamous social group, in much the same sense that Jews, the Mennonites, and any of the more primitive religious sects are endogamous."[22] Here the author seems to be very much in error.

Negroes are definitely not endogamous as the Jews or the tribe; in fact, Negroes are not endogamous at all. Such religious cultures as Judaism and Mohammedanism tend to oppose assimilation. Intermarriage is abhorrent to orthodox Jews; and sanctions against it come from within the group itself. This is also true of certain sects. Because white people are endogamous with respect to Negroes, it does not follow that Negroes are also endogamous. There are no primary sanctions among Negroes prohibiting outmarriage; there is too much color in the group for that. Negroes are probably the freest people in the United States, so far as attitudes against outmarriage are concerned, and this notwithstanding certain reactions against white endogamy. A recognition of this distinction should obviate many spurious comparisons between race relations and "culture-minority" problems.

The Mores and Race Relations

There is a definite ring of fatality and mysticism in Park's discussion of the stability of race relations in the South. This is evidently due to the false outlook derived from the caste belief and to an over-reliance upon the apparent extent to which race relations in the South are "in the mores," a static *laissez-faire* concept. The following illustrates his position:

The failure of reconstruction legislation to effect any fundamental change in the South's caste system is less an illustration of the recalcitrance

---

[20]Ibid., p. xxiii.
[21]Ibid., p. xxiv. (Italics added.) See also "Racial Ideologies," *American Society in Wartime,* William F. Ogburn, ed., p. 178.
[22]In Bertram W. Doyle, op. cit., p. xxii.

of the Anglo-Saxon than of Sumner's dictum that it is not possible to reform the mores by law.

People not reared in the southern tradition have sometimes assumed that southern people's insistence on racial segregation is evidence that they cherish some deep, instinctive antipathy for the Negro race. Anyone who accepts that conception of the matter is likely to be somewhat mystified when he learns that the Negro is quite all right in his place. And that place, like the place of everyone else, is the one which tradition and custom have assigned him.[23]

Here is an extraordinary mixture of ideas that is indeed "mystifying." What constructive thinking about race relations might one do when one is told that "custom" assigned the Negro to his place? If not custom, then one is left to choose between "Anglo-Saxon recalcitrance" and the "mores." At any rate, let us consider the mores. To what extent are race relations in the South in the mores? Here Park follows William G. Sumner's fatalistic ideology quite closely.

According to Sumner, "Each individual is born into [the mores] as he is born into the atmosphere, and he does not reflect on them, or criticise them any more than a baby analyzes the atmosphere before he begins to breathe it." When this concept is applied to race relations in the South, the prospects of change appear dismal indeed. Thus he asserts:

The whites have never been converted from the old mores. . . . Vain attempts have been made to control the new order by legislation. The only result is the proof that legislation cannot make mores. We see also that mores do not form under social convulsions and disorder. . . . Some are anxious to interfere and try to control. They take their stand on ethical views of what is going on. It is evidently impossible for any one to interfere. We are like spectators in a great natural convulsion. The results will be such as the facts and forces call for. We cannot foresee them. They do not depend on ethical views any more than the volcanic eruption on Martinique contained an ethical element.[24]

This is the passage from which Park took inspiration; it has also been the inspiration of the white ruling class of the South. Gunnar Myrdal is right when he asserts:

The theory of folkways and mores has diffused from the scientists and has in the educated classes of the South become a sort of regional political

---

[23]Ibid., p. xvi.

[24]*Folkways,* pp. 77–78. In the same vein he continues: ". . . nothing sudden or big is possible. The enterprise is possible only if the mores are ready for it. The conditions of success lie in the mores. That is why the agitator, reformer, prophet, reorganizer of society who has found out 'the truth' and wants to 'get a law passed' to realize it right away is only a mischief-maker." Ibid., p. 113.

credo. The characterization of something as "folkways" or "mores" or the stereotype that "stateways cannot change folkways"—which under no circumstances can be more than a relative truth—is used in the literature on the South and on the Negro as a general formula of mystical significance. It is expressed whenever one wants to state one's opinion that "what is, must be," without caring to give full factual reasons.[25]

At any rate, the question arises: What really is supposed to be "in the mores" and in whose mores? Clearly it could not be the whole social system of the South that is in the mores, and it would be difficult to accept the rationalization that it is the fear of intermarriage.

The "old mores," the slavery attitudes, were not the static phenomena which Sumner and Park have defined for us. They were never assimilated in the American society. Indeed, they might be compared with large stones in the stomach that were not only indigestible but also productive of increasing irritation, until at last they had to be disgorged. So, too, modern race relations keep the social system in a state of continual unrest. These race relations in the South have developed out of the immediate need of the white exploiting class to restore as far as possible the complete control over its labor supply, which it enjoyed during slavery. A high degree of restoration has been achieved, not through the force of "the mores," but through a continued and vigorous campaign of anti-Negro education and the creation of innumerable situations for the exercise of extralegal violence against Negroes or against whites who seek to intervene in their protection.[26]

The attitudes of the white ruling class in the South, called mores, are in fact conflict attitudes. The statement often heard in the South that "nothing, nothing will ever change the South" is like the statement, "They shall not pass." Both presume powerful antagonists; both are war cries. But whereas the general who takes the latter position may be fairly certain that he will stand his ground, the former is made by a class which recognizes that it is constantly losing ground. This class may be compared with a man rowing hard upstream, while his boat

---

[25] *An American Dilemma,* p. 1049; see also pp. 1045–57 for a good discussion of this subject.

[26] See Carey McWilliams, "Race Discrimination and the Law," *Science and Society,* Vol. IX, Winter, 1945, pp. 1–22, where the political and economic interests behind the laws which establish anti-racial "mores" are convincingly reviewed; also Frank E. Hartung, "The Social Function of Positivism," *Philosophy of Science,* Vol. 12, April 1945, pp. 120–33; and E. B. Reuter, "Southern Scholars and Race Relations," *Phylon,* Third Quarter, Vol. VII, 1946, pp. 232–33.

In fact, it may be an advantage to clear thinking, where social controls in modern society are being analyzed, to abandon altogether the concepts "folkways" and "mores" with their magical implications. Other terms may be devised to designate customary behavior that is more or less culturally mandatory in our highly dynamic social system.

moves slowly down with a powerful current. It gives him considerable encouragement to shout that he will never go down.

Then, too, the anti-Negro attitudes which the ruling class propagates among the white masses cannot be "in the mores" of the people of the South because at least half of them, all the Negroes and a considerable minority of whites,[27] reject them entirely. In reality race relations in the

---

[27]This point seems so significant that we shall illustrate it by quoting at length from a feature article published in a leading white newspaper of the Deep South. Probably no right is more desired by Negroes in the South than the right of free and equal access to the ballot; and none is more effectively denied them. Let us observe the state of the mores on this score:

"Next Tuesday is . . . July 4, the day we mark radiant on our calendar as the birthday of our nation, when our forefathers signed the great charter of American democracy. Fundamental to that charter, and on which every other claim rests, is the premise: 'All men are born equal, and are endowed by their Creator with certain inalienable rights.' Next Tuesday we celebrate this birthday of democracy by substituting 'white men' for 'all men,' as we eliminate Negroes from the right of self-government. We will do this with the slogan upon our lips, 'white supremacy.' In its final analysis it may be truly said that this war which we are fighting all over the world today is in protest against the claim of one race to be supreme over another race. Thus the Japanese began their rape of China, and the Germans their. slaughter of the Jews. What do we mean by race supremacy? Racial pride may be a wholesome emotion, or it may become a menace to the rights and welfare of mankind.

"Here in the South we are proud of our Anglo-Saxon blood, and basing our claims on the achievements of the race in the past, proclaim the dogma that our race must be supreme. This is a fatal fallacy. Any people, or individual who claims superiority on the achievements of the fathers, denies the fundamental principle of democracy by attempting to substitute the heresy of inheritance for the test of righteousness of achievement. We can only hope to claim any vestige of superiority for the Anglo-Saxon race by maintaining today the spirit and ideals by which our fathers won their place in the world of yesterday. What was that spirit, and what were their ideals?

"The foundation of Anglo-Saxon civilization was laid at Runnymede, when the English people won from the crown the right of trial by jury. It was the birthday of the English spirit of fair play. Out of that great charter was born years after our own great charter, which without discrimination of race, color or creed declares 'all men are endowed by their Creator with certain inalienable rights.' My Anglo-Saxon pride is in their record of fair play, their fine sense of chivalry, their disciplined obedience to their own laws, and their long history of protection of the weak against the strong.

"By that record the civilization of the South must be tested today. We have in our midst—by no choice of their own—a minority race absolutely dependent upon us for 'life, liberty and the pursuit of happiness.' The traditions of our past, and the very genius of our race, demand that we grant to them the 'inalienable rights' proclaimed in the Declaration of Independence, which we glorify next Tuesday.

"Of course, the slogan 'white supremacy' was born in the South during the terrible days of 'reconstruction,' when conscienceless 'carpetbaggers' and 'scallawags' mobilized an ignorant race, just freed from slavery, and voted them en masse against the welfare of both races. The fear of Negro supremacy produced the defense of white supremacy. But it is folly not to recognize the revolutionary change which has taken place among the Negroes in 65 years. Their progress educationally and commercially is really unmatched in the story of races. There has come an intelligent racial pride, and sense of responsibility, to their own leaders, which makes it impossible for conscienceless politicians to repeat the horrors of the reconstruction political nightmare.

"Of course, we must not shut our eyes to the truth that there is still a great mass

South are rather more in the trigger finger of the people than in their mores. Dr. Park might just as well argue that it is in the mores of the Germans, the "Aryan race," to rule over the peoples of central Europe. Even all the "convulsions and disorder" of World War I and all the attempts of the League of Nations to legislate did not disturb this attitude. Furthermore, anyone who had an opportunity in the early forties to observe the relations between the "German race" and the French people—how the crestfallen Frenchman grinned and reached for his cap as the proud German conquerors went by on the streets of Paris— cannot help concluding that it is in the mores of these people to be ruled by the master German race. Of course the utter nonsense of this hardly bears recitation, and yet it is not different from the antagonistic racial adjustment in the South. Park and Sumner see only the accommodation aspect of the interracial situation. The "convulsions and disorder" of which they speak are themselves the product of maladjustment. Convulsions and disorder do not develop out of social situations that are in the mores; moreover, the racial situation in the South remains pregnant with further possibilities for social eruptions.

Nothing is more discussed, nothing more provocative of heat, indeed, nothing more unstable than race relations in the South. The dominant attitudes supporting race relations are inconsistent with the fundamental democratic mores of the nation, and they are becoming increasingly so. The white ruling class is, to be sure, determined to keep the Negro exploitable, but it dares not rely upon "the mores" to do this. It must exercise "eternal vigilance" in maintaining an ever-present threat of interracial violence if it is to continue its exploitative social order. The Southern racial system "lives, moves, and has its being" in a thick matrix of organized and unorganized violence. As Myrdal observes, "There exists a pattern of violence against Negroes in the South

---

of ignorant irresponsibility among the Negroes, just as there is such a dead weight of ignorant and irresponsible mass of whites. But just here is our faith in democracy. It is not a form of government, but an educational process. It is in the exercise of freedom of choice, with its responsibility, that men develop in intelligence and character. To lose faith in this process is to lose faith in democracy.

"The story which Celestine Sibley told the other day of the schools of democracy established for Negro children was profoundly significant. It reveals the Negroes' faith in democracy, and also their faith that, despite their present attitude, eventually the white people will grant them the privileges of democracy. That is my faith also. Whatever may be the final legal interpretation of our present plan for a 'white primary,' it is so obviously an annulment of the purpose and spirit of our constitution, that it cannot stand against the growing sentiment of an enlightened democratic conscience. We cannot much longer continue to subject Negroes to 'taxation without representation' or draft them to jeopardize their lives in defense of a democracy which denies them the right of franchise." M. Ashby Jones, feature writer, in the Atlanta *Constitution,* July 2, 1944.

upheld by the relative absence of fear of legal reprisal. Any white man can strike or beat a Negro, steal or destroy his property, cheat him in a transaction and even take his life, without much fear of legal reprisal."[28] It may not be too strong an assertion to state that such a condition in America could never become stabilized.

Poor Whites

With respect to the role of poor whites, Park seems to have accepted the popular illusion that there is a fundamental antagonism between them and the colored people. For instance, he says:

It has been the violent . . . efforts of the New South, *in which the poor white man has become the dominant figure,* to enforce upon Negroes the ritual of a racial etiquette . . . that has been responsible for a good deal, including lynchings. . . . Negroes acquired in slavery the conviction that a poor white man was an inferior white man, and the course of events since emancipation has not increased the black man's respect for the white man as such.[29]

Might we not ask what "course of events" Park has in mind which might have resulted in an increase of the Negroes' "respect for the white man as such"? In what sense is the poor white man a dominant figure in the South? Indeed, even at a lynching we do not conceive of the poor white as being the dominant figure—unless, of course, we mean that in most of the lynch mobs lower- and middle-class whites are more numerous. But this could not be Park's meaning, because white mobs have always been thus constituted. As a matter of fact, both the Negroes and the poor whites are exploited by the white ruling class, and this has been done most effectively by the maintenance of antagonistic attitudes between the white and the colored masses. Could anything be more feared, is any aspect of race relations more opposed by this ruling class than a *rapprochement* between the white and the colored masses?

This, too, is consistent with Park's belief in the stability of race relations. Those who rely upon the mores for their interpretation of racial antagonism always seek to define their problem as an irrational upthrust of primitive folk attitudes; as having its roots in some instinctual drive toward repugnance between all biologically distinguishable peoples, a repugnance beyond the reach of cultural variations.

---

[28]Op. cit., p. 559.
[29]In Bertram W. Doyle, op. cit., p. xxi. Italics added.

An Estimate

Shorn of its censual and descriptive support, Park's theory of race relations is weak, vacillating, and misleading; and, to the extent that it lends "scientific" confirmation to the Southern rationalizations of racial exploitation, it is insidious.[30] His teleological approach has diverted him from an examination of specific causal events in the development of modern race antagonism; it has led him inevitably into a hopeless position about "man's inhumanity to man," a state of mind that must eventually drive the student into the open arms of the mystic.

It may seem puerile and even unfair to criticize Professor Park's ideas and views in this fashion. Puerile because one, knowing of Park's kaleidoscopic intellectual style, has no difficulty in finding inconsistencies and occasional contradictions in his writings; and unfair because the citations have been abstracted from their animated setting. But we have been especially careful not to distort these ideas and to consider only that part of Park's theory upon which he seems to put some continued reliance. In fact, this is apparently the whole substance of Dr. Park's contributions to the theory of race relations.[31] Moreover, it is easy to discover inconsistencies but not so easy to show that these inconsistencies are inevitable.

If we know that one believes that the cultural conflicts which existed in ancient times are in fact race conflicts, that race prejudice is caste prejudice, that "the mores" of the white man determine or even maintain the pattern of race relations, then we approach his work with assurance that there will be inconsistencies. Such theories do not explain the facts, and in order to achieve some semblance of logical exposition one must inevitably become inconsistent and contradictory.

Probably the crucial fallacy in Park's thinking is his belief that the beginnings of modern race prejudice may be traced back to the immemorial periods of human associations. As a matter of fact, however, if it is not recognized that color prejudice developed only recently among Europeans, very little, if any, progress could be made in the study of race relations. We must also recognize the peculiar socio-

---

[30]Consider, for instance, the manner in which David L. Cohn, one of the most rabid and effective apologists for racial discrimination in the South, brings Park into his service. Says Cohn: "Let those who would attempt to solve [the race] question by law heed the words of the distinguished sociologist, Dr. Robert E. Park: 'We do not know what we ought to do until we know what we can do; and we certainly should consider what men can do before we pass laws prescribing what they should do.'" See "How the South Feels," *Atlantic Monthly,* January 1944, p. 51.

[31]For a comprehensive bibliography of Park's writings, see Edna Cooper, "Bibliography of Robert E. Park," *Phylon,* Vol. VI, Winter, 1945, pp. 372–83.

economic necessity for race prejudice. Indeed, Park himself almost put his finger upon this. Thus he writes:

There was no such thing as a race problem before the Civil War, and there was at that time very little of what we ordinarily call race prejudice, except in the case of the free Negro. The free Negro was the source and origin of whatever race problems there were. Because he was free, he was at once an anomaly and a source of constant anxiety to the slaveholding population.[32]

Although we do not agree entirely with this statement, it might yet have been observed that in the United States the race problem developed out of the need of the planter class, the ruling class, to keep the freed Negro exploitable. To do this, the ruling class had to do what every ruling class must do; that is, develop mass support for its policy. Race prejudice was and is the convenient vehicle. Apparently it now becomes possible to give meaning to the phenomenon of race prejudice.

Race prejudice in the United States is the socio-attitudinal matrix supporting a calculated and determined effort of a white ruling class to keep some people or peoples of color and their resources exploitable. In a quite literal sense the white ruling class is the Negro's burden; the saying that the white man will do anything for the Negro except get off his back puts the same idea graphically.[33] It is the economic content of race prejudice which makes it a powerful and fearfully subduing force. The "peonization" of Negroes in the South is an extreme form of exploitation and oppression, but this is not caused by race prejudice. The race prejudice is involved with the economic interest. Indeed, "one does not feel prejudice against a beast of burden; one simply keeps him between the shafts." However, it is the human tendency, under capitalism, to break out of such a place, together with the determined counterpressure of exploiters, which produces essentially the lurid psychological complex called race prejudice. Thus race prejudice may be thought of as having its genesis in the propagandistic and legal contrivances of the white ruling class for securing mass support of its interest. It is an attitude of distance and estrangement mingled with repugnance, which seeks to conceptualize as brutes the human objects of exploitation.[34] The integrity of race prejudice must be protected and

---

[32] Ibid., p. xxi.

[33] In his second inaugural address President Lincoln arrived at a similar conclusion when he declared: "It may seem strange that any men should dare to ask a just God's assistance in wringing their bread from the sweat of other men's faces. . . ."

[34] It is some such idea Alexis de Tocqueville had when he wrote: "The European is to the other races of mankind, what man is to the lower animals; he makes them subservient to his use; and when he cannot subdue, he destroys them." *Democracy in America,* Vol. II, p. 182.

maintained by the exploiters, for it is constantly strained even at the very few points where sympathetic contact is permitted between the people.

Race prejudice, then, constitutes an attitudinal justification necessary for an easy exploitation of some race. To put it in still another way, race prejudice is the social-attitudinal concomitant of the racial-exploitative practice of a ruling class in a capitalistic society. The substance of race prejudice is the exploitation of the militarily weaker race. The slogan that the colored man shall never have social equality merely means that the colored man must be forever kept exploitable.

We should not be distracted by the illusion of personal repugnance for a race. Whether, as individuals, we feel like or dislike for the colored person is not the crucial fact. What the ruling class requires of race prejudice is that it should uniformly produce racial antagonism; and its laws and propaganda are fashioned for this purpose. The attitude abhors a personal or sympathetic relationship.[35] The following statement by Kelly Miller seems to be relevant:

Henry W. Grady, not only the mouthpiece, but also the oracle of the South, declared in one of his deliverances that he believed that natural instinct would hold the races asunder, but, if such instinct did not exist, he would strengthen race prejudice so as to make it hold the stubbornness and strength of instinct.[36]

This point may be illustrated further. As an American one might have a great hatred for the English; one might feel the Englishman decidedly repulsive. But normally such an attitude will be personal; it may even have to be private. There are no social sanctions for it. But if the United States should go to war with England, for what real reason the masses of people may not know, then Americans will be propagandized and made to feel dislike for every Englishman. The attitude thus becomes social, and public expressions of hatred for the English will merit the applause of the group. In this situation, to show friendship for the English is to be defined as a traitor, so that to live easily with one's fellows one should both hate and consequently fear the English. Above all, one should never seem to "fraternize" with them; and this even though one's personal experience contradicts the propa-

---

[35]Under feudalism there was no opportunity for the development of race prejudice, for the community of interest among vassals, subvassals, and serfs was based upon personal ties; in modern plantation slavery, race prejudice tends to be at a minimum when personal and sympathetic relationships between master and slave achieve a degree of stability in the process of accommodation.

[36]*An Appeal to Conscience,* p. 23.

ganda. Ordinarily, however, individual experience will tend to be consistent with social definitions and pressures.

Perhaps we can now begin to think constructively about race prejudice. The mystification is probably gone. Evidently race prejudice can never be wholly removed under capitalism, because exploitation of militarily weaker peoples is inherent in capitalism. However, within this system the form of race exploitation may be changed.

Ruth Benedict

Professor Ruth Benedict, the distinguished American anthropologist, is more careful in her study of race relations;[37] yet there remain some significant inconsistencies. She sees, as Dr. Park does not, that racial antagonism is a recent European development; moreover, she has examined with greater insight the intercultural relationships among the Grecian, Roman, and medieval peoples.[38] So far as we know, Mrs. Benedict has developed no theory which seeks to explain Negro-white relations in the United States as a relationship between two castes.

Both Benedict and Park, however, approach their problem with a concept which tends to weaken their whole discussion. "Ethnocentrism" is supposed to have some relationship to racial antagonism, but neither writer has been able to state clearly what this relationship is.[39] They seem to imply, at least, that ethnocentrism is incipient race prejudice. "Ethnocentrism," says W. G. Sumner, "is the technical name for this

---

[37] *Race: Science and Politics.*

[38] Ibid., pp. 157–66.

[39] In an article by an eminent student of Dr. Park which develops not only the letter but also the sermonizing spirit of Park's approach, "the genesis of race prejudice" is described fundamentally and in terms of universal, psychological human traits as follows: "Racial prejudice *is associated* with the disposition on the part of virtually every human group to think of itself as superior to outsiders. The notion of chosen people is quite widespread. We know of primitive communities the members of which call themselves 'men' or 'human beings' to distinguish themselves from all outsiders who are regarded as not quite human. We generally glorify the people whom we speak of as 'we,' whereas the 'others' or outsiders are depreciated and suspected. Although strangers do sometimes have a romantic fascination for us, more often than not we fear them and remain at a respectful distance from them, ready to believe almost anything about them to which we would not for a moment give credence if it concerned a member of our own group." Louis Wirth, "Race and Public Policy," *The Scientific Monthly*, April 1944, pp. 303–40. (Italics added.) This type of discussion of the behavior of "human beings" not only adds practically nothing to an understanding of race prejudice but also definitely distorts the subject. Is it really true that there is a "disposition on the part of virtually every human group to think of itself as superior to outsiders"? Do Negroes and Chinese and Indians feel superior to whites in the sense that whites feel superior to them? If they do not, it would seem that the significant problem lies in an explanation of the difference. As Emile Durkheim points out: "Social facts must be interpreted by social facts."

view of things in which one's own group is the center of everything, and all others are scaled and rated with reference to it."[40] Other sociologists have expressed this idea as a "we feeling" or a "consciousness of kind."

"Racism," asserts Dr. Benedict, "is essentially a pretentious way of saying that 'I' belong to the Best People. . . . The formula 'I belong to the Elect' has a far longer history than has modern racism. These are fighting words among the simplest naked savages."[41] Now it is very difficult to know what Professor Benedict means. She seems to say that modern race prejudice is merely "pretentious" ethnocentrism. But since ethnocentrism is a very ancient and rudimentary social attitude, must we conclude that race prejudice is as old as mankind? The latter conclusion is opposed to one of her basic hypotheses.

The fact is that one will be inevitably confused if he begins his study of the history of race relations by assuming that ethnocentrism precedes the phenomena. Ethnocentrism is a social constant in group association, hence it cannot explain variations in collective behavior. The "we feeling" may be present in the family, in the football team, as well as in the race or in the nation. Ethnocentrism exists today as ever, and it may continue indefinitely without evolving into race prejudice. In other words, ethnocentrism does not become anything else. When a group becomes race-conscious it will have achieved some degree of solidarity; therefore, we may expect it to show signs of ethnocentrism. But the ethnocentrism is immediately a function of its solidarity rather than of its racial antagonism. Indeed, the essential fact of ethnocentrism is not so much antagonism as it is a propensity in members of a cultural group to judge and estimate, in terms of their own culture, the cultural traits of persons in other cultures. John Linschoten, a sixteenth-century white stranger among the Africans at Mozambique, described this reaction among the natives:

. . . they take great pride, thinking there are no fairer people than they in all the world, so that when they see any white people, that wear apparell on their bodies, they laugh and mocke at them, thinking us to be monsters and ugly people: and when they will make any develish forme or picture, then they invent one after the forme of a white man in his apparell, so that . . . they think and verily persuade themselves, that they are the right colour of men, and that we have a false and counterfait colour.[42]

---

[40]Op. cit., p. 13.

[41]Op. cit., pp. 154–55. See also Robert E. Park in *Race Relations and the Race Problem,* E. T. Thompson, ed., pp. 10ff.

[42]Arthur Coke Burnell, ed., *The Voyage of John Huyghen von Linschoten to the East Indies,* from English trans., 1598, Vol. I, p. 271.

Ethnocentrism is always limited—both in intensity and in direction. A people's favorable conception of themselves may be affirmed by expressions of affection as well as by expressions of dislike for certain groups.[43] Therefore, to repeat, ethnocentrism may be thought of as indirectly derived from social attitudes which need not always be aggressive and antagonistic.[44] These may be (a) a friendly attitude: *We* like them; *they* are like us. We will give even our lives to help these friends when they are in serious difficulties—such as the attitude of the United States toward England in the two world wars. (b) A hostile attitude: They are barbarians, uncivilized people. We will not rest until they are subdued—such as the usual attitude of the Greek colonists toward the un-Hellenized peoples among whom they settled. (c) A conditional attitude of amiability: We like them; we are their best friends, if only they will stay in their place—such as the attitude of most white Southerners toward the colored people. (d) A defensive attitude: We have nothing against them; they are powerful, but we will fight back when they ill-treat us—such as the attitude of American Negroes toward whites. (e) An egocentric attitude: the common chosen-people conception of many groups.[45] There are other possibilities. For instance, in a single social situation, the "we" feeling of one group may be graded both in intensity and in quality toward other groups. In South Africa the social solidarity of the white English and Afrikander people assumes a different aspect as it is addressed to the Jews, or the "colored," or the Asiatics, or the natives. We should expect this because the solidarity itself is a function of the peculiar social interaction between one group and another in the total ethnic situation. Extremely isolated peoples may even express ethnocentrism with reference to the animals about them.[46]

---

[43] On June 28, 1943, at the meeting of the British Empire Parliamentary Association in Ottawa, Canada, attended by members of the American Congress, the Hon. Thomas Vien, Speaker of the Canadian Senate, referred to the assembly as "the two branches of the great Anglo-Saxon family."

[44] It is likely, however, that a common hostility toward an out-group may be more productive of in-group solidarity than a common friendship. Aristotle put it strongly when he said: "A common fear will make the greatest of enemies unite."

[45] The following is Aristotle's version of the Grecian variation of this attitude: "Those who live in cold countries, as the north of Europe, are full of courage, but wanting in understanding and the arts: therefore they are very tenacious of their liberty; but not being politicians, they cannot reduce their neighbors under their power: but the Asiatics, whose understandings are quick, and who are conversant in the arts, are deficient in courage; and therefore are always conquered and the slaves of others: but the Grecians, placed as it were between these two boundaries, so partake of them both as to be at the same time both courageous and sensible; for which reason Greece continues free, and governed in the best manner possible, and capable of commanding the whole world." *Politics,* p. 213.

[46] It is likely that not every primitive people would be so confident as were the early Hebrews that God gave man dominion over all the animals of the earth.

The following seem to be characteristic of the cycle of racial antagonism which includes ethnocentrism: first, a capitalist need to exploit some people and their resources; then the more or less purposeful development among the masses, the public, of derogatory social attitudes toward that particular group or groups whose exploitation is desired—here the strategy of the capitalists will depend upon the nature of the ethnic situation; a consequent public estrangement of sympathetic feeling for and loss of social identification with the exploited group—that is to say, a development of race prejudice; the crystallization of a "we feeling" and of social solidarity on the part of the propagandized group against the exploited group and a reaction of the latter; and, finally, the continual appeal to this "we feeling," consciousness of solidarity, or ethnocentrism as a means of intensifying race prejudice so that the exploitative purpose might be increasingly facilitated.[47]

Another shortcoming of Mrs. Benedict's study lies in its abstractness. It conceives of race prejudice as essentially a belief and gives almost no attention to the materialistic source of the rationalization. "Racism," she writes, "is the dogma that one ethnic group is condemned by nature to hereditary inferiority and another group is destined to hereditary superiority. . . . [Racism] is, like religion, a belief which can be studied only historically."[48]

This is the kind of approach which unwittingly deflects the view from the real impersonal causes of race prejudice. Indeed, from this position the author proceeds to identify race conflict with religious persecution. She recognizes no significant difference whatever between "persecution" and racial aggression. The fact that the Inquisition was a religious conflict "is a reflection of the times; from every other point of view religious persecutions and racial persecutions duplicate one another." Again: "In order to understand race persecution, we do not need to investigate race; we need to investigate persecution. Persecution was an old, old story. . . ."[49] This, obviously, is misleading.

As we have attempted to show in a previous chapter, in interracial antagonism it is not exactly intolerance which actuates the conflict. The

---

[47]This, of course, is an ideal statement. Race prejudice is a continuing, becoming, changing phenomenon. It is directly responsive to changes in the whole capitalist system. Moreover, people of all races are born into and ordinarily accept the system as they find it. In modern times capitalists never have to begin from scratch and create the social situation in which race prejudice is developed.

[48]Op. cit., p. 153. The following illustrates further the author's tendency in this respect: "To understand race conflict we need fundamentally to understand *conflict* and not *race*. . . ." Ibid., p. 237. (Italics Benedict's.)

[49]Ibid., pp. 230–31.

struggle is not one directed toward the achievément of enforced conversion; neither is there a secondary interest in the welfare of the group as in persecution situations. As a price of peace, the "inferior" group is not asked to recant or to renounce anything. The exploited race is all right so long as it remains contentedly exploitable;[50] the persecuted group is all right if it agrees to give up its beliefs.[51] Intolerance tends to cease with conversion or recantation, while race prejudice abhors the very idea of conversion. Therefore, religious persecution and racial domination are categorically different social facts. Indeed, during the first period of European transoceanic colonization, the interest of the Roman Catholic Church and that of the capitalist adventurers constantly came into conflict; and the predominance of the one or the other materially affected the form of interracial adjustment. This does not mean to say, however, that a capitalistically exploitative purpose may not be couched in a religious context.

Probably the most tentative thesis of Dr. Benedict is her conclusion that "racism was first formulated in conflict between classes. It was directed by the aristocrats against the populace."[52] In support of this, she relies principally upon the posthumous publications of Henry Boulainvilliers and Joseph Arthur de Gobineau's *Essay on the Inequality of Human Races,* written in the middle of the nineteenth century. Although Dr. Benedict elaborates this point considerably, further discussion of it could have only some remote academic significance if it did not give us an opportunity to observe the confluence of race, class, and nationality problems.

---

[50]The unvarnished purpose of all "racism" may be expressed as some variant of the following discourse delivered in 1859 by a New York advocate of the Southern system: "Now, Gentlemen, nature itself has assigned his condition of servitude to the Negro. He has the strength and is fit to work; but nature, which gave him this strength, denied him both the intelligence to rule and the will to work. Both are denied him. And the same nature which denied him the will to work, gave him a master, who should enforce this will, and make a useful servant of him. . . . I assert that it is no injustice to leave the Negro in the position into which nature placed him; to put a master over him; and he is not robbed of any right, if he is compelled to labor in return for this, and to supply a just compensation for his master in return for the labor and the talents devoted to ruling him and to making him useful to himself and to society." Quoted by W. E. B. Du Bois, *Black Reconstruction,* p. 52.

[51]Recently Hayim Greenberg introduced an article reporting persecution as follows: "Very alarming reports have reached us recently concerning the Jews in Yemen. A representative of the Yemenite Jews informed a press conference in Tel-Aviv that . . . the Jews of Yemen faced imminent prospects of extinction: they have been given the alternative of 'voluntary' conversion to Mohammedanism or of having to face such conditions as would lead to their natural death." See "In 'Arabia Felix,' " *Jewish Frontier,* July 1944, pp. 8ff; see also, for a good discussion of medieval persecution, Joshua Trachtenberg, *The Devil and the Jews,* 1943.

[52]Op. cit., pp. 174–75.

First, however, the meaning of the term "racism" calls for a word. Most people who use the term conceive of it as a racial ideology or philosophy of racial superiority; but, in addition, they usually make the implied or expressed assumption that racism is the substance of modern race antagonism. This almost always leads to confusion because it ordinarily resolves itself into a study of the origin and development of an idea rather than the study of social facts and situations. The study of racism is a study of opinions and philosophies. However, since students of racism are seldom, if ever, concerned with the peculiar type of social organization in which race antagonism develops, they are likely to produce an apparently consistent selection of verbalizations from promiscuous intergroup conflicts as the story of the development of racial antagonism. Such is the difficulty which confronts Dr. Benedict when she declares: "Fanatical racism . . . occurred in Israel long before the days of modern racism." She reaches this conclusion on the ground that the prophet Ezra advocated tribal endogamy and that the tribes themselves practiced group exclusiveness.[53] This protraction of "racism" into the distant past was made even though it is a thesis of Dr. Benedict's essay that racism has a recent beginning.

Although Boulainvilliers and Gobineau seem to have been expressing a similar racial philosophy, they were in fact reacting to two fairly distinct stages in the development of modern society. It is not by mere chance that Boulainvilliers (1658–1722) was a contempcrary of Louis XIV (1638–1715) and that Gobineau (1816–1882) was a contemporary of Metternich (1773–1859) and François Guizot (1787–1874). Nor should it be surprising that both Boulainvilliers and Gobineau are Frenchmen. It was Louis XIV, then the most divine and powerful monarch in Europe, who finally brought the French nobles to their knees and who derived very much of his power from the fluid wealth of the third estate. It was he who "domesticated" and pulled the teeth of the French feudal lords. It was Metternich of Austria who, after the Bourbon restoration in France, led the reactionary forces in Europe against the liberal and equalitarian philosophies which mothered the French Revolution. It was at that time also that liberal writers with Enlightenment ideologies were driven underground. Boulainvilliers and Gobineau, therefore, were reactionaries in highly reactionary social situations.

Boulainvilliers was the champion of the frustrated and weakened nobles; Gobineau was an antagonist of the Jacobins. Boulainvilliers

---

[53]Ibid., p. 163. Compare Num. 36:12 and Deut. 7:3–8.

stood between the monarch and the bourgeoisie, in which position he could develop no significant racial theory. Racism and nationalism are not ideologies of a nobility; superior right by conquest is the basis of feudal claims, and it is upon this ground that Boulainvilliers sought to rest his case for French feudalism.[54] But Gobineau's fire was directed squarely at the proletariat, especially at the exploited colored peoples of the world; he was a mature philosopher of racial antagonism. In grand style he declared, "The human race in all its branches has a secret repulsion to the crossing of blood, a repulsion which in many of its branches is invincible, and in others is only conquered to a slight extent." From the point of view of color prejudice, the *Essay* might have been written by William McDougall or Lothrop Stoddard.

There certainly is some justification for concluding that the *Essay* is anti-proletarian and, consequently, anti-democratic. But, if so, which class does it favor? Dr. Benedict thinks it is the "aristocrats." "Aristocrats" as such, however, are not a political class. Certainly Gobineau was not arguing for a return of feudalism. What he wanted was capitalism ruled by a superior bourgeoisie, probably a vestigial nobility as in England. This, together with his cult of ancestor worship as a basis of national power and aggression, his nationalism, which Dr. Benedict denies, rounds him out as the St. John of Fascism. The following excerpt might have been taken from *Mein Kampf:*

. . . a people will never die, if it remains eternally composed of the same national elements. If the empire of Darius had, at the battle of Arbela, been able to fill its ranks with Persians, that is to say with real Aryans; if the Romans of the later Empire had had a senate and an army of the same stock as that which existed at the time of the Fabii, their dominion would never have come to an end. So long as they kept the same purity of blood, the Persians and Romans would have lived and reigned.[55]

To understand Gobineau and his successors properly we shall have to inquire briefly into the relationship of modern class conflict, race relations, and nationality relations. Class conflict and capitalism are inseparable, modern race relations developed out of the imperialistic practices of capitalism, while offensive and defensive nationalism provides the *esprit de corps* necessary for solidarity in exploitative group action under capitalism. Leaders of nationalism must inevitably be opposed to modern political-class conflict; that is to say, they must be against the proletariat.

---

[54]For a brief discussion of Boulainvilliers and his contemporary Fénelon, see Jacques Barzun, *The French Race,* Chap. VII.

[55]Arthur de Gobineau, op. cit., p. 33.

These three social phenomena, all functions of capitalism, are progressive and, in given situations, they may combine with different degrees of intensity to produce different social effects. Ordinarily, the greater the imperialistic practice, the greater will be the nationalism and the less the class conflict. Therefore, the ruling capitalist class may seek to stimulate nationalism either for the purpose of suppressing class conflict or for the purpose of dividing a proletariat on racial lines so that both groups may be the more easily exploited. In recent times that imperialism which Europeans practiced so freely among the colored peoples of the world has been systematically attempted at home. In his characterization of fascism Maurice Dobb declares that we must see Hitlerism "as a monstrous system of exploitation of surrounding territories, treated as colonial regions for the exclusive benefit of privileged groups in the metropolis: a system of exploitation more ruthless than preceding ones, utilising more perfect and diabolic methods of repression, and essentially predatory in its economic effects."[56]

The modern nation itself is a product of capitalism; medieval peoples became nations as they developed a bourgeoisie. Moreover, the nationalism of the modern state is dynamic. The smaller nation that has become nationalistic[57] and rid itself of the immediate control of a great power tends to move from defensive to offensive nationalism.

Historically, racial ideologies were developed with reference to the relationship of Europeans with non-European peoples and subsequently refined to meet the needs of imperialism within Europe itself. Race problems and nationality problems, then, belong to the same species of social problem. However, we should not conclude, as Dr. Park does, that "language rather than color is the basis of . . . conflict" between nationalities; and it would be misleading to speak of nationality problems as a "phase of race conflict." Apparently the basis of international conflict must be sought either in the type of exploitative situation or in the competitive status of the international bourgeoisie.

---

[56]"Aspects of Nazi Economic Policy," *Science and Society,* Spring 1944, p. 97.

[57]In his famous book on the *National Question,* Joseph Stalin observes: "The bourgeoisie of the oppressed nation, repressed on every hand, is naturally stirred into movement. It appeals to its native folk and begins to cry out about the fatherland, claiming that its own cause is the cause of the nation as a whole." Pp. 20–21. To the same effect, see Leon Trotsky, *The History of the Russian Revolution,* trans. by Max Eastman, Vol. III, pp. 55–56.

A Restatement

We may restate in simple *outline* form the nexus between capitalism and race relations, with special reference to the American scene.

Capitalist, bourgeois society is modern Western society, which, as a social system, is categorically different from any other contemporary or previously existing society.

Capitalism developed in Europe exclusively; in the East it is a cultural adoption.

In order that capitalism might exist it must proletarianize the masses of workers; that is to say, it must "commoditize" their capacity to work.

To "commoditize" the capacity of persons to work is to conceptualize, consciously or unconsciously, as inanimate or subhuman, these human vehicles of labor power and to behave toward them according to the laws of the market; that is to say, according to the fundamental rules of capitalist society. The capitalist is constrained to regard his labor power "as an abstract quantity, a purchasable, *impersonal* commodity, an item in the cost of production rather than a great mass of human beings."

Labor thus becomes a factor of production to be bought and sold in a non-sentimental market and to be exploited like capital and land, according to the economic interest of producers, for a profit. In production a cheap labor supply is an immediate and *practical* end.

To the extent to which labor can be manipulated as a commodity void of human sensibilities, to that extent also the entrepreneur is free from hindrance to his sole purpose of maximizing his profits. Therefore, capitalism cannot be primarily concerned with human welfare. Slavery, in a capitalist society, presents an ideal situation for easy manipulation of labor power; but it is against free competition, a powerful desideratum of capitalism. Labor, under slavery, is of the nature of capital. It should be observed, however, that long-continued contact between slave and master may develop personal sympathies which tend to limit good business practice in the exploitation of slave labor.

It becomes, then, the immediate pecuniary interest of the capitalists, the bourgeoisie, not only to develop an ideology and world view which facilitate proletarianization, but also, when necessary, to use force in accomplishing this end.

So far as ideology is concerned, the capitalists proceed in a normal way; that is to say, they develop and exploit ethnocentrism and show by any irrational or logical means available that the working class of their own race or whole peoples of other races, whose labor they are bent upon exploiting, are something apart: (a) not human at all, (b) only part human, (c) inferior humans, and so on. The bourgeoisie in Europe were faced both with the problem of wresting the power from the agricultural landlords and at the same time keeping the workers from snatching any part of that power. Among the peoples of color, however, the Europeans had only the problem of converting virtually the whole group to worker status.

So far as force is concerned, we might illustrate. In the unrestrained process of "commoditizing" the labor of the American Indians the early European capitalist adventurers accomplished their complete extermination in the West Indies and deciminated them on the continent.

The rationalizations for their doing this were that the Indians were not human; they were heathens; they could not be converted to Christianity; therefore, they were exploited, like the beasts of burden, without compunction for infringements of natural human rights. At that time also the argument for the exploitation of the labor of white women and white children in Europe was that the long hours of labor kept them from the concern of the devil, from idleness, and that their supposed suffering was part of the price all human beings must pay for their sins either here or hereafter.

When the great resource of African black labor became available, Indians in the West were not so much relied upon. They were largely pushed back as far as possible from exploitable natural resources.

Slavery became the means by which African labor was used most profitably; hence Negroes were considered producers' capital.

As the tendency to question such overt capitalist exploitation of human beings increased, principally among some articulate persons ordinarily not immediately engaged in business, the rationalizations about the non-human character of Negroes also increased. Moreover, the priests, on the whole, pointed out that God amply sanctioned the ways of the capitalists. The greater the immediacy of the exploitative need, the more insistent were the arguments supporting the rationalizations.

At this time, the early nineteenth century, many white workers in Europe and in America were being killed, beaten, or jailed for attempting to organize themselves so that they might limit their free exploitation by the entrepreneurs. Their unions were considered conspiracies against "society," and thus against the bourgeois state.

In 1861 the Civil War was commenced partly as a reaction to certain social pressures to break the monopoly on black labor in the

South and to open up the natural resources of that region for freer exploitation.

At length, however, the Southern agricultural capitalists initiated a counterrevolution and re-established a high degree of control over their labor supply. To do this they had to marshal every force, including the emotional power of the masses of poor whites, in a fanatical campaign of race hatred, with sexual passion as the emotional core.

In support of this restoration the ruling class enacted black codes in which the principal offenses were attempts to whiten the black labor force by sexual contacts and tampering with the labor supply by union organizers or labor recruiters. All sympathetic contact between the white and black masses was scrupulously ruled out by a studied system of segregation. The whole Negro race was defined as having a "place," that of the freely exploitable worker—a place which it could not possibly keep if intermarriage was permitted.

At this time, also, the last quarter of the nineteenth century, the labor movement in the North was being driven underground. Labor had to organize in secret societies—sometimes terroristic societies. Troops, sometimes Federal troops, were being called out from east to west to put down strikes, and the Knights of Labor became a proletarian movement.

Today the ruling class in the South effectively controls legislation in the national Congress favorable to the continued exploitation of the Negro masses mainly by diplomatic bargaining with the politicians of the Northern capitalist exploiters of white labor. The guardians of the racial system in the South control or spend millions of dollars to maintain segregation devices—the most powerful illusory contrivance for keeping poor whites and Negroes antagonized—and to spread anticolor propaganda all over the nation and the world. For this expenditure they expect a return more or less calculable in dollars and cents.

Today it is of vital consequence that black labor and white labor in the South be kept glaring at each other, for if they were permitted to come together in force and to identify their interests as workers, the difficulty of exploiting them would be increased beyond calculation. Indeed, the persistence of the whole system of worker exploitation in the United States depends pivotally upon the maintenance of an active race hatred between white and black workers in the South.

The rationalizations of the exploitative purpose which we know as race prejudice are always couched in terms of the ideology of the age. At first it was mainly religious, then historico-anthropological, then Darwinian-anthropometrical, and today it is sexual, *laissez faire,* and mystical. The intent of these rationalizations, of course, must always be to elicit a collective feeling of more or less ruthless antagonism against and contempt for the exploited race or class. They could never have the meaning that, since the race or class is supposed to be inferior, superior persons ought to be humane toward it—ought to help it along the rugged road whereby full superior stature might be achieved. On the contrary, they must always have the intent and meaning that, since the race is inferior, superior people have a natural right to suppress and to exploit it. The more "inferior" the race is, the more securely the yoke should be clamped around its neck and the saddle fixed upon its back. The rationalizations are thus a defense; race prejudice is a defensive attitude. The obtrusiveness of certain social ideals developed under capitalism as concessions to the masses makes the rationalizations of racial exploitation necessary.

22. *The Modern Caste School of Race Relations*

D URING THE LAST DECADE A PROLIFIC SCHOOL OF WRITERS ON
race relations in the United States, led mainly by social anthropologists, has relied religiously upon an ingenious, if not original,
caste hypothesis. Professor W. Lloyd Warner is the admitted leader of
the movement, and his followers include scholars of considerable distinction.[1] We propose here to examine critically the position of this
school.

The Hypothesis

If we think of a hypothesis as a tentative statement of a theory which
some researcher sets out to demonstrate or to prove, then the school has
no hypothesis. But we shall quote liberally so that the authors might
have an opportunity to speak for themselves about the things which
they believe. These we shall call loosely the hypothesis. The school is
particularly interested in race relations in the Southern states of the
United States, and its members believe that they have struck upon an

---

[1] See the leading hypothesis by W. Lloyd Warner, "American Caste and Class,"
American Journal of Sociology, Vol. XLII, September 1936, pp. 234–37. See also,
by the same author, "Social Anthropology and the Modern Community," ibid., Vol.
XLVI, May 1941, pp. 785–96; W. Lloyd Warner and W. Allison Davis, "A Com-
parative Study of American Caste," in *Race Relations and the Race Problem,* pp.
219–40; W. Allison Davis and John Dollard, *Children of Bondage;* W. Lloyd
Warner, Buford H. Junker, and Walter A. Adams, *Color and Human Nature;*
W. Allison Davis, Burleigh B. Gardner, Mary R. Gardner, and W. Lloyd Warner,
Deep South; John Dollard, *Caste and Class in a Southern Town;* Buell G. Gal-
lagher, *American Caste and the Negro College;* Robert Austin Warren, *New Haven
Negroes;* Kingsley Davis, "Intermarriage in Caste Societies," *American Anthro-
pologist,* Vol. 43, September 1941, pp. 376–95; Robert L. Sutherland, *Color, Class
and Personality;* Edward A. Ross, *New-Age Sociology;* William F. Ogburn and
Meyer F. Nimkoff, *Sociology;* Kimball Young, *Sociology;* Robert L. Sutherland
and Julian L. Woodward, *Introductory Sociology;* Stuart A. Queen and Jeanette R.
Gruener, *Social Pathology;* Alain Locke and Bernhard J. Stern, *When Peoples
Meet;* Wilbert E. Moore and Robin M. Williams, "Stratification in the Ante-Bellum

unusually revealing explanation of the situation. In the South, they maintain, Negroes form one caste and whites another, with an imaginary rotating caste line between them. "The white caste is in a superordinate position and the Negro caste in a subordinate social position." The following definition of caste has been most widely accepted.

Caste . . . describes a theoretical arrangement of the people of a given group in an order in which the privileges, duties, obligations, opportunities, etc., are unequally distributed between the groups which are considered to be higher and lower. . . . Such a definition also describes class. A caste or organization . . . can be further defined as one where marriage between two or more groups is not sanctioned and where there is no opportunity for members of the lower groups to rise into the upper groups or of members of the upper to fall into the lower ones.[2]

A class system and a caste system "are antithetical to each other. . . . Nevertheless they have accommodated themselves in the southern community. . . ." The caste line is represented as running asymmetrically diagonally between the two class systems of Negroes and whites as in the following diagram.[3]

It is assumed that during slavery the caste line, AB in diagram, was practically horizontal but that since then, with the cultural progress of Negroes, it has rotated upward. It may become perpendicular so as to coincide with the line DE; indeed, though unlikely, it may swing over toward the whites. The point here is that it would be possible for the line to take a vertical position while the caste system remains intact.

It is thought further that the social disparity between Negro classes and white classes is particularly disconcerting to upper-class Negroes.

South," *American Sociological Review*, Vol. 7, June 1942, pp. 343–51; Allison Davis, "Caste, Economy, and Violence," *American Journal of Sociology*, Vol. LI, July 1945, pp. 7–15; James Melvin Reinhardt, *Social Psychology;* Guy B. Johnson, "Negro Racial Movements and Leadership in the United States," *American Journal of Sociology*, Vol. 43, July 1937, pp. 57–71; M. F. Ashley Montagu, *Man's Most Dangerous Myth;* "The Nature of Race Relations," *Social Forces*, Vol. 25, March 1947, pp. 336–42; Paul H. Landis, *Social Control;* Ina Corinne Brown, *National Survey of the Higher Education of Negroes*, U.S. Office of Education, Misc. No. 6, Vol. 1; Verne Wright and Manuel C. Elmer, *General Sociology;* W. Lloyd Warner, Robert J. Havighurst, and Martin B. Loeb, *Who Shall Be Educated;* St. Clair Drake and Horace R. Cayton, *Black Metropolis;* Mozell C. Hill, "A Comparative Analysis of the Social Organization of the All-Negro Society in Oklahoma," *Social Forces*, Vol. 25, 1946, pp. 70–77; and others.

The counterpart of this group of thinkers is another school which has with equal enthusiasm attempted to explain caste relationship in terms of racial antagonism. See chapter on the origin of caste.

[2]W. Lloyd Warner, "American Caste and Class," *American Journal of Sociology*, Vol. XLII, p. 234.

[3]Ibid., p. 235.

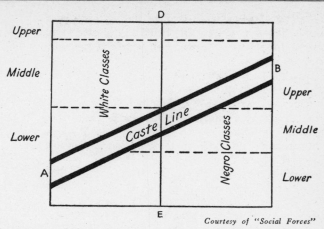

Position of "Caste Line" between Whites and Negroes
in the United States

The "emotional instability of many of the individuals in this group"
may be readily explained since:

> In his own personality he feels the conflict of the two opposing struc-
> tures, and in the thinking and feeling of the members of both groups there
> is to be found this same conflict about his position. . . . Although he is at
> the top of the Negro class hierarchy, he is constantly butting his head
> against the caste line.[4]

It is believed that in many countries of the world besides India there
are developed caste systems, but the school has never found it convenient to demonstrate this proposition. "Caste," Warner and Davis
assert without proof, "is found in most of the major areas of the world;
this is particularly true of Africa, Asia, and America. The Indians of
the southeastern United States and those of British Columbia have
well-developed, if not castes, then caste-like structures. We cannot take
time to examine those American systems, but we shall briefly summarize the material on East Indian caste. . . ."[5] Thus the caste system
in India has been taken as the criterion; nowhere has the school relied
upon any other system.

---

[4] Ibid., p. 236. See also *Deep South* by Davis, Gardner, Gardner, and Warner,
p. 13.

[5] "A Comparative Study of American Caste," in *Race Relations and the Race
Problem*, Edgar T. Thompson, ed. Observe, incidentally, this editor's own involvement with the ideas of the school: Ibid., p. xiii.

On the crucial question of marriage among castes Warner and Davis give Emile Senart credit for the belief that castes "isolate themselves to prevent intermarriage"; while they regard hypergamy as an example of "variations from the caste ideal."[6] Kingsley Davis, however, thinks that hypergamy distinguishes two major types of caste systems. In India hypergamy is possible because the Indian caste system is a "non-racial caste system"; in the United States and South Africa, on the other hand, hypergamy is impossible because there are in these situations "racial caste systems."[7] Warner and Davis depend further upon Senart and Bouglé for their significant conclusion that *"no one occupation has but one caste assigned to it."*[8]

Considerable emphasis is put upon the fact that a Negro or a white person, who is born Negro or white, could never hope to become anything other than Negro or white. "Children and grandchildren of Negroes will continue to be born into, live in, and only die out of the Negro 'caste.' "[9] Further, this biological fact of inheriting racial marks strikes Kingsley Davis as providing an ideal foundation for a caste system:

> The reason that race serves as an excellent basis of caste is that one gets one's racial traits by birth from parents having those traits, and one cannot change these traits during the rest of one's life.[10]

These, then, are some of the leading postulates of the caste school of race relations. Without continuing to introduce fragmentary statements at this point, we shall attempt an evaluation.[11]

Estimate of Basic Principles

Although the school has relied completely upon references to the caste system in India for its authority, it has nowhere made anything approaching a careful study of the caste system. Yet, even so, it has been difficult to determine which of their selected "essences" of the caste system will be controlling in given situations; and one is seldom certain about the degree of concentration of these extracts. For example, after

---

[6]Ibid., pp. 229, 230.

[7]"Intermarriage in Caste Societies," *American Anthropologist,* Vol. 43, July–September 1941, pp. 376–95.

[8]In *Race Relations and the Race Problem,* p. 231.

[9]W. Lloyd Warner, Buford H. Junker, Walter A. Adams, *Color and Human Nature,* pp. 11–12.

[10]Op. cit., note, p. 387. See also *Deep South,* p. 15.

[11]We should add that sometimes members of the school speak of "the American system of color-caste" with probable implication that the Indian system is not based upon color.

their most elaborate discussion of caste in India, the following conclusion is reached:

There has been no attempt in these last few paragraphs to demonstrate
that our caste structure and Indian caste structure are exactly the same,
but rather we have attempted to show that they are the same kind of
social phenomena.[12]

At this point the question may easily devolve upon the meaning of
the expression "same kind." At least the reader might have expected
that the authors would now attempt to show that the phenomena are
indeed commensurable. But they do not. From this point on they proceed to discuss race relations in the United States, totally oblivious of a
theory of caste or of whether caste ever existed in India. Apparently
their thin discussion of Indian caste is merely intended to provide subject atmosphere.

We have had considerable difficulty also in finding clear-cut statements of principle. Usually some such phrase as "for our purpose," "as
here used," "in so far as," or "generally" limits conclusions that are
forthwith given universal applicability. To be sure, one could hardly
question such a contrivance, yet it may be likened to the researcher
who says: "This animal before us is not a horse, but *for our purpose*
it is convenient to call it a horse. If you examine it closely, you will discover that it is a water buffalo. That does not matter, however, for we
are not going to use it in the water-buffalo sense. Obviously, you cannot
say the animal is not a horse; it is, in so far as it has four legs; and four
legs are generally understood to be the essence of all horses and water
buffaloes."

At points where clarity is most needed the school invariably becomes
obscure, impressionistic, or circuitous. It has been accepted that the
form of social organization in Brahmanic India constitutes a caste system. This system has certain distinguishing characteristics; hence we
shall consider these the norm.

Definitions of a society are difficult to formulate; they are usually insufficient. For example, A. L. Kroeber wrote an article on caste[13] and
came to the conclusion that a caste system is not possible in Western
society; notwithstanding this, Warner, without even so much as a reference to Kroeber's negative conclusion, adopted his definition of "a
caste" and reached the opposite position: "The social system of Old
City [in the South] fits this definition of Kroeber's and of most of the

---

[12]Warner and Davis, in *Race Relations and the Race Problem*, p. 232.
[13]"Caste," *Encyclopedia of the Social Sciences*.

ethnologists and social anthropologists."[14] A play with definitions usually results in debate rather than constructive interest in the social problem. At any rate, Warner's own definition of caste considers two factors as determining: (a) that intermarriage between groups is not sanctioned, and (b) that there is no opportunity for members of lower groups to rise into upper groups, nor for those of the upper groups to fall into the lower groups.

It should be emphasized that a definition of *a caste* does not describe the *caste system*. We have shown elsewhere that upper-caste men in India have always been able to marry women of lower castes without disturbing the caste system, a procedure which could not be sanctioned in the South. Then, too, endogamy may be an isolator of social classes, castes, tribes, sects, millets, or any other social groups which think they have something to protect; hence, the final test of caste is not endogamy but the social values which endogamy secures. Indeed, A. C. Mace sees marrying out of one's class as an offense second only to the commission of crime, while Bouglé speaks of the horror of misalliances and the belief in impurity of contact between upper and lower classes in Europe.[15] Endogamy is not the essence of caste; if there is an essence of caste, endogamy merely bottles it up.

Probably the most insidious analogy between race and caste relations resides in the idea of life membership in each group. The identity of these phenomena, however, is only apparent. It must be obvious that a man born in a certain race cannot have the choice of leaving it and going into another race. But it is not at all obvious that a person born in one caste could not become a member of another caste. The biological affiliation of persons belonging to a given race has not been the position of one caste-man with respect to another in India. In fact, this very distinction should raise the suspicion that different social forces are operating in the caste system from those in situations of racial adjustment.

But what really do we mean by saying that a white man cannot fall into the Negro group? To the extent that he can have sex relations with Negro women he can "fall" biologically. The mixed-blood children that are born are, in the long run, the most potent equilibrator of the races; and the lawmakers of the South are by no means unmindful of this fact. The Negro may "rise" biologically if he is able to pass.

From too much preoccupation with the unchangeableness of physical

---

[14]*Deep South,* p. 9.
[15]C. A. Mace, "Beliefs and Attitudes in Class Relations," in *Class Conflict and Social Stratification,* T. H. Marshall, ed., p. 159; C. Bouglé, *Essais sur le régime des castes,* 3d ed., p. 6.

inheritance, the conclusion is reached that the social status of Negroes and whites in the South may become identical, yet they will continue to constitute two castes. In explaining his diagram, Warner holds that there is a theoretical possibility of Negroes advancing to the point where they may become the dominant caste. And this makes his theory particularly illogical and sterile.

So far as its logic is concerned, it asserts that Negroes may become equal to whites, evidently in wealth, in learning, in opportunity to control the government of the state; in short, culturally equal. Yet Negroes and whites will still be unequal; unequal, obviously, in color. For a person born white could never have the privilege of becoming black. Clearly, it must be on the grounds of the latter disability that his caste system will still be maintained. And since, so far as we know, time will not alter the possibility of a man's changing his racial marks, we must expect the white caste and the black caste to remain indefinitely intact —an ideal leopard-and-spots theory of race relations.

The race-caste assumption is sterile because it has no way of confronting the real dynamics of race relations. It goes happily past the meaning of the racial dichotomy in the South. Engrossed with ideas of "social structure," the school remains oblivious of the physiology of the society. It presumes that the white man is protecting his color and that the Negro is equally interested in protecting his, so that with the ballot in the hands of Negroes and with the opportunity for cultural participation open to them as normal citizens, the black code which keeps the races segregated will still be the law of the South. Elsewhere we have attempted to show, however, that the greater the relative cultural advancement of Negroes, the less will be the need of the white man's protecting his color. The theory sees a caste system set up in the South in the interest of the white man's color and, for that matter, the Negro's also.[16] Nonetheless, it may be shown that the white man has no such obsession about his color. He will protect it only so long as it helps him to reserve a calculable cultural advantage.

The caste interpretation of race relations in the South cannot see that the intermarriage restriction laws are a social affront to Negroes;

---

[16]Guided by the idea of Warner's caste line, Guy B. Johnson goes into the following monstrosity: "The great question in the coming era of race relations in the South will be, how far and how fast can the horizontal line of caste shift toward the vertical line of a biracial society? That is, how much equality can Negroes secure in the separate order? In so far as the gradual revision of racial attitudes makes caste distinctions obsolete, there will be change with a minimum of conflict." In *Race Relations and the Race Problem*, p. 150. In other words, this writer reasons that changing social attitudes are making caste distinctions obsolete, and that when all caste distinctions become obsolete, the caste line will be vertical!

it cannot perceive that Negroes are smarting under the Jim Crow laws; it may not recognize the overwhelming aspiration among Negroes for equality of social opportunity; it could never realize that the superiority of the white race is due principally to the fact that it has developed the necessary devices for maintaining incontestable control over the shooting iron; and it will not know that "race hatred" may be reckoned in terms of the interests of the white ruling class. Hence, it is possible for the school to imagine the anomaly of Negroes fully assimilated culturally and yet living symbiotically apart from whites on the basis of some unexplained understanding that their colors should never be mixed. In other words, the races will, as Warner and Davis believe "isolate themselves to prevent intermarriage"! When this static approach is given up, the caste belief must also be given up.

In order that the authors might come to terms with the disturbing question of the relationship of occupation and caste, it is concluded that even in India there is no identification of every occupation with a caste. It is argued, in other words, that since many castes have the same occupation, occupation is no significant factor in the system.[17] The point to remember here, however, is that every caste has a traditional occupation or a limited number of cognate occupations, and not that every occupation has a caste.

Considerable importance is ascribed to interracial etiquette in the South as a social device supporting the supposed caste system there. Thus, according to Davis, Gardner, and Gardner:

> The most striking form of what may be called caste behavior is deference, the respectful yielding exhibited by the Negroes in their contacts with whites. . . . The behavior of both Negroes and white people must be such that the two are socially distinct and that the Negro is subordinate. Thus the Negro when addressing a white person, is expected to use a title such as "Sah," "Mistah," or "Boss," etc., while the white must never use such titles of respect to the Negro, but should address him by his first name or as "Boy."[18]

However, in the South there is also an etiquette intended to keep poor whites at a proper distance from the upper-class whites, and it is probably more severely non-reciprocating there than in other parts of the country. To upper-class Negroes, also, lower-class Negroes are very respectful. The titles "Boss," and so on, of themselves, may indi-

---

[17]See Warner and Davis in *Race Relations and the Race Problem,* p. 231.

[18]Op. cit., p. 22. Incidentally, we may observe that the authors present this passage concerning interracial etiquette with the implicit freshness of a discovery. No one reading it would ever suspect that *The Etiquette of Race Relations in the South,* by Bertram W. Doyle, had been on the bookshelves some years before.

cate only a recognition of superior rank. Indeed, a system of social etiquette which distinguishes superior persons or classes is no exclusive trait of the caste system. It is found in schools, in churches, among social classes, as well as among peoples and races who live in relationship of subordination and superordination.

The method of selecting and identifying isolatedly certain aspects of intercaste relationship, such as endogamy, non-commensality, or other marks of social distinction with their apparent counterparts in race relations, may at first seem convincing. In almost every case, however, the comparison is not between caste and race but merely a recognition of apparently common characteristics of all situations of superior-inferior or superordination-subordination relationships.[19] In conversation with the writer, one advocate of the caste school said: "No better illustration of the existence of caste in the South can be found than the practice of the races refusing to eat at the same table." But ordinarily only social equals eat, sleep, or play together. Army officers may not eat with privates, and medical doctors may resent sharing the same table with orderlies of the hospital; and so, too, a race bent upon maintaining a position of dominance can seldom engage in so socially leveling an act as that of eating together with members of the subordinate race.

The social-essence method of making comparisons between the caste system and other forms of social relationship makes it possible for different members of the caste school to choose different essences as their criterion of caste and yet not disturb the equanimity of the school. For example, according to John Dollard, the essence of caste is "a barrier to legitimate descent"; to W. Lloyd Warner, it is endogamy; to Guy B. Johnson, it is the achievement of "accommodation"; to Robert E. Park, "etiquette is the very essence of caste"; and to some, like Buell G. Gallagher, the criterion of analogy is not mentioned at all, the assumption evidently being that the identity of the phenomena should be taken for granted. Thus, it is possible for these writers to take hold of any one of a number of apparent analogues and proceed with it to identify caste and race relations.[20] If we study the

---

[19] It is this same kind of eclecticism which leads Gunnar Myrdal to conclude that the "status" and "problems in society" of women and children reveal, "striking similarities to those of Negroes." *An American Dilemma*, pp. 1073ff.

[20] As an illustration of this possibility, consider the following remarks by Jawaharlal Nehru concerning the Indian-European relations. "It was a notorious fact," he says, "that whenever an Englishman killed an Indian, he was acquitted by a jury of his own countrymen. In railway trains, compartments were reserved for Europeans; and, however crowded the train might be—and they used to be terribly crowded— no Indian was allowed to travel in them even though they were empty. . . .

caste system as the proverbial blind men studied the elephant, who will trust our conclusions?

Personality of Upper Class Negroes

It is a common belief, not peculiar to the caste school, that upper-class Negroes are especially maladjusted. The biracial system in the United States, it must be admitted, is a pathological situation; and to the extent that this is so, it affects adversely the personalities of both whites and blacks.[21] But sensitivity to social wrongs need not imply derangement or an "off-balance" personality. We may mention at this point, however, that although this assertion calls for explanation, the caste theorists evidently do not realize that it is most damaging to their hypothesis. A person belonging to a lower caste is not "constantly butting his head against the caste line." In fact, the absence of such a phenomenon is so vital to the persistence of a caste order that it would hardly be inaccurate to maintain that it is definitely incompatible with a caste system. Caste barriers in the caste system are never challenged; they are sacred to caste and caste alike.[22] The personalities developed in the caste system are normal for that society.

Negroes are moving away from a condition of extreme white domination and subjection to one of normal citizenship. The determinant of

---

Benches and chairs were also reserved for Europeans in the public parks and other places. I was filled with resentment against the alien rulers of my country who misbehaved in this manner; and, whenever an Indian hit back, I was glad." *Toward Freedom*, pp. 20–21.

It would seem possible, by some ingenious eclecticism, to use even this limited information to identify Indian-European relations with caste relations, but we should expect the dullest of Hindus to remain unimpressed with the suggestion that in India there are two castes: the one East Indian and the other European. And this even though another statement by the same writer is cited in apparent support of this caste theory: "What a great gulf divides the two races, and how they distrusted and disliked each other! . . . each side was a little afraid of the other and was constantly on its guard in the other's presence. To each the other appeared as a sour-looking, unamiable creature, and neither realized that there was decency and kindliness behind the mask." Ibid., p. 3.

[21] On this point Gunnar Myrdal observes: "The conservative Southerner is not so certain as he sometimes sounds. He is a split personality. . . . The Southern conservative white man's faith in American democracy, which he is certainly not living up to, and the Constitution, which he is circumventing, are living forces of decisive dynamic significance. Op. cit., pp. 461–62.

Another member of the school sees the inner strife as a personality difficulty of the whites. "With peculiar poignancy," says Buell G. Gallagher, "the individual white man feels within himself the warfare between profession and practice which he shares with his institutions. Two general streams of experience interweave in this shifting pattern of uneasiness." *Color and Conscience*, p. 24.

[22] Under the impact of Western culture the caste structure in India is being shaken, but it should be remembered that Western civilization is not attacking another civilization in the South, for this is itself Western civilization.

unrest or social dysphoria among a people is not so much their *state* of subjugation or seeming oppression; rather it is either the process of their changing from some accommodated stage of well-being to one of subservience, or some political-class movement itself determined by some fundamental economic change. At any rate, since the Civil War the situation among Negroes in the South has been culturally progressive. Hortense Powdermaker makes the significant observation that it is not difference in class so much as difference in age which determines the attitude of Negroes toward whites. "Among the younger [Negro] generation, those in their teens, twenties, and thirties, resentment is keen and outspoken."[23] Older Negroes were reared in an earlier school of racial beliefs; and, indeed, the younger are not infrequently very impatient with their elders' compromising attitudes toward whites. Among Negroes in the South the "Uncle Toms" are distributed all through the social classes.

Of course militance in the interest of racial progress should not be mistaken for personality imbalance. In fact, dissatisfaction with the status quo must necessarily be the common preoccupation of all Negro leaders. There is, furthermore, some compensation to upper-class Negroes. Frequently they meet whites in flattering situations, mostly in business relations. They have considerable prestige among their own people, sometimes even more than that which whites of similar attainments can hope for within their own group. This windfall may not only compensate for loss of respect from low-class whites, but it may even result in a sort of grandiose importance inconsistent with reality. The "big Negro," a recognized personality type, is usually indelicate and grossly lacking in humility; yet he is not pathological.[24]

Upper-class Negroes do not envy poor whites in the South because the latter are beyond the purview of the black code. One might as well argue that some human beings suffer severe personality traumas because they recognize that the dogs and cats of the rich have certain advantages that they cannot have. The resentment of upper-class Negroes is rather against the ruling class, the guardians of the status quo. Enlightened Negroes recognize clearly the cultural inferiority of the poor whites. As a youth, W. E. B. Du Bois says of himself: "I cordially despised the poor Irish and South Germans, who slaved in

---

[23] *After Freedom,* pp. 325, 331.

[24] Perhaps there should be no objection to a transient assertion of personality disorganization such as the following by Gunnar Myrdal. It makes no point as a basis for significant conclusions. "This national *ethos* [the American Creed] undoubtedly has a greater force in the North than in the South. . . . But . . . even the [white] Northerner has a split personality." Op. cit., p. 439.

the mills, and annexed the rich and well-to-do as my natural companions."[25] The power of sublimation and conceit to rescue persons from isolation and frustration must be reckoned with. Bitter as it is, therefore, the real conflict is usually between Negroes and their cultural equals or superiors. Sometimes it may seem to end in despair, as when Countee Cullen exclaimed:

> *Yet do I marvel at this curious thing:*
> *To make a poet black, and bid him sing!*[25a]

Ordinarily, however, it is a persistent challenge to Negroes, an integrating force in a cause which must be served. Claude McKay, in his *America,* symbolizes this situation.

> *Although she feeds me bread of bitterness,*
> *And sinks into my throat her tiger's tooth*
> *Stealing my breath of life, I will confess*
> *I love this cultured hell that tests my youth*
> *Her vigor flows like tides into my blood,*
> *Giving me strength erect against her hate.*
> *Her bigness sweeps my being like a flood.*
> *Yet as a rebel fronts a king in state,*
> *I stand within her walls with not a shred*
> *Of terror, malice, not a word of jeer.*[25b]

At this point we should mention another crucial misconception of Warner's. He believes that Dr. Du Bois has achieved leadership of a movement for "parallelism" among American Negroes.[26] However, the fact that Du Bois as an assimilationist had a secure following, yet on his advocating a compromise with segregation was speedily wound up in his position and left to the thankless and interminable business of explaining his policy,[27] should have led Warner to give a different significance to the place of "parellelism" in the social aspirations of Negroes. He might have been on safer ground had he referred to the open plan of white South Africans ostensibly to develop a nation of whites and one of blacks within the same economically competitive area.

---

[25]*Darkwater,* p. 10.

[25a]From "Yet Do I Marvel" in *Caroling Dusk,* an anthology by Countee Cullen, p. 182.

[25b]From Claude McKay, *Harlem Shadows,* 1922.

[26]"American Caste and Class," *American Journal of Sociology,* Vol. XLII, No. 2, September 1936, pp. 235-36.

[27]See W. E. Du Bois, *Dusk of Dawn,* pp. 301ff, for a recent defense.

At any rate, segregation is a white man's principal anti-color weapon of oppression; therefore, Negroes can have but one quite obvious attitude toward it. Du Bois's leadership was doomed—and is still so—when, as he says of himself, he "proposed that in economic lines, just as in lines of literature and religion, segregation should be planned and organized and carefully thought through."[28] We may assert, as a sort of social axiom, that, with population ratios approximately as they are, the Southern aristocracy could never yield to the Negro political equality—the right to vote and to campaign for votes without intimidation—and still maintain public segregation barriers. Therefore, it is nonsense to speak of political and economic equality of opportunity with segregation.

The Social Organization of Negroes

Symptomatic of the potentialities of the caste hypothesis of race relations is the classification of societies of the world by Warner and Davis.[29] From simple "theoretical" classless societies to "our own society [which] possesses ranked internal structures, class and caste orders, groups with diverse cultural [ethnic] traditions, as well as sex and age evaluations," all the types of societies in the world are included. Thus the dichotomized racial system in the South becomes a natural type of social ranking. "The ranking changes from a status situation in which there is little or no ranking to one in which almost all behavior is given an evaluation of rank."[30]

Unless clearly limited, the term "society" is very ambiguous. It is properly used with reference to Western society or to a consumers' cooperative society; however, the authors did not limit the concept. It becomes necessary, then, to settle upon some meaning of the term before discussing it. According to John Dewey:

Persons do not become a society by living in physical proximity any more than a man ceases to be socially influenced by being so many feet or miles removed from others. . . . Individuals do not even compose a social group because they all work for a common end. . . . What they

---

[28]Ibid., p. 305. Many years ago, when Alexis de Tocqueville said, "The Negroes and the whites must either wholly part or wholly mingle," he saw clearly the only possibilities of a stable racial adjustment; and it is doubtful whether today anyone will seriously question the inevitability of the latter alternative. See *Democracy in America,* Vol. II, p. 238.

[29]In *Race Relations and the Race Problem,* pp. 225–27.

[30]Ibid., p. 227. See also Emile Durkheim, *The Rules of Sociological Method,* trans. by Sarah A. Solovay and John H. Mueller, pp. 81–83, for a discussion of the misleading possibilities of such a typology of societies.

must have in common in order to form a community or society are aims, beliefs, aspirations, knowledge—a common understanding.[31]

Assimilation and consensus seem to be necessary. John S. Mackenzie emphasizes this:

> When a people is conquered and subject to another, it ceases to be a society, except in so far as it retains a spiritual life of its own apart from that of its conquerors. . . . So long as the citizens of the conquered state are merely in the condition of atoms externally fitted into a system to which they do not naturally belong, they cannot be regarded as parts of the society at all.[32]

Another way of looking at a society is in terms of its capacity to perpetuate itself. Hinduism, or the caste society of India, is a powerful form of social organization which may go on self-satisfiedly, so to speak, forever. It carries within itself no basic antagonisms. But the social aims and purposes of whites and Negroes in the South are irreconcilably opposed. If such a situation could be termed a society at all, it must be a society divided against itself. Sapir has used this idea in his analysis of culture. Thus he writes:

> The genuine culture is not of necessity either *high or low;* it is merely inherently harmonious, balanced, self-satisfactory. . . . If the culture necessitates slavery, it frankly admits it; if it abhors slavery, it feels its way to an economic adjustment that obviates the necessity of its employment.[33]

In like manner we may think of the larger American society as fundamentally antipathetic to the non-Christian, non-democratic, biracial system in the South; hence it is continuously "feeling its way" to something else. To put such a situation easily into a typology of societies which includes the caste system in India, indeed to identify it with the caste system, must be misleading to say the least. The caste system of India is a minutely segmented, assimilated social structure; it is highly stable and capable of perpetuating itself indefinitely. Castes in India constitute a natural status system in one society, while Negroes and whites in the South tend to constitute two status systems, i.e., two social-class systems in two societies that are in opposition.

---

[31]*Democracy and Education,* p. 5.

[32]Quoted by F. A. McKenzie, "The Assimilation of the American Indian," *Proceedings of the American Sociological Society,* Vol. III, p. 45; see also Emile Durkheim, op. cit., pp. 85–86. "By a society," says Robert Redfield, "is meant a recognizable system of human relations characterizing a group, the members of which are aware of their unity and of their difference from others." *The Folk Culture of Yucatan,* p. 80.

[33]"Culture, Genuine and Spurious," *American Journal of Sociology,* Vol. XXIX, January 1924, p. 410. See also Albert Bushnell Hart, *Slavery and Abolition, 1831–1841,* p. 32.

When two racial or nationality groups become more or less isolated from each other because of some continuing conflict situation or basic repugnance, we do not refer to them as forming a social-status hierarchy even though their relationship is one of superordination and subordination or of conqueror and conquered. As an illustration, Adolf Hitler says in his *My Battle:* "It must be held in greater honour to be a citizen of this Reich, even if only a crossing-sweeper, than to be a king in a foreign state."[34] Suppose now that this philosophy be made a reality in future German-Polish relationships; all Poles will then be considered inferior to the least of Germans, and an etiquette will be developed to implement the attitude. But there will be here no social-status hierarchy; neither would Hitler there and then have enacted a caste system. The Poles will seek a *modus vivendi* in some sort of society of their own; and the intergroup relationship will most likely be one of antagonism, a latent power-group relationship.[35]

So, too, Negroes and whites in the Deep South do not constitute an assimilated society. There are rather two societies. Thus, we may conceive of Negroes as constituting a quasi or tentative society developed to meet certain needs resulting from their retarded assimilation. Unlike the permanence of a caste, it is a temporary society intended to continue only so long as whites are able to maintain the barriers against their assimilation.[36] It provides the matrix for a universe of discourse in which members of the group give expression to their common sympathies, opinions, and sentiments, and in which their primary social institutions function. The political and economic

---

[34]E. T. S. Dugdale, trans., p. 182.

[35]Consider the following circular reasoning by Guy B. Johnson, a member of the caste school: "Caste may be thought of as an accommodation, since its very existence is evidence that two or more unlike groups have worked out some sort of *modus vivendi.*" In *Race Relations and the Race Problem,* p. 126.

[36]Professor Robert Redfield described the evolution of a racial dichotomy into a social class system. It is significant to note that no such process could be suggested as a means of liquidating the caste system. "It requires little special knowledge to assert that the contact of the Spanish with the Maya, as is generally the case with long-continuing interaction between diverse ethnic groups, began with the existence of two separate societies, each with its own racial and cultural characteristics, and moved toward the formation of a single society in which the original racial and cultural differences disappear. At the time of the Conquest there were two groups that looked across at each other, both aware of the marked ethnic differences that attended their sense of distinctness one from the other. As the two groups came to participate in a common life and to interbreed, the ethnic differences became blurred, so that other criteria of difference, such as occupation, costume, or place of residence, came to be relatively more significant signs of social distinctness than was race or general culture. . . . At first there were two societies, ethnically distinct. At last there is a single society with classes ethnically indistinct." Op. cit., p. 58.

structure is controlled by another and larger society to which the whites are assimilated and toward which all Negroes are oriented.

The "public" of the white society includes Negroes only in the broadest sense; and when Negroes in their institutional functions declare that "everybody is invited," white people who turn up must assume the role of strangers. The "we feeling" of the white and of the Negro society tends to be mutually exclusive. Says Robert E. Park: "Gradually, imperceptibly, within the larger world of the white man, a smaller world, the world of the black man, is silently taking form and shape."[37] Ray Stannard Baker reports an interview with a Negro store owner in Atlanta:

> "What do you mean by protection?" I asked.
> "Well, justice between the races. That doesn't mean social equality. We have a society of our own."[38]

One device for retarding Negro assimilation, which does not have to be resorted to in the caste system, is the policy of guarding against any development of an overt expression of indispensability of Negroes within the social organization. Whatever their *de facto* importance, they must never appear as an integral part of the society. Instead, they pay little taxes; hence little or none of certain public expenditures should be diverted to their benefit. The theory of taxation according to ability to pay and expenditure according to need does not include them. Crime, sickness, high mortality rates, and poverty almost characterize Negroes, hence they are a drag on "society" and may be ostensibly sloughed off to advantage. Whites are generally protected from contact with cultured Negroes. The successful practice of this contrivance tends to give the Negro a sense of worthlessness and unwantedness, which contributes finally to the retardation of his assimilation. In Brahmanic India, however, where the population is assimilated to the caste culture, it is openly admitted that low-caste men are indispensable to the system, and this admission does not conduce to any advancement in the latter's social status.

By using the caste hypothesis, then, the school seeks to explain a "normal society" in the South. In short, it has made peace for the hybrid society that has not secured harmony for itself; and in so far as this is true, its work is fictitious.

---

[37] "Racial Assimilation of Secondary Groups," *Proceedings of the American Sociological Society*, Vol. VIII, p. 77.

[38] *Following the Color Line*, p. 40. Cf. Carl C. Zimmerman, "The Evolution of the American Community," *American Journal of Sociology*, Vol. XLVI, May 1941, p. 812; Hortense Powdermaker, op. cit., p. 71.

Contribution of the School

An astonishing characteristic of this caste school of race relations is its tendency to conceive of itself as being original. It believes not only that it has made a discovery, but also that it has "created" something.[39] It is difficult, however, to determine wherein rests its originality. We do not know who first made the analogy between race relations and the caste system of India, but it is certain that the idea was quite popular during the middle of the last century. One of the most detailed and extended discussions of this hypothesis is that of the Hon. Charles Sumner published in 1869; and in 1904 William I. Thomas brought his full genius into play upon the subject.[40] Since then many textbooks have accepted the idea.[41] Some students, like Sir Herbert Risley, have used the hypothesis as the basis of extensive research.[42] Many writers, such as E. B. Reuter and Charles S. Johnson, have applied the term casually to the racial situation in the United States.[43] Donald Young has discussed the concept rather elaborately.[44] Among these we take somewhat at random from the writings of a journalist who in 1908 published in book form the findings of his study of race relations in the South.

In explaining the "class strata" among Negroes Ray Stannard Baker says:

I have now described two of the three great classes of Negroes: First, the worthless and idle Negro, often a criminal, comparatively small in

---

[39]"The view that the relationships of whites and Negroes in the South are systematically ordered and maintained by a caste structure, and that the status of individuals within each of these groups is further determined by a system of social classes existing within each color-caste, was the creation of Warner." Davis and Dollard, *Children of Bondage,* p. xvi. "The presence of caste and class structures in the society of the deep South was reported upon first by a member of our research group. . . ." Davis, Gardner, Gardner, and Warner, *Deep South,* p. 5. "An original interpretation of class and caste distinctions in the United States, providing a useful frame of reference for an appreciation of caste phenomena in this country." Ogburn and Nimkoff, *Sociology,* p. 343.

[40]Charles Sumner, *The Question of Caste.* William I. Thomas, "The Psychology of Race Prejudice," *American Journal of Sociology,* Vol. XI, March 1904, pp. 593–611. As early as 1828 Governor William B. Giles of Virginia referred repeatedly to the free Negroes as a "caste of colored population." See John H. Russell, *The Free Negro in Virginia,* p. 165.

[41]Among the best of them are C. H. Cooley, *Social Process,* p. 279, and *Social Organization,* pp. 209–28; Park and Burgess, *Introduction to the Science of Sociology,* pp. 205–06, 722.

[42]See, for example, *The Peoples of India,* p. 263, and *Census of India, 1901.*

[43]Reuter, *The Mulatto in the United States,* p. 360; Johnson, "Caste and Class in an American Industry," *American Journal of Sociology,* Vol. XLII, July 1936, pp. 55–65.

[44]*American Minority Peoples,* pp. 580–85. See also R. E. Park, "Racial Assimilation in Secondary Groups," op. cit., p. 73.

numbers but perniciously evident. Second, the great middle class of Negroes who do the manual work of the South. Above these, a third class, few in number, but most influential in their race, are the progressive, property owning Negroes, who have wholly severed their old intimate ties with the white people—and who have been getting further and further away from them.[45]

With respect to the color line, called a caste line by the modern school, Baker states:

When the line began to be drawn, it was drawn not alone against the unworthy Negro, but against the Negro. It was not so much drawn by the highly-intelligent white man as by the white man. And the white man alone has not drawn it, but the Negroes themselves are drawing it—and more and more every day. So we draw the line in this country against the Chinese, the Japanese, and in some measure against the Jews; and they help to draw it.[46]

Baker then proceeds to clinch the full idea of the caste hypothesis:

More and more they [Negroes] are becoming a people wholly apart—separate in their churches, separate in their schools, separate in cars, conveyances, hotels, restaurants, with separate professional men. In short, we discover tendencies in this country toward the development of a caste system.[47]

It is difficult to see what the modern caste school has added to this, unless it is perhaps publicity and "scientific" prestige.[48] Certainly anyone who has a taste for art might use the information given above to draw a caste line between the white and the black class structures. But Baker, like most other former advocates of the caste hypothesis of race relations in the United States, thinks almost fancifully of the idea and does not stipulate that his work should stand or fall with the belief. He realizes that the consideration of primary significance is not the "caste line" but the way in which that line holds. Thus he concludes:

This very absence of a clear demarcation is significant of many relationships in the South. The color line is drawn, but neither race knows just where it is. Indeed, it can hardly be definitely drawn in many rela-

---

[45]*Following the Color Line,* p. 65.

[46]Ibid., p. 218.

[47]Ibid., p. 300.

[48]It is true that sometimes members of the modern caste school have referred to race relations as "*color*-caste." But, so far as we know, they have never shown in what way "*color*-caste" is different from caste. In fact, some of the early theories on the origin of caste have sought to identify caste with racial antagonism. Therefore, the substitution of the term "color-caste" for caste does not seem to have relieved the fundamental confusion.

tionships, because it is constantly changing. This uncertainty is a fertile source of friction and bitterness.[49]

With respect to the scientific precision of the word "caste" the school insists: "By all the physical tests the anthropologists might apply, some social Negroes are *biologically* white," hence the term "race" cannot have meaning when applied to Negroes.[50] We should remember here, however, that the racial situation in the South never depended upon "physical tests of anthropologists." It developed long before anthropometry became of age. Furthermore, the sociologist is interested not in what the anthropometrists set up as their criteria of race, but in what peoples in interaction come to accept as a race. It is the latter belief which controls their behavior and not what the anthropometrist thinks.

But in reality the term "caste" does not economize thinking on this subject; it is a neology totally unjustified. Before we can know what the Negro caste means it is always necessary first to say what kind of people belong to the Negro caste. Therefore, in the course of defining "Negro caste" we have defined "Negro race," and the final achievement is a substitution of words only. One may test this fact by substituting in the writings of this school the words "Negroes" or "white people" wherever the words "Negro caste" or "white caste" appear and observe that the sense of the statement does not change.

For this reason the burden of the productions of this school is merely old wine in new bottles, and not infrequently the old ideas have suffered from rehandling. In other words, much that has come to us by earlier studies has taken on the glamour of caste, while the school seldom refers to the contributions of out-group students.[51]

One could hardly help recalling as an analogous situation the popularity which William McDougall gave to the instinct hypothesis. Without making any reference to William James, Lloyd Morgan, and others, who had handled the concept with great care, McDougall set out with pioneering zeal to bend all social behavior into his instinct theory. It was not long, however, before reaction came. And so, too,

---

[49]Ibid., p. 31.

[50]Davis, Gardner, Gardner and Warner, op. cit., pp. 7–8.

[51]As a typical example of this, see Davis and others, op. cit., pp. 15–136 and 228–539. Consider, in illustration, the weighty significance and originality with which the following commonplace is introduced: "The critical fact is that a much larger proportion of all *Negroes* are lower class than is the case with *whites. This is where caste comes to bear. It* puts the overwhelming majority of Negroes in the lowest class group, and keeps them there." (Italics added.) Davis and Dollard, op. cit., p. 65. This quotation also illustrates the mystical way in which real problems have been explained away.

until quite recently, the race-caste idea had a desultory career. This idea has now been made fashionable, yet already students who had once used the term "caste" are beginning to shrink from it.[52] However, we should hasten to add that this school has none of the anti-color complexes of the instinct school; its leadership merely relies a little too much upon sophistry and lacks a sociological tradition.

In the following chapter we shall consider the major contribution of the Carnegie Studies, which also relies upon a "caste hypothesis" but which seems important enough to justify separate discussion.

---

[52]See R. E. Park in the introduction to Bertram W. Doyle, *The Etiquette of Race Relations,* and Charles S. Johnson, *Growing Up in the Black Belt.* But observe Johnson's relapse. In speaking of Negro-white relationship in the United States he says: "A racial or caste division of labor is one type of adjustment growing out of economic conflict between racial groups." In *Sociological Foundations of Education,* Joseph S. Roucek, ed., p. 423; also in *Patterns of Negro Segregation,* pp. xvi *passim.* Professor Park has been toying with the idea. For instance, Dr. Donald Pierson gives him credit approvingly for the following simple and somewhat inadequate scheme. "In a caste system," Pierson writes, "the racial lines may run thus:

	White
Race Lines	Mixed-blood
	Black "

Negroes in Brazil, p. 337. For a similar diagram by Park, see "The Basis of Race Prejudice," *The Annals,* Vol. CXXXX, November 1928, p. 20. See also the preceding chapter.

23. An American Dilemma:[1] A Mystical Approach to the Study of Race Relations

*I*F THE THEORETICAL STRUCTURE OF OUR MOST ELABORATE STUDY of race relations in America, *An American Dilemma* by Gunnar Myrdal, is correct, then the hypotheses developed in the preceeding three chapters cannot be valid, for the two views are antithetical. It thus becomes incumbent upon us to examine carefully Myrdal's approach. In this examination some repetition is unavoidable, and it seems advisable to quote rather than to paraphrase the author. This critical examination, to be sure, is not intended to be a review of *An American Dilemma*. As a source of information and brilliant interpretation of information on race relations in the United States, it is probably unsurpassed.[2] We are interested here only in the validity of the meanings which Dr. Myrdal derives from the broad movements of his data. The data are continually changing and becoming obsolescent; but if we understand their social determinants we can not only predict change but also influence it. In fact, Myrdal himself directs attention to his social logic in saying: "This book is an analysis, not a description. It presents facts only for the sake of their meaning in the interpretation."[3]

In his attempt to explain race relations in the United States the author seems to have been confronted with two principal problems: (a) the problem of avoiding a political-class interpretation, and (b) the problem of finding an acceptable moral or ethical interpretation.[4]

---

[1]Gunnar Myrdal, *An American Dilemma*. Although this is a work of considerable scholarly collaboration, we shall, in this discussion of it, assume that it is entirely by Dr. Myrdal.

[2]Herbert Aptheker would disagree heartily with this, for he has published a small book devoted entirely to a criticism of Myrdal's factual data and of their interpretation. See *The Negro People in America*.

[3]Op. cit., p. li.

[4]Myrdal conceives of his problem—that is to say of race relations in the United States—as "primarily a moral issue of conflicting valuations" and of his "investiga-

In the first part of this discussion we shall attempt to show how his "value premise" and the caste theory are employed and, in the second part, how a shying away from the obvious implications of his data is contrived as solution for these problems. We shall not discuss the concept from which the book derives its title, for it seems quite obvious that none of the great imperialist democracies either can or intends to practice its democratic ideals among its subject peoples.[5] Myrdal does not bring to light the social determinants of this well-known dilemma; he merely recognizes it and rails against its existence. It is a long time indeed since Negro newspapers have observed: "The treatment of the Negro is America's greatest and most conspicuous scandal."[6] The dilemma is not peculiarly American; it is world-wide, confronting even the white masses of every capitalist nation.[7] At any rate, what seems to be of immediate significance is Myrdal's explanation of the basis of race relations.

"The Value Premise"

At the beginning of his study, in a chapter on "American ideals," Dr. Myrdal lays the atmosphere for his conclusions on race relations. The way in which the author handles this subject, as he himself recognizes with some contradiction, has been long ago in dispute among American historians. He considers certain national ideals as if they were phenomena *sui generis,* having an existence apart from and indeed determinative of the economic life of the people. Although he concedes that "the economic determinants and the force of the ideals can

---

tion" as "an analysis of morals." Ibid., p. xlvi. Cf. Leo P. Crispi, "Is Gunnar Myrdal on the Right Track?" *The Public Opinion Quarterly,* Summer, 1945.

[5]In a debate at an imperial conference in 1923 on the status of South African Indians, General Smuts faced the dilemma in this way: "I do not think our Indian fellow-subjects in South Africa can complain of injustice. . . . They have prospered exceedingly in South Africa. People who have come there as coolies, people who have come there as members of the depressed classes in India, have prospered. . . . They have been educated, and their children and grandchildren today are many of them men of great wealth. They have all the rights, barring the rights of voting for parliament and the provincial councils, that any white citizen in South Africa has. . . . It is only political rights that are in question. There we are up against a stone wall and we cannot get over it." Quoted in P. S. Joshi, op. cit., p. 107.

[6]Myrdal, op. cit., p. 1020. Dr. Myrdal understands clearly that expressions such as this have now achieved respectability; in fact, they are desirable, since "it is becoming difficult for even popular writers to express other views than the ones of racial equalitarianism and still retain intellectual respect." Op. cit., p. 96.

[7]Years ago Nathaniel Peffer entitled his book *The White Man's Dilemma* and sought to make it clear that "at bottom" the problem is economic—the problem of world-wide economic exploitation by "white capital," of which the American race problem is but one variation.

be shown to be interrelated,"[8] he is mainly concerned not with showing this interrelationship but rather with elaborating an implicit hypothesis that the "American Creed" is *the* vital force in American life.

> The unanimity around, and the explicitness of, this Creed is the great wonder of America. . . . The reflecting observer comes to feel that this *spiritual convergence,* more than America's strategic position behind the oceans and its immense material resources, is what makes the nation great and what promises it a still greater future.[9]

We need not be detained here with the question as to whether either of the foregoing alternatives is the sufficient explanation of the "nation's greatness"; our immediate purpose is to observe the author's abstract orientation. He seems never to recognize the determining role of class interest but rather sets his study against a backdrop of an apparently common American ideology which he says "is older than America itself." Thus:

> Americans of all national origins, classes, regions, creeds, and colors, have something in common: a social *ethos,* a political creed. . . . When the American Creed is once detected, the cacophony becomes a melody . . . as principles which *ought* to rule, the Creed has been made conscious to everyone in American society. . . . America is continuously struggling for its soul.[10]
> The cultural unity of the nation is this common sharing of both the consciousness of sin and the devotion to high ideals.[11]

Contrary to Myrdal's rhapsodic description of class and group unity, James Madison, one of the Founding Fathers of the United States, had this to say about the "sentiments" and beliefs of some of the interest groups:

> The most common and durable source of factions has been the various and unequal distribution of property. Those who have and those who are without property have ever formed distinct interests in society. Those who

[8]Op. cit., p. 6.

[9]Ibid., p. 13. (Italics added.) Myrdal describes "the American Creed" as follows: "These principles of social ethics have been hammered into easily remembered formulas. In the clarity and intellectual boldness of the Enlightenment period these tenets were written into the Declaration of Independence, the Preamble of the Constitution, the Bill of Rights, and the constitutions of the several states. . . . But this Creed is . . . no American monopoly. With minor variations . . . the American Creed is the common democratic creed. 'American ideals' are just humane ideals as they have matured in our common Western civilization upon the foundation of Christianity and pre-Christian legalism and under the influence of the economic, scientific, and political development over a number of centuries. The American Creed is older and wider than America itself." Ibid., pp. 4, 25.

[10]Ibid., pp. 3–4.

[11]Ibid., p. 22.

are creditors and those who are debtors fall under a like discrimination. A landed interest, a manufacturing interest, a mercantile interest, a moneyed interest, with many lesser interests, grow up of necessity in civilized nations and divide them into different classes, actuated by different sentiments and views. The regulation of these various and interfering interests forms the principal task of modern legislation, and involves the spirit of party and faction in the necessary and ordinary operations of government.[12]

The views of Myrdal and Madison are significantly different. Myrdal is seeking to detect the harmony and "melody" in American life, which he assumes are produced by unquestioned acceptance of certain generalized national symbols by all the people. Madison, on the other hand, is trying to see what fundamentally sets group against group within the nation—what it is that produces the "spirit of party faction." We think that Myrdal is abstract and unreal because he implicitly homogeneates the material interests of the American people and then declares animistically, "America is continually struggling for its soul." Madison recognizes the importance of group sentiments, but he does not say they are determined essentially by a creed. Probably if Myrdal had approached his problem from the point of view of group interests he might have recognized the irreconcilable inconsistency even in "these ideals . . . of the fundamental equality of all men, and of certain inalienable rights to freedom." It should be recalled here that the author's assignment was that of discovering the pertinent social factors entering into a situation of continuing social conflict and antagonism.

The following is an intimation of the significance of Myrdal's creedal analysis for his main problem: "From the point of view of the American Creed the status accorded the Negro in America presents *nothing more and nothing less* than a century-long *lag of public morals*. In principle the Negro problem was settled long ago. . . ."[13] Had this statement been a mere figure of speech, it should, of course, be of no consequence. It is, however, in this area of elated abstraction that our author intends to keep the subject. Probably it may be said rather conclusively that the Negro problem cannot be solved "in principle" because it is not basically an ideological problem. Indeed, speaking abstractly, we may conclude similarly that all the major social problems of the Christian world were solved "in principle" by the opening words of the Lord's Prayer—to say nothing of the whole Sermon on the Mount.

---

[12] *The Federalist*, No. 10. See, for a similar observation, Woodrow Wilson, *Constitutional Government of the United States*, pp. 217-18.

[13] Op. cit., p. 24. (Italics added.)

Many years ago Professor Charles A. Beard effectively criticized this romantic approach to the study of American society. He said: "In the great transformations in society, such as was brought about by the formation and adoption of the Constitution, economic 'forces' are primordial or fundamental and come nearer 'explaining' events than any other 'forces.'" And further: "Whoever leaves economic pressures out of history or out of the discussion of public questions is in mortal peril of substituting mythology for reality and confusing issues instead of clarifying them."[14] To be sure, social ideologies are always significant, but they are, on the whole, dependent social phenomena.

It is just such a relationship with which Abraham Lincoln was confronted when he declared: ". . . our fathers brought forth on this continent a new nation, conceived in liberty, and dedicated to the proposition that all men are created equal. Now we are engaged in a great civil war, testing whether that nation, or any nation so conceived and so dedicated, can long endure." Neither side in this civil war questioned the ideals, yet they were—and to this very day are—not fully agreed on the interpretation of the ideals.[15] The crucial circumstances, then, are not the presumed universal acceptance of the "Creed," but rather the interests which make its peculiar and divergent interpretations inevitable. In other words, each side had different material interests and, as is ordinarily the case, the ideals of each were made subservient to the material interests. To put it otherwise, the Creed, in its formative stage, was seriously debated and contested, but since it had become stereotyped, neither side questioned it. Each side, however, insisted upon a self-interested interpretation of it.

The Declaration of Independence and the Constitution have become national symbols, like the flag. It is quite another thing, however, to say that the content of these documents is accepted even as a creed

---

[14] *An Economic Interpretation of the Constitution of the United States,* 1st ed., pp. xii, xvii.

[15] In the Federal Constitutional Convention of 1787 General Pinckney of South Carolina intimated realistically the interests behind the contemporary Negro problem. Said he: "An attempt to take away the right [to import slaves] as proposed would produce serious objections to the Constitution." And he "declared it to be his firm opinion that if he himself and all his colleagues were to sign the Constitution and use their personal influence, it would be of no avail towards obtaining the assent of their constituents. South Carolina and Georgia cannot do without slaves. As to Virginia she will gain by stopping the importation. Her slaves will rise in value, and she has more than she wants. It would be unequal to require South Carolina and Georgia to confederate on such unequal terms. . . . He contended that the importation of slaves would be for the interest of the whole Union. The more slaves, the more produce to employ the carrying trade; the more consumption also, and the more of this, the more of revenues for the common treasury." See Max Farrand, ed., *The Records of the Federal Convention of 1787,* Vol. II, p. 371.

by the whole people. As E. E. Schattschneider points out: "The truth of the matter is that the American public has never understood the Constitution, nor has it ever really believed in it, in spite of the verbal tradition of Constitutionalism."[15a] One pertinent illustration is the non-acceptance of the Thirteenth, Fourteenth, and Fifteenth amendments either in spirit or in practice by the ruling class of the South. Again we cite a statement on this point by James Madison: "Neither moral nor religious motives can be relied on as an adequate control"; and, in another context: "Wherever there is an interest and power to do wrong, wrong will be done."[16]

The Constitution did not settle or remove the vitally conflicting interests of the infant capitalist system; it simply compromised or ignored them. In other words, it postponed for a later date the real solution of latent antagonisms—postponed it until such time as one side or the other developed sufficient power to force a solution in its favor. And yet the Constitution is so ample in its scope that with certain amendments and abrogations it may become the fundamental law of a consummate democracy.[17]

Moreover, Myrdal's "value premise" appears to be demonstrably weakened in consequence of its being built principally upon certain fictitious attributes of ideal types, such as "the citizen," "American popular thought," "the American soul," "the common good American." For instance, the foregoing concept is employed in this way: "Today it is necessary in everyday living for the common good American citizen to decide for himself which laws should be observed and which not."[18]

The Caste Hypothesis

The whole theoretical frame of reference of *An American Dilemma* is supposedly couched in a caste hypothesis. As Myrdal himself puts it: "Practically the entire factual content of . . . this book may be con-

---

[15a]*Party Government,* p. 53.

[16]*Documentary History of the Constitution,* Vol. V, p. 88.

[17]"The federal Constitution was a reactionary document from the point of view of the doctrines of the Revolution. Its bill of rights was a series of amendments added by dissatisfied elements after the instrument had been drawn up and submitted to the people. The rule of the few . . . soon began, and government lent its hand to the few who could invest in its financial paper and who gave their efforts to the building of cities and commerce and industry. . . . A new order of bourgeois acquisitiveness . . . was in the saddle. Democracy, like the rest of the hindmost, was left for the devil." Avery Craven, *Democracy in American Life,* p. 13. See also Woodrow Wilson, op. cit., p. 192.

[18]Myrdal, op. cit., p. 17.

sidered to define caste in the case of the American Negro."[19] However, it is evident that Myrdal—in spite of the lamentable use of such phrases as "in our view," "as we have defined it," and so on—does not intend to coin a new concept. In criticizing Charles S. Johnson's idea of caste he declares, "We do not believe that such a caste system as he has defined ever existed."[20] Therefore, in his explanation of race relations in the United States, our author means to accept the known concept as a norm. Of some significance is the way in which the term is selected. This is the reasoning:

The term "race" is . . . inappropriate in a scientific inquiry since it has biological and genetic connotations which . . . run parallel to widely spread false racial beliefs. The . . . term, "class," is impractical and confusing . . . since it is generally used to refer to a non-rigid status group from which an individual member can rise or fall. . . . We need a term to distinguish the large and systematic type of social differentiation from the small and spotty type and have . . . used the term "caste."[21]

Obviously, in arriving at this decision to use the term "caste" in explaining race relations in the United States, Dr. Myrdal employs the method of successive elimination. Without attempting to be facetious, it may be compared with that of the scientist who comes upon a strange animal and, having the necessity to classify it, says to himself: "This is not a cat, I am sure; neither is it a dog, I am positive of that; therefore, since I do not think of anything else, I am going to call it a duck."

There is no new theory of race relations in this study, but it develops the most elaborate defense of the caste belief. Dr. Myrdal has adopted not only the whole theory of the caste school of race relations in the United States but also its procedure. Like the leadership of this school, he appears to have taken some pride in regarding as worthless a study of Hindu society as a basis for making comparisons with Western society. Yet, as we should expect, he depends entirely upon the Hindu system for his orientation.

Thus the reader is asked to accept generalizations about the caste system in America when no other reference is made to the cultural norm than the following:

It should be pointed out . . . that those societies to which the term "caste" is applied without controversy—notably the ante-bellum slavery society of the South and the Hindu society of India—do not have the "stable equilibrium" which American sociologists from their distance are

---

[19]Ibid., p. 669.
[20]Ibid., p. 1375.
[21]Ibid., p. 667.

often inclined to attribute to them. . . . A Hindu acquaintance once told me that the situation in the United States is as much or more describable by the term "caste" as is the situation in India.[22]

From this, one thing is clear: Myrdal is very much in error in believing that it is recognized without controversy that slavery in the South constituted a caste system.[23] Moreover, it is difficult to see how one could avoid the conclusion that the author has descended to some vulgar means in referring to the hearsay of "a Hindu acquaintance" as authority for the sociology of caste.

The Biological Problem

Probably the crucial circumstance in attempts to use some term other than race in describing race relations is a desire to get around the biological implications in the term. Yet it has never been shown that there is a real necessity for this. In fact, those who verbally eschew the biological connotation of the term proceed, nonetheless, to make physical differences the crux of their discussion. This is particularly true of Myrdal. Says he, "Negro features are so distinct that only in the Negro problem does [belief in the desirability of a light skin and "good" features] become of great social importance."[24] And he proceeds, evidently without realizing it, to point out the relationship of skin color to caste:

. . . the average Negro cannot effectively change his color and other physical features. If the dark Negro accepts the white man's valuation of skin color, he must stamp himself an inferior. If the light Negro accepts this valuation, he places himself above the darker Negroes but below the whites, and he reduces his loyalty to his caste.[25]

Myrdal continues his biological interpretation of race relations with great clarity. "When we say that Negroes form a lower caste in America," he asserts, "we mean that they are subject to certain disabilities solely because they are 'Negroes,' "[26] manifestly; that is to say, solely because they are colored or black. Moreover, although the writer did not elaborate this point, he refers to Asiatics, Indians, and Negroes as

---

[22]Ibid., p. 668. See also note c.

[23]We cannot be certain, however, that Myrdal has a settled view on this point, for he says elsewhere: "After the [Civil] War and Emancipation, the race dogma was retained in the South as necessary to justify the caste system which succeeded slavery. . . ." Ibid., p. 88. See also pp. 221–24.

[24]Ibid., p. 669.

[25]Ibid., p. 669.

[26]Ibid., p. 669.

"the several subordinate castes."[27] It should be interesting to see how he fits these peoples into an American caste hierarchy. At any rate, with this conception of race relations, the author inevitably comes to the end of the blind alley: that the caste system remains intact so long as the Negro remains colored.

The change and variations which occur in the American caste system relate only to caste relations, not to the dividing line between castes. The latter stays rigid and unblurred. It will remain fixed until it becomes possible for a person to pass legitimately from the lower caste to the higher without misrepresentation of his origin. The American definition of "Negro" as a person who has the slightest amount of Negro ancestry has the significance in making the caste line absolutely rigid.[28]

Myrdal is so thoroughly preoccupied with the great significance of skin color that, although he realizes that in America Negroes of lighter complexion have greater social opportunities, he believes that they may as well be unmixed blacks so far as the "caste line" is concerned. Accordingly he asserts: "Without any doubt a Negro with light skin and other European features has in the North an advantage with white people when competing for jobs available for Negroes. . . . Perhaps of even greater importance is the fact that the Negro community itself has accepted this color preference."[29] This, however, has nothing to do with the rigidity of the caste line.

When Dr. Myrdal strays from his physical emphasis he becomes confused. For instance, he concludes that "being a Negro means being subject to considerable disabilities in practically all spheres of life."[30] Evidently it must follow logically from this that to the extent to which these "disabilities" are removed, to that extent also a person ceases to remain a Negro. The confusion is further deepened by the combination of a cultural and biological view of caste.

Caste . . . consists of such drastic restrictions to free competition in various spheres of life that the individual in a lower caste cannot, by any means, change his status except by a secret and illegitimate "passing" which is possible only to the few who have the physical appearance of members of the upper caste.[31]

In other words, caste consists in restrictions to free competitions, but restrictions to free competition are entirely limited by a man's

[27]Ibid., p. 670.
[28]Ibid., pp. 668–69.
[29]Ibid., p. 697.
[30]Ibid., p. 668.
[31]Ibid., p. 675.

physical appearance. Now, we may ask, what is the nexus between physical appearance and caste?

Rigidity of the Caste System

We may reiterate that the caste school of race relations is laboring under the illusion of a simple but vicious truism. One man is white, another is black; the cultural opportunities of these two men may be the same, but since the black man cannot become white, there will always be a white caste and a black caste: "The actual import of caste is gradually changing as the Negro class structure develops— except in the fundamental restrictions that no Negro is allowed to ascend into the white caste."[32] Yet, if this is so, what possible meaning could the following observation have? "We have been brought to view the caste order as fundamentally a system of disabilities forced by the whites upon the Negroes."[33]

Closely related to this amorphous concept of the rigidity of caste is the meaning given to interracial endogamy. Myrdal uses it to identify the races in the United States as castes.

> The scientifically important difference between the terms "caste" and "class" is . . . a relatively large difference in freedom of movement between groups. This difference is foremost in marriage relations. . . . The ban on intermarriage is one expression of the still broader principle . . . that a man born a Negro or a white is not allowed to pass from the one status to the other as he can pass from one class to another.[34]

Now it could hardly be too much emphasized that endogamy of itself is no final criterion of caste. Endogamy is an isolator of social values deemed sacrosanct by social groups, and there are many kinds of social groups besides castes that are endogamous. The final test of caste is an identification of the social values and organization isolated by endogamy. To say that intercaste endogamy in India means the same thing as interracial endogamy in the United States is like saying that a lemon and a potato are the same things because they both have skins.

An illustration of Myrdal's complete disregard of the nature of caste organization is his discussion of "caste struggle." This concept of "caste struggle," to be sure, is totally foreign to our norm, the Indian caste system. Moreover, this must be so because castes in Brah-

---

[32] Ibid., p. 693.
[33] Ibid., p. 669.
[34] Ibid., p. 668.

manic India do not want to be anything other than castes. There is no effort or logical need to homogeneate themselves. A caste is a status entity in an assimilated, self-satisfied society. Regardless of his position in the society, a man's caste is sacred to him; and one caste does not dominate the other. The following description of caste has absolutely no application to caste in India.

The caste distinctions are actually gulfs which divide the population into antagonistic camps. The caste line . . . is not only an expression of caste differences and caste conflicts, but it has come itself to be a catalyst to widen differences and engender conflicts.[35]

Mysticism

If the scientist has no clear conception of the norm which he is using to interpret social phenomena, the norm itself is likely to become lost in the data. When this happens he will ordinarily have recourse to mystical flights. In our case Myrdal seems to attribute magical powers to caste. Speaking of the cause of the economic position of Negroes in the United States he says: "Their caste position keeps them poor and ill-educated."[36] And, "Caste consigns the overwhelming majority of Negroes to the lower class."[37] Indeed, the whole meaning of racial exploitation in the United States is laid at the altar of caste. Thus it is observed: "The measures to keep the Negroes disfranchised and deprived of full civil rights and the whole structure of social and economic discrimination are to be viewed as attempts to enforce *the caste principle*."[38]

More immediately, this mysticism is due primarily to a misapprehension of the whole basis of race relations. Caste is vaguely conceived of as something, the preservation of which is valuable per se. "The caste system is upheld by its own inertia and by the superior caste's interests in upholding it."[39] It is no wonder, then, that Myrdal falls into the egregious error of thinking that the subordination of Negroes in the South is particularly the business of poor whites. In this light he reasons: "That 'all Negroes are alike' and should be treated in the same way is still insisted upon by many whites, especially in the lower classes, who actually feel, or fear, competition from the Negroes and who are inclined to sense a challenge to their status in the

---

[35]Ibid., pp. 676–77.

[36]Ibid., p. 669.

[37]Ibid., p. 71.

[38]Ibid., p. 690. (Italics added.)

[39]Ibid., p. 669.

fact that some Negroes rise from the bottom."[40] This, obviously, is a conception of race relations in terms of personal invidiousness. Surely, to say that "Southern whites, *especially in the lower brackets* . . . have succeeded in retaining [the] legal and political system" is to miss the point entirely. We shall return to this question in the following section.

One primary objection to the use of the caste belief in the study of race relations rests not so much upon its scientific untenability as upon its insidious potentialities. It lumps all white people and all Negroes into two antagonistic groups struggling in the interest of a mysterious god called caste. This is very much to the liking of the exploiters of labor, since it tends to confuse them in an emotional matrix with all the people. Observe in illustration how Myrdal directs our view: "All of these thousand and one precepts, etiquettes, taboos, and disabilities inflicted upon the Negro have a common purpose: to express the subordinate status of the Negro people and the exalted position of the whites. They have their meaning and chief function as symbols."[41]

It thus appears that if *white people* were not so wicked, if they would only cease wanting to "exalt" themselves and accept the "American Creed," race prejudice would vanish from America. "Why," asks Myrdal, "is race prejudice . . . not increasing but decreasing?" And he answers sanctimoniously: "This question is . . . only a special variant of the enigma of philosophers for several thousands of years: the problem of Good and Evil in the world."[42] Clearly, this is an escape from the realities of the social system, inexcusable in the modern social scientist.[43] At any rate, the philosophers' enigma ap-

---

[40]Ibid., p. 689.

[41]Ibid., p. 66.

[42]Ibid., p. 79. See W. Cunningham, *The Growth of English Industry and Commerce*, Vol. I, pp. 556–57, for a review of this tendency among sixteenth-century English moralists to explain social problems by attributing them to human sinfulness.

[43]Probably we should mention here another deplorable achievement of Myrdal's —his developed capacity for obscuring the basis of racial antagonism. Consider in illustration the following paragraph:

"Though the popular theory of color caste turns out to be a rationalization, this does not destroy it. For among the forces in the minds of the white people are certainly not only economic interests (if these were the only ones, the popular theory would be utterly demolished), but also sexual urges, inhibitions, and jealousies, and social fears and cravings for prestige and security. When they come under the scrutiny of scientific research, both the sexual and the social complexes take on unexpected designs. We shall then also get a clue to understanding the remarkable tendency of this presumably biological doctrine, that it refers only to legal marriage and to relations between Negro men and white women, but not to extra-marital sex relations between white men and Negro women." Ibid., p. 59.

This excerpt is not exceptional; it characterizes the writing. Its meaning is probably this: "The theory of color caste is a rationalization. Besides the economic

parently leads him directly into a mystical play with imponderables. As he sees it, "white prejudice" is a primary determinant in race relations. "White prejudice and discrimination keep the Negro low in standards of living. . . . This, in turn, gives support to prejudice. White prejudice and Negro standards thus mutually 'cause' each other."[44] Moreover, "the chief hindrance to improving the Negro is *the white man's firm belief in his inferiority*."[45] We shall discuss this controlling idea in a later section.

Poor Whites

It should be pointed out again that Myrdal not only closes his eyes to the material interests which support and maintain race prejudice but also labors the point that there is basic antagonism between poor whites and Negroes. Says he: ". . . what a bitter, spiteful, and relentless feeling often prevails against the Negroes among lower class white people in America. . . . The Marxian solidarity between the toilers . . . will . . . have a long way to go as far as concerns solidarity of the poor white American with the toiling Negro."[46] In fact, the author goes further to intimate that the poor whites may assume a dominant role in the oppression of Negroes in the South, because the interest of the poor whites is economic, while that of the ruling class is a feeling for superiority:

Lower class whites in the South have no Negro servants in whose humble demeanors they can reflect their own superiority. Instead, they feel actual economic competition or fear of potential competition from the Negroes.

interests upon which this rationalization is based, we should take into account certain appetites and instinctual drives common to all human beings." The conclusion in the last sentence is incorrect. It is contrary to both the logic of race relations and the data as recorded in the literature including some of the earliest court records on white-man, Negro-woman sex relations. The deplorable fact about this writing is not so much that it is obscure as that it seeks to maneuver the reader into accepting the rationalization as the real reason for racial antagonism. We could hardly emphasize too much that "sexual urges, inhibitions," and so on, traits common to Negroes as well as, whites, cannot explain why certain whites dominate Negroes. Moreover, the author does not show that anyone has ever argued that the mere fact that a rationalization is recognized for what it is destroys it. This, obviously, is a straw man set up to cover the author's obsession with abstractions.

[44]Ibid., p. 75.

[45]Ibid., p. 101. (Italics added.)

[46]Ibid., p. 69. In almost identical terms André Siegfried interprets the racial situation: "In the wealthy families some of the old-time sentimentality still survives from the slave days, but the 'poor white' sees in the Negro nothing but a brutal competitor who is trying to rob him of his job. His hatred is unrelenting, merciless, and mingled with fear. To understand the South, we must realize that the lower we descend in the social scale, the more violent the hatred of the Negro." *America Comes of Age*, p. 97. See also Edwin R. Embree, *Brown America*, p. 201.

They need the caste demarcations for much more substantial reasons than do the middle and upper classes.[47]

The author hesitates to come to that obvious conclusion so much dreaded by the capitalist ruling class: that the observed overt competitive antagonism is a condition produced and carefully maintained by the exploiters of both the poor whites and the Negroes. Yet he almost says this in so many words: "Plantation owners and employers, who use Negro labor as cheaper and more docile, have at times been observed to tolerate, or co-operate in, the periodic aggression of poor whites against Negroes. It is a plausible thesis that they do so in the interest of upholding the caste system which is so effective in keeping the Negro docile."[48] And even more strikingly he shows by what means white workers are exploited through the perpetuation of racial antagonism. Says he: "If those white workers were paid low wages

---

[47]Op. cit., p. 597. This social illusion concerning the naturalness of racial antagonism between Negroes and poor whites, a mirage ordinarily perpetuated by the white ruling class, is deeply embedded in the literature. For instance, Professor Louis Wirth declares with finality: "It has been repeatedly found by students of Negro-white relations in the South that the so-called white aristocracy shows less racial prejudice than do the 'poor whites' whose own position is relatively insecure and who must compete with Negroes for jobs, for property, for social position, and for power. Only those who themselves are insecure feel impelled to press their claims for superiority over others." See "Race and Public Policy," *The Scientific Monthly,* April 1944, p. 304.

Now, we may ask, why should competition be more natural than consolidation in the struggle for wealth and position? Why should insecurity lead more naturally to division than to a closing of ranks? Suppose the Negro and the white proletariat of the South decide to come together and unite for increasing power in their struggle for economic position, what are the sources of opposing power—disorganizing power—that will be immediately brought into action? Wirth might just as well argue that the antagonism and open conflicts which ordinarily develop between union strikers and scabs are caused by a feeling of insecurity among the scabs. In the end this argument must be put into that category of vacuus universals which explain nothing, for who in this world does not feel insecure? And if it is a matter of the degree of insecurity, then we should expect Negroes to take the initiative in interracial aggression since they are the most insecure. In the theoretical discussion of race relations "human nature" or the behavior of human beings as such should be taken for granted.

Sometimes thought is effectively canalized by such apparently objective statements by social scientists as the following: "A standard saying among the southern common folks is that we ought to treat the Negro as we did the Indian: kill him if he doesn't behave and, if not, isolate him and give him what we want to." Howard W. Odum, "Problem and Methodology in an American Dilemma," *Social Forces,* Vol. 23, October 1944, p. 98. Clearly the implication here is that the Southern aristocrats and their university professors are the protectors of the Negroes against the pent-up viciousness of the "southern common folks"—a complete perversion of reality.

[48]Ibid., p. 598. In another context he recognizes that "there had been plenty of racial competition before the Civil War. White artisans had often vociferously protested against the use of Negroes for skilled work in the crafts. But as long as the politically most powerful group of whites had a vested interest in Negro mechanics, the protesting was of little avail." Ibid., p. 281.

and held in great dependence, they could at least be offered a consolation of being protected from Negro competition."[49]

At any rate, Myrdal refuses to be consistent. Accordingly, he asserts, attitudes against interracial marriage "seems generally to be inversely related to the economic and social status of the informant and his educational level. . . . To the poor and socially insecure, but struggling, white individual, a fixed opinion on this point seems an important matter of prestige and distinction."[50] It would not do, of course, to explain the situation realistically by concluding that if the revised black codes written by the white exploiting class against intermarriage were abrogated an increasing number of marriages between the white and the black proletariat would take place, the consequence of which would be a considerably reduced opportunity for labor exploitation by this class.[51]

The Ruling Class

Myrdal does not like to talk about the ruling class in the South; the term carries for him an odious "Marxist" connotation. Yet inevitably he describes this class as well as anyone:

The one-party system in the South . . . and the low political participation of even the white people favor a *de facto* oligarchic regime. . . . The oligarchy consists of the big landowners, the industrialists, the bankers,

[49]Ibid., p. 286. In the South African situation Lord Olivier makes a similar observation: "When the capitalist employer comes on the scene, making discriminations as to the labor forces he must employ for particular work in order to make his profits, which is the law of his activity to do, then, and not till then, antagonism is introduced between the newly-created wage-working proletarian white and the native—who, in regard to the qualifications which properly determine wage contracts, are on exactly the same footing." *The Anatomy of African Misery*, p. 135.

[50]Op. cit., p. 57.

[51]Hinton R. Helper, the renegade Southerner who never bit his tongue in his criticism of the white ruling class of the South and who, however, never concealed his prejudices against the Negroes, spoke more than a grain of truth when he described the position of the poor whites. It is essentially applicable to present-day conditions. "Notwithstanding the fact that the white non-slaveholders of the South are in the majority as five to one, they have never yet had any part or lot in framing the laws under which they live. . . . The lords of the lash are not only absolute masters of the blacks . . . but they are also the oracles and arbiters of all the non-slaveholding whites, whose freedom is merely nominal and whose unparalleled illiteracy and degradation is purposely and fiendishly perpetuated. How little the 'poor white trash,' the great majority of the Southern people, know of the real conditions of the country is indeed sadly astonishing. . . . It is expected that the stupid and sequacious masses, the white victims of slavery, will believe and, as a general thing, they do believe, whatever the slaveholders tell them; and thus it is that they are cajoled into the notion that they are the freest, happiest, and most intelligent people in the world, and are taught to look with prejudice and disapprobation upon every new principle or progressive movement." *The Impending Crisis*, pp. 42–44 *passim*.

and the merchants. Northern corporate business with big investments in the region has been sharing in the political control by this oligarchy.[52]

And he stresses the ineffectiveness of the exploited masses. "The Southern masses do not generally organize either for advancing their ideals or for protecting their group interests. The immediate reason most often given by Southern liberals is the resistance from the political oligarchy which wants to keep the masses inarticulate."[53] Furthermore, he indicates the desperate pressure endured by Southern workers when he says: "The poorest farmer in the Scandinavian countries or in England . . . would not take benevolent orders so meekly as Negroes and white sharecroppers do in the South."[54]

Sometimes Myrdal shakes off the whole burden of obfuscation spun about caste, creeds,[55] and poor-white control to show, perhaps without intending to do so, the real interest of the ruling class and how it sets race against race to accomplish its exploitative purpose:

The conservative opponents of reform proposals [that is to say the ruling class in the South] can usually discredit them by pointing out that they will improve the status of the Negroes, and that they prepare for "social equality." This argument has been raised in the South against labor unions, child labor legislation and practically every other proposal for reform.

It has been argued to the white workers that the Wages and Hours Law was an attempt to legislate equality between the races by raising the wage level of Negro workers to that of whites. The South has never been seriously interested in instituting tenancy legislation to protect the tenants' rights . . . and the argument has again been that the Negro sharecropper should not be helped against the white man.[56]

It seems clear that in developing a theory of race relations in the South one must look to the economic policies of the ruling class and not to mere abstract depravity among poor whites. Opposition to social equality has no meaning unless we can see its function in the service of the exploitative purpose of this class. "When the Negro rises socially," says Myrdal, "and is no longer a servant, he becomes a stranger to

---

[52]Op. cit., p. 453.

[53]Ibid., p. 455.

[54]Ibid., p. 466.

[55]This statement is made advisedly. The following unreal conflict between status and ideals may indicate further the nebulous level at which the theoretical part of this study is sometimes pitched: "The American Creed represents the national conscience. The Negro is a 'problem' to the average American partly because of a palpable conflict between the status actually awarded him and those ideals." Ibid., p. 23.

[56]Ibid., p. 456.

the white upper class. His ambition is suspected and he is disliked."[57] Again: "The ordinary white upper class people will 'have no use' for such Negroes. They need cheap labor—faithful, obedient, unambitious labor."[58] And the author observes further: "In most Southern communities the ruling classes of whites want to keep Negroes from joining labor unions. Some are quite frank in wanting to keep Negroes from reading the Constitution or studying social subjects."[59]

In the South the ruling class stands effectively between the Negroes and the white proletariat. Every segregation barrier is a barrier put up between white and black people by their exploiters. Myrdal puts it in this way: "On the local scene the accommodation motive by itself does not usually encourage Negro leaders to such adventures as trying to reach behind the white leaders to the white people."[60] Moreover, it is not the poor whites but the ruling class which uses its intelligence and its money to guard against any movement among Negroes to throw off their yoke of exploitation. "In many communities leading white citizens make no secret of the fact that they are carefully following . . . all signs of 'subversive propaganda' and unrest among the Negroes in the community, and that they interfere to stop even innocent beginnings of Negro group activity."[61]

The reasoning which we are now following, it may be well to state, is not Myrdal's; we are merely culling those conclusions which the data seem to compel the author to make but which he ordinarily surrounds with some mysterious argument about caste.

From one point of view the masters did not have so great a need for racial antagonism during slavery. Black workers could be exploited in comparative peace; the formal law was on the side of the slave owner. As Myrdal observes: "Exploitation of Negro labor was, perhaps, a less embarrassing *moral conflict* to the ante-bellum planter than to his peer today. . . . Today the exploitation is, to a considerable degree, dependent upon the availability of extralegal devices of various kinds."[62] Obviously, among these extralegal devices are race prejudice, discrimination, and violence—especially lynching and the threat of lynching. "Discrimination against Negroes is . . . rooted in this tradition of economic exploitation."[63]

---

[57]Ibid., p. 593.
[58]Ibid., p. 596.
[59]Ibid., p. 721.
[60]Ibid., p. 727.
[61]Ibid., p. 459.
[62]Ibid., p. 220. (Italics added.)
[63]Ibid., p. 208.

Emphasis upon Sex

In spite of this, however, Myrdal refuses to accept a realistic interpretation of race relations. Throughout these volumes he warns his readers not to put too much reliance upon a socioeconomic explanation. Thus he declares: "The eager intent to explain away race prejudice and caste in the simple terms of economic competition . . . is an attempt to *escape from caste to class.*"[64] The reasoning here, of course, is unrelieved nonsense. Incidentally, it illustrates the hiatus in understanding which an inappropriate use of the concepts "caste" and "class" might entail. At any rate, our author thinks it is more revealing to take sex as our point of reference. In fact, Myrdal presents a scheme of social situations in which he ranks intermarriage and sexual intercourse involving white women as the highest in motives for discrimination, while he ranks economic conditions sixth and last.

(1) Highest in this order [of discrimination] stands the bar against intermarriage and sexual intercourse involving white women (2) . . . several etiquettes and discriminations . . . (3) . . . segregations and discriminations in use of public facilities such as schools . . . (4) political disfranchisement . . . (5) discrimination in the law courts . . . (6) . . . discriminations in securing land, credit, jobs . . .[65]

This rank order evidences the degree of importance which "white people" attach to certain social facts calculated to keep the Negro in his place, and it is "apparently determined by the factors of sex and social status."[66] The Negroes' estimate, however, is just the reverse of this: "The Negro's own rank order is just about parallel, but inverse, to that of the white man."[67] Here, then, is a perfect example of social illusion, an illusion that must inevitably come to all those who attempt to see race relations in the South as involving two castes.

In reality, both the Negroes and their white exploiters know that

---

[64] Ibid., p. 792. (Italics added.)

[65] Ibid., p. 61. In similar vein he asserts: "It is surely significant that the white Southerner is much less willing to permit intermarriage or to grant 'social equality' than he is to allow equality in the political, judicial and economic spheres. The violence of the Southerner's reaction to equality in each of these spheres rises with the degree of its relation to the sexual and personal, which suggests that *his prejudice is based upon fundamental attitudes toward sex and personality.*" (Italics added.) Ibid., p. 61.

[66] Ibid., p. 61. It is further emphasized: "The concern for 'race purity' is *basic* in the whole issue; the primary and essential command is to prevent amalgamation. . . . Rejection of 'social equality' is to be understood as a precaution to hinder miscegenation and particularly intermarriage. The danger of miscegenation is so tremendous that segregation and discrimination inherent in the refusal of 'social equality' must be extended to all spheres of life." Ibid., p. 58.

[67] Ibid., p. 61.

economic opportunity comes first and that the white woman comes second; indeed, she is merely a significant instrument in limiting the first. Moreover, these selected elements of social discrimination should not be thought of as discrete social phenomena; they are rather inter-meshed in a definite pattern supporting a dominant purpose. If the white ruling class intends to keep the colored people in their place —that is to say, freely exploitable—this class cannot permit them to marry white women; neither can it let white men marry Negro women. If this were allowed to happen Negroes would soon become so whitened that the profit makers would be unable to direct mass hatred against them[68] and would thus lose their principal weapon in facili-tating their primary business of exploiting the white and the black workers of the South.[69] If a Negro could become governor of Georgia it would be of no particular social significance whether his wife is white or colored; or, at any rate, there would be no political power presum-ing to limit the color of his wife. But if, in a "democracy," you could insist that his wife must be black, you could not only prevent his be-coming governor of Georgia, but you could also make him do most of your dirty and menial work at your wages.[70] Sexual obsession, then, functions in the fundamental interest of economic exploitation.

As a matter of fact, Myrdal is apparently so concerned with his sexual emphasis that he is here led to compare incommensurable

[68]It should be made crystal-clear that the design of the ruling white people is not primarily to keep the blood of the white race "pure," but rather to prevent race mixture; it is therefore definitely as frustrating to their fundamental purpose of economic exploitation to infuse white blood into the Negro group. Their purpose can be accomplished only if the Negroes remain identifiably colored.

[69]Decades ago George W. Cable observed: "The essence of the offence, any and everywhere the race line is insisted upon, is the apparition of the colored man or woman as his or her own master; that masterhood is all that all this tyranny is in-tended to preserve. . . . The moment the relation of master and servant is visably established between race and race there is a hush of peace. . . . The surrender of this one point by the colored man or woman buys more than peace—it buys amity." *The Negro Question*, pp. 22–23.

And, as if it were in confirmation of this, C. R. Goodlatte writes, "It may be said of us that we welcome the native as a servant: as a rule we treat him individually in a fairly humane fashion; we often win his esteem and trust; but in any other capacity than that of a docile servant we consider him intolerable." "South Africa: Glimpses and Comments," *Contemporary Review*, CXXXIII, 1928, p. 347.

[70]In order to support his specious argument Myrdal relies pivotally upon such sour-grape expressions as the following by R. R. Moton: "As for amalgamation, very few expect it; still fewer want it; no one advocates it; and only a constantly diminishing minority practise it, and that surreptitiously. It is generally accepted on both sides of the color line that it is best for the two races to remain ethnologically distinct." Op. cit., p. 62. This, from a Negro, is assumed to be evidence that Negroes do not want intermarriage. On its face, Myrdal might have asked: Why should something that is not wanted be practiced "surreptitiously"? Moreover, would the white ruling class be obsessed with the prevention of intermarriage if the natural likelihood of its occurring were exceedingly remote?

arrays: the "white man's" system of rationalization with the real basis of race relations, as the Negroes react to it. If he had been consistent in dealing with economic reality, he would probably have been able to extricate its superstructure of rationalization with sex as its emotional fundament. Indeed, this very approach might have led him to discover the pith of the problem, for Negroes "resist" least that which is of comparatively little moment and most that which is of crucial significance. Sex is not "basic" in race relations, but it is basic in the system of rationalization which supports racial antagonism.

Again our author sees the problem in this light: "It is inherent in our type of modern Western civilization that sex and social status are for most individuals the danger points, the directions whence he fears the sinister onslaughts on his personal security."[71] This passage is intended as an explanation of the "white man's theory of color caste," determined by sexual fears. However, it seems inadequate for two reasons: (a) it is not significantly characteristic of "Western civilization" and (b) it tends to conceive of race prejudice as a personal matter. In all societies "sex and social status" are "danger points" to the individual. In apparently most of them they are much more so than in Western society; in Brahmanic India, for instance, they are infinitely more so, but there has been no race prejudice in Brahmanic India. Then, too, we could hardly overemphasize the fact that race prejudice is not a personal attitude. The individual in the South is not allowed to exercise personal discretion in this matter. Indeed, it is obviously the very fear of sexual attraction between individual members of the races which caused the ruling class to make laws supported by propaganda for its control.

The Vicious Circle

Capitalist rationalizations of race relations have recently come face to face with a powerful theory of society and, in order to meet this, the orthodox theorists have become mystics. This evidently had to be so because it is exceedingly terrifying for these scientists to follow to its logical conclusion a realistic explanation of race relations; and yet they must either do this or stultify themselves. Here the social scientist is "on the spot"; he must avoid "the truth" because it is dangerous, regardless of how gracefully he eases up to it. In illustration, Myrdal advises Negroes not to become too radical and to think of many causes as of equal significance with the material factor: "Negro strategy would

---

[71] Ibid., p. 59.

build on an illusion if it set all its hope on a blitzkrieg directed toward a basic [economic] factor. In the nature of things it must work on the broadest possible front. There is a place for both the radical and the conservative Negro leaders."[72] This, obviously, will lead to a situation in which the ideas of one group of leaders will tend to offset those of another.

Although Myrdal overlays his discussion of race relations with a particularly alien caste belief, his controlling hypothesis has nothing whatever to do with caste. His "theory of the vicious circle"[73] is his controlling idea. This theory is essentially an abstract formulation, inspired by a largely inverted observation of "a vicious circle in caste" by Edwin R. Embree,[74] and rendered "scientific" by the application of certain concepts which Myrdal seems to have used to his satisfaction in his study, *Monetary Equilibrium*.

As we have seen in a previous section, the vicious circle runs as follows: "White prejudice . . . keeps the Negro low in standards of living. . . . This, in turn, gives support to white prejudice. White prejudice and Negro standards thus mutually 'cause' each other." These two variables are interdependent, but neither is consistently dependent; a change in either will affect the other inversely. If we initiate a change in Negro standards, say, by "giving the Negro youth more education," white prejudice will go down; if we change white prejudice, say, by "an increased general knowledge about biology, eradicating false beliefs concerning Negro racial inferiority," then Negro standards will go up.

It is this kind of mystical dance of imponderables which is at the basis of the system of social illusions marbled into Myrdal's discussion. In the first place, Myrdal does not develop a careful definition of race prejudice. He does say, however: "For our purpose [race prejudice] is defined as discrimination by whites against Negroes."[75] But he does not use this definition, in fact we do not see how he can, for race prejudice is a social attitude, an acquired tendency to act; it is not some act or action which is the meaning of discrimination.[76] Myrdal's studied analysis would lead us rather to deduce the following definition of race

---

[72]Ibid., p. 794.

[73]Ibid., pp. 75–78, 207–09, and Appendix 3.

[74]Ibid., p. 1069, note.

[75]Ibid., p. 78.

[76]In another connection Myrdal seems to give a different meaning to the concept: "If for some reason . . . white workers actually came to work with Negroes as fellow workers, it has been experienced that *prejudice* will often adjust to the changed amount of *discrimination*." Ibid., p. 1067. (Italics added.) See also pp. 1141ff.

prejudice: a feeling of bitterness, especially among poor whites, aroused particularly by a standing sexual threat of Negro men to white women. As he sees it, the white man's "prejudice is based upon fundamental attitudes toward sex and personality."

If, according to Myrdal's "rank order of discrimination," the whites are most concerned with sex and the Negroes with economic advancement, his fundamental equilibrium of social forces should be a direct correlation between white prejudice and Negro sexual aggression—not Negro standards, which are clearly basically economic. In this way white prejudice will tend to vanish as Negro men give up their interest in white women; Negro standards will also go up, but only incidentally. If, for instance, Negro men would relinquish their desire to marry white women, "white people" would no longer be prejudiced against Negroes; the latter would be encouraged, say, to vote and campaign for political office and to demand their share of jobs and public funds in the Deep South.[77] To be sure, Myrdal does not demonstrate any such proposition. We may put it in still another way: If Negro standards go up and at the same time Negroes increase their interest in white women, then, to be consistent with Myrdal's sexual emphasis, white prejudice must increase. From this it follows that Negro standards are a non-significant variable.

The point which the author seems to have avoided is this: that both race prejudice and Negro standards are consistently dependent variables. They are both produced by the calculated economic interests of the Southern oligarchy. Both prejudice and the Negro's status are dependent functions of the latter interests. In one variation of his theory of the "vicious circle" Myrdal reasons:

Assuming . . . that we want to reduce the bias in white people's racial beliefs concerning Negroes, our first practical conclusion is that we can effect this result to a degree by *actually improving Negro status*. . . . The impediment in the way of this strategy is . . . that white beliefs . . . are active forces in keeping the Negroes low.[78]

Here beliefs are assumed to be prime movers; they "keep the Negroes low." This is mysticism. If we can "improve Negro status" the reason

---

[77]"Negroes are in desperate need of jobs and bread. . . . The marriage matter [to them] is of rather distant and doubtful interest." Ibid., p. 6. The Negroes, thus goes the logic, want jobs and the white men want to protect their women from Negro men. But white men are rather willing to let Negroes have jobs, while Negro men are not particularly interested in white women. If this is so, if these two admittedly antagonistic groups are vitally interested in different things, why is there antagonism at all? It would seem that men fight only when they are possessed of conflicting interests in the same object.

[78]Ibid., p. 109. (Italics added.)

for the existence of derogatory beliefs about Negroes is, to the extent of the improvement, liquidated. With a rise in the standard of living of Negroes there tends to be merely a concomitant vitiation of the rationalizations for the depressed conditions of Negroes. The belief is an empty, harmless illusion, like beliefs in werewolves or fairies, without the exploitative interest with which it is impregnated. If the economic force could be bridled, the belief would collapse from inanition. There is a vested interest in anti-racial beliefs.

The effective interest is a need for slaves, or peons, or unorganized common laborers—a need for "cheap, docile labor." The latter interest, of course, is involved in a complicated web of feeling established by both immemorial and recent rationalizations. If beliefs, per se, could subjugate a people, the beliefs which Negroes hold about whites should be as effective as those which whites hold about Negroes.

This assumption of Myrdal's, that racial beliefs are primary social forces, leads him to conclude almost pathetically that the "white man's" beliefs are only a "mistake," which he would gladly correct if only he had truthful information. Accordingly our author suggests the following attack upon the beliefs themselves:

A second line of strategy must be to rectify the ordinary white man's observations of Negro characteristics and inform him of the specific mistakes he is making in ascribing them wholesale to inborn racial traits. . . . People want to be rational, to be honest and well informed.[79]

Evidently the misapprehension in this presentation inheres in Myrdal's moral approach. He does not recognize consistently that the propagators of the ruling ideas, those whose interest it is to replace debunked beliefs with new ones, are not mistaken at all, and that they should not be thought of merely as people or white people. They are, in fact, a special class of people who fiercely oppose interference with the established set of antagonistic racial beliefs. The racial beliefs have been intentionally built up through propaganda. They are mass psychological instruments facilitating a definite purpose; therefore, they can best be opposed by realistic aggressive propaganda methods.[80] It is, to repeat, consummate naïveté to assume that the ruling class in the South will permit a free, objective discussion of race relations in its schools or public places.[81] Today such a practice can succeed only as a hazardous underground movement.

---

[79] Ibid., p. 109.

[80] This view also holds against certain popular conceptions of race prejudice as "superstition" or "myth."

[81] On this point, see Stetson Kennedy, *Southern Exposure*, p. 349.

Furthermore, the author's unstable equilibrium between race prejudice and Negro standards is evidently too simple. For instance, if Negro standards go up because of interference from some outside force, say the Federal Government, the cultivated race prejudice among the poor whites may tend to diminish, but at the same time the hostility of the ruling-class whites may increase. The reason for this is that, because of the interference, the status and problems of Negroes and those of the poor whites may be made more nearly to coincide and thus enhance the possibility of an establishment of a community of interest between these two groups, a process diametrically opposed to the purpose and interests of the white ruling class. Therefore, it becomes incumbent upon the latter class to re-establish its position by bringing into play those very well-known means of reaffirming racial antipathy.

Although Myrdal never permits himself to accept a consistently realistic approach to the study of race relations, he recites as historical fact that which his theory confutes. For instance, the following historical passage says quite clearly that race prejudice is an attitude deliberately built up among the masses by an exploiting class, using acceptable rationalizations derogatory to the Negro race, so that the exploitation of the latter's labor power might be justified.

The historical literature of this early period . . . records that the imported Negroes—and the captured Indians—originally were kept in much the same status as the white indentured servants. *When later the Negroes gradually were pushed down into chattel slavery* while the white servants were allowed to work off their board, *the need was felt* . . . for some kind of justification *above mere economic expediency and the might of the strong.* The arguments called forth by this need . . . were broadly these: that the Negro was a heathen and a barbarian, an outcast among the peoples of the earth, a descendant of Noah's son Ham, cursed by God himself and doomed to be *a servant* forever on account of an ancient sin.[82]

Now there is no mysticism here—nothing about "sexual drives," "fears," "inhibitions," "labile balance," and so on—the historical process is clear. The exploitative act comes first; the prejudice follows. It explains unequivocally that a powerful white exploiting class, by "the might of the strong" and for "economic expediency," pushed the Negroes down into chattel slavery and then, as a justification and facilitation of this, utilized the means of propaganda, which are ordinarily in its control, to develop racial antagonism and hate in the white public for the Negroes.[83]

---

[82]Op. cit., p. 85. (Italics added.)

[83]It is interesting to observe with what anonymity Myrdal uses such key concepts as "imported," "captured," "kept," "pushed down," and so on. One would think

Attacking beliefs by negation is obviously a negative procedure—
sometimes even a futile one. In an essay of epoch-making significance,
written in about the year 1800, Henri Grégoire[84] demonstrated, probably as clearly as ever, that the white man is "making a mistake in
ascribing Negro characteristics to inborn racial traits"; yet this assignment is still freshly advocated. As a matter of fact, Count Arthur de
Gobineau almost put men like Grégoire out of existence.[85] In like
manner, Dr. W. T. Couch, formerly editor in chief of probably the
most influential Southern press, proceeds to "gobinize" Myrdal.

Couch, in a caustic criticism of Myrdal, referring to him as "silly"
and "ignorant," says the white man cannot make concessions to
Negroes because these will ultimately lead to Negro men's marrying
white men's daughters. "One concession will lead to another, and ultimately to intermarriage."[86] Here the thinking of both authors is bogged
down in the slough of sexual passion from which we may not hope for
light on race relations. Moreover, in this unrealistic world of beliefs
Couch has Myrdal where he wants him; he seems to triumph with
such intuitive declarations as: "The assertion of equality is an assertion
of values."[87] And, in a characteristically pre-Civil War, slaveholders'
contention about the meaning of the Declaration of Independence, he
becomes involved with Myrdal's moral orientation. "I believe," says
Couch, *"An American Dilemma* was written under gross misappre-

---

that the subject referred to by these terms of action would be of primary concern in
the investigation. It is, however, highly impersonalized, and the whole social situation tends to remain as if it were an act of Nature.

[84]*An Inquiry Concerning the Intellectual and Moral Faculties, and Literature
of Negroes,* trans. by D. B. Warden, Brooklyn, 1810.

[85]After Professor Donald Young had completed his examination of the conditions
of American minority peoples he made the following conclusionary statement:
"Action, not cautious and laborious research, is demanded of those who would lead
the populace. Thus a Chamberlain, a Gobineau, or a Stoddard attracts myriads of
followers by a pseudo-scientific program based on a doctrine of God-given white
supremacy . . . while the very names of Franz Boas, Eugene Pittard, Herbert A.
Miller, E. B. Reuter, Friedrich Hertz, and other scholarly students of the peoples
of the world are unknown outside of a small intellectual circle. 'Give us the solution
and let sterile scholars while away their time with obscure facts which lead but to
quibbling books!' is the cry of the masses." Yet the reason that Gobineau *et al.* have
been widely accepted by the white ruling classes of the world is not that they presented a course of "action" but that they had the timely ingenuity to contrive a system of plausible logic which justified an accomplished act: the white racial mastery
of the world. Explanations and justifications were desperately needed. For the most
part the scholars mentioned have been able only to point out flaws in the anti-racial
arguments; they had already lost their conviction when they innocently accepted
the spurious grounds of discussion which the apologists of racial exploitation had
chosen. They apparently did not recognize that both the racial antagonism and its
pseudo-scientific rationalizations are products of a peculiar social system.

[86]*What the Negro Wants,* Rayford W. Logan, ed., p. xvi.

[87]Ibid., p. xvii.

hensions of what such ideas as equality, freedom, democracy, human rights, have meant, and what they can be made to mean."[88] Thus, without restraint and without enlightenment, the mystics, steeped in metaphysical truck, set upon each other.

A positive program, on the other hand, calls for an attack upon the source of the beliefs, so that it might be divested of its prestige and power to produce and to substitute anti-racial beliefs among the masses. In other words, the problem is that of converting the white masses to an appreciation and realization of the ruling-class function of the beliefs and their effect as instruments in the exploitation of the white as well as of the black masses. Then, not only will the old beliefs lose their efficacy, but also the new ones will die aborning.

A positive program calls for the winning of the white masses over to a different system of thinking—not merely a campaign of scholarly denials of spectacular myths about creation, stages of biological progress, cultural capacity, and so on. Indeed, such negation may even play into the hands of the "racists," for they may not only divert attention from the realities of race relations but also help to spread and implant the myths among the public. However, the effectuation of such a program, the intent of which must be to alienate public support of the aristocracy, will undoubtedly evoke terrific opposition from this class. To be sure, this fact merely demonstrates further the basis of racial antagonism in the South and the correctness of the suggested positive program. At the same time, of course, Negroes must learn that their interest is primarily bound up with that of the white common people in a struggle for power and not essentially in a climb for social status.

At any rate, it is precisely this realization which Dr. Myrdal constantly seeks to circumvent. Accordingly he argues inconsistently that the ruling class in the South is the Negroes' best friend.

Our hypothesis is similar to the view taken by an older group of Negro writers and by most white writers who have touched this crucial question: that the Negroes' friend—or the one who is least unfriendly—is still rather the upper class of white people, the people with economic and social security who are *truly a "non-competing group."*[89]

The author, by one symptom or another, cannot help showing of what he is really apprehensive: the bringing into consciousness of the

[88]Ibid., p. xv.

[89]Op. cit., p. 69. (Italics added.) It is interesting to observe how Dr. Myrdal has finally become almost reactionary in the sense of the incorrigible segregationist, W. T. Couch, who also says: "Nothing is more needed in the South today than rebirth of [Booker Washington's] ideas, restoration of the great leadership that he was giving." Op. cit., p. xxiii.

masses the identity of the interests of the white and the black workers. In accordance with this attitude he takes a superficial view of the economic order and asks Negroes to go to the labor market and see who is their real enemy. Thus he asserts:

> The aim of [the theory of labor solidarity] is to unify the whole Negro people, not with the white upper class, but with the white working class. . . . The theory of labor solidarity has been taken up as a last solution of the Negro problem, and as such is escapist in nature; its escape character becomes painfully obvious to every member of the school as soon as he leaves abstract reasoning and goes down to the labor market, because there he *meets caste* and has to talk race, even racial solidarity.[90]

As a justificatory illustration of the validity of his principle of "cumulative causation," the summatory interaction of the elements of Negro standards and other social factors, Myrdal says: "The philanthropist, the Negro educator, the Negro trade unionist . . . and, indeed, the average well-meaning citizen of both colors, pragmatically applies the same hypothesis."[91] In reality, however, this is not a confirmation of a sound theory of race relations; it is rather an apology for reformism. Within the existing system of power relationship this is the most that is respectably allowed. Reformism never goes so far as to envisage the real involvement of the exploitative system with racial antagonism. Its extreme aspiration does not go beyond the attainment of freedom for certain black men to participate in the exploitation of the commonalty regardless of the color of the latter. This aspiration is the prospect which the Southern oligarchy with some degree of justification ordinarily refers to as "Negro domination."

Then, too, with reformation as an end, the logical "friend" of the Negro leader must necessarily be this same white aristocracy; for he must ultimately become, like the aristocracy, the inevitable economic adversary of the exploited masses; he must become, in other words, a "black Anglo-Saxon." Indeed, assuming bourgeois proclivities, his very appeal to the masses for support in his struggle for "equality" is an unavoidable deception. The reformer seeks to eliminate only the racial aspects of the exploitative system; he compromises with the system which produces the racial antagonism. But the white ruling class cannot willingly accept even this compromise, for it knows that the whole system is doomed if Negroes are permitted to achieve unlimited status as participating exploiters. In such an event there would be no racial scapegoat or red herring to brandish before the confused white com-

---

[90]Myrdal, op. cit., p. 793. (Italics added.)
[91]Ibid., p. 1069.

monalty as a means of keeping them and the Negro masses from recognizing the full impact of political-class oppression.

Today "conservative" theories of race relations are not merely denied; they are confronted with a countertheory, the theory that racial antagonism is in fact *political-class* antagonism and that race prejudice is initiated and maintained by labor exploiters. It is not, it would seem clear, that the aristocracy is less antagonistic to the Negroes but that this class uses more respectable weapons against them, which are also infinitely more powerful and effective. As a matter of fact, the poor whites themselves may be thought of as the primary instrument of the ruling class in subjugating the Negroes. The statement attributed to a great financier, "I can pay one half of the working class to kill off the other half," is again in point.

As we have seen, Myrdal does not favor this explanation. He declares that all the Negro's troubles are due to the simple fact that "white people" want to be superior to colored people; or, indeed, merely to the fact that the Negro is colored. His argument follows:

> We hear it said . . . that there is no "race problem" but only a "class problem." The Negro sharecropper is alleged to be destitute not because of his color but because of his class position—and it is pointed out that there are white people who are equally poor. From a practical angle there is a point in this reasoning. But from a theoretical angle it contains escapism in a new form. It also draws too heavily on the idealistic Marxian doctrine of the "class struggle." And it tends to conceal the whole system of special deprivations visited upon the Negro *only because he is not white.*[92]

Throughout the study the author has frequently found it sufficient simply to mention the name of Karl Marx in order to counter views based upon the determining role of the "material conditions of production" and distribution.[93] After a studied agrument in favor of the futility

---

[92]Ibid., p. 75. (Italics added.)

[93]And yet Myrdal has shown himself to be vitally wanting in an understanding of the difference between status rivalry and class struggle. Observe, for instance, the following typical confusion: "Our hypothesis is that in a society where there are broad social classes and, in addition, more minute distinctions and splits in the lower strata, the lower class groups will, to a great extent, take care of keeping each other subdued, thus relieving, to that extent, the higher classes of this otherwise painful task necessary to the monopolization of the power and the advantages.

"It will be observed that this hypothesis is contrary to the Marxian theory of class society. . . . The Marxian scheme assumes that there is an actual solidarity between the *several lower class groups* against the *higher classes,* or, in any case, a potential solidarity. . . . The inevitable result is a 'class struggle' where all poor and disadvantaged groups are united behind the barricades." Ibid., p. 68. (Italics added.) Myrdal thinks that Marx thinks the *upper class* and the *lower class,* mere social illusions, are in conflict. No wonder he seems to conclude that Marx is rather foolish. And he does not trouble himself at all to explain how the "higher classes" exercise the "necessary painful task" of keeping the lower classes subdued when, per-

of Negroes adopting a Marxian view of society, he concludes: " 'Even after a revolution the country will be full of crackers' is a reflection I have often met when discussing communism in the Negro community."[94] The least we could say about this is that it is very crude. On this kind of thinking John Stuart Mill is emphatic: "Of all the vulgar modes of escaping from the consideration of the effect of social and moral influences on the human mind, the most vulgar is that of attributing the diversities of conduct and character to inherent natural differences."[95] More especially it expresses the fatalism upon which the whole orthodox school of race relations inevitably rests.

Myrdal, as a confirmed moralist, is not concerned with problems of power but rather with problems of "regenerating the individual" by idealistic preachments. If only the individual could be taught to accept the morality of the Creed, then society would lose its fever of racial pathologies and settle down to a happy existence. However, the point we are trying to make is that, in a feudal system, serfdom is natural and the serf will be treated like a serf regardless of whether the lord is a bishop or a secular noble; in the slavocracy of the South the slave was treated like a slave, whether his master was white or black; in modern capitalism black workers are exploited naturally and race hatred is a natural support of this exploitation. In other words, morality is a function of the social system, and a better system can change both morality and human nature for the better.

There will be no more "crackers" or "niggers" after a socialist revolution because the social necessity for these types will have been removed. But the vision which the capitalist theorist dreads most is this: that there will be no more capitalists and capitalist exploitation. If we attempt to see race relations realistically, the meaning of the capitalist function is inescapable. At any rate, although Myrdal criticizes Sumner and Park for their inert and fatalistic views of social change, he himself contends that any revolutionary change in the interest of democracy will be futile:

. . . a national policy will never work by changing only one factor, least of all if attempted suddenly and with great force. In most cases that would either throw the system entirely out of gear or else prove to be a wasteful expenditure of effort which could be reached much further by being

---

chance, the latter stop fighting among themselves and turn their attention to their common enemy. This is, to use the term so frequently employed by Myrdal, "escapism."

[94] Ibid., p. 509.

[95] *Principles of Political Economy*, Vol. 1, p. 390. Long before this John Locke had said quite as much; see *Essay Concerning Human Understanding*.

spread strategically over various factors in the system and over a period of time.[96]

This is not the place to discuss the theory of revolution, but it must be obvious that the purpose of revolution is not to "throw the system out of gear." It is to overthrow the entire system, to overthrow a ruling class; and the cost of revolution did not frighten the capitalists when it became their lot to overthrow the feudalists.

An American Dilemma, the most exhaustive *survey* of race relations ever undertaken in the United States, is, for the most part, a useful source of data. In detail it presents many ingenious analyses of the materials. But it develops no hypothesis or consistent theory of race relations; and, to the extent that it employs the caste belief in interpretations, it is misleading. Clearly, the use of "the American Creed" as the "value premise" for his study severely limits and narrows Dr. Myrdal's perspective. Even though we should grant some right of the author to limit the discussion of his subject to its moral aspects, he still develops it without insight. He never brings into focus the two great systems of morality currently striving in our civilization for ascendancy, but merely assumes a teleological abstraction of social justice toward which all good men will ultimately gravitate. Moreover, since we can hardly accuse him of being naïve, and since he clearly goes out of his way to avoid the obvious implications of labor exploitation in the South, we cannot help concluding that the work in many respects may have the effect of a powerful piece of propaganda in favor of the status quo. If the "race problem" in the United States is pre-eminently a moral question, it must naturally be resolved by moral means, and this conclusion is precisely the social illusion which the ruling political class has constantly sought to produce. In this connection we are conscious of the author's recognition that "social science is essentially a 'political' science." One thing is certain, at any rate: the work contributes virtually nothing to a clarification of the many existing spurious social theories of race relations—indeed, on the latter score, Myrdal's contribution is decidedly negative. And for this reason evidently he has been able to suggest no solution for the dilemma, but, like the fatalists whom he criticizes, the author relies finally upon time as the great corrector of all evil.

---

[96]Op. cit., p. 77.

24. The Area of Caste Society and Practical Value of the Concept

*W*E NOW COME TO THE QUESTION: WHERE IN THE WORLD OUT-side of Brahmanic India do caste systems exist? And the answer must be briefly: Practically nowhere. The caste system is an Indian cultural invention, and the fact that it did not diffuse may be due to the comparative isolation and sedentariness of the Hindus, besides the probable difficulty of reorganizing other societies under the peculiar aegis of godlike priests. An economic system in which occupational specialization is presumed to inhere in corporate social groups producing out of a sense of religious duty in the interest of social peace—in which leadership is atomized and loyalty passionately bestowed upon the producing unit—is to be found only in India.[1] A number of authorities, among them Bouglé, Hutton, Senart, and Risley,[2] have reached a similar conclusion.

---

[1]There are evidently some real vestiges of the caste system among the islands off the coast of southern India. The caste culture was carried there by early migrations. See Miguel Covarrubias, *Island of Bali,* pp. 52–57; Jane Belo, "A Study of a Balinese Family," *American Anthropologist,* New Series, Vol. 38, 1936, pp. 12–31. See also Clive Day, *The Dutch in Java,* p. 9, and Raymond Kennedy, *The Ageless Indies,* pp. 32–36.

[2]"Even from ancient times," says Bouglé, "western civilization has set its face against such a system." Op. cit., p. 11. J. H. Hutton, census commissioner of India, thinks that the caste system is a form of social organization unique in the world, for "there is no other country or nation which possesses anything approaching the elaborate caste system of India, nor is there any other country known to have possessed one of the same kind." *Census of India, 1931,* Vol. I, Pt. 1, p. 433; see also for a similar statement by Hutton, *Caste in India,* pp. 41–42. And Senart concludes: "Caste exists only in India. It is therefore in the situation peculiar to India that we must seek its explanation. . . . We must turn to the facts themselves . . . to . . . study the characteristic elements of the system. . . ." Op. cit., p. 174. See also p. 32. Although Risley reached some rather astonishing conclusions in support of his race-caste theory, he writes: "Nowhere else in the world do we find the people of a large continent broken up into an infinite number of mutually exclusive aggregates, the members of which are forbidden by an inexorable social law to marry outside the group to which they themselves belong." Op. cit., p. 24. To the same effect, see also Max Weber, *Gesammelte Aufsatze zur Religionssozi-*

Many others, however, think that caste systems have existed at various periods and in different areas of the world. Yet none of this group has ever gone to the pains of assuring himself that the system under consideration stood up in careful comparison with Hindu society. Consider, in illustration, the treatment of this subject by the eminent anthropologist, Robert H. Lowie. In a discussion of caste among the Natchez Indians he asserts:

> The Natchez evidently had a most interesting caste system. . . . The common herd were designated by the unflattering term *Stinkards* and were sharply set off from the nobility. This latter group was subdivided into three ranks of Honored People, Nobles and Suns, the ruler standing at the head of the scale as Great Sun. . . . The Natchez were not only permitted but prescribed the marriage of Suns with commoners, the regulation affecting both sexes. When a Sun woman espoused a Stinkard, the customary patriarchal arrangements of the tribe were suspended, the husband occupying the status of a domestic not privileged to eat in his wife's company and being liable to execution for infidelity. The working of the scheme has been thus summarized by Swanton: "The Suns comprised children of Sun mothers and Stinkard fathers; the Nobles were children of Noble mothers and Stinkard fathers, or of Sun fathers and Stinkard mothers; the Honored People included children of Honored women and Stinkard fathers, and of Noble fathers and Stinkard mothers; finally, the large class of Stinkards was recruited from plebeian intermarriages or from unions of Stinkard mothers and Honored men."[3]

We have quoted at length from Dr. Lowie, for we know of no other discussion of caste systems independent of India which improves significantly upon his. Critically, however, it may be said that this whole description appears irrelevant to basic principles of caste organization. From the foregoing description, the Natchez society appears to be a type of matriarchate with some sort of estate system.[4]

Some students have been very much troubled about the tendency to limit caste society to India. Thus it has been said to the writer: "If you require, for a society to be characterized by 'caste,' that it resemble the Indian situation in every important particular, then of course there is

---

ologie, Vol. II, Sec. 1. Weber thinks that Jews in Europe have been a caste similar to the outcastes of India, "a Pariah folk." He distinguishes the Jewish situation, however, with the modifications that the Jews lived in a casteless milieu, that they were never spiritually resigned, and that they possessed a rational religion. Ibid., pp. 2–7. Notwithstanding these modifications, the analogy remains questionable.

[3]Robert H. Lowie, *Primitive Society,* pp. 351–52.

[4]For a discussion of the estate systems of the Aztecs and Incas, see Bailey W. Diffie, *Latin-American Civilization,* pp. 165–78. It should be observed that although the caste system of India is very ancient it involves a highly developed civilization, and in consequence we should not expect to find it in decidedly primitive cultures.

no instance of caste in the world except that found in India; and it further follows that 'caste' cannot be the name of a class of phenomena and is no concept."[4a] Clearly, such a view opens the way for endless debate. At any rate, we feel rather like Professor MacIver, who explains: "If we are to study a thing together we must, when we use a word or phrase, be denoting, mentally pointing out as it were, the same object."[5]

At any rate, this contention should be met directly. It is not so much an insistence that every social fact in the caste system of Brahmanic India must be identical or duplicated in detail in the social structure of race relations in the United States as it is absolutely necessary that at least every detail, which the race-caste hypothesis itself considers significant enough to mention in its own support, should be tested and compared to the social norm. We should consider the race-caste hypothesis invalid if its postulates are inconsistent with the caste system of India. If not India, then the theorist is obviously limited to two alternatives: (1) He should state explicitly which other caste system or systems he is using as a social prototype, or (2) he should indicate clearly that his assumed caste system is a fictitious construct. In either case the validity of his reasoning will depend upon the acceptability of his criteria and assumptions. Thus far, however, no race-caste theorist known to us has followed either of these two procedures.

The caste system is not a social concept in the sense that social status is one. Social status is a universal attribute of human societies. Just as, for instance, warm blood does not differentiate species of Mammalia, so also social status of itself does not differentiate types of societies. But the caste system is not merely an attribute of society; it is itself a type of society. It will make no sense at all to speak of a caste society as an attribute of a capitalist society. These two are distinct social systems, with entirely independent cultural histories and with mutually antagonistic social norms. It is beyond all social logic, moreover, to conceive of a caste system developing spontaneously within a capitalist

---

[4a] For a rather loose discussion of this point, see M. F. Ashley Montagu, "The Nature of Race Relations," *Social Forces*, Vol. 25, March 1947, p. 339.

[5] R. M. MacIver, *Society, Its Structure and Changes*, p. 5. Moreover, to conceive of a social concept as definitive of a type of social organization, which the concept of a caste system must necessarily imply, and to impute this concept to some social fact in a totally different type of social organization can hardly be a valid procedure. Raymond Bauer makes this point when he observes: "To study culture one must study it as a complete pattern of functionally related institutions. As a matter of fact, even individual institutions should not be studied apart from an explicitly stated cultural framework, since the significance of any one institution lies in its functional relationship to the entire pattern." Review of *The Social Systems of American Ethnic Groups* by W. Lloyd Warner and Leo Srole in *Science*, Vol. 103, February 1, 1946, p. 150.

system. We cannot even conceive of social status, as it manifests itself in the caste system, having an identical or similar manifestation in the capitalist system.

A concept which changes its meaning according to the convenience of the student may complicate rather than clarify thinking on the subject. The sociologist who says that the caste system of India represents a unique form of social organization is evidently on better ground than he who asserts that wherever you find a society whose social-status structure is rigid with one or more in-marrying groups, there you have a caste system. And this admission of uniqueness does not mean that Hindu society is an anomalous social phenomenon, for this pattern of culture reveals social situations which might have developed in other societies. Its very uniqueness should present a tempting field for study. The caste system, like capitalism, is a form of social organization; both of these are types of societies. Clearly, it is as logical to think of the caste system as having developed independently in India as it is for us to realize that modern capitalism is exclusively a European-culture development.

Furthermore, the indiscriminate use of a concept naturally tends to limit its effectiveness. If, according to the predilection of the writer, he might extract any one or a selection of attributes of the caste system to verify his hypothesis that castes exist in Haiti, or in England, or in the United States, or, for that matter, in the Army, or in the Church, then indeed we have a concept of wide serviceability but at the same time sociologically meaningless.

Another tendency, which should rather be deplored among sociologists and anthropologists, is that of using the term "castelike" when an accurate description of the social situation evidently seems too abstruse. The term "castelike," even more so than the term "caste," confuses the problem. Obviously a castelike society may be defined only by saying that it represents a social system which looks like or behaves like a caste system. This done, however, we are faced with the query, How does a caste system look? The ocular connotation of this type of adjective apparently detracts from its value in describing societies. When we say a thing is manlike, or doglike, or redlike, our meaning is ordinarily quite clear. There is no mistaking the gorilla for a man, or the dog for a wolf, or purple for red; acceptance of the one when the other is desired may mean all the difference in the world. But in the case of abstract phenomena, the common assumption seems to be that "likes" may be identified *for all practical purposes*.

In his study of race relations in the United States Dr. Sutherland explains that "the term 'castelike' is used in describing the relations of the Negro and white groups. This has been done because the separation of the two groups is neither complete nor uniform."[6] Before this statement, however, Sutherland prepared his readers with the following postulate: "In a class system individuals can move from one level to another by acquiring the proper symbols. In a *caste society* mobility is *not permitted* so long as the individual possesses the symbol which has been used to separate the groups."[7]

Here, then, reappears the "symbol" criterion of caste society. Evidently this standard of social mobility excludes the possibility of degrees of effective caste systems. Just how much prevention of symbol acquisition constitutes "castelike" and what determines the permitting agency are questions, unfortunately, left to the reader. Probably one might say that Negro-white relationship in the North is not so "castelike" as it is in the South. But the question arises: Who prevents whites in the United States from acquiring any of the symbols which Negroes now possess? And if perchance the answer is, "Obviously nature," then we have again returned quite smugly to the leopard-and-spots hypothesis of caste society. According to the interest of the person who derives the meaning, the term "castelike" may be interpreted as racelike, guildlike, labor-union-like, classlike, and so on. Its value to the sociologist seems to lie principally in its power to obscure social problems.

Practical Value of the Concept

In conversation some thoughtful persons have suggested to the writer that although the American application of the term "caste" may not be "scientific," it is nonetheless a very effective word in the service of the orator or the journalist. Since we have built up negative stereotypes about the caste idea, the use of the term "caste" in describing the racial system in this country may have a quite desirable result. We should remember, however, that truth is on the side of colored people and that they probably need few, if any, artificialities to support it. Ray Stannard Baker says well: "The situation in the South has made some people afraid of the truth."[8]

Furthermore, there is usually some unexpected, distasteful rebound in compromising with untruth. For instance, it is not unlikely that the propagandists will awaken to discover that they have played into the

---

[6]Robert L. Sutherland, *Color, Class, and Personality,* p. xix.
[7]Ibid., p. xviii–xix.
[8]Op. cit., p. 258.

hands of the ruling class in the South. It has been an old practice of the Southern aristocracy to stifle any incipient discontent among the un-privileged whites by pointing to a two-class system—all whites above and all blacks below. By this method they have been able to strengthen their political-class position. It worked well with the slaveholders and has continued to function admirably. As Roger W. Shugg says: "To parry the thrusts of Abolitionists, Free Soilers, and Republicans, the southern planters consolidated support at home by spreading their mantle over all classes and denying the existence of any class except the white and black races."[9]

To be sure, no one need be overmeticulous about an offhand use of the term "caste" in discussions of race relations. In formal sociological writings, however, its indiscriminate use may be insidiously misleading. Indeed, attempts to give the vulgar use of this term scientific precision have probably divested it of much of its former odium. In the sociology books it has been objectified and desiccated so that race relations in the Southern states, for instance, are sometimes made to appear as one of the natural forms of social organization. The idea of a "type of society" obscures the actual pathological racial antagonism, leaving some dif-fused impression that it is socially right, even as the caste system in India is right.[10]

The terms "race prejudice" and "racial discrimination" have already been defined in the world view of Western society as social sins per se. However, such subjects as race prejudice and discrimination call for delicate handling in the textbooks. Consequently many writers will find it more incommodious to discuss and explain these phenomena than to couch the situation in the euphonious terminology of "American caste."

If we have caste among blacks and blacks in Haiti,[11] among peoples of color in India, and among whites and whites in England,[12] then there may be all the more reason and justification for having caste be-tween whites and blacks in the South. The implication of the "natural-ness" of caste provides a comforting blanket assumption.

---

[9]*Origins of Class Struggle in Louisiana,* p. 33.

[10]Observe, in illustration, with what nicety of reasoning Guy B. Johnson gets around his problem: "There has lately been much agitation for the suppression of lynching by Federal law. Some people, with characteristic faith in the magic of legislation, imagine that Federal law can stop lynching. Any custom which is as deeply rooted in caste consciousness as lynching is, will not be eradicated easily." See "Patterns of Race Conflict," in *Race Relations and the Race Problem,* p. 146.

[11]John Lobb, "Caste in Haiti," *American Journal of Sociology,* Vol. XLVI, July 1940, pp. 23–34.

[12]*The University of Chicago Round Table,* December 8, 1940, p. 20.

25. The Race Problem in the United States——

WE SHALL LIMIT THIS DISCUSSION TO NEGRO-WHITE RELATION-ships; these are the races ordinarily referred to when the race problem is considered. Moreover, we shall consider mainly the situation in the South because it is more obvious; that in the North differs mainly in degree. The "race problem" includes all the immediate or short-run instances of overt friction between Negroes and whites; maladjustments due to disparity in population characteristics, such as death rate, disease, unemployment, poverty, illiteracy, and so on, and innumerable conflicts of opposing attitudes and policies. The whites determine the pattern of these problems and the grounds upon which they must be thrashed out. Broadly speaking, the general policy of the nation follows the scheme developed in the South, and the ruling-class whites in this area are explicitly devoted to the ideal that Negroes shall never be assimilated. The race problem, then, is primarily the short-run manifestations of opposition between an abiding urge among Negroes to assimilate and a more or less unmodifiable decision among racially articulate, nationalistic whites that they should not.

The Problem of Assimilation

The solidarity of American Negroes is neither nationalistic nor nativistic. The group strives for neither a forty-ninth state leading to an independent nation nor a back-to-Africa movement; its social drive is toward assimilation. In this respect Negroes are like most other American immigrants; it is well known that the social tendency toward assimilation is an American cultural trait. Therefore, the solidarity of Negroes is defensive and tentative only, while their social orientation is centrifugal. For them social solidarity is not a virtue in itself. Their society is not designed for self-perpetuation; it will endure only so long as the white ruling class is successful in opposing their assimilation.

The urge toward assimilation and away from group solidarity is so compelling among Negroes that few, if any, of the organizations maintained by whites which offer reasonably unrestricted participation to Negroes can be developed by Negroes for Negroes. As a rule, only those types of white enterprises which discriminate against Negroes can be developed among Negroes. If the white society were to be impartial to Negro participation, no business, no school, no church would thrive among Negroes. Negroes are old Americans. The businesses of Negroes are mainly those of catering; their church had its birth in reaction to white discrimination, and their separate schools belong to the system of white race segregation. In short, Negro business enterprises and social institutions may be thought of as crystals of reaction to white race discrimination.

One of the most powerful techniques utilized by the white ruling class for retardation of assimilation of the races is segregation. Segregation obviously limits the opportunity for communication and interracial understanding and makes possible an easy exploitation of antagonistic stereotypes. The refined Negro is most carefully guarded against, so that in the South the principal racial contact is between the white upper class and Negro domestic servants.

If the races live in protected residential zones and are kept apart in schools, in churches, in cemeteries, on the playgrounds, in hotels and restaurants, on transportation vehicles, and so on, they will tend to believe in a disparity of every possible group interest and purpose, a social fact which is basically antipathetic to assimilation.

In the United States white foreigners are ordinarily encouraged to assimilate, but peoples of color are not. The Christian democratic world view of the nation, however, is not thus selective. In fact, this world view is a prepotent force tending to counteract and subordinate the immediate anti-assimilation attitudes of the white racially articulate class. Therefore, with respect to the basic ideals of Western civilization, the position of this class must necessarily be defensive; and this, even though its rationalizations may seem aggressive.

The Meaning of Assimilation

According to Albert Ernest Jenks: "Only when the individuals or ethnic groups are emotionally dead to all their varied past, and are all responsible solely to the conditions of the present, are they assimilated people."[1] To be assimilated is to live easily and unobtrusively in the society. One must be at home, so to speak, with the dominant social organization. So long as a group is identified or remembered as alien, it will be forced to have a divided allegiance. Naturally, the assimilation ideal of American Negroes is to be recognized as unqualified Americans.

It would seem paradoxical, however, to assume that the more assimilated Negroes become, the more socially maladjusted they are. According to Ogburn and Nimkoff:

> The Negroes today are largely assimilated, yet as a group they are now less well adjusted to the white man's world than they were in the earlier period of slavery. . . . The more thoroughly assimilated Negroes become, the more they realize the limitations and discriminations under which they must live and the more resentful they become. The more assimilated the Negro, the more nearly he approaches the white man in competitive skill; hence the greater becomes the white man's resentment against him.[2]

Apparently there are two questions raised in this conclusion: (a) What do we mean by the term "largely assimilated"? and (b) To what extent does interracial conflict represent mutual maladjustment? It is possible that Negroes are farther away from ultimate oneness and belonging in the general American social order than any white European group that might currently enter the country. If this is so, then Negroes in America are less well assimilated than any conceivable white immigrant group. According to Robert E. Park, "Assimilation may in some senses and to a certain degree be described as a function of visibility. As soon as an immigrant no longer exhibits the marks which identify him as a member of an alien group, he acquires by that fact the actual if not the legal status of a native."[3] Thus acculturation alone may not be sufficient for assimilation; in other words, the mere assumption of the dominant cultural patterns has not been sufficient to assure complete integration of the group.

In fact, the dominant attitude in the South is that cultural disparity is of exceedingly minor significance when compared with difference in skin color. So great indeed is the alleged alienating power of the latter that it is sometimes believed that difference in color forever precludes the possibility of the two groups achieving cultural parity. In his argument that the Negro is not assimilated, Park concludes: "This distinc-

---

[1]"Assimilation in the Philippines," *Proceedings of the American Sociological Society*, Vol. VIII, 1913.

[2]*Sociology*, pp. 385–86.

[3]"Assimilation," *Encyclopedia of the Social Sciences*.

tion which sets him apart from the rest of the population is real, but it is based not upon cultural traits but upon physical and racial characteristics."[4] The Negro is very much more assimilated today than in 1860 in the sense that if it now becomes possible to overthrow the Southern oligarchy with its racial ideologies by extirpating it, then Negroes would be in a much better position to assume the role of normal citizens in harmony with the rest of the population.

With respect to the point that Negroes are becoming increasingly less well adjusted, it is significant to observe that increasing interracial conflict is a problem of both races. A race riot may result in the death of both blacks and whites, while a lynching is a disturbing event as well for white people. Booker Washington's aphorism that "you can't hold a man down in the ditch without staying down there with him" is homely but eminently suggestive.

Much of the racial aggressiveness of white people runs counter to the basic ideals and social ethics of Western society. Its satisfactory operation necessitates a relegation of the laws and a reliance upon spontaneous elemental force. In this sense whites may be thought of as culturally maladjusted. The most significant of these acts of racial aggression is the well-known practice of lynching. At this point we shall attempt an analysis of this phenomenon; it is the fundamental reliance of the white ruling class in maintaining its racial superiority.

Lynching

Quite frequently lynching has been thought of as a form of social control consisting in the taking of the life of one person or more by a mob in retribution for some criminal outrage committed by the former. This method of unceremonial punishment is assumed to be common on the frontier where there is no constituted juridical machinery and where, in the interest of social order, the group finds itself constrained to act spontaneously. Furthermore, it is known to occur in organized society where some crime is of such a heinous and socially revolting nature that an angry crowd gathers spontaneously and passionately mangles the criminal to death. Even in this situation, however, the police may be ineffectively organized, as is ordinarily the case in rural communities.

---

[4]Ibid. However, this statement by Park should not be taken too literally; the fact is that the Negro is marked by his color for the purpose of achieving an ulterior cultural advantage.

At any rate, these two situations do not involve significant social problems in America; in fact, they hardly refer to lynching as a social institution.[5] They have no racial, nationality, or political-class significance. Justice among frontiersmen has never been a pressing problem for the nation. Furthermore, lynching must not be confused with the "hue and cry" of the general mob in medieval times. Here indeed was a recognized method of arrest, with its system of sanctuaries and sanctuary law.

Lynching may be defined as an act of homicidal aggression committed by one people against another through mob action for the purpose of suppressing either some tendency in the latter to rise from an accommodated position of subordination or for subjugating them further to some lower social status. It is a special form of mobbing— mobbing directed against a whole people or political class.[6] We may distinguish lynching from race rioting by the fact that the lynching mob is unopposed by other mobs, while it tends to be actuated by a belief that it has a constituted right to punish some more or less identified individual or individuals of the other race or nationality.

Lynching is an exemplary and symbolic act. In the United States it is an attack principally against all Negroes in some community rather than against some individual Negro.[7] Ordinarily, therefore, when a lynching is indicated, the destruction of almost any Negro will serve the purpose as well as that of some particular one. Lynchings occur mostly in those areas where the laws discriminate against Negroes; sometimes, in these areas, the administrative judicial machinery may even facilitate the act. However, the lynching attitude is to be found everywhere among whites in the United States.

A lynching, as the definition given above suggests, is not primarily a spontaneous act of mob violence against a criminal. Where the interracial situation is not agitated, it will not occur. There seems to be a recognizable lynching cycle, which may be described as follows:

---

[5] We may mention incidentally that a rather puerile approach to a study of the institution of lynching is to derive hypotheses from an examination of the history of *the term* "lynching."

[6] Recently there has been a tendency, especially among journalists, to call any kind of mobbing a lynching. This, however, gives us no basis for an understanding of lynching as an intergroup problem.

[7] Francis W. Coker says well that "as violent manifestations of a racial antagonism mixed with economic rivalry the pogroms of czarist Russia and the terrorist activities against Jews in Germany and the states of southern Europe are in a class with lynching. Similarly, the conflicts between labor and capital [political class action] often give rise to what are in essence lynching." "Lynching," *Encyclopedia of the Social Sciences.*

(a) A growing belief among whites in the community that Negroes are getting out of hand—in wealth, in racial independence, in attitudes of self-assertion, especially as workers, or in reliance upon the law. An economic depression causing some whites to retrograde faster than some Negroes may seem a relative advancement of Negroes in some of the latter respects.

(b) Development, by continual critical discussion about Negroes among whites, of a summatory attitude of racial antagonism and tension.

(c) The rumored or actual occurrence of some outrage committed by a Negro upon some white person or persons. The ideal act is the rape of a white girl. But if the tension is very high, whites will purposely seek an incident with the Negroes.

(d) The incident having occurred, the white mob comes into action, lays hands upon the Negro, and lynches him. He is burned, hanged, or shot in some public place, preferably before the courthouse, and his remains dragged about the Negro section of the community. Ordinarily, in the heat of mob action, other Negroes are killed or flogged, and more or less Negro property is destroyed—houses are burned, places of business pillaged, and so on. There is usually a scramble among the mob for toes, fingers, bits of clothing, and the like, which are kept as souvenirs of the lynching occasion.

(e) During a lynching all Negroes are driven under cover. They are terrified and intimidated. Many put themselves completely at the mercy of their non-militant "white friends" by cowering in the latter's homes and pleading for protection from the enraged mob. Sometimes they leave the community altogether.

(f) Within about two or three days the mob achieves its emotional catharsis. There is a movement for judicial investigation, and some of the "best white people" speak out against lynching. On the following Sunday a few ministers of great courage declare that lynching is barbarous and un-Christian; and in time the grand jury returns its findings that "the deceased came to his death by hanging and gunshot wounds at the hands of parties unknown."

(g) There is a new interracial adjustment. Negroes become exceedingly circumspect in their dealing with whites, for they are now thoroughly frightened. Many are obligated to their "white friends" for having saved their lives, and few will dare even to disagree with white persons on any count whatever. The man who does so is not considered a hero by the majority of Negroes; rather he earns their censure.

(h) In a more or less short period of time Negroes begin to smile broadly and ingratiatingly over the merest whim of white men.[8] They are eager to show that they bear no malice for the horrible past.[9] The lynching has accomplished its purpose, social euphoria is restored, and the cycle is again on its way.

Some lynchings may appear to have a high degree of spontaneity. It should be remembered, however, that in the South the threat of lynching is continually impending, and this threat is a coercive force available to white people as such. Says Arthur F. Raper, "Lynching is resorted to only when the implied threat of it appears to be losing its efficacy."[10] Both the overt threat of lynching and prevented lynchings function to maintain white dominance. They provide, in fine, the socio-psychological matrix of the power relationship between the races.

Lynching in the South is not a crime, and this notwithstanding the fact that a few state statutes apparently proscribe it.[11] It is quite obvious that the constitutions of the Southern states and their supporting black codes, the system of discriminatory laws intended to keep Negroes in their place, intentionally put the Negro beyond the full protection of the law, and that the former take precedence over any contravening statute. Furthermore, it is clear that the political power of the area aims

---

[8]Gunnar Myrdal makes an observation in point: "Much of the humor that the Negro displays before the white man in the South is akin to that manufactured satisfaction with their miserable lot which the conquered people of Europe are now forced to display before their German conquerors. The loud, high-pitched cackle that is commonly considered as the 'Negro laugh' was evolved in slavery times as a means of appeasing the master by debasing oneself before him and making him think that one was contented." Op. cit., p. 960.

[9]"Law and order" in the South implicitly but resolutely insist that the family or, worse still, Negroes of the community upon whom this appalling atrocity has been committed do nothing to show that they harbor resentment. The lynching, to be successful, must have so cowed the Negroes that even a gratuitous offer of possible legal assistance would be rejected by them. In a recent Mississippi lynching a white Northern reporter tactfully avoided interviewing the colored family of two lynched boys "because a man in Quitman told me quietly, 'It wouldn't do them niggers any good to be seen talking to you.'" (Victor H. Bernstein, in the Pittsburgh *Courier,* October 31, 1942.) The overwhelming terror among Negroes in the lynching situation is evoked principally by the awareness that there is in effect no legal power presuming to question the free violence of the lynchers.

It is to this social attitude which Mrs. Atwood Martin, Chairman of the Association of Southern Women for the Prevention of Lynching, refers when she says: "Knowing at the start that if we went too fast . . . it would be the Negro population that would suffer, we have refrained from overzeal until sure of our support." See Jessie Daniel Ames, *The Changing Character of Lynching,* p. 68.

[10]*Preface to Peasantry,* p. 23. In discussing a lynching situation Raper says also: "While these seventy-five thousand people were members of actual mobs but one day in the year, they were most probably mob-minded every day in the year. Millions of others were mob-disposed, and under provocation would have joined a mob, killing or standing sympathetically by while others killed." *The Tragedy of Lynching,* p. 47.

[11]Cf. James H. Chadbourn, *Lynching and the Law,* Chapter III; James E. Cutler, *Lynch Law,* pp. 1–12; and Frank Shay, *Judge Lynch,* p. 8.

at class exclusiveness. Consider, for example, the following not uncommon public threat to Negroes of South Carolina by a United States
senator—the normal attitude of the Southern politician:

Whenever the Constitution comes between me and the virtue of the
white women of South Carolina, I say, "To hell with the Constitution" . . .
When I was governor of South Carolina you did not hear me calling out
the militia of the State to protect Negro assaulters.
In my South Carolina campaigns you heard me say, "When you catch
the brute that assaults a white woman, wait until the next morning to
notify me."[12]

It is certainly true that all white people in the South will not thus
express themselves, and some are decidedly opposed to this view. But
where a leading politician could hold himself up for election on the
grounds that he is a potential lyncher, the presumption is inevitable
that lynching is not a crime.

The dominant opinion of the community exalts the leaders of the
mob as "men of courage and action."[13] Raper reports an incident in
point:

Women figured prominently in a number of outbreaks. After a woman
at Sherman had found the men unwilling to go into the courtroom and
get the accused, she got a group of boys to tear an American flag from the

---

[12]Cole Blease, quoted in Arthur F. Raper, *The Tragedy of Lynching*, p. 293. In
November 1942, at the national poll-tax filibuster, Senator Doxey said confidently,
"Mississippi and the other Southern states will uphold Anglo-Saxon supremacy
until the lofty mountains crumble to dust." No one has the slightest doubt about
the means which the senator and the entire legal machinery of the Southern states
employ and will continue to employ in the interest of this brand of democracy.
Doxey knows that he has behind him the firmly established and effective Southern
institution of interracial violence; hence he speaks to the nation with conviction.
Moreover, he is able to speak with this degree of finality because he is assured that
the United States Senate dares not challenge his position—at least he knows that
the moral level of the Senate is far below that necessary to cope with the probable
cost of instrumenting such a challenge.
Nothing serves to bring the Southern congressmen so solidly in opposition as a
national movement to pass legislation making lynching a crime. We should expect
this because to make lynching a crime would be to strike at the pivot of white
dominance in the South; to make lynching a crime would be to indict the political
leadership of the South; indeed, to make lynching a Federal crime would be to bring
before the nation the full unfinished business of the Civil War. An effective anti-
lynching law must inevitably inculpate the deepest intent of Southern constitutions.
Remarkable as it may seem, the most sacred and jealously guarded right of the
Southern states is undoubtedly the right to lynch Negroes; consequently, any Federal law seeking to limit this right will be promptly construed to be an infringement
upon the sovereignty of states. It is in this light that the impotence of the Fourteenth Amendment in protecting the life and liberty of Negroes in the South must
be estimated.
[13]Walter White, *Rope and Faggot*, p. 4.

wall of the courthouse corridor and parade through the courthouse and grounds, to incite the men to do their "manly duty."[14]

To be a crime lynching must be an offense against the local state, but the propagandized sentiment of the community registered by votes determines what offenses shall be. "Mobs do not come out of the nowhere; they are the logical outgrowths of dominant assumptions and prevalent thinking. Lynchings are not the work of men suddenly possessed of a strange madness; they are the logical issues of prejudice and lack of respect for law and personality."[15] To be sure, the law loses respect naturally when it seems to contravene the powerful interests which lynching protects.

Moreover, the sense of penal immunity which pervades the mob, amounting frequently to elation in performance of a social service, tends to belie the theory that lynching is criminal. A story of crime does not read like the following:

Shortly before midnight, with an acetylene torch and high explosives, a second story vault window was blown open and the Negro's body was thrown to the crowd below. It was greeted by loud applause from the thousands who jammed the courthouse square. Police directed traffic while the corpse was dragged through the streets to a cottonwood tree in the Negro business section. There it was burned.[16]

A person or group of persons committing crime might be expected to go to great pains in relieving themselves of any trace of the act. Lynchers, however, expect to be glorified in identifying themselves. In reviewing one case Ray Stannard Baker writes: "They scrambled for the chains before they were cold, and the precious links were divided among the populace. Pieces of the stump were hacked off, and finally one young man . . . gathered up a few charred remnants of bone, carried them uptown, and actually tried to give them to the judge."[17]

The mob, then, is seldom, if ever, apprehensive of punishment. The law stands in a peculiar relationship to lynching. Nowhere is lynching advocated on the statute books; yet there is a prepotent sanction in the South that whites may use force against any Negro who becomes overbearing. According to Raper, "The manhunt tradition rests on the assumption of the unlimited rights of white men and the absence of any

---

[14]Arthur F. Raper, op. cit., p. 12; see also p. 323.

[15]Ibid., p. 47.

[16]Ibid., p. 7. Sometimes the scheduled lynching of a Negro is announced in the newspapers. See William H. Skaggs, *The Southern Oligarchy*, p. 300.

[17]*Following the Color Line*, p. 187.

rights on the part of the accused Negro."[18] Negroes can ordinarily be taken from police custody because there is a controlling assumption that the formal law is not available to Negroes. The mob is composed of people who have been carefully indoctrinated in the primary social institutions of the region to conceive of Negroes as extralegal, extrademocratic objects, without rights which white men are bound to respect. Therefore, most Southern official criticism of mob action against Negroes must necessarily be taken largely as pretense. The jury and courts could hardly be expected to convict, since their "hands are even as dirty."[19] Mrs. Jessie Daniel Ames puts it in this way:

Newspapers and Southern society accept lynching as justifiable homicide in defense of society. When defenders of society sometimes go too far in their enthusiasm, as in the Winona, Mississippi, torch lynchings of 1937, public opinion regrets their acts, deplores them, condemns, but recognizes that too much blame must not be attached to lynchers because their provocation is great and their ultimate motives are laudable.[20]

Such functionaries as the sheriff, mayor, or prosecuting attorney have not only been known to take part in lynchings, but also the court sitting formally has answered the purpose of the mob. "Mobs do not loiter around courtrooms solely out of curiosity; they stand there, armed with guns and threats, to see that the courts grant their demands— death sentences and prompt executions. Such executions are correctly termed 'legal lynchings,' or 'judicial murders.' "[21]

We should make the distinction between that which is socially pathological and that which is criminal. Although these two phenomena may converge, they are nevertheless capable of separate existence. All criminal acts indicate some form of social maladjustment, but not vice versa. In illustration, certain types of speculation on the stock and commodity exchanges may be socially pathological and yet not crimes. If the economic system and supporting laws are such that unwhole-

---

[18]Op. cit., p. 9.

[19]The tables of convictions for lynchings and attempted lynchings presented by Chadbourn, op. cit., pp. 14–15, are not very revealing. They may include contempt cases and cases falling within the two possible meanings of lynching suggested in the introduction to this analysis. The situations may be further complicated by lynchers doing more or less serious violence to white persons who may attempt to protect the Negro.

[20]Op. cit., p. 51.

[21]Arthur F. Raper, op. cit., p. 46. See also page 13, and Walter White, op. cit., p. 32. In this connection Mrs. Ames observes: "In more than one prevented lynching a bargain was entered into between officers and would-be lynchers before the trial began in which the death penalty was promised as the price of the mob's dispersal." Op. cit., p. 12.

some speculation cannot be but inevitable, then clearly it will not be criminal. In like manner, although the lynching of a Negro involves some social wrong against Negroes besides some increment of degeneracy among the lynchers, statutory impotency or even implied encouragement may necessarily exclude it from the category of crime.

Lynching is socially pathological only in the sense that it is incompatible with the democratic Christian spirit of the Western world. The spirit of the age is antipathetic to both the Southern system of social values and its stabilizer, lynching; but lynching happens to be the more obtrusive. Like a society of head-hunters or cannibals where the individual hunter is never inculpated in terms of the values of his society, the Southern lyncher can be considered criminal and degenerate only in the judgment of an out-group.

Lynching is crucial in the continuance of the racial system of the South. From this point of view lynching may be thought of as a necessity.[22] This is not to say, however, that lynching is "in the mores"; it is rather in the whip hand of the ruling class. It is the most powerful and convincing form of racial repression operating in the interest of the status quo. Lynchings serve the indispensable social function of providing the ruling class with the means of periodically reaffirming its collective sentiment of white dominance. During a lynching the dominant whites of the community assume an explicit organization for interracial conflict. By overt acts of aggression they give emotional palpability to their perennial preoccupation with racial segregation and discrimination. Their belligerency tends to compel the conformity of possible indifferent whites in the community, and it defines opposing whites as unpatriotic and traitorous to the cause of white dominance.

Furthermore, there is an inseparable association between Negro disfranchisement and lynching. Disfranchisement makes lynching possible, and lynching speedily squelches any movement among Southern Negroes for enfranchisement. In the South these two are indispensable instruments in the service of the status quo. Indeed, as Jessie Ames concludes: "Negroes, as a voteless people in a Democracy, [are] a helpless people."

Clearly, the lynching would be of no particular concern to Negroes if custom in the South prescribed, as punishment for certain offenses, public hanging and mutilation. We should not expect Negroes to be

---

[22]In criticizing the policy of Southern newspapers, Jessie Daniel Ames declares: "They cannot defend lynching as a necessary form of violence to insure white supremacy. All the country holds the philosophy of white supremacy . . . but nationally it is not good sales talk to advertise that white supremacy can be maintained in the South . . . only by force, coercion, and lynching." Op. cit., p. 54.

any more occupied with problems of such a practice than they are, say, with the current question of capital punishment. Indeed, there is a sense in which Negroes may prefer public retribution for such a crime as rape. The act of penalizing is itself a factor contributing to social cohesion.[23] If Negroes were permitted to attend in concert with whites the public execution of a white or a Negro rapist, we should expect the event to engender a degree of solidarity between them. Such interracial action, however, is not at all intended by a lynching. Lynching is not punishment; it is racial aggression.

"In the states where most lynchings have occurred, white people generally justified slavery. . . . They justified methods of terror employed to intimidate and disfranchise the Negroes; and they later enacted laws and perfected party procedures to restore and preserve 'white supremacy.' "[24] Through the instrumentality of these laws and political contrivances the Southern aristocracy returned to power and relegated the protection of the Negro to the benevolence of white people as individuals. Having defined Negroes basically as extralegal objects, some sort of informal means of violent coercion, ranging all the way from an occasional blow to floggings, mutilations, and lynchings, had to be relied upon.

Lynchings were excluded, *ipso facto,* from the category of criminal offenses when Negroes were disfranchised by the Southern state constitutions; the black codes support the constitutions. As we have attempted to show in our chapter on situations of race relations, the type of racial situation determines the pattern of white-colored relationship, while some sort of political-class interest is fundamental. The planter, exploitative class interest dominates the social life of the South, and lynching is bound up with the latter interest.[25] In South Africa, where the racial situation is in many respects similar to that of the South, the same need for extralegal violence against the colored people presents itself. As one writer concludes: "The history of the century [in South

---

[23]For a general discussion of the nature of negative sanctions, see Emile Durkheim, *The Division of Labor in Society,* Chap. II.

[24]Arthur F. Raper, op. cit., p. 50.

[25]"The Black Belt lynching is something of a business transaction. . . . Negroes are in least danger in these plantation counties. The whites, there, chiefly of the planter class and consciously dependent upon the Negro for labor, lynch him to conserve traditional landlord-tenant relations rather than to wreak vengeance upon his race. Black Belt white men demand that the Negroes stay out of their politics and dining rooms, the better to keep them in their fields and kitchens." Ibid., pp. 57–58.

This inherent requirement of Southern economy tends to set the dominant theme of race relations, so that even poor whites may seem to exploit the advantage in their competitive contacts with Negroes.

Africa] would hardly show an instance of a single white man awarded capital punishment for the murder of a native. But it will bring to light scores of cases in which the white murderer escaped scot-free or only with nominal punishment. . . . [The natives] get nominal wages and heaps of insults. The white farmer could . . . whip them and make them slave for him."[26] In South Africa, however, the lynching pattern is not exactly duplicated because personal violence against the natives is, to a considerable extent, permitted in the formal law.

This is a consideration of highest importance in understanding the determining force in the pattern of race relations in the South. The insistence upon a personal right of white men to control Negroes has its roots in the Southern system of slavery. The landlords had achieved such a right over their Negro slaves, and their vision of losing it was clearly the most galling aspect of the Civil War. As Hinton R. Helper says with acrimony: "All slaveholders are under the shield of a perpetual license to murder."[27] It is this right which the counterrevolution of the aristocracy practically restored. Its brilliant self-satisfying outer covering was extended to the white commonalty as a reward for their counterrevolutionary support.[28] The aristocracy retrieved this right of personal control over the Negro at greater cost than that of any other right known to their constitutions. This class is naturally sensitive about it and cannot be expected either to accept or to make laws which will abrogate it.[29] Then, too, the rights secured by belonging to a dominant race must necessarily be personal.

Lynching, besides, is integral in the Southern system. To remove the threat of it is to overthrow the ruling class in the South and to change the basis of Southern economy. "Threats, whippings, and even more serious forms of violence have been customary caste sanctions utilized

---

[26] P. S. Joshi, *The Tyranny of Colour*, pp. 18, 20.

[27] Op. cit., p. 140.

[28] Even before Emancipation the white commonalty was allowed a superior right of violence over Negroes. This had to be done, for it was upon the white masses that the slaveholders depended for protection against insurrection. The practice involved the poor whites in deep antagonism with the Negroes, while the masters held the property right to sue these whites for damages in case of "unreasonable" injury to the slave.

[29] At a recent court hearing in Mississippi, prosecuted by the Federal Government, the Southern attorney defending the lynchers of Howard Wash said: "The people of this great Southland are on trial. We may as well face the truth. This is not a trial to vindicate the lynching of Howard Wash, the Negro, nor is it a trial only to convict the three defendants. . . . It is just another effort to see how much we of the South will permit invasion of state rights." The newspaper reported that "a popular subscription, conducted by leading citizens of southeastern Mississippi, was launched for a defense fund." The jury, of course, did not convict. See Pittsburgh *Courier,* May 1, 1943.

to maintain a strict discipline over Negro labor."[30] Where the system is functioning most effectively, lynching tends to become natural even to Negroes. Arthur F. Raper observes a case in point: "The Negroes were not greatly disturbed by the lynching, being already inured to the undisputed domination of whites. In Bolivar County, with an average of one lynching every four years, such occurrences are part of the normal picture."[31] One is in error, then, in thinking that it is possible to eradicate mob action in the South, as it may be possible to stamp out, say, the crime of kidnaping, without also questioning the foundations of the Southern social order. Jessie Daniel Ames, Executive Director of the Association of Southern Women for the Prevention of Lynching, sees the alternatives thus: "To those who believe lynchers are criminal devils, inherently wicked and depraved, then punishment, swift, severe, and sure, appeals; to those who believe lynchers are born into a social and economic system which turns them to acts of brutal violence, then change of the system appeals."[32]

We have seen that lynching is a form of interracial conflict facilitated by the fundamental laws of the Southern states. By lynching, Negroes are kept in their place; that is to say, kept as a great, easily exploitable, common-labor reservoir.[33] It is not essential, therefore, that the victim be actually guilty of crime. When the situation of interracial tension is sufficiently developed, a scapegoat will do.[34] Negroes have been lynched for such apparent trivialities as "using offensive language," "bringing suit against white men," "trying to act like white men,"[35] "frightening women and children," "being a witness," "gambling," "making boastful remarks," and "attempting to vote."[36]

Yet there is a peculiar and consistent association of the crime of rape committed by Negroes upon white women and lynching. Indeed, the

[30]Gunnar Myrdal, op. cit., Vol. I, p. 229.

[31]Op. cit., p. 97.

[32]Op. cit., p. 59.

[33]In the period of early Reconstruction, Judge Humphrey of Alabama expressed the fundamental economic purpose of the ruling class. "I believe," he said, "in case of a return to the Union, we would receive political co-operation so as to secure the management of that labor by those who were slaves. There is really no difference, in my opinion, whether we hold them as absolute slaves or obtain their labor by some other method." Quoted by W. E. B. Du Bois, *Black Reconstruction,* p. 140.

[34]"Two of the 1930 mob victims were innocent of crime (they were not even accused), and there is grave doubt of the guilt of eleven others. In six of these eleven cases there is considerable doubt as to just what crimes, if any, were committed, and in the other five, in which there is no question as to the crimes committed, there is considerable doubt as to whether the mobs got the guilty men." Arthur F. Raper, op. cit., pp. 4–5.

[35]Ibid., p. 36.

[36]From Tuskegee Institute's unpublished records on lynching.

arguments in favor of lynching have consistently justified it on the grounds that Negroes can be deterred from venting their asserted vicious sexual passion upon white women only by the constant threat of lynching.[37] Our problem here is not to disprove this position (many Negro women have been lynched), but rather to indicate further the relationship between lynching and the social system.

There are two principal reasons why the accusation of rape is apparently the best available defense of lynching. In the first place, rape, especially when committed upon a child, is probably the most outrageous of crimes in modern society. Mob action against a rapist, then, tends to be excused in the mores. In fact, the lynchers of such a criminal, like the men of the New Testament who threw stones, expect some sort of social approbation as a reward for their chivalry. Hence supporters of lynching find it expedient to hold out the crime of rape to a censuring world and to focus all discussion upon it. On this ground they are able to develop any degree of eloquence and heat in justification of the institution.

In the second place, as we have attempted to show in a previous chapter, the white woman holds a strategic position in the interracial adjustment of the South. To the extent that the ruling interest in the South can maintain eternal watchfulness over her, to that extent also the system may be perpetuated. The belief that Negroes are surreptitiously using white women to "mongrelize" the population produces a bitter sense of frustration, calling for practically unlimited violence against Negroes. It is principally on the latter score that the white ruling class has been able to corral the white masses for expressions of mob violence. Clearly a "mongrelized" South will ultimately mean not only a non-segregated South but also a non-aristocratic South, the perennial nightmare of the Southern oligarchy.

Therefore, in order that the Negro-man, white-woman emotional set might be exploited, lynchers and their defenders always seek to manipulate the story of a lynching to include rape as a crime of the victim. Success in this would disarm almost any Southern judge, jury, or defending attorney. The latter, like the majority of the propagandized population, are naturally predisposed and receptive to arguments

---

[37]"Regardless of the cause of the particular lynching there were always those who defended it by the insistence that unless Negroes were lynched, no white woman would be safe, this despite the fact that only one-sixth of the persons lynched in the last thirty years were even accused of rape. Regardless of the accusation, an example must be made of the accused Negro for the sake of womanhood." Arthur F. Raper, op. cit., p. 20. Says Walter White, "Sex and alleged sex crimes have served as the great bulwark of the lyncher." Op. cit., p. 55.

founded upon sexual precaution. In the final analysis, then, the shibboleth of white womanhood provides the most effective rationale of the interests of the Southern aristocracy.

Since the act of lynching is directed particularly against the Negroes of the community, wide publicity and exemplary cruelty are desirable. The purpose of the lynching is not merely the elimination of a dangerous individual from society; rather the ideal is to make the occasion as impressive as possible to the whole population.[38] To Negroes it involves a challenge and a setting at naught of all that they might have held as rights to integrity of person and property, while to whites it is a demonstration and reaffirmation of white dominance. As one Southern writer asserts: "Lynching is a symptom of weak, inefficient rule. . . . Lynching will disappear when the white race is satisfied that its supremacy will not be questioned. . . ."[39]

Sometimes outsiders wonder at the presence of women and children at lynchings. For instance, Arthur F. Raper quotes the Raleigh *News and Observer* on a 1930 lynching as follows:

It was quite the thing to look at the bloody dead nigger hanging from the limb of a tree near the Edgecombe-Wilson County line this morning. . . . Whole families came together, mothers and fathers bringing even their youngest children. It was the show of the countryside—a very popular show. Men joked loudly at the sight of the bleeding body . . . girls giggled.[40]

However, as a means of schooling white children in the Southern principles of race relations, there could hardly be a more effective method. On the other hand, the custom of mutilating, burning, or dragging the victim's body in the Negro community produces the obverse side of the lesson.

Recently there have been considerable discussions among statisticians and lawmakers concerning the exact definition of a lynching. Persons who tabulate the number of lynchings per year feel a great need for accuracy and reliability, while lawmakers want to be certain that the concept is limited so as to exclude other forms of violence and homicide. Thus far, however, these problems have not been settled—and for good reason. Everyone knows what an ordinary lynching is, but

---

[38]The following is a report on one lynching: "In Baker County, Ga., a Negro killed a white bootlegger at a Negro dance. When the 'right man' could not be found, two unaccused Negroes were lynched as an object lesson." Jessie D. Ames, op. cit., p. 66.

[39]Allen Tate in *The American Review,* II, February 1934, quoted by Sterling A. Brown in *What the Negro Wants,* p. 323.

[40]Op. cit., p. 114.

there are marginal cases difficult to define. What is a mob? Two or ten times two people? In Mississippi a Negro and a white man are gambling. The white man kills the Negro in a fight and goes free. Is that a lynching?

The reason why lynching is difficult to define for purposes such as those mentioned above is that the lynching, the culminating act of continuing white aggression against Negroes, cannot be completely extricated from the social matrix which produces it. In the South the lyncher is involved in the dominant theme of the society. Indeed, lynching should be thought of as homicidal but not necessarily homicide. Any one of the unnumbered insults, slaps, cuffs, and kicks which white persons deal to Negroes daily in the South may be described as a lynching situation.[41] So far as its effect upon Negroes of the community is concerned, the flogging of a Negro boy by a few white men is not very much different from a full-blown lynching. Specifically, we may think of a lynching situation as one in which one Negro or several encounter one white or more and in which they find themselves exposed to coercion, insult, or violence, their rightful reaction to which, as normal citizens, threatens to lead either to their being beaten or killed by one white or by a mob of white persons; and, for this impending exercise of arbitrary violence, there is a consciousness on both sides that the law will not punish and that the organized ruling class in the community will show condonement.

We do not mean to say that every act of violence by whites against Negroes in the South, without exception, has gone unpunished. Ordinarily such acts do go unpunished; yet there are situations unfavorable to lynchers. The following are some of them: (a) a lynching motivated by a highly personal controversy in a community where the Negroes are well behaved; that is to say, where they are working honestly and industriously for the "big white folk"; (b) where the occasion for the killing, the lynching, is clearly a "drunken prank" of "white trash" in a "peaceful" Negro community; and (c) where uninformed whites accidentally become involved with and lynch some trusted and dependable Negro leader of the community. In the border states, especially, there is some remote likelihood that such lynchers may be sentenced to prison.

---

[41]Gunnar Myrdal observes graphically the summatory character of interracial violence in the South: "A Negro can seldom claim the protection of the police and the courts if a white man knocks him down, or if a mob burns his house or inflicts bodily injury on him or on members of his family. If he defends himself against a minor violence, he may expect a major violence. If he once 'gets in wrong' he may expect the loss of his job or other economic injury; and constant insult and loss of whatever legal rights he may have had." *Op. cit.*, p. 485.

On the periphery of the Deep South the definition of acts of extralegal violence which contribute to the support of white dominance and exploitation tends to contract.

It is sometimes believed that all the "best white people" in the South are opposed to lynching. Nothing is farther from the truth. In fact, we should expect the leading Southern citizens to be most deeply affected by a policy so significant to the continuance of the social system as mob violence.[41a] When it is possible for a sheriff, in answer to an accusation of non-feasance, to declare that "nearly every man, woman and child in our community wanted the Negro lynched,"[42] it is difficult to exculpate the leading citizens from the charge of mob sentiment or condonement of it. In reality lynching is an institution maintained by leading white people of the South; it serves as a powerful support of the ruling class.

The "best white people" may be classified into the following groups:

(a) Those who are convinced of the wrongness of lynching and speak directly against it. This group does not see the place of lynching in the Southern system. There are, naturally, degrees of enthusiasm among them.[43]

(b) Those who recognize that white violence and general aggression against Negroes is determined by the political-class system but who, confronted with the magnitude of the problem involved in attacking the system, remain silent.

(c) Those who understand the relation of the system to lynching and actually speak out against the system. These constitute a very small minority of white people who live precariously in the South.[44]

[41a]As Bernard Shaw puts it satirically: ". . . when a Negro is dipped in kerosene and set on fire in America at the present time, he is not a good man lynched by ruffians: he is a criminal lynched by crowds of respectable, charitable, virtuously indignant, high-minded citizens." *Man and Superman*, p. 214.

[42]Walter White, op. cit., p. 25.

[43]The following excerpts are intended to represent types of reaction for these groups:

"It was the average man," declares the Macon *Telegraph* editorially, "who took the vicious Negro, James Irwin, from the sheriff and mutilated and lynched him. For their crime there is not a shadow of excuse. . . . By their deed they wiped their bloody feet on society's rule of law. By their deed they lynched justice in Georgia and did almost as terrible a thing to society as did the Negro." Quoted by Arthur F. Raper, op. cit., p. 154.

For a discussion of duplicity in Southern newspaper practice concerning lynching, see Jessie D. Ames, op. cit., pp. 51-58.

[44]Among these, William H. Skaggs is typical. This critic writes: "Both social and economic conditions in the South are conducive to propagation of crime. Punishment alone will not prevent crime, so long as the economic and social causes remain. . . .

"The revival of lynching after the [Civil War] was caused by economic condi-

(d) Those who attack lynching as a means of restoring the good name of the community in the eyes of critical outsiders. This procedure is essentially a matter of good business policy.[45]

(e) Those who are convinced about the rightness of lynching and who either silently approve of or openly justify it as inevitable. Sometimes these people actually attend the lynching ceremony. Evidently this group is in the overwhelming majority.[46]

During a lynching it would be foolhardy for Negroes of the community to seek the protection of the police station, the sheriff's office, or the courthouse; to be sure, they will never dream of seeking shelter in a white church. To enter the police station on the assumption that their persons would be defended against the mob is to infuriate the mob. In other words, such a course would symbolize to the white mob that Negroes expect to utilize the machinery of the law to protect their rights, which is the antithesis of the lynchers' objective. The custom of Negroes is rather to go to the homes of "white friends," who would be able to certify to the lynchers that they are *"hard-working,* well-behaved niggers." In discussing one case Raper writes: "Most of the Negroes had gone to the homes of white friends, or had left town. . . . At midnight when other Negroes called the police-officers and Rangers and militia men for protection, they were told that nothing could be done for them, that they had better get out of town or stay at the homes of 'white friends.' "[47]

---

tions; the claim that it was for the protection of white women was an afterthought." Op. cit., pp. 309, 319.

[45]"Mob-law . . . struck . . . at the sensitive pocket of the business interests of the county. . . . It was just at the beginning of the cotton picking season, when labor of every sort was much needed, Negro labor especially. It will not do to frighten away all the Negroes. . . . Some of the officials and citizens of Statesboro got together, appointed extra marshals, and gave notice that there were to be no more whippings, and the mob-spirit disappeared." Ray Stannard Baker, op. cit., p. 188.

[46]"At Scooba, Mississippi, where a double lynching occurred, the two men reported to have organized and engineered the mob from start to finish were leading people in the community and prominently identified with the local church, school and other community activities.

"In every community where lynching occurred in 1930 there were some people who openly justified what had been done. All walks of life were represented among the apologists: judges, prosecuting attorneys, lawyers, business men, doctors, preachers, teachers." Arthur F. Raper, op. cit., pp. 11, 19. As an example of studied justification for lynching among the better class, see also David L. Cohn, *God Shakes Creation,* pp. 92ff. Here one may observe with what elfish art the case for lynching is built up, and how pointedly lynchers and those who, like this writer, provide the rationale of lynching direct their antagonism against colored people as a whole rather than against any allegedly offending Negro person.

[47]Op. cit., p. 438. In a pamphlet issued by the Southern Conference of Human Welfare, *The Truth about Columbia Tennessee Cases,* 1946, describing a lynching situation in Columbia, Tennessee, Clark H. Foreman observes: "The people of

This act of relying upon white friends for primary security has a double significance. It demonstrates to the lynchers that the Negro is willing to accept the personal authority and guardianship of white people as the final guarantee of any possible rights which he may have. It is a sort of admission that he has divested himself of any hope of reliance upon institutions intended to safeguard the rights of citizens as such. He prostrates himself, as it were, before white men in recognition that Negroes may enjoy a degree of well-being only by sufferance of their white neighbors.

In the second place, the practice is significant in that it provides an invaluable lesson to possible intractable Negroes. Negroes who have been saved by their white friends are indebted to the latter, and subsequently such Negroes tend to act as a check upon any of their fellows who might harbor ideas of revolt. Most Negroes come to know these "sympathizers" as the "good white folk" of the community. The combined effect is to make Negroes aware of their dependence upon whites and to put at rest any tendency to criticize the whites for their partiality in government, education, economic dealings, and so on. Out of this situation is produced the finally accommodated Negroes known as "Uncle Toms."

We have considered at some length the problem of lynching because mob violence against Negroes occupies a dominant role in the interracial adjustment. We have mentioned also the fact that Negroes have great difficulty of access to the law. One secondary reason for this is that Negro legal talent is practically excluded from the South. Of all functions among Negroes, with the possible exception of the Negro politician, the Negro lawyer is most insufferable. He is an affront to the courts, and it is a decided humiliation for white advocates to debate the law with him. Most of the authorities in the Southern states hold Negroes presumptuous merely on application for admission to the bar, and by devious means they are fairly well excluded from the practice of law. An effect of this is that the ruling-class whites are able to keep the Negro under their surveillance by denying him a sympathetic access to the forum of justice.

The National Conscience

Recently social scientists have been giving considerable attention to "the national conscience." To be sure, this is an analogical concept, the

---

Columbia are not responsible for this outrage. . . . It was the State forces sent in from outside that organized the armed invasion and pillaging of the Negro business section. Even the killing in the jail was done by state officers."

use of which is subject to the dangers of its being identified with reality. In the person, conscience may be thought of as the personality disturbance produced by conflicting definitions of ethical or moral situations. There is, therefore, no conscience unless there is conflict. In modern democracies the conflict develops principally between the ideals of the two great political classes; that is to say, between the democratic and the oligarchic ideals. But these ideals are functions of distinct types of economic organization and are not in themselves primary social determinants. To believe that they are is to run the risk of becoming mystical. In the stable feudal system of Europe the serfs did not conceive of certain ideals of Christianity as ideological weapons for their liberation, for the social and economic system was such that they did not want liberation. Serfdom per se was not conceived of as oppression. To the extent that the feudal system was superseded by a new economic order, however, serfdom became oppression.

So, too, the greater the decline of the bourgeois social order, the more intense the ideological conflict in the "democracies."[48] Probably one reason for whites dealing so brutally with Negroes in interracial conflicts is the necessity for their summoning of passions sufficient to overcome possible inhibitions of conscience—sufficient to overcome the distracting proletarian world view. The frantic, orgiastic behavior at lynchings may testify to this. Unceasing racial aggression becomes a necessary opiate. Both the black and the white schoolboy have an opportunity to hold up Thomas Jefferson as an ideal. The little black boy is on reassuring ground when he reads "that justice is the fundamental law of society; that the majority, oppressing an individual, is guilty of crime, abuses its strength, and by acting on the law of the strongest breaks up the foundation of society."[49] The white boy, however, has a life question for decision; a dilemma which Gunnar Myrdal has made the theme of his discussion. Should he accept the policy of white dominance, then the weaker his rationalizations, the more ferocious he is likely to become toward Negroes. There is only one position for him to take if he dares discuss this question with the little black democrat;

---

[48]Indeed, in all capitalist countries there is an incurably and increasingly affected "national conscience." It is, in fact, the unconscious internalization of the conflict of ideals of the two major political classes by the most sensitive, "disinterested" thinkers. The high bourgeoisie, the defenders of the status quo, do not have a troubled conscience, for they are convinced that the system is right. The exploited proletariat does not have a troubled conscience, for it is the object of the "social injustice." A troubled conscience is mainly the lot of the undecided participators in the spoils of the system, whose social position is mainly that of a public of the ruling class.

[49]Thomas Jefferson, *Democracy,* ed., Saul K. Padover, p. 29.

hence, in order to avoid it, he ordinarily defends himself by segregation, from which position he strikes mercilessly at his challengers.

But the white rulers of the South must be forever watchful, because the sands of a false position are always moving under them. According to John Stuart Mill:

> The real advantage which truth has consists in this, that when an opinion is true, it may be extinguished once, twice, or many times, but in the course of ages there will gradually be found persons to rediscover it, until some one of its appearances falls on a time when, from favorable circumstances, it escapes persecution until it has made such head as to withstand all subsequent attempts to suppress it.[50]

Although in practice Negroes in the South have no opportunity to claim rights, privileges, and duties on an equal footing with whites, they nevertheless *possess the right* to believe that they have a claim to rights equal to those of whites.

This is vouchsafed them by the democratic orientation of the dominant culture, which obviously transcends local and current practice; and which increases in force as the masses rise in social importance. Even in the darkest of the Deep South, where Negroes are most accommodated to discrimination, there is always this powerful group expectation. It articulates the race problem and prevents the vicissitudes of race relations from attaining concensus or crystallizing. It never gets into what Sumner calls the mores.

One is amazed at the strength of the simple faith of the older, unlettered, rural Negroes. Powerless in the hands of their white exploiters, they go beyond them directly to their omnipotent God, almost happy in the assurance that retribution will come. Indeed, the sense of being wronged suffuses the thinking of the entire people. Powdermaker puts it in this way:

> The Negro feels guiltless with regard to the racial situation, and deeply wronged; whereas the white feels guilty, sometimes consciously and sometimes—perhaps more injuriously—without admitting it to himself. Even though he accepts the *status quo* and feels the Negro essentially inferior, he still cannot quite escape the realization that his actions run counter to the professed beliefs of democracy and Christianity. . . . The Negro's bitterness is intensified by a scorn for what he considers white hypocrisy, but this makes him feel all the more in the right.[51]

---

[50] *On Liberty and Other Essays,* pp. 34–35.

[51] Hortense Powdermaker, *After Freedom,* pp. 361–62. See also Robert E. Park, "Racial Assimilation in Secondary Groups," *Publications of the American Sociological Society,* Vol. VIII, 1913, p. 82.

Respect for law is indispensable in a democracy. But a very large part of the social thinking in the South is in terms of lawlessness. Racial domination and respect for law are incompatible. Almost any day one may read in some of the more liberal Southern newspapers such expressions of qualms as the following:

> The spectacle of more than a dozen bombings of Negro homes in Dallas in the last six months without a single arrest is a shameful commentary on our respect for civil rights. If anyone thinks that this condition would have persisted in a residential area occupied by leading citizens, he is either naïve or has a poor understanding of the American police system.
> Citizens, black or white, have a right to expect protection from lawless acts. If this is withheld from Negroes, the rights of the rest of us are in jeopardy. The difference as to vigilance of protection may involve the color of skin in one case, and in another the poverty or wealth of the victim. . . . Local democratic self-government cannot live in such weed-infested soil.[52]

It may be said finally that no system which depends for its existence principally upon anti-social acts, upon inevitable violence, can hope to perpetuate itself indefinitely.

Changing Social Status

It seems quite evident that the status of Negroes in the United States has changed considerably since 1865. It is exceedingly infrequent, however, that we are able to observe the immediate incidence of change. Sometimes it is difficult to determine whether the race is advancing toward a more favorable position within the larger society, for the apparent solution of some one of the innumerable race problems usually precipitates a multiplicity of them. Symptoms of the changing social status are many and divergent. However, any socially significant act or condition is an index of relative readjustment of racial position only in so far as it limits or enhances freedom of participation of Negroes in the general culture. Hence it is toward the fretting away of such limitations as segregation, intergroup etiquette and deferences, economic restrictions, intermarriage prohibitions, and political ostracism that Negroes continually address themselves.

A people may derive a conception of itself only by invidious comparisons of its cultural and physical attainments and attributes with those of other competitively related groups. When the frame of reference is the general American culture, however, Negroes cannot revert to a cultural history and mythology of such a character as would inspire

---

[52]C. P. Brannin, letter to the Dallas *Morning News,* April 17, 1941.

a significant in-group sentiment of nativistic pride.[53] Thus the race is not oriented toward its past but toward its present capacity and "right" to participate freely in the culture. The American Negro's past seems to be no longer a cause. The teachings of democracy, science, and Christianity evidently afford a more consistent basis for the group's achievement of a new conception of itself than a knowledge of the past cultural contribution of the race to world civilization. Moreover, this is largely true because American Negroes have no social urge for nationalism. René Maunier has made a similar observation in his conclusion that American Negroes are influenced by an idea of progress, while the cultural aspirations of such peoples as the Chinese, Hindus, and North African whites tend to regress toward earlier civilizations.[54]

At the basis of assimilation is the social phenomenon of persons attaining new conceptions of themselves. A people's conception of itself is a social force which constantly seeks expression, and it may be extinguished only after considerable struggle with opposing ideas. Even after this it may unexpectedly return to life, especially among those who possess a written history. "The role of the controlling ideas," says Gustave le Bon, "has always been so significant that peoples have never been able to change them without changing also the whole course of their history. And if in our day some benevolent divinity wanted to transform Europe, he would have only to modify the conceptions which orient certain peoples."[55]

Before any real increment of status advancement can be attained, therefore, the group must be able to conceive of itself as meriting it. Accommodation may be so nearly complete that even slaves may rest contented with their status. There is probably a grain of truth in Edward B. Reuter's statement: "Slavery did not rest upon force except in the early stages of the institution. . . . The forces that controlled the slaves were within the slaves themselves."[56] The white masters, of course, were, in a sense, also resigned to their own position. In fact, to this day there is a degree of naïve adjustment of superordination and

---

[53]Cf. Melville J. Herskovits, *The Myth of the Negro Past.*

[54]"Among Negroes of the United States it is the idea of advancement which actuates them today. While among the Chinese and even among the whites of Africa, among the Arabs and the Berbers, it is the idea of regress and not the idea of progress that determines their behavior. It is an aspiration toward the past, a desire to go backwards, a need for restoration and reconstruction. . . . These attitudes are especially striking in the teachings of Gandhi. We should differentiate, then, between the black and the yellow movement." *Sociologie coloniale,* pp. 77–78.

[55]*Premières Conséquences de la guerre,* p. 324.

[56]*The American Race Problem,* p. 105. For an elaborate discussion of continuing unrest among slaves in the United States, see Herbert Aptheker, *American Negro Slave Revolts.*

subordination between the races in the South. The situation, however, is extremely unstable. Both groups are constantly preoccupied with it.

An advance in social status of a subordinate group involves a concession to it, the result of which is a reciprocal redefinition of intergroup position. This concession to status may be voluntary or involuntary, but it is always an admission that the "distanced" group merits the right to be included further in the "we" feeling of the dominant group. In the United States, Negroes strive constantly to obtain these admissions.

A people without a culture peculiar to itself, but having only a truncated pattern of the general culture within which it lives, might be expected to rely upon decisions of the privileged group for estimates of its own achievements. In most parts of the South, therefore, the Negro leader is one who is "liked" by white people; and the first Negro to go beyond some barrier of the status quo almost invariably has prestige within his group. He is a symbol presaging the group's formation of a new conception of itself; he has attained recognition among those having access to the vertex of the culture; he has wrested a voluntary or involuntary concession leading to wider cultural participation for his group.

Although comparatively isolated achievements of Negroes may result in some form of redefinition of group position, the situation which produces the more radical changes is success in direct competition, rivalry, or conflict. For this reason, especially in the South, some whites have found it necessary to prohibit any situation involving a direct matching of abilities between the races. At any rate, the process of assimilation involves a psychological narrowing of intergroup estimations of themselves. Hence, of major significance to a true advance in status for Negroes is a conscious realization on their part that they have an unquestionable right to some immediate social position.

Negroes in the North

It may seem paradoxical that Negroes suffer less from race prejudice and discrimination in the North where capitalism is farther advanced. A friendly critic of the writer put the question thus: "Why does anti-Negro, anti-Semitic, anti-alien activity not attain quite the same ferocity in the highly industrialized North, with its need for an 'exploitable labor force,' as in the South?" The answer is, apparently, not far to seek. In the North the proletariat is farther advanced than it is in the South. In fact, we may think of advanced capitalism as a state in which the proletariat has attained some considerable degree of power. In other words, the farther the progress of capitalism, the greater the relative power of the proletariat.

In the North democracy, the proletarian system of government, is much more developed than in the South, where the white and the black proletariat has been consistently suppressed. The first great aim of the proletariat in all countries has been the capture of the ballot. In the North the workers now have the ballot, but in the South it is still limited among whites and virtually denied to Negroes. It must be obvious that if the common people, regardless of color, were as free to vote in Mississippi as they are, say, in Illinois, Mississippi could never be the hotbed of racial antagonism that it is.[57]

Industrialization creates the need for an exploitable labor force, but it is in this very need that the power of the proletariat finally resides. The factory organization not only provides the basis for worker organization but also facilitates the development of a consciousness of class power and indispensability. Social equality is not an aspiration unique among Negroes; it has been an explicit objective of the whole proletariat, regardless of color or country, almost from the dawn of industrial capitalism. Therefore, as the stronger white proletariat advanced toward this end in the North, Negroes have advanced also. In the South the white proletariat is weak and Negroes, almost totally proletarian,— that is to say, propertyless wage workers with a very small upper crust holding relatively insignificant productive property precariously—are weaker still. To the extent that democracy is achieved, to that extent also the power of the ruling class to exploit through race prejudice is limited.[58]

---

[57]Stetson Kennedy puts it in this way: ". . . short of another civil war, the southern Negro must be emancipated economically and politically before he can be emancipated socially. This means that he must first join democratic unions and beat a democratic path to the polls. Once these two things have been accomplished —gains in one will facilitate gains in the other—the abolition of Jim Crow will be as inevitable as was the abolition of chattel slavery after civil war broke out. Once the economic and political functions of Jim Crow have been negated, its social function will vanish as the subterfuge that it is." "Total Equality, and How to Get It," *Common Ground,* Winter, 1946, p. 66.

[58]On this point Gunnar Myrdal makes a pertinent observation: "The South, compared to the other regions of America, has least economic security, the lowest educational level, and is most conservative. The South's conservatism is manifested not only with respect to the Negro problem but also with respect to all other important problems of the last decades—woman suffrage, trade unions, labor legislation, social security reforms, civil liberties—and with respect to broad philosophical matters, such as the character of religious beliefs and practices. . . . There are relatively few liberals in the South and no radicals." Op. cit., p. 73.

Negroes' Approach to the Problem

Because the racial system in the United States is determined largely by the interests of a powerful political class, no spectacular advance in status of Negroes could be expected. This, of course, might happen if the Southern oligarchy were liquidated in revolution. Revolution, however, cannot be initiated by Negroes. If it comes at all, it will be under the aegis of the democratic forces of the nation. Basically, therefore, Negroes as a whole are not radical. They tend to be conservative and forgiving, though not resigned. Their policy is that of whittling away at every point the social advantages of the whites. By continual advances, no matter how small, the Negro hopes to achieve his status of complete equality as an American citizen.

With the exception of the power philosophy of Marcus Garvey,[59] the racial rationale of Negroes is based upon Western ideas of right and justice. Considerable reliance is put upon simple logic in exposing the inconsistencies of race prejudice. Consider, for instance, the following few sentences by Kelly Miller:

They sometimes tell us that America is a white man's country. The statement is understandable in the light of the fact that the white race constitutes nine-tenths of its population and exerts the controlling influence over the various forms of material and substantial wealth and power. But this land belongs to the Negro as much as to any other, not only because he has helped to redeem it from the wilderness by the energy of his arm, but also because he has bathed it in his blood, watered it with his tears, and hallowed it with the yearnings of his soul.[60]

Two principal ideas of racial policy seem to divide the allegiance of Negroes, the one that "Negroes should stick together" and the other that "Negroes should shift for themselves individually, since the individual can advance more easily than the group as a whole." In reality, however, these two plans of action are correlated. The first is a necessity, the second an aspiration. Negroes "stick together" when, in attempting to act as individuals, they are rebuffed or disadvantaged. Nevertheless, there is a continuing ideal that they should be free to act on their individual merits. As social pressure about them is relieved, they automatically become individualists. Negro leaders who do not perceive the latter aspiration and advocate solidarity as an ideal readily loose favor among Negroes.

---

[59]For a discussion of Marcus Garvey, see Ira De A. Reid, *The Negro Immigrant,* pp. 147–56.

[60]*An Appeal to Conscience,* pp. 72–73.

The Problem of Negro Leadership

One of the most persistent laments among Negroes in the United States is that the race has no great leader. There is a sort of vague expectation that someday he will arise. But Negroes will not have a "great leader" because, in reality, they do not want him. The destiny of Negroes is cultural and biological integration and fusion with the larger American society. Opposition by the latter society is generally directed against this aspiration of Negroes. Therefore, a great leader, whose function must be to bring about solidarity among Negroes, will facilitate the purpose of the opposition. The old-fashioned great leader of the post-slavery period, the almost unreserved appeaser of the Southern aristocracy, is gone forever. To develop a powerful leader Negroes must retract themselves, as it were, from their immediate business of achieving assimilation, and look to him for some promised land or some telling counterblow upon their detractors. At present, however, the most that the race can hope for is many small torchbearers showing the way upon innumerable fronts.

These leaders cannot give Negroes a "fighting" cause. None can be a Moses, George Washington, or Toussaint L'Ouverture; he cannot even be a Mohandas Gandhi[61]—a Lenin will have to be a white man. The task of leaders of the race is far more delicate. They must be specialists in the art of antagonistic co-operation. Their success rests finally in their ability to maintain peace and friendship with whites; yet they must seem aggressive and uncompromising in their struggle for the rights of Negroes. They dare not identify all whites as the enemy, for then they will themselves be driven together into a hostile camp.

This tentative nature of Negro solidarity presents a particularly baffling problem for the Negro leader. He must be a friend of the

---

[61]In commenting upon the wonderful power which Gandhi wields in India, the noted Negro publicist, George S. Schuyler, inquires despairingly: "Can the American Negro use soul force to win his battle for equal rights? Have we any leader who is ready to starve himself to death that freedom may live? Or to be beaten or shot for his convictions?" The Pittsburgh *Courier*, February 27, 1943. The answer is evidently yes; there are probably hundreds who will be ready to do so, if only for the glory of it. But, alas, even glory is not available to such a martyr. Unlike the East Indians, Negroes will not achieve their liberty through these methods. Leaders are in large measure produced by their followers; therefore, the question may be put thus: "Will American Negroes arise solidly in revolt behind a Negro holy man starving to death, say, for the purpose of having the modern black codes abrogated in the South? Or will they be aroused in a body to take action against American whites because a Negro offers himself to be shot in the interest of the race?" By putting the query in this way the answer becomes obvious. Surely the Negroes might make Father Divine a universal symbol if such a prospect would not make their cause seem ridiculous.

enemy. He must be a champion of the cause of Negroes, yet not so aggressive as to incur the consummate ill will of whites. He knows that he cannot be a leader of his people if he is completely rejected by whites; hence no small part of his function is engaged in understanding the subtleties of reaction to the manipulations of the whites of his community.

No contemporary Negro leader of major significance, then, can be totally void of at least a modicum of the spirit of "Uncle Tom"; ingratiation, compromise, and appeasement must be his specialties. Hence, "a great leader," who might with one blow realize the racial dreams of Negroes, will never appear; he is destined to remain a fantasy of Negroes. Booker T. Washington symbolizes the old Southern Negro leader. He was placed between a victorious counterrevolutionary South and an apathetic North; he could not help compromising. At least the alternative of compromise must have been an unproductive, unexpressed, sullen hate.[62] Those Negro leaders who advocate Negro solidarity for purposes of nationalistic aggression will be short-lived. Indeed, in the South, the Negro who addresses his attack directly to the status quo may be feared by Negroes and marked by whites.

Probably this technique of alternate smiling and sulking will never be sufficient to reduce the obdurate racial antagonism of whites in the South. Yet it is certain that open hostility on the part of Negroes alone will not accomplish the latter end. If there is to be an overthrow of the system, it will be achieved by way of a political-class struggle, with Negroes as an ally of white democratic forces of the nation. It will not come by way of an open interracial matching of power. As a matter of fact, the struggle has never been between all black and all white people —it is a political-class struggle.

But just at this point Negro leadership seems to be weakest. Today very few of those who have the ear of the public appear to appreciate the significance of the modern political-class movement. Some, like W. E. B. Du Bois, are frightened by the prospects of violence.[63] Others,

---

[62] Yet it should be remembered that Washington was completely void of any sense of a social mission in the common people; he stands out as the ideal Negro bourgeois, who apparently miscalculated the implacable purpose of the white ruling class in the South to keep the whole race proletarianized. He believed that Negroes, by their sweat, upon the soil especially, could unobservedly slip off their yoke of exploitation to become companion exploiters with the white oligarchy. In this, to be sure, he underestimated the intelligence of the ruling class.

[63] See *Dusk of Dawn*, pp. 301–02. This citation also shows the extent to which intelligent Negroes have absorbed even the comic anti-proletarian propaganda of the ruling class. See, however, "Prospects of a World without Race Conflict," *American Journal of Sociology*, March 1944, where Du Bois takes a more serious attitude toward the potentialities of socialism; *What the Negro Wants*, Rayford W. Logan, ed., pp. 60–62; and his *Color and Democracy*.

like George S. Schuyler, think, as the ruling class would have them, that communism and fascism are bedfellows; therefore, they declare that good Negroes should have nothing to do with either.[64] And still others, like most of the college presidents and bishops, believe that it is safer not to talk about "isms" at all. Of course, that small group, *le petite bourgeoisie noire,* the successful Negro businessman, cannot be expected to harbor proletarian ideas. In so far as we know, none of the leading newspapers seems to realize even remotely the significance of the social movement for the future welfare of Negroes.

And yet Negroes as a whole are not anti-communist; they are indeed more decidedly potentially communists than whites. At present they seem to sense some deep meaning and value in the movement, but under the tremendous weight of anti-communist propaganda they tend to remain somewhat bewildered. Then, too, they cannot be expected to take the initiative in this movement. Probably most of them would express some such basic sympathy as the following by Congressman Adam Clayton Powell, Jr.: "Today there is no group in America including the Christian church that practices racial brotherhood one tenth as much as the Communist Party."[65] Indeed, in New York, com-

---

[64]See Şchuyler's column in the Pittsburgh *Courier,* where he criticizes communism interminably. The following illustrates the rash criticism which some Negro journalists reserve for the communist system of the USSR: "Here is a state in which lackeyism is carried to the nadir of nausea; in which bureaucracy is elevated to a tragic absurdity; in which integrity is a dangerous addiction. In the Kremlin sits the Russian Gremlin, a crude, ignorant, egotistic, ruthless monster who has violated every human law, killed the revolution, slaughtered millions of his loyal followers; jailed ten times as many, and whose policies brought Russia and the world to the brink of disaster. . . . Only American Lend-Lease saved Russia—that, and the tremendous distances, plus ice, snow and mud." George S. Schuyler, in a favorable book review of *One Who Survived,* by Alexander Barmine, a Russian political refugee, in the Pittsburgh *Courier,* October 20, 1945.

To this group of thinkers socialism is not a social movement, in the sense that the bourgeoisization of Western society was a social movement, but rather a problem of conflicting personalities. Their common approach to the subject centers about a criticism of "those communists whom I have met" as unscrupulous or insane; therefore, at best, the movement must be described as the rantings of a cult of charlatans. To be sure, this is not a peculiarity of Negroes; it is merely their adoption of current propaganda.

More specifically, there is a large number of journalists and popular writers, white and black, who are sincere in their beliefs that they have reached some ultimate in an understanding of the social movement. The fact seems to be, however, that they have attained only to the personality or "gossip" stage of perception. Socialism to them involves an analysis of the character and foibles of certain leaders, or of the idiosyncrasies of certain "little commies" within their acquaintance, or of immediate practices, many of which must necessarily be underground and dissimulative. These persons are obviously buried under the very transpiration of a social movement more gigantic and significant than any—in so far as human initiation is concerned—that the world has ever seen. Compare, however, a responsible reporter's account: John Scott, *Europe in Revolution.*

[65]*Marching Blacks,* p. 69.

munism among Negroes has made some tangible headway; they have recently elected a Negro communist to the city council of Manhattan.

The Problem of White Leadership

The problem of extending democracy to Negroes in the South involves one of the most frightful prospects in American social life. The Southern oligarchy has set its jaws against any such plan, which necessarily holds for them revolutionary economic consequences. The prospects are frightful because, like a true political class, the rulers of the South are prepared to hold their position even at a high cost in blood. Confronted with this terrible decision, the minority of liberal whites in the South are easily overwhelmed. Here too, therefore, as in the case of the white common people, democracy involves a conquest of the bourgeois oligarchy.

To be sure, at a certain cost the articulate leaders in this region can be overthrown. Without them the masses will soon reach a satisfactory way of living, consistent with democratic principles. Modern democracy is something to be won; it has always been *withheld* by some ruling class. We should miss an understanding of the political-class interest in the racial situation of the South if we were to think as some writers that:

Underlying all is the great need of every man, however humble and stupid, to feel that there is some one or some group still lower than he is. Thus only can the craving for a sense of superiority be fed. In the case of the Negro, it is notoriously the poor whites who are bitterest, who most tenaciously hold to the doctrine that he must be kept down at any cost either to himself or to the community.[66]

This kind of reasoning is common, and it has the significant—though frequently unintended—function of exculpating the Southern ruling class. But clearly, we could never explain the social order in the South by resorting to some socio-psychological constant in human nature. That which is assumed to be common to all human behavior cannot explain behavior variations; therefore, "the craving for a sense of superiority" tells no crucial story. The attitude of the poor whites is rather more an effect than a cause. "The Poor White, in his occasional expressions of race antagonism, acts for those Whites who tacitly condone and overtly deplore such behavior."[67] We may take it as axiomatic

---

[66]Edwin R. Embree, *Brown America*, p. 201.

[67]Hortense Powdermaker, op. cit., pp. 334–35. The makers of the laws of the South ingeniously set the stage for the encouragement and perpetuation of racial antagonism. "If there were more real contact between [poor whites and Negroes]

that never in all the history of the world have poor people set and maintained the dominant social policy in a society.

The Civil War was a war between two dominant political classes; it resulted in a partial limitation of the scheme of life of the Southern aristocracy, yet it neither extirpated nor defeated the essential purpose of this class. The South is still very much aristocratic and fascist. "The present white aristocratic party in the South is defending itself exactly after the manner of all aristocracies. . . . Having control of the government it has entrenched itself with laws."[68] From her recent study of a Southern community Hortense Powdermaker refers to the aristocracy as follows:

This class and the old South are inseparable, and both play an enormous part in sanctioning the beliefs by which the middle class today guides and justified its course. The superiority of the white man is the counterpart of Negro inferiority. And the aristocrat is a superior white *par excellence,* for his own qualities and because he is associated with the glory of the old days when the South was not at a disadvantage.[69]

The present Southern aristocracy is not that natural aristocracy among men, "the most precious gift of nature," of which Thomas Jefferson spoke. Rather it is represented by such classic expounders of conservative, nationalistic, social philosophy in the South as Governor James K. Vardaman and Senator Theodore G. Bilbo of Mississippi, Senator Jeff Davis of Arkansas, Governors Hoke Smith and Eugene Talmadge of Georgia, and Senators B. R. Tillman and Ellison D. (Cotton Ed) Smith of South Carolina.

This is the same ruling class that has condoned lynching, disfranchised most Negroes, kept the Negroes confined to work as share-croppers, laborers, and domestics, retained the racial pollution laws, and used the news-

---

some of the fierce hatred might be drained off, or even converted into fellow-feeling based on the similarity of their positions as agricultural workers struggling against great disadvantages." Ibid., p. 29. In these dichotomized racial situations the poor whites are always a danger to the position of the ruling class. Says Brookes: "The economic pressure to which the Bantu has been increasingly subjected since 1924 arises principally from solicitude for the class known as 'Poor Whites.' This solicitude is the result . . . of a feeling on the part of nationalist thinkers that the Poor Whites represent a submerged part of the South African nation. Bantu encroachment is to be resisted, not only because the Poor White may starve, but also because he may, under pressure of living conditions, betray his colour and mix his blood with the members of the Bantu proletariat. . . . A great part of the driving force which leads parties and governments to restrict fields of employment for the Bantu in favour of the Poor Whites is nationalism." Edgar H. Brookes, *The Colour Problems of South Africa,* pp. 28–29.

[68]Ray Stannard Baker, op. cit., p. 245. See also William H. Skaggs, op. cit., pp. 20, 58.

[69]Op. cit., p. 26.

papers, radio and school books to mould the minds of the white masses against equality of Negroes.[70]

The "aristocrats" maintained their power not only by their exploitation of Negroes but also by their exploitation of poor whites, who are artfully played against colored people.

It should be emphasized that the guardians of the economic and social order in the South are not poor whites; indeed, it is sheer nonsense to think that the poor whites are the perpetuators of the social system in the South. The fierce filibustering in the national Congress against the passage of an anti-lynching bill, or against the abolition of the poll tax; the hurried conferences of governors to devise means of emasculating a Supreme Court decision for equal educational opportunities; the meeting of attorneys general for the purpose of sidetracking an anti-Jim Crow decision for railroads; the attitude of Southern judges toward Negroes in courtrooms—these are obviously the real controlling factors in the Southern order.[71] The poor whites are not only incapable but evidently also have no immediate interest in the doing of such things.

Moreover, in the very amiability which upper-class whites sometimes seem to have for Negroes lies a most powerful attitude of social distance. It is a condescending, patronizing attitude, which is the complete expression of racial superiority and prejudice. This attitude is hardly available to poor whites. The Southern "aristocracy," as the modern capitalist ruling class of this area is sometimes called, could not endure without the hatred which it perpetuates among the white and black masses, and it is by no means unmindful of that fact. No single social problem, whether of war or of peace, is as important to the Southern aristocracy as that of keeping the Negro in his place.[72]

---

[70]George Schuyler in the Pittsburgh *Courier,* March 15, 1942.

[71]On almost any day we may clip such declarations as the following from newspapers in the South: "If the Supreme Court of the United States rules that Negroes must be admitted [to the Democratic primaries of Texas]," says W. S. Bramlett, Dallas County Democratic Chairman, "I will contribute all my experience as a lawyer and as a Democrat to nullify the ruling; and I believe most county and state party leaders will feel the same way." Reported in the Dallas *Morning News,* December 1, 1943.

[72]It is questionable whether such off-color statements as the following by Dr. Louis Wirth contribute to our understanding of race relations: "In a period of war we realize more clearly than ever . . . that racial, religious, and other prejudices constitute a danger to our national unity and it begins to dawn upon us that, however deep-seated our own internal conflicts may have been, they are as nothing compared with the conflicts between us and our enemies." *The Scientific Monthly,* April 1944, p. 305. The textbooks put the latter idea in this way: The greater the intensity of conflict between two groups, the greater the internal solidarity of each. But Wirth seems to be very much in error when he applies this concept unrefinedly

The problem of the democratic white leadership of the nation, then, is not to think of the exploitative order in the South as a Negro problem but rather as a political-class problem of the first magnitude for the nation. The Southern "aristocrats" should be understood in the light of what they really are, and the cost of reducing them should be estimated in the light of political-class practice. The alternative is a continued divided nation, for a political class has never been known to give up its position because of logical conviction. The interest of the ruling class rests in the Negroes' and poor whites' being and feeling inferior and antagonistic. This class insists that any plan for improving Southern conditions must first satisfy the latter interest.

It is not possible to speak with any degree of comprehensiveness about the problem of white leadership without reviewing somewhat its more inclusive world context. In our chapter on race relations we attempted to develop the hypothesis that modern race prejudice is rooted in certain attitudes and economic needs of the white race and that race prejudice has been diffused throughout the world by the white race. We should reiterate, however, that we do not mean to say that race prejudice has a somatic determinant. Commercial and industrial capitalism, which involved the organized movement of Europeans to distant lands, created the cultural situation favorable for the development of white race prejudice.

In our own day this very capitalism has undoubtedly passed the noontide of its vigor and is giving place to another basic form of social organization. With the change of the dominant economic organization of the world, we should expect fundamental changes in social attitudes.

In a previous chapter we have attempted to show also that two

---

to that situation. In this war, World War II, Quislings and fifth columnists were political-class leaders and members who were natural friends of the "enemy." Moreover, it is misleading to say, "We realize that prejudices constitute a danger to our national unity." The Southern prejudice against Negroes was not given up. There was "unity" only so long as Negroes did not demand that the South give up its prejudice. If such a demand had threatened to become effective, the ruling class in the South would have done exactly what the leaders of a number of European nations did; that is to say, make a choice between the Negroes, i.e., the proletariat, and Hitler; and the likelihood of Hitler's being chosen was great indeed. Anyone, for instance, might have tested this by trying to put through an anti-lynching bill in the national Congress. In such an event it would soon have become evident that matters concerning the war were quite secondary in importance.

For a realistic approach to this problem, see Stetson Kennedy, *Southern Exposure*, pp. 107–08 and 341ff.; also Theodore H. White and Annalee Jacoby, *Thunder Out of China*, pp. 45–47. It is reported that Chiang Kai-shek declared in 1941: "You think it is important that I have kept the Japanese from expanding during these years. . . . I tell you it is more important that I have kept the Communists from spreading. The Japanese are a disease of the skin; the Communists are a disease of the heart." Ibid., p. 129.

major systems are contending for primacy in the suppression of the present hybrid social order: fascism and communism. Fascism must obviously be transitory; it is an aggravation of the worst aspects of capitalism. We may think of fascism as the deathbed attendant of a moribund system, or indeed as the last great spasm in the death throes of capitalism.[73] "The chills and fever of capitalism, observed since its infancy, shake and burn its whole body more drastically as it approaches old age."[74] In degenerating into organized fascism, capitalism surrenders very much of its adopted ideals of political democracy, but it has no alternative. Fascism is the only significant device developed by the established political class for the purpose of both reinvigorating capitalism and combating the democratic forces which are naturally antipathetic to capitalism.

Fascism, then, is defensive and, to repeat, necessarily exalts the worst traits of capitalism. So far as race relations are concerned, it makes a fanatic religion of white race superiority. But this is merely a function of its imperialistic obsession, which in turn stimulates nationalism. Those persons, then, who are honestly concerned with the elimination of race prejudice and race exploitation by the white ruling class must be concerned also with the elimination of world imperialism. It will probably not be inaccurate to state that the world stronghold of imperialism and colonialism is symbolized by the British Crown supported finally by the military and economic power of the United States.

The British Crown is a device kept sacrosanct by the great capitalists of the British Empire principally to overawe and exploit the larger part of the colored peoples of the world.[75] It is a putative institution serving as cover and shock absorber for the great imperialists and is completely

---

[73]Cf. J. Kuczynski and M. Witt, *The Economics of Barbarism,* and John Strachey, *The Coming Struggle for Power.* "It is our fate to live in one of those times in history when a whole economic system is in decay. History teaches us that once that process has begun there is no way of saving the dying economic system. The only way out is to put a new one in its place. That is what we must, can, and will do." John Strachey, *Socialism Looks Forward,* p. 100.

[74]George Soule, *The Coming American Revolution,* p. 148.

[75]Probably no historical situation illustrates better than the semi-bourgeois interlude of the Russian Revolution the great value of a decadent and impotent monarchy to a rising bourgeoisie. Behind the controlled divinity of the royal family the bourgeoisie is able to put into effect schemes of mass exploitation, both at home and abroad, that would be otherwise unthinkable.

In his discussion of another situation, John Scott makes the following observation: "Russian prestige among eastern peoples is today higher than ever before, owing to an inexcusable American blunder at San Francisco. Having raised the issue of the ultimate independence of colonial peoples, the American delegation joined the British in voting for a sterile formula promising colonial peoples little, and allowing the Russians to stand before the world as champions of the hundreds of millions of dependent eastern peoples. This single action quite unnecessarily de-

without purpose in a non-capitalist democracy. As Mr. Laski puts it: "British imperialism has deliberately elevated the prestige of the Crown as a method of protecting the ends it seeks to serve."[76] About fourteen out of every hundred people in the British Empire are white. Without reviewing the imperialistic practices of other nations[77] it should be apparent that race exploitation cannot be eliminated from the world without first eliminating capitalism and attacking vigorously the imperialism of Great Britain.

It should be emphasized, however, that the capitalism and imperialism of Great Britain could not survive without the sustaining hand of the American ruling class. Mr. Winston Churchill, in his Fulton, Missouri, address, might have gone even farther to say that not only *must* the United States and Britain establish a permanent military alliance— which for all practical purposes is already in effect—but also an economic brotherhood. The burden of making a capitalism, collapsing all over the world, work rests squarely on the shoulders of the American ruling class; and since capitalism no longer has a morality, the people of the United States will have to keep it resuscitated and defended by pouring into it an endless stream of wealth. In a very real sense the United States today must finance world capitalism, for it cannot convince peoples by any logical argument of the social and economic value of capitalism to them. Churchill knows that the United States must pay for capitalism or speedily become aware that it is "encircled" by a socialist world, hence he speaks with oracular confidence. Capitalism cannot offer to the masses of people that better world for which they now hunger and thirst; it can give them only reaction supported by military might and a strategic distribution of a relatively few full bellies.

The American ruling class, in its own interest, must make "lend lease" permanent, even though it is disguised in the form of loans or outright gifts to "suffering humanity." This class will have to see that food and "supplies" are rushed all over the world to strengthen the position of the various national bourgeoisies as the common people

---

prived America of its historic rôle as champions of liberty [?] in the eyes of millions, and turned this invaluable asset over to the Russians.

"Unfortunately the same blunder has occurred repeatedly in Europe on less spectacular issues. We have given in to pressure from the British, and from our own reactionaries, and have identified ourselves with the dusty little kings and equally dusty outmoded ideas from the nineteenth century, allowing the Russians to champion progress." Op. cit., pp. 233–34.

[76]*Parliamentary Government in England*, p. 330.

[77]For broad views on this question, see Parker Thomas Moon, *Imperialism and World Politics*, and Benjamin H. Williams, *Economic Foreign Policy of the United States*.

gather about them to exact an accounting of the use of their resources. In a sense, then, the United States is already fighting its own proletarian revolution on foreign battle fields.

The new economic system which will naturally supplant the old is socialism, the system whose normal emphasis is upon human welfare. The relation of socialism to racial exploitation may be demonstrated by the fact that the greater the immediacy of the exploitative practice, the more fiercely socialism is opposed. In other words, in those areas where whites live by the immediate exploitation of colored people, in those areas also socialism is most abhorred. For instance, a white communist in the Deep South is regarded in about the same light as a Negro man with a white wife. They are both threats to the exploitative system, and the ruling class has provided for their violent dispatch.[78] Indeed, the method of "solving the race issue" is identical with the method by which capitalism is being liquidated by proletarian action.

There is an increasing number of people all over the world who are willing to accept socialism with all its implications for the abandonment of mass exploitation. Some of these people understand that there will be no possibility of giving up race prejudice while still retaining the system which produced it. They recognize consequently that the problem of white leadership is no longer that of appeasing plantation capitalists but rather that of striking decisively at the very root of the social order, and they are under no illusions about the fact that the "capitalist power will not surrender its privileges without fighting for them."[79]

In the process of bringing the Southern Negro into full manhood and citizenship, therefore, the white leader has a responsibility of considerable importance. It involves the liberation of the Southern poor whites as well. A great leader of Negroes will almost certainly be a white man, but he will also be the leader of the white masses of this nation; and of

---

[78]It may be observed further that the pith of the argument that race prejudice will not exist in a socialist society necessarily rests on the fact that this indispensable economic drive of capitalism—exploitation, and human exploitation especially—will also cease to exist. In a capitalist system human beings live and labor in the interest of private enterprise; and the fact that a goodly number of them are impersonally degraded and consumed in the latter interest is consistent with the ethics of the system. On the contrary, in a socialist system human welfare becomes the dominant purpose of production, and the ethics of that system abhor the idea of such human degradation. In other words, increasing productivity is made dependent upon increasing development of the human intellect, tastes, and ambition. Human beings are freed and elevated beyond the elevation of their material resources.

[79]On this Daniel Guerin remarks advisedly: "Although socialism utilizes all the legal methods supplied by the law or the constitution, it does so, without the slightest illusion; it knows that the victory in the end is a question of force." *Fascism and Big Business*, p. 109.

course, whether they are permitted to recognize him or not, he will eventually prove to be the emancipator of the poor whites of the South. For example, without any considerable attention to the "Negro problem" particularly, President Franklin D. Roosevelt undoubtedly did more to elevate the status of Negroes in the United States than all other leaders, white and black together, over a period of decades before him. Negroes are auxiliary in the American proletarian struggle for power. James Madison probably had more vision than he thought when he referred to Negroes as that "unhappy species of population abounding in some of the states who, during the calm of regular government, are sunk below the level of men; but who, in the tempestuous scenes of civil violence, may emerge into human character and give a superiority of strength to any party with which they may associate themselves."[80]

In the Deep South, ruling-class whites have taught Negroes to look to them personally for guidance; in fact, these whites have controlled Negroes through their own black leaders. The successful Negro leader has learned to be sensitive to the wishes of whites. In any political-class struggle in the South, therefore, this attitude should be capitalized by the radical white leadership.

Although Negroes have become increasingly intractable to being thus indirectly led, they have yet a certain faith in "what the white man says." It is this faith to which the white radical leader, interested in breaking up the Southern social order, has access. Many overcautious and conservative Negro leaders, who have no patience with militant Negroes, become readily animated when white functionaries speak to them of equal rights. When the time comes for the South to be purged of its present political-class leadership, it will surely be easier for most Negroes to follow convinced whites than to tread behind the uncertain feet of their familiar black leadership.

Moreover, it is also the responsibility of white leaders to conduct the struggle according to principles of political-class conflict. That is to say, the aristocratic Southern ruling class must be defeated not only in an open matching of power but also broken in spirit, a social aspiration which the military victors of the Civil War failed to achieve.[81]

In this we should not be mistaken as to the source of antagonism against any serious attempt to extend democracy in the South. The

---

[80] *The Federalist*, No. 43.

[81] The same necessity for psychological defeat which the Hon. Henry A. Wallace recommended in dealing with foreign countries should also prove effective in dealing with domestic fascists. "A special problem that will face the United Nations immediately upon the attainment of victory over either Germany or Japan," he said, "will be what to do with the defeated nation. . . . We must make absolutely sure that

standard bearers of the area have repeatedly and most bluntly stated that the issue could be settled only by open violence. Thus the noted Southern writer, David L. Cohn, declares: "I have no doubt that in such an event [that is to say, an attempt to abolish the terrible segregation laws] every Southern white man would spring to arms and the country would be swept by civil war."[82] Again, when the United States Supreme Court decided eight to one that Negroes should be allowed to vote in state primaries, the South Carolina General Assembly passed a number of bills to emasculate the decision, and "the House . . . applauded a speech by Representative John Long . . . who said he was willing to 'bite the dust as did my ancestors' to prevent Negroes from participating in the white Democratic primaries."[83] In many parts of the modern world democracy is feverishly seeking to get such a hold of itself as to be able to say to this characteristic, anachronistic challenge: "You shall have your wish."

The problem of racial exploitation, then, will most probably be settled as part of the world proletarian struggle for democracy; every advance of the masses will be an actual or potential advance for the colored people. Whether the open threat of violence by the exploiting class will be shortly joined will depend upon the unpredictable play and balance of force in a world-wide struggle for power.

---

the guilty leaders are punished, that the defeated nation realizes its defeat and is not permitted to rearm. The United Nations must back up military disarmament with psychological disarmament—supervision, or at least inspection, of the school systems of Germany and Japan, to undo so far as possible the diabolical work of . . . poisoning the minds of the young." Radio address, December 28, 1942.

[82]"How the South Feels," *The Atlantic Monthly,* January 1944, p. 50.

[83]The Dallas *Morning News,* April 18, 1944.

Bibliography

Bibliography

THIS IS A LIST OF MOST OF THE WORKS REFERRED TO IN THE TEXT.

ACTON, LORD. *The History of Freedom and Other Essays,* London, 1909.

ADAMIC, LOUIS. *Dynamite: The Story of Class Violence in America,* New York, 1931.

ADAMS, GEORGE BURTON. *Civilization during the Middle Ages,* New York, 1900.

ADAMS, ROMANZO. *Interracial Marriage in Hawaii,* New York, 1937.

ALLEN, CLIFFORD. "Has Britain Turned Socialist?", *The Western Socialist,* Vol. XII, Sept. 1945.

AMES, JESSIE DANIEL. *The Changing Character of Lynching,* Atlanta, 1942.

ANDERSON, ELIN L. *We Americans,* Cambridge, Mass., 1937.

ANDREWS, C. F. *Mahatma Gandhi's Ideas,* New York, 1930.

Annals, The, "Present-Day Immigration with Special Reference to the Japanese," Vol. 93, Jan. 1921.

APTHEKER, HERBERT. *American Negro Slave Revolts,* New York, 1943.

ARENDT, HANNAH. "Race-Thinking before Raceism," *The Review of Politics,* Vol. 6, Jan. 1944.

ARNOLD, THURMAN W. *The Folklore of Capitalism,* New Haven, 1937.

AZURARA, GOMES EANNES DE. *The Discovery and Conquest of Guinea,* trans. by C. R. Beazley and E. Prestage, London, 1896–99.

BADEN-POWELL, B. H. *Village Communities of India,* London, 1899.

BAKER, RAY STANNARD. *Following the Colour Line,* New York, 1908.

BANERJEA, PRAMATHANATH. *A Study of Indian Economics,* 2d ed., London, 1916.

BARNES, HARRY ELMER. *An Economic History of the Western World,* New York, 1937.

———. "Democracy," *The Encyclopedia American,* 1940.

———. *The History of Western Civilization,* Vol. II, New York, 1935.

BARON, SALO WITTMAYER. *A Social and Religious History of the Jews,* Vol. III, New York, 1937.

———. "Nationalism and Intolerance," *The Menorah Journal,* Vols. XVI, XVII, Jun. 1929 and Nov. 1929.

BARZUN, JACQUES. *Race, A Study of Modern Superstition,* New York, 1937.

BATESON, MARY. *Medieval England,* New York, n.d.

BEARD, CHARLES A. *An Economic Interpretation of the Constitution of the United States,* New York, 1943.

BEARD, CHARLES A., and MARY R. *The Rise of American Civilization,* New York, 1930.

BECKER, CARL L. *Freedom and Responsibility,* New York, 1945.

BEK-GRAN, ROBERT. "5 Keys to Europe," *Politics,* Nov. 1944.

BENEDICT, RUTH. *Race: Science and Politics,* New York, 1943.

———. *Patterns of Culture,* Boston, 1934.

BENSON, EDWIN. *Life in a Medieval City,* London, 1920.

BENTON, A. H. *Indian Moral Instruction and Caste Problems,* London, 1917.

BERNSTEIN, SAMUEL. "Jefferson and the French Revolution," *Science and Society,* Vol. VII, No. 2, Spring, 1943.

BEVERIDGE, SIR WILLIAM H. *Full Employment in a Free Society,* New York, 1945.

BEYNON, E. D. "The Southern White Laborer Migrates to Michigan," *American Sociological Review,* Vol. III, Jun. 1938.

BHATTACHARYA, J. H. *Hindu Castes and Sects,* Calcutta, 1896.

BINGHAM, ALFRED M. *Insurgent America,* New York & London, 1935.

BLUNT, E. A. H. *The Caste System of Northern India,* Oxford, 1931.

BOEHM, MAX HILEBERT, "Minorities," *Encyclopedia of the Social Sciences.*

BÖHTLINGK, O., and ROTH, R. *Sanskrit-Worterbuch,* Petrograd, 1855–75.

BOISSONNADE, P. *Life and Work in Medieval Cities,* London, 1927.

BOUGLÉ, CELESTIN C. A. *Essais sur le régime des castes,* 3d ed., Paris, 1935.

BOUSQUET, GEORGES HENRI. *A French View of the Netherlands Indies,* trans. by Philip E. Lilenthal, Oxford, 1940.

BOWEN, TREVOR. *Divine White Right,* New York & London, 1934.

BRADY, ROBERT A. *Business as a System of Power,* New York, 1943.

———. *The Spirit and Structure of German Fascism,* New York, 1937.

BRIEFS, GOETZ A. *The Proletariat,* New York, 1937.

BRIFFAULT, ROBERT. *The Decline and Fall of the British Empire,* New York, 1938.

———. *Reasons for Anger,* New York, 1936.

BRIGGS, GEORGE W. *The Chamars,* Oxford, 1920.

BROCKWAY, FENNER. *Workers' Front,* London, 1938.

BROOKES, EDGAR H. *The Colour Problems of South Africa,* London, 1934.

BROWN, FRANCIS J., and ROUCEK, JOSEPH S., eds. *One America: Our Racial and National Minorities,* New York, 1945.

BROWN and ROUCEK. *Our Racial and National Minorities,* New York, 1937.

BROWN, J. F. *Psychology and the Social Order,* New York, 1936.

BRUFORD, W. H. *Germany in the Eighteenth Century,* Cambridge, 1935.

BRYCE, JAMES. *The Relations of the Advanced and Backward Races of Mankind,* 2d ed., Oxford, 1903.

BUCHER, CARL. *Industrial Evolution*, trans. by S. M. Wickett, New York, 1907.

BÜCHER, KARL. *Die Bevölkerung von Frankfurt am Main im XIV. und XV. Jahrhundert*, Tübingen, 1886.

BUELL, RAYMOND LESLIE. *The Native Problem in Africa*, New York, 1928, Vols. I, II.

BUKHARIN, NIKOLAI. *Historical Materialism*, New York, 1925.

BULLITT, WILLIAM C. *The Great Globe Itself*, New York, 1946.

BURKE, EDMUND. *Reflections on the Revolution in France*, The Works of Edmund Burke, Vol. II, London, 1855.

BURNHAM, JAMES. *The Machiavellians*, New York, 1943.

BURNS, C. DELISLE. *Political Ideals*, London, 1936.

CABLE, GEORGE W. *The Negro Question*, New York, 1903.

California and the Oriental: Report of the State Board of Control of California, Jan. 1, 1922.

Cambridge History of India, Vol. I, Cambridge, 1922.

Cambridge Medieval History, Vols. I, III, VII, Cambridge, 1924.

CAMPBELL, MILDRED. *The English Yeoman*, New Haven, 1942.

CARR, EDWARD HALLETT. *The Twenty Years' Crisis*, London, 1939.

CARR-SAUNDERS, A. M., and JONES, D. CARADOG. *A Survey of the Social Structure of England and Wales*, London, 1927.

CARTER, JOHN FRANKLIN. *The New Dealers* (Published anonymously by "Unofficial Observer"), New York, 1934.

CATTELL, RAYMOND B. "The Concept of Social Status," *The Journal of Social Psychology*, Vol. 15, May 1942.

Census of India, 1921, Vol. I, Pt. 1.

CHAMBERS, JOHN S. "The Japanese Invasion," *The Annals*, Vol. XCIII, Jan. 1921.

CHANDLER, ALBERT R. *The Clash of Political Ideals*, New York, 1940.

CHANG, SHERMAN H. M. *The Marxian Theory of the State*, Philadelphia, 1931.

CHEYNEY, EDWARD POTTS. *European Background of American History*, New York, 1904.

CLARKE, M. V. *Medieval Representation and Consent*, London, 1936.

COHN, DAVID L. *God Shakes Creation*, New York, 1935.

COLE, G. D. H. *What Marx Really Meant*, New York, 1934.

COMMONS, JOHN R., and Associates. *History of Labor in the United States*, Vol. II, New York, 1926.

COREY, LEWIS. *The Decline of American Capitalism*, New York, 1934.

COULTON, G. G. *The Medieval Scene*, Cambridge, 1930.

———. *The Medieval Village*, Cambridge, 1926.

CRAVEN, AVERY. *Democracy in American Life*, Chicago, 1941.

CROOKE, WILLIAM. *Things Indian*, London, 1906.

CUNNINGHAM, W. *The Growth of English Industry and Commerce*, 5th ed., Vol. I, Cambridge, 1915.

DANVERS, FREDERICK CHARLES. *The Portuguese in India*, London, 1894.

DAS, ABINAS CHANDRA. *Rigvedic Culture*, Calcutta & Madras, 1925.

DASGUPTA, SURENDRANATH. *A History of Indian Philosophy*, Cambridge, Vols. I, II, III, 1922.

DAUGHERTY, CARROLL R. *Labor Problems in American Industry*, New York, 1941.

DAVIES, JOSEPH E. *Mission to Moscow*, New York, 1943.

DAVIS, GARDNER, GARDNER, and WARNER. *Deep South*, Chicago, 1941.

DAVIS, KINGSLEY. "A Conceptual Analysis of Stratification," *American Sociological Review*, Vol. 7, Jun. 1942.

DAY, CLIVE. *The Dutch in Java*, New York, 1904.

DE GRE, GERARD. "Freedom and Social Structure," *American Sociological Review*, Vol. XI, Oct. 1946.

DELEVSKY, J. *Antagonismes sociaux et antagonismes Proletraiens*, Paris, 1924.

DE MOTTE, MARSHALL. "California—White or Yellow," *The Annals*, Vol. XCIII, Jan. 1921.

DE RUGGIERO, GUIDO. *The History of European Liberalism*, trans. by R. G. Collingwood, London, 1927.

DETWEILER, FREDERICK G. "The Rise of Modern Race Antagonisms," *The American Journal of Sociology*, Vol. 37, Mar. 1932.

DE VERTUIL, L. A. A. *Trinidad*, 2d ed., London, 1884.

DEWEY, JOHN. *Liberalism and Social Action*, New York, 1935.

DIES, MARTIN. *The Trojan Horse in America*, New York, 1940.

DIFFIE, BAILEY W. *Latin American Civilization*, Harrisburg, 1945.

DOLBEER, MARTIN LUTHER. *The Movement for the Emancipation of Untouchable Classes in South India*, Master's Thesis, University of Chicago, 1929.

DOLLARD, JOHN. *Caste and Class in a Southern Town*, New York, 1937.

DOVER, CEDRIC. *Half-Caste*, London, 1937.

DOYLE, BERTRAM W. *The Etiquette of Race Relations*, Chicago, 1937.

DRACHSLER, JULIUS. *Democracy and Assimilation*, New York, 1920.

DRAKE, ST. CLAIR, and CAYTON, HORACE R. *Black Metropolis*, New York, 1945.

DU BOIS, W. E. B. *Black Reconstuction*, New York, 1935.

———. *Darkwater*, New York, 1921.

———. *Dusk of Dawn*, New York, 1941.

DUBOIS, ABBÉ JEAN ANTOINE. *Hindu Manners, Customs, and Ceremonies*, 3d ed., Oxford, 1906.

DURKHEIM, EMILE. *The Rules of Sociological Method*, trans. by Sarah A. Solovay and John H. Mueller, Chicago, 1938.

DUTT, NRIPENDRA KUMAR. *Origin and Growth of Caste in India*, London, 1931.

DUTT, R. PALME. *Fascism and Social Revolution*, New York, 1935.

EAVES, LUCILE. *A History of California Labor Legislation*, Berkeley, 1910.

Economic Power and Political Pressures, Monograph No. 26, Temporary National Economic Committee, Washington, D.C., 1941.

EMERTON, EPHRAIM. *Medieval Europe, 814–1300*, Boston, 1894.

ENGELS, FRIEDRICH. *Socialism Utopian and Scientific* (fortieth anniversary ed.), New York, 1935.

Essays Related to the Habits, Character, and Moral Improvement of the Hindoos, London, 1823.

EVANS, MAURICE S. *Black and White in South East Africa*, London, 1911.

FAIRCHILD, HENRY PRATT. *Profits or Prosperity*, New York, 1932.
———. *Dictionary of Sociology.*
FAIRCHILD, MILDRED. "Social-Economic Classes in Soviet Russia," *American Sociological Review*, Jun. 1944.
FARIS, ELLSWORTH. *The Nature of Human Nature*, New York & London, 1937.
FARQUHAR, J. N. *The Religious Quest of India: An Outline of the Religious Literature of India*, Oxford, 1920.
———. *Modern Religious Movements in India*, New York, 1915.
———. *The Crown of Hinduism*, Oxford, 1913.
FERGUSON, W. K., and BRUNN, G. *A Survey of European Civilization*, Boston, 1942.
FINER, HERMAN. *Road to Reaction*, Boston, 1945.
FLEURE, H. J. *The Dravidian Element in Indian Culture*, London, 1924.
FORM, WILLIAM H. "Social Stratification in a Planned Community," *American Sociological Review*, Vol. 10, Oct. 1945.
FOSTER, LAWRENCE. *Negro-Indian Relationships in the Southeast*, Philadelphia, 1935.
FRANKLIN, BENJAMIN. *Autobiography*, ed. by John Bigelow, New York, 1916.
FREYER, HANS. *Einleitung in die Soziologie*, Leipzig, 1931.
FROMM, ERICH. *Escape from Freedom*, New York, 1941.
FUNK, ARTHUR LAYTON. *The Movement of Reform and Revolt in Mid-Fourteenth-Century France*, Ph.D. dissertation, University of Chicago, 1940.
FURNISS, EDGAR S. *The Position of Labor in a System of Nationalism*, Boston, 1920.
GAIT, EDWARD ALBERT. "Caste," *Encyclopedia of Religion and Ethics*, 1911.
GALLAGHER, BUELL G. *Color and Conscience*, New York & London, 1946.
GAMBLE, W. H. *Trinidad: Historical and Descriptive*, London, 1866.
GANDHI, MAHATMA. *Young India, 1924–1926*, New York, 1927.
GAXOTTE, PIERRE. *The French Revolution*, trans. by Walter A. Phillips, London & New York, 1932.
GELLERMANN, WILLIAM. *Martin Dies*, New York, 1944.
GERTH, H. H., and MILLS, C. WRIGHT. "Class, Status, Party," *Politics*, Oct. 1944.
———. *From Max Weber: Essays in Sociology*, New York, 1946.
GHURYE, G. S. *Caste and Race in India*, New York, 1932.
GIDE, CHARLES. *Political Economy*, Boston & New York, 1913.
GINSBERG, MORRIS. "Class Consciousness," *Encyclopedia of the Social Sciences.*
GIRKE, OTTO. *Political Theories of the Middle Ages*, trans. by F. W. Maitland, Cambridge, 1900.
GLOTZ, GUSTAVE. *Ancient Greeks at Work*, New York, 1926.
GOBINEAU, ARTHUR DE. *The Inequality of Human Races*, trans. by Adrin Collins, New York, 1915.
GOMPERS, SAMUEL. *Seventy Years of Life and Labor*, Vol. I, New York, 1925.

GOWEN, HERBERT H. *A History of Indian Literature,* New York & London, 1931.

GRAEBER, ISACQUE, and BRITT, S. H., eds. *Jews in a Gentile World,* New York, 1942.

GREEN, MRS. J. R. *Town Life in the Fifteenth Century,* London, 1894.

GRIFFITH, RALPH T. H. *Hymns of the Rigveda,* Benares, 1896–97.

GRINKER, ROY R., and SPIEGEL, JOHN P. *Men under Stress,* Philadelphia, 1945.

GRISWOLD, H. D. *The Religion of the Rigveda,* Oxford, 1923.

GUERIN, DANIEL. *Fascism and Big Business,* trans. by Frances and Mason Merrell, New York, 1939.

GULICK, SIDNEY L. *The American-Japanese Problem,* New York, 1914.

HACKER, LOUIS M. *The Triumph of American Capitalism,* New York, 1940.

HALL, JOSEF W. (Upton Close). *The Revolt of Asia,* New York & London, 1927.

HAMMOND, J. L., and HAMMOND, BARBARA. *The Town Labourer, 1760–1832,* London, 1917.

HAYEK, FRIEDRICH A. *The Road to Serfdom,* Chicago, 1944.

HAYES, CARLTON J. H. *Essays on Nationalism,* New York, 1926.

HECKSCHER, ELI FILIP. *Mercantilism,* trans. by Mendell Shapiro, London, 1935.

HEDGER, GEORGE A. *An Introduction to Western Civilization,* New York, 1939.

HEIMANN, EDUARD. *Communism, Fascism or Democracy,* New York, 1938.

HELPER, HINTON ROWAN. *The Impending Crisis,* New York, 1860.

HITLER, ADOLF. *Mein Kampf,* New York, 1940.

HOBHOUSE, L. T. *Liberalism,* New York & London, n.d.

HOBSON, J. A. *Democracy and a Changing Civilization,* London, 1934.

HOLCOMBE, A. N. *The New Party Politics,* New York, 1933.

HOLLAND, W. E. S. *The Indian Outlook,* London, 1927.

HOOVER, HERBERT. *American Individualism,* New York, 1922.

HOPKINS, EDWARD W. "The Social and Military Position of the Ruling Caste in Ancient India," *Journal of American Oriental Society,* Vol. XIII, 1888.

HOWARD, HARRY PAXTON. *America's Role in Asia,* New York, 1943.

HUGHES, PHILIP. *The Popes' New Order,* New York, 1944.

HUME, ROBERT ERNEST. *The Thirteen Principal Upanishads,* 2d ed., Oxford, 1934.

HUNT, WILLIAM S. *India's Outcastes,* London, 1924.

HUXLEY, JULIAN. *Race in Europe,* Oxford Pamphlets on World Affairs, No. 5, Oxford, 1939.

IBBETSON, DENZIL. *Panjab Castes,* Lahore, 1916.

ICHIHASHI, YAMATO. *Japanese Immigration,* San Francisco, 1915.

Indian Year Book, The, Bombay, 1939–40.

Institutes of Vishnu, trans. by Julius Jolly, Vol. II of *The Sacred Books of the East,* F. Max Müller, ed., Oxford, 1880.

IRISH, JOHN P. "The Japanese Issue in California," *The Annals,* Vol. XCIII, Jan. 1921.

JOHNSEN, JULIA E., ed. *Japanese Exclusion,* New York, 1925.

JOHNSON, CHARLES S. *Growing Up in the Black Belt,* Washington, D.C., 1941.

JOHNSON, GERALD W. *Roosevelt, Dictator or Democrat?,* New York & London, 1941.

JOHNSON, JAMES WELDON. *Negro Americans, What Now?,* New York, 1935.

———. *The Book of American Negro Poetry,* New York, 1931.

JONES, CHESTER LLOYD. *Caribbean Backgrounds and Prospects,* New York, 1931.

JONES, JOHN P. *India, Its Life and Thought,* New York, 1908.

JOSHI, P. S. *The Tyranny of Colour,* Durban, 1942.

KANZAKI, KÜCHI. "Is the Japanese Menace in America a Reality?" *The Annals,* Vol. XCIII, Jan. 1921.

KARANDIKAR, S. V. *Hindu Exogamy,* Bombay, 1929.

KAWAKAMI, K. K. "The Japanese Question," *The Annals,* Vol. XCIII, Jan. 1921.

KENNEDY, RAYMOND. *The Ageless Indies,* New York, 1942.

KENNEDY, STETSON. *Southern Exposure,* New York, 1946.

KETKAR, SHRIDHAR V. *The History of Caste in India,* New York & London, 1909–11.

KNIGHT, FRANK H. "The Meaning of Freedom," and "The Ideal of Freedom," *The Philosophy of American Democracy,* ed. by Charner M. Perry, Chicago, 1943.

KOHN, HANS. *The Idea of Nationalism,* New York, 1944.

KORNHAUSER, A. W. "Analysis of Class Structure of Contemporary American Society," in *Industrial Conflict,* ed. by George W. Hartmann and Theodore Newcomb, New York, 1939.

KRUEGER, E. T., and RECKLESS, WALTER. *Social Psychology,* New York and London, 1934.

KUMARAPPA, J. C. "Handicrafts and Cottage Industries in India," *The Annals,* May 1944.

LANDIS, PAUL H. *Social Control,* Philadelphia, 1939.

LANDTMAN, GUNNAR. *The Origin of the Inequality of the Social Classes,* London, 1938.

LANGE, OSKAR, and TAYLOR, FRED M. *The Economic Theory of Socialism,* Minneapolis, 1938.

LANGSAM, WALTER C. *Documents and Readings in the History of Europe since 1918,* Philadelphia, 1939.

LASKI, HAROLD F. *Where Do We Go from Here?,* New York, 1940.

———. *Parliamentary Government in England,* New York, 1938.

———. *Reflections on the Revolution of Our Time,* New York, 1943.

———. *The Rise of Liberalism,* New York & London, 1936.

Laws of Manu, The, trans. by G. Bühler, Vol. XXV of *The Sacred Books of the East,* F. Max Müller, ed., Oxford, 1886.

LE BON, GUSTAVE. *Premières Conséquences de la guerre,* Paris, 1917.

LECKY, W. E. H. *History of the Rise and Influence of the Spirit of Rationalism in Europe,* London & New York, 1904.

――――. *Democracy and Liberty,* New York, 1899.

LENIN, NIKOLAI. *The State and Revolution,* New York, 1929.

LEVINTHAL, LOUIS E. "The Case for a Jewish Commonwealth," *The Annals,* Vol. 240, Jul. 1945.

LINDLEY, ERNEST K. *The Roosevelt Revolution,* London, 1934.

LINTON, RALPH. *The Study of Man,* New York, 1936.

LIPPINCOTT, BENJAMIN EVANS. *Victorian Critics of Democracy,* Minneapolis, 1938.

LOBB, JOHN. "Caste in Haiti," *American Journal of Sociology,* Vol. XLVI, Jul. 1940.

LOGAN, RAYFORD W., ed. *What the Negro Wants,* Chapel Hill, 1944.

LORWIN, LEWIS L. "Class Struggle," *Encyclopedia of the Social Sciences.*

――――. *The American Federation of Labor,* Washington, D.C., 1933.

LOWIE, ROBERT H. *Primitive Society,* New York, 1920.

LUNDBERG, FERDINAND. *America's 60 Families,* New York, 1937.

LUXEMBURG, ROSA. *Reform or Revolution* (2d ed., 1908), New York, 1937.

MACDONELL, ARTHUR ANTHONY. *India's Past,* Oxford, 1927.

MACDONELL, ARTHUR ANTHONY, and KEITH, ARTHUR BERRIEDALE. *Vedic Index,* London, 1912.

MACIVER, R. M. *Society, A Textbook in Sociology,* New York, 1937.

MACKENZIE, FINDLAY, ed. *Planned Society,* New York, 1937.

MACNUTT, FRANCIS AUGUSTUS. *Bartholomew De Las Casas,* New York & London, 1909.

MAINE, SIR HENRY SUMNER. *Popular Government,* New York, 1886.

MAITLAND, F. W. "The History of a Cambridgeshire Manor," *The English Historical Review,* Vol. IX, 1894.

MANGUM, CHARLES S., JR. *The Legal Status of the Negro,* Chapel Hill, 1940.

MANNHEIM, KARL. *Man and Society, in an Age of Reconstruction,* trans. by Edward Shils, London, 1940.

――――. *Ideology and Utopia,* trans. by Louis Wirth and Edward Shils, New York, 1936.

MANTOUX, PAUL. *The Industrial Revolution in the Eighteenth Century,* trans. by Marjorie Vernon, New York, 1928.

MARLIO, LOUIS. *Can Democracy Recover?,* New York, 1945.

MARX, KARL. *A Contribution to the Critique of Political Economy,* trans. by N. I. Stone, New York, 1904.

MARX, KARL, and ENGELS, FRIEDRICH. *Communist Manifesto,* trans. by Friedrich Engels, 1888.

MASUOKA, JITSUICHI. "Race Preference in Hawaii," *The American Journal of Sociology,* Vol. XLI, Mar. 1936.

MATHIES, ALBERT. "French Revolution," *Encyclopedia of the Social Sciences.*

MAUNIER, RENÉ. *Sociologie coloniale,* Paris, 1932.

MAYNE, JOHN D. *A Treatise on Hindu Law and Usage,* 8th ed., Madras, 1914.

McKENZIE, R. D. *Oriental Exclusion,* Chicago, 1928.
McWILLIAMS, CAREY. *Prejudice,* Boston, 1944.
———. *Brothers under the Skin,* Boston, 1943.
MEAD, ELWOOD. "The Japanese Land Problem in California," *The Annals,* Vol. XCIII, Jan. 1921.
MEARS, ELIOT GRINNELL. *Resident Orientals on the American Pacific Coast,* Chicago, 1928.
MEES, GUALTHERUS H. *Dharma and Society,* The Hague, 1935.
MELISH, WILLIAM HOWARD. "Religious Developments in the Soviet Union," *American Sociological Review,* Jun. 1944.
———. "The Western Catholic Bloc," *The Nation,* Vol. 162, Jun. 29, 1946.
MERRIAM, CHARLES E. *What Is Democracy?,* Chicago, 1941.
MEUSEL, ALFRED. "Middle Class," and "Revolution and Counter-Revolution," *Encyclopedia of the Social Sciences.*
MICHELS, ROBERT. *Political Parties,* trans. by Eden and Cedar Paul, New York, 1915.
MILL, JAMES. *The History of British India,* Vol. I, London, 1840.
MILLER, HERBERT A. *The Beginnings of Tomorrow,* New York, 1933.
MILLER, KELLY. *An Appeal to Conscience,* New York, 1918.
MILLIS, HARRY A. *The Japanese Problem in the United States,* New York, 1915.
MOHL, RUTH. *The Three Estates in Medieval and Renaissance Literature,* New York, 1933.
MOMBERT, PAUL. "Class," *Encyclopedia of the Social Sciences.*
MONTAGU, M. F. ASHLEY. *Man's Most Dangerous Myth: The Fallacy of Race,* New York, 1942.
MOON, PARKER T. *Imperialism and World Politics,* New York, 1932.
MOREL, E. D. *The Black Man's Burden,* New York, 1920.
MORRIS, RICHARD B. *Government and Labor in Early America,* New York, 1946.
MOSCA, GAETANO. *The Ruling Class,* trans. by Hanna D. Khan, New York, 1939.
MUIR, JOHN. *Original Sanskrit Texts on the Origin and History of the People of India,* London, 1872–74.
MUKERJEE, RADHAKAMAL. *The Foundations of Indian Economics,* London, 1916.
MUSSBAUM, FREDERICK. *A History of the Economic Institutions of Modern Europe,* New York, 1933.
MYRDAL, GUNNAR. *An American Dilemma,* New York, 1944.
NEHRU, JAWAHARLAL. *Toward Freedom,* New York, 1942.
NEHRU, SHRI SHRIDHAR. *Caste and Credit,* London & New York, 1932.
NESFIELD, JOHN C. *The Caste System of the North-Western Provinces and Oudh,* Allahabad, 1885.
NICOLAY, JOHN G., and HAY, JOHN. *Abraham Lincoln Complete Works,* Vol. I, 1894.
OGBURN, WILLIAM F., and PETERSON, DELVIN. "Political Thought of Social Classes," *Political Science Quarterly,* Vol. 31, 1916.
OLDHAM, J. H. *White and Black in Africa,* London, 1930.

OLIVIER, LORD. *The Anatomy of African Misery,* London, 1927.

O'MALLEY, L. S. S. *Modern India and the West,* London, 1941.

OVIEDO, GONZALO FERNANDEZ DE. *Historia General y Natural de las Indias,* Madrid, 1885.

PAGE, CHARLES HUNT. *Class and American Sociology,* New York, 1940.

PAGE, FRANCES M. *The Estates of Crowland Abbey,* Cambridge, 1934.

PAL, BIPIN CHANDRA. *The Soul of India,* Madras, 1923.

PARK, ROBERT E., and BURGESS, ERNEST W. *Introduction to the Science of Sociology,* Chicago, 1924.

PARMALEE, MAURICE. *Bolshevism, Fascism, and the Liberal-Democratic State,* New York, 1924.

PARSONS, TALCOTT. "Capitalism in Recent German Literature: Sombart and Weber," *The Journal of Political Economy,* Vol. 36.

———. *The Structure of Social Action,* New York & London, 1937.

———. "An Analytical Approach to the Theory of Social Stratification," *American Journal of Sociology,* Vol. XLV.

PAYNE, E. J., ed. *Burke Selected Works,* Vol. III, Oxford, 1926.

PEFFER, NATHANIEL. *The White Man's Dilemma,* New York, 1927.

PETHNICK-LAWRENCE, EMMELINE. *My Part in a Changing World,* London, 1938.

PETIT-DUTAILLIS, CH., and LEFEBVRE, GEORGES. *Studies and Notes Supplementary to Stubbs' Constitutional History,* Manchester, 1930.

PHELAN, JAMES D. "Why California Objects to the Japanese Invasion," *The Annals,* Vol. XCIII, Jan. 1921.

PHILLIPS, GODFREY E. *The Outcastes' Hope,* London, 1912.

PIERSON, DONALD. *Negroes in Brazil,* Chicago, 1942.

PIGOU, A. C. *Socialism versus Capitalism,* London, 1938.

PINKHAM, MILDRED WORTH. *Women in the Sacred Scriptures of Hinduism,* New York, 1941.

PIRENNE, HENRI. *Economic and Social History of Medieval Europe,* New York, 1937.

———. *Medieval Cities,* trans. by Frank D. Halsey, Princeton, 1925.

POSTGATE, R. W. *Revolution from 1789 to 1906,* London, 1920.

POWDERMAKER, HORTENSE. *After Freedom,* New York, 1939.

POWICKE, F. M. *Medieval England,* London, 1931.

RADER, MELVIN. *No Compromise: The Conflict between Two Worlds,* New York, 1939.

RAPER, ARTHUR F. *Preface to Peasantry,* Chapel Hill, 1936.

———. *The Tragedy of Lynching,* Chapel Hill, 1933.

RAWLINSON, H. G. *India, A Short Cultural History,* London, 1938.

READE, W. H. V. *The Revolt of Labor against Civilization,* Oxford, 1919.

REED, LOUIS S. *The Labor Philosophy of Samuel Gompers,* New York, 1930.

REES, J. F. "Mercantilism and the Colonies," *Cambridge History of the British Empire,* Vols. I, II.

REINHARDT, JAMES MELVIN. *Social Psychology,* Philadelphia, 1938.

Report of the Age of Consent Committee, 1928–1929, Calcutta: Government of India Central Publication Branch, 1929.

Report of the Committee on Emigration from India to the Crown Colonies and Protectorates, London, 1910.
REUTER, EDWARD BYRON. *The Mulatto in the United States,* Boston, 1918.
REUTER, EDWARD BYRON, ed. *Race and Culture Contacts,* New York & London, 1934.
REVES, EMERY. *A Democratic Manifesto,* New York, 1942.
REYNOLDS, REGINALD. *The White Sahibs in India,* London, 1937.
RHYS, ALBERT. "Meet the Russian People," *Survey,* Feb. 1944.
RICE, STANLEY. *Hindu Customs and Their Origins,* London, 1937.
RIDLEY, F. A. *The Papacy and Fascism,* London, 1937.
Rigveda Brahmanas, trans. by Arthur B. Keith, Harvard Oriental Series, Vol. 25, Charles R. Lanman, ed., Cambridge, Mass., 1920.
RISLEY, SIR HERBERT HOPE. *The People of India,* Calcutta, 1908.
ROBERTSON, E. WILLIAM. *Scotland under Her Early Kings,* Edinburgh, 1862.
ROBERTSON, H. M. *Aspects of the Rise of Economic Individualism,* Cambridge, 1933.
ROBINSON, JAMES HARVEY. *The Mind in the Making,* New York & London, 1921.
———. *Readings in European History,* Boston, 1906.
ROGERS, JAMES HARVEY. *Capitalism in Crisis,* New Haven, 1938.
ROSENBERG, ARTHUR. *Democracy and Socialism,* New York, 1939.
ROSENMAN, SAMUEL I., ed. *The Public Papers and Addresses of Franklin D. Roosevelt,* New York, 1938–41.
ROSS, E. A. *Principles of Sociology,* New York, 1930.
ROY, ANILBARAN, ed. *The Message of the Gita,* Madras, 1938.
RUGGLES, THOMAS. *History of the Poor,* London, 1793.
RUSSELL, R. V. *The Tribes and Castes of the Central Provinces of India,* London, 1916.
RYDER, DAVID WARREN. "The Japanese Bugaboo," *The Annals,* Vol. XCIII, Jan. 1921.
SABINE, GEORGE H. *The Works of Gerard Winstanley,* New York, 1941.
SANDMEYER, ELMER CLARENCE. *The Anti-Chinese Movement in California,* Urbana, 1939.
SAPIR, E., "Culture, Genuine and Spurious," *American Journal of Sociology,* Vol. XXIX, Jan. 1924.
SAYERS, MICHAEL, and KAHN, ALBERT E. *The Great Conspiracy,* Boston, 1946.
SCHMOLLER, GUSTAV. *The Mercantile System,* New York, 1897.
SCHUMAN, FREDERICK L. *Soviet Politics,* New York, 1946.
———. *The Nazi Dictatorship,* New York, 1935.
SCHUMPETER, JOSEPH A. *Capitalism, Socialism, and Democracy,* New York & London, 1942.
SCHWEITZER, ALBERT. *Indian Thought and Its Development,* New York, 1936.
SCOTT, JOHN. *Europe in Revolution,* Boston, 1945.
SCOTT, JONATHAN F., HYMA, ALBERT, and NOYES, ARTHUR H. *Readings in Medieval History,* New York, 1933.

Sée, Henri. *Modern Capitalism,* trans. by Homer B. Vanderblue and George F. Doriot, New York, 1928.

———. *La France économique et social en XVIII° siècle,* Paris, 1925.

Seldes, George. *Facts and Fascism,* New York, 1943.

———. *The Catholic Crisis,* New York, 1939.

Senart, Émile. *Caste in India,* trans. by Sir E. Denison Ross, London, 1930.

Shapera, I., ed. *Western Civilization and the Natives of South Africa,* London, 1934.

Shay, Frank. *Judge Lynch,* New York, 1938.

Sherring, M. A. *Hindu Tribes and Castes,* Calcutta, 1879.

Shridharani, Krishnalal. *Warning to the West,* New York, 1942.

Shugg, Roger W. *Origins of Class Struggle in Louisiana,* Baton Rouge, 1939.

Skaggs, William H. *The Southern Oligarchy,* New York, 1924.

Smith, Vincent A. *The Oxford History of India,* Oxford, 1920.

Smith, William C. "Minority Groups in Hawaii," *The Annals,* Vol. 223, Sept. 1942.

Smith, William Roy. *Nationalism and Reform in India,* New Haven, 1938.

Snyder, Carl. *Capitalism the Creator,* New York, 1940.

Sombart, Werner. *Der Moderne Kapitalismus,* II, 2, München & Leipzig, 1937.

———. *The Quintessence of Capitalism,* trans. by M. Epstein, New York, 1915.

———. *Socialism and the Social Movement in the 19th Century,* trans. by Anson P. Atterbury, New York, 1898.

Sorokin, Pitirim A. *Social Mobility,* New York, 1927.

Sorokin, Pitirim A., and Zimmerman, Carle C. *Principles of Rural-Urban Sociology,* New York, 1929.

Sorokin, Pitirim A., Zimmerman, Carle C., and Galpin, Charles J. *A Systematic Source Book in Rural Sociology,* Minneapolis, 1930.

Spahr, Walter E. "Full Employment in Exchange for What?", *The Commercial and Financial Chronicle,* Sept. 27, 1945.

Spann, Othmar, "Klasse und Stand," *Handworterbuch Der Staatswissenschaften,* Vol. 5, Jena, 1923.

Spellman, Francis Cardinal, "Communism Is Un-American," *The American Magazine,* Jul. 1946.

Stalin, Joseph. *Leninism,* New York, 1942.

Stark, Herbert Alick. *Hostages to India,* Calcutta, 1926.

Steiner, Jesse Frederick. *The Japanese Invasion,* Chicago, 1917.

Stephenson, Gilbert. *Race Distinction in American Law,* New York, 1910.

Stonequist, Everett V. *The Marginal Man,* New York, 1937.

Strachey, John. *Socialism Looks Forward,* New York, 1945.

Stubbs, William. *The Constitutional History of England,* Oxford, 1883–84.

Sullivan, Louis R. "The Labor Crisis in Hawaii," *Asia,* Vol. XXIII, No. 7, Jul. 1923.

SUMNER, WILLIAM G. *Folkways,* Boston, 1906.

SUTHERLAND, ROBERT L. *Color, Class, and Personality,* Washington, D.C., 1942.

SUTHERLAND, ROBERT L., and WOODWARD, JULIAN L. *Introductory Sociology,* Philadelphia, 1940.

SWEEZY, PAUL M. *The Theory of Capitalist Development,* New York, 1942.

SWINTON, JOHN. *A Momentous Question: The Respective Attitudes of Labor and Capital,* Philadelphia, 1895.

TAWNEY, R. H. *Equality,* New York, 1929.

THOMAS, EDWARD J. *The Life of Buddha,* London, 1927.

THOMPSON, JAMES WESTFALL. *The Middle Ages,* New York, 1931.

THOMPSON, WARREN S. *Danger Spots in World Population,* New York, 1930.

THURSTON, EDGAR. *Castes and Tribes of Southern India,* Vol. II, Madras, 1909.

TOCQUEVILLE, ALEXIS DE. *Democracy in America,* 3d ed., trans. by Henry Reeve, London, 1838.

TOWNSEND, MARY EVELYN. *European Colonial Expansion since 1871,* Philadelphia, 1941.

TOYNBEE, ARNOLD J. *A Study of History,* Vol. IV, London, 1939.

TRACHTENBERG, JOSHUA. *The Devil and the Jews,* New Haven, 1943.

TROTSKY, LEON. *History of the Russian Revolution,* Vol. III, New York, 1922.

UNDERWOOD, A. C. *Contemporary Thought of India,* London, 1930.

VALENTIN, HUGO. *Antisemitism,* trans. by A. G. Chater, New York, 1936.

VEBLEN, THORSTEIN. *The Theory of the Leisure Class,* New York, 1899.

VINCENT, GEORGE E. "The Rivalry of Social Groups," *American Journal of Sociology,* XVI, 1910–11.

WALKER, E. A. *South Africa,* Oxford, 1940.

WALLACE, HENRY A. *Whose Constitution?,* New York, 1936.

WALLACE, KENNETH E. *The Eurasian Problem,* Calcutta, 1930.

WALSH, JOHN RAYMOND. *C.I.O.,* New York, 1937.

WARNER, W. LLOYD, and LUNT, PAUL S. *The Status System of a Modern Community,* New Haven, 1942.

———. *The Social Life of a Modern Community,* New Haven, 1941.

WARNER, LLOYD, and SROLE, LEO. *The Social Systems of American Ethnic Groups,* New York, 1945.

WASHINGTON, BOOKER T. *Working with the Hands,* New York, 1904.

WEALE, PUTNAM B. L. (Bertram L. Simpson). *The Conflict of Color,* New York, 1910.

WEBB, SIDNEY and BEATRICE. *Industrial Democracy,* London, 1920.

———. *Soviet Communism: A New Civilization,* New York, 1936.

WEBER, MAX. *The Protestant Ethic and the Spirit of Capitalism,* trans. by Talcott Parsons, London, 1930.

———. *Gesammelte Aufsatze zur Religionssoziologie,* Tübingen, 1921.

———. *Wirtschaft und Gesellschaft,* Tübingen, Vol. I, 1922.

WEINREICH, MAX, *Hitler's Professors,* New York, 1946.

WESTERMARCK, EDWARD. *The History of Human Marriage,* New York, 1922.

WHITE, WALTER. *Rope and Faggot,* New York & London, 1929.

WILSON, WOODROW. *Constitutional Government in the United States,* New York, 1918.

WINTERNITZ, MAURICE. *A History of Indian Literature,* trans. by S. Ketkar, Calcutta, 1927.

WISER, WILLIAM HENRICKS. *Social Institutions of a Hindu Village of North India,* abstract of Ph.D. dissertation, Cornell University, 1933.

WISER, WILLIAM HENRICKS, and CHARLOTTE V. *Behind Mud Walls,* New York, 1930.

WOOLF, LEONARD. *Imperialism and Civilization,* New York, 1928.

WRISTON, HENRY M. *Challenge to Freedom,* New York & London, 1943.

YAT-SEN, SUN. *Le triple Demisme,* French trans. by Pascal M. d'Elia, Shanghai, 1930.

YELLEN, SAMUEL. *American Labor Struggles,* New York, 1936.

YINGER, J. MILTON. *Religion in the Struggle for Power,* Durham, 1946.

YOUNG, ARTHUR. *The Farmer's Tour through the East of England,* Vol. IV, London, 1771.

YOUNG, DONALD. *Research Memorandum on Minority Peoples in a Depression,* Bulletin No. 31, 1937.

YOUNG, KIMBALL. *An Introductory Sociology,* New York, 1934.

YUTANG, LIN. *Between Tears and Laughter,* New York, 1943.

ZWEIG, STEFAN. *Erasmus,* trans. by Eden and Cedar Paul, London, 1934.

Index

Index

(Index by C. P. and E. C. Chadsey)

Modern Reader Paperbacks